THE UNHCR AND WORLD POLITICS

OTHER BOOKS BY THE AUTHOR

Beyond Charity: International Cooperation and the Global Refugee Crisis
The Global Refugee Crisis: A Reference Handbook (co-author)
Refugee Movements and International Security
Refugees and International Relations (co-editor)
The Moral Nation: Humanitarianism and US Foregin Policy (co-editor)
Calculated Kindness: Refugees and America's Half-Open Door, 1945 to Present (co-author)

The UNHCR and World Politics

A Perilous Path

GIL LOESCHER

OXFORD
UNIVERSITY PRESS

OXFORD

UNIVERSITY PRESS

Great Clarendon Street, Oxford OX2 6DP

Oxford University Press is a department of the University of Oxford.
It furthers the University's objective of excellence in research, scholarship,
and education by publishing worldwide in

Oxford New York

Athens Auckland Bangkok Bogotá Buenos Aires
Cape Town Chennai Dar es Salaam Delhi Florence Hong Kong Istanbul
Karachi Kolkata Kuala Lumpur Madrid Melbourne Mexico City Mumbai
Nairobi Paris São Paulo Shanghai Singapore Taipei Tokyo Toronto Warsaw
and associated companies in Berlin Ibadan

Oxford is a registered trade mark of Oxford University Press
in the UK and in certain other countries

Published in the United States
by Oxford University Press Inc., New York

British Library Cataloguing in Publication Data
Data available

Library of Congress Cataloging in Publication Data

Loescher, Gil.
The UNHCR and world politics: a perilous path/Gil Loescher.
p. cm.
Includes bibliographical references and index.
1. Office of the United Nations High Commissioner for Refugees—History.
2. Refugees—Governmental Policy. 3. Refugees--International cooperation. I. Title.
HV640.3.L64 2001   362.87'56—dc21   2001021839
ISBN 0–19–829716–5
ISBN 0–19–924691–2 (pbk.)

1 3 5 7 9 10 8 6 4 2

Typeset in Stone Sans and Stone Serif by
Cambrian Typesetters, Frimley, Surrey
Printed in Great Britain
on acid-free paper by
Biddles Ltd., Guildford & Kings Lynn

In Loving Memory
of
my mother
Helene Achen Loescher

ACKNOWLEDGEMENTS

I have wanted to write a book about the UNHCR since I first became interested in the refugee issue in the 1980s. The UNHCR is unique among UN agencies. It has a long-standing mandate to protect the human rights of refugees. Yet it is also the most politically active UN agency. Its work is constrained by the national interests of sovereign states but the office also at times takes independent decisions that are either unanticipated or opposed by states. Consequently, the UNHCR has always trod a perilous path between its mandate to protect refugees and the demands placed upon the agency by states to be a relevant actor in world politics.

During the 1990s, I had considerable experience with the UNHCR. I served as chair of the External Academic Advisory Board of the UNHCR, which oversaw the production of the biennial *State of the World's Refugees*. I also served as an adviser and rapporteur for the UNHCR's Partnership in Action (PARINAC) efforts with NGOs. During 1996, I worked for nine months as a senior adviser for the agency at its Geneva headquarters where my task was to help the office set up a policy research unit. While these first-hand experiences have greatly influenced my thinking about the strengths and weaknesses of the UNHCR, I received no financial support from the agency for this book. My book does not represent the official history of the UNHCR. Indeed, it is likely that some people in the agency will be unhappy with some of my criticisms of policies and programmes. I have tried to write an honest, independent, and critical assessment of the UNHCR and its history over the past 50 years.

I am grateful to the Open Society Institute in New York and the US Institute of Peace in Washington, DC, for generously supporting this study. The Institute for Scholarship in the Liberal Arts at the University of Notre Dame provided initial travel funds that permitted me to begin work at the UNHCR archives in Geneva before I received external research support for this project. I also benefited from a four-week stay as a Scholar in Residence at the Rockefeller Study Centre at the Villa Serbelloni in Bellagio.

This book has relied on archival research, particularly for the period up to the late 1970s. For the more recent decades, I have relied on secondary sources, personal interviews with UNHCR staff and others, and on primary documents shared with me on an unofficial basis. Numerous institutions have offered me their support and hospitality during the research for this book. I would like to thank especially the staff of the UNHCR archival unit in Geneva, in particular, Ann Newhall, Ineke Deserno, and Joseph Jesuthasan;

the UNHCR Documentation and Research Centre in Geneva; the British Foreign Office archives at Kew Gardens, London; the US State Department archives at the National Archives in College Park, Maryland; the National Security Council archives at the National Archives in Washington, DC; and the Documentation Centre at the Refugee Studies Centre in Oxford.

For this book, I have interviewed many of the former UN High Commissioners for Refugees as well as scores of past and present UNHCR staff members. While serving as High Commissioner, Sadako Ogata took the time to be encouraging and helpful in many ways. Over the last two decades, I have visited numerous refugee camps in Africa, Asia, and Central America as well as refugee holding and detention centres in Europe and North America. In preparing this study and in writing about UNHCR and refugee issues over many years, I have interviewed or spoken with hundreds of officials, human rights and humanitarian aid agency workers, researchers, refugees, and asylum-seekers on every continent.

It is impossible for me to list all the names of individuals who have helped me either directly or indirectly in the research and writing of this book. Special thanks go to Dennis McNamara, Jeff Crisp, Jacques Cuenod, Gilbert Jaeger, Michel Moussalli, Irene Kahn, Philip Rudge, and Soren Jessen-Petersen. Without the assistance of these individuals who spent hours talking with me and sharing their insights, this book could not have been written. Sergio Vieira de Mello, Mahendra Lama, Mark Cutts, Bela Hovy, Wilbert van Hovell, Bernard Alexander, Elizabeth Ferris, Michael Barnett, Arthur Helton, Nicholas Van Hear, Johan Cels, Nicholas Morris, Eric Morris, Filippo Grande, John Horekens, Francois Fouinat, Milton Moreno, Ron Redmond, Kris Janowski, Patricia Weiss-Fagen, Erika Feller, Kirsten Young, Cathy Sabety, Anne Fati, Michelene Saunders-Gallemand, and many others were also helpful in various ways. The staff at the John Knox Centre in Grand-Saconnex, Geneva provided me with a home away from home during my frequent visits to Geneva. I am grateful to many others who helped me along the way—whether at Notre Dame, Oxford, Geneva, London, Washington, DC, or in refugee camps in Africa, Asia, or Central America—and to those who provided information, documents, and personal comments and observations while requesting anonymity.

Some passages in the present work originally appeared in *Beyond Charity: International Cooperation and the Global Refugee Crisis, Calculated Kindness: Refugees and America's Half-Open Door, 1945 to Present*, and the International Migration Review. I am grateful to The Century Fund, the Free Press, and to the Centre for Migration Studies for allowing me to use them here.

The editorial assistance I received from Oxford University Press was especially helpful. Dominic Byatt, Amanda Watkins, and Mark Taylor piloted the book to publication and were generous in a number of ways. Finally, I could not have finished this book without the encouragement, prodding, and inestimable assistance of my wife. Annie read and edited the entire manuscript, reorganized and retyped the endnotes and bibliography, and literally gave over most of the summer 2000 to seeing this book through to completion. This was a very difficult book to call finished and I was updating the manuscript well into the copyediting process. By the end of the project, everyone concerned, especially my family, wanted to lock up the computer and throw away the key!

G.L.

South Bend, Indiana
November 2000

CONTENTS

ABBREVIATIONS

ACVA	American Council for Voluntary Agencies in Foreign Service
CCAI	Argentine Catholic Commission
CIREFCA	International Conference on Central American Refugees
CONAR	National Committee for Aid to Refugees [Chile]
CPA	Comprehensive Plan of Action [on Indo-Chinese refugees]
DHA	Department of Humanitarian Affairs [of the UN—later OCHA]
DP	Displaced Person
EOCWAS	Economic Community of West African States
ELF	Eritrean Liberation Front
EPLF	Ethiopian People's Liberation Front
Excom	UNHCR Executive Committee
FAO	Food and Agricultural Organization [UN]
FLN	Algerian National Liberation Army
FMNL	Farabundo Marti National Liberation Front [El Salvador]
FNLA	National Front for the Liberation of Angola
FRELIMO	Front for the Liberation of Mozambique
IASC	Inter-Agency Standing Committee [UN]
ICEM	International Committee for European Migration [later IOM]
ICRC	International Committee of the Red Cross
IDP	Internally Displaced Person
IGCR	Intergovernmental Committee on Refugees
ILO	International Labour Organization
IOM	International Organization for Migration
INS	Immigration and Naturalization Service [US]
INTERFET	International Force in East Timor
IRO	International Refugee Organization
KLA	Kosovo Liberation Army
LRCS	League of Red Cross Societies
MPLA	Movement for the Liberation of Angola
NGO	Non-Governmental Organization
NPFL	National Patriotic Front of Liberia
OAU	Organization of African Unity
OCHA	Office for the Co-ordination of Humanitarian Affairs [UN]
ODP	Orderly Departure Program [for refugees leaving Vietnam]
OSCE	Organization for Security and Co-operation in Europe
PAFMECA	Pan African Freedom Movement for East, Central, and South Africa

PICME	Provisional Intergovernmental Committee for the Movement of Migrants from Europe [Later ICEM]
PRC	People's Republic of China [mainland China]
PRODERE	Development Programme for Displaced Persons, Refugees, and Repatriates [Programme of the UNDP]
ROC	Republic of China [Taiwan]
RPF	Rwanda Patriotic Front
SPLA	Sudanese People's Liberation Army
SWAPO	South West African People's Organization
TPLF	Tigray People's Liberation Front
UN	United Nations
UNAMIR	UN Assistance Mission for Rwanda
UNBRO	UN Border Relief Operation
UNDP	UN Development Programme
UNDRO	UN Disaster Relief Organization
UNHCR	UN High Commissioner for Refugees
UNICEF	UN International Children's Emergency Fund
UNITA	National Union for Total Independence of Angola
UNKRA	UN Korean Reconstruction Agency
UNPROFOR	UN Protection Force [Balkan crisis]
UNREF	UN Refugee Emergency Fund
UNRRA	UN Relief and Rehabilitation Agency
UNRWA	UN Relief and Works Agency for Palestine Refugees in the Near East
USEP	United States Escapee Program
UNTAET	UN Transitional Administration in East Timor
WFP	World Food Programme
WHO	World Health Organization

1

The UNHCR at 50: State Pressures and Institutional Autonomy

For the past half century, the Office of the United Nations High Commissioner for Refugees (UNHCR) has been at the heart of many of the gravest breakdowns of social and political order and tragic human loss in recent history. These events have propelled the Office into the maelstrom of world politics. From the1956 Hungarian Uprising at the height of the Cold War to the mass exodus of Albanians from Kosovo in 1999, the UNHCR has been central to the international debates about human rights and international responsibility, conflict resolution, preventive diplomacy, and the delivery of humanitarian assistance. From focusing almost exclusively on protection and humanitarian relief for refugees in host countries, the UNHCR has progressively taken on additional responsibilities that involve it in a myriad of activities for refugees and non-refugees alike.

Scholars and practitioners of international relations have been slow to recognize either the rationality or significance of the United Nations High Commissioner for Refugees in world politics. Among UN agencies, the UNHCR is unique. It is both an individual, represented in the High Commissioner, and a bureaucracy with its own distinct culture and value system. The High Commissioner has little or no political authority but is vested with considerable moral authority and legitimacy dating back not just the Office's founding in 1951 but to 1921 when Fridtjof Nansen was appointed as the first High Commissioner for Refugees by the League of Nations. The UNHCR is an organization with its own identity, comprising over 5,000 individuals of different nationalities who share similar values. One cannot fully understand the UNHCR without a knowledge of its organizational culture. There exists no other UN agency where values and principled ideas are so central to the mandate and *raison d'être* of the institution or where some committed staff members are willing to place their lives in danger to defend the proposition that persecuted individuals need protection. As the UNHCR itself claims, if the Office did not exist, hundreds of thousands, if not millions, of refugees would be left unassisted and unprotected.

However essential the agency is, it is important not to take the rhetoric and self-presentation of the UNHCR at face value. While the UNHCR has had many successes over the past 50 years, it has also had many failures. Slow and inadequate responses to refugee emergencies and protection crises have sometimes risked the lives of countless numbers of refugees. A number of internal and external constraints inhibit the organization from achieving its full impact. The Office has an organizational culture that makes innovation and institutional change difficult. Some UNHCR senior management are arrogant and insensitive to the real needs of refugees. The UNHCR is confronted with persistent problems of lack of learning and policy effectiveness.

The UNHCR also has endemic political problems. The High Commissioner has the almost impossible task of trying to influence states to protect and find solutions for refugees without challenging the prerogative of states to deal independently with their own internal affairs. The UNHCR was created by UN member states to be both a strictly non-political agency and an advocate for refugees.[1] From its beginning, it was clear that the agency's role would be an intensely political one. As defined in the 1951 Refugee Convention, refugees are people who have a well-founded fear of persecution and cannot return to their home countries for fear of placing their lives in jeopardy. The UNHCR's primary mandate is to protect refugees from government repression. This often requires the Office to directly challenge governments and places the agency in a conflictive relationship with states. However, the UNHCR is not just an advocacy organization; it also exists to facilitate state policies towards refugees. States did not establish the UNHCR from purely altruistic motives, but from a desire to promote regional and international stability and to serve the interests of governments. Governments created the Office to help them resolve problems related to refugees who were perceived to create domestic instability, to generate interstate tensions, and to threaten international security. The UNHCR is an intergovernmental organization and part of the UN system and therefore cannot always act in a strictly neutral fashion. Thus the UNHCR often walks a tightrope, maintaining a perilous balance between the protection of refugees and the sovereign prerogatives and interests of states.

The UNHCR and Refugee Crises at the beginning of the Twenty-First Century

As the UNHCR celebrates its fiftieth anniversary, refugee crises around the world continue to create instability, demonstrating the inadequacy of current approaches to dealing with all kinds of international conflict. During the last year of the twentieth century, a series of humanitarian and political disasters shocked most observers and gave the world a foretaste of what is likely to be in store for the international community at the beginning of this century. In

Kosovo, over 850,000 people were driven out of the country in a massive and brutal ethnic cleansing the like of which Europe had not experienced since World War II. In Indonesia, gangs of armed thugs, with the active support of the military and police, waged a campaign of terror against the East Timorese people and against UN staff who were stationed there to monitor the referendum that would confirm East Timor's independence. Thousands of people were killed and as many as half of East Timor's 800,000 population fled their homes. The strategies of the respective authorities in both East Timor and Kosovo were to lay waste to the countries, depopulate them, and let the international community deal with the consequences. One and a half years later, despite large-scale international involvement in both countries, Kosovo and East Timor remained highly unstable.

While these examples happened to be the ones attracting the most headlines at the end of the twentieth century, they were far from the only humanitarian disasters. According to the *World Refugee Survey*, 35 million people—including refugees and internally displaced people—remained displaced worldwide at the end of the century.[2] Conflict and systematic human rights violations were the root cause of most displacements. Many of these displacements attracted little or no international attention. For example, during the past decade, the number of people killed in Colombia was four times the number killed in the Balkans and the number of internally displaced was at least 2 million people. The Russian army's brutal assault on Chechnya, which forced hundreds of thousands of people into exile, generated only muted Western complaints. Similarly, until recently, the international community ignored the violence, atrocities, and massive displacement occurring in Sierra Leone. As all-out conflict returned to Angola in 1999, 1.6 million people were displaced, with 950,000 civilians having been made refugees during the year. In the war between Ethiopia and Eritrea, over 50,000 people were killed and several hundred thousand were made homeless. Four million people in Sudan remained displaced after 16 years of endless fighting.

Indeed, the future is likely to represent a period of massive displacement in which most regions of the world will experience forced population movements. Armed conflict is no longer always identified with the clash of armies across borders but often with the assault by a government and its military on its own population or by rebel forces terrorizing their own society. While the crises with which the world has had to deal in recent years are not new,[3] conflict does seem to be increasingly brutal, endangering more civilians and aid workers than ever before. Widespread availability of high-powered arms has affected the intensity and duration of today's conflicts. Currently over 90 per cent of the casualties of armed conflicts are civilians. Wherever there is conflict, the most fundamental tenets of humanitarian law are being flagrantly abused and violated on a daily basis. In such conflicts, international conventions on the laws of war mean very little to the perpetrators of

atrocities. Children and women are particularly vulnerable in these circumstances. In Sierra Leone, rebels cut off the hands of teenaged boys and other
children, routinely raped teenaged girls, and trapped families in their houses
and torched them. A report by the Fondation de France on the 1994 genocide
in Rwanda suggested that almost all women and girls past puberty who had
not been massacred had been raped by the militias. In late 1998, the Special
Representative to the UN Secretary-General on Children in Armed Conflict,
Olara Otunnu, reported that some 9 million children were killed, injured,
orphaned, or separated from their parents during such conflicts in the past
decade.

The Role of the UNHCR in World Politics

The escalating plight of refugees at the beginning of the twenty-first century
underlines the need to re-evaluate both traditional and current practices and
the role of the High Commissioner. To clarify the new historical situation
facing the UNHCR—and to generate consensus for innovative responses to
the global refugee problem—it is essential to trace the roots and earlier experiences of the Office. International policy-makers and programme developers
who want to be prepared to deal with future refugee interventions need to be
familiar with the experiences of previous interventions and co-ordination
efforts in refugee crises. However, surprisingly little systematic research has
been done into the past policy responses of the UNHCR to international political and refugee crises.[4] Even within the UNHCR there is little knowledge or
appreciation of the past 50 years of working with refugees or its impact on
present policy and doctrine.[5] Much of the UNHCR's past experiences, both its
successes and failures, have been largely forgotten or ignored because of the
Office's preoccupation with more recent refugee crises. As a result, the
UNHCR lacks institutional memory and is always reinventing itself.

The evolution of the UNHCR has not taken place within a political
vacuum. While the international refugee problem has always been linked to
the political and security interests of states, the extensive literature on international relations hardly mentions the refugee question at all and attaches
little or no importance to it. There does not exist a recent comprehensive and
independent history of the UNHCR, its role in world politics, the nature of
the pressures upon it, and the impact it has made on the treatment or resolution of the world's refugee crises since its creation. This gap is all the more
remarkable given the rise on the international political agenda of the refugee
issue and the complex political, legal, and moral problems of forced displacement with which the organization attempts, and has been mandated, to deal.

This book situates the UNHCR within the context of world politics. In the international political system today, states remain the predominant actors. But this does not mean that international organizations like the UNHCR are completely without power or influence. Most High Commissioners have realized that in order to have had any impact on the world political arena they had to use the power of their expertise, ideas, strategies, and legitimacy to alter the information and value contexts in which states made policy. The Office has tried to project refugee norms into a world politics dominated by states driven by concerns of national interest and security. Successful High Commissioners have convinced states to define their national interests in ways compatible with refugee needs.

The UNHCR not only promotes the implementation of refugee norms; it also monitors compliance with international standards. Both the UNHCR Statute and the 1951 Refugee Convention authorize the organization to 'supervise' refugee conventions. This opens up the possibility for the UNHCR to make judgements or observations about state behaviour under refugee law and to challenge state policies when they endanger refugees.

For most of its history, the Office has acted as a 'teacher' of refugee norms.[6] The majority of the UNHCR's tactics have mainly involved persuasion and socialization in order to hold states accountable to their previously stated policies or principles. Past High Commissioners have frequently reminded Western states that as liberal democracies and open societies they are obliged to adhere to human rights norms in their asylum and refugee admissions policies. Because the UNHCR possesses specialized knowledge and expertise about refugee law, states often deferred to the Office on asylum matters. This was particularly the case before the 1980s when the UNHCR had a monopoly on information about refugee law and refugee movements. During the early decades of its existence, the Office enjoyed maximum legitimacy as it simultaneously tried to define the refugee issue for states, to convince governments that refugee problems were soluble, to prescribe solutions, and to monitor their implementation. In recent decades, as a result of increasing restrictionism on the parts of states, the UNHCR has lost its monopoly on information and expertise. Consequently, its authority and legitimacy in the realm of asylum has declined.

The UNHCR not only acted as a transmitter and monitor of refugee norms but also socialized new states to accept the promotion of refugee norms domestically as part of becoming a member of the international community. This socialization occurred first in the 1960s and 1970s in the newly independent countries of Asia, Africa, and Latin America, and later in the 1990s in the republics of the former Soviet Union. The political leaders of most newly independent governments in Africa, Asia, and the Commonwealth of Independent States care deeply about their international image and sought international legitimacy through co-operation with the UNHCR. High Commissioners sought to maximize their influence or leverage to affect the behaviour of states towards refugees, and different High Commissioners have used different strategies with varying degrees of success to accomplish these ends. In addition to exercising moral leverage to gain influence with states, the High Commissioner has repeatedly tried to link the refugee issue to states' material interests. Material assistance programmes have provided the UNHCR with significant leverage. Many new states were willing to adapt their behaviour to UNHCR pressures for purely instrumental reasons. International humanitarian assistance has provided resource-strapped governments with the means to cope with influxes of refugees. Thus, through a mixture of persuasion and socialization, the UNHCR has communicated the importance of refugee norms and convinced many new states that the benefits of signing the refugee legal instruments and joining the UNHCR Executive Committee—either as a member or an observer—outweighed the costs of remaining outside the international refugee regime.

The UNHCR has not just been an agent in world politics but a principal actor. This has been particularly true in situations where there has been a coincidence of humanitarian with political factors. While the UNHCR is constrained by states, the notion that it is a passive mechanism with no independent agenda of its own is not borne out by the empirical evidence of the past half-century. For example, it seems clear that the autonomy and authority of the UNHCR in world politics has grown over time and the Office has become a purposeful actor in its own right with independent interests and capabilities. This was especially the case in the formative phase of the organization but it is also the case that the UNHCR has not been solely an instrument of state interests in the last decade of the twentieth century. Rather it is more correct to say that UNHCR policy and practice have been driven both by state interests and by the Office acting independently or evolving in ways not expected nor necessarily sanctioned by states.

Realpolitik of Refugee Policy: The Impact of State Interests on the UNHCR

There has hardly ever been a time in the UNHCR's history when governments' foreign policies or strategic interests did not affect their stance towards the Office. And there has hardly ever been a time when states offered asylum and accepted refugees without some form of political calculation or discrimination. When the UNHCR opened its doors in January 1951, there was a remarkable symmetry in world politics. In the conflict between communism and capitalist democracy, each camp's view of good and evil was unquestionably identifiable. From its founding, the UNHCR was enmeshed in the international politics of the East-West conflict and refugees were perceived as elements of power in the bipolar rivalry.

In some respects, Cold War politics made life easy for the UNHCR and for Western governments. In a Manichaean political world, there was a clarity and simplicity in deciding refugee status. Recognizing persecution and identifying its perpetrators caused no headaches and the grant of asylum was generally used to reaffirm the failures of communism and the benevolence of the West. The UNHCR proved valuable to the West as an agency able to handle flows out of Eastern Europe for resettlement in the 'Free World', particularly after the 1956 Hungarian Uprising. International refugee policy not only saved many individuals who were subject to repression in commu- nist dictatorships, but it also clearly served the geopolitical interests of the United States and its allies.[7]

During the 1950s, Europe was the principal area of refugee concern as the Cold War intensified and new refugee flows moved from East to West. While the Eurocentric orientation of the UNHCR reflected the international polit- ical environment, it also reflected the foreign policy priorities of the United States and the other major Western governments. Two things critically affected the lens through which Washington viewed both its own refugee policy and the UNHCR. One was the reconstruction and rehabilitation effort in Europe after World War II and the other was the rapidly developing Cold War. US policy makers considered refugee issues within the same policy framework as national security and even limited refugees by definition as only those fleeing Communism. US generosity of asylum towards refugees from Eastern Europe was in part motivated by a desire to 'roll back' or at least contain Communism by encouraging East European citizens to escape their homelands. Refugees became instruments of the Cold War, representing increments of power and sources of espionage and information. Refugees also became important symbols in the ideological rivalry of the Cold War. 'Escapees' who crossed over to the West 'voted with their feet' and repres- ented a significant political and ideological asset for the West. This, in turn, contributed to the determination of Communist regimes to impose severe barriers on exit.

At the height of the Cold War, American leaders considered refugee policy too important to permit the United Nations to control it and they did not want their freedom of action in the refugee field to be constrained by the UN. To this end, the United States sought to limit severely the functional scope and independence of the UNHCR and instead created two other US-led organ- izations which were parallel to and outside the purview of the United Nations. These were the International Committee of European Migration (ICEM) and the US Escapee Program. The United States was also instrumental in establishing specially created UN agencies in the Middle East and the Korean Peninsula, which handled refugee populations that were located in strategic conflict areas where US geopolitical interests were significant. The United States funded all of these organizations much more generously than it did the UNHCR, and for a time these organizations provided the United States with a pretext for completely withholding financial support from the UN-based refugee regime.

The denial of American financial and diplomatic support directly affected the UNHCR's ability to define an independent role and to implement its goals and programmes. Even five years after its founding, and despite large refugee flows around the world, governments deliberately kept the UNHCR small and confined it to providing legal protection for displaced persons who had not been resettled by the International Refugee Organization (IRO).

The UNHCR Strives for Autonomy

Despite the opposition of Western governments, the UNHCR began to exercise power autonomously in ways unintended by states at its creation. The first High Commissioner, Gerrit van Heuven Goedhart, initially enlarged the scope of his Office by obtaining the capacity to independently raise funds and by assuming material assistance responsibilities. A grant from the Ford Foundation enabled the UNHCR to take the lead role in responding to a refugee crisis in West Berlin in early 1953, thereby demonstrating its usefulness to the major powers and raising the Office's international profile. These early successes legitimized the need for UNHCR material assistance to refugees and directly led to the establishment of a UNHCR programme for permanent solutions and emergency assistance. This paved the way for the UN to designate the UNHCR as the 'lead agency' directing the international emergency operation for Hungarian refugees in 1956, despite initial American opposition.

The Hungarian operation demonstrated the important diplomatic role that the High Commissioner could play in events at the centre of world politics. In the midst of the first major Cold War refugee crisis, the UNHCR played an essential mediating role between East and West involving the repatriation of nearly 10 per cent of the Hungarian refugees. This operation was extremely controversial and was initially opposed by Western governments who considered repatriation to socialist countries unthinkable.

Thus, largely on its own initiatives, UNHCR grew from a strictly non-operational agency with no authority to appeal for funds, to an institution with a long-range programme emphasizing not only protection but, increasingly, material assistance. This remarkable transition not only demonstrated the tension between state interests and the drive for relative autonomy on the part of an international organization, but it also underlined the capacity of the UNHCR to have an independent influence on events at the centre of world politics.

During the 1950s, the UNHCR took initial steps to lay the groundwork for an expansion of its activities to the developing world. This new approach was the 'good offices' formula which involved the UN General Assembly granting the UNHCR the authority to raise funds or to initiate assistance programmes for operations outside its usual mandate.

The first major expansion of the UNHCR into the developing world occurred as a result of refugees from the Algerian war of independence fleeing to neighbouring Tunisia and Morocco. The second High Commissioner, Auguste Lindt, felt assistance to the Algerian refugees presented an opportunity for the UNHCR to use the new international support and goodwill it had earned in its response to the Hungarian refugee emergency to confirm its position as the leading international refugee agency. Lindt feared the UNHCR would be accused of discriminatory treatment if it neglected the Algerians, and he did not want to be perceived as the 'High Commissioner for European refugees only'. He felt that the UNHCR mandate as defined in its statute was worldwide and that his Office had a responsibility for dealing 'with completely different people and not only refugees from communism'.[8] He was concerned that to refuse assistance to Tunisia and Morocco would estrange the organization from a growing bloc of developing nations and would weaken the more favourable attitude that the Soviet bloc had recently adopted towards the agency.

The decision to aid Algerian refugees was politically difficult, however, and the UNHCR had to overcome strong government opposition. The French government denied the authority of the UNHCR to give assistance in this case, fearing its involvement would internationalize the crisis. Only through persistent and courageous diplomacy on the part of the High Commissioner was French resistance to UNHCR involvement overcome. Indeed, it was one of Lindt's most noteworthy diplomatic accomplishments.

The UNHCR initiated and capitalized on international political developments to expand its scope both operationally and geographically. In the view of many developing states, the UNHCR's action on behalf of Algerians signified a turning point in the Office's geographical reach and function. The Algerian operation was a bridgehead leading to a period of both global and institutional growth for the UNHCR.

The 1960s to the 1980s: the Cold War, the Third World, and the UNHCR

During the 1960s and 1970s the Cold War extended beyond Europe into parts of the third world. Violent decolonization, as well as post-independence civil strife and warfare in Africa, generated vast numbers of refugees and underscored the strategic importance of conflicts outside Europe. Both the East and West vied for influence in Africa and Asia, trying to minimize the possibilities of their ideological and strategic opponents gaining political advantage in these regions. Throughout the third world, the US and USSR competed to build up local allies and, through economic aid, political support and weapons deliveries, constructed a range of client regimes which included not only governments but also liberation movements. The United States perceived refugee problems in developing countries as sources of instability which the Soviet Union could exploit for its own advantage in extending hegemony in the third world. In the face of an escalating Cold War struggle, Western governments came to perceive assistance to refugees as a central part of their foreign policy towards newly independent states, thus using foreign aid as one of the principal tools in this East–West struggle for influence. International action on the refugee issue was also now viewed as a way to deal with potential sources of instability in the third world. At the same time, a number of newly independent African and Asian member states joined the United Nations making it possible for the UN to pass resolutions that authorized the UNHCR to assist a broad category of people displaced by conflict outside of Europe. Consequently, by the 1980s virtually all of the UNHCR's activity occurred in the developing world.

The UNHCR capitalized on these 'winds of change' that heralded the new international political developments in Africa and the rest of the developing world to expand its scope both operationally and geographically. The two High Commissioners during this period were Felix Schnyder and Sadruddin Aga Khan. Both were politically astute and anticipated major political transformations in the international system, namely decolonization and the emergence of newly independent states in Africa and Asia. Neither was surprised by the mass exoduses of refugees in the developing world. Schnyder and Sadruddin realized that the traditional concepts and legal definitions that the Office had used in Europe would not apply in the less developed countries and took steps to adapt the international refugee instruments to the new environment.

After its expansion into Africa in the 1960s, the UNHCR, under Sadruddin Aga Khan, rapidly evolved into a truly global organization during the next decade. Refugee emergencies emerged on all continents, multiplied, and took on numerical proportions hitherto unknown. The UNHCR embarked on new assistance programmes in a number of refugee and 'refugee-like' situations around the world. Sadruddin, an expansionist High Commissioner, was determined to make the UNHCR the most important international humanitarian organization and he largely accomplished this objective.

In the 1971 Bangladeshi crisis, the UNHCR's assumed the role of 'focal point' for the overall relief effort for some 10 million refugees. This would be the first of many refugee crises in which UNHCR would be called upon by the

Secretary-General to act as the UN lead agency for the co-ordination of international humanitarian assistance. As a result, the UNHCR developed an enormous agenda and became an indispensable and autonomous actor in many of the major political developments in Africa, Asia, and Latin America.

During most of the 1960s and 1970s, the UNHCR experienced few of the kinds of asylum problems in the industrialized states that would confront the Office in later decades. Most governments acknowledged the UNHCR Protection Division's unrivalled specialized knowledge and expertise concerning refugee and asylum law and deferred to the Office's authority on asylum policy. The UNHCR played an active role in the refugee determination procedures of many industrialized states—with the notable exception of the United States—and exerted a considerable influence over government decisions. Hence, the UNHCR's authority and autonomy was enhanced, and most governments in Western Europe demonstrated a generally liberal attitude towards asylum-seekers.

The New Cold War, Proxy Conflicts, and the UNHCR

The intensification of the Cold War during the late 1970s and the 1980s shifted the structure of the bipolar conflict. The rivalry between the United States and the USSR caused both powers to build up client states across the globe and to arm and supply local and regional conflicts.

As a result, internal wars in Indochina, Afghanistan, Central America, the Horn of Africa, and Southern Africa became globalized. These conflicts perpetuated endemic violence which, in turn, generated large outpourings of refugees. Some of these refugees were resettled in other regions or continents but most remained in neighbouring countries from where they continued to actively participate in the conflicts. During the 1980s, 'refugee warriors' used refugee camps in Pakistan, along the Thai-Cambodian border, in Central America, in Southern Africa, and in the Horn of Africa to provide themselves with food and medicines, to forcibly recruit new soldiers, and to raise revenue. These refugee warrior communities served as important instruments and proxies both in the interventionist policies of the external powers and in regional power struggles.[9]

UNHCR involvement with militarized refugee camps presented the Office with considerable headaches. Because combatants were present in refugee camps, the armed forces of sending governments viewed these settlements as legitimate military targets. Relief supplies provided by humanitarian organizations ended up feeding refugee warriors, thus helping to sustain and prolong conflicts.[10]

The UNHCR under Sadruddin's successor, Poul Hartling, found it difficult to maintain an impartial and humanitarian approach to its work. Virtually all of its funding came from Western governments who had a geopolitical interest in supporting UNHCR camps, which housed anti-communist refugees. In a situation similar to the 1990s, states used UNHCR and humanitarian assistance as an excuse for political inaction in resolving long-standing regional conflicts. This cost the UNHCR the relative autonomy it had developed during the Sadruddin era.

The UNHCR's protracted care and maintenance programmes caused annual UNHCR expenditures to explode. The annual budget of the UNHCR doubled each year from 1978 to 1980. Conditions in countries of origin rarely permitted repatriation, either because of conflict or because the refugee-sending state discouraged the return of exiles. In addition, as the 'second' Cold War froze political relations between Moscow and Washington, the international community failed to devise comprehensive or long-term political solutions or to provide any alternatives to prolonged camp existence.

At the same time, a growing number of third world refugees appeared on the doorsteps of Western countries to seek asylum. Unlike in earlier periods, these 'jet age' refugees were no longer confined to their region of origin and now travelled directly to Western countries by air transport. The asylum crisis in the industrialized world further raised the overall financial cost of the global refugee problem for the donor state community. The ensuing asylum crisis put Western governments into direct conflict with the UNHCR, which struggled but ultimately lost the fight to maintain its position as the principal source of legitimacy and influence over refugee and asylum policy in Europe.

By the mid-1980s, the UNHCR became identified with costly long-term care and maintenance in refugee camps around the world. To relieve the costs that protracted, large-scale, forced displacements imposed, donor governments began to promote alternative approaches to the refugee problem, particularly repatriation. Governments also appointed a new High Commissioner, Jean-Pierre Hocke, whom they felt could help them break out of this deadlock and to make the Office more relevant to the contemporary refugee problem. Hocke advocated a new strategy that required the UNHCR to deal not only with asylum countries but also with countries of origin and with the 'root causes' of refugee exoduses. In particular, the High Commissioner identified repatriation as 'the only realistic alternative to indefinite subsistence on charity'.[11] This analysis of the refugee crisis and the UNHCR's role presaged many of the policies and practices that the Office would try to put into effect in the post-Cold War period of the 1990s. However, Hocke's ideas were clearly too far ahead of his time. Throughout most of the 1980s, Cold War politics continued to paralyse diplomatic initiatives to break the deadlock of regional conflicts in most of Africa, Asia, and Central America. Consequently, most refugees were destined to remain trapped in camps for most of the decade. Donor governments soon became disillusioned with the UNHCR and Hocke in particular. This led to a major financial crisis for the agency by the end of the decade.

The Post-Cold War Era and UNHCR: International Security and Refugees

The 1990s ushered in a new era in which humanitarian issues played a historically unprecedented role in international politics. Refugee movements assumed a new degree of political importance in the discourse about global and regional security and were the subject of increasing discussion in political and military fora such as the UN Security Council and the North Atlantic Treaty Organization. The new security importance of refugee movements, combined with greatly increased global media coverage, forced the international community to focus more urgently on refugee issues. In the early 1990s, a political consensus prevailed for the first time since 1945, which enabled the UN Security Council to support collective interventionist policies previously thought to be impossible.

In the 1990s, refugees came to be viewed as posing threats to international security, thus providing a basis for action under Chapter 7 of the UN Charter. In northern Iraq, Somalia, former Yugoslavia, and Haiti, international intervention across borders and in the domestic affairs of states was authorized in response to refugee flows. Moreover, forced displacements were also at the centre of crises in the African Great Lakes region, Liberia, Sierra Leone, Albania, Kosovo, and East Timor. In most of these cases, the UN, or regional or national forces acting with UN authorization, directly intervened in intrastate conflicts in an attempt to tackle these crises which led to mass displacement.

At the same time, without a clear ideological divide in the post-Cold War conflicts, the major powers, including the United States, were reluctant to become directly involved. This was particularly true in Africa where their strategic interests were limited. Refugees were no longer of symbolic or instrumental value to the US. Rather, refugees were perceived increasingly as burdens, particularly if they made a claim for asylum in the West. In response, governments became more restrictionist and pushed for a comprehensive international refugee policy which sought to modify the causes of refugee flows through conflict resolution, peacemaking, and peacekeeping. At the same time, governments felt compelled to respond to refugee disasters, especially those covered extensively by the media, and therefore repeatedly tasked the UNHCR and other international agencies to provide relief aid. For the world's most powerful states, the provision of humanitarian assistance was financially and politically a relatively low risk option because it satisfied the demands of the media and public opinion for some kind of action to alleviate human suffering. But it was also used repeatedly by governments as an excuse for refusing to take more decisive forms of political and military intervention.

The UNHCR's Broadened International Agenda

For the UNHCR, these shifts in attitudes about intervention meant greater involvement in situations of internal armed conflict. The Office was often involved in sharing responsibility with UN mandated military forces for the assistance of displaced people, and a renewed emphasis on encouraging early repatriations despite the uncertainties and dangers for refugees. Under Sadako Ogata, the UNHCR made a concerted effort to frame its policies in terms of state interests in resolving conflicts and refugee problems. The high priority given to humanitarian operations and the increasing recognition of a link between refugees and international security meant that UNHCR played an increasingly important role in international political negotiations and exerted material leverage over states. The High Commissioner showed a sophisticated awareness of the political opportunities that the post-Cold War environment presented her agency. She sought to raise the salience of the global refugee problem, and the Office's international profile and credibility, by skilfully using the media to affect public opinion and to mobilize government support for her agency.

During the 1990s, fundamental changes occurred in the international refugee regime. Many of the changes concerned the way in which the UNHCR operated. During the Cold War, in-country assistance and protection involved violation of state sovereignty and therefore was taboo for UN agencies. In the post-Cold War period, by contrast, the UNHCR attempted to tackle refugee-producing situations at or near their source. This major change in the handling of refugee issues included an increased focus on working in countries of origin—even in countries at war—to reduce the likelihood of massive refugee flows across borders. In addition, the UNHCR was also frequently asked to take part in comprehensive and integrated UN peace-keeping or peacemaking operations that involved political and military actors of the UN. In response, the UNHCR extended its services to a much wider range of people who were in need of assistance including returnees, internally displaced people, war-affected populations, the victims of mass expulsions, and unsuccessful asylum-seekers, as well as refugees. For example, 'war-affected populations'—people who have not been uprooted but need humanitarian assistance and protection—comprised a substantial proportion of the

UNHCR's beneficiary population during the height of the 1990s Bosnian conflict. As a result, the numbers of displaced people and war-affected populations receiving UNHCR assistance increased dramatically. The number of people of concern to the UNHCR increased from 15 million in 1990 to a peak of 26 million in 1996. Of this total of the UNHCR's beneficiaries, refugees constituted only about 50 per cent. Consequently, the UNHCR expanded from a refugee organization into a more broadly-based operational agency driven by emergencies.

With these momentous changes, the UNHCR became synonymous with large-scale international relief programmes to victims of armed conflict and ethnic cleansing. Successes and failures of humanitarian action were judged primarily in terms of technical standards of aid delivery and in fulfilling the material needs of refugees and threatened populations. Under pressure to ensure the very survival of several hundreds of thousands, if not millions of people, the central importance of human rights protection of displaced and threatened populations was frequently neglected.

Not only did the new humanitarian emergencies diminish the UNHCR's core role in affording protection, but they also compromised its scope and effectiveness as refugee crises became more intractable. The UNHCR and other humanitarian actors found themselves enmeshed in highly militarized and politicized situations such as was found in the African Great Lakes after the Rwandan genocide. Critics maintained that, in the former Zaïre, the UNHCR exacerbated the situation there by providing assistance to militants in the camps, thereby contributing to greater humanitarian crises in the long run.

In almost every refugee crisis in the 1990s, camps were subject to some sort of military pressure. There was bombardment by the Turkish air force of Kurdish camps in northern Iraq, forced military recruitment from camps in Sierra Leone, which also aided the movement of militias between Sierra Leone and Liberia, raids by rebel forces of Sudanese camps in northern Uganda, and pressured recruitment by the Kosovo Liberation Army of refugees out of camps in Albania and Macedonia. Few active steps were taken to prevent the militarization of refugee camps. The main focus of the international humanitarian response to refugee crises remained material assistance at the expense of the human rights protection of refugees.

The UNHCR and the International 'Asylum Crisis'

Increasing humanitarian action to respond to refugee crises coincided with a weakening of traditional protection and asylum mechanisms in most states. In the face of growing numbers of illegal migrants and abuse of asylum procedures, Western governments became increasingly reluctant to grant asylum. They enacted severe controls on immigration which reduced the scope of appeals from decisions on refugee eligibility and erected barriers to those seeking refuge from war and persecution as well as those looking for jobs and new homes. The closure of borders to prevent unwanted refugee and migrant influxes became much more widespread than it was during the Cold War. In place of asylum, various forms of 'temporary protection' were utilized to deal with those fleeing war and ethnic cleansing. Thus, at the end of the twentieth century, refugees became a symbol of system overload, instead of a symbol of what was always best in the Western liberal tradition.

The trend towards excluding asylum-seekers spread to governments in the South as well as the North. For developing countries, the growing numbers of displaced people entering already overloaded economies presented problems that threatened governmental authority. Alarmed by the economic, environmental, social, and security costs of hosting mass influxes of refugees, a number of governments across the world took steps to exclude asylum-seekers from their territory and to ensure the rapid—and in some cases involuntary—repatriation of refugees. Diminishing donor government support for long-term refugee assistance, coupled with declining levels of official development assistance, and the imposition of structural adjustment programmes on many poorer and less stable states, reinforced this attitude and contributed to the hostility towards refugees.

The UNHCR and its Focus on Repatriation as the Pre-eminent Solution to Refugee Problems

Accompanying the 'asylum crisis' was a renewed emphasis by states on repatriation as the 'pre-eminent solution' to the refugee problem. Governments insisted that refugees return to their homes at the earliest opportunity, often with the assistance of the UNHCR, whether or not conditions were conducive to such returns. Before the late 1980s, the UNHCR's Western donors actively discouraged repatriation as most of the world's refugees originated from communist countries. When repatriation did occur, to a large extent, refugees themselves decided when to return and under what conditions. The precondition for the involvement of the UNHCR in repatriations included such factors as 'fundamental change of circumstances, voluntary nature of the decision to return, tripartite agreements between the state of origin, the host state and the UNHCR and return in safety and dignity'.[12] With the ending of the Cold War, repatriation was increasingly perceived as the only effective solution to refugee problems. As the superpowers with-

drew from long-standing regional conflicts, the numbers of refugees returning home increased dramatically. During the 1990s, some 12 million
refugees returned home either on their own initiative or under the auspices
of the UNHCR.[13] By this time too, governments everywhere were also
becoming more restrictionist and were exerting pressure on the UNHCR to
encourage and promote the return of refugees to their home countries as
quickly as possible.

State pressure to promote repatriation was accompanied by new thinking
about repatriation within the UNHCR.[14] To respond to the new international
political environment of the early 1990s, repatriation became a central part of
the UNHCR's new global strategy of preventive protection. In the UNHCR's
eyes it was far better for most refugees to return home at the earliest opportunity to benefit from the UNHCR's repatriation programmes than to remain
in refugee camps that could offer them no future. The Office posited that
conditions in the home country did not have to improve substantially but
only enough to allow refugees to return home in safety. This shift in terminology made it much more likely that the UNHCR would promote repatriations under less than strict conditions of voluntary repatriation. For the
UNHCR this was a dramatic shift from its traditional position that repatriation had to be a strictly voluntary decision on the part of refugees. Rather, it
would now be the UNHCR and states that would make the assessment as to
whether conditions were safe enough for refugees to return. Moreover, there
was a growing view that refugee safety did not necessarily and always
outweigh the security interests of states or broader peace building and conflict
resolution goals. Thus, in the early 1990s, repatriation came to be perceived
as part of the Office's emphasis on preventive protection and encouraging the
responsibility of countries of origin toward their own citizens. Unfortunately,
repatriation did not always serve refugees' interests. The return of refugees
from Bangladesh to Burma and from Tanzania and former Zaïre to Rwanda
and Burundi are only two illustrations of situations in which the UNHCR co-
operated with host governments to return refugees home before conditions
had become safe.

Because the UNHCR focused almost entirely on repatriation during the
past decade, it virtually ignored other possible solutions, often to the detriment of refugees. With less donor funding for operations other than repatriation and emergency relief, a range of traditional solutions—local
integration projects, educational programmes, income-generating projects,
and the promotion of refugee participation—disappeared from the Office's
possible options for long-staying refugee populations. Instead, believing that
return provided the only humane solution to refugee problems, the UNHCR
essentially ran long-term programmes in an emergency mode, which was
damaging to the long-term welfare of refugees stuck in protracted camp situations.

The UNHCR at the Beginning of the
Twenty-First Century

An era of relative simplicity and generosity in refugee affairs has long ago passed and we are in the midst of a more complex and difficult period. The decline in generosity and openness towards the uprooted and persecuted has occurred because of a radically different international political environment and 'compassion fatigue' brought about by overexposure to humanitarian crises. The present reality is that the Cold War interest in taking refugees from the Communist world has passed with the collapse of European Communism and has now been replaced by a growing state interest in keeping refugees out, or in sending them back home. This is a worldwide trend.

These crises are placing the UNHCR under growing pressure in regard to both its functions and identity. A radically transformed UNHCR aimed at preventing conditions that generate refugee flows, assisting many of those caught in brutal civil conflicts, and promoting refugee return has also emerged in recent years. But these new developments in UNHCR policy directions raise questions about the adequacy of the agency's mandate given recent changes in international relations. What is the appropriate role of an intergovernmental agency in balancing the protection of individual and group rights against the sovereign prerogatives and interests of states? There is a widespread concern as to whether the UNHCR's expansion into humanitarian assistance will be at the further expense of protection of refugees and displaced people. Indeed, many persons within the UNHCR, governments, and the non-governmental community fear for the survival of the Office's traditional mandate, namely the international protection of refugees.

Never has there been a more appropriate time to ask fundamental questions about the UNHCR and the future directions and objectives of the Office. The UNHCR functions with an imperfect mandate, under circumstances necessitating competition with other agencies for limited resources, and in political environments that are inhospitable to crisis management and refugee protection. The Office is frequently expected to work within exceedingly complex and insecure situations with little or no backing from the international community. The UNHCR has an organizational culture that makes it extremely difficult to learn from past mistakes and therefore some of the same errors are repeated from one operation to another. The UNHCR can occasionally act in expedient but irresponsible ways, such as when it coerces refugees by closing down camps or reducing food rations and services in an effort to get refugees to repatriate. The agency is largely unaccountable for programmes and policies that are insensitive or damaging to the protection and assistance needs of refugees. The Office lacks strong policy research and strategic thinking capacities.

While there are no simple solutions to such endemic problems, it is necessary for the UNHCR to begin to confront these difficulties by examining its history as a refugee protection agency. The following chapters examine patterns of refugee problems during the last half century and how these were addressed by the UNHCR and the international community. The book concludes with an overall assessment of the agency and its High Commissioners and provides suggestions for how the UNHCR might perform more effectively and humanely in the future.

NOTES

1. *Statute of the United Nations High Commissioner for Refugees*, HCR/INF/Rev.3, para. 2, United Nations, 1950.
2. US Committee for Refugees, *World Refugee Survey 2000* (Washington, DC: US Committee for Refugees, 2000).
3. Mark Frohardt, Diane Paul, and Larry Minear, *Protecting Human Rights: The Challenge to Humanitarian Organizations*, Occasional Paper 35 (Providence, RI: Watson Institute for International Studies, Brown University,1999); and Gil Loescher, *Beyond Charity: International Cooperation and the Global Refugee Crisis* (New York, NY: Oxford University Press, 1993).
4. The last attempt at writing an overall history of the UNHCR, Louise Holborn's *Refugees: A Problem of Our Time: The Work of the United Nations High Commissioner for Refugees* (Metuchen, NJ: Scarecrow Press, 1975), was published in 1975. However, this is largely a UNHCR sponsored account of the Office's early operations and not an independent policy analysis. It also does not place the Office within the larger context of international relations.
5. The UNHCR, *State of the World's Refugees: Fifty Years of Humanitarian Action* (Oxford: Oxford University Press, 2000) is a welcome exception but it is understandably limited in its criticism of the agency and its operations as well as of governments' policies.
6. There is a growing literature on the impact of ideas and norms in international politics and international organizations. See: Martha Finnemore, 'Norms, Culture, and World Politics: Insights from Sociology's Institutionalism', *World Politics*, i/2 (Spring 1996): 325-48; Thomas Risse, Stephen Ropp, and Kathryn Sikkink, eds., *The Power of Human Rights: International Norms and Domestic Change* (Cambridge: Cambridge University Press, 1999); and Margaret Keck and Kathryn Sikkink, *Activists Beyond Borders: Advocacy Networks in International Politics* (Ithaca, NY: Cornell University Press, 1998).
7. The economic and employment situation of the 1950s also posed few problems which could not be overcome through greater international co-operation. Economic recovery and productivity were spurred by postwar reconstruction. States in Europe and the New World rebuilding for the future and beset by manpower shortages actively sought refugees and migrant workers. While it has never been easy to promote refugee relief and resettlement, the hostility and

resistance to refugee movements which exist among many states today was nearly unknown.

8. UNHCR interview with Auguste Lindt, Bern, Switzerland, 4 February 1998.

9. For further elaboration of these points see: Astri Suhrke, 'Uncertain Globalization: Refugee Movements in the Second Half of the Twentieth Century,' in Wang Gungwu, ed., *Global History and Migrations* (Boulder, CO: Westview Press, 1997): 217–37; Aristide Zolberg, Astri Suhrke, and Sergio Aguayo, *Escape from Violence: Conflict and the Refugee Crisis in the Developing World* (New York, NY: Oxford University Press, 1989); and Peter Koehn, *Refugees from Revolution: U.S. Policy and Third World Migration* (Boulder, CO: Westview Press, 1991).

10. This was not an entirely new problem for the UNHCR. During the 1970s, the camps for South African refugees in Mozambique and Tanzania, for Rhodesian refugees in Mozambique and Zambia, and for Namibian refugees in Angola were all controlled by their respective liberation movements and were consequently subject to raids by the South African and Rhodesian armed forces.

11. These views were expressed in Jean-Pierre Hocke, 'Beyond Humanitarianism: The Need for Political Will to Resolve Today's Refugee Problem,' in Gil Loescher and Laila Monahan, eds., *Refugees and International Relations* (Oxford: Clarendon Press, 1989): 37–48.

12. B. S. Chimni, 'The Meaning of Words and the Role of UNHCR in Voluntary Repatriation', *International Journal of Refugee Law*, 5 (1993): 442.

13. Richard Black and Khalid Koser, eds., *The End of the Refugee Cycle: Refugee Repatriation and Reconstruction* (New York, NY: Berghahn Books, 1999): 3

14. Michael Barnett, 'Humanitarianism with a Sovereign Face: UNHCR in the Global Undertow', *International Migration Review* (forthcoming).

2

International Recognition of Refugees

People today are inclined to perceive refugees as a relatively new phenomenon that primarily occurs in Africa or Asia, and in war-torn countries in the Balkans and the former Soviet Union. Certainly during the past few decades most refugees have fled violent conflicts or persecution in the developing countries but mass refugee movements are neither new nor exclusive to the third world. They have been a political as well as a humanitarian issue for as long as mankind has lived in organized groups where intolerance and oppression have existed. The difference is that, before this century, refugees were regarded as assets rather than liabilities. Countries granted refuge to people of geopolitical importance and religious or ideological views similar to their own, and rulers viewed control over large populations—along with natural resources and territory itself—as an index of power and national greatness.[1]

While most refugees of earlier eras found it possible to gain safe haven outside their countries of origin, this has not been the case for many refugees in the twentieth century. After both World Wars, Europe experienced refugee flows similar to those taking place in the third world today. Like most contemporary refugee movements, people left their homes for varied and complex reasons, including the severe economic disruption and starvation that accompanied war and the upheaval of political and social revolution that followed the breakup of multi-ethnic empires and the creation of new nation-states. The majority of these people were members of unwanted minority groups, political fugitives, or the hapless victims of warfare, communalism, and indiscriminate violence. Essentially, the refugee problems of the period from 1921 to 1951 were political ones, as they are today.

The international responses to mass expulsions, compulsory transfers of population, mass exits, and arbitrary denial of return were often weak and inconsistent. In circumstances similar to those that exist today, mass influxes threatened the security of European states, particularly when many refugee crises became protracted affairs that surpassed the capability of humanitarian agencies and individual states to resolve.

Organized international efforts for refugees began in 1921 when the League of Nations appointed the first High Commissioner for Refugees. Over the next twenty years, the scope and functions of assistance programmes gradually expanded, as efforts were made to regularize the status and control of stateless and denationalized people. During and after World War II, two expensive and politically controversial refugee organizations with radically different mandates further developed the international organizational framework. They were the United Nations Relief and Rehabilitation Agency (UNRRA) and the International Refugee Organization (IRO). Since 1951, an international refugee regime—composed of the UN High Commissioner for Refugees and a network of other international agencies, national governments, and voluntary or non-governmental organizations—has developed a response strategy that permits some refugees to remain in their countries of first asylum, enables some to be resettled in third countries, and arranges for still others to be repatriated to their countries of origin. Although unevenly applied, there are international laws that designate refugees as a unique category of human rights victims who should be accorded special protection and benefits. These have been signed, ratified, and in force for several decades.

Causes of the 1920s Refugee Movements

During the late nineteenth and the early twentieth centuries, the causes and dimensions of the refugee problem assumed a modern character not too different from the present era. The changing nature of international warfare, the dissolution of the old multinational empires in Eastern Europe and the Balkan region, and the expansion of nation-states, accompanied by the deliberate persecution of minority and stateless groups and the elimination of former ruling classes and opposition groups, were the immediate causes of most refugee movements during the first several decades of the twentieth century.

Although war has always generated some refugees, it is only in the twentieth century that international conflict began to affect entire populations.[2] With the advent of wider technological, economic, and social changes, the scale and destructiveness of military conflict has grown enormously; enemy civilians as well as opposing armed forces have become military targets. This elimination of the distinction between combatants and non-combatants has resulted in vast numbers of refugees desperate to escape the ravages of indiscriminate violence.

A second cause of refugee movements during the early part of this century was the formation, consolidation, and expansion of the nation-state system. In Europe, the multinational Habsburg, Romanov, Ottoman, and Hohenzollern empires all succumbed to the pressures and conflicts that accompanied the transition from imperial social and political orders to successor nation-states.[3] As World War I accelerated the dismantling of these multi-ethnic empires into nation-states, masses of people were excluded from citizenship on grounds of language, location, ethnicity, or religious affiliation. Claudena Skran notes that newly formed governments in Austria, Czechoslovakia, Estonia, Hungary, Latvia, Lithuania, Poland, and Yugoslavia tried to eliminate the old order and consolidate their power by creating culturally and politically homogeneous populations.[4] Approximately two million Poles migrated to Poland, and one million ethnic Germans moved to Germany from their previous homes in the Russian and Austro-Hungarian Empires.[5] Hungary received several hundred thousand Magyar refugees driven out by the successor states of Romania, Czechoslovakia, and Yugoslavia.

In a continuation of a policy of 'ethnic cleansing' begun in the late nineteenth century, the Turks intensified their massacres and genocide of the Armenians. During 1914–19, between 500,000 and 1 million Armenians died, and survivors fled to Soviet Armenia, Syria, and other parts of Europe and the Middle East.[6]

At the end of World War I, in a series of Minority Treaties, Western powers attempted to provide for the elementary rights of the ethnic minorities who were threatened as a result of the redrawing of national boundaries.[7] However, as the global economic situation deteriorated following the initial postwar recovery, minorities quickly became scapegoats. Governments defined broad categories of people as belonging to the nation-state and relegated others to the ranks of outsiders and aliens who threatened national and cultural cohesion. Many national minority groups were immediately naturalized by their new country, but some groups were not so fortunate.

As nations redefined their borders and identities and the 'unmixing of peoples' was imposed on sometimes reluctant populations, millions of people were rendered stateless. The Balkan Wars and the transformation of the ethnically heterogenous Ottoman Empire into a number of more homogeneous nation-states generated mass refugee movements in the Balkans. Hostilities between Turkey and Greece resulted in the Greco–Turkish War of 1922, which displaced 1 million more Anatolian Greek and Armenian refugees.

To the chaos in southeastern Europe and Asia Minor were added huge refugee movements generated by the collapse of tsarist Russia, the Russian civil war, the Russo-Polish war, and the Soviet famine of 1921.[8] These cataclysmic events dispersed between 1 and 2 million people—mainly Russians— from the Russian Empire mostly to Germany and France but also as far away as China in the east and North America in the west. The Russian refugees included many people that the Communist Party perceived to be obstacles to achieving revolutionary change in the new Soviet Union. The migration also included the soldiers of the defeated White Russian armies who had participated in the Russian Civil War, civilians fleeing the chaos and famine brought about by the revolution and civil war, ethnic Russians fleeing newly independent Poland and the Baltic states, and Russian Jews facing persecution.[9]

The cumulative result of these events was the largest displacement of peoples in Europe in modern times. By the early 1920s, the Soviet Union issued decrees that revoked the citizenship of many of its nationals. Without national identity papers or passports, expelled Russians could not legally stay, move on, or return to their homes. Unlike other refugee groups joining new nation-states, the Russians were not quickly naturalized by their host governments. They were said to threaten the national homogeneity of states where an explosive ethnic balance already existed.[10] Moreover, the emigres, particularly the ex-soldiers among them, were also perceived to pose a destabilizing political threat to the newly formed regimes.[11]

Vast numbers of Russians wandered all over the European continent, where they became a source of interstate friction. The sheer numbers of these refugees, their virtual expulsion from their homeland, and the long years of their displaced wanderings made their collective fate in the twentieth century qualitatively different from that of other groups forced into exile by earlier political or religious upheavals. Fearful of further mass influxes of unwanted refugees, governments rushed to erect protective barriers and close borders. Most responded to the plight of refugees by simply expelling as many displaced persons as they could round up. Hundreds of thousands of people were consequently plunged into an endless cycle of illegal entry, clandestine existence, expulsion, and yet another illegal entry.

The problem of refugees became a source of interstate tension that far exceeded the limited capacity of individual governments to ameliorate. By 1921, the resources of the voluntary agencies that assisted the stateless Russians were exhausted. The principal humanitarian organizations of the period, headed by the International Committee of the Red Cross, prevailed upon the League of Nations to create international machinery for dealing with at least some of the refugees.

The High Commissioner for Refugees

In 1920, Fridtjof Nansen, the world famous Norwegian explorer, was given the task of negotiating the repatriation of Russian war prisoners and a year later he was appointed the first High Commissioner for Refugees with specific responsibilities for Russian refugees only.

The League established strict guidelines within which refugee work had to take place. Governments mandated that aid be limited to Russian refugees, that League funds be spent only on administration and not on direct relief, and that refugee assistance be considered temporary.[12] For most of the inter-war period, the international refugee regime ran on extremely limited *ad hoc* budgets, put together without benefit of long-range planning. Financially the

League provided only for administrative costs: aid to refugees and host governments depended on direct financial assistance from individual states or voluntary agencies. The refugee regime lacked the political and financial support of most League members and later proved to be totally ineffective in responding to the Holocaust. There simply was no widespread agreement that refugee aid should be institutionalized much less that it should be administered through a permanent international agency. Despite the much-publicized shortcomings of the interwar refugee regime, the appointment of Nansen as High Commissioner constituted the first formal acknowledgment of an international responsibility toward refugees. Nansen proved to be a highly innovative and successful advocate for them particularly in facilitating assistance to certain groups of refugees. The interwar period also saw the development of legal norms about the protection of refugees and the establishment of refugees as a special category of migrant within municipal and international law.

Initially, Nansen was concerned in general with the practical problems of Russian refugees, and in particular with the problems of refugee travel. Through skilful diplomacy, Nansen tackled the problem head-on by persuading fifty-one governments to recognize travel documents termed 'Nansen passports' for stateless Russians. With these documents, not only former Russian refugees but also others could legally move from areas where their stays were temporary and often illegal to more hospitable areas in Europe and elsewhere.

Governments moved quickly to adopt the Nansen passport system and co-operated in the exchange and repatriation of massive numbers of refugees following the Greco-Turkish War of 1922.[13] Nansen negotiated agreements involving the exchange of 1.1 million Turkish nationals of the Greek Orthodox religion for 380,000 Greek Muslim nationals. Similar population exchanges involving well over 100,000 refugees took place between Greece and Bulgaria.

The number of activities Nansen undertook on behalf of refugees mushroomed and the functions of the High Commissioner expanded. Following the exchanges between Bulgaria, Greece, and Turkey, governments and voluntary agencies—under the auspices of the League—financially assisted in resettling, finding employment for, and making economically self-sufficient hundreds of thousands of Greek, Bulgarian, and Armenian refugees.[14] Skran notes that the international refugee regime grew to encompass refugee settlement, employment opportunities, emigration, and the linkage of refugee assistance with economic development.[15] Viewing refugees as part of the problem of general unemployment in Europe, Nansen believed that by targeting assistance towards the creation of employment opportunities for refugees, the international refugee regime would also contribute to solving Europe's economic problems. With direct encouragement from Nansen, the

International Labour Organisation (ILO) established a Refugee Section that acted as a clearing house for information on employment opportunities for refugees, matching prospective employers in one country with those in another.[16]

In addition to developing a more comprehensive set of provisions covering employment and social services, governments reached agreements to create a more stable and secure legal status for refugees. This included assigning regular consular services to be carried out by the High Commissioner and the certifying of refugee identity and civil status. In 1928, governments agreed to accept a series of legal provisions relating to the economic, social, and legal status of Russian and Armenian refugees. These initiatives were eventually codified into international law in the 1930s.

In 1933, a convention was drafted that attempted to limit the practice of repatriation and to grant Russian and Armenian refugees rights in their countries of asylum.[17] A number of rights to which refugees were entitled were specified, including education and employment in the receiving country and travel documents. A similar convention was promulgated in 1938 for the benefit of refugees exiting Germany,[18] which was extended in 1939 to those fleeing Austria.[19]

While neither convention received the signatures of more than eight nations, they were first international efforts to elaborate a body of treaty law designed to afford protection to refugees. Although the language of these conventions was purposely limited to benefit narrowly-defined national groups and provided only minimal protection for the members of these groups, they were a step toward the formation of more permanent international laws and institutions.

At best, however, the measures were only partly successful. Providing identity documents allowed refugees to cross international borders legally, but it did not ensure that a foreign government would actually grant them entry visas. The right to grant or deny admission remained the prerogative of sovereign states—as it still does today—and even those that granted asylum did not necessarily acknowledge any legal obligation to do so. Moreover, many refugees were not covered under international arrangements and continued to lack any travel and identity system.

The Politicization of Refugee Policy

The emerging international refugee regime operated within a highly politicized context in which governments supported refugee assistance programmes for security and foreign policy concerns as much as out of humanitarian concern.

Although the High Commissioner for Refugees was formally independent, Nansen always depended on governments for donations. Without official funding to undertake any relief programmes, the ability to intervene actively was largely determined by Nansen's ability to raise funds and to convince governments to increase refugee aid, ease immigration barriers, and provide more legal protection for refugees within their borders. And these attempts were made at a time when assistance and protection of refugees was intensely political and thus directly influenced by governments' foreign policy and strategic interests.

The refugee assistance programmes of the 1920s especially depended on the financing of the two Great Powers, Britain and France, and on the support of the smaller European countries. However, the decisions as to which refugees qualified for aid were political ones made by the Council and the Assembly of the League of Nations. Governments were more likely to aid refugees fleeing from their enemies than from their friends. Governments in Eastern Europe, for example, aided refugees from the Soviet Union but not those from Germany. Great Britain aided its strategically important allies, Greece and Bulgaria. Refugees fleeing important political states, on the other hand, were a source of embarrassment and League members sought to avoid arousing the hostility of other members by refraining from criticizing their human rights records. As a consequence, some major refugee groups—such as refugees from fascist Italy and Spain—were excluded from League assistance altogether. All governments were more willing to act in a non-political, non-discriminatory fashion toward refugees when they needed immigrant labour.

Aid for Russian exiles was perhaps the most politicized refugee problem dealt with by the League in the 1920s. The concern for Russian refugees resulted at least partly from the fact that the Soviet Union was not a member of the League at that time and was regarded with extreme hostility and suspicion by most of its members. Moreover, Great Britain and France felt themselves to be financially and morally responsible for the thousands of defeated White Russian army soldiers they had supported during the Russian Civil War. The Soviet Union, in contrast, sharply objected to any international efforts aimed at helping refugees, especially White Russians. Interstate co-operation over the issue was impossible. Furthermore, the League of Nations had been at the forefront of economic and diplomatic efforts to isolate the Soviet Union. For the Russians, the Nansen office was a creature of the League of Nations and of the Western powers that they so profoundly distrusted.

These political difficulties underscored the limitations of humanitarian work. Close co-ordination between political bodies and humanitarian agencies was needed to ensure that the capabilities as well as the limitations of humanitarian work were taken into account. However, not only did governments keep the mandate of the High Commissioner deliberately narrow throughout this period, but they also refrained from adopting a universal definition of the term *refugee* for fear of opening the door to international recognition of political dissidents in any state, including the Great Powers.

Anti-Fascist Refugees

In the 1930s, Europe became flooded with new groups of refugees, this time fleeing fascism in Germany, Italy, Portugal, and Spain. The rise of totalitarian governments that demanded the total allegiance of the people to the state produced millions of refugees. Perceiving minority groups as threats to internal control, the fascist regimes that rose to power in Europe in the 1920s and 1930s adopted state policies that forced out those that they considered unassimilable. In a radical attempt to create a homogeneous and 'racially pure' society, the Nazis purged the country of unwanted elements. The main targets were political opponents, such as Communists, Social Democrats, anti-fascist intellectuals, and pacifists but also members of 'racially inferior' population groups—mainly Jews, Slavs, and Gypsies.

As anti-Semitic legislation and brutal agitation and discrimination were stepped up under the Nazis, the group most severely affected was the Jews. Major waves of emigration took place after the initial Nazi takeover in 1933, again after the passage of the Nuremberg Laws in 1935, and a third time after the devastation of *Kristallnacht* in 1938. Increased pressure was placed on Jews to leave. The German government expelled Jews of Polish origin across the Polish border, and after the conquest of Poland, Jews in areas annexed by the Nazis were forced to move to other parts of the country. In 1940, the Nazis began deporting German Jews to Poland and in October 1941 the 'Final Solution' to exterminate the Jewish people was adopted as state policy.

The rise of fascism elsewhere in Europe also created refugee movements. In Italy, the reign of Benito Mussolini generated a steady but relatively small flow of refugees, made up mainly of anti-fascists and political opponents whose departure the government encouraged. In general, however, Italy made it extremely difficult for its citizens to emigrate and severe penalties were set for illegal emigration.[20] In Portugal, some 2,000 political opponents of Antonio Salazar fled the country. Much larger refugee movements were generated by the Spanish Civil War and by the creation of a fascist government there. At the conclusion of the war, about 400,000 defeated Spanish Republicans fled to neighbouring France.

Refugee movements during this period would have been far greater had it not been for the exit controls and emigration restrictions imposed by a number of governments. Only a trickle of people were fortunate to be able to leave the Soviet Union compared with the estimated 20 to 40 million people who died there under the purges, famines, and forcible deportations during

Stalin's murderous 'Red Terror'.[21] Outside of Europe, there were huge displacements of people in Asia and the Pacific, but most of these population movements involved internal flights and migrations.

The Closing of Borders

Refugees fleeing Italy, Spain, and Portugal generally found temporary asylum in neighbouring countries. Some 10,000 Italians who fled the Mussolini regime found refuge in France among the community of Italian migrants already living there. Similarly, 400,000 Spanish Republicans were given temporary asylum by the French government, which had supported their cause against Franco.

In contrast to refugees from other fascist regimes, Jews from Germany scattered throughout the world. In the early 1930s, most either went to countries bordering Germany or resettled permanently in Palestine or the United States. Jews who fled later in the decade found it almost impossible to locate a country willing to give them temporary asylum. In writing about this period, Hannah Arendt graphically described the refugee's plight: 'Once they had left their homeland, they remained homeless; once they had left their state, they became stateless; once they had been deprived of their human rights, they were rightless, *the scum of the earth*'.[22] This absence of a place of refuge and the impossibility of finding a new home distinguished the plight of Jewish refugees from refugees of earlier eras.

The lack of international co-operation regarding refugees during the 1930s is traceable not only in the weakness of the League of Nations and the refugee organizations under its auspices, but also to the absence of any consistent or coherent international commitment to resolving refugee problems. Instead, there was a broad consensus in almost every industrialized nation, particularly during the years of the Great Depression, that national interests were best served by imposing and maintaining rigid limits on immigration; that humanitarian initiatives on behalf of refugees had to be limited by tight fiscal constraints and the need to employ their own citizens; and that no particular foreign policy benefits would accrue from putting political and moral pressure on refugee-generating countries, or from accepting their unwanted dissidents and minority groups.

These views operated in the United States and in Commonwealth countries like Canada and Australia which, prior to World War I, had accepted a substantial majority of the world's emigrants and had acted as a safety valve for Europe's forced migrants. Between the two World Wars, more and more governments instituted highly restrictive immigration laws to keep out all but selected national groups. In the United States, the Immigration Acts of 1921 and 1924 established a quota system designed to limit total immigration and to ensure a certain ethnic composition among each year's newcomers. The

British Dominions enacted restrictions aimed at keeping their populations British.[23] Australia restricted immigration by non-British migrants, excluded Asians altogether, and promoted schemes to bring in British settlers. In Canada and Latin America, restrictive policies became general policy.

Restrictionism was exacerbated by deepening worldwide economic depression and massive unemployment. Wherever they went, Jewish refugees encountered a world that was closing its frontiers and reducing its immigrant quotas. Even the United States refused to adjust its quota system to accommodate more of these refugees. About half of the very limited 150,000 places were for the English and Irish, and most of these openings went unfilled. To make matters worse, Presidents Hoover and Roosevelt instructed US consuls to withhold visas from any persons likely to become 'a public charge'—a restrictive clause that had been introduced in the Immigration Act of 1917. The effect of these measures was to severely limit the number of refugees who could enter as immigrants.[24]

Other states resorted to tortuous legal interpretations to prevent the entry of these doomed people. Pleas by representatives of public and private international refugee organizations went unheeded. Isolationism was still a factor in the Western hemisphere and encouraged a growing antipathy to aliens of all kinds. In particular, however, the pervasiveness of anti-Semitism worldwide made immigration almost impossible for Jews fleeing the Third Reich. Potential host governments feared that welcoming Jewish fugitives from Nazism might open the floodgates and provoke the flight of hundreds of thousands more Jews from Eastern Europe.

The High Commissioner of Refugees from Germany

Fritdjof Nansen died in 1930. During the next ten years, the international refugee regime he had almost single-handedly established proved totally incapable of dealing with the problem of Jewish refugees. In 1930, duties involving protection for refugees was placed under the aegis of the League Secretariat, while responsibility for administering the remaining limited assistance programmes was transferred to an agency that became known as the International Nansen Office. Responding to the initial outflow of Jewish refugees following Hitler's accession to power in Germany in 1933, the League established yet another fragile refugee organization, the High Commissioner for Refugees from Germany. Out of concern for German sensibilities, the High Commissioner was instructed to avoid discussing causes or stressing the political dimension of the refugee problem. His tasks were restricted to negotiating with host governments concerning settlement and emigration plans and the questions of work permits and travel documents. To avoid antagonizing

Germany at a time when it was still a member of the League, this organization was set up outside the formal structure of the League of Nations.[25] In
contrast to its predecessors, the organization did not even receive funding for
the administrative expenses of the High Commissioner from the League.

Similarly, in 1938, the Soviet Union objected to any kind of League protection for the few Russian citizens who were able to flee Stalin's purges and
collectivization campaigns. These events occasioned relatively little attention
from the outside world and the League was hardly inclined to take action.

As the scale of the Jewish refugee problem grew, any will to resolve it faded.
Despite the limited international recognition of the rights of refugees granted
at the time, states were unwilling to extend new legal protections to refugees,
particularly when these would limit the right of sovereign nations to exclude
or deport aliens. In addition, virtually no state was willing to accept refugees
as migrants even when all other means of affording protection had failed.

In the face of such international reluctance to accept Jews or to confront
the German government on the refugee issue, the High Commissioner for
Refugees from Germany, James G. McDonald, could do little. Frustrated, he
quit his post in 1936; but in his letter of resignation he underscored the political roots of the problem and the limitations of the international response:

The efforts of the private organizations and of any League organization for refugees can
only mitigate a problem of growing gravity and complexity. In the present economic
conditions of the world, the European States, and even those overseas, have only a
limited power of absorption of refugees. The problem must be tackled at its source if
disaster is to be avoided   (Cited in Gervase Coles, 'Approaches to the Refugee Problem
Today', in Gil Loescher and Laila Monahan, eds., *Refugees and International Relations*
(Oxford: Clarendon Press, 1989): 409–10.)

McDonald believed that it was not enough simply to assist those who fled
from the Third Reich. Efforts had to be made to confront the causes that
created the refugees and to negotiate with the country that was responsible
for the exodus. This was not a function of the High Commissioner's office; it
was a political function that belonged to the League of Nations itself, and
particularly the Great Powers. At the time, however, all major governments
considered such action to be politically inexpedient.

The High Commissioner's attempt to draw attention to human rights
abuses in Germany as the immediate cause of the Jewish refugee problem did
not spur international action against the Nazis. Simply put, Western governments viewed the refugee problem as an internal matter of the German
government, particularly since Germany was still a member state of the
League. Even after Germany withdrew from the League in 1938, France and
Britain sought to appease Germany and, therefore, were reluctant to criticize
its persecution of the Jews. Western statesmen could not master the challenge
of political events in Europe.

In his letter of resignation, James McDonald referred to the need to set aside state sovereignty in favour of humanitarian imperatives and to resolve the Jewish refugee problem at the level of international politics: '[When] domestic politics threaten the demoralization and exile of hundreds of thousands of human beings, considerations of diplomatic correctness must yield to those of common humanity.'[26] They did not.

After Germany quit the League, the two offices for refugees—the International Nansen Office and the High Commissioner for Refugees from Germany—were consolidated into what became the fourth High Commissioner for Refugees and this functioned until after the end of World War II in 1946. The new High Commissioner was Sir Herbert Emerson and his powers were even more rigidly limited than had been the case in the past. He was denied the power to enter into any legal commitment whatsoever on behalf of the League of Nations, and the League assumed no responsibility, legal or financial, for his activities. He had no power to engage in material assistance and was assisted only by a skeleton staff. The severe limits on the High Commissioner were also evident in the unwillingness of member states to assume greater responsibility for dealing with the rapidly worsening refugee crisis. As political conditions deteriorated in the late 1930s, and as an increasingly restrictionist political and economic environment emerged, the influence of Nansen's successors on government behaviour and attitudes towards refugees evanesced.

The Evian Conference

The only significant international effort to resolve the problem of Jewish refugees reflected and subsequently strengthened the restrictive attitudes and policies of governments that were already in force at the time. Under considerable pressure from Jewish groups and private voluntary agencies, Franklin Roosevelt called an international conference at Evian, France, in 1938 to consider ways of resettling Jews who fled Germany and Austria. Up to that time, the United States had taken little notice of the existing international refugee structures or of refugee norms of the League of Nations. It had failed to ratify either refugee convention and it had refused to modify its own immigration law even to the extent of permitting the entry of Jewish refugee children.[27] At Evian, the United States made no new pledges for increased quotas. Other government delegates noted that the movement of Jewish refugees was 'disturbing to the general economy', since those in flight were seeking refuge at a time of serious unemployment. Jewish refugees posed a 'severe strain on the administrative facilities and absorptive capacities of the receiving nations', racial and religious problems were rendered more acute, international unrest increased, and 'the processes of appeasement in international relations' might be hindered.[28] Although Germany had favoured emigration as one way to rid itself of its minorities, the Evian Conference yielded no new resettlement places and merely reaffirmed the extreme reluctance of the United States and the rest of the world to offer a lifeline to Jewish refugees.

The Intergovernmental Committee on Refugees (IGCR)

The only concrete measure taken at Evian was the creation of a new refugee mechanism outside of the League of Nations structure—the Intergovernmental Committee on Refugees (IGCR)—to negotiate with Germany about Jewish migration. For the next eight years until 1946, the IGCR existed alongside the League of Nations' Office of the High Commissioner for Refugees, and the two staffs shared common facilities.[29]

Despite this augmentation of the institutional framework for dealing with the problem, the international community's response to the plight of Jews in Europe remained limited and ineffectual. The IGCR tried to work with Germany to achieve an orderly exodus of Jews, who would be allowed to take their property and possessions with them. But Germany would not agree to let Jews exit without sacrificing most of their possessions. Western states were not willing to finance a resettlement programme or increase immigration quotas and the migration of Jews to Palestine was sharply curtailed by the British. Avenues of exit from Germany and entrance to western countries were closed. Germany regarded Evian and the Western nations' policy of closing their doors against refugees as exonerating its policies and began to use more draconian measures to rid the Third Reich of its Jewish population. The subsequent mass murder of Jews by the Nazis was tacitly tolerated by most of the Western world until it was too late for effective counteraction. In 1943, the United States and Great Britain convened yet another conference in Bermuda to mollify voices of concern for European Jews, but no effective steps were taken to alter a Western policy towards refugees which was based on rigid barriers to immigration.

The Breakdown of the International Refugee Regime

Unlike many earlier refugee movements, twentieth century refugee problems defied quick solutions. The majority of these refugees could not simply return home; nor could they settle in Europe or travel across the Atlantic to a new home. A solution to their problem had to be found in the prevailing political, economic, and social climate of the interwar period in Europe. During the

1930s, the world's statesmen were essentially impotent in confronting Europe's dictators, and the response to the refugee problem by governments and international organizations was inevitably politicized and selective. Throughout the period, assistance and protection was temporary and limited to certain groups. As the League's political effectiveness and credibility declined—particularly after the withdrawal of Germany, Japan, and Italy from the League, and after its failure to resolve the Manchurian and Ethiopian conflicts—its competence to deal with refugee problems also decreased.

The institutions created to respond to refugee problems during the inter-war period did leave one lasting legacy. Twenty years of organizational growth and interstate collaboration had firmly established the idea that refugees were victims of human rights abuses for whom the world had a special respons-ibility. Moreover, the first international co-operative efforts on behalf of refugees and the establishment and evolution of the international refugee agencies of the period, had constructed the foundations on which successor institutions would build.

The Postwar Crisis

By the end of World War II, millions of people were outside of their countries of origin and in need of assistance.[30] A State Department report prepared in early 1945 described the situation in Europe at the end of the war as '[one] of the greatest population movements of history taking place before our eyes. As the German retreat has rolled westward before the oncoming Soviet troops and as the Allies have pushed eastward on the western front, millions of people have been uprooted and are fleeing toward the center of Germany.'[31] The report estimated that this flow not only included the 20 to 30 million people uprooted during the war, but also 'some 9.5 million displaced Germans returning from outside the Reich, and 4 million and probably more war fugitives who fled before the oncoming Soviet and Allied troops'.[32]

As the concentration camps in Eastern Europe were liberated, some 60,000 starved and psychologically damaged Jewish survivors joined this huge group of homeless people.[33] Postwar conflicts and political changes in Eastern Europe generated millions of additional fugitives, most notably about 12 million ethnic Germans driven out of the countries of eastern and central Europe who surged westwards into the British, French, and American zones of military occupation.[34] The bulk of Europe's displaced population was absorbed by Germany. Concurrently, tens of thousands of new refugees were being generated by the civil war in Greece as well as by post-liberation conflicts in Eastern and Southern Europe.

The influx of so many refugees and displaced people in such a short time into an area where most of the physical infrastructure had been destroyed put immense strains on Western European states, particularly Germany, and on the Allied military authorities responsible for administering significant areas of former enemy territory. Scores of private voluntary agencies[35] sprang up and new intergovernmental organizations were created to relieve the misery of the war victims.

United Nations Relief and Rehabilitation Agency (UNRRA)

In November 1943 the Western powers set up the UNRRA[36] to provide immediate relief when the anticipated anti-Axis counter-offensive occurred. In 1944 and 1945, UNRRA provided temporary emergency assistance for millions of displaced persons (DPs) who fell into allied hands, thus following the pattern set in the interwar period. UNRRA, however, was not strictly a refugee organization in that it aided all those who had been displaced by the war but only incidently dealt with refugees with political fears.

Working directly under Allied military command, UNRRA was given a very limited mandate. It was to extend aid to civilian nationals of the Allied nations and to DPs in countries liberated by the Allied armies. UNRRA had no power to resettle refugees and DPs to third countries. Its goal was simply to return to their homes as soon as possible all the people who had been uprooted and displaced by the war. Relief and rehabilitation in Europe were to be for the short term only. Once people were repatriated and adequate resources for rebuilding were provided, it was widely assumed that Western European states could stand on their own feet again and deal with their own problems.

Unlike the interwar period, however, enormous amounts of money were donated by UNRRA's forty-four member-states for relief purposes. From its inception in November 1943 until its disbandment in June 1947, UNRRA expended nearly $3.6 billion—of which the United States contributed $2.8 billion—and at the peak of its activity it employed 27,800 people. Because it was not strictly a refugee assistance agency, UNRRA's functions also included rehabilitation of agricultural and industrial production and the support of basic social infrastructure including public health, public education, and other social services.

One of UNRRA's principal functions was to promote and oversee repatriation. The great majority of the dislocated people in UNRRA's care were anxious to go home to rebuild their lives. The overburdened countries of asylum—such as Germany, Austria, and Italy—were anxious that these people be repatriated quickly. At the Yalta Conference in February 1945, the big powers paved the way for large-scale repatriations to the Soviet Union.[37] At the Potsdam Conference in August 1945, they provided for the return of the ethnic German minorities in Poland, Czechoslovakia, and Hungary.[38] The solution agreed on by the Allied Powers was that all displaced citizens would, without delay after liberation, be separated from enemy prisoners of war and alien members of the national population until they were handed over to their national authorities. At this time UNRRA authorities still generally expected that refugees would voluntarily seek repatriation to, and re-habilitation in, their own countries; this sensitive issue, later to play such an important a role in United Nations debate, did not trouble UNRRA at its inception. UNRRA devoted a substantial part of its efforts to aiding Allied military forces in identifying displaced persons, separating them into broad national categories, putting them into trucks and boxcars, and shipping them back to the countries from which they had originally come, without regard to their individual wishes. So successful were these methods that in the first five months after the war, UNRRA and the Allied military command managed to repatriate three-quarters of the displaced people in Europe.

Among those repatriated were large numbers of Soviet and Eastern European citizens, many of whom ended up in Stalin's labour camps when they returned.[39] Some who convinced the Western authorities that they faced political persecution and possible execution if returned were put into camps until decisions could be reached about what to do with them. Among them were Baltic and Polish nationals whose territory had been annexed by the Soviet Union, Ukrainians, and Jewish refugees who were considered ineligible for immediate repatriation. However, the Western Powers initially yielded to the Soviet insistence that all its nationals be repatriated, and were slow to acknowledge that many of those who resisted being sent back home faced possible persecution. Thus, the great majority of Soviets and Eastern Europeans were not the beneficiaries even of the limited protection of camps.[40] Before long, the fate of those people who refused to return became the focus of sharp international political debate between East and West.

Refugees as an East–West Issue

After World War II, relations between the Western powers and the Soviet Union rapidly deteriorated, and the problem of refugees in the West who either did not want to return or were hesitant about returning home erupted into a major East–West controversy. Several dramatic suicides in the displaced persons camps and bloody confrontations between Western military officials and Russians resisting forced repatriation finally convinced the United States military command that the fears of many of those remaining in their custody were genuine. As the Western powers became increasingly reluctant to return displaced persons to areas under Soviet control, the mass repatriations of 1945 slowed and then came to an almost complete halt by the end of 1946.[41] By this time, less than one quarter of the estimated 2.5 million Soviet nation-als in the British, American, and French zones had not been handed over to

Soviet authorities, and over 1 million demoralized people remained in camps. They presented a relief and security problem which UNRRA was not in a position to solve. None the less, it had to continue to support them. The situation was made worse by Soviet complaints that the Western powers were refusing to fulfil their obligations under the Yalta agreements and were encouraging Soviet nationals to resist repatriation.

After the War, East and West quarrelled bitterly over the issue of forcible repatriation and about what the international community's responsibility was for those who refused to go home. In the 1920s, it had been customary to regard refugees as persons who could not return home because their own governments were unwilling to have them. In the mid-1940s by contrast, many hundreds of thousands of persons were unwilling to return to their countries although their governments were anxious to have them back.

The question of repatriation, coloured by the emerging East–West conflict, became a major political issue within the United Nations.[42] The status of refugees and displaced persons was among the most contentious of all the issues discussed at these early UN sessions, and on few subjects were more prolonged and exhaustive negotiations occurred between the Soviet Union and the Western countries.[43] Repatriation touched on the fundamental ideological conflicts dividing East and West. The core of the conflict concerned the rights of people to choose where they wanted to live, to flee from oppression, and to express their own opinions. Although Soviet representatives privately acknowledged that many of the displaced persons rejected the Communist system and that it was unrealistic to force them all to go home, in public the Soviet Union and the Eastern European countries rejected outright the idea that their citizens could have any valid reason for opposing return, and maintained that those who resisted return were war criminals or traitors.[44]

A major dispute arose over whether UNRRA was obligated to provide assistance to displaced persons who refused repatriation. The Eastern bloc asserted that assistance should be given only to displaced persons who returned home, while the Western countries insisted that each individual should be free to decide whether or not to return home, without prejudicing his right to assistance. An immediate blow-up was avoided when the Western and Eastern delegations agreed to a compromise plan which permitted such aid to be continued for a maximum of six months, while acknowledging that UNRRA was entitled to repatriate displaced persons and would be prepared to do so in the future.[45]

The International Refugee Organization (IRO)

The United States remained strongly critical of UNRRA operations, particularly its repatriation policies and its rehabilitation programmes in Eastern bloc countries, which the US felt only served to consolidate Russian political control over Eastern Europe. Toward the end of 1946, the United States, which provided 70 per cent of UNRRA funds and much of its leadership, took action to kill UNRRA by refusing either to grant it additional aid or to extend its life beyond 1947.[46] In its place, and in the face of adamant opposition from the Eastern bloc, the United States worked to create a new International Refugee Organization (IRO) which had as its chief function not repatriation but the resettlement of refugees and displaced persons uprooted by World War II and its aftermath.

From the beginning of the UN General Assembly debates on the formation of IRO, it was apparent that the question of a new refugee organization would generate additional tension between East and West.[47] The Soviet bloc favoured the retention of UNRRA, because of the aid it channelled to Eastern Europe, and because of its limited mandate which favoured repatriation over resettlement and accorded well with the official Soviet view that all those resisting repatriation were criminals or traitors. The subsequent debates within the General Assembly on the mandate of the IRO were embittered by the American determination to terminate UNRRA which the Soviet Union regarded as a decision to deny Eastern Europe economic aid.

The debates covered various topics including the length of term of the new organization, its method of selecting a director, and its means of raising funds. But the principal East–West split centred on the definition of refugees within the IRO's mandate and on the related issue of resettlement versus re-patriation. The Western bloc insisted that the mandate of the IRO be broad enough to offer protection to individuals with 'valid objections' to repatri-ation, including objections based on 'persecution, or fear, based on reason-able grounds, of persecution because of race, religion, nationality or political opinions' and objections 'of a political nature, judged by the organization to be valid.'[48] Previously, international organizations had dealt only with specific groups of refugees, such as Russians or Germans and governments had never attempted to formulate a general definition of the term *refugee*. For the first time, therefore, the international community made refugee eligibil-ity dependent upon the individual rather than the group and accepted the individual's right to flee from political persecution.

As a gesture to assuage Communist bloc objections, the IRO constitution included the assertion that its principal objective was 'to encourage and assist in every way possible early return [of refugees and displaced persons] to their countries of origin', and that 'no international assistance should be given to traitors, quislings and war criminals, and that nothing should be done in any way to prevent their surrender and punishment'.[49] Despite this concessionary statement, the Soviet Union saw the IRO as a tool of the West and criticized the organization for preventing DPs from repatriating. The eastern bloc reit-erated its charges that 'the refugee camps of the West had become centers of anti-communist propaganda; that the refugees were being used as forced laborers and as mercenaries; and that the West intended to enrich itself by resettling the so-called refugees to the countries of the world making the highest bid for their labor'.[50] More plausibly, the Soviet Union claimed that the West used refugee organizations to recruit spies and anti-Soviet intelligence experts from the large numbers of pro-Nazi East Europeans who had fought against the Soviet Union during the World War II.[51] Regarding the IRO as an 'immigration bureau' and as an instrument of the US bloc, the Soviet Union and its allies refused to join the new organization and made no contribution of any kind towards its operation.

Given the depth of East–West hostilities at the time, it is hardly surprising that the IRO's policies should have been caught up in the politics of the day. Initially, persons unwilling to return to their countries of origin became the concern of the IRO only if they could present a valid case against repatriation on the grounds of racial, religious, or political persecution. But following the outflow of refugees from Czechoslovakia after the Communist coup of 1948, the IRO's programme was expanded beyond displaced persons from World War II to include escapees from Eastern European Communist regimes. Moreover, perceiving refugees to be of symbolic and instrumental use in the Cold War between East and West, Western governments—especially the United States—prevailed upon the IRO to apply the refugee eligibility criteria more liberally, to accommodate larger numbers of escapees. The United States underwrote over two-thirds of the IRO's costs, controlled its leadership, and played the key role in investing the organization's refugee protection with specific ideological content.

Resettlement over Repatriation

Resettlement seemed the only practical policy option for resolving the refugee problem. Germany and the nations of Western Europe were in favour of it, since their chief interest was to minimize relief problems during a period of intensive reconstruction. Resettlement also served the broader political interests of the West by discrediting and embarrassing the newly established Communist regimes.

With the opening up of a major resettlement programme, the number of repatriations was reduced to a trickle. During the four and a half years of the IRO's existence, no more than 54,000 people returned to Eastern and Central Europe. By 1949, all Eastern European repatriation missions were asked to leave the areas under Western control, and the IRO was requested by host governments to close offices in their capitals. Repatriation as a possible solution to refugee problems became entirely discredited in Western eyes, tainted by the forcible returns of the immediate postwar period.

Because the war-torn countries of Western Europe were incapable of accepting all displaced persons, pressure was put on the United States, Canada, Australia, and other non-European countries to make available at least some admission slots. The United States admitted nearly 400,000 displaced persons during the period 1949–54, through a series of *ad hoc* legislative and administrative measures, collectively known as displaced persons legislation.[52] US refugee admissions policy reflected intensive lobbying and constituency pressures from ethnic groups both to aid surviving victims of Nazi and fascist persecution and to open up new immigration channels from the Old World.[53] Even more importantly, foreign policy concerns, such as anti-communism and the need to restore stability to Western Europe, were employed by refugee advocates such as the Citizens Committee for Displaced Persons, to overcome the restrictionist attitudes and policies of the American Congress. Labour recruitment programmes enabled large numbers of displaced persons to emigrate to Canada, Australia and New Zealand, South America, and even parts of the Middle East and Africa.

The IRO resettled the majority of the refugee caseload it had inherited from UNRRA within the first year of its existence. It was able to accomplish this because Western European nations as well as the overseas resettlement countries saw practical advantages for themselves in alleviating labour shortages by recruiting from the camps. Mainly single men, childless couples, and manual labourers could agree to several years' government designated labour—mostly in coal mines, road building, and construction work—in return for being granted the opportunity to apply for citizenship. During the four and a half years of IRO operations, the United States received 31.7 per cent of the refugees resettled, Australia took 17.5 per cent, Israel 12.7 per cent, Canada 11.9 per cent, Britain 8.3 per cent, the rest of Western Europe 6.8 per cent, and the countries of Latin America 6.5 per cent.

After this initial surge of resettlement activity, the IRO encountered patterns of discrimination against certain groups of immigrants who, for one reason or another, were considered undesirable. For example, Chile, Argentina, and Brazil refused to take Jews. European states generally discriminated against intellectuals and members of professional classes, and no one wanted to take the unemployable—particularly the sick, elderly, and handicapped.[54] By the end of IRO's tenure, those whom selective admissions policies had left unsettled became known as the 'hard core' cases. These totalled some 400,000 people, most of whom were still in camps scattered throughout Western Europe. The scandal of these camps was to be the subject of criticism in the West until the early 1960s. In addition to the hard-core group, the numbers of refugees continued to grow, with large numbers of persons fleeing Eastern European countries for resettlement in the West.

Despite the achievements of the IRO, refugee problems showed few signs of disappearing. Resettlement of the remaining wartime displaced persons had become more difficult, as European states that had once welcomed new arrivals now claimed that their economies could handle no more. With the onset of the Cold War, new groups of refugees from the East began to make their way westward which compounded the problem. A series of East–West crises—including the Communist seizure of Czechoslovakia, the explosion of the first Soviet atomic bomb, the Berlin blockade and airlift, the victory of Mao Zedong in China, and the beginning of the Korean conflict in 1950— greatly increased political tensions between the two blocs. These events consequently brought about a series of reactions: the Truman Doctrine which proclaimed that the United States would 'support free peoples who are resist- ing attempted subjugation by armed minorities or by outside pressures';[55] the Marshall Plan; the North Atlantic Treaty Organization (NATO); and Comecon as the central economic organization for Eastern European communism and the Warsaw Pact military alliance. Europe became divided, and the opposition of each side to the other hardened considerably. In this tense international environment, Europe was being pressed between the remains of one refugee problem and the emergence of another.

The IRO recognized the threat the refugee problem posed for Europe and in one of its final reports to the UN General Assembly it warned that the temporary problem it was assigned to deal with was rapidly becoming permanent. Despite the IRO's successes in resettlement, there remained a large camp population in Western and Central Europe, an urgent caseload of some 5,000 European refugees (mainly White Russians) in China, groups in Turkey, Spain, Portugal, and the Middle East as well as a tense international situation in Europe that was daily generating large numbers of new refugees. It seemed that the problem of refugees in numerical terms was almost as serious when IRO closed down as when it came into existence.

A widespread perception grew among governments that there were limits to the numbers of immigrants resettlement countries would accept. The United States and Great Britain were concerned that continued reliance on the IRO would serve to institutionalize the refugee problem as an indefinite responsibility of overseas resettlement countries, particularly themselves. Despite its success, the IRO proved to be an extremely expensive operation spending over $428.5 million—three times the amount spent by the combined budgets of the rest of the UN and at its peak.[56] The United States was weary of the vast scale and expenses of the refugee problem. Having spent huge sums of money on the operations of the IRO, the US was content to leave the burden of the refugee problem largely to countries of asylum. The US State Department believed that European governments should assume responsibility for the remaining refugee problem in Europe:

The Western European Governments, accustomed since 1945 to have indigent refugees on their territories cared for out of international funds, are now reluctant upon the termination of IRO to resume unilateral care for these persons and hold the view that they should continue to be provided for out of international assistance funds. The

United States Government holds the opposite view: that the burden of caring for indigents among the residual refugees should not fall so heavily on any one country as to justify international assistance funds. Congress has made it clear that it does not propose to appropriate funds annually hereafter to cover United States contributions to such a fund. (US State Department, 'Refugees and Stateless Persons', *Foreign Relations of the United States* (Washington, DC: UGPO, 1950): 539–40).57

By 1950 the United States had also turned decisively to the direct economic assistance of the European countries through the Marshall Plan, a strategy which Washington believed would make it easier for governments in Europe to absorb the remaining refugees. Implicitly, this policy shift assumed that the need for exceptional or urgent relief and resettlement measures for European refugees has passed, and that the problems which remained were temporary and could be dealt with by a small successor agency to the IRO. Many governments, particularly the United States, believed that the refugee problem had been virtually solved, and all that was needed now was in effect a 'mopping up' operation.

Financial considerations alone do not explain the fundamental change in the American support for international refugee organizations after 1950. From 1943 to 1950, the US had been the leading financial and political supporter of international co-operation of refugees. By 1950, however, US refugee policy was reoriented toward exposing the inadequacies of the Soviet Union and its allies, and for exploiting unrest behind the iron curtain. With accentuation of these Cold War themes, US perceptions of international organizations dedicated to resolving refugee problems underwent a monumental shift. As World War II faded into the past and with the displaced persons crisis largely resolved, conservative members of the US Congress reasserted their control over refugee and immigration policy. International refugee relief operations were curtailed, unilateral initiatives were encouraged, and international organizations unwilling to subordinate themselves to US foreign policy objectives were denied American aid.

Concurrent with the shifts in the American mood towards refugees, new flows were moving from east to west in Europe and massive displacements were occurring on the Indian subcontinent, the Korean peninsula, in China, and in Palestine. It seemed that the world refugee problem would be virtually unending. Against this background, discussions took place within the United Nations Third Committee, the General Assembly, and the Economic and Social Council from 1948 to 1950 regarding the termination of IRO and the creation of a new international refugee organization—the Office of the United Nations High Commissioner for Refugees (UNHCR). What emerged from these discussions was a compromise between the US and European positions. While governments debated matters such as the longevity of the proposed agency, its relationship to the Secretary-General, and its sources of funding and general functions, the need for a new UN refugee agency was never questioned. There was also strong support for safeguarding the protection of refugee rights within the framework of a convention that the UN legal advisers had under preparation. The core rights included the right of return or resettlement of refugees and the desirability of safeguarding against forcible return, or *refoulement,* of refugees. Nevertheless, the initial efforts to establish a successor agency to the IRO were fraught with political problems and disagreements among the major powers. The debates over the refugee issue were contentious and politicized, revealing significant differences and policy preferences among the various governments regarding the authority and financing of the new refugee organization as well the definition of *refugee.*

The Inauspicious and Uncertain Beginnings of the UNHCR

The Soviet Union and its allies did not take part in the negotiations leading to the establishment of the UNHCR and the United Nations Convention Relating to the Status of Refugees. The socialist bloc objected to protection for refugees whom they considered 'traitors who are refusing to return home to serve their country. . . .'[58] The planning and drafting of the major refugee legal instrument and organization were therefore conducted solely by Western powers and non-Communist members of the developing world. Despite the exclusion of Communist participants, Western governments were not entirely like-minded about the potential scope of the new organization and serious differences arose among participating governments regarding the authority and financing of the new agency and the refugee definition.

The United States was tired of financing international refugee programmes. With the expensive experiences of UNRRA and the IRO fresh in their minds, US policy-makers were principally interested in limiting rather than expanding their financial and legal obligations to refugees. The Americans had the support of the British who were concerned that the UK would inevitably be called upon to help finance new relief efforts for refugees in Europe. In drafting the refugee convention, the US and the UK worked hard to ensure that the United Nations did not have resources at hand to commit itself to unspecified and future responsibilities towards refugees.

The United States and most European governments differed on what they believed the UNHCR's scope and functions should be. The United States sought a temporary refugee agency with narrow authority and limited functions. In particular, the United States sought to deny the UNHCR a relief role by depriving it of the authority and the funding to carry out material assistance operations for refugees. American officials believed that the sole function of the proposed Office should be international legal protection. The American delegate, Mrs Eleanor Roosevelt, contended that the United Nations as a deliberative body should not assume responsibility as an international relief agency. She argued that it should be limited in size and responsibility, should respond to each problem on an *ad hoc* basis, and should not be required to provide material assistance. Western European governments, on the other hand, took different positions. The principal countries of asylum such as France and the Benelux countries opposed the American view and were anxious to secure large-scale operational funds for the refugees they were assisting. Other states such as the UK were largely protected from influxes of refugees by geographic factors and felt that refugees should be the responsibility of host states. Finally, the occupied territories of Germany, Italy, and Austria which bore the bulk of asylum-seekers from Eastern Europe, sought international assistance but had no voice at this time in United Nations deliberations. In addition, non-European states—particularly India and Pakistan, which were in the throes of one of the most massive and disorderly population exchanges of modern times as a result of the British partition of the Indian subcontinent—argued that the UNHCR should be a strong, permanent organization with the ability to raise funds for material assistance on a voluntary basis.[59] In the end the United States, supported by the UK, succeeded in making UN General Assembly approval a precondition of all appeals for voluntary contributions. The UNHCR thus became totally dependent on a small administrative annual budget granted by the UN General Assembly and on a small 'emergency fund' to which the United States made no contributions at all until 1955.

The drafters of the December 1950 UNHCR statute and the July 1951 Convention Relating to the Status of Refugees were deeply influenced by the experience of post-World War Europe. Both documents defined a refugee as a person who had a 'well-founded fear of being persecuted for reasons of race, religion, nationality, membership of a particular social group or political opinion'. The adoption of persecution as the main characteristic of a refugee was made to fit a Western interpretation of asylum-seekers. The Western states who were chiefly responsible for the persecution-centred definition perceived refugees to be victims of oppressive, totalitarian, and specifically Communist regimes. The definition had the added advantage that it would serve ideological purposes by stigmatizing the fledgling Communist regimes as persecutors. It was also perceived to be an appropriate way of dealing with the concerns of religious and ethnic minorities in Europe—especially the Jews—who were anxious to ensure that in the event of future persecutions, international arrangements existed for facilitating departure and resettlement elsewhere.

Although governments agreed on a general, universally applicable refugee definition, they were divided over whether the term should apply to refugees worldwide or whether it should be restricted to European refugees. The British, supported by Scandinavia, Belgium, and the Commonwealth countries, argued for a broad general definition which would adequately cover present and future refugee flows.[60] The United States, backed belatedly by France,[61] argued for a narrow definition which enumerated clearly the categories needing protection. In the end, the US position regarding the definition of refugee in the UNHCR's mandate prevailed, but only after the Americans exerted considerable pressure on the Latin American and other delegations to change their positions. Governmental representatives also debated in late 1950 whether 'internal refugees'—internally displaced people—should be included in the refugee definition and decided to exclude these groups from the UNHCR mandate.[62] However, the United States offered a significant concession authorizing the High Commissioner to intervene on behalf of other groups of refugees pending consideration by the General Assembly as to whether such groups should be brought under his mandate, thus opening the way for future expansion of the Office.[63]

Only twenty-six countries participated in the subsequent negotiations regarding the writing of the 1951 refugee convention, and none except Yugoslavia, were from the Soviet bloc. During these negotiations Western governments, led by the United States and France, argued for limiting the responsibilities of states who were signatories to the refugee convention. The British again took the lead in arguing for a broad global definition covering all refugees, wherever located, who were then seeking asylum and others who might require asylum in the future. The United States and France considered that if governments were expected to adhere to the convention they should know in advance precisely for which refugees, in what numbers, and in what places they were to undertake commitments.[64] In the end, the view that the refugee convention should serve mainly as an instrument for the legal protection of European refugees prevailed. Thus, whereas the Statute of the UNHCR placed no geographical limits on the High Commissioner's mandate, the UN Refugee Convention defined the obligations of signatory nations more narrowly. The Convention covered only those who were refugees as 'a result of events occurring before January 1, 1951', and governments were given the discretion to apply it to those who were refugees 'owing to events in Europe or owing to events in Europe and elsewhere'.[65]

Thus the Convention and its definition were not universal. They were not intended to apply to refugees from every part of the world, nor to people fleeing from any international or civil conflicts. The Convention was intended to be used by the Western states in dealing with arrivals from the East, and largely reflected the international politics of the early Cold War period. In addition, the scope and extent of the authority of the High Commissioner were limited by the importance attached by states to the international norms of sovereignty and non-intervention in the domestic affairs of states. The

UNHCR statute restricted the authority of the High Commissioner to assist refugees in flight, not to address those factors and forces likely to produce large-scale movements of people across international borders. During most of the Cold War, these norms limited the scope of UNHCR activity and, with few exceptions, restricted the Office to work in countries of asylum rather than countries of origin.

NOTES

1. Michael Marrus, *The Unwanted: European Refugees in the Twentieth Century* (New York, NY: Oxford University Press, 1985).
2. Independent Commission on International Humanitarian Issues, *Modern Wars: the Humanitarian Challenge* (London: Zed Books, 1986).
3. Aristide Zolberg, 'The Formation of New States as a Refugee Generating Process', in Gil Loescher and John Scanlan, eds., *The Global Refugee Problem: U.S. and World Response*. Special issue of *Annals of the American Academy of Political and Social Science*, 467 (May 1983): 24–38.
4. Claudena Skran, *Refugees in Inter-War Europe: The Emergence of a Regime* (Oxford: Clarendon Press, 1995): 31–2.
5. Ibid. and Marrus, *The Unwanted*.
6. For general background, see: Leo Kuper, *Genocide: Its Political Uses in the Twentieth Century* (New Haven, CT: Yale University Press, 1981).
7. For background, see Inis Claude, *National Minorities: An International Problem* (Cambridge, MA: Harvard University Press, 1955).
8. John Hope Simpson, *The Refugee Problem* (London: Oxford University Press, 1939) and Marrus, *The Unwanted*.
9. For more details see Marrus, *The Unwanted*, and Simpson, *The Refugee Problem*.
10. C. A. Macartney, *National States and National Minorities* (New York, NY: Russell and Russell, 1968).
11. Simpson, *The Refugee Problem*, and Marrus, *The Unwanted*.
12. Simpson, *The Refugee Problem*: 192.
13. Skran, *Refugees in Inter-War Europe*. Unless otherwise indicated, information on the League of Nation's activities on refugees is drawn from this work.
14. Ibid.
15. Ibid.
16. Ibid.
17. League of Nations, *Convention Relating to the International Status of Refugees*. League of Nations, Treaty Series, clix/3363 (28 October 1933).
18. League of Nations, *Treaty Series*, cxcii/4461.
19. League of Nations, *Treaty Series*, cxcviii/4634, and by a resolution of the League Council to the Sudeten Germans on 19 January 1939, League of Nations, 1939/72.
20. Alan Dowty, *Closed Borders: The Contemporary Assault on Freedom of Movement* (New Haven, CT: Yale University Press, 1987): 76–8.
21. Robert Conquest, *The Great Terror: Stalin's Purge of the Thirties* (Harmondsworth: Penguin Books, 1971).

22. Hannah Arendt, *The Origins of Totalitarianism* (New York, NY: Harcourt Brace Jovanovich, 1958): 267.

23. For background see: Richard Plender, *International Migration Law* (Leiden: A.W. Sijthoff, 1989).

24. These policies are discussed, among other places, in David Wyman's *Paper Walls: America and the Refugee Crisis, 1938-1941* (Amherst, MA: University of Massachusetts Press, 1968); and in his *Abandonment of the Jews: America and the Holocaust, 1941–1945* (New York, NY: Pantheon Books, 1984).

25. When Germany subsequently resigned from the League of Nations, the High Commissioner was once again made responsible to the Assembly.

26. Cited in Coles, 'Approaches to the Refugee Problem Today', 410.

27. Gil Loescher and John Scanlan, *Calculated Kindness: Refugees and America's Half-Open Door, 1945 to Present* (New York, NY, and London: The Free Press and Macmillan, 1986), xvi.

28. *League of Nations Journal* (1938), 19 (8–9): 676–7 cited in Guy Goodwin-Gill, 'Different Types of Forced Migration Movements as an International and National Problem', in Goran Rystad, ed., *The Uprooted: Forced Migration as an International Problem in the Post-War Era* (Lund, Sweden: Lund University Press, 1990).

29. The most authoritative work that covers the IGCR is Tommie Sjoberg, *The Powers and the Persecuted: The Refugee Problem and the Intergovernmental Committee on Refugees, 1938-1947* (Lund: Lund University Press, 1991).

30. Eugene Kulischer, *Europe on the Move. War and Population Changes, 1917– 1947* (New York, NY: Columbia University Press, 1948): 305.

31. J. P. Clark Carey, 'Displaced Populations in Europe in 1944 with Partial Reference to Germany', *Department of State Bulletin* 12/300 (25 March 1945): 491 cited in Loescher and Scanlan, *Calculated Kindness:* 1.

32. Ibid.

33. According to Leonard Dinnerstein—*America and the Survivors of the Holocaust, 1941–1945* (New York, NY: Columbia University Press, 1982): 28—twenty thousand of the sixty thousand survivors died within one week of liberation.

34. Jacques Vernant, *The Refugee in the Post-War World* (New Haven, CT: Yale University Press, 1953): 94–5 and Marrus, *The Unwanted.*

35. For example, the US government urged the creation of an umbrella organiza-tion, The American Council for Voluntary Agencies in Foreign Service (ACVA), to promote co-operative planning among voluntary agencies for the postwar relief and rehabilitation effort. See: Bruce Nichols, *The Uneasy Alliance: Religion, Refugee Work, and U. S. Foreign Policy* (New York, NY: Oxford University Press, 1988).

36. George Woodbridge, *The History of UNRRA* (New York, NY: Columbia University Press, 1950), and Kim Salomon, *Refugees in the Cold War: Toward a New International Refugee Regime in the Early Postwar Era* (Lund: Lund University Press, 1991).

37. See Nikolai Tolstoy, *The Silent Betrayal* (New York, NY: Scribners, 1977) and Nicholas Bethell, *The Last Secret: Forcible Repatriation to Russia, 1944–47* (London: Andre Deutch, 1974).

38. See Alfred de Zayas, *Nemesis at Potsdam: The Anglo-Americans and the Expulsions of the Germans* (London: Routledge and Kegan Paul, 1979).

39. See Mark Elliot, *Pawns of Yalta* (Champaign, IL: University of Illinois Press, 1982):

104; and Malcom Proudfoot, *European Refugees, 1930–1952: A Study in Forced Population Movement* (London: Faber and Faber, 1957): 229.

40. For background see Proudfoot, *European Refugees.*
41. Elliot, *Pawns of Yalta.*
42. See, for example, the debates over repatriation at the United Nations Third Committee during January and February 1946.
43. Edith Penrose, 'Negotiating on Refugees and Displaced Persons, 1946', in Raymond Dennet and Joseph Johnson, eds., *Negotiating with the Russians* (Boston, MA: Little Brown,1951): 144–7.
44. Ibid.
45. John Stoessinger, *The Refugee and the World Community* (Minneapolis, MN: University of Minnesota Press, 1956): 41–2.
46. Dean Acheson, *Present at the Creation* (New York, NY: Norton, 1966): 201.
47. Louise Holborn, *The International Refugee Organization: A Specialized Agency of the United Nations, Its History and Work, 1946–1952* (London: Oxford University Press, 1956).
48. Annex to the Constitution of the International Refugee Organization, Part 1, Sec. C., Part 1(a), reprinted as Appendix to Senate Report 950, 80th Congress, 2nd Session (1948).
49. *IRO Constitution*, Art. 2; Annex, Art. 1(c). Also see Annex, Part II.
50. Proudfoot, *European Refugees:* 401.
51. See John Loftus, *The Belarus Secret* (New York, NY: Alfred A. Knopf, 1982) and Tom Bower, *The Pledge Betrayed: America, Britain and the De-Nazification of Postwar Germany* (Garden City, NY: Doubleday, 1982) cited it Marrus, *The Unwanted:* 349.
52. For a detailed history of US refugee policy during this period see: Loescher and Scanlan, *Calculated Kindness*, and Dinnerstein, *America and the Survivors of the Holocaust.*
53. Dinnerstein, *America and the Survivors of the Holocaust* and Robert Divine, *American Immigration Policy, 1924–1952* (New Haven, CT: Yale University Press, 1957).
54. One of the best treatments of resettlement during the IRO period is Stoessinger, *The Refugee and the World Community.* In contrast to the prevalent policy of self-interest on the part of governments during this period was the decision by Turkey to admit all Muslim refugees irrespective of sex, marital status, health, or profession; and the policy of Norway to receive a large number of sick and handicapped refugees, apparently without taking the labour market or political effects into consideration.
55. Raymond Dennett and Robert K. Turner, *Documents on American Foreign Relations 1947* (Princeton, NJ: Princeton University Press, 1949): 7.
56. Stoessinger, *The Refugee and the World Community:* 145. Other governments, particularly France and Belgium, maintained that the refugee problem in Europe was likely to continue, particularly as East-West flows grew and that there was a need for institutionalized international cooperation on refugees after the IRO ceased its work.
57. Cited in Emily Copeland, 'Paths to Influence: NGO Networks and Refugees'. Conference paper, International Studies Association meeting, Washington, DC (1999).
58. Statement by Mr. Soldatov of the USSR in UN Doc A/1682 (1950).
59. Neither the IRO nor UNRRA aided victims of war and political upheavals outside

of Europe. When a massive refugee crisis involving some 14 million people accompanied the partition of India in 1947, the IRO refused to help. Unlike the refugee situation in Europe which attracted huge sums of money, the governments of India and Pakistan received almost no international assistance and had to rely on their own meagre resources and that of a few NGOs.

60. See: British Public Records Office, Foreign Office Files, FO 371/87400, July 1950.

61. Up to August 1950, the French supported the British position regarding a broad definition. According to the UK Foreign Office files, the French delegation changed to support the American position for a narrow definition in the belief that the United States would be unlikely to ever provide material assistance if the refugee definition was so broad that 'even large-scale financing from the US could hardly be expected to meet the needs'— ibid. The British also opined that the French sudden swing to the American position may have been connected with the chief French delegate, Robert Rochefort's ambition to be appointed to a high position in the newly formed UN refugee agency—ibid: FO 371/87408, 28 November 1950.

62. An appraisal of the debate over inclusion of the *Volksdeutsche* is included in UNHCR Archives, HCR/15/4, 22 GRE, 4 June 1957. The US delegation wished to 'exclude from the High Commissioner's competence persons involved in mass movements of population due to frontier changes, who possess the same rights as the inhabitants of the country in which they were currently living. Such was the case of the German minorities which totaled approximately nine million persons.' The French delegate strongly supported the proposal to exclude the 'Volksdeutsche refugees' arguing that the reason for such action was 'to exclude some 8–10 million members of former German minorities who had entered Germany either as a result of international agreements or of population transfers'. France feared that if the German government should refuse to consider them as Germans *de jure*, millions of such persons might stream into France illegally, claim refugee status and invoke the protection of the Convention or the High Commissioner's Office. Although the proposal was opposed by governments of several developing countries, including Pakistan whose refugees were excluded with this provision, a text was finally approved which excluded from the High Commissioner's mandate 'a person who has the same rights and obligations as the nationals of the country in which he has taken residence.'

63. This concession by the United States which had been promoted by the United Kingdom would prove to be especially significant in the future expansion of the Office's activities and would open the way for the 'good offices' resolutions of the UN General Assembly during the 1950s and 1960s.

64. George Warren, *The Development of United States Participation in Inter-governmental Efforts to Resolve Refugee Problems* (Mimeo, 1967).

65. The authoritative account of the Refugee convention is Guy Goodwin-Gill, *The Refugee in International Law* (Oxford: Clarendon Press, 1998).

3

The Cold War Origins of the UNHCR under Gerrit Jan van Heuven Goedhart

When the first United Nations High Commissioner for Refugees, Gerrit Jan van Heuven Goedhart of the Netherlands, first assumed his duties in January 1951, he said he 'found three empty rooms and a secretary and had to start from scratch'.[1] He had a mandate to protect refugees and to provide solutions to refugee problems, but he had practically no funds with which to carry out these functions.

No international organization has had such an unpromising beginning. It started as a temporary body with only three years to run. The Office of the United Nations High Commissioner for Refugees (UNHCR) had to provide legal protection to more than one million people across the world who were refugees within the terms of the High Commissioner's mandate. However, the Office was denied virtually all means for enforcing the international legal norms of which it was named the guardian. Determined to keep the UNHCR a strictly limited agency and to restrict their own obligations to costly refugee resettlement, states denied the High Commissioner all financial resources save administrative costs. Goedhart was given a paltry sum to run the Office and to make ends meet, he is reported to have to sold the gold bar the inter-war refugee office had received in 1938 when it won the Nobel Peace Prize. At the end of his first year, the UNHCR had a staff of thirty-three officers. At the staff Christmas party in 1951 the UNHCR was still so small that the entire staff could gather around to sing carols while the High Commissioner played the piano.

Lean Times and Early Constraints on the UNHCR

Not only did Goedhart have few resources at his disposal, but the UNHCR was also conceived in an extremely unfavourable international political environment. Intense and unremitting hostility existed between the United States and the Soviet Union and their respective allies. For separate reasons, both the

Soviet Union and the United States resisted participation in this emerging UN refugee regime. The Soviet Union opposed all efforts that did not have repatriation as the prime goal and viewed the UNHCR as an instrument of the Western powers and of anti Soviet propaganda. The United States, on the other hand, recognized that the UNHCR was not under its control, as the International Refugee Organization had been, and took initiatives that effectively marginalized the new UN agency. Realizing that it was unlikely to convert the UNHCR wholeheartedly to the American foreign policy agenda, the US erected organizational barriers to contain and control the High Commissioner's influence. It sought to implement its own independent, principally anti-Communist, refugee policy through agencies created outside of the UN system and under direct US influence. At its creation, the UNHCR was severely disadvantaged and without any powerful supporters.

Given an initial annual budget of only $300,000—compared to IRO's annual income of $150 million—and operating without any material assistance budget, the High Commissioner was severely restricted in his activities and had a minimal impact on the situation of refugees in Europe in the early Cold War period. Yet, the problems initially confronting the new UN High Commissioner for Refugees were far more complicated than simple lack of funds. At the start of his tenure, Goedhart found himself confronted by personal hostility on all sides, particularly from the United States, France, and from the leadership of the IRO who still remained influential despite the fact that the organization was in the process of closing its operations.

American hostility to Goedhart originated in the election of the first High Commissioner. The United States had initially expressed a preference for having the High Commissioner appointed by the UN Secretary-General and not, as desired by most other states, elected by the General Assembly. When this proposal was eventually defeated, the United States was disappointed because it could have expected to heavily influence, if not veto, the Secretary-General's choice. The United States had in fact exercised absolute control over the appointment of the three Directors General of the IRO, all of whom were Americans, and of the UNRRA, whose Director was also an American. The US candidate in the election for the new UN High Commissioner for Refugees was Donald Kingsley, the American Director General of IRO. Opposition to Kingsley was led by the British and the Commonwealth countries who felt that he would be too much a servant of the US State Department and the 'worst elements in Congress'.[2] The British considered it desirable to have a High Commissioner from a 'neutral' country such as the Netherlands or a Scandinavian country and therefore backed the Netherlander, Gerrit Jan van Heuven Goedhart.[3] He was the only High Commissioner ever to have been a refugee himself. For two years during World War II, van Heuven Goedhart had been a leader in the Dutch resistance. After the Nazis had listed him as a state enemy in 1944, he escaped to England where he became Minister of Justice in the Netherlands Government-in-Exile. The Germans executed his brother and scores of close friends. After the War, Goedhart acted as the Netherlands delegate to the Fourth and Fifth Sessions of the United Nations General Assembly and chaired the Third Committee which oversaw the creation of the UNHCR. As a Netherlander, he supported the vision that Western European states had for the organization. Unfortunately, this made him a natural enemy of the United States.

Goedhart was a cultivated man who was a product of interwar European culture and a fine orator whose speeches drew people to UN meetings. A well-known publicist, Goedhart had been a very good political fighter in the domestic political arena. He was strongly committed to human rights and refugee causes. Later, as High Commissioner, Goedhart often drove himself in his own car to visit refugee camps in Europe.

Despite strong lobbying for Kingsley by the American delegation to the UN, Goedhart was elected on 14 December 1950 in a secret ballot by thirty votes, against twenty-four for Kingsley, in the only contested election of a High Commissioner in the General Assembly. While Kingsley was subsequently appointed Agent General for the United Nations Korean Reconstruction Agency, both he and the US State Department remained bitter about his failure to secure election as High Commissioner and the failure of the British and the dominions to support his candidacy.[4] France had also supported Kingsley over Goedhart, not least because Robert Rochefort, *Chef de Cabinet* of the French Foreign Minister, M. Schuman, reportedly aspired to be the first Deputy High Commissioner under Kingsley.[5] After Goedhart took office, Rochefort continued to seek the Deputy High Commissioner post but was offered instead a Director's post within the Office which he flatly refused.[6] Finally, Goedhart chose an American educationalist, James Read, a Quaker, without any strong connections to the State Department, as his Deputy.[7] Feeling slighted, Rochefort became a formidable opponent of Goedhart and because he was the French representative on all bodies concerned with refugees and migration, he was, according to the British, 'in a position to do a lot of damage'.[8] Rochefort aligned himself with Kingsley at IRO to obstruct any co-operation between the two agencies and both men actively lobbied their respective governments against Goedhart. At the Council of Europe in Strasbourg, Rochefort instigated a plan for a European Refugee Service to supplant UNHCR and later pushed for a new migration agency to take over all refugee problems. His point of view was that international protection for refugees was not required.[9]

As the IRO did not expire until early 1952, the UNHCR and IRO overlapped for over a year during which a fierce inter-agency rivalry broke out between Kingsley and Goedhart. During its tenure, the IRO had had responsibilities in legal protection, care and maintenance, and overseas resettlement, but in practice the organization had focused on resettlement and on maximizing the numbers of people who were to be transported overseas. Although IRO had a department of legal protection, these staff members felt marginalized and believed that the IRO's priority was to empty the displaced persons camps as quickly as possible rather than to provide protection.[10] Not surprisingly, this caused ongoing conflict within the IRO between the Director-General's office and the IRO protection staff.[11] With the establishment of the UNHCR, most of the IRO legal protection staff moved to join Goedhart and subsequently formed the core of the UNHCR. The rift within IRO was thus carried over to the UNHCR and served to continue to poison relations between Kingsley and Goedhart and to accentuate the initial differences and difficulties between the two organizations.[12] Throughout the first year of the High Commissioner's existence, the IRO and the UNHCR fought over their respective spheres of activities and responsibilities. The IRO continued to claim the protection function for displaced persons and non-German refugees in Germany and opposed the UNHCR assuming the protection functions of IRO. The IRO also tried to thwart the establishment of a UNHCR representative in Germany and refused to hand over the thousands of IRO protection files of displaced persons to the UNHCR's legal protection division, thus making it almost impossible for the High Commissioner to assume an effective operational and protection role there.[13]

Almost from the beginning of his time as High Commissioner, Goedhart was isolated. The Americans still harboured resentment that Goedhart had defeated their candidate and did little to ensure the UNHCR's success. Rather, the US avoided the UNHCR in favour of institutional arrangements that it could more readily control. Great Britain and the Benelux and Scandinavian governments offered the High Commissioner backing and advice but he made little effort to utilize this support. Indeed, for the most part, UNHCR was confronted from the very beginning by a hostile international environment. Summarizing the first six months of the High Commissioner, the British Foreign Office noted:

Dr. Van Heuven Goedhart finds himself in a far from enviable position at the moment. He faces the implacable hostility of the French as a result of his very proper refusal to make Rochefort his Deputy; he appears to exercise no influence in Washington, despite his appointment of an American deputy; his relations with IRO are far from happy; the governments from which he formerly drew his support have been given no opportunity of helping him and he is far from well served by his own subordinates   (British Public Records Office, Foreign Office Files, FO 371/95942, 28 June 1951.)

The UNHCR as a Side-show

By far the biggest obstacle to UNHCR's development as an international organization was American hostility towards the High Commissioner. Throughout

Goedhart's tenure, the United States treated the UNHCR as a side-show and as a mostly irrelevant organization. According to Goedhart's Deputy, James Read, the United States kept the UNHCR as non-operational as possible and State Department officials frequently let UNHCR officials know where the power really lay. They 'could make the UNHCR feel like they were a lot of little boys'.[14] From the American perspective, the High Commissioner's clients were of little political value to the United States in the emerging Cold War. The UNHCR case load comprised approximately 400,000 'hard-core' refugees left over from the IRO period. These were displaced persons who, because of age, illness, or the wrong profession, were considered undesirable to resettlement countries.

The United States was primarily interested in the refugees who were fleeing Communist regimes. For most of the 1950s, thousands of refugees from Eastern and Central Europe left their homes to seek asylum in the West. They emigrated illegally or in flagrant contravention of government policy and felt unable to return to their homes because of the likelihood of persecution. Because refugees constituted visible rejection of their domestic policies, Communist authorities lashed out at the receiving states and refused to co-operate with the UNHCR.

For Western governments, refugees exposed the inadequacies of the Communist system. Therefore, these governments encouraged the flow from East to West in order to weaken their ideological rivals and gain political legitimacy in their Cold War struggle. For American policy-makers, the acceptance of such migrants served clear ideological ends; a series of decisions made between 1947 and 1952 established an official, albeit unacknowledged US policy of exploiting the symbolic and instrumental value of mass migration and defections.[15] The US and the UK sought to use sabotage, guerrilla tactics, and propaganda behind the Iron Curtain as a way of encouraging the local populations in Russia and the Soviet bloc to rise up.[16] As part of this general strategy, Russian and Eastern European exiles were employed in a variety of propaganda exercises and covert military operations. Thus, special US legislation approving the recruitment of up to a hundred defectors a year was included in the 1949 act that created the Central Intelligence Agency.[17] In 1950, the State Department and the CIA launched the National Committee for a Free Europe, a nominally private organization dedicated to promoting the policy of 'liberation' and the 'rollback of communism'. With the authority of the *Mutual Security Act* of 1951, President Truman set up the United States Escapee Program (USEP) to facilitate defections from the Communist bloc. By 1952, the Psychological Strategy Board, charged with coordinating US intelligence and propaganda activities, was actively monitoring the influx of East Europeans and was organizing the recruitment of a substantial number as intelligence operatives or as staff of US clandestine radio stations.[18] In fact, United States policy until 1980 was that refugee admissions were limited by law to those fleeing Communist countries or countries in the Middle East. Of the 233,436 refugees admitted between 1956 and 1968, all but 925 were from Communist countries.[19] Thus, for political and ideological reasons, refugees from communism were welcomed—even encouraged to vote with their feet.

The nature of the American commitment to refugees, which became increasingly regional and unilateral, continued to evolve during the 1950s and reflected the mania of anti-Communism and McCarthyism that gripped the nation. The UNHCR was the chief victim of this new approach. US officials strongly opposed funding UN organizations involved in refugee or labour movements because they thought the US would have more control and influence over the kinds of refugees and migrants assisted and the programmes carried out outside the UN framework. Despite the fact that the UNHCR received no more support from the Eastern bloc than did the IRO, the Office was adversely affected by the upsurge of suspicious anti-UN sentiment in the United States during the early 1950s. The power of the Soviet Union in the UN Security Council, the representation of Communist countries in the UN Secretariat and in UN Specialized Agencies, and UN advocacy of human rights conventions were all deemed suspect by the conservatives who controlled the US Congress at the time. The Senate debates over the Bricker Amendment[20] and over US support for the ILO revealed a deep distrust of all internationalism which was not employed to serve clear American interests as defined by the dominant coalition of Republicans and conservative Southern Democrats. The 1951 refugee convention may well have been suspect because it gave an international body the implicit right to identify and comment on at least some human rights violations. The UNHCR was clearly suspect because, as a UN organization, it was not amenable to direct American control. When van Heuven Goedhart was selected as first High Commissioner over active US opposition, the validity of this concern was confirmed.

The United Nations became a very low priority for US foreign policy, and the United States eschewed the UNHCR, deliberately choosing not to contribute to its programmes. Rather, America concentrated its resources heavily in its own military and economic programmes, beginning with the Marshall Plan and followed by the *Mutual Security Acts* of 1951 through 1961. The Mutual Security legislation also provided funding for humanitarian programmes and refugee assistance came to be viewed within this framework. Special modifications were made in American immigration law to facilitate the admission of more Germans, primarily on the grounds that West Germany was afflicted with a 'surplus population' problem which could destabilize that nation, and promote the spread of communism.[21] Provision was also made for the admission of more 'escapees' from Iron Curtain countries. It was of paramount interest to the United States that international attention remain firmly focused on refugees from Communist countries. From the American perspective, the UNHCR's programmes and expenditures might benefit refugees who were of little political interest to the US and might create more demands for their resettlement into the United States. Thus, wherever possible, the United States sought to support only refugee agencies created outside the UN, where the US and its allies would be directly involved.

The United States was instrumental in creating two specially created United Nations refugee organizations which were outside the mandate of the UNHCR and were funded generously by US administrations. Both organizations were situated in regions of key geopolitical interest to the United States: the Middle East and the Korean Peninsula. In the period leading up to the declaration of the State of Israel by the Jewish community of Palestine in May 1948, and immediately following the subsequent invasion by the armies of neighbouring Arab countries, some 700,000 Palestinians fled or were expelled from areas under Jewish control to surrounding countries. In this case, the United States supported the United Nations and helped establish the United Nations Relief for Palestine Refugees, soon to be replaced by the United Nations Relief and Works Agency for Palestine Refugees in the Near East (UNRWA). Its mandate was to provide aid—but no resettlement opportunities in Western countries—to Palestinian refugees. It was to foster the economic integration of the refugees in their host countries, but was not called upon to provide legal protection to Palestinians nor to seek a political solution to the Arab–Israeli conflict.[22] While some refugees were absorbed into Arab states and others repatriated, the majority of Palestinians remained in camps in the region. This was necessitated by the foreign policy objectives of the Arab states, as the resettlement or assimilation of Palestinian refugees would have made it difficult if not impossible to contest the legitimacy of the establishment of a Jewish state or to construct a Palestinian state in the future.

At the insistence of Arab states, Palestinians registered with UNRWA were purposely excluded from the competence of the UNHCR, both in its Statute and in the 1951 Refugee Convention. American support for a separate UN agency for Palestinians reinforced the anti-Communist impulse behind US refugee policy. The UNRWA provided stability in a strategically important region by materially assisting the refugees and preserving the internal security of the Arab states as a bulwark against Communist subversion. This view was emphasized in testimony before Congress given by US Assistant Secretary of State George McGhee:

The political loss of the Middle East would be a major disaster . . . the political strategic position of the Soviet Union would be immeasurably strengthened by the attainment of its objectives in the Near East, and the Cold War materially prolonged. . . . Against this background, our solicitude for the Palestine refugees, partly based on humanitarian considerations, has additional justification. As long as the refugee problem remains unsolved . . . attainment of a political settlement in Palestine is delayed . . . [and] the refugees . . . will continue to serve as a natural focal point for exploitation by communist disruptive elements which neither we nor the Near Eastern governments can afford to ignore. (US House of Representatives, Committee on Foreign Affairs, 81st Congress, 2nd Session, *Hearings on Palestine Refugees*, 16 February 1950: 9).[23]

The second UN agency that received significant American funding was the United Nations Korean Reconstruction Agency (UNKRA). Like the UNRWA, the UNKRA provided a similar limited service to the millions of people displaced by the Korean War and assisted South Korea to relocate refugees from Communist North Korea and to repatriate Koreans from Japan.[24] Although the 1951 Refugee Convention only applied to Europeans and therefore excluded Koreans, Korean refugees nevertheless benefited from a massive UN relief effort. The provision of material assistance to those who had fled from North Korea or who had been displaced by the war was perceived to be integral to the anti-Communist war effort by the American forces who were fighting on the South Korean side under the UN flag. Like the Palestinian refugee situation in the Middle East, the plight of Korean refugees had the foreign policy attention of the United States, and a special UN organization, outside of the UNHCR, was created to administer to their needs. In setting up the UNKRA, the United States agreed to fund up to 70 per cent of its operations and insisted on the appointment of the former IRO Director, Donald Kingsley, as the first Agent-General of the UNKRA.[25] In both Korea and Palestine, refugee assistance programmes were viewed as supporting larger American interests in strategically important regions and the United States provided the bulk of financing for these organizations.

The massive displacement of peoples in other regions of Asia in the early post-World War II years did not generate such large-scale international responses and was largely met with the indifference of the United States and the Western Powers. Despite Indian and Pakistani appeals for material assistance from the UN for the 14 million refugees who were generated after the British partition of the Indian subcontinent in 1947, very little aid from the international community was forthcoming. The governments which had drafted the 1951 Refugee Convention purposely excluded refugees on the Indian subcontinent. Unlike the Koreans or the Palestinians, they were not viewed by the United States and the West as refugee populations in a geopolitically important region of the world. Hence, the material needs of the displaced Hindu and Muslim communities were not recognized as constituting a legitimate demand on the emerging international refugee regime, and no special international agency was created for them.

'Surplus Populations' and the Creation of the Intergovernmental Committee for Migration

World War II had left Europe in a state of economic prostration, which was greatly exacerbated by large-scale population movements. Several years after the war, many European countries still experienced high rates of unemployment.

Many countries were overpopulated as a result of involuntary migrations and high birth rates. Fearful that a large, unemployable and discontented population would threaten economic recovery in Europe and would be exploited by Communists for political gain, the United States sought the establishment of an international migration agency to replace the IRO in order to move refugees and other elements of surplus population out of Western Europe to final resettlement sites in skill-starved Latin America, Australia, Canada, and other less-populated parts of the world.[26]

One of the prime movers behind this effort was the powerful Chairman of the House Judiciary Committee, Congressman Francis Walter, who voiced his concern that overpopulation in central and western European countries threatened order and security in western Germany and Austria.[27] Walter was alarmed at the electoral success of Western European Communist parties and argued that such a migration initiative was in the US interest since it would help prevent the spread of Communism in Europe.[28] He also maintained that the establishment of a new migration agency would relieve resettlement pressure on the US by opening doors for future migrants in Australia, Canada, and Latin American countries. Moreover, Walter was concerned that since there was not enough land and industrial production in Western European countries to support all their inhabitants, there was a danger that Marshall Plan aid to these countries could be substantially dissipated in continuing welfare support to unemployed persons. If the US ever hoped to cut future foreign aid appropriations to Europe, the Congressman argued, it had to establish an international migration office to resolve the problem of overpopulation in Europe. Walter also believed that if the new organization was to be effective, it had to be under American control and be created outside the orbit of the United Nations system because 'of the known hostility of the eastern European governments to projects of this nature'.[29] Walter's proposal quickly gained the support of the Truman administration and US allies.

International pressure for some kind of new machinery to deal with surplus populations, precipitated an intense rivalry among the refugee and migration organizations. Donald Kingsley, backed by the US State Department, wanted to utilize the vast transport organization built up by the IRO along with its army of trained officers and its experience in the mass movement of manpower across oceans to create a new permanent international migration organization. Opposing Kingsley was Bradford Morse, the Director-General of the International Labour Organization (ILO) who sought to assume all international migration activities within his agency. Even the Council of Europe held discussions about setting up a European Migration Office to deal with such issues.

The UNHCR perceived such moves as a further threat to its already precarious international position. The Office was concerned that the new emphasis on migration in terms of manpower would mean that it would be increasingly difficult for the High Commissioner to get governments to do anything for refugees.[30] Goedhart did not think that refugees would have their fair share in any opportunities for migration and that the new agency would simply duplicate current international efforts and create new problems of co-ordination.[31] He also feared that any new agency would intrude on his own Office's activities and interests.[32] The UNHCR's opposition to a new migration organization was strongly supported by the UK, who argued that the surplus population problem was the responsibility of the German and Austrian governments and could best be resolved through local integration, and by an improvement in their economic, financial, and social structures, and not by emigration.[33]

At first the ILO tried to seize the initiative to head this new migration agency despite the fact that the US Congress signalled opposition to locating the new organization within the UN. In October 1951, the ILO organized a conference on migration in Naples at which it presented a specific proposal to establish a Migration Council to be responsible to the Director General of the ILO. The United States, along with other governments, opposed the ILO plan, arguing that the agency did not have the experience necessary to function successfully as an operating agency in the transport of migrants.[34] The United States favoured the establishment of a new intergovernmental agency concerned solely with the transport of migrants and refugees, making use of the resettlement machinery of the IRO. A few days after the failed Naples conference, the US Congress passed the 1951 *Mutual Security Appropriations Act* which allocated $10 million to fund a new international migration initiative led by the US. Several weeks later at a migration conference in Brussels on 26 November 1951, the United States presented its own plan for a Provisional Intergovernmental Committee for the Movement of Migrants from Europe (PICME). In contrast to the UNHCR, the PICME, later to be renamed the Intergovernmental Committee for European Migration (ICEM), was designed to be operational in order to enable national states to manage and structure migration flows. By including both labour migrants and refugees under its mandate, the establishment of ICEM also killed any prospects for the creation of a labour migration programme at the ILO. As the creator and principal supporter of the new organization, the United States promoted the agency as the successor to the IRO and ensured that the ICEM was financed to the full extent of its requirements and received the IRO's fleet of ships to fulfil its transportation and resettlement functions. The ICEM was established as a multilateral institution outside of the United Nations, with an American Director, and a board composed entirely of democratic nations friendly to the United States.[35]

Communist Bloc Defectors and the Establishment
of the US Escapee Program

In addition to giving full support to the ICEM, the United States was specifically interested in assisting refugees who continued to flood into Western
Europe from the East. In the early 1950s, between 1,000 and 1,500 Eastern
European refugees were arriving monthly in Austria, Germany, Greece, Italy,
and Turkey. For host countries, this movement assumed crisis proportions
because there existed no adequate reception or care facilities, particularly in
Austria, Germany, and Greece where the return of hundreds of thousands of
their own ethnic refugees was taking place simultaneously.

The largest flow out of the Eastern bloc during the 1950s was created by
the mass exodus of East Germans into West Germany. Until the early 1950s,
the lines between the occupation zones in Germany could easily be crossed.
Taking advantage of this route, in 1950 some 197,000 East Europeans applied
for political asylum in West Germany; in 1951 the number was 165,000; in
1952, 182,000; and in 1953, 331,000.[36] Although cultural similarities made
for relatively easy integration into the host West European countries, and
refugees provided labour for the expanding Western economies, not all were
spontaneously welcomed. By 1952, nearly 200,000 were jammed into camps
and centres in Berlin and West Germany, sometimes living in appalling
conditions.[37]

To respond to this crisis and to take advantage of the political opportunities presented by the refugees from the Communist bloc countries, the US
took a series of unilateral initiatives in the early 1950s to encourage and
provide for mass defections from the East. On March 22, 1952, President
Harry Truman sent a message to Congress describing the inadequate and
unsatisfactory conditions of reception and care confronting the escapees from
eastern European countries. He reported that 15,000–20,000 German
expellees were crossing the border monthly from the Soviet zone of Germany
to western Germany. In addition 1,000 refugees were coming each month
from the eastern European countries to add to the 18,000 who had already
arrived at the time in the west. To relieve these pressures, Truman asked
Congress to authorize additional immigration of refugees to the United States
and to establish a special programme of assistance for escapees. Over the next
several years, the United States increased its resettlement admissions quotas[38]
and granted the Attorney-General the power to 'parole' refugees—that is, to
admit those outside the national origins quota system for 'emergent reasons',
and for those who were deemed to be in the 'public interest'.

In April 1952, the United States formally established the United States
Escapee Program (USEP), which was essentially the national governmental
arm of the United States for the resettlement of Communist bloc refugees.

Although it had been a covert programme that had existed since at least 1949, the USEP was regarded by its Congressional supporters as part of a 'new American foreign policy' dedicated to the 'liberation of Poland and other captive nations'.[39] The USEP was administered within the Department of State by the Office of Refugee and Migration Affairs, an integral part of the Bureau of Security and Consular Affairs. Country field units of the programme to assist and resettle 'iron curtain refugees' were attached to US Missions in Germany, Austria, Italy—both Rome and Trieste—Greece, and Turkey with a regional co-ordinating unit in Frankfurt.[40] With an annual budget of $4.3 million, the USEP reached agreements with the ICEM and with voluntary agencies to carry out its programmes and operations.[41] The USEP programmes excluded German refugees and expellees (*volksdeutsche*), ethnic Turks from Bulgaria, ethnic Greeks from Romania, and Yugoslav refugees.

Escapees from the East were encouraged to flee and were used to gain intelligence and information about life on the other side of the Iron Curtain, to destabilize the regimes they fled, and to reveal the political, moral, and economic bankruptcy of life under Communism. US intelligence agencies collaborated closely with their Austrian and German counterparts to debrief individual defectors and to share information. These programmes and institutions played a major role in shaping American refugee policy and investing it with specific ideological content.

The UNHCR's Bid to be Relevant and to End 'Administering Misery'

From its inception, the UNHCR had to demonstrate its relevance to the international community. In order for his Office to increase its influence, the High Commissioner had to overcome the financial and operational limitations imposed upon the UNHCR by its founding members. Goedhart realized that without a bigger budget the Office would have no programme worthy of the name and would exercise little clout in the international system. The High Commissioner sought almost immediately to assume material assistance responsibilities and to change the organizational ideology of the Office. From the outset, Goedhart stressed that protection would be worthless without the resources necessary to provide material assistance to people who were in need of both physical assistance as well as legal protection. However, the obstacles the High Commissioner faced were numerous and difficult.

Perhaps the biggest problem confronting the High Commissioner was the fact that donor governments were hostile to the idea of granting the UNHCR the capacity to raise funds for operational purposes and considered such activities as 'empire building' on the part of the High Commissioner.[42]

Despite the fact that governments repeatedly told the High Commissioner that he could only operate 'within the resources at his disposal', Goedhart tenaciously fought to obtain the capacity to independently raise funds and to increase his budget. Not only did the UNHCR find itself virtually excluded from all American aid as the US generously funded the ICEM and its own refugee office, the US Escapee Program. But European states also were reluctant to spend large sums of money on local refugee settlement, especially if it meant diverting any of the economic aid they were receiving from abroad. Moreover, local populations feared competition from refugees and displaced persons for jobs and services. Thus, from the inception of his office in January 1951, the High Commissioner had to fight constantly for more funds and political support to carry out his programmes.

The High Commissioner felt boxed in and repeatedly appealed to the international community to help him solve his dilemma. The UNHCR was forbidden to have any programmes of material assistance, despite the existence of an estimated 400,000 'hard core' displaced persons who were the UNHCR's direct responsibility. The UNHCR was restricted to concerning itself with international protection and the promotion of permanent solutions without actually contributing anything of a concrete nature to their realization. There also remained some 5,000 European refugees in Shanghai, groups in Turkey and the Middle East, and Eastern European refugees streaming into Germany and Austria.[43] The most difficult groups involved those displaced persons who had been passed over for resettlement during the IRO period because of poor health or economic non-productivity. The High Commissioner repeatedly drew attention to the plight of a 'hard core' of unwanted people who were still in camps many years after the end of the war. They included TB victims, the blind and elderly, paralytics, and increasing numbers of those attempting suicide.[44] In his speeches before the UN, Goedhart hammered home the view that there was an urgent need to integrate these refugees. The High Commissioner observed that, if these conditions persisted, the problems of refugees would fester and there was a very real danger that his office would simply 'administer misery'.

American Opposition to the UNHCR's Refugee Emergency Fund

Almost immediately upon assuming office, Goedhart made the first step to enlarge the scope of his Office beyond legal protection to include the planning and co-ordination and, to some extent, the financing of relief and material assistance.[45] The High Commissioner worked hard to convince the General Assembly of the seriousness of the European refugee problem. He drew the General Assembly's attention to the disgrace of the camps in which displaced people had been living for several years and argued that 'one can hardly speak of a solved problem'.[46] As he saw it, expanded programmes of emigration would not alleviate the problem because the refugees left in his care could not satisfy the requirements of the countries of immigration and would be overlooked in any new international migration programme. Finally, Goedhart pointed out that the General Council of the IRO had itself foreseen the need for continuing material assistance to large numbers of refugees. The problem, according to the High Commissioner, 'although certainly one of international protection, is more than legal protection in the limited sense of the word',[47] and required for its resolution complete assimilation which necessitated economic aid as well as legal protection.

Goedhart also sought help from prominent outsiders in his campaign to garner funds. In 1951, he persuaded the Rockefeller Foundation to fund a comprehensive survey of the refugee populations under his care. The study by Jacques Vernant[48] documented that these refugees were in need of material assistance as much as legal protection. In September 1951, Queen Juliana of the Netherlands, in a letter to President Truman, inspired by Goedhart, argued that 'international protection is not enough' and that 'the best way to help them (the refugees under the care of the UNHCR) is by integrating them into economic life'.[49] Goedhart then went before UN member states to ask for a limited relief fund to carry out these expanded functions. In November 1951, he requested the General Assembly to authorize him to undertake the necessary negotiations and appeals to raise voluntary contributions for this fund.[50]

On 2 February 1952, the General Assembly narrowly passed a resolution backing Goedhart's proposal for a limited relief fund of $3 million and authorized him to launch an appeal for government donations.[51] However, money received could only be used for emergencies and not for the long-range solutions he was beginning to promote. Moreover, the United Nations Refugee Emergency Fund (UNREF) proved to be largely undersubscribed, principally because the United States refused to give it any diplomatic and financial support. According to Eleanor Roosevelt, the US delegate to the United Nations at the time, the US delegation could not vote for a resolution authorizing the issuance of yet another appeal which would place the United Nations in the position of administering relief on a world-wide basis and which set the precedent of 'authorizing a United Nations official to collect funds for a rather indefinite program in competition with other and more definite ... programs'.[52] The US government's public justification for not funding the UNREF was that American contributions to European economic reconstruction, through Marshall Plan aid and its own refugee programmes, more than supplemented the UNHCR's activities. Washington also felt that the UNREF duplicated and therefore conflicted with its own refugee programmes. The USEP operated in most of the same European countries as the UNHCR and performed many of the same services, often for people who usually also fell under the jurisdiction of the High Commissioner. Yet the terms of reference and operating procedures of the USEP were far more exclusionary than were those of the UNHCR, and they were totally political in character. The USEP only assisted anti-Communist refugees, except those from Yugoslavia, excluded national refugees, and did not take those expelled from the western zones of Germany and Austria. Most importantly, the USEP only aided refugees who had escaped after 1948, thereby excluding the hard core IRO residuals under UNHCR care.

The ICEM's principal objective was to move people from the overpopulated countries of Germany, Austria, Greece, and Italy—the very countries for which the High Commissioner had requested permission to launch his international funding appeal. The UNREF included local integration projects, but it also emphasized overseas resettlement, which was identical to the function of the ICEM. At least part of the reason why the United States chose not to view the work of the two organizations as complementary and deserving of support was that they radically differed in political composition. As has been noted, the membership of the ICEM was composed entirely of nations friendly to the United States, and its statute forbade the participation of Communist states. In addition, the United States made its funding to the ICEM contingent on that agency assisting only those persons who met American security clearances. It was not possible for the United States to impose these kinds of conditions on a UN agency.

Until the end of 1954, the United States opposed funding any part of the UNHCR's programme although the Office regularly conferred and collaborated on operational issues with the two American-funded organizations which were parallel to and outside the United Nations. Their existence diverted resources from an agency that desperately needed American support to succeed. From 1952–5 when the UNHCR was vainly trying to raise $3 million, the United States allocated $45 million to the USEP and the ICEM—which carried out many USEP programmes. What was particularly demeaning to the UNHCR was that this was virtually the only United Nations fund to which the United States did not contribute.

American opposition to the High Commissioner, coupled with the fact that the United States perceived the UNHCR to be largely irrelevant to American interests, led the US to pursue its independent course. This negative attitude adversely affected the responses of practically all other potential donor governments to UNREF. By March 1954, only a little over one-third of the $3 million had been collected, and only eleven of sixty UN members had contributed. While refusing to give a penny to the UNHCR, the United States became the principal donor of two other special UN refugee agencies. The US gave over $150 million for the UNRWA and around $75 million for the UNKRA.

Goedhart was not easily deterred. He mounted a vigorous public defence of his programmes and continued to urge the US to become more supportive of the UNHCR. In a March 1953 letter to President Eisenhower, Queen Juliana of the Netherlands again urged the United States to support a new approach which 'creates the necessary economic conditions permitting the assimilation of refugees in the countries of their present residence'.[53] In his reply, Eisenhower outlined steps taken by the US Government, the ICEM, and the US Escapee Program to assist refugees but made no specific mention of the UNHCR or the High Commissioner's UN Refugee Emergency Fund.[54] At the same time, in a separate letter to the ICEM, and in what must have appeared a deliberate snub to the UNHCR, the President pledged full US support for an expanded international programme of aiding European migrants.[55] In March 1954, the High Commissioner complained that of all the refugee and migration agencies then in existence, the UNHCR was the most neglected and poorly funded:

. . . the program of emergency aid for the neediest refugees was the only one to which the United States had so far made no contribution. Both the United Nations Relief and Works Agency for Palestinian Refugees, and the United Nations Korean Reconstruction Agency had programs which dwarfed his Office's program, and to which the United States was the largest single contributor. Moreover, in no other field . . . did the fact that the United States Government was engaged in a program of its own prevent it from contributing, and contributing generously, to United Nations programs. A final consideration was that, given its present role of world leadership, the attitude taken by the United States of America on any question had a very real influence on the attitude taken by other countries. There was in his mind no doubt at all that if the United States Government made a contribution to UNREF, other countries which had so far held back would follow suit. (UN Refugee Emergency Fund Advisory Committee, Fourth Session. Documents A/AC.36/SR.26 and SR.27. 3 March 1954).

Goedhart not only felt the US neglect of the UNHCR was malign but he also believed that the establishment of numerous international refugee and migration organizations created unnecessary and expensive duplication and overlapping of programmes. According to the High Commissioner:

One of the most unfortunate aspects of this development in the refugee field is that every international or governmental organization for refugees operates on the basis of its own definition of 'refugee'. That of the United Nations differs from that of the Intergovernmental Committee for European Migration, the US 'Escapee Program' has in its turn a completely different definition and so has the Council of Europe. All these definitions are again different from that of the Convention relating to the Status of Refugees. The consequences of this situation are obvious. A man can be a refugee within the mandate of my Office, but, nonetheless, not qualify for the services of the Migration Committee. A man can live in the same barracks with a fellow-refugee and be in the same circumstances, but one is eligible for international assistance and the other is not. . . . It is clear that this development also militates against the interests of the refugees themselves in that it tends to introduce political considerations into a humanitarian problem.   (G. J. van Heuven Goedhart, *The Problem of Refugees* (Leiden: A. W. Sijthoff, 1953)).

America's opposition to the UNHCR also had a deleterious effect on the willingness of the major voluntary agencies—many of them American—to co-operate with the UNHCR. According to the terms of its mandate, the UNHCR was not an operating agency and had to find voluntary agencies to implement its meagre programmes. Many of the US voluntary agencies were reluctant to serve as implementing partners, particularly when the ICEM and the USEP could provide them with lucrative refugee contracts.[56] Moreover, the US government, fully recognizing the political significance of the refugee issue in the Cold War, encouraged voluntary agencies to act as its surrogates in the field. In this highly politicized environment, most agencies willingly utilized American government funds and implemented programmes that, although undoubtedly humanitarian, also benefited refugees of direct political interest to the United States.[57] Thus, the UNHCR and the ICEM engaged in an intense competition for ties with NGOs.

While the UNHCR met regularly with the ICEM and the USEP during the 1950s to co-ordinate the technical aspects of refugee policy in Europe, including the co-ordination of the activities of NGOs, the conflict between the UNHCR and these two agencies continued throughout the decade. As an international organization concerned about its institutional survival, the UNHCR resented the ICEM's attempts to expand its organizational priorities beyond transport to areas where it directly competed with the UNHCR. In particular, the UNHCR perceived the ICEM as seeking overall co-ordination of policy responses among NGOs and international organizations. These initiatives were strongly opposed by the UNHCR which was very suspicious of the ICEM's motives. For example, in a June 1955 letter concerning ICEM's co-ordination of refugee activity in Austria, Goedhart challenged its expansion into the UNHCR's mandate activities, particularly co-ordination of NGO activities. The UNHCR believed its Statute gave NGOs an official place in its work.[58] In a letter to the Director of the ICEM, Goedhart asserted that ICEM's interest in the refugees in Austria 'is directly the concern of my office under Article 8 of its Statute, and it really has little or nothing to do with the migration of refugees which is the legitimate concern of ICEM'.[59]

A Lifeline from the Ford Foundation and the Initiation of UNHCR Assistance Programmes

Faced with US opposition, a void of governmental support, and intense competition for funds from other agencies, the High Commissioner turned to the private sector for help. In July 1952, limited financial assistance for local integration programmes came from a 1952 Ford Foundation grant for $2.9 million[60] which enabled the Office to actively involve itself for the first time in administering assistance to refugees in West European asylum states and in co-ordinating the activities of major NGOs.

The Ford grant proved significant for the UNHCR's further expansion in several respects. The grant mandated that no funds were to be spent on direct relief. The funds were to be used for pilot projects to promote the integration of the refugees in the communities in which they lived. For the first year and a half of its existence, the Office had been able to focus only on legal protection so this constituted an exciting new programme direction for the UNHCR. The Ford Foundation programme's emphasis on local integration and self-help projects in areas such as housing, agriculture, youth projects, and vocational training constituted a significant departure from the international community's prior emphasis in refugee work on emergency relief and overseas resettlement. Acting as trustee and administrator of the grant enabled the UNHCR to develop closer relations with a number of NGOs and laid the groundwork for future international responses to refugee crises in Europe and elsewhere. The UNHCR relied on NGOs to plan and implement the Ford programmes and pilot projects and in this way NGOs became the 'operational arm' of the UNHCR in the field. Perhaps most importantly, the grant inspired and encouraged other contributions, especially from governments. A year after it had begun to operate, some $2.6 million of Ford Foundation money had been supplemented by almost $8 million from other sources. The Ford grant was the kick-start the UNHCR needed and it had far-reaching consequences for subsequent international refugee work and broadened the scope and functions of the UNHCR for the future. The programme demonstrated both the value of funding aimed at local integration and the multifaceted role the UNHCR could play in co-ordinating NGOs and encouraging financial contributions, mainly from governments, that were not necessarily directed at emergency relief or overseas resettlement.

The Ford grant also allowed the High Commissioner to demonstrate his usefulness to the major powers and to raise his Office's international profile. An opportunity to do so arose in the form of a refugee crisis which occurred in Berlin in early 1953. This crisis presented the UNHCR for the first time with an opportunity to relate its task and operations directly to future social and political stability in Europe. Berlin was considered the key Western outpost in Central Europe and from the beginning of his tenure as High Commissioner, Goedhart had singled out the refugee problem in Germany as being the key to international peace and security.[61] During the early 1950s, there was a constant stream of East Germans into West Berlin and West Germany. The federal, state, and local governments of West Germany were overwhelmed with coping with these refugees from the East. Because there was an acute shortage of housing, many of the refugees lived in the open. There was wide-spread concern that the internal instability created in Germany as a result of embittered and homeless refugees would have strategic implications for all of central Europe.[62]

The beginning of 1953 saw the inauguration of Dwight Eisenhower who had campaigned on a platform committed to exercising US power to combat communism globally. Early 1953 also witnessed an intense power struggle within the Kremlin as an increasingly paranoid Stalin eliminated those around him until he himself suddenly died of a stroke in March 1953. Not only were Stalin's actions becoming more terrifying at home, his foreign policies were failing abroad. East German citizens became frightened that the increased Sovietization of East Germany and Stalin's unpredictable behaviour at home would make access to West Berlin much more difficult in the future. Thus, the numbers of refugees crossing from Eastern Germany into West Berlin escalated sharply in early 1953, rising from over 15,000 in December 1952 to 28,000 in January 1953, and peaking at 48,000 in March 1953. As existing camps and other reception facilities became inundated, an acute social and political crisis enveloped West Berlin. Despite the fact that these refugees were clearly not within the mandate of his Office, Goedhart tried to exert leadership in responding to the crisis. On 30 January 1953, he cabled sixty UN member governments proposing housing relief in Western Germany and appealing for assistance. Hoping to position the Office as the leading refugee agency, Goedhart dispatched one of his immediate staff to Berlin to preside over a co-ordinating meeting of voluntary agencies, the representa-tives of the three Allied High Commissioners, and Western German govern-ment authorities. Anticipating criticism from donor governments that he was overstepping his mandate, Goedhart justified his action on the basis that the UNHCR would use funds for housing from the Ford grant which were not restricted as to their use. He also justified his action on the grounds that the influx of refugees from the East through Berlin would take away all the avail-able accommodation in the proximity of industrial areas of employment and thus retard the economic integration of the UNHCR's own refugees, who were deteriorating in camps in rural areas.[63] It is clear that Goedhart perceived the crisis as an opportunity both to demonstrate that his Office's interests converged with those of governments and to outshine his rivals in the refugee assistance field. In an interoffice memorandum to the High Commissioner, one of Goedhart's assistants, G. Kullman, outlined a number of advantages for the Office provided by the Berlin initiative:

... it was sound policy to be on the look-out for an opportunity of assisting non-mandated refugees in a somewhat spectacular way which would impress public opin-ion and governments and which, in the long run, might improve our relations with some governments, thus strengthening the High Commissioner's standing and ulti-mately benefitting our own refugees. ... Should this bold move come off without recrimination, it might, in the first place facilitate further approaches to Adenauer on behalf of our own categories. Should the American High Commissioner react positively, it might improve our relations with Washington . . . Last, but not least, the new move should help to bring about a first-class funeral of the attempt made in the Council of Europe to appoint a Special Representative for Refugees and Overpopulation. (UNHCR Archives, HCR/G/XV.L/13/6a. Geneva Chron: 27, 3 February 1953).

In the end, the Berlin crisis was an important success for the UNHCR. The Office administered a large-scale inter-agency programme which laid the foundation for a future expanded role for itself in the international refugee regime. The Ford Foundation provided the initial funds for relief and housing programmes for East German refugees but other governments, including the United States, contributed considerable extra funds for the effort.[64] The UNHCR was most anxious to get the maximum publicity for itself out of the Berlin crisis. But most of all, it wanted to highlight the message that the Berlin situation certainly illustrated how efficiently the High Commissioner's Office could function in dealing with all such matters if the tools to do the job were at its disposal.[65]

The Establishment of the UNREF

The UNHCR's success in the Berlin crisis and the pilot projects of the Ford programme legitimized the need for UNHCR material assistance to refugees. It demonstrated what could be accomplished with available funds and at last opened the door for the Office to become involved in permanent solutions for refugees. When Goedhart reported to the UN General Assembly in January 1954,[66] he argued that in the future the UNHCR had no choice but to support local integration projects, emphasizing not only the financial cost to governments of maintaining unsettled refugees, but also the political and security costs of not providing lasting solutions for them. He believed that, if governments were expected to offer long-term asylum, the international community had to provide material assistance to countries such as Germany, Austria, Greece, and Italy, where geopolitical circumstances resulted in unusually heavy refugee burdens. He then proceeded to outline a programme intended to accelerate the integration or resettlement of a large proportion of the 350,000 refugees who were still unsettled. The first priority was given to those who were still in the camps. He considered a sum of $12 million subscribed over a period of five years would make it possible to implement the plan.

A key to gaining General Assembly approval of the proposal and of ensuring adequate financial support for the new programme lay in finally overcoming American opposition to funding the High Commissioner's programmes. Both the United Kingdom[67] and the United States were initially opposed to the establishment of a permanent solutions fund, but a softening of hard-line American opposition to the UNHCR was becoming evident by mid-1954. Goedhart seemed for the first time hopeful about a gradual change in the American attitude toward the UNHCR. In May 1954, Goedhart had persuaded the Eisenhower administration to seek the approval of Congress for a $500,000 contribution to the UNREF.[68] The High Commissioner had actively lobbied American NGOs and had been received by John Foster Dulles, the American Secretary of State, in Washington, DC. In June 1954, the British Mission in Geneva reported Goedhart's views regarding the prospects for garnering support for his permanent solutions fund:

He could hardly expect any explicit support from the Americans, but nor did he think they would come out in opposition to his plan. He detected a change of attitude on their part: when his office was first set up, they had been the prime exponents of the thesis that refugees should be made part of the responsibility, in every respect except the narrow one of legal protection, of the governments of the countries of residence. Subsequently, they had discovered for themselves that external aid was essential and the very strong case now submitted by the State Department to Congress for a contribution to UNREF seemed an earnest change of heart. He found it difficult to believe in these circumstances that the Americans, having said yes to UNREF, would say no to a plan for a permanent solution. That did not mean they would contribute financially to the latter, but only that they would not seek to obstruct it.   (British Public Records Office, Foreign Office Files, FO 371/112621, 24 June 1954).

Goedhart was disappointed when Congress removed the State Department's request for a contribution to the UNHCR in a last minute, across-the-board cut of $17.9 million from the administration's budget for the 1955 Mutual Security Program in July 1954. Despite this cut, the United States's delegation co-sponsored a UN General Assembly resolution on 21 October 1954 calling for a four year plan for permanent solutions, known as the United Nations Refugee Fund. The overall target for the four years 1955–8 was $16 million, which it was hoped would be provided by voluntary governmental contributions. This was a significant breakthrough for the UNHCR. However, the United States made its support for the Fund contingent on definable limits to American contributions, matching support from other governments, and the assumption of responsibility for the refugees by the countries of asylum at the termination of the Fund in four years time.

At the 6–10 December 1954 meeting of the UNHCR's Advisory Committee on Refugees, Goedhart hailed the US decision to support his four year programme for permanent solutions to refugee problems.[69] At the meeting, governments also decided to reconstitute the Advisory Committee as the UNREF Executive Committee. Since governments would be footing the bill for the UNHCR's expansion into operations, states sought a more direct oversight role over the Office's finances. The terms of reference for the new governmental Executive Committee would include giving directions to the

High Commissioner in carrying out his programme for permanent solutions and emergency assistance, and exercising controls over the funds allotted to the High Commissioner.[70] Thus the UN Refugee Fund placed the UNHCR under direct government control for the first time. Unlike the former Advisory Committee which only had an advisory capacity, the new Executive Committee gave directions to the High Commissioner in carrying out the programme. It had overall control over spending by setting the annual target, approving the annual operation planning, and ensuring the close co-operation of the High Commissioner with governments and other intergovernmental and non-governmental agencies. With the establishment of the UNREF Executive Committee and more secure funding, the UNHCR increasingly came to depend on contributions from governmental rather than private sources like the Ford Foundation. For the next 12 years, governments contributed about 80 per cent of the voluntary contributions available to the UNHCR while NGOs provided only 20 per cent of such funds.[71]

By insisting on preconditions and assuming an active role on the new UNREF Executive Committee, the United States was able to spread the financial burden and at the same time to assume some degree of international control over the use of funds through its dominant position as the principal donor and most powerful government on the new Executive Committee. The stipulations that financial assistance to the UNHCR would be limited and subject to close intergovernmental supervision, as well as the knowledge that the Executive Committee of the Fund would be composed entirely of non-Communist governments, helped to finally convince the US Congress in mid-1955 to approve the $500,000 contribution to the UNHCR.

This American about-turn was also the result of increasing visibility given to the UNHCR by the international community. There was growing recognition that the refugee problem was not simply a temporary problem but a permanent one requiring sustained international attention. In 1955, the UNHCR was awarded the Nobel Peace Prize. These events had a cumulative effect in slowly changing the United States's perception of the High Commissioner and his Office.

By this time too the UNHCR had taken on a more permanent structure. In setting up the organization of the Office, Goedhart had drawn on the experience of earlier refugee agencies, particularly the Nansen Office. At his headquarters in Geneva, the High Commissioner had a team of administrators who advised him on policy developments and administered UNHCR programmes in assistance and protection. In addition, the UNHCR had field missions and representatives in the major European states, the US, Latin America, and Asia. As the agency expanded worldwide during the next several decades, the number of representatives and field missions would increase dramatically. At the same time, the assistance and protection divisions would become the core pillars in Geneva but the Office would also develop regional divisions with powerful directors to oversee the agency's ever-expanding international operations.

Soviet Re-Defection Campaigns and the American About-Turn

In the 1953 Berlin refugee crisis, the High Commissioner had demonstrated his capacity successfully to lead an inter-agency effort in a major Cold War crisis region. The US came to perceive the UNHCR as a useful political instrument. The convergence of the UNHCR's operations with US security interests in Europe was a key factor in the State Department's efforts to secure Congressional support for the High Commissioner's programme. During 1955, a new 'Soviet re-defection campaign' sought, with limited success, to persuade recent escapees to abandon the West and to return to their homelands. Moscow granted general amnesties, rehabilitation, the release of political prisoners, and reforms of the judiciary and police in Eastern Europe. US Embassy dispatches from Vienna[72] at that time described several Communist campaigns to lure refugees back home. One report noted,

Generally speaking the intelligence services of the Soviet satellites display an unusual interest in the activities and whereabouts of their nationals who have sought refuge in the Western occupied zones of Austria. The intelligence services appear to attach a good deal of importance to such persons whom they consider to be dangerous to the satellite governments either because of their espionage potential or, more likely, because they make for bad publicity and injure the prestige of the satellite countries concerned. (US National Archives, Diplomatic Branch, 863.411/3-2555. American Embassy, Vienna, 'Events of Interest to Displaced Persons Section—through March 24, 1955', 25 March 1955).

In response to these developments, the US outlined a policy to monitor closely the conduct of Communist bloc repatriation missions and to prevent frequent returns to the Iron Curtain countries.[73] The UNHCR also stepped up its monitoring of Eastern European officials by accompanying repatriation missions in Austria.[74]

Apparently influenced by the stepped-up propaganda efforts of the Communist bloc countries, some refugees, particularly Hungarians and Czechs in Austria, voluntarily returned home. Some refugees made their decision on the basis that they wanted to escape the 'sterile atmosphere of a DP camp' and 'would risk whatever reprisals [they] might incur in returning'.[75] The United States perceived these Communist re-defection campaigns to be a direct threat to its own intelligence and psychological warfare programmes, and to its escapee programme.

There was also concern, especially after the Occupation Powers withdrew from Austria following the 1955 Austrian State Treaty, that Eastern bloc refugees would no longer enjoy secure asylum status there. During the Allied occupation of Austria, Communist bloc refugees enjoyed the protection of the Allied High Commissioners. Following independence, the US felt that Austria applied too rigid and restrictive criteria with regard to determining refugee status, particularly to new arrivals from Yugoslavia. Austrian local officials often proved unsympathetic and even hostile to refugees. Burdened with a huge post-World War II refugee population and located on the frontiers of the Communist World, Vienna was under constant pressure from Moscow to repatriate all refugees from neighbouring satellite countries. As economic and political conditions improved in neighbouring Communist countries, Austrian authorities claimed that many of the new arrivals fled for economic reasons rather than because of political persecution and periodically repatriated some of the border-crossers and rejected asylum-seekers. The matter was made worse because Austria rejected UNHCR guidance and remained determined to retain full control over determination of refugee status.[76] Sensitive to any actions which would render it vulnerable to accusations of breach of neutrality by the Eastern powers, Austrian officials were guided in making their eligibility decisions primarily by considerations of their own internal security.

The entry into force on 27 July 1955 of the Austrian State Treaty not only brought to an end the Allied Control Agreement and, with it, the responsibility of Allied High Commissioners over displaced persons in Austria, but also required the Western Occupation Powers to relinquish to Austria the surveillance and intelligence aspects of the reception of newly arrived refugees. The United States perceived these developments and the Soviet re-defection campaign to be a direct threat to its own escapee, intelligence, and psychological warfare programmes. According to the US Embassy in Vienna:

During the past ten years, US direct control over refugees has provided US agencies having interests in intelligence...and psychological warfare objectives with unlimited access to a constant source of individuals and information. A refugee, upon reaching Vienna or the US Zone of Austria, was generally channeled by either Allied or Austrian representatives to the USFA refugee reception facilities operated by Military Intelligence Service, where a thorough screening of the refugee could take place without interference over as long a period as the individual was of interest. During this period the refugees were usually made available not only to US intelligence groups, but also to agencies interested in their exploitation for psychology warfare purposes, such Voice of America and Radio Free Europe. (US National Archives, Diplomatic Branch, 863.411/8-1155. American Embassy, Vienna, 'Embassy Analysis of the Post-Occupation Status of Displaced Persons and Refugees in Austria'. Appendix, 'Intelligence and Psychology Warfare Aspects', 11 August 1955.)

Austria feared that the continuation of these activities as well as the programmes of 'foreign-sponsored psychological warfare agencies, such as

Radio Free Europe or Voice of America, would risk creating a public issue between Austria and her Eastern neighbors',[77] and the Austrian Secretary of Interior went so far as to warn, 'Propaganda agents, such as Radio Free Europe, had better stop encouraging the politically dissatisfied persons in the Peoples' Democracies to escape to Austria.'[78] At the same time, the Austrian government requested that the activities of the USEP in Austria be confined to welfare and resettlement operations, thus ruling out 'any attempts of [US] agencies to lean on the USEP as a source of exploitable refugee material as they have done in the past'.[79]

In order to shore up its deteriorating position in Austria, American foreign policy officials felt that the US had to be more generous not only to recent escapees from East Europe but also to the IRO residuals who had been left behind in camps and who were coming under increasing pressure from Communist propaganda campaigns to return home. The US Embassy in Vienna, therefore, proposed a series of measures including not only increased funding for its own refugee programmes but also a US contribution to the UNHCR's programme for permanent solutions, the UNREF. It aimed at integrating refugees in Austria through a series of schemes for housing and agricultural assistance, the establishment of a refugee credit institution, vocational counselling programmes, and student aid.[80] It was the State Department view that support of UNHCR projects such as the UNREF would help to renew Austrian trust in US refugee programmes such as the USEP.[81]

Thus, for the first time, the US began to perceive UNHCR programmes as being potentially useful in the ideological struggle between East and West. Indeed, in an appeal to Congress for an American contribution to this new UN Refugee Fund in 1955, the State Department had warned that the Communists under the Soviet re-defection campaign were 'finding fairly fertile minds in those camps where these people have been festering for a very long time' and that the United States 'cannot afford to have refugees returning to communist countries because, in view of their experience as refugees, they come to believe that conditions of living behind the Iron Curtain are better than in the free world'.[82] Therefore, US Congressmen were advised that the UN Refugee Fund would support refugee projects in those 'countries closely linked in interest to the United States—Austria, Germany, Italy and Greece' where 'it is also in our own self-interest to encourage those countries to maintain liberal asylum policies'.[83] Assured that the UN Refugee Fund constituted an important part of the American struggle against Communism, the US Congress finally approved the first American financial contribution to the UNHCR.

Despite the American decision to contribute to the UN Refugee Fund, the flow of contributions from other governments was slow and insufficient to enable the programme to be fully implemented in its first two years of operation. In the first year of the Fund's activities, government contributions to the approved target of $4.2 million fell short by over 30 per cent. The target for 1956 was almost $6 million but less than half was pledged. It was not until after the November 1956 Hungarian uprising and the subsequent refugee crisis that the international community fully committed itself to the UN Refugee Fund. By the end of the programme in 1958, unlike the disastrous lack of contributions to the earlier United Nations Refugee Emergency Fund, the new fund received almost $14.5 million of its $16 million goal.[84] The establishment of the UN Refugee Fund was the first major recognition of the centrality and importance of UNHCR to the resolution of refugee problems. It also changed the emphasis of the High Commissioner's work. The new fund was not intended to deal with refugees on an emergency basis but was to concentrate on permanent solutions, particularly through local integration in countries of first asylum in Europe. The UN Refugee Fund thus represented a continuation of the effort begun under the Ford Foundation programme to assist refugees who could not meet the standards laid down for overseas migration. It was aimed at putting an end to the existing refugee camps, which, by the end of 1955, still housed some 70,000 refugees. It also sought to empty some 30,000 to 50,000 others from unofficial camps where conditions were often debilitating and demoralizing. 'These camps', van Heuven Goedhart had noted, 'are black spots on the map of Europe and should burn holes in the consciences of those who are privileged to live in better conditions'.[85] It would take another decade of work and millions of dollars of expenditures before these camps were finally cleared.

In July 1956, Gerrit Jan van Heuven Goedhart died suddenly of a heart attack. James Read, the Deputy High Commissioner took over his duties temporarily until the UN General Assembly could elect a new High Commissioner at the end of the year. Goedhart's main achievements had been to develop a broader international conscience regarding the plight of displaced persons and refugees and to begin to establish an independent niche for the Office. Despite the inauspicious beginnings of the UNHCR and the adamant opposition of the United States and some other governments, Goedhart had begun to convince the major powers that their interests converged with those of the UNHCR. By gradually enlarging the scope of his office, by obtaining the capacity to independently raise funds, and by assuming material assistance responsibilities, the High Commissioner began to exercise power autonomously in ways unintended by states at the UNHCR's creation. These developments would pave the way for the UNHCR to assume a leadership role in responding to the first major Cold War refugee crisis in Hungary in 1956 and to the first major Third World refugee crisis in Algeria beginning in 1957. These events would lead to the UNHCR becoming the centrepiece of the emerging international refugee regime.

NOTES

1. UNHCR Archives, HCR/INF/21. Statement of the United Nations High Commissioner for Refugees at the Meeting of the Third Committee during General Assembly VIII, 3 October 1953: 3.
2. British Public Records Office, Foreign Office Files, FO 371/87443, 23 September 1950.
3. Ibid.
4. British Public Records Office, Foreign Office Files, FO 371/95935, 8 January 1951. See also the unofficial memoirs of the senior American refugee official at the time: George Warren, *The Development of United States Participation in Inter-governmental Efforts to Resolve Refugee Problems* (Mimeo, 1967).
5. John Alexander of the UNHCR, in a letter to the British Foreign Office during the election of the High Commissioner, alleges that Kingsley had promised the post of Deputy High Commissioner to Rochefort if he were elected in return for French support for his candidacy. The Americans likewise felt indebted to Rochefort for the *volte face* the French delegation had taken a few weeks before the Summer 1950 ECOSOC session to support the US position regarding the definition of refugee and the description of the scope of the mandate of UNHCR. British Public Records Office, Foreign Office Files, FO 371/95936, 27 June 1951.
6. Ibid.
7. George Warren of the State Department was reluctant at first to agree to Goedhart's request for an American deputy and he advised him that he should accept Rochefort instead. According to the Foreign Office, the British doubted whether 'Mr Read cut much ice in Washington'. British Public Records Office, Foreign Office Files, FO 371/95942, 28 June 1951. Warren expressed the view that Rochefort's appointment would secure the full co-operation of the French government in bringing into force the Draft Convention relating to the Status of Refugees. He also wanted to rid Goedhart of the hope that the appointment of an American would assist him in securing US support for a large operating relief fund which both the US State Department and Congress believed unnecessary. US National Archives, Diplomatic Branch, 320.42/3-1551, 12 March 1951.
8. British Public Records Office, Foreign Office Files, FO 371/95942, 28 June 1951.
9. Ibid.
10. Interview with Bernard Alexander, former UNHCR assistant to G. van Heuven Goedhart and former IRO official, Great Hasely, England, December 1986.
11. British Public Records Office, Foreign Office Files, FO 371/95935, 8 January 1951.
12. Kingsley reportedly fired his entire legal protection staff with one month's notice and without any consultation with Goedhart. British Public Records Office, Foreign Office Files, FO 371/95935, 8 March 1951.
13. Ibid. FO 371/95943, 12 July 1951.
14. Bruce Nichols interview with James Read, New York, November 1983 cited in Bruce Nichols, *The Uneasy Alliance: Religion, Refugee Work, and U.S. Foreign Policy* (New York, NY: Oxford University Press, 1988): 88.
15. For background see: Gil Loescher and John Scanlan, *Calculated Kindness: Refugees*

and America's Half-Open Door, 1945 to Present (New York, NY, and London: The Free Press and Macmillan, 1986).

16. Peter Grose, *Operation Rollback: America's Secret War Behind the Iron Curtain* (Boston, MA: Houghton Mifflin Co., 2000).

17. US Congress, *Central Intelligence Act* (July 1949).

18. Harry S. Truman Library, David D. Lloyd Collection, Box 3 File: Immigration Memo No. 4, Psychological Strategy Board, Policy Guidance No D-18/a, 'Psychological Operations Plan for Soviet Orbit Escapees, Phase A,' 20 December 1951: 5.

19. Arthur Helton, 'Political Asylum Under the 1980 Refugee Act: An Unfulfilled Promise,' *University of Michigan Journal of Law Reform*, 17 (1984): 243–6.

20. Conservatives and ultra-nationalists within the US Congress feared that Executive Branch support for international human rights conventions would impose unwanted international legal obligations on the federal government and on state governments. Congressional members therefore championed the US Constitution over international treaty law. The Bricker Amendment sought to undermine the Executive's authority to ratify self-implementing international treaties. Because of Congressional support for the Bricker Amendment, the Eisenhower administration agreed to back away from open support for human rights treaties and sacrificed its leadership on international human rights issues.

21. US Congress, *Refugee Relief Act* (7 August 1953).

22. For background see: Edward H. Buehrig, *The United Nations and the Palestinian Refugees: A Study in Non-Territorial Administration* (Bloomington, IN: Indiana University Press, 1971); David Forsythe, 'UNRWA, the Palestinian Refugees, and World Politics', *International Organization*, 25 (Winter 1971): 26–45, and 'The Palestine Question: Dealing with a Long-Term Refugee Situation', *Annals of the American Academy of Political and Social Sciences*, 468 (May 1983): 89–101; Howard Adelman, 'Palestine Refugees, Economic Integration and Durable Solutions', in Anna Bramwell, ed., *Refugees in the Age of Total War* (London: Unwin-Hyman, 1988); and Benny Morris, *The Birth of the Palestinian Refugee Problem: 1947–1949* (Cambridge: Cambridge University Press, 1987).

23. The Special Representative of the US Secretary of State to the Near East, Ambassador Edwin Locke, Jr., also stressed the political importance of the Palestinian refugees in the context of US–Soviet competition in the Middle East. See Larry Newman, 'Locke Sees Reds Playing Cosy Game in the Middle East', *The Daily Star* (Beirut, Lebanon: 2 December 1952): 1.

24. Gene M. Lyons, *Military Policy and Economic Aid: The Korean Case* (Columbus, OH: Ohio University Press, 1961).

25. US National Archives, Diplomatic Branch, 320.52/10-1050, 'Korean Relief and Rehabilitation', 10 October 1950.

26. A 13 May 1950 statement from the Foreign Ministers of France, the United Kingdom, and the United States stated that 'the excess of population from which several countries in western Europe are suffering is one of the most important elements in the difficulties and disequilibrium of the world'. Warren, *The Development of United States Participation*: 136.

27. Ibid: 135–68.

28. The *New York Times* reported US officials, including Walter, who believed that the 'communists are capitalizing on unrest and unemployment in overpopulated

countries' and pointed out that 'it is impossible for a middle of the road political party to succeed where there is no large segment of moderately well off population'. 'Parley on Agency Set', *New York Times* (24 August 1951).

29. Ibid.
30. British Public Records Office, Foreign Office Files, FO 371/95938, 18 October 1951.
31. European Office of the United Nations, Information Centre, Geneva. Press Release No. REF/56. Speech by UN High Commissioner for Refugees to the Conference on Migration at Brussels, 29 November 1951.
32. British Public Records Office, Foreign Office Files, FO 371/95934, 4 December 1951.
33. Ibid: FO 371/95938, 18 October 1951.
34. Warren, *The Development of United States Participation*: 147–8.
35. Ibid: 149.
36. Michael Marrus, *The Unwanted: European Refugees in the Twentieth Century* (New York, NY: Oxford University Press, 1985): 354.
37. Ibid.
38. This was accomplished primarily through passage in the US Congress, of the *Refugee Relief Act* of 1953, the *Refugee Escapee Act* of 1957, and the *Fair Share Refugee Act* passed in 1960.
39. For a detailed account of the evolution of these programmes see: Loescher and Scanlan, *Calculated Kindness*.
40. Warren, *The Development of United States Participation*: 171–4.
41. In a written statement provided the US Congress, the State Department described the relationship between USEP and NGOs: 'Operating primarily through contracts with the nonprofit American and international voluntary agencies, the U.S. Escapee Program reimburses these agencies for actual expenses incurred under individually approved projects that implement escapee program objectives, yet still are in keeping with the humanitarian objectives of the agencies themselves. All projects, closely supervised by the USEP staff, are developed with an eye to the overall operational objective of establishing the escapees as useful and self-sustaining citizens of the free world community. All Americans and local employees are carefully screened on a level which assures dedicated personnel oriented along free world concepts and sympathetic to U.S. objectives.' US Senate, Committee on Foreign Relations, *Migration and Refugee Assistance Act* of 1961, 87th Congress, 1st Session (11 September 1961): 12.
42. George Warren, writing in March 1951, criticized the expansionist tendencies of Goedhart and reiterated the US view that the creation of an international fund could not be justified. US National Archives, Diplomatic Branch, 320.42/3-1551, 12 March 1951. Information on the early formation of the UNHCR relies to an extent on Ronald Scheinman, *The Office of the United Nations High Commissioner for Refugees and the Contemporary International System*, Mimeo, 1974.
43. Jacques Vernant, *The Refugee in the Post-War World* (New Haven, CT: Yale University Press, 1953).
44. For a brief account of the conditions of displaced persons in camps, see UNHCR Archives, HCR/INF/7, 1953—a series of personal statements collected from them by voluntary agencies in early 1953.
45. United Nations General Assembly (VI), Document E/2036 (27 June 1951).
46. Ibid.

47. Ibid: paragraph 25.
48. Vernant, *The Refugee in the Post-War World.*
49. The text of a letter from her Majesty the Queen of the Netherlands to the President of the United States (22 September 1951). In his reply, Truman stressed the official American position that integration and assimilation must take place within each individual country of residence and that in Germany this effort could not be isolated from the effort to improve the total economy of Germany.
50. United Nations General Assembly (VI), Document E/2036/Add.2 (13 November 1951).
51. United Nations General Assembly Resolution 538B (VI) (1952): Paragraph 1
52. United Nations General Assembly (VI), Third Committee, 382nd Meeting, 10 January 1952.
53. Letter dated 18 March 1953 from Her Majesty Queen Juliana of the Netherlands to the President Dwight Eisenhower of the United States.
54. Letter dated 4 April 1953 from President Dwight Eisenhower of the United States to Queen Juliana of the Netherlands.
55. *New York Times* (23 April 1953).
56. Interview with Bernard Alexander, former chief assistant to G. J. van Heuven Goedhart, Great Hasely, England, December 1986.
57. See Bruce Nichols, *The Uneasy Alliance*, and Loescher and Scanlan, *Calculated Kindness* for more detailed accounts of the relationship between the US government and voluntary agencies during this period.
58. Article 8 of the Statute of UNHCR specifies the means by which the High Commissioner shall provide for the protection of refugees under his mandate, requires that the High Commissioner shall establish 'contact in such manner as he may think best with private organizations dealing with refugee questions', and facilitates 'the coordination of the efforts of private organizations concerned with the welfare of refugees'.
59. International Organization for Migration Archives, letter from G. J. van Heuven Goedhart to Harold Tittman, ICEM, 6 June1955.
60. Louise Holborn, *Refugees: A Problem of Our Time* (Metuchen, NJ: Scarecrow Press, 1975).
61. European Office of the United Nations, Information Centre, Press Release No. REF/48, 'Dr. G. J. van Heuven Goedhart, High Commissioner for Refugees, in Speech before Social Committee of ECOSOC Warns Stability of Central Europe Depends on Solving German Refugee Problem' (3 September 1951).
62. Final Report on the Ford Foundation Program for Refugees, Primarily in Europe, July 1968, 40–68.
63. UNHCR Archives, HCR/G/XV/13/1/23, 6 February 1953; and HCR/G/XVL/1/3, Geneva Chron: 49, 2 March 1953.
64. For a breakdown of these contributions and programmes see: Holborn, *Refugees: a Problem of Our Time*, 365–96.
65. UNHCR Archives, HCR/G/XV.L/13/1/23, 3 March 1953.
66. UN General Assembly, Advisory Committee (IV), A/AC.36/32, 29 January 1954.
67. The British view was that 'the programme represents a major shift of responsibility for refugees from the governments of their countries of residence to the member governments of the United Nations (and in practice to those governments such as

the United Kingdom, the United States, Australia and Canada who might be expected to furnish funds on the scale envisaged'. British Public Records Office, Foreign Office Files, FO 371/112624, 4 March 1954.

68. Ibid.
69. Goedhart was so anxious to obtain US support that he offered to appoint an American to head the UNHCR unit that would handle the UNREF program. US National Archives, Diplomatic Branch, 1954. 320.42/12-1454, 14 December 1954.
70. US National Archives, Diplomatic Branch, 320.42/12-1054, 20 December 1954.
71. Holborn, *Refugees: A Problem of Our Time*, Annex 50.4, 1419
72. US National Archives, Diplomatic Branch, 863.411/3-2155. American Embassy, Vienna, 'Recent Soviet-Satellite Attempts to Induce Escapees to Return From Austria to Iron Curtain Countries', 21 March 1955.
73. Ibid., 7.
74. US National Archives, Diplomatic Branch, 863.411/3-2555. American Embassy, Vienna, 'Events of Interest to Displaced Persons Section - through July 11, 1955', 5 July 1955.
75. Ibid., 3.
76. UNHCR Archives, HCR/6/1 Aus and 22/1 Aus, 1955.
77. US National Archives, Diplomatic Branch, 863.411/11-1755. American Embassy, Vienna, 'Recent Developments in Austria Affecting Refugees', 17 November 1955.
78. Ibid. Concerned about the effect the changeover was expected to have on US intelligence operations, the US extracted from the Austrian Ministry of Interior an agreement 'to permit U.S. intelligence agencies to remove particularly interesting refugees to Germany provided that the U.S. accepted full responsibility for the care and maintenance of the refugees and agreed that they would not be returned to Austria after screening'.
79. Ibid.
80. Ibid.
81. US National Archives, Diplomatic Branch, 863.411/8-956. American Embassy, Vienna, 'Recent Developments in Austria Affecting Refugees', 9 August 1956.
82. US Congress. Subcommittee on Foreign Operations Appropriations of the House Committee on Appropriations. 84th Congress, 1st Session. Hearing on 28 June 1955: 428, 433.
83. Ibid.: 428.
84. The United States finally contributed $5.3 million to the UN Refugee Fund.
85. G. J. van Heuven Goedhart, *Refugee Problems and Their Solutions* (Geneva: UNHCR, 1955). Lecture given at the Nobel Institute in Oslo on the occasion of the award of the Nobel Prize for Peace 1954 to the Office of the UN High Commissioner for Refugees.

4

The Emerging Independence of the UNHCR under Auguste Lindt

Two political events at the centre of world politics in the late 1950s—the Hungarian Revolution and the Algerian War of National Independence—transformed the UNHCR. The roles played by the UN High Commissioner for Refugees in both ensuing refugee crises resulted in fundamental changes in the Office's orientation and in its international reputation. Because of the successful roles it played in these crises, the UNHCR became the centrepiece of the international refugee regime.

The man who steered the UNHCR through these momentous events was Auguste Lindt, a Swiss diplomat who was elected second UN High Commissioner for Refugees by the General Assembly in December 1956, at the beginning of a massive refugee exodus from Hungary. Lindt, a personal friend of Dag Hammarskjöld, was hand picked by the Secretary-General to succeed Goedhart.[1] Before taking up his position as the new High Commissioner, Lindt had been the Permanent Observer of Switzerland to the United Nations. Unlike his predecessor, Lindt was on good terms with the United States and consequently, under his leadership the UNHCR's orientation became clearly pro-American. Not everyone at the UNHCR was pleased with this change, particularly some former senior members of Goedhart's staff who still chafed at past American snubbing of the agency. Yet, because the UNHCR was fully supported for the first time by the US government, the new High Commissioner was able to consolidate the good will the UNHCR earned as a consequence of its own actions in Hungary. This allowed the Office to initiate policies which would have been unthinkable under Goedhart. Lindt was also a very capable pragmatist and a skilled diplomat. He had a strong personality and constitution, and a determined approach to difficult problems. These qualities served him well when dealing with the immediate problems confronting the UNHCR—particularly the repatriation of Hungarian refugee minors and the opening up of the Office to the developing world in response to the Algerian refugee crisis.

The Hungarian Revolution and the Consolidation of International Support for UNHCR

The UNHCR really came into its own as the most important actor within the international refugee regime with the rapid and totally unexpected eruption of a major Cold War refugee crisis that accompanied the 1956 Hungarian Revolution. The invasion of Hungary by the Soviet army on 4 November 1956 precipitated a mass exodus of refugees to neighbouring Austria and Yugoslavia. Lines of struggling refugees with battered suitcases and wheelbarrows were shown on live television to Western audiences who were not yet affected by compassion fatigue. The emergency also presented the UNHCR with a rare opportunity to demonstrate that it was the only agency capable of taking large-scale international action for refugees. The Office successfully handled its first mass asylum crisis, helped engineer a major resettlement effort, and played an important mediating role between East and West involving the repatriation of large numbers of Hungarians to their homeland.

By 21 November, some 7,000 people were crossing the frontier daily and within a few weeks of the outbreak of the Hungarian Revolution, 21,000 persons had entered Austria. In December, a few days after his appointment as High Commissioner, Auguste Lindt travelled to Austria to assess the needs of the Hungarian refugees. By March 1957, approximately 171,000 Hungarians entered Austria and another 20,000 crossed over into Yugoslavia. Neither country had the physical infrastructure to deal with this mass influx and thus they were initially hesitant to take action on behalf of the Hungarians for fear of provoking a hostile Soviet reaction.[2]

The West was caught completely off-guard by these developments and was totally unprepared for the massive refugee outflows. The Hungarian crisis had been precipitated by internal developments in the Soviet bloc following Stalin's death in 1953 and was influenced by a major international crisis in the Middle East. At the Twentieth Party Congress in February 1956, Nikita Khrushchev had stunned the Communist World by detailing and denouncing Stalin's past crimes. This 'liberalization' set off a series of internal protests in Soviet Georgia, Poland, and Hungary in which popular demonstrations demanded the appointment of more liberal officials. Soviet concessions to Wladyslaw Gomulka in Poland were followed by demonstrations in Hungary demanding the removal of Soviet troops and the replacement of the Stalinist Erno Gero regime by Imre Nagy. He was a critic of collectivization and forced industrialization. Hungarian protestors were also encouraged in part by the clandestine support given to them by CIA covert operations and by Radio Free Europe which promised American support to the country's freedom fighters.[3] Initially, the Soviet Union appeared to recognize the need for reform, withdrew their tanks and permitted Imre Nagy to take the reins of power in

Budapest. On 27 October 1956 Nagy formed a coalition government that excluded Communist hard-liners, and a few days later he promised to withdraw Hungary from the Warsaw Pact and to declare the country neutral.

Unfortunately, the United States, Britain, and France were almost totally preoccupied at this time with a major political crisis in the Middle East. In July 1956, Nasser had seized the Suez Canal by nationalizing the British-controlled Universal Suez Canal Company in retaliation for the cancellation of US support for the planned Aswan Dam. On 29 October, the Israeli Army made a lightning attack on Egypt and conquered most of the Sinai Peninsula. The next day, Britain and France, anxious to safeguard the supply route for their oil in the Middle East, delivered ultimatums to Egypt and Israel, warning both nations to keep their troops away from the canal. When Nasser rejected the note, British and French planes began bombing Egyptian military targets.

The confrontation in the Middle East provided Khrushchev with the perfect opportunity to reverse his policy on Hungary. Alarmed by Nagy's announcement that Hungary was withdrawing from the Warsaw Pact and under pressure from hard-liners within the Soviet leadership to pull in the reins on liberalization in eastern Europe, Khrushchev decided to crack down on the Nagy regime. As Anglo-French troops moved into the Suez Canal area on 4 and 5 November, Russian tanks re-entered Budapest to crush the Hungarian uprising and to replace Nagy with a more compliant regime. Nagy and thousands of his supporters were deported or executed. The United States, which was distracted by its involvement in the Suez crisis and preoccupied with the 1956 presidential election that occurred just two days after the Soviet invasion, watched on helplessly as Hungarian 'freedom fighters' were crushed. Despite heart-rendering appeals from Hungarian leaders for America to intervene, the United States was paralysed, fearing that overt action to follow through on their promise to 'liberate' Soviet satellites might provoke a war with the Soviet Union.[4]

Refugees began to arrive in Austria several days before the brutal suppression of the Hungarian uprising. Initially, Austria was reluctant to receive the refugees crossing their frontier for fear of provoking a Soviet attack. On 2 November, Moscow Radio made threatening remarks alleging that Austria had violated its neutrality by allowing the US to channel weapons and ammunition to the Hungarian rebels across Austrian territory.[5] Austrian authorities were also anxious not to open their borders to massive numbers of refugees, especially just after they had largely resolved the long-standing refugee problem they had inherited following World War II.

The international community took immediate steps to reassure Austria and to provide assistance. Both Britain and the United States signalled to the Soviet Union that they would consider a Soviet attack on Austria as a *causus belli* that might risk the outbreak of World War III.[6] In response, Moscow gave orders to its military forces stationed along the Austrian-Hungarian border to take extra precautions not to violate the frontier. Reassured by such developments, Austria soon took a more relaxed attitude towards receiving Hungarian refugees.

The dramatic exodus of refugees from Hungary served to internationalize the Hungarian crisis and to embarrass the Soviet Union. The UN General Assembly refused to accept Hungary's characterization of its revolution as an internal matter and the UNHCR started its work immediately, even before it had been asked to do so by the General Assembly. Overwhelmed by the influx of refugees, on 5 November 1956 Austria formally requested the UNHCR and the ICEM to appeal to their member governments for assistance in meeting the emergency. The UN General Assembly also appealed for international assistance for the Hungarian people, in cash or kind, from all member states. On 9 November, the General Assembly asked Dag Hammarskjöld to call upon the UNHCR to consult with other agencies 'with a view towards making speedy and effective arrangements for emergency assistance to refugees from Hungary'.[7] In response, the High Commissioner's Office immediately established a co-ordinating group. This included the ICEM for transport for tens of thousands of Hungarians to new homes, the League of Red Cross Societies for most of the fieldwork in Austria, the International Committee of the Red Cross (ICRC), the USEP, and a number of NGOs. In both Austria and Yugoslavia, the High Commissioner's local representative chaired the groups that administered the emergency aid.[8] As the flood of refugees continued, the General Assembly called on the many governments and agencies involved to co-ordinate their assistance efforts through the UNHCR. It not only asked the Secretary-General to make an immediate appeal 'to meet the minimum present needs as estimated in the UNHCR's latest report' but also to make subsequent appeals on the basis of the High Commissioner's future plans and estimates.[9] For the first time in its history, the UNHCR was specifically designated by the international community as the 'lead agency' to direct a large-scale emergency operation. Even more significant was the fact that earlier American opposition to the UNHCR and preference for unilateral solutions were abandoned in the Hungarian case. The US advocated that all relief should be planned and co-ordinated by a single organization and that the most suitable organization for this task was the UNHCR.[10]

Austria emphasized both the need for financial assistance and the need for the international community to share the burden of providing asylum for the refugees. The US and other Western governments were concerned that if the refugees were left in Austria, they might have a destabilizing effect on that key country which bordered the Communist bloc. Thus, the UNHCR's appeals to governments for the resettlement of Hungarians and for funds generated numerous generous offers from governments all over the world. Apart from the obvious political and ideological importance of the Hungarian refugees, a tremendous groundswell of sympathy and support arose for them. As this was the first refugee crisis covered by television, this new visual medium was extremely influential in portraying both the dramatic events of the revolution and the plight of the refugees. Spurred by extensive television coverage of students hurling paving stones and Molotov cocktails at Soviet tanks, the Western public viewed the Hungarians as heroes who deserved their help. More than any other event in the 1950s, the Soviet suppression of the Hungarian Revolution symbolized the brutality of the Soviet Union and vindicated Western descriptions of life behind the Iron Curtain. Expressing guilt over its failure to do more to back its policy of the 'rollback of Communism' with direct assistance to the Hungarian 'freedom fighters', the United States and other Western governments believed that it owed these recent victims of Communism safe haven and a fresh start.

In addition to the 171,000 Hungarian refugees in Austria, some 20,000 Hungarians also fled to Yugoslavia. This was also a Communist state but one that had split from Stalinist domination in 1948 to pursue an independent path to socialism under Tito. Earlier, in 1953, Goedhart had made the first ever visit of a High Commissioner to a Communist country, to brief Yugoslav officials on the Office's activities. This subsequently made it easier for Auguste Lindt to approve assistance to Yugoslavia despite the initial opposition of some senior UNHCR staff members. Belgrade was alarmed that Soviet action in Hungary might be the prelude to a general Soviet crackdown and reassertion of Russian hegemony in the region.[11] At first Yugoslavia turned back refugees from Hungary but eventually it opened its borders after it received assurances that the US would not escalate the situation into a major US–USSR confrontation. The Yugoslav authorities were initially reluctant to request international assistance and lacked any government structure to carry out any refugee processing. At first, resettlement of Hungarian refugees from Yugoslavia to the West was complicated for two main reasons. Yugoslavia was not a member government of the ICEM and US refugee policy made it difficult to resettle refugees from first asylum countries that were Communist. Eventually, Yugoslavia agreed to the presence of the UNHCR and the ICEM resettlement teams, which were allowed to operate in much the same way as they did in Austria. However, resettlement of Hungarian refugees out of Yugoslavia proved much more difficult than out of Austria[12] and there was glaring discrimination in the treatment of Yugoslavia's needs as compared with those of Austria. Whereas the international community paid for most of the estimated $17.3 million costs of the care and maintenance operations in Austria, it paid for almost none of the $7.5 million spent on care and maintenance operations in Yugoslavia.[13]

From the beginning of the crisis, it was assumed that all Hungarians fleeing persecution were *prima facie* refugees and deserved asylum. However, the 1951 Refugee Convention applied only to refugee 'events occurring before

1 January 1951'. Therefore, it was not immediately clear that the Convention would cover the Hungarian refugees. But it was the height of the Cold War and Western policy-makers did not seriously consider the Hungarians would be motivated to leave for any reason other than a desire to escape genuine political persecution. Moreover, most observers felt that in such a mass exodus situation, judging each individual's motive for flight was administratively impossible.

The UNHCR quickly had to devise a legal justification for considering the Hungarians as refugees under the Convention and the UNHCR mandate. Paul Weis, the Legal Adviser to the High Commissioner, outlined the UNHCR position in a memorandum in January 1957.[14] He argued that it was reasonable to relate the departure of these refugees not merely to the events which took place in Hungary beginning in October 1956 but also to fundamental changes which took place in the country following the establishment of a peoples' republic, dominated by the Communist Party, in 1947–8. The 1956 refugee exodus was in a sense 'an after effect of this earlier political change'.[15] The UNHCR therefore determined to grant all Hungarians in Austria and Yugoslavia *prima facie* group eligibility as refugees.

One of the most striking aspects of the international response to Hungarian refugees was the speed with which the process of resettlement was begun. The first resettlement operations began in Austria on 7 November 1956 and proceeded so rapidly that the daily rate reached 800 within a two-week period. In a period of less than eight weeks, outward resettlement movements amounted to 84,000. In a remarkable demonstration of solidarity with the Hungarian refugees, many governments abandoned their customary restrictionist policies, lowered their immigration barriers, and granted visas to entire families—including the ill and the disabled—without regard to quotas. Western Europe immediately began to provide resettlement opportunities. Great Britain took approximately 21,000 Hungarians, West Germany 15,000, Switzerland 13,000, France 13,000, Sweden 7,000, and Belgium 6,000. Similar generosity was displayed by some of the less heavily populated countries of Europe such as Denmark and Norway, and was matched by the actions of a number of non-European nations. Canada accepted 37,000, Australia 11,000, and Israel 2,000. Several thousand more were allowed into Latin America by the governments of Honduras, Guatemala, Venezuela, Argentina, and Brazil.[16]

Initially, West European countries resettled Hungarians at a much quicker pace than did the United States. From the beginning of the crisis, the Eisenhower Administration's objective to admit large numbers of refugees was constrained by restrictionist immigration laws and by opposition from conservative leaders in Congress who feared the threat refugees posed to internal security and the economy. These obstacles were finally overcome when President Eisenhower took advantage of a small loophole in the law which gave the Attorney-General the authority to temporarily 'parole' aliens into the US 'for emergent reasons or for reasons deemed strictly in the public interest'.[17] Eventually, the United States admitted approximately 38,000 Hungarians and spent $71 million on that refugee problem.[18] Nearly 200,000 Hungarian refugees were permanently resettled in third countries in less than two years at a global cost of more than $100 million—a sum that far surpassed and dwarfed the amount channelled through the UN Refugee Fund to the postwar refugees.

The relative success in resettling so many refugees so quickly was not due entirely to Western geopolitical interests and the emotional overtones and the anti-Communist sentiment prevalent at the time. It was also attributable to the personal qualifications of many of the Hungarians and to the favourable economic conditions that prevailed in their new home countries. In many ways, Hungarians were a model immigrant group. A large percentage of them were young, skilled, and educated, and they entered labour markets at a time when unemployment rates were low. The National Academy of Sciences in the United States estimated that the value of the education of university graduates among the recent Hungarian immigrants alone represented an investment of over $30 million. The US Secretary of Labor, James Mitchell, noted that 'America's instinctive reply to the call for help has enriched her own economy in many ways. . . . . It is now clear that America has received a valuable economic bonus'.[19] Receiving countries benefited greatly from what amounted to a Hungarian brain drain.

Auguste Lindt and Promoting Return to a Communist State

Perhaps the most politically difficult issue facing the High Commissioner was the question of repatriation of some of the Hungarian refugees to their Communist homeland. Almost from the beginning of the Hungarian refugee crisis, Hungary and the Soviet Union pressed Austria to return refugee minors.[20] The new Kadar regime in Hungary had serious misgivings about the scale of the refugee exodus. Concerned about the loss of thousands of educated professionals and young people, and fearful of the possibility that a resistance force could be formed outside the country, the government offered a limited amnesty to those who had fled and made appeals as early as December 1956 for Hungarians to return home. Hungarian officials also made diplomatic approaches to Auguste Lindt to help them resolve this problem.

Hungarian officials charged that many people under 18 years of age had left the country during the crisis without their parents' knowledge or consent, and that some of the asylum and resettlement states were refusing to help in determining whether any of these persons wanted to return home to rejoin their families. There was some truth to these allegations but the issue of repatriation to a Communist state was highly contentious and politically divisive. This was a period of heightened Cold War tensions and there were Western charges of a reign of terror in Budapest and mass deportations from Hungary. Any action on the part of Austria or the UNHCR that even hinted at forced repatriation would have caused an immediate uproar by the United States and other Western governments.[21] Despite the political sensitivity of the issue, Lindt felt strongly that families should be reunited and did not hesitate to involve the UNHCR in the repatriation of Hungarian minors.[22] As a first step, the High Commissioner proposed the creation of mixed commissions to visit refugees to determine whether there was a desire on the part of minors to return home. Within these commissions, UNHCR representatives were to be present at meetings between the refugees, the authorities of the countries concerned, and Hungarian repatriation missions. Lindt sought to use the principle of family reunion as a means to establish a two-way flow into and out of Hungary. The UNHCR not only sought to open up repatriation to Hungary, but also sought to secure exit permits for family members still in Hungary who wished to join up with relatives living in countries of asylum or resettlement outside Hungary. As was to be expected, repatriation efforts moved ahead slowly. But Lindt remained strongly committed to the principle of family unity and to the best interests of the individual child. In order to expedite repatriation of minors, the UNHCR urged host countries to establish legal procedures for deciding contested repatriations.[23] At the same time, Lindt also ensured that a Hungarian observer was present at the meeting of the UNHCR's Executive Committee to put forward his government's views, especially on repatriation. Initially, negotiations between Austria, the International Committee of the Red Cross (ICRC), and Hungary concerning the establishment of repatriation arrangements foundered.[24] But sympathy grew for the Hungarian government's efforts to repatriate children and young people who remained abroad without family or guardians.[25] Through painstaking diplomacy and personal interventions with both Hungary and the countries of residence, Lindt was eventually able to gain the co-operation of Western asylum and resettlement countries and the Hungarian authorities in embarking on what became the first successful repatriation programme to an East European Communist state. More than 13,000 persons returned to Hungary during the first year, and by the end of the crisis, approximately 18,000—10 per cent of those resettled abroad—had gone home. When the High Commissioner reported to the General Assembly in November 1957, the Hungarian delegation showed appreciation for the efforts that had been made by the office and, in fact, voted in favour of the resolution renewing the UNHCR's tenure. This vote on the part of a country of origin of refugees signalled recognition and widening acceptance of the UNHCR among Eastern bloc governments. In January 1958, Lindt went to Budapest at the invitation of the Hungarian government and while there he visited many of the returnees.

In his handling of the Hungarian refugee operation, Lindt strengthened the organizational standing, mandate, and influence of the UNHCR. The Office proved itself capable of dealing effectively with a Cold War political crisis and a refugee problem of major proportions. It had worked quickly to defuse the refugee crisis so as to open up both resettlement and repatriation opportunities. For the first time, it had earned the respect of some of the socialist governments and opened doors for future UNHCR involvement both in Yugoslavia and in Hungary. It was the only actor having a positive impact on the crisis surrounding the Hungarian uprising. Its actions were of considerable importance for the reputation and credibility of the United Nations and the major Western powers. As a result of its initiatives during this crisis, the UNHCR now had the full backing and support of the United States and other Western powers. The Office had clearly come of age and had won international acceptance and recognition.

Clearing the 'Camps of Misery' in Europe

The generous and rapid response of the international community to the Hungarian exodus stood in marked contrast to the attitude of governments toward the displaced people within Europe who were still in need of resettlement. In the mid-1950s, there still remained over 200 refugee camps in Austria, Italy, Germany, and Greece, in which over 70,000 'hard core' refugees had been living since the late 1940s. 25 per cent of the camp population consisted of children under 14 years of age, most of whom had been born and raised in the camps. There were also tens of thousands of refugees living outside these camps and thousands more in China and the Middle East. This was the most serious and embarrassing residual social and humanitarian problem of the Second World War. The worldwide publicity given the Hungarians drew international attention again to the shameful conditions in which these stateless people were still living.

In 1957, the General Assembly passed a series of resolutions which gave the UNHCR a wider and more flexible role in coping with the old refugees as well as with any emergency relating to new refugees not only in Europe but also elsewhere. The Office, which was due for redundancy in 1958, was extended for another five years. The High Commissioner was authorized to appeal to governments and UN specialized agencies for funds to clear the refugee camps in Europe and to seek solutions for those outside of the camps. Further, the scope of the High Commissioner's authority and programmes were considerably expanded to 'provide assistance to all refugees under his mandate, in whatever part of the world they might be'.[26]

Even more importantly, the Hungarian emergency had also significantly changed popular perceptions about the global refugee problem. The successful resettlement of Hungarian refugees had established a pattern of action that Lindt hoped could be used to solve the residual problem of refugees in Europe. In an attempt to exploit this change in attitude and greater international generosity towards refugees, in 1959, the United Nations gave its full backing to the establishment of a 'World Refugee Year' during which member nations pledged to finally resolve the problem of Europe's remaining refugees by resettling them.

Lindt was determined to use the impetus of Hungary and the World Refugee Year to clear the 'camps of misery' in Europe. In an address before a US audience, the High Commissioner emphasized the importance he attached to finally resolving this issue.

One particularly distressing aspect of the remnants, in camps and outside camps, of previous refugee waves, is that of the residual groups left behind after successive selection missions have picked those people who were young and healthy and met rigid resettlement criteria. Frequently, whole families were thus confronted with an agonizing choice: separation, so that the young and the healthy could get away; or stay together—and stay behind. . . . It is now nearly two years since I was appointed High Commissioner; and during this period, I have seen much misery, and a great deal of wrong that should and could be put right. (UNHCR Archives, HCR/1/7/5/USA/CAN, 'High Commissioner's Statement at Meeting of American Immigration Conference', 28 October 1958).

Despite the determination of Lindt and other High Commissioners to resolve this problem, the UNHCR's camp clearance programme turned out to be the single most stubborn problem the UNHCR had to face during the 1950s. In the decade between 1954 and 1964, the UNHCR's programme funds and extra-budgetary contributions were almost entirely concentrated on this protracted refugee problem. While Lindt was able to initiate action and programmes to deal with this, it took several more years beyond Lindt's tenure and tens of millions of dollars to finally resolve the long-standing problem of the remaining non-settled European refugees.

The World Refugee Year and the camp clearance programme reflected a fuller and wider appreciation of the refugee problem in Europe than had previously existed among governments. The publicity accorded the UNHCR during these years enabled the office to strengthen and expand its role in the international refugee regime and to make it possible for the High Commissioner to seek funds for material assistance for new groups of refugees.

The UNHCR under Lindt began to take greater responsibility for refugees in the developing world and to *de facto* widen the UNHCR's refugee definition.

During the late 1950s, the UNHCR expanded its scope to include Chinese escaping to Hong Kong, Tibetans fleeing to India and Nepal, and Algerians fleeing to Morocco and Tunisia. By the early 1960s, the major powers themselves began to recognize the changing nature of the global refugee problem. The US, for one, no longer perceived the refugee problem as one confined almost exclusively to Europe and realized the UNHCR had a significant role to play in responding to refugee problems in other regions of the world. In testimony before the US Congress in 1961,[27] for example, the State Department noted that while considerable progress had been made in reducing the total number of escapees on the USEP caseload in Europe, 'experience has shown that the refugee problem is anything but static. It is continually changing in its nature, in its dimensions, and in its location. It is constant in only one respect, it will continue to exist as long as conditions exist which create it—political tyranny, international conflicts, and tensions.' Stating that international refugee programmes were of 'utmost importance' to its foreign policy, the State Department listed a number of refugee programmes outside of Europe which affected US interests, including 'the Tibetans in India and Nepal, Angolan refugees and refugees from Rwanda-Burundi in the Congo, Meo Tribe refugees in Laos, the Khmer Krom refugees fleeing from South Vietnam into Cambodia, Cuban refugees in Central and South American countries, and the question of the ultimate status of Algerian refugees in Morocco and Tunisia'.[28] Recognizing the political importance of many of these new, non-European refugee groups, the United States encouraged the High Commissioner's Office to get involved in these situations. In testimony the following month before the US Senate, the State Department noted, 'We believe that the spread of unrest in Africa and southeast Asia attaches growing importance to the High Commissioner's good offices function....Our national interest dictates that we should continue our leading role in support of the High Commissioner.'[29]

By 1960, therefore, Western governments saw that refugee problems were occurring no longer solely in Europe but now also in Africa and Asia, and they encouraged the UNHCR to respond to these new movements. The UNHCR had to reorient its programme and priorities from Europe to the Third World.

The Expansion of the UNHCR into the Developing World

Even while the UNHCR was preoccupied with problems in Europe, the Office was taking initial steps to lay the groundwork for an expansion of its activities to the developing world. Since the end of World War II, demands for independence from European colonies in Africa and Asia increased dramatically.

In most of the developing world the process of decolonization was a peaceful one and the various nationalist movements attained their independence without resorting to force on a large scale. Britain was committed to the evolution of its colonial territories towards independence within a loose framework of attachment to the Commonwealth. In contrast, the continental powers perceived their colonies largely as overseas parts of the metropolitan territory and foresaw a gradual evolution towards a common citizenship and self-government within these territories. The drive towards independence, especially in parts of Africa, was resisted by European settlers. For example, France remained intransigent in Algeria and was willing to use harsh means to support its settlers and to keep Algeria under French rule. Moreover, in Portuguese-ruled Africa, the intransigence of Lisbon with regard to independence for its colonies led nationalists to follow a strategy of armed resistance. In both Algeria and in the Portuguese colonies of Angola, Guinea-Bissau, and Mozambique, the decolonization process was violent and involved massive displacements of refugees. In addition, the British colony in Hong Kong attracted large numbers of refugees from the Communist regime in China.

The UNHCR began to feel mounting pressures to give these new refugees international assistance. However, the Office faced acute political problems arising from these new groups. In Europe where refugee problems were perceived in an exclusively East–West context, a political consensus among Western nations regarding international approaches was assured. In dealing with third world refugees, however, the situations encountered were considerably different. In many cases, refugee situations directly involved either the political interests of the Western colonial powers who were also among the founding members of the international refugee regime, or the security concerns of newly independent states who were the newest members of the United Nations. In such cases, the UNHCR and UN member states sought a means to avoid the embarrassment of treating refugees involving their supporters and close allies, as victims of persecution. In the end, a distinctly new way of responding to refugee problems emerged within the United Nations. Whenever refugee situations appeared with political dynamics and problems that did not correspond with those of the European situation, which were not covered in the UNHCR Statute, or which involved one or more of the Western powers, the UN General Assembly simply granted the High Commissioner new authority so that he could take action. Thus, for the next two decades, UN member governments were willing to turn to the UNHCR whenever its services could be usefully applied to meet the needs of new and different groups of refugees and displaced persons.

The Use of 'Good Offices' to Aid the Chinese in Hong Kong

As the UNHCR moved into uncharted territory, the limitations of the 1951

UN Refugee Convention became all too apparent. A way had to be found to get around the limited scope of the international legal instruments for dealing with refugees. This new approach was the 'good offices' formula. It was applied in the first instance to give assistance to Chinese refugees in Hong Kong.

In January 1952, the Chinese government in Taiwan raised the issue of Chinese refugees at the UN General Assembly. For the next several years, the Chiang Kai-shek government strenuously lobbied the UNHCR to provide limited material assistance to some 700,000 Chinese refugees who had flooded into Hong Kong in the two years after the establishment in 1949 of the People's Republic of China (PRC). Fleeing the introduction of revolutionary social and economic programmes in China, hundreds of thousands of Chinese piled into the already tightly packed British colony. This mass influx constituted over a quarter of Hong Kong's population and placed an enormous financial strain on British colonial authorities. The arrival of newcomers created huge housing and social problems in Hong Kong. In 1950, the British authorities declared most new arrivals to be illegal immigrants, subject to immediate expulsion. Despite the fact that these were refugees fleeing Communism, they lacked strong external patronage. At the time Britain was keen to develop a closer political relationship to the new Chinese regime and did not wish to harm those relations by accepting large numbers of Chinese refugees. The Nationalist government on Taiwan, itself home to over a million and a half Chiang Kai-shek supporters and refugees from China, was not large nor rich enough to take all the newly arriving Chinese. And although the anti-PRC lobby was very strong in Washington, the Chinese refugees were too numerous and too poor for the United States to do anything more than provide humanitarian assistance. Consequently, Hong Kong, and to a lesser extent, the Portuguese colony of Macau, became the places of refuge for most Chinese leaving the mainland.

Goedhart, who was the High Commissioner at the time, let it be known that his Office had a universal mandate to assist refugees everywhere and that he was prepared to help if he were given the authority and funds to do so. The major roadblock to UNHCR assistance, however, was the complex political dimension of the Chinese refugee problem in Hong Kong. Britain didn't consider them legally to be refugees. In addition, when the United Kingdom adhered to the international refugee instruments, it did not extend the application of the 1951 Refugee Convention to its colony, Hong Kong. Thus, the British were not obliged to treat the Chinese newcomers as refugees and strenuously opposed UNHCR involvement.

As important as British opposition to UNHCR involvement, however, was the fact that the Chinese revolution had led to the creation of two Chinas, Chiang Kai-shek's Republic of China (ROC) and Mao Zedong's Peoples Republic of China (PRC). The ROC represented China at the UN. It claimed that the refugees from the PRC were entitled to protection by the Nationalist government despite the fact that it accepted relatively small numbers for resettlement. The ROC was principally interested only in those refugees who would be politically useful to the government in its conflict with the PRC. Nevertheless, the ROC expended great propaganda efforts on behalf of all Chinese refugees, particularly through non-governmental agencies with close links to its government, such as the China Free Aid Relief Association. The ROC representatives at the UN raised the Hong Kong refugee issue at the General Assembly in 1951 and 1952. The problem was further complicated by the fact that governments which recognized the ROC as the legitimate government of China maintained that the Chinese refugees were outside the UNHCR's mandate, since only persons who lack the protection of their government can be considered refugees according to the UNHCR Statute. However, the UK government had recognized the PRC, and not the ROC, as the legitimate government of China and rejected the ROC's claim that the refugees were entitled to its protection. Moreover, the UK had been one of the first Western governments to recognize the PRC and had consistently sought to improve its relations with the Communist regime. Thus, the British considered the possibility of direct UNHCR assistance to refugees in the Colony as politically embarrassing to Beijing and potentially harmful to Sino-British relations.[30] The UNHCR, as a UN organization, was required to accept the ROC as the official government of China. As long as the Chiang Kai-shek government remained China in the eyes of the United Nations, it could not very well recognize the new arrivals in Hong Kong as refugees without offending the government in Taiwan. Yet without a declaration that the Chinese in Hong Kong were within the UNHCR's mandate, the Office had no authority to seek assistance for them.

Before taking firm decisions on this issue, the UNHCR sought and obtained $50,000 from the Ford Foundation in November 1953 for an investigation of the eligibility status of the Chinese refugees in Hong Kong and the possibility of starting pilot projects for their resettlement. After a series of difficult negotiations with London, the UK government accepted that an independent assessment of the refugee situation in Hong Kong could be made. Edvard Hambro, a former registrar of the International Court of Justice in The Hague, was appointed the chief investigator. The so-called Hambro Report,[31] which was completed in 1955, focused on the social and economic conditions in Hong Kong and on the prospects for resettlement initiatives. It discussed the question of refugee eligibility but it did not take a definitive position on this difficult political issue. The report did argue, however, that although from a strictly legal point of view the Chinese refugees might fall outside the High Commissioner's mandate, they should be considered *de facto* refugees because the ROC was incapable of protecting and resettling them. As a result, the question of eligibility remained unresolved. When the matter was finally taken up at the UNREF Executive Committee in 1956, the High Commissioner suggested that the issue be referred to the UN General Assembly for consideration. It was evident that if the UNHCR was to assist Chinese refugees in Hong Kong, a basis for action had to be found other than the UNHCR Statute.

The political and legal problems over the refugee eligibility of the Chinese in Hong Kong were finally sorted out in November 1957, when the UN General Assembly made it possible for the UNHCR to assist Chinese refugees in Hong Kong without making an evaluation of the political conditions in either of the two Chinas and without seeming to take sides between two rival governments. The UN General Assembly acknowledged that 'the problem of Chinese refugees in Hong Kong . . . is such as to be of concern to the international community' and requested the High Commissioner to 'use his good offices to encourage arrangements for contributions' to the Chinese refugees in Hong Kong.[32]

The 'good offices' mandate for Chinese refugees in Hong Kong was never fully exploited by the UNHCR, largely because the political problems blocking international action persisted and because donations to the UNHCR for the Chinese in Hong Kong never amounted to enough to maintain a viable programme. The colonial authorities in Hong Kong continued to resist what they considered to be international interference in a local problem in Hong Kong. For several years after the passage of the UN General Assembly Resolution, the British refused permission for the High Commissioner, August Lindt, to visit Hong Kong on the grounds that such a visit would raise expectations and might provoke demonstrations that 'might be considered provocative by the Chinese government'.[33] The British also sought to limit discussion of the Hong Kong issue at the UNHCR Executive Committee (Excom) meetings. It vehemently opposed ROC membership in Excom, believing that Taiwan's objective in seeking election was 'to obtain a locus standing in Hong Kong which will enable her to foment intrigue in the colony which could well lead to difficulties for us and the government of Hong Kong with the Chinese government in Peking'.[34]

The Geopolitics of Assisting Tibetan Refugees

Under Lindt, the UNHCR also became interested in another group of refugees from the PRC: Tibetans. The Chinese Communists had forcibly occupied Tibet in 1950, but it was not until 1959 that the Dalai Lama and several thousand Tibetans fled. This was the beginning of a sustained outflow of Tibetan refugees to neighbouring Nepal and India. Initially, the Indian government did not cope well with the influx and the Tibetans lived in bad conditions in very hot areas of the Ganges Plain where dysentery was rife and many refugees died. India refused to accept any international assistance, and rebuffed Lindt's offer of UNHCR assistance. Both India and Nepal feared that by internationalizing the Tibetan refugee issue, they would endanger their relations with their powerful neighbour, China. Lindt did not attempt to deal with the Tibetans in the way he had with the Chinese refugees in Hong Kong, by obtaining a UN General Assembly resolution authorizing him to use his good offices.[35] The High Commissioner felt that the legal difficulties arising from the disputed international status of Tibet made it difficult for him to intervene officially.[36] The situation was particularly complicated by the fact that the PRC claimed that Tibet had always been an integral part of China and that, therefore, the international community had no right to interfere. Furthermore, the Indian government strongly opposed any such initiative, preferring to deal with the influx of refugees as an internal and domestic matter and without UN assistance. New Delhi discouraged UNHCR initiatives to aid the Tibetans and refused Lindt permission to personally visit the Tibetan refugee settlements in India.

Throughout the 1950s and 1960s, the Tibetan cause generated much political sympathy throughout the world and in some quarters Tibetan refugees were accorded the same heroic status as the Hungarian 'freedom fighters' of 1956. The UN General Assembly passed several resolutions calling upon China to respect the rights of Tibetans to pursue their own way of life and their own traditional religion. These resolutions were accompanied by generous support for the Tibetan refugees by the international community.

The Tibetans also had powerful political and military patrons who were anxious to use Tibetan refugees in their geopolitical struggles against the PRC. The Dalai Lama and the Tibetans soon became enmeshed not only in the regional conflict between India and China but also in the globalization of the Cold War. The Indian military trained and supported Tibetan refugee warriors to cross over from Nepal into Tibet to engage Chinese forces. These activities severely strained Indian-Nepalese relations. A 1964 UNHCR field investigation in Nepal revealed that 'there was a militant group of three to four thousand Tibetans called Khampas in the area called Mustang. They were armed, fed, and led by India and were undertaking forays into Tibet against the Chinese. This was another reason for the present bad relations between Kathmandu and Delhi.'[37]

The United States also championed the cause of the Tibetans believing that it had 'an important political interest in seeing that they survive as a vital symbol representing a better alternative to Chinese Communist imperialism and genocide'.[38] Perhaps most importantly, the US perceived the refugees to be Cold War allies in their effort to undermine the Chinese Communists.[39] Beginning in 1959, the CIA provided the Tibetan exile movement with $1.7 million a year and they paid the Dalai Lama a subsidy of $180,000 annually during the early 1960s. The CIA also trained a small number of Tibetans in guerrilla warfare in the Rocky Mountains in Colorado and sent them back into Tibet by parachute and on foot from Nepal and Mustang. As with the CIA-led irregular forces in Vietnam and Laos in the early 1960s, the objective of the US effort was to mobilize groups of guerrillas to harass the Chinese army. CIA support for Tibetans lasted until the late 1960s when suddenly the clandestine operation stopped as Washington moved toward an eventual *rapprochement* with Beijing in 1971–2.

Fortunately, most Chinese refugees were absorbed by the rapidly growing Hong Kong economy of the 1960s, and, in the end, only a small amount of international assistance was ever provided through the UNHCR.[40] Likewise, Tibetan refugees started their own businesses and integrated successfully in India and Nepal. Perhaps the most long-standing outcome of the UNHCR's involvement in Asia was the initial UN General Assembly resolution for Chinese refugees in Hong Kong. This set an important precedent that led to a steady expansion of the High Commissioner's authority and competence to mount assistance programmes throughout the developing world during the next decade.

UNHCR's Expansion into Africa: Assistance to Algerian Refugees

While the UNHCR cautiously expanded its programmes to Asia, refugee crises in Africa dominated the attention of the Office. The Algerian refugee crisis was significant to the UNHCR's expansion into the developing world.[41] The Algerian War of 1954–62 demonstrated the shift in world politics away from Europe to the developing states. The Algerians were the first non-Western refugees to be assisted by the UNHCR and thus, for the first time, symbolized the Office's universality. In the view of many, the UNHCR's action on behalf of Algerians signified a turning point in the Office's geographical scope and function. The Algerian operation, therefore, was a bridgehead leading to a period of great institutional growth for the UNHCR. Its involvement with Algerians had long term effects on its role and image in the world that were of greater importance than any previous operation, including Hungary.

The Algerian war of independence presented the UNHCR with a huge political dilemma. It was the first African struggle against European colonial rule in the postwar period to produce significant numbers of refugees. The presence of a large number of European settlers led France to take an intransigent position against all demands for change in Algeria, thus radicalizing the Algerian nationalist movement. As a result, the Algerian War was one of the most violent decolonizations in history, involving terror campaigns directed against civilian populations and ransacking of entire villages by both French forces and the Algerian National Liberation Army (FLN). An estimated one million Muslim Algerians were killed and at least the same number of peasants were forcibly resettled to French, barbed wire encampments (*regroupement*) as part of counter-revolutionary strategy to cut off the population from FLN guerrillas. As *regroupement* proceeded, large numbers of Algerians fled to neighbouring Tunisia and Morocco. These two countries had only recently won their independence from France in 1956 and so they willingly supported the FLN's armed struggle. They provided asylum for Algerians fleeing the fighting and tolerated military bases for armed refugees—so-called 'refugee warriors'—on their territories.

The Algerian issue involved the principle of national self-determination in the developing world and therefore was among the most politically divisive items on the UN General Assembly agenda during the late 1950s. There was a clear political line-up on every vote regarding Algeria. The Western hemisphere countries supported France and the Arab countries; Africa and Asia, together with the Soviet bloc, voted in favour of Algerian self-determination. For Africa and Asia, the Algerian question was crucial in their struggle against colonialism. Algeria also became important in the East–West conflict, and was one of the reasons why the Cold War was extended to Africa and the developing world in the 1960s.

In May 1957, while the UNHCR was still in the throes of responding to the Hungarian emergency, Tunisia requested material assistance from the UNHCR for the 85,000 Algerian refugees who had fled across the border during the previous two and a half years. This was the first occasion on which UNHCR emergency assistance was requested in the third world, and it marked an important step in the development both of the political conditions under which the UNHCR had to act and of the functions it was permitted to perform. However, the decision to offer assistance for Algerian refugees was politically difficult and engendered an intense debate within the UNHCR about its future role in the developing world. Lindt felt that the Tunisian request presented an opportunity for the UNHCR to use its new international support to confirm its position as the leading international refugee agency. Moreover, the UNHCR's decision to intervene in the Hungarian refugee emergency without examining individual asylum claims had established a precedent for action which was difficult for the UNHCR to ignore in the Algerian case. Lindt feared that the UNHCR would be accused of discriminatory treatment if, after helping the Hungarians, it neglected the Algerians and he did not want to be perceived as the 'High Commissioner for European refugees only'.[42] He felt that the UNHCR mandate as defined in its Statute was worldwide and that his Office had responsibility for dealing 'with completely different people and not only refugees from communism'.[43] He was concerned that to refuse assistance to Tunisia would estrange the organization from a growing bloc of developing nations and would weaken the more favourable attitude that the Soviet bloc had recently adopted towards the agency.

Not everyone within the UNHCR agreed with these views. Bernard Alexander, who had been Goedhart's right-hand man, argued that it was politically impossible for the UNHCR to declare the Algerians refugees, because such action would imply that France—one of the great powers within the United Nations, and a member of the High Commissioner's Executive Committee with a history of liberal asylum policies and support for international assistance to refugees—was persecuting some of its own subjects.[44] To make matters more difficult, the French government denied the authority of the UNHCR to give assistance in this case, claiming that Algeria was an integral part of the state of France, and that the eventual solution could only be the return to Algeria of the people who had taken refuge in Tunisia and Morocco. France also feared UNHCR involvement would internationalize the crisis. Some UNHCR staff members supported the French position and maintained that the Algerians did not meet the terms of the legal refugee definition included in the Statute. Others felt strongly that the UNHCR should limit its activities to European refugees and argued against UNHCR expansion to the developing world.[45]

Lindt's views prevailed within the UNHCR, but crucial decisions concerning the Office's response to Tunisia were taken through informal negotiations between the High Commissioner and the most influential Western governments.[46] The major Western powers were unwilling to take a public position on the Algerian refugee issue. Lindt was keenly aware of what kinds of initiatives had a chance of succeeding and he skilfully used the international political situation in order to give the UNHCR the necessary space to manoeuvre. The United States, which had already started a bilateral aid programme to Tunisia in 1956, tacitly supported the UNHCR initiative and was willing to give Lindt considerable discretion to handle the matter in the way he saw fit. Washington believed North Africa to be vulnerable to Communist influence and believed that, by channelling assistance to Algerian refugees through UNHCR programmes, it could win the good will of African states and at the same time avoid damaging its political relations with France. The British were less supportive of UNHCR action and feared offending Paris. Lindt also informally consulted with Dag Hammarskjöld, the UN Secretary-General, who backed him in his plan to initiate an investigation.[47]

With the backing of the Secretary-General and the tacit support of the most important donor government, Lindt dispatched one of his representatives, Arnold Rorholt, to investigate the situation in Tunisia and to determine whether the Algerians who had taken refuge there could be considered eligible as refugees under the UNHCR mandate. On his return, Rorholt reported that there was indeed a case for considering some of the Algerians as eligible for protection under the UNHCR's mandate. Lindt then reported Rorholt's findings to the French Foreign Minister, Christian Pineau, detailing for him the atrocities carried out by French forces against Algerian civilians.

According to Lindt, Pineau acknowledged the correctness of Rorholt's findings and replied, 'I am the last to contradict the marvels of the Army!'[48] Lindt
then said that he was personally convinced that Algerians in Tunisia were
refugees and he intended to reply positively to Tunisia's request for aid.
Pineau responded simply, 'Okay, but don't make too much of a fuss!'[49]
Having secured French acquiescence to UNHCR action for Algerian refugees
that was confined to material assistance, Lindt then obtained assurances from
the Tunisian authorities that they would not exploit UNHCR assistance for
their own political purposes.

The UNHCR began its work for Algerian refugees in Tunisia in the summer
of 1957 and initially employed the International Committee of the Red Cross
(ICRC) as its operational partner and later the League of Red Cross Societies
(LRCS). For the first eighteen months, the Office worked in principle on the
basis of the Statute's refugee definition, but it did not make any clear determination of refugee eligibility so as to avoid a direct confrontation with the
French government. Not only did the UNHCR and the League have difficulty
providing food and medical assistance to the primitive camps situated in the
Tunisian desert but the refugee camps harboured militants of the FLN and
were occasionally subject to attack by French aircraft. The problem of refugee
warriors among the other refugees increased as the war continued, presenting
the UNHCR with operational difficulties that persist in other parts of the
world today.

By late 1958, however, nearly 200,000 Algerians had fled to Tunisia and
Morocco and the influx showed no sign of diminishing. Lindt felt that there
was a need to firm up the basis for UNHCR action and to extend UNHCR
assistance to Morocco. In December 1958, the UN General Assembly finally
approved UNHCR assistance to Algerians in a text that recommended 'the
United Nations High Commissioner for Refugees to continue his action on
behalf of the refugees in Tunisia and to undertake similar action in
Morocco.'[50]

A year later, the UN General Assembly freed the UNHCR from the necessity of seeking further authorizations for each new refugee group.[51] Unlike
the first good offices resolution which had been adopted specifically for the
Chinese in Hong Kong, this resolution gave the UNHCR the future right to
determine which groups to assist under the good offices function without
further consultation with the General Assembly.

A distinctive feature of the joint UNHCR-LRCS operation was that both
Western and Eastern governments made contributions to the international
relief effort. The United States not only provided the UNHCR important
diplomatic and political support, but it was also the largest donor to the joint
operation. The Soviet Union and its Eastern European allies also contributed
significantly to the Algerian refugee aid operation. Neither East nor West
regarded refugee relief as solely a non-political humanitarian effort. Quite to

the contrary, refugee assistance was given to the UNHCR and LRCS as a direct result of East–West competition for influence in North Africa. The Soviet Union and its allies perceived Algeria as a key event in the anti-colonial struggle in the developing world and for geopolitical and ideological reasons were anxious to tangibly demonstrate their support through economic and relief assistance. Since one of the primary objectives of US aid for Algerian refugees was to minimize Soviet influence in North Africa, the US pressured other Western governments to contribute to the operation. Even the UNHCR took advantage of East–West competition to persuade the US to increase its contributions. In 1959, Lindt told US officials that he was concerned that if the United States did not commit itself to continued participation in the relief operation, the Soviet bloc might step in with contributions.[52] Although the Algerian War would not be successfully concluded until nearly two years after his departure as High Commissioner, Lindt's decision to assist the Algerian refugees was one of his most noteworthy diplomatic achievements and provided another example of the UNHCR acting in ways counter to powerful state interests at the time.

In just four short years, Lindt had overseen a remarkable transition in the UNHCR from its being a sideshow to centre stage in world politics. The crises in Hungary and Algeria constituted a bridgehead leading to future global and institutional growth and autonomy for the UNHCR. In his final address to his Executive Committee in 1960, Lindt noted that the UNHCR had to remain flexible and elastic in responding to new refugee situations. Little did he realize the momentous challenges that would confront both his successor and the UNHCR in the 1960s, particularly in Africa.

NOTES

1. Interview with Auguste Lindt, UNHCR Oral History Project.
2. Austria had only regained its independence in July 1955 and the last occupation troops had been withdrawn only a year earlier. Austria had pledged itself to permanent neutrality and was initially concerned that it would violate that neutrality by welcoming Hungarian refugees. Austria was also still caring for some 30,000 refugees and 150,000 volksdeutsche who had not yet been fully integrated and many of whom still lived in camps. Yugoslavia, under Marshall Tito, maintained a precarious balance between East and West.
3. For background see: Gil Loescher and John Scanlan, *Calculated Kindness: Refugees and America's Half-Open Door, 1945 to Present* (New York, NY, and London: The Free Press and Macmillan, 1986): 49–60.
4. Interview with Robert Murphy, Dulles Oral History Project, Dulles Papers, Princeton, NJ.
5. British Public Records Office, Foreign Office Files, FO 371/124082 (22 December 1955–22 December 1956).

6. British Public Records Office, Foreign Office Files, FO 371/124087.
7. United Nations General Assembly Resolution 1006 (ES11) (9 November 1956) and United Nations General Assembly Resolution 1039 (XI) (23 January 1957).
8. Author's interview with Bernard Alexander, Great Hasely, England, December 1986.
9. United Nations General Assembly Resolution (21 November 1956).
10. UN General Assembly, Official Records, Session II, Plenary meeting 578 (21 November 1957): para. 77 cited in Cecelia Ruthstrom-Ruin, *Beyond Europe: The Globalization of Refugee Aid* (Lund: Lund University Press, 1993): 214.
11. According to Robert Murphy, Yugoslavia's ambassador to the US 'believed his country was trembling on the thin edge of war against the Soviet Union, and urged that everything be done to confine the conflict to Hungary'. Robert Murphy, *Diplomat Among Warriors* (Garden City, NY: Doubleday, 1964): 430.
12. British Public Records Office, Foreign Office Files, FO 371/129950-52.
13. US National Archives, Diplomatic Branch, 324.8411/11-1557, *Visit of Dr. Lindt*, 15 November 1957; and Elfan Rees, 'Century of the Homeless Man', *International Conciliation*, 515 (New York, NY: Carnegie Endowment for International Peace, November 1957): 235.
14. UNHCR Archives, HCR/22/1/HUNG, Paul Weis, 'Eligibility of Refugees from Hungary', 9 January 1957.
15. Ibid.
16. See Loescher and Scanlan, *Calculated Kindness*, 49–67.
17. For background to the parole provision see Loescher and Scanlan, *Calculated Kindness*, chapter 3; and Deborah Anker and Michael Posner, 'The Forty Year Crisis: A Legislative History of the Refugee Act of 1980', *San Diego Law Review*, 19 (Winter 1981): 9–89.
18. US Library of Congress. 'Chronology of the Hungarian Refugee Program'. Typescript. 14 May 1975.
19. The *New York Herald Tribune* (10 May 1957) cited in Rees, 'Century of the Homeless Man': 236.
20. UNHCR Archives, HCR/6/9/HUNG/AUS. 24 December 1956.
21. Protests claiming forced repatriation of Hungarian minors were frequently made. For example, see a letter from Bela Fabian, Member of the Executive Committee of the Hungarian National Council, New York, which alleged that repatriated children were sent to concentration camps in the Soviet Union. *New York Times* (6 August 1957).
22. Lindt's policy was outlined for the first time at the UNREF Executive Committee meeting on 31 January 1957.
23. UNHCR's policy concerning Hungarian unaccompanied minors was laid down in the High Commissioner's statement to the UNREF Executive Committee, 31 January 1957.
24. UNHCR Archives, HCR/6/9/HUNG/AUS and HCR/3/1/2/HUNG/AUS, 1956-8.
25. See US National Archives, Diplomatic Branch, 864.411/3-657: 6 March 1958 and 3 October 1958.
26. United Nations General Assembly Resolution 1166 (XII) (26 November 1957).
27. US House of Representatives, Judiciary Committee, *Migration and Refugee Assistance*, 87th Congress, 1st Session (3 August 1961): 39.

28. Ibid., 40.
29. US Senate, Committee on Foreign Relations, *Migration and Refugee Assistance Act* of 1961, 87th Congress, 1st Session (11 September 1961): 11.
30. British Public Records Office, Foreign Office Files, FO 371/103827, 25 February 1953.
31. Edvard Hambro, *The Problem of Chinese Refugees in Hong Kong* (Leiden: A.W. Sijthoff, 1955). Author's interviews with Gilbert Jaeger, the UNHCR member of the investigation team to Hong Kong, in Oxford in December 1986 and January 1989.
32. United Nations General Assembly Resolution 1167 (XII) (26 November 1957).
33. British Public Records Office, Foreign Office Files, FO371/145394, 20 January 1959.
34. Ibid: FO371/137034-35, 3 January 1958. Despite intensive British lobbying, particularly with the US government authorities that supported the ROC, the government in Taiwan was elected to the Excom in June 1958.
35. Ibid: FO371/145404, 'Refugees from Tibet', 22 September 1959.
36. UNHCR Archives, HCR/15/72/INDIA, 'Meeting between the High Commissioner and Mr. T. J. Norbu, the brother of the Dalai Lama', 11 September 1959.
37. British Public Records Office, Foreign Office Files, FO371/178263, 1 May 1964.
38. US National Archives, Diplomatic Branch, Ref and Mig Tibet, Box 3187A, 27 October 1966.
39. John Kenneth Knaus, *Orphans of the Cold War* (Washington, DC: Public Affairs, 1999) and Tsering Shakya, *The Dragon in the Land of Snows* (London: Pimlico/Random House, 1999).
40. The United States had established the US Far East Refugee Program in 1954 which mainly assisted voluntary agencies in Hong Kong and Macao to provide food, clothing, housing, hospitals, and schools to needy Chinese including refugees.
41. The most comprehensive treatment of UNHCR's response to the Algerian refugee crisis can be found in Ruthstrom-Ruin, *Beyond Europe*. The following analysis draws on this study as well as on documentation contained in UNHCR archives in Geneva, US State Department archives in Washington, DC, British Foreign Office archives in Kew Gardens, London, and on interviews with UNHCR officials.
42. US National Archives, Diplomatic Branch, 320.42/6-557, 5 June 1957.
43. Interview with August Lindt, Berne, Switzerland, 4 February 1998.
44. Lindt asked for and received Alexander's resignation from the UNHCR as a result of his opposition. Interview with Bernard Alexander, Great Hasely, England, December 1986.
45. Interview with August Lindt, Berne. According to Bernard Alexander, 'Lindt was very keen to get involved in every refugee problem under the sun'. Interview with Bernard Alexander.
46. These negotiations between the UNHCR and Western powers are outlined in Ruthstrom-Ruin, *Beyond Europe*.
47. Interview with Lindt.
48. Ibid.
49. Ibid. Defiance of French opposition by persistent and courageous diplomacy was

a great personal accomplishment for Lindt and required considerable political courage. In an interview over 40 years later, he noted: 'I must say . . . I was proud of it.'

50. United Nations General Assembly Resolution 1286 (XIII) (5 December 1958).

51. UN General Assembly Resolution 1388 (XIV) (20 November 1959).

52. US National Archives, Diplomatic Branch, 320.42/8-1159, 11 August 1959. Cited in Ruthstrom-Ruin, *Beyond Europe*: 183.

5

'The Good Offices' and Expansion into Africa under Felix Schnyder

In Africa during the 1960s, violent decolonization, and post-independence strife underscored the strategic significance of conflicts outside Europe.[1] These conflicts generated vast numbers of refugees. The easing of East–West tensions led to the lessening of refugee problems in Europe but political and strategic concerns continued to dominate international refugee policy. The Cold War moved from Europe to Africa and Asia where refugees and refugee assistance were viewed as part of the East–West struggle for hegemony in the developing world. The UNHCR's programmes were viewed by the United States and other Western states as providing stability in a region rife with conflict and potential for Communist expansion. The UNHCR's own work in Africa became part of the total UN effort to assist developing countries with their modernization and development.

The decade brought fundamental changes to the UN system of refugee assistance and protection. The expansion of the UNHCR coincided with major political transformations in world politics: primarily decolonization and the ensuing emergence of newly independent states in Africa and Asia. The developing world replaced Europe as the central focus of the UNHCR's world. Mindful of its non-political role, the UNHCR avoided directly criticizing the behaviour of Western colonial authorities during national liberation wars in Africa but reminded European governments of their responsibilities as liberal democracies to uphold international refugee and human rights norms and to permit the UNHCR access to assist refugees. After obtaining their independence, developing states asserted themselves as the UNHCR's chief constituents and the Office began to reshape its programmes to accommodate them. A *de facto* expansion of the UNHCR's refugee definition occurred allowing it to provide assistance to displaced people who did not strictly qualify as refugees under the 1951 UN Refugee Convention or the UNHCR Statute. Also, the Office progressively increased the range of the services it provided both to refugees and to host governments. The UNHCR acted as a transmitter of international refugee norms to the newly independent states of Africa. Aspiring to join the community of nations, Africa's political leaders were eager to raise their status and improve their image in the international political system. The agency taught new states the value and utility of belonging to the international refugee regime and of adhering to international refugee norms. A major function of the UNHCR during this time was to socialize new states to accept the promotion of refugee norms as part of becoming law-abiding members of the international community.

Felix Schnyder and the Algerian Repatriation

In December 1960, the UN General Assembly elected the Swiss diplomat, Felix Schnyder, to become UN High Commissioner for Refugees. Auguste Lindt had resigned to become the Swiss Ambassador to Washington, DC. Schnyder had been Switzerland's Permanent Observer at the United Nations since the beginning of 1958. He served as Swiss delegate to the UN Technical Assistance Committee and chaired the Executive Committee of the UNICEF. While in New York, he had developed close relationships with several African delegates. He was well liked by African delegations who often sought his advice and crowded around him after meetings. Schnyder understood well the seismic shifts that were occurring in international relations in the 1960s. He foresaw decolonization and was not taken by surprise by mass exoduses of refugees in Africa. Realizing that the traditional concepts and legal definitions that the Office had used in Europe would not apply in the less developed countries, Schnyder had to both adapt the traditional tools of the Office and to invent new mechanisms to deal with new refugee situations confronting the UNHCR. Schnyder made clear from the very start that he foresaw a shift in the UNHCR away from programmes involving European refugees to a focus on assistance to refugees in the developing world. He made it known that he would rely on the authority of the 'good offices' resolutions to respond to new refugee emergencies and to undertake new tasks.[2] In a press release on the day he assumed office, Schnyder said there would be 'a shift in emphasis to groups in other continents' and stated that 'in his opinion the "good offices" concept was elastic enough to permit him, when asked, to bring effective aid to nearly any group of refugees provided there was sufficient interest and support on the part of the international community'.[3]

Algeria was by far the most important issue confronting Schnyder when he took office. From the beginning of its aid operation for Algerian refugees, the UNHCR believed that repatriation, not resettlement, was the only feasible approach to the problem. Refugees were held in camps in anticipation of a successful, organized repatriation at the end of the war. In preparation for this, the UN General Assembly in late 1961 requested that the High Commissioner 'use the means at his disposal to assist in the orderly return of those refugees to their homes and consider the possibility, when necessary, of facilitating their resettlement in their homeland as soon as circumstances permit'.[4]

By the early 1960s, developments began to unfold quickly in Algeria. Political opposition to the war had grown not only in France and Africa but in much of the rest of the world. Peace talks were initiated between the French government and the Provisional Government of the Algerian Republic in Evian on 21 May 1961. At first, French President Charles de Gaulle promoted local autonomy for Algeria, but when this failed, he advocated its full independence. The Evian Peace Agreements of 19 March 1962 called for the return to Algeria of all the refugees from Tunisia and Morocco. At the insistence of the Provisional Government of Algeria, France agreed to include the UNHCR in forming the tripartite repatriation commission. This body supervised the return of some 181,000 Algerian refugees between May and July of 1962.

The UNHCR and the LRCS assumed the task of transporting the refugees from the asylum countries of Tunisia and Morocco to the border. There, a UNHCR official was present to facilitate the refugees' actual crossing into Algeria. Despite the tense relations between French and Algerian forces and the militarized conditions existing along the border, the repatriation was successfully completed within three months. The operation proceeded quickly because there was no individual screening of returning refugees. People simply seized the opportunity to accept international assistance to return home after the conclusion of a successful war of national liberation.

Once the repatriation operation had been concluded, it became clear to Schnyder that the returning refugees had to be integrated into a country largely devastated by eight years of bloody conflict.[5] For the most part, the refugees had come from areas where there had been intense fighting and from where most of the inhabitants had either fled or been evacuated. The reinstallation of these people into Algerian society could not come about simply through return. The problems of reintegration were exacerbated by the sudden departure from Algeria of over a million European settlers, mostly to France. International assistance was desperately needed to keep alive both the repatriated refugees and the community who had stayed behind during the conflict. According to Schnyder, the repatriation of refugees would only succeed if it was 'accompanied by . . . the actual reintegration of these refugees in the economy of their country, so that they can once again become self-supporting'.[6] Consequently, the UNHCR launched a small reconstruction programme for the populations of war affected regions in Algeria which included rebuilding schools and medical dispensaries, and other community projects. In addition, Schnyder placed the new Algerian authorities in contact with other UN agencies that could support larger development efforts. This established the basis for the seeds of the 'zonal development' concept which was one of the major developments in UNHCR programmes in Africa during the 1960s.[7]

The Algerian repatriation and reconstruction efforts were the first of their kind for the agency and established a significant precedent for further operations beyond the 1960s. Each phase of the Algerian operation was unique for the UNHCR. It was the first time the agency had worked outside Europe and the experience gained was to influence greatly the future operations of the UNHCR. The Office's operating procedures became a blueprint for UNHCR actions and policies in practically all subsequent repatriations. The use of tripartite arrangements involved the participation of host state, country of origin, and the UNHCR. The provision of reintegration and reconstruction assistance, not only to returning refugees but to the community at large, in countries of origin was also a model for future repatriations. The UNHCR's policies towards Algerian refugees changed the entire approach and perspective of the international community to refugee problems.

Of even greater significance was the fact that the Algerian operations opened the door to Africa for the UNHCR. Because the Algerian War of Independence was so important symbolically to other anti-colonial struggles in Africa, the UNHCR's operations in North Africa had a major impact on its relations with other African governments and liberation movements. By being willing to defy the French in Algeria over aid to refugees in Tunisia and Morocco and to offer assistance to the new regime in Algiers, the UNHCR earned the trust of most Africans elsewhere. This became increasingly evident as the UNHCR developed relations with the nascent Organization of African Unity (OAU) and the African Commission for Refugees within the OAU.[8] The foothold that the UNHCR had gained in Africa through its operations for Algerian refugees enabled the Office to promote refugee norms at the regional level and to help African states organize, direct, and expand their refugee programmes.

Schnyder felt that the Algerian refugee problem seemed likely to be the type of situation to command more of the UNHCR's attention in the future.[9] This was the first real test of the usefulness of the UNHCR in the highly volatile atmosphere created by the emergence of new states. It was also evident that the Algerian case could be used as a precedent for future UNHCR action in the developing world. The Algerian operation demonstrated that the UNHCR's future lay in the developing world and not in Europe, and from then onwards the UNHCR began to take on a much more universal character. The High Commissioner believed that the Office needed to be not only flexible enough to respond to new refugee problems in the developing world but also capable of co-ordinating solutions to highly politicized problems. In this context, the good offices approach could legitimize flexibility for the Office in the new refugee crises.

Seizing the Concept of Good Offices and Extending it Everywhere

As the centre of the international refugee problem moved from Europe to Africa and Asia during the early 1960s, Schnyder pushed his Office into new programmes and new regions. However, in taking on new refugee problems, the UNHCR was handicapped by some serious weaknesses, particularly in staff and resources. In 1961, the UNHCR was still a predominantly European organization. The staff still comprised mainly people who had worked with refugees during World War II or its immediate aftermath. The eighty professional staff were mainly British, French, and Americans with little, if any, Asian or African experience and included no individuals from Africa or Asia.[10] There was no thought given at the time to hiring African or Asian specialists who might better understand the cultural and political contexts of new refugee situations in the developing world.[11]

While Schnyder realized the need to change the face of the Office from that of 'a paternalistic European agency' to one that reflected better its 'universal character', he did not feel that he could simply fire his staff and replace them with new people from the developing world.[12] Early on, however, he did seize the one opportunity open to him to strengthen Afro-Asian representation on his staff and that was to appoint a Third-World national as his Deputy High Commissioner. Prince Sadruddin Aga Khan from Iran, a man with good contacts in the Middle East, Asia, and Africa, became the Deputy High Commissioner. Sadruddin was instrumental in opening up new regions in the developing world for the UNHCR. Schnyder also expanded his Executive Committee during his term to include five new African nations: Algeria, Madagascar, Nigeria, Tanzania, and Tunisia. The shift to the Third World was also reflected by changes in the allocation of the UNHCR funding. In 1963 for the first time, African and other Third-World projects were included in the UNHCR's annual programme and in 1964, they came to constitute one-half of the High Commissioner's budget. Schnyder had a forceful personality and was more of a visionary than the previous two High Commissioners.[13] The most far-reaching decisions Schnyder took concerned the use and further expansion of the good offices concept—the tool he had inherited from Auguste Lindt's period. According to one former UNHCR senior staff member, during his term as High Commissioner, 'Schnyder seized the concept of good offices and extended it everywhere'.[14]

During his first months in office, Schnyder was confronted with a series of problems involving new groups of refugees in Africa and Asia. In some ways these refugees were similar to those with whom the Office had dealt in the past: Most were fleeing political disturbances in their home country, had sought asylum in neighbouring states, and were without any national protection.

While they seemed to be refugees within the mandate of the UNHCR, it was not possible to determine their individual eligibility for refugee status. However, unlike in Europe, many refugees were scattered in remote regions and the countries in which they sought refuge did not have the administrative apparatus to carry out individual determinations. Thus, these new groups of refugees presented legal and political problems that the UNHCR had never had to confront in the past. While Schnyder felt that it was not practical for the UNHCR to make individual refugee determinations in these new situations, he did strongly believe that the Office had a role to play in providing emergency assistance to these refugees. The High Commissioner had at his disposal an Emergency Fund of $500,000 for unexpected refugee crises and he was determined to use these resources when the need arose.

The first subsequent refugee crisis to emerge was in Cambodia. In 1961, Prince Norodom Sihanouk of Cambodia requested assistance from the UN Secretary-General for some 30,000 refugees who had arrived in Cambodia from Laos. Schnyder was told by both his Legal Adviser and Dag Hammarskjöld that the Emergency Fund could only be used to assist persons whom the High Commissioner considered to be at least *prima facie* within his mandate and not for good offices functions.[15] But he was so impressed by the gravity of the refugee situation as described to him in a staff member's on-site report that he decided to allocate $10,000 from his Emergency Fund to Phnom Penh. This was the first time since the Algerian programme that a disbursement had been made from the Emergency Fund. Thus, the High Commissioner's grant to Cambodia represented a significant precedent and would be cited increasingly in the future to assist non-mandate refugees. Schnyder also used the good offices function to expand the UNHCR's activities into South Asia, particularly to assist the Tibetan refugees in Nepal and India. Following the 1962 Sino–Indian border war, the government of India no longer felt the need to appease China and gradually opened up international relief channels for the Tibetans. Schnyder visited India in 1963 and reached an agreement with the Indian authorities on the terms of UNHCR assistance to these long-term refugees. While the Indian government did not want assistance to Tibetans to be part of the normal public programme of the UNHCR, it did welcome assistance, which would be made available without publicity and within the framework of the good offices of the High Commissioner.[16] India also agreed to permit UNHCR field investigations on Indian Territory. However, further negotiations between the UNHCR and India dragged on for several years and it was not until 1969 that a UNHCR branch office was established in New Delhi. It was not until 1970 that a UNHCR programme of assistance was started for Tibetans. In Nepal, on the other hand, the UNHCR played a role from the early stages of the Tibetan refugee crisis. In 1964, the UNHCR opened a branch office in Kathmandu to provide liaison between the Office and NGOs, and set aside $50,000 from its Emergency Fund for aid to Tibetan refugees in Nepal.

Responding to Refugees from Portuguese-Ruled Angola

The UNHCR was confronted with a number of difficult refugee problems in Africa during the early 1960s. The national liberation struggle in Angola was the first of several anti-colonial conflicts fought against Portugal in Africa. The anti-colonial war initiated in Angola in 1961 was followed by guerrilla wars in Guinea-Bissau in 1962 and in Mozambique in 1964. Like the French colonial situation, the Portuguese colonies were still integrated parts of the mother country and Lisbon strenuously objected to any international criticism of its colonial policy as an interference in its domestic affairs. As in Algeria, there was a large and inflexible white settler community in Angola who were opposed to decolonization. Moreover, Portugal's colonial policy was closely linked to the domestic situation in the home country where it was believed that decolonization could mean the collapse of the Salazar regime. Finally, Portugal was a member of NATO and provided the United States with air bases on the Azores, making it politically difficult for the Western powers to exert pressure on Lisbon to negotiate an end to the conflict with the liberation movements in Angola. As Portuguese troops embarked on a campaign of terror, including forcibly uprooting and relocating civilians, the national liberation struggle in Angola attracted considerable international attention. The anti-colonial movement was particularly important for African states who provided refuge for the displaced and sanctuaries for the guerrilla resistnce forces. When 150,000 refugees from the border region of Angola crossed into the Congo in 1961, the UNHCR was soon confronted with another request for emergency assistance. The UN Security Council declared the situation in Angola to be 'an actual and potential cause of international friction and is likely to endanger the maintenance of international peace and security'.[17] As in Algeria, the logistical, legal and political ramifications of UNHCR action were complex. Since this was a mass influx of people into a remote area of the Congo, it was virtually impossible for the UNHCR to determine how many of the refugees met the legal criteria laid down in the Statute. More significantly, Portugal was opposed to any UNHCR action that implied Portugal persecuted its subjects.[18] The Portuguese Foreign Minister, for example, charged that the 'UNHCR assistance was an attempt to internationalize and make a political issue out of the Angolan problem'.[19] In addition, the Western governments were unwilling to openly criticize their ally. In light of the political explosiveness of the issue, Schnyder believed that 'it is particularly important to avoid letting the problem become a political issue, thus making cooperation with Portugal impossible'.[20]

The UNHCR, therefore, handled the Angolan issue with the greatest possible discretion. Following a request from Dag Hammarskjöld to assist the

Angolan refugees, Schnyder agreed to take an 'active interest based on good offices resolutions visualizing [his] role as one of coordinating aid and mobilizing international support in cooperation with League [of Red Cross and Red Crescent Societies]'.[21] After obtaining an investigation report of the situation from one of his staff,[22] Schnyder announced that he was earmarking $100,000 from the UNHCR's Emergency Fund for the Angolan refugees. However, when some governments questioned the legal basis of the High Commissioner's use of his Emergency Fund to assist the Angolans and expressed the view that in the future he should consult with Excom members before making such distributions, Schnyder felt that he needed to clarify his authority to expend emergency funds to non-mandate refugees.[23]

To maximize his discretionary power to determine when and where to use his Emergency Fund, Schnyder sought General Assembly approval to further increase the flexibility of the UNHCR and to widen its field of action. Schnyder felt strongly that, because refugee emergencies emerged quickly and in large numbers in Africa, it was impossible for the UNHCR to make individual determinations of eligibility for refugee status under the Office's Statute. More importantly, he also realized that the new refugee situations would be compounded with political difficulties. He observed that persecution 'was at the root of many misunderstandings with countries of origin, whose susceptibilities were offended by eligibility decisions which they tend to regard as more or less open criticisms of themselves'.[24] From the Algerian experience, the High Commissioner had learned that it had been essential 'to keep the humanitarian work of the Office from the political contexts which lay at the origins of the problems he was called upon to help solve'.[25] Schnyder maintained that it was important for the international community to have an agency like the UNHCR which could act as a channel for governments who were thus able to assist in resolving problems, in a way otherwise denied to them. According to the High Commissioner, the UNHCR acted like a 'detergent' in the many conflicts arising in the world.[26] He would later successfully apply this approach to his relations with the Portuguese colonial authorities as well as to other Third World refugee situations.[27]

Schnyder considered it essential to the operation of his Office that he avoid any dispute about the refugee eligibility of these new groups or any question about his competence to deal with them. In light of the changing nature of refugee problems, Schnyder felt that the legal basis on which his Office functioned should be reconsidered. In the future, he considered that all his actions in 'new' refugee situations should be based on his good offices function and not on his mandate.[28] The UNHCR mandate, he felt, should only be applied when refugees needed legal protection. Schnyder sought to have this view accepted by the UN General Assembly.

In December 1961, the United Nations passed a resolution giving the High Commissioner the authority to assist both 'refugees within his mandate and those for whom he extends his good offices',[29] effectively removing the legal and institutional barriers to future UNHCR action for non-mandate refugees. This measure allowed the UNHCR to consider Angolans who were fleeing Portuguese repression and other African refugees as *prima facie* eligible for assistance, without accusing Portugal or any of the newly independent states of persecution of their subjects. In effect, the resolution, basing its practice on the precedent established for the Hungarian refugees, avoided the need for the UNHCR to make individual determinations of eligibility. It also left the High Commissioner free to decide which groups of refugees should benefit from his good offices. It made it clear that he could use the Emergency Fund both for these groups and for refugees who come within his mandate. This resolution gave the High Commissioner the authority and discretion to use his funds to fit the needs of the moment without first having to consult his Executive Committee, thus laying the groundwork for UNHCR expansion into Africa. The distinction between mandate and good offices refugees was completely abandoned in 1965 when the General Assembly requested the High Commissioner to provide protection and permanent solutions to all groups within his competence.[30] Henceforth, both refugees within the UNHCR mandate and refugees covered by the High Commissioner's good offices were entitled to receive protection and assistance from the High Commissioner's Office.

The good offices approach was both pragmatic and provisional. It enabled the UNHCR to avoid the undesirable political consequences of making refugee determinations in the developing world that might damage relations with some of the principal Western supporters of the international refugee regime or of newly independent governments. The good offices basis for action contained no assumption of persecution and avoided most of the limitations for action in the international refugee legal instruments. It also allowed the High Commissioner quickly to extend financial and emergency assistance to people in need who were not statutory refugees.[31] But at the same time the UNHCR disclaimed any intention of seeking a long-term solution to these problems or of assuming ongoing legal protection for these groups.

While Schnyder was liberal in expanding the presence of the UNHCR everywhere, he did so with limited funds and resources. His office operated on an annual budget of between three and four million dollars for most of the decade. The UNHCR remained conscious that it was not the intention of the states that had created the Office that the High Commissioner should launch ambitious programmes of material assistance. During the 1960s, the UNHCR initially viewed its role in assistance as a relatively passive one. The Office waited for host states to ask for assistance and advice. Indeed, it was a point of doctrine with the UNHCR during the 1950s and the early 1960s that the material welfare of refugees should be basically the responsibility of the host country and not of the UNHCR. The agency would provide material assistance only upon request from the host governments and even then only to supplement as modestly as possible the host government's own efforts.[32] In fact, the majority of Africa's refugees in the 1960s were self-settled and widely dispersed. The UNHCR provided some emergency relief and established programmes to support organized rural settlements, but most refugees had to fend for themselves without any international assistance.[33] Because the Office's annual programmes during this time did not exceed a few million dollars, the High Commissioner maintained that its material assistance was catalytic, supplementary and, at best, modest in scope. As a non-operational agency, the UNHCR relied on NGOs and other UN agencies to carry out relief programmes, principally, to get refugees to help themselves.[34]

UNHCR Strategy and Programmes in Africa

Resistance to armed struggles for national liberation from colonial rule accounted for many African refugee problems. Refugees were also generated as a consequence of conflicts arising within or between newly independent African states. In Togo in 1960 there was an estimated 10,000 refugees, including some 4,000 Togolese nationals from the Ivory Coast, and over 5,700 refugees from Ghana. Between 1959 and 1961, over 120,000 refugees of the Tutsi ethnic community fled post-independence violence in Rwanda. The Hutu majority overthrew the Tutsi monarchy, gained control of the government, and then set out to destroy any remaining political power of the Tutsi minority. This conflict initiated an exodus of Tutsis to neighbouring Burundi, Tanzania, Uganda, and the Kivu province in eastern Congo (Leopoldville) where their numbers swelled to approximately 150,000.[35] Internal conflict in the newly independent state of Congo resulted in movements of refugees to Burundi, Central African Republic, Sudan, Uganda, and Tanzania. By 1966 their numbers had reached more than 80,000.[36] In 1956, major waves of refugees from newly independent Sudan resulted from the policies adopted by successive Arabic-speaking Islamic regimes in Khartoum. They sought to forcibly incorporate into Sudan the mainly Christian and animist southern region. As widespread resistance to northern rule developed, the south became engulfed in civil war. Conflict between Sudanese government forces and southern rebels, such as the guerrilla force known as Anya-nya, resulted in major refugee flows into the Central African Republic, Uganda, and the Congo, and smaller flows into Ethiopia, Chad, and Kenya.[37]

New African governments often viewed refugees as a national security threat because they frequently caused severe interstate tensions. The presence of large numbers of disaffected refugees in border areas served to strain relations between sending and receiving states. Sending states were concerned that refugee warriors would use receiving states as bases of operation for attacks against them. Angola, Rwanda, and Sudan, for example, believed that rebel groups would exploit refugees who had fled from their home countries. Sending states correctly foresaw that refugees could become a reservoir from which subversive forces could be drawn.

The presence of Angolan refugees in the Congo led Portugal to accuse the Congo of protecting 'terrorists' and of providing material and moral support as well as safe bases for Angolan rebel movements. There was considerable truth to these allegations. Not only did the Congolese government provide refuge to Angolans fleeing Portuguese military campaigns but it also permitted the Angolan government-in-exile and other nationalist organizations to operate in the Congo. The Congo also allowed opposition groups to establish military training camps on its territory and provide supplies and some funds to the Angolan political opposition.

The dispersal of Tutsi refugees throughout central Africa created political and military tensions between several governments in the region.[38] Many Tutsi exiles never relinquished their aim of returning to their homeland to restore the former regime and to re-establish their earlier dominance. Therefore they constituted a seedbed of discontent along Rwanda's borders. In December 1963 and January 1964, organized bands of armed refugees made several incursions into Rwanda from Burundi and the Congo. These raids were repulsed. They were followed by renewed reprisals against the Tutsi minority in Rwanda, including the mass slaughter of thousands of civilians. Tutsi-ruled Burundi encouraged and supported Tutsi exiles in their subversive activities. Subsequently, political tensions between Rwanda and Burundi almost led to the outbreak of war between the two countries. In Kivu in the Congo, secessionist rebel movements recruited Rwandan refugees as reinforcements, promising to support them in their efforts to regain power in Rwanda. These events precipitated a mass arrest of Tutsis, and authorities in Leopoldville ordered their expulsion from the Congo.

During the early 1960s, the large numbers of refugees from the southern part of Sudan who fled to neighbouring countries became embroiled in the separatist struggle against Khartoum. Among the refugees were members of the militant Anya-nya guerrillas whose objective was to achieve self-determination for southern Sudan. The countries hosting Sudanese refugees, therefore, became directly and indirectly involved in the secessionist guerrilla campaigns launched by the Sudan Army of National Union (SANU) against the Sudanese government. Neighbouring countries became alarmed by the security threats against their own internal stability by the presence of Sudanese refugees. On several different occasions, the Sudanese military entered border areas in neighbouring countries such as Uganda and Ethiopia, seized refugees, and returned them to Sudan. Uganda gave direct and indirect assistance to the southern Sudanese refugees and rebels. Consequently, relations between Uganda and Sudan became stretched to the breaking point.[39]

Mozambican refugees in Tanzania closely identified with the Mozambican Liberation Front (Frelimo) and its freedom fighters in their fight against Portuguese colonial authorities and occasionally engaged in political and military activities.[40] In fact, the Tanzania government permitted and encouraged Frelimo forces to use refugees as resources in their anti-colonial struggle and allowed Frelimo bases to be established in Tanzania. The Tanzanian government permitted refugees from Mozambique to enter or remain in the country only if they were registered members of Frelimo. A large number of Mozambican young people were sent to other countries in Africa or to countries within the Soviet bloc for further educational training, while other refugees were trained in Tanzania by Frelimo in military and guerrilla warfare. In retaliation, Portugal made punitive incursions against Tanzania and heavily mined the Mozambique-Tanzania border.

Refugees also caused tensions with local communities in receiving countries. This often made it difficult for the UNHCR to promote and help to achieve 'permanent solutions' to refugee problems. Achieving a permanent solution to a refugee crisis meant that the refugees should be helped to achieve a situation in which they were socially integrated with the local population and could stand on their own feet economically after the UNHCR withdrew and ended its assistance. The UNHCR rural resettlement programmes really only provided food for an initial period in order to give refugees time to clear and cultivate land so as to become self-sufficient. These programmes worked satisfactorily only in host countries where there was political and social stability. This was rarely the case in most of Africa. While there were some positive instances of refugees spontaneously integrating with their host population, newcomers were not equally welcome everywhere. This was particularly true where they put strains on food supplies and other local resources. In some situations refugees were unwilling to settle in UNHCR rural resettlement programmes because they believed that a possible change in the political situation in their own country would make an early return home possible. Reluctance on the part of some Sudanese and Rwandan refugees to make any efforts toward settlement and integration led to tensions in parts of Kivu province in Zaïre and in Uganda for example.[41] Lasting settlement, including naturalization, was not a real possibility for most refugees. Thus, the results achieved by many UNHCR programmes were less than satisfactory and did not lead to permanent solutions. After the UNHCR withdrew from programmes, some refugees found permanent solutions of their own that were often different from those intended. In some cases, refugees relapsed into situations of poverty and insecurity, as was the case with many Rwandan refugees in Tanzania.[42]

Protection vs. Assistance in Africa

Schnyder believed that in situations such as those in Africa, the major and immediate need of refugees was for emergency assistance rather than international legal protection. Thus, for political reasons, the *de facto* extension of international action to non-European refugees was confined to categories of emergency relief and material assistance only. Nevertheless, UNHCR staff attempted to provide minimal legal and physical protection for refugees on several specific occasions. Sometimes, UNHCR staff in Africa intervened in other countries to secure protection for refugees and to promote the maintenance of generous asylum policies. At other times, individual staff members took initiatives to physically protect refugees. This frequently involved the UNHCR in the internal security affairs of host countries. In Burundi and in Kivu province in eastern Congo, for example, the UNHCR attempted to move refugees out of danger,[43] and even organized the transfer of several thousand Rwandan refugees from Burundi and Kivu to Tanzania.[44] In one attempt to transfer refugees to safety in 1964, François Preziosi, a UNHCR representative, was killed by rebel soldiers in the kind of incident that would recur frequently in later decades. UNHCR reporting and monitoring often provided the grounds for diplomatic intervention from UN political authorities and foreign embassies. UNHCR staff in the field had close contacts with the refugee communities, local and international organizations, and governments, as well as with foreign embassies.[45] Unlike in Europe, UNHCR personnel in Africa worked as intermediaries with both countries of origin and of asylum. On some occasions UNHCR staff were the eyes and ears for Western embassies and were able to alert them to developing problems.[46]

While UN and Western policy-makers frequently encouraged the High Commissioner to mediate between countries of origin and asylum, the UNHCR's political role in defusing violent confrontations involving refugees was extremely limited. Schnyder felt that it was not the job of the High Commissioner to resolve the bigger political problems at the root of most refugee emergencies.[47] He believed that the refugee problem was essentially a political problem to be resolved by governments, and not by the UNHCR. He stressed that the High Commissioner's role was to ease tensions between states by assisting refugees and to help governments resolve refugee problems. But Schnyder firmly believed that there was a danger in overstating the role of the UNHCR. Therefore, UNHCR initiatives tended to deal with the symptoms rather than with the causes of conflicts.

These limitations inhibited the UNHCR from taking a more active role in resolving Africa's refugee problems. In December 1963, the US asked the UNHCR to defuse the political crisis between Rwanda and Burundi when agitators among the refugees threatened to invade Rwanda.[48] The State Department sought Schnyder's help because the UNHCR had access to both governments. The US also felt that the UNHCR's interest in the resettlement and integration of Tutsi refugees gave it a legitimate basis for informally approaching both the sending (Rwanda) and host (Burundi) countries. Schnyder, however, was reluctant to involve the UNHCR directly in this political problem. Instead of directly intervening with the governments himself, he requested the UN Secretary-General to respond to the breakdown in security in the region by seeking a political solution in order to stabilize the position of the Rwandan refugees in Burundi.[49] Unfortunately, there was insufficient political will among UN member states at that time to fully address the Rwandan refugee crisis. The UN was focused at that time on the civil war in neighbouring Congo in the early 1960s. Not enough attention was devoted to finding a political accommodation between Tutsi and Hutu that would have permitted a repatriation of the refugees. But the international community also neglected to provide sufficient funds to host countries to promote stability and local settlement of refugees. These were costly political mistakes which, at least indirectly, would lead to renewed genocide in the Great Lakes region of Africa 30 years later.

Despite some courageous work on the part of some individuals, the *modus operandi* of the UNHCR in Africa focused on material assistance and not on protection issues. In the 1960s, there were conflicting views within the UNHCR about whether or not material assistance should have priority over legal protection. Schnyder, along with his Assistance Division, believed the problems raised by the new groups of refugees were essentially those of material assistance. For the most part, assistance to refugees was in the nature of emergency relief and aimed at preventing starvation, and not at securing legal protection for them.[50] Those running the UNHCR Assistance Division argued that the provision of material assistance to refugees would improve the economic position of newcomers and eventually improve their legal position in their new society. According to mainstream UNHCR thinking at that time, it was perfectly normal for UNHCR representatives to give priority to material assistance programmes in refugee settlements. In Africa, the normalization of the legal and social position of refugees was seen to be largely dependent on the possibilities of settlement and assimilation into the host culture. In the best circumstances, protection in Africa meant obtaining access for refugees to local health care and education.[51]

The Legal Protection Division did not agree with this viewpoint and was disappointed by the failure of some African governments receiving UNHCR assistance to observe the legal obligations they had incurred by ratifying the 1951 Convention. The Legal Division argued that legal status for refugees was as important for their integration in host societies as material assistance. They maintained that material assistance and legal rights should develop simultaneously and that, if either of the two should take precedence, it should be legal rights.

In fact, legal protection was of little interest to many African host countries. Most governments were more concerned about the security risks
refugees posed to their interests. The African refugee situations were too politically explosive for the Office to do much more than respond through material assistance programmes. Protection was also constantly underemphasized
in Africa because the UNHCR had too few staff on the ground. The UNHCR
office for East and Central Africa had five staff members to cover the entire
region from Tanzania to Senegal. There were no Africans on the staff and the
UNHCR relied almost entirely on its operational partners who also lacked
expertise about Africa.[52] The UNHCR usually reacted to refugee crises in an *ad
hoc* fashion and had little time to think systematically about protection problems. Upon returning from an inspection trip to Africa in 1964, the UNHCR's
legal adviser noted, 'The staff of UNHCR branch offices is heavily overworked
[and the] branch offices are almost exclusively concerned with program
implementation.'[53] The report concluded that, not only did the UNHCR
branch offices in Africa give little time to the legal problems of protection but,
in fact, UNHCR material assistance programmes usually did not lead to the
assimilation of the refugees in host countries. The senior UNHCR Legal
Adviser at that time complained that most African countries sought UNHCR
involvement only for the money and that they viewed UNHCR concerns over
legal protection as unwanted interventions.[54]

The UNHCR's Role in Developing Countries:
Development of Rural Settlement Schemes and
'Zonal Development'

The UNHCR's expansion in the developing world coincided with the growing
membership in the United Nations of the developing countries and the
increasing recognition of the economic and political problems of the Third
World. Decolonization radically changed the composition of the United
Nations. In 1945, two-thirds of the globe was under colonial rule. There were
only fifty-one UN member states, most of which were European, North
American, and South American countries. There were only four African
member states: Egypt, Ethiopia, Liberia, and South Africa. By 1956, there were
eighty members, and in 1960 UN membership reached one hundred, with
seventeen new members from developing countries.

With the rapid increase in UN membership, the period of absolute Western
hegemony in the UN ended and the Third World preponderance of voting
power within the General Assembly began. The new nations acted as a pressure
group for increased international assistance. The desire on the part of the developing countries to present their problems to the international community and

to attract greater attention to their economic problems was reflected in the creation of many new UN institutions. Of greatest symbolic importance was the emergence of the Group of 77 in 1963. Determined to use its numerical weight in the councils of the United Nations to raise a broad range of development and trade issues, this bloc of developing states pressed for fundamental reforms of the international economic system and for redistribution of wealth. While the developed countries were unwilling to grant preferential treatment in international trade, development aid was one area where the north felt that concessions could be made to the south.

During the early 1960s, the amounts spent on development aid were increased dramatically. Development aid became big business.[55] In 1960, the World Bank created the International Development Association, which granted long-term, low interest loans to developing countries. Bilateral aid programmes were also increased during this period. US development assistance per annum increased from $2.0 billion in 1956 to $3.7 billion in 1963.

The UNHCR was also affected by the rise in power of developing countries and by the new UN ideology of global redistribution. During the 1960s, the refugee issue became linked to claims by the developing world for greater aid. The UNHCR took advantage of these events to enhance its own institutional growth and to expand its refugee programmes in Africa. As the Third World gained voting strength in the United Nations, the UNHCR transformed itself to meet the interests of the developing countries. Schnyder came to envisage the Office's own work in Africa as part of the total UN effort to assist these countries with their modernization and development.

The UNHCR's material assistance programmes to refugees provided the office with leverage over host countries.[56] The newly independent states in Africa were clearly more interested in the relief and economic assistance that the UNHCR and development agencies could supply, than they were in ensuring the adequate protection of refugees. Aid, therefore, became one of the Office's means to persuade governments to accept the validity of international refugee norms and to eventually institutionalize those norms in African domestic practices.

While material assistance became its central function during the 1960s, the UNHCR initially emphasized a pragmatic approach to African refugee problems. This was very modest in scope and cost, involving little more than self-sufficiency at a subsistence level. A forceful proponent of this approach was Thomas Jamieson, the long-time Director of Operations at the UNHCR. He believed that the Office's sole responsibility was to help refugees become self sufficient—primarily through basic minimal assistance—and to leave when this was achieved. Anything more that subsistence level assistance would step beyond the UNHCR's mandate. For example, in responding to the Angolan refugee emergency in the Congo, the UNHCR had provided land, tools, and seeds with a view towards local settlement of the refugees in the country of asylum. However, in many cases, including that of Angolan refugees in the Congo, economic self-sufficiency was not achieved by the UNHCR's minimal approach to assistance.[57]

Some within the UNHCR argued for a more expansive approach to assistance that would be linked to broader UN development efforts. Schnyder himself came to believe that the UNHCR needed to provide more than emergency assistance targeted at meeting the basic needs of refugees. Local host communities, as well as refugees, needed assistance. Otherwise, frictions would develop with local communities who were often as poor as the newcomers. However, most African countries lacked the infrastructure, the resources, and the technical ability to deal with their own impoverished nationals let alone with the indigent refugees they hosted. To overcome some of these problems, Schnyder encouraged the organization of rural resettlement schemes where refugees would be able to re-establish themselves in their accustomed way of life and simultaneously contribute to their host country's economies.[58] Settlements were planned and services provided so that refugees could become self-sufficient at a standard of living comparable to—but not markedly better than—that of the surrounding local population. Recognizing that the African refugee situations were but one aspect of the overall economic and social problem of development, Schnyder believed that for refugee assistance programmes to be effective, they had to be part of the larger development programme in a country of asylum. In a report to his Executive Committee, he outlined his new thinking:

. . . efforts should also be encouraged to provide a wider basis for the solution of refugee problems within the framework of the social development of the country. Seen against this background, the international efforts for assistance to refugees could be regarded as a useful element in the field of international development aid. (Felix Schnyder, *Report on New Refugee Situations*, submitted to the 7th session of Excom (1962): UN doc A/AC.96/158).[59]

The UNHCR would now not only aim 'to save the lives of refugees and to enable them to support themselves on a subsistence level, but also to give them a chance to improve their living conditions within the development of the country of asylum'.[60]

Schnyder also acknowledged that this broader developmental approach would necessitate an active primary role for UN agencies and NGOs other than the UNHCR. The High Commissioner, therefore, began to develop inter-agency co-operation with other UN bodies engaged in multidimensional development programmes. Schnyder envisioned the UNHCR's role to act as a catalyst or as 'a drop of oil' to engage the interest and to promote the involvement of other specialized UN agencies and NGOs in refugee issues.[61] As Schnyder explained:

Although the role the High Commissioner can play in the face of the new refugee problem is modest by definition, experience has nevertheless proved it is one of real usefulness. In fact, the High Commissioner in many cases is the initiator as well as the catalytic element, capable of mobilizing and making the best use of the available energies and resources. The High Commissioner must also intervene to coordinate the activities of governments and voluntary agencies assisting refugees. Finally, it is essential that in fulfilling its task, my office be enabled to work in close liaison with the Technical Assistance services and the specialized agencies of the United Nations. (United Nations Doc. A/C.3/SR. 1112, 22 November 1961: 10).

The UNHCR was inspired by World Bank-guided 'integrated rural development land settlement schemes'. In collaboration with various international agencies, including the International Labour Organization (ILO), the UN Development Programme, and the Lutheran World Federation, the Office sought to integrate its refugee schemes into broader national rural development strategies throughout the continent.[62] The strategy of 'integrated zonal development' was first promoted in Burundi for Rwandan refugees and in the Central African Republic for Sudanese in the mid-1960s, and later in Tanzania, Uganda, and other African states.[63]

The UNHCR thus sought a crucial role for itself in Africa's development. By assisting host governments in the emergency phase of refugee situations, the UNHCR hoped to attract more sizeable investments by other UN agencies in long term projects involving not only refugees but also local residents. In this way, UNHCR programmes awakened government interest in development possibilities that otherwise might have remained on a lower level of importance in national priorities. For several years, rural settlement schemes became standard UNHCR solutions for Africa. Unfortunately, many of the UNHCR's efforts to introduce a more developmental framework into refugee relief proved unsuccessful in the long term. Most African host countries lacked social and political stability and the majority of refugees settled spontaneously outside UNHCR programmes anyway. Nevertheless, these programmes were viewed by several host countries as important UNHCR contributions to their development.

The UNHCR Policy in the Global Context

The growth in foreign aid budgets during the 1960s was by no means stimulated by generosity alone. Western donor governments were willing to support the UNHCR's operational expansion into the developing world because international action on the refugee issue was now also viewed as a way to deal with potential sources of instability in the Third World.[64] During the 1960s, the South gained greater visibility as the Cold War extended beyond Europe to parts of the Third World. Randolph Kent, a relief aid specialist, noted that the developing world was no longer isolated in a framework of Western colonial interests but was now part of the broader arena of international relations.[65] By the 1960s, each superpower believed that the future of its ideological, economic, and strategic systems depended upon 'winning' the Third World.

Both East and West vied for influence in Africa and Asia and tried to minimize the ability of their opponent to gain political advantage in these regions. As the Cold War extended to Asia and Africa, the struggle to end colonialism and to draw attention to the economic and political disparities between rich states and poor states gained importance within the international political system. Anti-colonialism became a political weapon for the Soviet Union to use in its ideological conflict with the West and it joined a number of African and Asian states to form an anti-colonial coalition in the United Nations. Growing Soviet involvement in the developing world, the socialist rhetoric of newly independent states, and their turn towards 'non-alignment' from the mid-1950s on, heightened the geo-strategic attention of the United States to developments in Africa and the rest of the developing world.[66]

The US and other Western governments began to perceive refugee situations in developing countries as a source of instability, which the Soviet Union could exploit for its own advantage in extending Communism in the Third World. Consequently, the West came to view assistance to refugees as a central part of their foreign policies towards newly independent states. In this way they used foreign aid as one of the principal tools for influence in the East–West struggle. Governments made little distinction between military aid, development assistance, and refugee relief aid. More importantly, because the UNHCR was a donor-dependent organization, dominated by the West and with no Communist state representation on Excom, there was little risk of multilateral refugee aid being used in ways unacceptable to the United States and other major Western governments.

Strengthening the Legal Underpinnings of the UNHCR

At a time when the majority of the world's refugees originated in and stayed in the developing world, Western states had little difficulty in extending UNHCR's capacity to assist a much broader category of refugees. The developed states were not in danger of confronting masses of Third World arrivals, and therefore, could avoid the question of whether these groups were in fact formally within the High Commissioner's mandate. In Europe, meanwhile, the 1951 Convention served that continent's refugees well. It provided the legal underpinnings for a liberal asylum system that was strengthened by the financial resources and resettlement quotas of the United States and other

resettlement countries. Thus, the refugee situation evolved into one characterized by a lack of state consensus on a single refugee definition for all
regions of the world and requiring multiple definitions for multiple purposes.

For a while, this pragmatic and principally non-legalistic approach served
the interests of both developed and developing states. However, as new
refugee groups emerged in the 1960s whose circumstances could not be
related to events prior to 1951, the Refugee Convention's time limitation
became a growing handicap for the High Commissioner.[67] Schnyder was well
aware that existing international legal norms were not suitable for dealing
with refugee issues in the Third World. The 1951 Refugee Convention had
been developed to respond to a largely European refugee problem of the late
1940s and early 1950s. The 1960s Third World refugees did not fall within the
classic definition in the Convention. That is, they had not fled as a result of
conditions in Europe before 1951 nor could many of them meet the individual persecution criteria outlined in the international legal instruments. Large
groups of destitute people fleeing violence and conflict associated with decolonization, national liberation struggles, and the establishment of nation
states in the Third World were in need of a wide variety of special kinds of
emergency assistance. While the General Assembly good offices resolutions
made many new refugee groups the concern of the UNHCR, the measures
were recommendations only and could not impose fresh or greater obligations on sovereign states. Consequently, Schnyder and his Executive
Committee sought to delete the geographic and time limitation provisions
from the 1951 Convention by means of a 'protocol'.

A group of experts met in Bellagio, Italy, in 1965 and issued a report urging
the international community to re-examine the convention and the statute
in the light of new refugee situations. In 1967, after Schnyder had left his
post, a protocol was signed by many nations including some that were not
parties to the original Convention.[68] Rather than simply amending the
Convention, the new Protocol Relating to the Status of Refugees was drafted
in such a way that a government signing it would in effect undertake all the
obligations of the original Convention. The High Commissioner was thus
able to secure ratification by a number of governments that had not signed
the original convention including the United States.[69] In contrast to the slow
pace with which states accepted the 1951 Convention, the Protocol was
quickly ratified by a large number of governments.[70] The most important
effect of the 1967 Protocol was that it brought the 1951 Convention on
Refugees into line with the universal mandate of the statute of UNHCR.

During the 1960s, African states expressed dissatisfaction that the international refugee instruments did not reflect the realities of the refugee situation
in Africa and that inadequate attention was given to taking measures to
defuse the political tensions refugees created in their region. For several of
Africa's new governments, especially those in central and eastern Africa,

refugee movements constituted a source of serious political and military tension between governments. In 1964, the OAU-formed a Commission on Refugee Problems in Africa made up members from the interior ministries of African governments to investigate ways to deal with the political nature of the continent's refugee problems. It drew up a series of 'guiding principles' that involved actions by all African countries concerned with refugees, including the receiving countries, countries of origin, and third countries. Several of the principles dealt directly with the security concerns of interior ministers. For example, asylum countries were encouraged to settle refugees as far as possible from the borders of the country of origin and to not allow refugees to attack their country of origin. Asylum countries were also supposed to prohibit all subversive activity by refugees. Similarly, countries of origin were admonished neither to view the granting of asylum as an unfriendly gesture nor to attack the countries of refuge through the media, press, or radio or by resorting to arms. Finally, the host countries were told to try to promote voluntary repatriation as soon as possible.

When OAU states considered the establishment of a regional High Commissioner for Refugees, the UNHCR became alarmed. The Office felt that the Africans' efforts to set up their own refugee organization would duplicate and compete with their own agency and programmes. Most importantly, however, Schnyder felt the UNHCR had a universal mandate and that refugees in Africa should remain the UN's concern. Moreover, the UNHCR feared that the establishment of a separate OAU refugee office would unduly politicize the African refugee problem.

The UNHCR was also concerned that the OAU sought to formulate its own regional refugee convention. Finding that many of the provisions in the early draft of the convention were far less liberal than the 1951 Convention, the Office stepped up its efforts to promote international refugee norms in the region. The UNHCR opened a liaison office in Addis Ababa, Ethiopia—the site of the OAU headquarters—and during the next several years, the UNHCR actively collaborated with the OAU Refugee Commission to formulate the 1969 OAU Refugee Convention.[71] The UNHCR offered itself as a source of knowledge and expertise to OAU ministers. The Office was initially concerned that African governments attached more importance to protect themselves against the security threat posed by refugee movements than to protect the welfare of refugees.[72] The UNHCR hoped that its participation in reviewing the draft of the OAU Convention would ensure that refugee legal and organizational efforts in Africa would supplement the international refugee instruments. In fact, the preamble to the OAU convention acknowledged that the 1951 Refugee Convention and the Protocol of 1967 constituted the basic and universal instrument relating to the status of refugees, thus embedding African states in the international refugee regime. However, the OAU Convention also had many unique features. Unlike the 1951 Convention, the

OAU Convention stressed the right of asylum and prohibited the rejection of asylum-seekers at the frontiers of African states. The most important feature of this first regional refugee convention, however, was that the OAU extended the definition of refugee to include 'every person who, owing to external aggression, occupation, foreign domination or events seriously disturbing public order . . . is compelled to leave his place of habitual residence'.[73] By covering individuals seeking refuge from the violence and devastation of war, the OAU offered a significantly broader interpretation of 'refugee' than did the Convention and the Protocol, and set an important precedent for future regional refugee legal instruments.

The UNHCR and US Foreign Policy Interests

The increasingly positive US attitude towards the UNHCR was one of the main factors influencing the Office's development during this time. The United States generally supported the UNHCR's expansion into Africa and Asia, as the Office was perceived as a vehicle for providing order and stability in the developing world.[74] By the early 1960s the major powers themselves began to recognize the changing nature of the global refugee problem. The US, for one, no longer perceived the refugee problem as one confined almost exclusively to Europe and realized that the UNHCR had a significant role to play in responding to refugee problems in other regions of the world.

Felix Schnyder's appointment as High Commissioner had coincided with the inauguration of the John F. Kennedy Administration in the United States. Although the new US administration still gave strategic priority to Europe, American policy-makers began to take note of refugee developments in Africa, Asia, and Latin America. In particular, Kennedy sought to counter the increased Soviet interest in new nations and believed that the developing world would be the new arena of the Cold War. Naturally, the new US interest in the developing world also caused the Americans to foster close relations with the UNHCR.

In Africa, the US State Department saw considerable political advantage in working through the UNHCR. For example, Sudanese refugees had fled to several nearby African countries in the 1960s, damaging relations between African countries and endangering regional security. Many of these refugees were closely aligned to the resistance movements in southern Sudan, and the government in Khartoum perceived any assistance to refugees as support for the rebels. American security interests in the region dictated maintaining good relations with both Khartoum and the southern Sudanese rebels. But direct US assistance to the refugees would be perceived by Khartoum as criticism of its human rights and domestic policies. In this situation, the UNHCR provided the perfect cover for US policy-makers. Providing assistance to refugees from southern Sudan using the UNHCR 'umbrella' rather than US bilateral programmes 'defused and deflected' any criticism by Sudan of American action.[75]

American policy regarding African refugees was driven by the increased Soviet interest in these groups. In the Sudanese case, for example, the Soviet Union offered the Sudan African National Union extensive aid in exchange for bases in the country.[76] The US perceived the political upheaval and diaspora of so many people in Africa as providing fertile ground for Communist propaganda and opportunism. The Department of State informed the Senate Committee that, '...the communists do seek to dominate Africa. They are actively attempting to destroy independence on that continent'.[77] The State Department then outlined the ways in which the Communist bloc exploited the refugee situation:

In the case of the Rwandan refugees, for example, there is reasonably reliable evidence that communist powers, particularly communist China, have involved themselves to the detriment of a peaceful solution. This involvement has included encouragement of extremist agitators who stir up the refugees to pursue a militant policy toward Rwanda, extending to terrorist raids across Rwanda's borders. Communist assistance to refugee extremists reportedly encompassed financial support to the ex-King of Rwanda and his close adherents, advice on organizing terrorist raids, some arms aid, and the training of guerrilla instructors in mainland China. It is believed that this assistance in recent months probably has been coordinated by the Chinese Communist Embassy in Bujumbura, Burundi, with its similar assistance given to the rebels in the Congo.

In Dar-es-Salaam and other refugee centers, the Soviet Union, China, and other communist countries actively seek to influence and gain footholds in refugee groups. Their efforts take several forms which include offering scholarships to refugee students, flooding offices of exiled nationalist groups and student groups with propaganda literature, providing arms and other material assistance to nationalist refugee organizations, and offering the leaders short-term visits to communist countries. (US National Archives, Diplomatic Branch, REF SUDAN. Pol. 30-2 Sudan, 20 March 1964: 8).

Africa's national liberation struggles presented the United States with some difficult policy choices during the 1960s. Washington felt that, if the US did not support national liberation fronts in Africa, Africa's freedom fighters would then turn to the Communist bloc countries for help. America had military and economic interests in the region, such as US miliary bases in the Portuguese Azores and large-scale American investment in the mines and industries of southern Africa. Backing southern African liberation movements would endanger these. A State Department analysis of US policy options regarding national liberation fronts in Africa outlined the problems likely to confront American policy-makers in southern Africa.

. . . the members of Pan African Freedom Movement for East, Central and South Africa (PAFMECA) and other African states will exert increasing pressure on the West for support of freedom movements in southern Africa. . . . Intensified pressure upon the US and other nations also is clearly in prospect for sanctions against the Republic of South Africa, Portugal, and possibly Southern Rhodesia. But the most serious threat will be the infusion of Bloc influence as growing frustration turns Africans increasingly to the East for aid. . . . Thus PAFMECA activities will sharpen the horns of the dilemma facing the West in southern Africa; to balance Western strategic interests against ties with present and future African leaders and at the same time to counter and expanding Bloc influence in the nationalist movements of this area. (US National Archives, Diplomatic Branch, Record Group 59, Central Policy Files, 1963, Box 3789, 25 March 1963).

One way to signal support to African national liberation movements and to forestall the advance of Communist influence in African countries was to increase US assistance to refugees in the region. Consequently, the United States channelled most of its refugee aid through multilateral organizations — chiefly the UNHCR—as a way of gaining good will in recipient countries and with liberation fronts. Multilateral refugee assistance also satisfied the wishes of most African states. As the State Department explained to the US Congress,

. . . the African countries sometimes do not want the assistance to have too close US identification. They often like voluntary agency assistance handled quietly, in view of the political problem . . . [Therefore] . . . the United States has not tried to establish a separate refugee program of its own in Africa . . . African countries generally prefer to get assistance through international organizations. (US Senate, Judiciary Committee, Subcommittee to Investigate Problems Connected with Refugees and Escapees, *African Refugee Problems*, 89th Congress, 1st Session, 21 January 1965: 38–9).

The United States gave most of its assistance through the UNHCR, principally by providing surplus food for distribution—PL-480 Food for Peace Program— and assistance to African students. US assistance to a UNHCR-supported multilateral effort made the American policy acceptable in the eyes of the Portuguese and the South African governments. In effect, the UNHCR became an indirect vehicle for US foreign objectives in Africa.

Refugees and the Decline ofCold War Tensions in Europe

While the US supported the UNHCR programme in Africa, tension continued to exist between them over refugee and asylum issues in Europe and North America. The US preferred to maintain near absolute control over its own refugee and asylum programme in Europe and rebuffed any UNHCR criticisms, however mild, of American asylum policy. In Europe, geopolitical concerns and anti-Communist programmes continued to dominate American interests.

A special task force set up by the State Department in 1960 to review US refugee policy drew attention to the continuing strategic importance that the United States attached to assisting refugees from Communist bloc countries. The annex to the resulting report outlined clearly the political and ideological significance of US refugee policy in Europe:

The intelligence community is vitally interested in the maintenance of the United States escapee program for the encouragement of escapees from Sino-Soviet bloc countries and particularly of those who may, because of their specialized background and knowledge, qualify as defectors. It is obviously in the best interests of the United States that this flow of intelligence information be continued and increased if possible.

While persons falling within this 'special interests' category constitute a small proportion of escapees and refugees arriving in the West, a considerably larger number may be of incidental intelligence value, some having provided highly useful intelligence information. Regardless of their personal knowledgeability, the majority of escapees and refugees have a certain amount of psychological and propaganda value both individually and collectively. It is imperative that the advantage thus gained be prevented from turning into adverse propaganda which is likely to result if conditions met with in the West are such as to encourage redefection.

The USEP may be considered to have two broad objectives: [1] to care for and maintain all eligible persons from the Sino-Soviet bloc seeking asylum, with the assistance of U.S. charitable ('voluntary') agencies, and to assist in resettling such persons in a Western country in circumstances which will make it possible for them to become useful citizens within the country of resettlement; and [2] to encourage, by the example thus set, additional escapees and refugees, particularly those who are able to add valuable new or confirmatory information to existing knowledge of the Soviet world. (US National Archives, Diplomatic Branch, 324.8411/2-1860 CS/RA, Annex, 'The Intelligence Value of Defectors, Escapees and Refugees', 8 February 1960).

While recognizing the continuing geopolitical importance of assisting Communist bloc refugees, the authors also noted that the numbers of refugees in Europe were radically declining and foresaw that US financial contribution to European refugees would be reduced gradually in the years ahead:

... within two years the refugee problem in Western Europe will be reduced to an endemic level. At this level it will no longer be an economic problem of international concern (except possibly in Austria and Greece) but will remain one of political, psychological and intelligence concern. The United States should use its influence to speed the final solution of the European refugee backlog, as far as possible through the existing programs of the UNHCR. After this backlog is removed (hopefully by 1962) our support of UNHCR should be directed primarily to the legal and political protection aspects of his work in Europe; but should recognize the possible desirability of his maintaining operational capabilities elsewhere in the world.

As the European problem diminishes, the U.S. should aim correspondingly to reduce its organizational and financial contributions in Europe and place the emphasis of its refugee efforts in such other areas of the world as the needs and U.S. national interest dictate. (Ibid.)

The US *Migration and Refugee Assistance Act* of 1962[78] simplified and codified government refugee relief operations and centralized them in the State Department, under a separate budget. However, detaching refugee assistance from the foreign aid budget had a significant impact on the levels of annual US contributions to the UNHCR during the 1960s. When the new refugee legislation was enacted, US government annual contributions to the UNHCR were $1.2 million. Two years later the American contribution was halved. This level of contribution continued throughout most of the rest of the 1960s, causing significant problems for the UNHCR. Similarly, US efforts to assign the State Department with the primary responsibility of supervising refugee affairs did not have the intended effect. Despite the change in the name of the US Escapee Program to the US Refugee Program in 1962 and the appointment of a Special Assistant for Refugee Affairs to the Secretary of State in 1966, the US continued to lack a focal point for refugee affairs for most of the decade.

Throughout the 1960s, the United States also maintained the Cold War priorities of the former USEP. The ideological and propaganda importance of Communist bloc refugees continued to be tied to larger American foreign policy concerns. In an accompanying letter to the 1962 refugee legislation, President Kennedy summarized the continuing foreign policy rationale for US refugee programmes:

The successful re-establishment of refugees (he said in part) is importantly related to free world political objectives. These objectives are: (a) continuation of the provision of asylum and friendly assistance to the oppressed and persecuted; (b) the extension of hope and encouragement to the victims of communism and other forms of despotism, and the promotion of faith among the captive populations in the purposes and processes of freedom and democracy; and (c) the exemplification by free citizens of free countries, through actions and sacrifices, of the fundamental humanitarianism which constitutes the basic difference between free and captive societies. (Quoted a US State Department mimeo, *The US Government and Refugee Relief*, August 1972).

President Kennedy also identified the following categories of refugees, which he believed would contribute to the defence, security, or foreign policy interests of the United States:

[1]refugees from Soviet bloc countries; [2]Yugoslav refugees; [3]refugees from Communist China; [4]Tibetan refugees; [5]Cuban refugees in foreign areas; [6]Algerian refugees repatriating to or displaced within Algeria; [7]African refugees in Central Africa; [8]selected refugees from North Africa; [9]selected exiles who have rendered valuable service to the United States; [10]selected students from uncommitted countries who have been studying in communist countries; and [11]Cuban refugees in the United States who are in need of loans to attend institutions of higher education. (US National Archives, Diplomatic Branch,, S/R:ORM: Grossman X 21479: 12/4/72.16, August 1962).

The Berlin Wall and the Decline of East European Refugees

Throughout the 1950s, the mass exodus of East Germans into West Germany principally via Berlin had captured the attention of American and other Western policy-makers. An estimated 3.5 million East Germans—about 20 per cent of the population—resettled in West Germany during these years. Ethnic Germans were automatically accepted as citizens under West German law. Communist bloc refugees—Hungarians, Czechs, and East Germans among others—were accepted into the West with little scrutiny into their motives of departure. In August 1961, however, the flow of refugees into West Germany was staunched with the construction of the Berlin Wall and the tightening of border controls in East Germany. Despite the introduction of barbed wire and electrified fencing around the Berlin Wall and of a 'death strip' along the East German border, there continued to be infrequent but well-publicized escapes. Nevertheless, after 1961, the numbers of escapees fell dramatically. The number of refugees from Warsaw Pact countries to West Germany was reduced from 1,173 in 1961 to 458 in 1962.[79] As a result, the caseload of the USEP dropped from a high of 44,197 at the end of 1958 to only 4,112 at the end of 1962.[80]

In light of the fact that Western Europe was now economically strong enough to deal with the fewer numbers of Communist bloc refugees fleeing East Europe, the United States began to attach less importance to the problem of refugees in Europe. While the USEP remained operational throughout the decade, the US significantly cut back its financial support for both USEP and ICEM activities. By 1963, the US share of total governmental contributions to the ICEM fell to 33 per cent from 45 per cent in 1960 and its total contributions to the USEP amounted to $1.25 million, down from $9.3 million in 1959.[81]

The reduction in American support for refugees in Europe also adversely affected US financial support for the UNHCR's key remaining programmes in Europe. At the beginning of 1961, there were still some 13,800 long-standing refugees in camps and 65,000 out-of-camp, nonsettled refugees in Europe. Schnyder was determined to successfully complete the Camp Clearance Programme he had inherited from Lindt. However, the costs of completing the programme were considerable. Unlike the emergency programmes for 'new refugee groups' in Africa, the programmes for 'old refugee groups' in Europe required sustained funding over several years. In 1962 the UNHCR asked for $5 million and in 1963, for $5.4 million.[82] During a period of relative calm in Europe, it was difficult to focus US attention on old refugee problems on the continent. When Schnyder requested the United States to contribute more generously to this programme, he was told that

Congressmen in Washington were somewhat skeptical regarding appeals made for concluding the old refugees programme, as during the past five years, the

Administration has stated that the Office of UNHCR had almost completed the programme and despite this, each year more money was required for this purpose. (UNHCR Archives, HCR/USA/'Notes on Washington Talks', 27 February 1963).

The US Congress was only interested in funding refugee situations in which the United States was most actively engaged. At that time the Kennedy Administration was focused on events in the Caribbean. Moreover, for the first time in history, the United States faced a major asylum crisis in Florida which swallowed up practically all available funds for refugees.

The Cuban Asylum Crisis: A No-Go Area for the UNHCR

Nearly one quarter of a million Cuban refugees entered the United States from 1959 through October 1962. With the overthrow of the Fulgencio Batista regime and the radicalization of the Cuban state under Fidel Castro, US–Cuban relations were marked by continuous mutual hostility and distrust. American policy was to isolate diplomatically, deprive economically, discredit ideologically, and overthrow violently the Castro regime.

The US response to the Cuban refugees was very similar to the response given Eastern European escapees throughout the 1950s. In both instances, the refugees were characterized as victims of totalitarianism whose departure constituted a 'ballot for freedom'. Refugees from Cuba were part of these larger American foreign policy objectives. Until the Bay of Pigs fiasco in May 1961, Cuban exiles were in the vanguard of US efforts to unseat Castro.[83] US Government policy was to accept all persons fleeing from Cuba, regardless of their status.[84] Resettlement of Cubans was initially based on the premise that the Cubans were temporary exiles in the United States, likely to topple Fidel Castro with CIA training and assistance, and then return home. All Cuban entrants received generous public welfare allowances provided by the federal Government. By the end of 1963, expenditures from US government sources on the programme for Cuban refugees amounted to an astounding $100 million, completely dwarfing the annual UNHCR budget of $3 million for all refugees worldwide.

For the UNHCR, the Cuban asylum crisis in the United States was a no-go area. Since the early 1950s, the US had made clear that it did not see any role for an international agency in overseeing American asylum policy. Despite US obstruction, the UNHCR did in fact make several *demarches* to the US government during the 1950s regarding deportation policy and practice in the United States. For example, the UNHCR pointed out on numerous occasions that there was a serious discrepancy between the terms of the 1951 Convention and the US *Immigration and Naturalization Act*. The latter permitted the US Attorney General to deport individuals who should have been protected from forcible return under the terms of the 1951 Convention. However, these consultations did not result in a substantial change in US policy.

The UNHCR did not have an office in Washington DC until 1980. The only point of direct contact in the United States between the US government and the UNHCR was through its liaison office at UN headquarters in New York. The UNHCR monitored refugee protection problems through this office but the US did not welcome this activity and did not provide any help to the UNHCR in fulfilling its protection role.

During the 1960s, the expansion of the UNHCR's practical mandate would have permitted it to involve itself in the large flow out of Cuba. At the start of the crisis, the UNHCR debated whether it should intervene in the US to decide on the eligibility of Cuban asylum-seekers or at least to send a Representative to Washington DC for more direct contact with US government officials.[85] Because the United States offered sanctuary to all who fled and sought no assistance from the UNHCR, the organization, well aware of its own limited resources and mindful of following a policy that would not put it in conflict with a major power on Excom, took no action.[86] In the end, the UNHCR decided to restrict its role to simply collecting information about the asylum problem,[87] and played no effective protection role in the US. The State Department even refused any role for the UNHCR in cases of family reunion involving the US and another state.[88]

Although the UNHCR was deliberately excluded from dealing with Cuban refugees in the US, the Office did become involved in assisting Cuban refugees who fled to Spain.[89] The great majority of the refugees living in Spain arrived after the cessation of flights from Havana to Miami in October 1962. Few of the Cubans in Spain had relatives or other real links with Spain. Virtually all of them wanted to emigrate, mostly to the US. While the US was willing to accept large numbers of Cubans from Spain for resettlement, the slow process of obtaining a visa from the US Consulate in Spain created a backlog of potential emigrants.

The UNHCR initiated an emergency assistance programme for these refugees through a local NGO to provide limited care and maintenance until they could be resettled outside Spain. The UNHCR avoided making a deter-mination of mandate status for the Cubans in Spain on the grounds that they could be assisted under the good offices responsibility. Schnyder believed it would be wise to avoid involving the question of UNHCR assistance in the political controversy over Cuba, since many Cubans arrived in Spain with Cuban documents and it would be difficult in many individual cases to prove political persecution.[90] In April 1964, the UNHCR Executive Committee approved a programme for $159,000 to help Cuban refugees integrate in Spain. The US government also encouraged the UNHCR to co-operate with the ICEM to resettle Cubans. Although the US tried to get other countries to share the burden, the great majority of Cubans were in fact resettled in the US. Latin American governments and other resettlement countries were unwilling to accept Cubans from the United States and Spain. Most countries viewed the Cuban refugee crisis to be a direct consequence of the US–Cuban political rift and therefore as solely an American responsibility.

The Next Stages of UNHCR Expansion

From its expansion into Africa in the 1960s, refugee emergencies during the next decade would emerge on all continents, multiply, and take on numerical proportions hitherto unknown. Faced with mass exoduses from East Pakistan, Uganda, and Indochina; highly politicized refugee crises in Chile and Argentina; the repatriation and reintegration of refugees and internally displaced persons in Southern Sudan, the UNHCR would embark on new assistance programmes in a number of refugee and 'refugee-like' situations around the world. In the process, the UNHCR, under an ambitious new High Commissioner, would develop an enormous agenda and become an indispensable actor in world politics.

NOTES

1. For background see Aristide Zolberg, Astri Suhrke, and Sergio Aguayo, *Escape from Violence: Conflict and Refugee Crises in the Developing World* (New York, NY: Oxford University Press, 1989).
2. US National Archives, Diplomatic Branch, 324.8411/4-661. Speaking in New York in January 1961, even before he took up his post as High Commissioner, Schnyder said that, 'although the [UNHCR] mandate was useful in Europe, it had much less relevance to Asian conditions. . . .', and that 'given the increased Afro-Asian representation in the UN, he thought that the refugee problem in these areas would receive increasing attention'. US Mission Geneva to Department of State Washington, 'Possible Shift of Emphasis in Program of UNHCR', 6 April 1961.
3. UNHCR Archives, Press Release, No. Ref. 638, Geneva, 1 February 1961.
4. UN General Assembly Resolution 1672 (XVI) (18 December 1961).
5. Interview, Jacques Cuenod, Geneva, January 1999. Cuenod was one of the UNHCR officials responsible for UNHCR's repatriation programme for Algerians.
6. Felix Schnyder, Statement to the Third Committee of the UN General Assembly, 19 November 1962.
7. Louise Holborn, *Refugees: A Problem of Our Time: The Work of the United Nations High Commissioner for Refugees* (Metuchen, NJ: Scarecrow Press, 1975): 1025–7.
8. Interview with Michel Moussalli, Geneva, January 1999. Moussalli took part as a UNHCR official in the Algerian repatriation and in developing early relations between UNHCR and the OAU in Addis Ababa.

9. US National Archives, Diplomatic Branch, 324.8411/2-2161. US Mission Geneva to Secretary of State, 21 February 1961.

10. Interview with Michel Moussalli.

11. Interview with Jacques Cuenod, Geneva, January 1999. Cuenod was responsible for helping to develop and implement UNHCR policy and programmes in Africa during Schnyder's period.

12. Interview with Felix Schnyder.

13. Interview with Jacques Cuenod.

14. Interview with Gilbert Jaeger, Oxford, 1988. Jaeger was a senior member of staff under Schynder. The theory of using the 'good offices' of UNHCR is fully developed in Schnyder's lectures in the Hague. Another senior member of staff, Jacques Colmar, was instrumental in developing the 'good offices' doctrine. See Felix Schnyder, 'Les Aspects Juridiques Actuel du Probleme des Refugies', *Recueil*, 114 (Leiden: Academie de Droit International, 1965).

15. UNHCR Archives, HCR/15/82, 27 February 1961 and HCR/15/82, 20 March 1961.

16. UNHCR Archives, HCR/15/72/INDIA, Folio 168B, 3 December 1963.

17. United Nations Security Council Resolution S/4835, adopted on 9 June 1961.

18. Portugal regularly protested any implied criticism of its policies. For example, a communication from the Portuguese Embassy to the Department of State argued, 'Such displaced persons in the Congo fled from the violent activities of the terrorists in northern Angola rather than from the action of the Portuguese security forces. Most of them would have already returned to Angola, had they not been victims of threats and intimidation by the anti-Portuguese terrorist organizations based in the Congo which have systematically used the plight of the refugees for political propaganda purposes. Many others, classified as refugees by such terrorist organizations, are neither refugees nor have they fled from Angola.' Portugal was also critical of international aid arguing that 'none of this help, not even the smallest portion does in fact reach these people, because it is all deviated for the personal gain of the small group that heads the terrorist movement'. See Appendix to US Senate, Committee on the Judiciary, Subcommittee to Investigate Problems Connected with Refugees and Escapees, 89th Congress, 1st Session (21 January 1965): 41–2.

19. US National Archives, Diplomatic Branch, Reference 3, Box: Organizations and Conferences/UN, 8 February 1963.

20. UNHCR Archives, HCR/ANG/30, 2 June 1961.

21. UNHCR Archives, HCR/ANG/30, 21 May 1961.

22. UNHCR Archives, HCR/ANG/30, J. D. R. Kelly, *Report on Refugees from Angola*, 26 June 1961. US National Archives, Diplomatic Branch, 324.8411/7-2861, *Angolan Refugees in the Congo, Report by the UN High Commissioner for Refugees*, 28 July 1961.

23. US National Archives, Diplomatic Branch, 324.8411/9-3061, 30 September 1961. According to Paul Weis from the legal department, the use of the Emergency Fund was limited to mandate refugees only. See: UNHCR Archives, HCR/ANG/29/5, *Refugees from Angola*, 26 May 1961.

24. Holborn, *Refugees*: 441.

25. The High Commissioner's report to the General Assembly, United Nations General Assembly (XIII), Official Record, Annex: 2.

26. Interview with Felix Schnyder, Locarno, 1988.

27. Commenting on his discussions with Portuguese Prime Minister Salazar in Lisbon, Schnyder noted: 'I pointed out that in helping refugees we do not only contribute to the elimination of a source of misery but of a source of friction, too.' *Note for the File Concerning the High Commissioner's Visit to Lisbon* (Geneva: UNHCR/POR, 19 November 1963).

28. British Public Records Office, Foreign Office Files, FO371/161014, 1 November 1961.

29. United Nations General Assembly Resolution 1673 (XVI) (18 December 1961).

30. United Nations General Assembly Resolution 2039 (XX) (1965).

31. As Schnyder explained, 'Prompt and effective action is the only way of preventing refugee problems . . . from getting rapidly out of control . . . and thus becoming a cause of serious concern to the governments of host countries. That means that the steps taken to remedy them must be as simple, flexible and effective as possible. Thanks to the resolutions adopted by the General Assembly, it has been possible in recent years, on the basis of the "good offices" idea . . . to develop a new procedure adapted to the special conditions applying in he countries where the new refugee problems are to be found.' Statement by Felix Schnyder, UN High Commissioner for Refugees to the Third Committee of General Assembly XX. UNHCR Archives, HCR/4/66, GE.66-157, November 1965.

32. Interview with Gilbert Jaeger. According to Jaeger, the attitude of UNHCR staff and many donor governments was that, if governments of asylum did not ask for assistance from the UNHCR, no international aid would be given.

33. For the problems of self-settled refugees, see Robert Chambers, 'Rural Refugees in Africa: What the Eye Does Not See', *Disasters*, 3 (1979): 381–92.

34. Interview with Felix Schnyder.

35. For background see Rene Lemarchand, *Rwanda and Burundi* (London: Pall Mall Press, 1970); Yefime Zarjevski, *A Future Preserved: International Assistance to Refugees* (Oxford: Pergamon Press, 1988); and Zolberg, Suhrke, and Aguayo, *Escape from Violence*.

36. Zolberg, Suhrke, and Aguayo, *Escape from Violence*, and Holborn, *Refugees*.

37. Mohamed Awad, 'Refugees from the Sudan' in Hugh C. Brooks and Yassin El-Ayouty, eds., *Refugees South of the Sahara: An African Dilemma* (Westport, CT: Negro Universities Press, 1970).

38. Lemarchand, *Rwanda and Burundi*.

39. UNHCR Archives, HCR/KAM-Gen-49. *Recent Influx of Refugees from Congo and Sudan into Uganda,* 21 September 1964.

40. UNHCR Archives, HCR/2/MOZ, 62, *Refugees from Mozambique*, 9 November 1964.

41. Jacques Cuenod, 'The Problem of Rwandese and Sudanese Refugees', in Sven Hammel, *African Refugee Problems* (Uppsala: The Scandinavian Institute of African Studies, 1966): 345–53.

42. Pierre Coat, 'Material Assistance: Some Policy Problems Reviewed in Light of Robert Chambers' Evaluation Reports' (Geneva: UNHCR, 1977). Box 19, Refugee Studies Programme Documentation Centre, Oxford.

43. In reporting to the UNHCR on the problem of transferring Rwandan refugees in Burundi to Tanzania, the UNHCR's regional representative, Jacques Cuenod, commented, 'The Secretary-General, as well as the OAU, should be requested to intervene with the Burundi government to control the agitators and to implement

the plan. . . . While it is true that security is not our major concern, the refugees will suffer if a security risk becomes a reality. The Office is not responsible for security in itself but it is certainly responsible for the repercussions of insecurity on the refugees. An interest, even marginal, in security aspects, is perfectly in line with the purposes and principles of the United Nations, and indirectly, is related to the protection function of the Office.' UNHCR Archives, HCR/BUR/RWA/1619. *Problem of 'New' Refugees from Rwanda in Burundi*, 12 December 1964.

44. UNHCR Archives, HCR/KIVU/15/81. *Report on the First Moves of Refugees from Central Kivu to Tanganyika via Goma*, 20 November 1964.

45. The US Embassy in Burundi commented on the diplomatic abilities of UNHCR staff and their usefulness to the United States. 'I believe Cuenod has done superb job as UNHCR delegate for Black Africa. He has earned high respect for his organization in both Burundi and European quarters and by combined persuasion and firmness proved a consummate diplomat in getting Burundi to act when many others would have failed miserably. I know of no other UN official who has been as frank and cooperative with this embassy as Cuenod.' US National Archives, Diplomatic Branch, Organizations and Conferences/UNHCR, Box 3178, REF 3 UNHCR, 29 June 1965.

46. For example, UNHCR staff were the first to alert the US Embassy in Burundi to the Tutsi attack on Rwanda. UNHCR and State Department archival records indicate that there existed a reciprocal exchange of information between the Office and the US embassies in African countries. In interviews with the author, several former UNHCR staff members who worked in Africa during the 1960s also mentioned that the US Embassy would be the first stop in a visit or mission to a country and that information was freely exchanged.

47. Interview with Felix Schnyder.

48. US National Archives, Diplomatic Branch, Ref: Rwanda/Ref.3 UNHCR, 20 December 1963.

49. UNHCR Archives, HCR /5/81 BUR, 4 February 1964.

50. Interview with Gilbert Jaeger.

51. Interview with Jacques Cuenod.

52. Ibid.

53. UNHCR Report, *Mission to Algiers, Central and Western Africa* (May 1964).

54. Interview with Paul Weiss, Geneva, 1984.

55. Randolph Kent, *The Anatomy of Disaster* Relief: *The International Network in Action* (London: Pinter Publications, 1987).

56. Interview with Felix Schnyder.

57. Barbara Harrell-Bond, *Imposing Aid: Emergency Assistance to Refugees* (Oxford: Oxford University Press, 1985).

58. Interviews with Felix Schnyder and with Jacques Cuenod.

59. A year earlier, UNHCR staff member, Jean Heidler, had recommended to UNHCR senior staff that a World Bank-funded regional development plan in Togo be used to integrate refugees from Ghana. He was rebuffed because the idea of seeking the help of UN and other agencies to engage in development projects for refugees was too new for an organization still oriented toward European solutions like resettlement. Interview with Jacques Cuenod. See also: US National Archives, Diplomatic Branch, 324.8411/10-2761, *Findings of UNHCR Representative on Refugee Problems in*

Togo, 27 October 1961; 324.8411/11-1561, *Refugees in Togo,* 15 November 1961; and 324.8411/11-2461, 24 November 1961.

60. UNHCR Archives, HCR/IOM/15/63/ and HCR/BUR/17/63. *Attitude of the High Commissioner's Office in New Refugee Situations,* 29 March 1963. This policy memorandum for all UNHCR staff reflected the tensions between those who advocated the limited subsistence approach and those who promoted a more development-oriented approach.

61. Interview with Schnyder.

62. See T. F. Betts, 'Zonal Rural Development in Africa', *Journal of Modern African Studies,* 7 (1966): 149–53; and *Integrated Rural Development: Reports 1–4* (Geneva: International University Exchange Fund, 1969).

63. For an assessment of these programmes, see T. F. Betts, 'Evolution and Promotion of the Integrated Rural Development Approach to Refugee Policy in Africa', *Africa Today,* 31 (1984): 7–24; Robert Chambers, 'Rural Refugees in Africa': 381–92; Gaim Kibreab, *Reflections on the African Refugee Problem: A Critical Analysis of Some Basic Assumptions* (Uppsala: Scandinavian Institute of African Studies, 1983): 123–40; and Robert Gorman, *Coping with Africa's Refugee Burden: A Time for Solutions* (Dordrecht: Martinus Nijnoff, 1987).

64. Interview with Felix Schnyder.

65. Kent, *Anatomy of Disaster Relief.*

66. Fritz Schatten, *Communism in Africa* (New York, NY: Praeger, 1966) and Samuel Huntington, *Political Order in Changing Societies* (New Haven, CT: Yale University Press, 1968) are representative of Western thinking at the time.

67. In 1960, Auguste Lindt had convened a committee of experts to study the ways and means by which the UNHCR Statute might be updated. The High Commissioner had wished to bring general language into the Statute which would permit assistance to refugees under his mandate. However, the experts opposed this on the ground that it could convert UNHCR into an international relief agency. The committee's recommendations regarding amendments to the Statute were discussed at the 1960 Excom meeting but were not proposed to the UN General Assembly. Lindt resigned as High Commissioner at that time and the proposals were shelved. US National Archives, Diplomatic Branch, 324.8411/6-1560, 15 June 1960.

68. *The 1967 Protocol Relating to the Status of Refugees.* A number of countries, most notably Italy and Turkey, maintained geographic limitations.

69. The State Department was able to present the Protocol to the US Senate for accession because persons who were previously in the State Department and US Congress who had a negative attitude toward the UNHCR had been replaced by James Wine, Special Assistant to Secretary of State Dean Rusk, Senator Edward Kennedy, and others. The US refugee NGOs also actively lobbied for US accession to the Protocol.

70. According to Holborn, *Refugees:* 199–200, the number of ratifications and accessions to the 1951 Convention and the 1967 Protocol almost quadrupled between 1960 and 1970.

71. These concerns were forcefully expressed to the OAU by Prince Saddrudin Aga Khan. See text of speech by Deputy High Commissioner at OAU Conference, 27 October 1965.

72. Interviews with Felix Schnyder, Michel Moussalli, and Gilbert Jaeger.

73. OAU Refugee Convention (1969).

74. According to the US, refugee 'problems will be seedbeds of instability, probable prey to agitators, and potential reservoirs of political and quasi-military opposition to existing regimes.' US Senate, Judiciary Committee, Subcommittee to Investigate Problems Connected with Refugees and Escapees, *Refugees and Escapees*, 87th Congress, 2nd Session, (6 June 1963): 7.

75. US National Archives, Diplomatic Branch, REF SUDAN. Pol. 30-2 Sudan, 20 March 1964.

76. Ibid., 29 February 1964.

77. Ibid.: 4–5

78. United States Public Law 87-510, 'The Refugee and Migration Act of 1962'.

79. US National Archives, Diplomatic Branch, State, Refugees and Migration, Germany, Box 3184, 1964, 1 April 1964.

80. US House of Representatives, Judiciary Committee, *Study of Population and Immigration Problems* (Washington, DC: US Government Printing Office, 1963): 38.

81. Ibid.: 21.

82. US National Archives, Diplomatic Branch, 324.8411/7-2062, 20 July 1962.

83. John Scanlan and Gilburt Loescher, 'US Foreign Policy, 1959-1980: Impact on Refugee Flow from Cuba' in *The Annals of the American Academy of Political and Social Science* (May 1983): 116–37.

84. According to one source, 'U.S. authorities have taken unusual steps to facilitate the entry of disaffected Cubans, even going so far as to allow the majority to enter without visas. No other potential exile group in the hemisphere has been so advantaged. If Castro's policies created the potential for mass exodus, U.S. policies made the exodus possible.' R. F. Fagen, R. A. Brody, and T. J. O'Leary, *Cubans in Exile: Disaffection and the Revolution* (Stanford, CA: Stanford University Press, 1968): 102.

85. UNHCR Archives, HCR/USA/Note for the File, 'Cuban Nationals in the US', 22 November 1960.

86. Interview with Gilbert Jaeger, Brussels, January 1985.

87. UNHCR Archives, HCR/66/USA/Interoffice Memorandum/ 'Refugees from Cuba', 22 December 1960.

88. UNHCR Archives, HCR/USA/Interoffice Memorandum/'Cuban Refugees', 30 January 1961.

89. For background see: UNHCR Archives, HCR/USA/SPA/ J. B. Woodward, *Cuban Refugees in Spain*, September 1964.

90. US National Archives, Diplomatic Branch, 324.8411/10-1062, 10 October 1962.

6

The Global Expansion of the UNHCR under Prince Sadruddin Aga Khan

Prince Sadruddin Aga Khan became the fourth UN High Commissioner for Refugees in late 1965, succeeding Felix Schnyder, under whom he had served as Deputy High Commissioner since 1962. Unlike his predecessors, Sadruddin had a truly global vision and perhaps his greatest accomplishment during his long, 12-year tenure was to plant the UNHCR flag in all regions of the world. Sadruddin took the UNHCR into previously unchartered territories, opening offices in Asia and Latin America, administering massive repatriation programmes, and acting as the focal point for large-scale UN relief efforts. He oversaw further enlargement of refugee law and good offices doctrine, making the UNHCR the co-ordinator of international assistance to refugees and victims of 'man-made' disasters and opening up assistance channels for the internally displaced. With these developments, the UNHCR became a player in the major political developments in Africa, Asia, and Latin America.

Under Sadruddin, the UNHCR developed a degree of independence and credibility it had not enjoyed before. Its autonomy and authority derived from its status as the guardian of international refugee norms and as the holder of specialized knowledge and expertise on refugee issues. As the representative of the Office and the embodiment of its rules and norms, the High Commissioner claimed to stand above power politics. Sadruddin sought to influence and shape state practices and to define what constituted acceptable and legitimate state behaviour regarding the treatment of refugees. Consequently, the UNHCR under Sadruddin acquired considerable legitimacy and authority in the eyes of most states during the 1960s and 1970s.

Sadruddin was the second son of the Aga Khan of Iran and his mother was French. Some members of his extended family had reputations for high living but Sudruddin was a more serious man and he was a deeply committed member and respected leader of the Ismaeli community. On his visits throughout the world, Sadruddin kept in close contact with the Ismaelis, always encouraging them to assimilate with local communities and to work to develop the countries they lived in.

Sadruddin's manner was urbane and cosmopolitan. He had several passports, spoke fluent French and English, and had been educated at Harvard where he had been a roommate of Edward Kennedy's. He was an intellectual and extremely well spoken. However, one of his greatest weaknesses was his inclination to rely solely on a few trusted staff and family members for advice and counsel, particularly towards the end of this career as High Commissioner.

Sadruddin was a true internationalist with a high profile. Through his family and religious connections, Sadruddin had contacts throughout the world. He had direct access to many of the world's political leaders and frequently used these contacts to achieve considerable diplomatic and political successes for the UNHCR. He could also be fiercely independent and contemptuous of the great powers. Sadruddin viewed impartiality as a core principle of the High Commissioner's action. He felt that his moral standing, authority, and ability to engage in effective international diplomacy rested on this principle. Despite his strong American connections, Sadruddin did not share identical views with the US on every issue and, depending on the circumstances, he could and did differ with the US government. As a result, during Sadruddin's tenure, the UNHCR shed its image of being a tool of the United States and gained credibility as an independent global actor. Also, the United States did not always give Sadruddin full rein in handling refugee problems. These tensions occasionally led to stormy relations between Washington and the UNHCR headquarters in Geneva.

Sadruddin was an expansionist High Commissioner with expansionist advisers. He perceived his Office to be first among equals within the UN agencies and successfully fought off rivals who encroached on the UNHCR's turf. As a technique for institutional growth, relief assistance rather than protection became the Office's central function. The UNHCR adapted itself to the needs of governments by expanding into emergency assistance and becoming the principal UN co-ordinator of relief projects. In this way, the provision of emergency relief assistance became the pivot of UNHCR assistance or failure as an institution in world politics, and it remains so today.

Sadruddin was also politically ambitious. During his last years as High Commissioner, Sadruddin steadfastly sought the job of UN Secretary-General, a goal which eluded him and led to great personal disappointment. Unfortunately, this failure tarnished somewhat his reputation and legacy as High Commissioner. Nevertheless, Prince Sadruddin Aga Khan was widely viewed as one of the most effective High Commissioners and one of the strongest leaders in the UNHCR's history.

UNHCR under a New High Commissioner

Sadruddin was not the unanimous choice of all governments to succeed Felix Schnyder as High Commissioner. The United States was initially reticent to support his candidacy and tried very hard to quash his nomination and to find a candidate more amenable to American interests. The State Department thought that Sadruddin was 'too young and inexperienced and lack[ed] executive ability and overall stature to successfully direct a specialized and complex program' and felt that his 'private interests were so extensive as to interfere substantially with his position as High Commissioner.'[1] The US also objected because it felt that Sadruddin

. . . would be weak on asylum matters insofar as refugees in Europe were concerned . . . Sadruddin is Afro-Asian oriented and over the years has displayed little or no interest in refugees and asylum seekers in Europe who remain of special interest to the U.S. (US Archives, Diplomatic Branch, Ref 3, Organizations and Conferences UN, Box 3178, 9 October 1965).

However, the Secretary-General, U Thant, strongly supported Sadruddin. When no other candidate emerged to challenge his nomination, the US reluctantly supported his candidacy and Sadruddin was elected High Commissioner. To assuage the US, Sadruddin chose Albert Bender, an American, to be his Deputy. In 1969 Bender was replaced by another American, Charles Mace, thus firmly establishing a tradition of appointing American nationals to that position.

Upon assuming office, Sadruddin initially pursued the same approach to refugee problems as Schnyder had. When he visited Washington DC in January 1966, the new High Commissioner outlined the major problems confronting his Office.[2] He told the State Department that the refugee problem had completely changed course in the past several years, and that the most 'burning and difficult problem' confronting the UNHCR was in Africa. Later that year, in a speech to the United States Refugee Committee annual meeting,[3] Sadruddin noted that out of the 222,558 refugees assisted under UNHCR programmes throughout the world in 1965, 208,000—94 per cent— were in Africa. Moreover, this trend was continuing. He told his audience that during the first half of 1966, 75,000 of the 90,000 new refugees of concern to the UNHCR were in Africa. In both 1965 and 1966, one-half of the UNHCR's regular budget had gone to help refugees in Africa, in addition to the lion's share of allocations made from the High Commissioner's Emergency Fund. By the end of the decade, the total number of refugees in Africa would exceed one million, and two-thirds of the UNHCR's budget would be spent on Africa's refugee problems.

In light of these circumstances, Sadruddin was inclined to follow the same kinds of policy approaches for Africa as his predecessor. Initially ruling out repatriation[4] and resettlement as being impractical solutions for Africa's refugees, Sadruddin noted that his Office concentrated on 'integration on the spot', with NGOs and other UN agencies providing the funds and resources to implement the programmes. The UNHCR's policy would be to incorporate refugee settlements into broader regional development programmes which would be carried out by governments or other UN development agencies. Essentially this meant the continuation of the integrated zonal development schemes. Unfortunately, this policy never received the full support of the development agencies because of the high capital outlay of some of these schemes, and languished as a result of a lack of adequate funding. Instead of becoming self-sufficient, many refugee camps and their inhabitants continued to rely on international assistance. The limitations of the integrated zonal development approach did not become fully evident until the late 1970s when the idea was rejuvenated in another form.

It is not surprising that UNHCR policy during the last half of the 1960s was not all that different from the first half of the decade. Sadruddin had been Deputy High Commissioner since 1962, had helped develop the UNHCR's Africa programmes, and had a stake in their continuation. In addition, the Office experienced considerable resource constraints, which at first made further expansion difficult, if not impossible. With annual budgets of $3 to $4 million, the UNHCR had to take a cautious approach. Throughout the 1960s, the UNHCR experienced chronic financial difficulties. Despite a steady rise in the number of refugees, especially in Africa, donor governments never contributed more than the bare essentials and frequently there was not enough to fully cover needs. The US contribution during the decade averaged about $600,000 per annum, a smaller percentage than to other international refugee programmes—US contributions to ICEM averaged $3 to $4 million per annum—and an amount very little higher than French, British, Canadian, German, and Swedish contributions. The UNHCR staff had not grown appreciably since the 1950s, and in the mid-1960s there still were only eight professional staff members in all of Africa south of the Sahara. The UNHCR relied to a great extent on NGOs as their operational partners during this time. Conditions were not immediately conducive to rapid organizational expansion.

Initial Caution of Sadruddin

Initially, the High Commissioner was unwilling to take on major new commitments that extended beyond the traditional scope of his office. When Sadruddin took over the UNHCR, the US made overtures for the UNHCR to get involved in assisting internally displaced people and war victims in South Vietnam, a task that would have overwhelmed the UNHCR. At that time, Vietnam was awash with refugees and displaced persons. Approximately 900,000 to 1 million people had fled Communist North Vietnam in 1954 and 1955. Although these refugees had all resettled quickly in the new Republic of Vietnam, the resurgence of conflict within South Vietnam during the early 1960s had generated another million displaced persons, mostly South

Vietnamese residents fleeing from Vietcong controlled or threatened areas.[5] These numbers increased markedly as US forces progressively intervened in the conflict. After US B-52 bombers strafed the rural provinces of Vietnam, US military personnel systematically removed civilians from war zones to provincial capitals where they were looked after by American humanitarian agencies. From early in the conflict, refugee flows and the displacement of people became one of the war objectives of the US. According to the American military strategist, Robert Komer, the US perceived the increased flow of refugees as 'a plus. It helps deprive VC [the Vietcong] of recruiting potential and rice growers, and is partly indicative of growing peasant desire to seek security on our side'.[6]

As the war in Vietnam created larger numbers of displaced people, their plight and poor camp conditions drew the attention of Senator Edward Kennedy and the Senate Judiciary Committee. The refugee resettlement centres were poorly organized, suffered from a shortage of medical supplies, and had no schools for children. Refugees in the camps were frequently in poor health, and there was a marked increase in the incidence of malaria and cholera among the displaced. Kennedy was convinced that a broad international effort was needed to cope with the refugee problem in Vietnam and appealed for help from America's allies. However, other governments were reluctant to assist with the refugee problem in Vietnam because they viewed this as principally an American responsibility.

Kennedy also appealed to the UNHCR in early 1966 to assist refugees within South Vietnam. Sadruddin turned down the request stating that the Vietnamese were internally displaced people, not refugees, and therefore beyond the mandate of his Office.[7] He felt that if the UNHCR were to become involved in South Vietnam, it would be vulnerable to other requests to assist displaced persons outside the Office's mandate. Senator Kennedy and his staff also had discussions with UN agencies, including the UNHCR, about the possibility of UN co-ordination of an international programme for Vietnam.[8] The UNHCR made it clear, however, that such a programme would have to be non-political and include both North and South Vietnam. These terms were clearly unacceptable to both North Vietnam and the US. It was also clear to the High Commissioner that the Vietnam War was a politically sensitive issue. Sadruddin knew that to launch a programme in Vietnam would require an authorizing resolution from the General Assembly. After consultation with the Secretary-General, U Thant, the High Commissioner concluded that the Soviet and Afro-Asian blocs would not approve such a resolution.[9] Consequently, the UNHCR did not get involved in the US refugee programme in South Vietnam. Rather, at a later stage in the Indo-Chinese conflict in the early 1970s, Sadruddin would open up his own independent programmes for internally displaced persons in Laos and North and South Vietnam. He would reach out to all sides in the conflict and even have a presence with the

Vietcong. Sadruddin skilfully exploited political openings while still remaining neutral, thereby laying the foundation for further expansion of the Office in the region after 1975.

During the 1960s, the UNHCR was restricted by the international norms then prevalent in world politics, especially concerning the sovereign rights of states and the principle of non-interference in the domestic affairs of states. The international human rights treaties had not yet been ratified or entered into force and no international human rights network had yet emerged. While Amnesty International was founded in 1961, it was practically the only major international human rights NGO. International human rights norms and institutions were weak and were subordinate to anti-Communism during the Cold War. The UNHCR did not challenge the traditional notions of sovereignty and non-intervention.

Despite the fact that the UNHCR was in essence a human rights organization, Sadruddin did not consider it legitimate to concern himself with the treatment of the people who had not crossed international borders. The UNHCR dealt only with persecuted persons and human rights victims after they had left their countries. The High Commissioner did not feel it was his place to intercede with governments in countries of refugee origin to secure modification or elimination of human rights abuses or military actions that generated the forcible displacement of people. For such purposes, other agencies, such as the International Committee of the Red Cross (ICRC), had primary responsibility. During the 1960s, Sadruddin felt bound by these conventional norms and constantly reinforced traditional notions of sovereignty.

Sadruddin was reluctant to become involved in the major internal conflicts of the 1960s: the Indonesian *coup* of October 1965 which brought General Suharto to power and resulted in a slaughter of Indonesian Communists; and the 1967–70 Nigerian civil war, which resulted in the deaths of about one million people and displaced some 2 million people on both the Federal and Biafran sides. Despite massive human suffering in both conflicts, the UNHCR assumed a policy of strict non-involvement. In both Indonesia and Nigeria, the displacements were largely internal rather than external. The Office took a legalistic position, arguing that these situations were not a matter within the competence of the High Commissioner and were not a matter of direct concern to the UNHCR for 'constitutional' and legal considerations.[10] Sadruddin was careful not to take the Office into areas where he would be criticized by UN member governments for taking sides on controversial political issues. Therefore, the UNHCR took pains not to intervene in either conflict.

In October 1965, a military *coup d'état* in Indonesia brought General Suharto to power. During that *coup*, the Indonesian Communist Party (PKI), with support from China, allegedly attempted to seize power. In the bloody aftermath, hundreds of thousands of PKI supporters were rounded up, incarcerated, and murdered. A virulent anti-Chinese campaign was also initiated. The Chinese embassy and Chinese schools were attacked by mobs and new onerous political and economic restrictions were also imposed on all Chinese residents in the country. Thus, the 2.5 million Chinese minority in Indonesia were targeted and made the scapegoat for the attempted *coup*. Consequently, hundreds of Chinese reportedly left the country and fears were expressed for a massive outflow of Chinese into neighbouring South-East Asian countries and back to the PRC.[11]

There was surprisingly little international protest to the mass killings and human rights abuses in Indonesia. Indonesia was geopolitically important and protected from criticism by the might of the Cold War Western military alliance. Because of his Muslim connections, Sadruddin might have been expected to play an active role in trying to moderate Indonesian behaviour. However, there is very little evidence that the UNHCR exerted any leverage on Indonesia but rather took the position that it could not intervene in the domestic affairs of a nation no matter how horrendous its human rights violations were. In a letter to Peter Benenson of Amnesty International in London, Sadruddin wrote 'the internal problems of Indonesia fall by definition outside my competence'.[12] Instead of acting himself, the High Commissioner chose to refer the matter to the ICRC and the International Commission of Jurists.

The 1967–70 civil war in Nigeria—Africa's most populous country—generated millions of refugees, most of whom remained within either the Federal or the Ibo-dominated Biafran zone. In one of the bloodiest civil wars in Africa during the decade, the combatants were left to fight to the finish. The Nigerian government imposed a blockade of food and relief supplies to the territory of Biafra, effectively employing starvation as a weapon of war. Most outsiders stayed well away and sat on their hands while nearly one million civilians were killed or died as a result of widespread famine. The UN remained paralysed by political constraints and refused to intervene in what was a highly sensitive political situation involving all aspects of a complex disaster: famine, refugees, and threat to civilian populations. U Thant took the position that the war in Nigeria was a civil war and, according to the UN Charter, therefore completely outside the competence of the UN. The Secretary-General was unwilling to take any initiative that might have offended either the African states or the major powers. This reflected the common UN practice of avoiding taking sides in a conflict over contested sovereignty, or antagonizing governments by favouring opposition groups. Both the UK and the US sought to distance themselves from assisting non-combatants in Biafra because their paramount interest was to preserve the territorial integrity of Nigeria. The Organization of African Unity (OAU) decided unanimously to regard the Biafran conflict as an internal Nigerian affair and felt that the UN therefore had no right to interfere. U Thant could have appealed to the Soviet Union and Britain to stop supplying weapons to the federal government, and to Israel, Portugal, and South Africa to stop arming Biafra. Instead, the Secretary-General stuck to the strictest interpretation of the UN Charter and chose almost complete inaction.

Despite the gravity of the humanitarian crisis in Nigeria, no state sought to involve the UNHCR. With no such support, the ability of the UNHCR to lend material assistance and even to exert moral pressure was severely limited. Moreover, since no other UN agency was willing to intervene, Sadruddin did not feel threatened with being outmanoeuvred by another agency encroaching on an area that the UNHCR considered its own domain. Thus, fearing that he might step beyond what was acceptable, the High Commissioner fell back on a conservative reading of his mandate. With no encouragement from the UN Secretariat or the major powers, Sadruddin refused to assist the displaced in Nigeria claiming that his Office was not in a position to deal with situations affecting nationals who find themselves displaced within a territory of their country.[13] Rather, it was the ICRC, in their largest undertaking since World War II, who assisted some 2 million internally displaced people, both on the Biafran and Federal sides.[14] It was only very late in the conflict, that the UNHCR temporarily set up a regional office in Lomé and made aid available to Nigerians who found themselves in neighbouring Equatorial Guinea with no means of support. At the end of the conflict, the UNHCR also repatriated over 5,000 children who had been evacuated to Gabon and the Ivory Coast during the hostilities. For the most part, however, the UNHCR was not involved directly in the repatriation of many of the tens of thousands of refugees who had fled Nigeria during the conflict. A number of the West African governments refrained from recognizing Nigerians of Ibo origin in their territories as refugees, and as a consequence did not seek UNHCR assistance.

The UNHCR's Initiatives in Sudan

Early in his first term as High Commissioner, Sadruddin chose Sudan as the country on which to focus his diplomatic efforts. One of his first missions abroad as High Commissioner was to the Sudan. The continuous outflow of refugees from southern Sudan into the neighbouring countries of Uganda, Kenya, Ethiopia, and the Central African Republic constituted UNHCR's biggest refugee caseload in Africa. Although Sadruddin had shown great interest in the Sudanese refugee problem during his time as Deputy High Commissioner, Sudanese authorities had refused to discuss their refugee problem with the UNHCR, fearing that contact with any outside authority would internationalize the issue. With the advent of a civilian government anxious

to solve the conflict in southern Sudan, the way finally became clear for inviting the High Commissioner to visit Khartoum to discuss the possibilities for
the repatriation of Sudanese refugees.

From the mid-1960s, Sudan had taken a series of policy initiatives to
encourage the return of Sudanese living in neighbouring countries and in
December 1964, the government proclaimed an amnesty for returning
Sudanese. This was expanded and clarified in the Indemnity Acts of 1966 and
1967. The amnesty also provided for the settlement of repatriated Sudanese
in new 'peace villages' under army supervision. The peace villages were
loosely patterned on the strategic hamlet concept then being used by the US
and South Vietnamese armies in South Vietnam. The new villages were
designed not only to encourage the return of refugees from neighbouring
countries but also to inspire the return home of internally displaced people
and to cut off rebels from their source of supply or support. In addition,
Sudan had concluded a series of bilateral agreements on repatriation—with
Uganda in 1964 and the Congo in 1967—and an extradition treaty with
Ethiopia in 1964. However, none of these initiatives had resulted in large
numbers of Sudanese repatriating.

Frustrated by their lack of progress in encouraging more returns, the
Sudanese government sought the assistance of the UNHCR. Khartoum
believed that UNHCR assistance programmes for Sudanese refugees in neighbouring countries encouraged people to stay put and provided a disincentive
for return. During the conflict, perhaps a quarter of the population of Sudan's
three southern provinces had been driven from their homes and was either
hiding in the forests or living in exile in neighbouring countries. A total of
194,000 had officially been registered by the UNHCR as refugees in neighbouring countries where the Office had spent some $10 million during the
1960s to promote their settlement in organized rural communities. The
UNHCR was concerned about the continuing high cost of maintaining the
Sudanese refugees in camps and settlements in neighbouring countries and
the security risks presented by these refugees to the host countries. The
UNHCR, therefore, shared an interest with Khartoum in seeing the refugees
return home. In a report on Sadruddin's visit to Sudan, A. K. Sadry, the High
Commissioner's cousin and personal assistant, noted the objectives of the
UNHCR in seeking a settlement of the conflict in South Sudan:

The continuous influx of refugees from southern Sudan into the neighbouring countries, i.e., Uganda, Kenya, Ethiopia and the Central African Republic, and the
programme of assistance in which the High Commissioner's Office is involved in
response to requests from some of these governments has been in the past years a
matter of concern to the Office. The cost of relief operations and emergency assistance
to refugees in Uganda and the Central African Republic represent a very high percentage of the total cost of the assistance programme to refugees in Africa in general. For
these reasons the office of the High Commissioner was anxious to establish contact

with the Sudanese authorities in order to discuss this problem as a whole and see what could be done in the way of restoring stability and security and an atmosphere in which an eventual voluntary repatriation would be possible and the problem thus resolved. (UNHCR Archives, HCR/1/7/75/SUD, 15 September 1966).

During Sadruddin's visit to Sudan, the Sudanese Prime Minister, Sadik el-Mahdi informed the High Commissioner that Sudan was embarking on a 'crash programme' for southern Sudan to restore security so that refugees could return in safety. During the war, southern Sudan had also witnessed the wholesale destruction of its infrastructure. Four out of every five dispensaries had been destroyed or shut down, scores of primary schools had been forced to close, and education at the secondary level had been all but abandoned. Agricultural production had also been disrupted and malnutrition was rife throughout the south. In addition to those who had fled to the country, a further half million persons had been internally displaced within Sudan. Sadik el-Mahdi hoped to initiate reconstruction and development programmes with international assistance and a gradual withdrawal of the army in an attempt to restore normal conditions in the south as an incentive for repatriation.[15]

Sadruddin warmly welcomed Sudan's initiatives and in the following months and years he became closely involved in promoting these developments. The High Commissioner took it upon himself to act as an intermediary for Sudan with the international community. Only a month after his visit to Sudan, Sadruddin visited the United States where he briefed U Thant and Ralph Bunche—Under-Secretary for Political Affairs—on his Khartoum visit. He encouraged them to respond favourably to Sudanese requests for the involvement of the UN Specialized Agencies in a social and economic development effort for the south. He also consulted with the State Department and Senator Edward Kennedy asking for US support for any new Sudanese initiatives for the southern provinces.[16] In 1968, in an unusual diplomatic move for a High Commissioner, Sadruddin consulted with members of the Sudanese opposition parties, as well as the Chief of Staff of the Sudanese Army to determine their views on repatriation. With UNHCR encouragement, Sudan also expanded on its information activities. Sudanese government ministers were sent to neighbouring countries to explain to Sudanese refugees the political changes that had taken place in the south since their departure and to offer them the opportunity to return to their homes. Even the President of Sudan personally visited refugee centres in neighbouring countries to explain the terms of the amnesty and to encourage repatriation. Small groups of refugees were also brought back to their homes on fact-finding missions to the Sudan in order to advise fellow refugees about conditions in the south and consequently about repatriation.

Although Sadruddin laid the groundwork for a mass repatriation and a comprehensive UN reconstruction effort in South Sudan from 1966 on, a peace agreement between the Sudanese government and the South Sudan

Liberation Movement was not reached until February 1972. The Peace Agreement put an end to 17 years of devastating conflict—the longest continuous war that Africa had known in the twentieth century. It also removed a major source of political tension that had existed among half a dozen African states and provided for the repatriation of hundreds of thousands of refugees and internally displaced persons.

In May 1972, the UN Secretary-General entrusted the UNHCR with the responsibility of co-ordinating operations in southern Sudan on behalf of the entire UN system. The UNHCR's purpose went far beyond simply resettling the repatriates and the much greater number of internally displaced persons. Its further purpose was to lead a UN effort to improve the economic condition of South Sudan and to ensure a longer-term programme of development aid to be carried out under the aegis of the United Nations Development Programme. With governmental funds and $17 million from UNHCR appeals, the UNHCR and other UN agencies provided for the repair of thousands of miles of roads and for the upgrading of the crucial river transport system. The only road bridge in the entire region was eventually thrown across the Nile at Juba, and provided spectacular improvement in regional communications. But supplies had to reach returning villagers long before these undertakings could be completed. For more than a year starting in July 1972, the UNHCR operated an airlift involving several aircraft flying from Khartoum to the three southern provincial capitals of Juba, Malakal, and Wau from whence distribution could best be organized. Refugees soon came pouring back across the Sudanese border, most in a spontaneous fashion. Within the first eight months of its relief operation, many refugees ready and willing to return had made it back home.

The South Sudan Operation established important precedents for the UNHCR and was the prototype for later mass repatriation movements. Most significantly, it provided for a further stretching of the original concepts developed around the 'good offices' approach and permitted the UNHCR to assist not only refugees but also others in 'refugee-like' situations, including returnees and internally displaced persons. These concepts laid the groundwork for UNHCR involvement in other refugee emergencies and humanitarian disasters in Africa, Asia, and Latin America.

The Expansionist Phase of the UNHCR in the 1970s: Developing a Role as UN Co-ordinator and Seeing Off its Rivals

In the 1970s, Sadruddin seized opportunities to adapt the UNHCR to meet the needs of states. By daring executive management he progressively expanded the UNHCR's mandate and organizational ideology. Realizing that without a sizeable budget the Office would exercise little clout in the international political system, Sadruddin embarked on ambitious assistance programmes in a number of refugee-like situations, intervening in a number of tense political and security situations around the world. Africa continued to be a focus of concern, but it was in Asia, and to a lesser extent in Latin America, that UNHCR operations increased substantially during the 1970s. A large number of refugee situations, often occurring in close succession, led to a substantial increase in the staff of the UNHCR, its working budget, and above all the amount spent on assistance programmes. Annual programme expenditure, which amounted to $8.3 million at the beginning of the 1970s, leapt to $69 million in 1975. In addition, to its regular activities, the UNHCR also acted as co-ordinator or the focal point for UN-wide humanitarian and development assistance programmes, sometimes involving budgets in the hundreds of millions of dollars. Consequently, the UNHCR's special operations budget in 1975 had grown thirtyfold since 1966 as it co-ordinated massive repatriations and UN programmes throughout the Third World.

During the 1970s, Sadruddin oversaw a tremendous growth in both the international prestige and the operations of his Office. In 1971, he campaigned hard to succeed U Thant as Secretary-General. When this attempt was vetoed by the Soviet Union, and Kurt Waldheim, the Austrian candidate, became the new Secretary-General, Sadruddin was gravely disappointed. When Sadruddin was reappointed for a second term as High Commissioner, he became determined to make the UNHCR the most important international humanitarian organization. With the help of highly ambitious personal assistants, Sadruddin pushed his mandate to the extreme and embarked on a deliberate programme of expansion that led his Office into practically every corner of the globe.

Sadruddin expanded the UNHCR during a period of heightened international awareness of both man-made and natural disasters. The Nigerian civil war, a devastating earthquake in Peru, and the East Pakistan cyclone with its subsequent civil war and refugee exodus awakened both governments and the UN to the need for a more effective international response to such disasters.[17] In an effort to improve international relief capacity, member governments established the Office of the United Nations Disaster Relief Co-ordinator (UNDRO) in 1971.[18] Its task was to integrate the various UN activities surrounding assistance to countries suffering the consequences of natural disasters. From its inception, however, the UNDRO was severely limited by lack of authority, bureaucratic competition, limited funding, and inadequate staff planning. It faced considerable competition for funding from the UN agencies in the field and the co-ordinator was unable to assemble a qualified staff.[19] Moreover, fierce inter-agency competition greatly hindered the UNDRO's effectiveness. UN agencies resisted all efforts to subordinate them to UNDRO control. The UNHCR in particular, fought fiercely to maintain absolute control over its operations.[20]

The UNHCR expansion also coincided with a period of institutional crisis within the ICEM, the UNHCR's main rival. In the early 1970s, the ICEM no longer had large numbers of European refugees and migrants to transport overseas. The Latin American members promoted migration for development but most donor states did not see the need for new ICEM programmes. Hence, during the late 1960s and early 1970s, several prominent donor governments—United Kingdom, France, and Sweden—withdrew their membership from the ICEM. Australia's decision to build up its own immigration offices and programmes overseas and its withdrawal in 1973 from the ICEM was particularly serious since Canberra contributed 22.5 per cent of the total of the organization's budget.[21] It also deprived the ICEM of a large part of its essential character, namely the movement of European emigrants to overseas countries. During this period the ICEM was also accused of being used as a cover for CIA activities in Latin America which further alienated some member governments.[22] There was even discussion about the possibility of the ICEM becoming 'a permanent support organization of the High Commissioner for Refugees'.[23] For a brief period, until the ICEM found a major role for itself in the Indo-Chinese resettlement effort, the UNHCR benefited from its rival's travails.[24]

The ascendancy of the UNHCR also coincided with increased prominence given to the refugee issue by the Nixon administration. By 1973, the US began to refocus the emphasis of its refugee programme away from Europe to the rest of the world, principally to accompany the global expansion of its foreign policy and security commitments. In the eyes of the State Department, 'situations which generate refugees are inseparably bound up with specific problems within or between nations—for us, foreign policy problems'.[25] Secretary of State Henry Kissinger noted: '. . . disaster relief is becoming increasingly a major instrument of our foreign policy. The assistance we can provide to various nations may have a long-term impact on US relations with those nations and their friends'.[26] Relief assistance, therefore, was a means to 'ease tensions among nations'[27] and to consolidate bonds with friendly states. In order to broaden its operations to enable it to assist refugees beyond Eastern Europe and the People's Republic of China, as stipulated in the *Immigration and Refugee Act* of 1962, President Nixon authorized the State Department to assist refugees anywhere in the world when it deemed it was in the interest of the US to do so.[28] One of the principal beneficiaries of increased US attention to the global refugee issue was the UNHCR. During the early 1970s, the Office's budgets soared as Sadruddin took action everywhere. Big budgets reflected the international community's confidence in the UNHCR's ability to carry out refugee relief programmes and to be the primary humanitarian actor in the global arena.

Under Sadruddin in the early 1970s, the UNHCR became the pre-eminent international humanitarian and relief organization.

In order to lay the legal groundwork for this expansion, Sadruddin followed the path of preceding High Commissioners. He sought to broaden his authority to assist a growing number of persons claiming to be refugees or in refugee-like situations through successive UN resolutions. In southern Sudan and elsewhere, UNHCR came into contact with people who were displaced in their own country or who otherwise did not obviously fit the Refugee Convention's definition. Yet in most respects they resembled refugees, fleeing possible or actual persecution, war, or political upheaval. To facilitate the repatriation of Sudanese refugees who had taken refuge in neighbouring countries and to help those who had fled to the interior to return to their homes after the 1972 Addis Ababa Agreement, the UN General Assembly mentioned refugees and displaced persons side by side for the first time in the history of the UNHCR.[29] In 1975 and in 1979, the UN General Assembly again unequivocally requested the High Commissioner to promote lasting and speedy solutions for refugees and displaced persons 'wherever they occur'.[30] Sadruddin interpreted these resolutions to mean that:

the High Commissioner's Office could take action on behalf of large groups of people who may not all conform to conventional definition of a refugee but are in a situation analogous to that of refugees. For example, they are victims of man-made events over deprivation or uprootedness as a result of sudden upheaval and separation from their homes. The reasoning behind this evolution would appear to be that cut off from their origins and scattered or brought together again by circumstances in one place, or another, these displaced persons clearly need some form of international assistance. (Sadruddin Aga Khan, *Legal Problems Related to Refugees and Displaced Persons*, (The Hague: Academy of International Law, 1976): 49–50).

The legal expansion of his authority gave Sadruddin tremendous scope to involve UNHCR in massive material assistance programmes throughout the world. The objective in many cases was repatriation.

Perhaps the most prominent feature of the UNHCR's activities in the 1970s was the increase in repatriation. During the 1950s, repatriation had played virtually no part in the organization's activities. During the Cold War in Europe, the great majority of refugees fled Communist states and Western powers considered it out of the question that these refugees should want to return to their homes. During the 1960s, the principal repatriation operation had been for Algerians who had taken refuge in Tunisia and Morocco during the events which led up to the independence of Algeria in 1962. In 1961, the General Assembly had asked the High Commissioner not only to facilitate the return of refugees from Algeria but also, 'when necessary', their resettlement.[31] This precedent was used again from the beginning of the 1970s when repatriation operations followed in rapid succession, in particular the East Bengalis (1972) and the Sudanese (1972–3). In each of these cases, the General

Assembly requested not only the return of refugees but also their 'rehabilitation and resettlement'. A 1974 General Assembly Resolution identified repatriation as the preferred solution to refugee problems in certain circumstances, particularly where the principle of self-determination was involved, and urged the international community to provide rehabilitation assistance.[32] Thus, when the independence of the former Portuguese territories in Africa led to the return of hundreds of thousands of persons to Guinea-Bissau (1974–5), and to Mozambique and Angola (1975–6), it was accompanied by rehabilitation programmes. Later, repatriation and rehabilitation programmes were instituted for the Zaïrians in Angola, the Burmese Rohinga in Bangladesh, the Zimbabweans, and the Nicaraguans.

The UNHCR enjoyed much success in bringing about repatriation agreements during this period and thereby enhanced its reputation of playing an instrumental role in resolving refugee crises. Nevertheless, in all of these repatriation operations the UNHCR played a limited role in the reintegration and rehabilitation process. The UNHCR provided refugees with transport to their country of origin, as well as an assistance package consisting of foodstuffs, blankets, cooking equipment, tools, and occasionally housing material. Usually the UNHCR would also encourage other UN agencies such as the UN Development Agency to provide longer-term assistance targeted at the returnees. Otherwise, returnees were considered to be the responsibility of the country of origin. Despite the UNHCR's circumscribed role, by the late 1970s the understanding that the UNHCR would not only assist refugees to return but also facilitate their resettlement and rehabilitation, was regarded as a well-established principle.

Another characteristic of several of the 1970s refugee crises was that the international programmes were so large that the entire UN system was compelled to play a part. Therefore the High Commissioner had to assume the role of co-ordinator of the programmes of the various agencies concerned. This happened first in 1956 in response to the Hungarian refugee emergency, when the UN General Assembly invited governments and NGOs participating in aid and resettlement work to co-ordinate their programmes in consultation with the UNHCR. By the 1970s, the scale of disasters and the numbers of NGOs and specialized agencies within the UN system had grown so significantly that overall co-ordination of relief work was essential if international humanitarian action was to be effective. During the 1970s, the UN Secretary-General, Kurt Waldheim, repeatedly called on Sadruddin to co-ordinate UN humanitarian and rehabilitation programmes. Sadruddin seized the initiative to fill this role for the international community and thereby to expand greatly the functions and size of his Office.

The first expansion of UNHCR activities occurred in response to the 1971 war between West Pakistan and secessionist East Pakistan and the subsequent flight of East Bengalis to India. From its New Delhi office, the UNHCR directed the joint efforts of the international and voluntary agencies to help the displaced Bengalis and later to repatriate them to their homeland. At the conclusion of this operation, the General Assembly requested that the High Commissioner 'continue to participate, at the invitation of the Secretary-General, in those humanitarian endeavours of the United Nations for which his Office had particular expertise and experience'.[33] In 1973, the General Assembly noted 'the increasingly useful cooperation between the High Commissioner and other members of the United Nations system, resulting in better co-ordination of action and greater efficiency in fields of common interest',[34] and in 1974 included among the High Commissioner's duties 'his special humanitarian tasks', and requested that he report to the Executive Committee on these tasks in the same manner as on his regular programme.[35] By this time, the UNHCR was also co-ordinating other large-scale operations such as the repatriation of the Sudanese and the programme of humanitarian assistance in Cyprus. By 1976, the UN Economic and Social Council confirmed the UNHCR's new co-ordinating function as an integral part of its enlarged competence when it requested the High Commissioner 'to continue his activities in cooperation with governments, UN bodies, appropriate inter-governmental organizations and voluntary agencies, to alleviate the suffering of all those of concern to his Office'.[36] The same resolution identified persons of concern to be 'refugee and displaced persons, victims of man-made disasters, requiring urgent humanitarian assistance'.[37]

The UNHCR as 'Focal Point' for the Bangladesh Operation

The flight of refugees to India occurred in early 1971 as a consequence of a classic national liberation struggle between East Pakistan and the Pakistan military. Pakistan was a nation geographically and ethnically divided into two entities, West Pakistan and East Pakistan. Widespread political and economic discrimination and lack of representation at the hands of West Pakistan caused deep resentment in East Pakistan. East Pakistan's demands for regional autonomy dated back at least to the 1960s. In February 1971, the Awami League of East Pakistan won 167 out of 169 parliamentary seats reserved for East Pakistan, and the Bengalis thus obtained a majority of seats in the elections for Pakistan's National Assembly. The Awami League called for a national federation in which the federal government would be responsible only for defence and foreign affairs, with the two federal states maintaining their own militia, currencies, revenue, and foreign trade. President Yahya Khan immediately construed these actions as a threat to the territorial integrity of Pakistan. When negotiations between West and East Pakistan failed, the Pakistani military arrested Sheikh Mujibur Rahman and other Awami League leaders on 25 March 1971. The Awami League reacted by declaring the independence of East Pakistan and fighting broke out between the Pakistani army and Bengali units known as the *Mukhti Bahini*. Bengali Hindus—as well as Muslim nationalist politicians, intellectuals, and students—became the major target of arrests, torture, and death at the hands of the Pakistani Army. The UN and the great powers proved unable to address, let alone stop, the massacres in East Pakistan.

Following the Pakistani military crackdown and the indiscriminate killings of unarmed civilians in East Pakistan, refugees first started crossing the border into the Indian states of West Bengal, Tripura, and Assam in April 1971. By the middle of the month, some 30,000 refugees had arrived in India. A week later there were 600,000 and the refugee flow soon became a torrent. The one-million mark was reached on 1 May 1971. By the end of that month there were 4 million refugees; two weeks later 6 million; by September 8 million, and at the peak of the emergency some 10 million East Bengalis were in India. Of these 6.8 million lived in 825 camps scattered through four north-eastern states of India, while the remainder found homes with friends and relatives.

The continuing influx placed severe strains on the Indian government and local authorities, which bore the brunt of feeding and sheltering the refugees. Indira Gandhi, the Indian Prime Minister, perceived the mass influx of refugees to pose a major security threat to her country. The majority of refugees were Bengali Hindus. India believed that Pakistan sought to bring East Pakistan under control by reducing East Pakistan's population to a minority within Pakistan by forcibly expelling Bengali Hindus to India. Gandhi warned that 'Pakistan cannot be allowed to seek a solution of its political or other problems at the expense of India and on Indian soil'. By forcing millions of refugees into India, Pakistan was committing external aggression against India. Indian authorities were also alarmed at the demographic and political consequences of the mass inflow and, in particular, the internal threat that the refugees posed to Indian security. Since 1948, India had already absorbed some 5 million East Bengali migrants, causing serious overcrowding and contributing to communal tension and growing political extremism. Not surprisingly, the Indian government perceived the settlement of refugees in Assam and the north-east tribal hill states, where there were already conflicts between the indigenous populations and Bengalis, as potentially explosive. Indian authorities were convinced from the beginning of the crisis that the refugee flow not only had to be halted but reversed. They maintained that the refugee situation was 'temporary'; these were 'evacuees', not refugees; and they were housed in 'transit relief camps' not refugee camps. Indira Gandhi insisted that the refugees could not remain as permanent residents in India but would be returned as soon as conditions in their homeland would permit.

India initially tried to cope with the refugee influx on its own but it was soon overwhelmed. Outbreaks of cholera and other infectious diseases in refugee camps exhausted medical stocks in India and the economic burden on the country was monumental. The involvement of the UNHCR began in response to a request from the Indian authorities to the UN Secretary-General, U Thant, for assistance on 23 April 1971. U Thant immediately agreed to this request and appealed to the international community for assistance. He also took the unusual step of asking Sadruddin to act as the 'focal point' for the co-ordination of relief activities without first referring this highly politicized issue to the UN General Assembly. The size of the operation was beyond the technical and administrative capacity of any one agency and necessitated the involvement of several of the UN specialized agencies.

In many ways the 1971 war between West Pakistan and secessionist East Pakistan, and the subsequent flight of East Bengalis to India marked a watershed in the history of the UNHCR. After Sadruddin was called upon to co-ordinate relief efforts, the UNHCR embarked on the biggest operation in its history. The costs of mounting a relief effort of this size dwarfed its already stretched budget. It was a huge leap from administering an annual global general programme of around $7 million to organizing a special operation in one country involving over sixty times that amount.[38]

As focal point for the entire operation, the UNHCR dealt with various agencies within the UN system—notably UNICEF, WHO, and the World Food Programme (WFP)—as well as with NGOs outside it, such as the Indian Red Cross, private voluntary agencies and the Indian Government. The operation rested on two pillars. In New Delhi, a UNHCR office provided liaison with the Government of India, other UN agencies, and the embassies of donor countries. Their findings and requests were transmitted to the UNHCR headquarters in Geneva and were placed before a Standing Inter-Agency Consultative Unit, composed of UN agencies and NGOs, where decisions were made on the policy action to be taken.

While the international response to the refugees' plight was immediate, it was always recognized that assistance measures in the camps were at best palliatives and the only real solution to the problem would be the refugees' repatriation. The Indian government was never disposed to accept the permanent resettlement of the Bengali refugees. As early as April 1971, the High Commissioner's representative in New Delhi reported that 'nobody speaks of resettling these refugees'. In his 19 May 1971 appeal for relief assistance the Secretary-General spoke of emergency assistance 'pending repatriation'. Following a visit by Sadruddin to Pakistan in June 1971, it was agreed he would provide assistance to Pakistan in arranging the return and rehabilitation of the refugees. Pakistan also agreed that a representative of the High Commissioner would be stationed in Dhaka to maintain contact with the authorities in the source country. Their work closely co-ordinated with the

UN East Pakistan Relief Operation (UNEPRO) which provided relief to the population inside East Pakistan.

The refugee crisis generated intense diplomatic activity on the part of the UN, the UNHCR, and Western governments. U Thant perceived the crisis to be much more than just a humanitarian concern or an internal affair.[39] The refugee crisis spilled over borders and not only threatened the security of India but also threatened to precipitate a regional conflict between India and Pakistan. In order to avert such an outcome, the Secretary-General remained in continuous contact with the governments of Pakistan and India throughout the crisis. Nevertheless, the UN was unable to address satisfactorily the political crisis. U Thant took several unsuccessful initiatives to prevent the crisis from deteriorating into a full-scale regional war, including separate proposals first to station UNHCR representatives on both sides of the border in order to facilitate repatriation and later to place civilian UN observers on the border to prevent the outbreak of war between Pakistan and India. He also used Sadruddin to try to initiate a dialogue between the two countries and to act as a diplomatic intermediary.

The United States was also extremely concerned about the security implications of the refugee crisis and tried to impose restraint on both countries. In Washington, a Special Action Group on the Indo–Pakistan Situation was formed. Its focus was to identify:

(a) ways to convince India that it should act with restraint despite the enormous burden the refugee inflow from East Pakistan is posing for the Indian economy and polity, (b) ways to persuade the Pakistanis to stop and if possible reverse the refugee outflow, (c) efforts to achieve a political settlement in East Pakistan, and (d) steps to involve third parties in the solution of these problems. (US National Archives, Diplomatic Branch, Pol 23-9 PAK/XR REF PAK, 26 May 1971).

A memorandum for President Richard Nixon outlined US security concerns over the refugee crisis in South Asia and the policy measures adopted by the US government:

The principal danger of escalation of India-Pakistan tensions now comes from the burden imposed on India by the very substantial flow of refugees from East Pakistan. We are encouraging India to manage the refugee problem by getting international assistance rather than by taking direct action against East Pakistan as some Indians are urging. In order to support these tactics, we have told India of our private efforts to get Pakistan to accept international relief in East Pakistan, to establish peaceful conditions there, to urge the refugees to return, and to seek political accommodation. It is important that we also offer to provide as part of an international effort substantial assistance to meet the cost of refugee relief. (US National Archives, Diplomatic Branch, SOC 10 PAK/XR REF PAK, 29 May 1971).

In letters to President Yahya Khan of Pakistan and to Prime Minister Indira Gandhi of India,[40] Nixon stressed the fact that it was in no one's interest to permit political unrest in East Pakistan and internationalization of the refugee crisis, and cautioned restraint.

Not only were these diplomatic efforts largely unsuccessful but the authorities in New Delhi viewed UN and US diplomacy with great scepticism. While Pakistan responded favourably to U Thant's offer of his good offices to mediate, India perceived the move as an attempt to save the Pakistani regime which was responsible for the refugee exodus rather than as an effort to find a political solution which took into account the wishes of the East Pakistani people.[41] India also felt that Sadruddin's diplomacy tilted towards Pakistan, endorsing Pakistani efforts to woo the refugees home without trying first to stabilize the situation in East Pakistan. Officials in New Delhi also felt that the UNHCR did not sufficiently appreciate the economic burden imposed on India, and India complained that international assistance was both inadequate and slow in arriving. Consequently, relations between the UNHCR and India soured.

By the autumn 1971, it was evident that the prospects for repatriation were bleak and India was leaning towards seeking a military solution to the refugee problem. Despite diplomatic efforts for restraint and reconciliation and several appeals by Yayha Khan to the refugees to return home, the brutality of the Pakistani military continued unabated, forcing people to flee to India as late as November 1971. Pakistan refused to remove the ban on the Awami League and proceeded to try Sheik Mujibur Rahman. Judging from its actions, Pakistan clearly did not intend to allow more than a token number of refugees—and none of them Hindus—to return to East Pakistan. It was also certain that few refugees would return voluntarily until the Pakistani Army withdrew and a representative government in East Pakistan was established. The prospect was that India would remain host to some 10 million refugees indefinitely.

India believed that only armed intervention could liberate East Pakistan and enable refugees to return home. In preparation for such an eventuality, the Indian government supported the functioning of a Bengali government-in-exile on Indian soil and the Indian Army trained and armed the *Mukhti Bahini* refugee warriors. However, Indian forces did not wait for the East Pakistani freedom fighters to defeat the Pakistani Army alone. In late November, the Indian Army invaded East Pakistan, and on 6 December war was declared between India and Pakistan. Despite condemnation of the Indian intervention and last minute appeals by the UN Security Council for a cease-fire, India continued its military offensive until the Pakistani military surrendered on 16 December. India immediately recognized the newly independent state of Bangladesh, and the fighting stopped completely on 17 December 1971.

With independence for Bangladesh, the stage was set for the largest voluntary repatriation in the UNHCR's history. Thousands of refugees did not wait for an organized movement, but started to trek back home as soon as they heard of the cease-fire. Subsequently, mass repatriation proceeded, both in a spontaneous and in an organized manner. Once the massive return movement had begun, the responsibility of mobilizing international resources needed to facilitate repatriation was assigned to the UNHCR. On 22 January, Sadruddin appealed to UN member states for funds to cover the repatriation. During the month of January 1972, a daily average of 210,000 returning refugees crossed the Bangladesh border, with the assistance and encouragement of the UNHCR and the Indian and Bangladeshi authorities.[42] By the end of March that year, all but 50,000 of the 10 million refugees had returned home and the camps were closed.

The UNHCR had risen quickly to its new challenge of overseeing the massive repatriation that returned the 10 million refugees to their homes. In the process it gained valuable experience that was to stand it in good stead for future special programmes in other parts of the world.

Dealing with Stranded Populations and the Aftermath of the Bangladeshi War for Independence

While some 10 million Bengalis successfully repatriated to the newly independent Bangladesh, hundreds of thousands of others were left stranded in various parts of the subcontinent. Among the stranded populations were Pakistani prisoners of war and civilian internees in India, all Bengalis then in Pakistan, and a substantial number of Biharis—Indian Muslims originally from the Indian state of Bihar who had migrated to East Pakistan at the time of partition in 1947. In March 1973, Prime Minister Sheikh Mujibur Rahman of Bangladesh requested the assistance of UN Secretary-General Kurt Waldheim in repatriating these groups. Waldheim used Sadruddin to try to negotiate between the parties. The High Commissioner's family had long-standing links to Pakistan and he was therefore able to play an essential mediating role.[43] Negotiations were not easy, however, as Pakistan still had refused to recognize Bangladesh. Nevertheless, on 28 August 1973, the governments of Bangladesh, India, and Pakistan signed the New Delhi Agreement which included provisions for the repatriation of all the major stranded populations. The UNHCR, along with the ICRC, was asked to co-ordinate the repatriation process. A massive UNHCR-led air repatriation operation, with aircraft on loan from Britain, East Germany, and the USSR, was launched to return some 250,000 people from Pakistan to Bangladesh and from Bangladesh to Pakistan. This was the largest airlift of refugees ever organized. But several hundred thousand Biharis who wanted to move to Pakistan were left behind in refugee camps in Bangladesh. Their fate remains largely unresolved to this day and constitutes one of the most heart-rending human tragedies in the world.

The UNHCR and Humanitarian Assistance to Cyprus

As a result of the UNHCR's success in the Bangladesh Operation, Sadruddin was called upon to co-ordinate both the UN relief effort in southern Sudan in 1972 and the administration of UN humanitarian assistance to Cyprus in 1974. During the early 1970s, assistance to people displaced by conflict—including those who did not cross national borders—became an integral part of the High Commissioner's programmes. Perhaps the clearest example of such expansion can be seen in the international response to the mass displacement of Greek Cypriots during the *coup d'état* against the government of President Makarios and the subsequent invasion of the island by Turkish forces. When tens of thousands of Greek Cypriots fled their villages, Secretary-General Kurt Waldheim asked Sadruddin to co-ordinate assistance to the internally displaced persons. As with earlier UN efforts in South Sudan and Bangladesh, the UNHCR co-ordinated the international humanitarian response, raising over $20 million, and resettling most of the displaced persons.

Repatriation to Angola, Guinea Bissau, and Mozambique

During the 1960s and early 1970s, major refugee flows were linked to the struggles for national liberation in southern Africa. Apart from Sudanese and Rwandan refugees, the majority of Africa's refugees were from the Portuguese colonies of Angola, Guinea-Bissau, and Mozambique and from the white minority-ruled regimes in Rhodesia, South Africa, and South West Africa. For the most part, refugees remained in the region either in liberated zones inside their own country or in neighbouring countries where they supported the liberation fighters and were often linked to the military struggles.

Violent decolonization in Southern Africa generated huge numbers of refugees. Numbering nearly a million in the early 1970s, they formed large concentrations in neighbouring states where the UNHCR set up camps with millions of dollars in international funds. Despite UNHCR efforts to ensure the civilian nature of these camps, in many instances they became recruiting centres and bases for liberation movements. Consequently, the camps frequently became targets for attack by the military forces of colonial authorities. Militarized refugee camps became the norm in Southern Africa. During the 1970s, camps for South African refugees in Mozambique and Tanzania were controlled by the military wing of the African National Congress and the Pan African Congress and were regularly attacked by South African armed forces. In Angola, Namibian refugee camps headed by the South West Africa People's Organization (SWAPO), were bombed by the South African air force. In Zambia and Mozambique, refugee camps for those fleeing the anti-colonial struggle in Rhodesia were controlled by the Zimbabwean liberation movements and were attacked by Rhodesian forces.[44]

Following a military *coup* in Portugal in 1974 and the new Portuguese junta's appeal to the liberation movements of the Portuguese African territories for a cessation of hostilities, refugees started returning home in large numbers. The former Portuguese territories had been devastated by long years of war. In Guinea-Bissau, eleven years of war had devastated the countryside, uprooted one quarter of the population, and driven 80,000 people to seek refuge abroad, mostly in neighbouring Senegal and the Gambia. When liberation was completed in the fall of 1974, only one hospital, one secondary school, a single modern industrial plant, and less than one hundred kilometres of usable paved roads remained. Facing an immense task of reconstruction and development, the Republic of Guinea-Bissau turned for assistance to the international community. On 12 March 1975, Sadruddin appealed for aid to assist the repatriation and resettlement not only of the refugees but also of the 60,000 internally displaced persons in Guinea-Bissau. In response to this appeal, the UNHCR drew up a $4 million programme for that purpose. The UNHCR financed a variety of small-scale projects aimed at facilitating the social and economic integration of these refugees in rural areas.

The repatriation to Guinea-Bissau, like the returns to Angola and Mozambique, were complicated by political and economic factors. The new government in Guinea-Bissau required security clearance for all returning refugees. The UNHCR was required to provide the necessary documentation and to forward it to the authorities in Guinea-Bissau. Several thousand former Guinean members of the Portuguese army who had fled to Senegal chose not to return home.

In Mozambique, as soon as a transitional government under the control of the Front for the Liberation of Mozambique (FRELIMO) was installed in September 1974 as a result of the Lusaka Agreement, those who had taken refuge in neighbouring countries such as Malawi, Tanzania, Zambia, and Rhodesia, began to return spontaneously. Large parts of the Mozambican infrastructure had been destroyed by war. The Portuguese had pursued a scorched earth policy in the north and had forced civilian populations into 'protected villages'. In order to meet the needs of the first returnees, the High Commissioner allocated, in December 1974, an amount of $100,000 from his Emergency Fund. A few months later, a $7 million UNHCR assistance programme was drawn up for the repatriation and resettlement of the refugees who had already returned or were expected to repatriate. The programme provided medical care, seeds, tools, and mechanized agricultural equipment. It also covered some of the specific and immediate needs of the internally displaced persons in Mozambique. Overall, some 500,000 persons were assisted by the UNHCR. The repatriation was not without political problems. Some of the refugees were opposed to the new FRELIMO government and were reluctant to return home. In August 1975, the new government had passed citizenship legislation denying entry to any foreigner who had stayed outside the country for more than 90 days without valid reason. In March 1976 the Mozambican authorities published new procedures for those wishing to return. Thousands of Portuguese effectively lost their right to return and those allowed to return had to provide evidence of their Mozambican origin. Repatriation slowed as some refugees opposed return, alleging that returnees would be subject to compulsory 're-education'. Eventually, the great majority of refugees returned to Mozambique, although the UNHCR did continue to assist some of the refugees who opted to stay in their places of exile.

In Angola, international efforts to assist nearly one million Angolans and to repatriate hundreds of thousands proved largely unsuccessful. The struggle for independence in Angola had been extremely destructive. The Portuguese had forcibly displaced hundreds of thousands of people, mostly to neighbouring states. Unlike in Guinea-Bissau and Mozambique, international factors played an important role in the Angolan conflict, complicating the UNHCR's repatriation efforts and the country's transition to post-independence.

From the mid-1960s on, Angola had been part of the global East–West struggle. Fearing the rise of black nationalism in the region, South Africa had provided assistance to the Portuguese colonial authorities. The Soviet Union had supported the Movement for the Liberation of Angola (MPLA) who were allied with the Portuguese Communist Party. The United States, despite its NATO alliance with Portugal, countered Soviet involvement by providing covert support to the National Front for the Liberation of Angola (FNLA) headed by Roberto Holden. US aid to the FNLA had been channelled through Zaïre where the CIA had installed Sese Seko Mobuto in 1965 and where the FNLA had its base. The FNLA had also been supported by the People's Republic of China who viewed it as a counterweight to the Soviet-backed MPLA. The third significant Angolan party was Jonas Savimbi's National Union for Total Independence of Angola (UNITA). While agreements were quickly reached for the independence of Guinea-Bissau and Mozambique, negotiations on Angola were hindered by the failure of the Angolan liberation movements to form a common front and by general hostility and rivalry among the three groups. This inter-party conflict greatly complicated repatriation and the initiation of any international humanitarian aid programme for Angola. Armed conflict broke out again in Luanda in March 1975 and quickly spread to other regions of the country. Insecurity in the countryside made it impossible for the UNHCR to establish the necessary reception and resettlement facilities for the returnees. The conflict was extended to the UNHCR Executive Committee meeting in Geneva in October 1975 where the MPLA representative accused UNITA and FNLA of using refugee aid as assets for obtaining electoral, financial, and even military advantages.[45] It was only in August 1976 that the UN Secretary-General was able to designate the UN High Commissioner for Refugees as co-ordinator of UN humanitarian assistance in Angola. Later that month, Sadruddin launched an appeal for $32.5 million and 48,000 tons of food.

Despite UN and UNHCR initiatives, Angola quickly plunged back into full-scale war. The situation was greatly exacerbated by the internationalization of the conflict. In October 1975, South African forces, with the tacit support of the US, crossed into Angola to bolster Savimbi's UNITA army. The Soviet Union, meanwhile, expedited military supplies to its MPLA client, including the dispatch of several thousand Cuban troops. Consequently, new mass displacements occurred in Angola as the MPLA, FNLA, and UNITA, trained and equipped by foreign patrons, resumed their struggle. Under these conditions, very few refugees chose to return to Angola at that time.

Neither Angola nor Mozambique achieved peace with independence. Both countries became caught up with the Cold War and larger geo-strategic battles in southern Africa during the late 1970s and 1980s. Renewed conflict in Angola and Mozambique and instability along their borders as well as mass outflow of refugees from Namibia, South Africa, Zaïre, and Rhodesia severely compounded the difficulties inherent in reconstructing these war-torn countries.

Overseas Resettlement of Ugandan Asians and Latin Americans

Another prominent feature of the 1970s was the renewed importance of resettlement. During the decade, overseas resettlement was used as almost the sole solution for Ugandan Asians and Latin American refugees. The resettlement of several thousand Ugandan Asians who were expelled from their homes by Idi Amin in 1972 marked a return to resettlement in permanent homes overseas. After the 1973 *coup d'état* in Chile, several thousand Latin Americans who had taken refuge there had to be sent to other countries on the American continents and to Europe. The resettlement operation was repeated for refugees from Argentina and Peru, which had not wished to give asylum to all of the applicants. The largest resettlement operation occurred after Sadruddin left office in 1977. The end of the war in Vietnam in 1975 led to the exodus of the Indo-Chinese. What started as a trickle became a flood by 1978, inundating the countries of South-East Asia. Thailand, Malaysia, Indonesia, the

Philippines, and Hong Kong accepted these refugees only on a temporary basis, subject to UNHCR assistance, and on the condition that they be resettled elsewhere.

The resettlement of refugees from repressive regimes in Africa, Asia, and Latin America during this time was seen as a rescue effort to help victims of massive human rights violations. Military *coups d'état* and repression in such countries as Argentina, Chile, Greece, the Soviet Union—mainly of Jews and dissidents—Uganda, Uruguay, and Vietnam increased global awareness of human rights violations and spurred greater human rights advocacy. International consciousness about human rights expanded enormously in the 1970s as membership in human rights organizations in the US and Europe grew and new organizations were created. The US section of Amnesty International expanded from 3,000 to 50,000 members between 1974 and 1976.[46] The human rights network grew in the less developed countries as well, both in repressive regimes and among refugee exile communities. Human rights actors across the world began to develop links with each other and a transnational human rights network emerged.[47]

National and international policy-makers also grew interested in human rights issues. In 1973, the US Congress promoted hearings on human rights abuses around the world and began to pass legislation linking human rights criteria to American foreign and security policies. The administration of President Jimmy Carter gave human rights an even higher profile by directly incorporating human rights considerations into the US foreign policy agenda.[48] In 1976, the international human rights covenants came into effect, and new institutions such as the UN Human Rights Committee emerged.

In this new international political environment, there was strong support for rescuing human rights victims through overseas refugee resettlement programmes. The growth of the international human rights movement directly affected most states' willingness to co-operate with the UNHCR and to contribute generously to its resettlement programmes.

The Ugandan Asians

When Uganda obtained independence in 1962, large numbers of Asians were given the option of becoming Ugandan citizens. Not all, however, chose to avail themselves of this opportunity within the stipulated time limit. In August 1972, President Idi Amin issued an order expelling all Asians who did not possess Ugandan nationality. Although these persons had lived and worked in Uganda for generations, they were given just 90 days—until 7 November 1972—to get out of the country. About 40,000 people were affected by President Amin's decree in 1972 and most were totally unprepared for a rapid departure.

While Asians had been bullied and subjected to extortion for some time by Idi Amin's soldiers, most were confused and surprised by the expulsion order. Only some were able to make advance arrangements and resettle elsewhere. Unlike other groups of refugees in Africa who were pushed out of their countries by war or repression, Ugandan Asians were suddenly and arbitrarily uprooted and then thrust into a completely different region of the world. It was an early example of 'ethnic cleansing' and was the first of a series of mass expulsions carried out by authoritarian or Communist regimes in the next 25 years, including Vietnam, Cuba, Bosnia, Croatia, Kosovo, and East Timor.

There were different categories of Ugandan Asians. 55,000 held British passports and a majority among them eventually went to the United Kingdom and Canada. There were an estimated 2,000 who held Indian, Pakistani, or Bangladeshi passports. These travelled to their countries of origin, in many cases for the very first time in their lives. Others, and theirs were the most difficult cases, were classified as Asians of undetermined nationality.

In principle, Asians of Ugandan nationality were not affected by the expulsion order as originally formulated. However, it soon appeared that many were being denied their claim to Ugandan nationality and were made to meet the forced departure deadline. Furthermore, all remaining Asians were ordered by the Ugandan Government to leave the urban areas where they lived and earned their livelihood, and to move to rural villages. In despair many joined the queue of those seeking resettlement elsewhere.

Initially, the Ugandan Government held that Ugandan Asians were a British rather than an international responsibility and refused to allow any United Nations involvement. The UK government position was that if Asian holders of UK passports were deported or expelled and no other country would accept them, then, as a last resort, the UK would accept them. In fact, British policy-makers feared the political and social consequences of large-scale immigration and were extremely reluctant to admit all of the Ugandan Asian expellees. John Kelly, the UNHCR Representative in London at the time, described the situation thus:

Among the general population in the UK there is considerable reluctance to accept a further large group of immigrants, particularly in view of the shortage of housing and the presence of a million unemployed. Undoubtedly, it is hard for a native-born Englishman, who may have been on a waiting list for Council housing for years, or may have been trying to get employment for himself, to see newly arrived immigrants get priority over him in his own country for housing and employment. The purpose of the Commonwealth Immigrants Act 1968, agreed to by the commonwealth countries concerned, was to slow the movement of immigration to an orderly progress so that the persons concerned could be absorbed in the UK community without causing undue strains. (UNHCR Archives, HCR/1/UK/ASI, 14 September 1972).

Nevertheless, the UK decided to accept the Asian expellees and made arrangements for their orderly reception by the establishment of a Government Uganda Resettlement Board and a committee of NGOs to co-ordinate welfare for the evacuees from Uganda and by the provision of funds to local authorities for resettlement costs. Some 27,000 Ugandans with British passports went directly to the United Kingdom. However, there were some 7,000 Asians of undetermined status—in that they were not recognized as nationals by any country. Some of these stateless people arrived in Britain at the time of the expulsion order and were put in camps, pending future British or UNHCR action. Others were forcibly returned to Uganda.[49] Fearful of a negative domestic political fallout from the refugee crisis, the UK government appealed to its allies to help out through resettlement pledges. The British Foreign Secretary, Sir Alec Douglas Home, appealed personally to the United States. The Nixon administration agreed to admit 1,000 Ugandan Asians on an emergency basis under the Attorney General's parole authority.[50] The United States, along with Switzerland, Canada, and Denmark, dispatched missions to Kampala before the expulsion deadline and selected thousands of immigrants on the spot. Norway, the Netherlands, and Sweden came forward to offer permanent settlement opportunities. A number of Latin American states announced their readiness to consider applications from candidates satisfying their regular immigration criteria. But in spite of this goodwill, it soon became evident to all concerned, including the Government of Uganda, that a co-ordinated international effort was necessary to secure entry visas for all those expelled.

At a meeting held in Kampala in late October 1972, it was decided to organize an emergency evacuation operation under the responsibility of the Resident Representative of the United Nations Development Programme. The International Committee of the Red Cross (ICRC) agreed to issue one-way travel documents to those requiring them and ICEM arranged transportation out of Uganda. Meanwhile, Sadruddin sent messages to capitals around the world appealing for permanent resettlement opportunities and, where these could not be made available immediately, for temporary transit facilities. The UNHCR also asked governments to contribute some funds to provide for the care and maintenance of refugees in transit and, wherever necessary, for their transportation.

Throughout the operation, the UNHCR was careful to maintain good working relations with the Ugandan Government and, at no time during this crisis, did Sadruddin publicly condemn Idi Amin for the expulsion of Asians. He had good reason for this. Apart from Ugandan Asians still awaiting depart-ure, there were at the time some 180,000 refugees from Zaïre, Rwanda, and the Southern Sudan in the country, all of direct concern to the UNHCR. The UNHCR was also in the middle of a massive repatriation operation in Southern Sudan which involved the co-operation of Ugandan authorities. Finally, Sadruddin's own community, the Ismaelis in Uganda, were affected, and their wealth made them a potential target for Ugandan Army corruption and greed.[51] Thus, the High Commissioner remained silent about Uganda's human rights abuses while at the same time he was extremely active on the diplomatic front in trying to find resettlement places for the stateless refugees.

The response to the High Commissioner's plea for transit accommodations was quick and within 12 days, over 3,600 Ugandan Asians were flown to Austria, Belgium, Italy, Malta, and Spain. The evacuation itself did not resolve the crisis. The UNHCR had to find permanent places of resettlement. Here again, the international community responded generously. By January 1973, more than 1,500 persons in the transit centres had found new homes. But further efforts were required to find resettlement places for over 2,000 more.[52] During the next two months, Sadruddin visited capitals,[53] including London, and Ottawa, and Washington, and the UN in New York in an effort to find places for stateless Ugandan refugees and to encourage governments to be generous in permitting family reunifications. His interventions for greater burden-sharing led several countries to raise their admission quota or to set up special schemes for Ugandan Asian applicants. The UK agreed to take some of the stateless Asians.[54] In what was viewed as a key to 'breaking the back of the problem',[55] the United States agreed to admit a further 500 Ugandan Asians. This set off a kind of humanitarian chain reaction and, at the end of the year, fewer than 100 persons were still awaiting resettlement. By the autumn of 1974, every refugee had been placed in one of 25 receiving countries.

In 1972 and 1973 the Government of Uganda promulgated several decrees providing a legal and procedural framework for claiming compensation for assets left behind by Asians who had been forced to hurriedly leave Uganda. The British and Indian Governments registered compensation claims on behalf of their nationals and the UNHCR undertook to negotiate claims on behalf of Asians of undetermined nationality.

Fleeing Pinochet's Chile and other Southern Cone Military Dictatorships

In the 1970s, Latin America, a region renowned for its long-standing tradition of asylum, underwent a series of internal crises. Political and civil unrest resulted in widespread political repression. Between 1973 and 1976, military juntas took power from civilian regimes in Chile, Uruguay, and Argentina. States of emergency were proclaimed and arbitrary detentions, lack of due process, systematic use of torture, physical disappearance of opponents, prohibition of political parties and unions, and censorship of the press became the norm. These policies produced major waves of refugees. Estimates are that over one million people departed these three countries during the 1970s.[56] The military *coups* in Chile, Argentina, and Uruguay were catalytic events for the international human rights movement. Because Chile had been one of the first democracies in Latin America, the fact that such brutal events could take place there suggested that it could happen anywhere. These events gripped the attention of Western publics and generated an outpouring of sympathy for the victims of these military juntas.

The first wave of Latin American refugees included those who fled violence during the overthrow of the Salvador Allende Grossens government in Chile in 1973. Some 15,000 refugees had previously escaped from Brazil, Argentina, Uruguay, Paraguay, and other authoritarian regimes in Latin America had been granted asylum in Chile during Allende's presidency. These were groups immediately targeted for persecution by the new military junta of Augusto Pinochet. Many were detained and tortured. Others were forced to seek political asylum in foreign embassies in Santiago or go underground. Large numbers were executed. In addition, thousands of Allende supporters were summarily imprisoned and tortured, or shot.

The acute refugee problem which surfaced in Chile necessitated an emergency response. Most Latin American governments responded by filling their embassies to capacity with refugees seeking diplomatic asylum. Many Western governments, with the notable exception of the United States, also provided asylum in their Santiago embassies.

After the initial siege, the new military authorities became concerned about the extensive negative coverage in the Western press and media given to the *coup* and subsequent repression in Chile. Concerned that negative publicity would damage the legitimacy and economic prospects of the new regime, the junta believed that the best way to handle this problem and to get rid of former Allende supporters and potential dissidents was to involve the international agencies.[57] Sadruddin sensed that the new authorities in Chile were vulnerable to external criticism and opted to try to hold them to their word rather than criticize them for their human rights abuses. Reminding the Chilean government that it had signed international refugee instruments and therefore had obligations to implement them, Sadruddin appealed to Chile's Minister of Foreign Affairs not to return these foreign refugees to their countries of origin where they feared persecution.[58] Chile's Foreign Minister, Ismael Huerta, responded positively, assuring the UNHCR that:

1) Refugees who have entered the country in regular fashion and are not implicated in offences are fully protected according to the laws of the country.
2) Refugees who have committed offences will be tried in Chile and, in case of expulsion, there is no purpose whatsoever of returning them to their country of origin leaving open the choice of their place of destination.
3) Concerning those whose situation is irregular, it is necessary for them to regularize it soonest. (UNHCR Archives, HCR/1CHL/GEN/600/CHL, 16 September 1973).

On 20 September 1973, the UNHCR established an emergency office in

Santiago and arranged with the Chilean government to establish a National Committee for Aid to Refugees (CONAR). On 3 October, the ruling junta issued a degree officially recognizing CONAR defining its scope and activities and providing legal sanction to 'safe havens'. These sanctuaries were centres of lodging and assistance for refugees where they could remain inviolate and were an innovation of great significance in the law and practice relating to asylum and human rights. From September 1973 to March 1974 more than 3,500 refugees availed themselves of the protection of the UNHCR and the services of CONAR in the safe havens.[59]

Despite the fact that they could now seek legal protection as well as direct assistance from CONAR and the UNHCR, most of the foreign refugees sought to resettle either in other Latin American countries or in Europe. The resettlement effort was led by the UNHCR, the ICEM, and the ICRC. The UNHCR initially concentrated on foreign refugees stranded in Chile, and under its auspices some 2,500 refugees from Latin American countries left Chile for 39 destinations abroad. Intensive media coverage of the atrocities and massive human rights violations surrounding the Chilean *coup* aroused the widespread attention and sympathy of Western public opinion. Labour unions and the European left campaigned vigorously in order to get their governments to react positively. In response to UNHCR appeals for resettlement places, France, Sweden, and West Germany each took in between 800 and 1,100 refugees while the United States accepted only 26 out of about 150 people who had applied for admission to the US through the UNHCR. By the end of March 1974, the emergency phase of the resettlement operation was completed. The number of refugees of Latin American origin still in need of urgent resettlement was reduced to 18 and they were all in safe havens.

The end of the emergency did not, however, mean the end of the resettlement process. After the *coup*, there were tens of thousands of Chileans who wanted to leave the country. The ICEM and the ICRC negotiated with government authorities to help move the thousands of Chileans held in prisons and in detention centres who sought to resettle in third countries. Of even greater magnitude was the problem of Chilean nationals who had themselves left the country to seek refuge elsewhere. Argentina received the highest number of the Chilean refugees, approximately 15,000 of them. A considerable proportion succeeded in integrating independently with little or no UNHCR assistance. However, the increasing number of new arrivals, coupled with problems of national security and public order in Argentina, created difficulties for the authorities, for the refugees themselves, and for those concerned with refugee work in Argentina. As a result, Argentina was unable to continue its policy of granting permanent asylum to all Chilean refugees arriving in the country in the wake of the events of September 1973.

Concerted efforts, therefore, had to be made to resettle several thousand Chilean refugees elsewhere. In response to the High Commissioner's urgent appeal for resettlement places, several countries outside the region agreed to accept Chilean refugees. The Federal Republic of Germany, France, Great Britain, Italy, the Netherlands, Spain, and Sweden as well as the German Democratic Republic, Hungary, Romania, and Yugoslavia all took large numbers. In sharp contrast to its European allies, the United States remained singularly unresponsive to the plight of Chilean refugees. It virtually ignored appeals for resettlement, and it even refused to provide any funding to support ICEM programmes to finance resettlement.

A year after the *coup*, in August 1974, the UNHCR appealed to the US to grant asylum to a substantial number of the 4,000 Chilean exiles in Peru. In September 1974, the Chilean government also announced that it would release most of its political prisoners if foreign governments would offer them asylum. In response to these appeals, the US Office of Refugee and Migration Affairs urged its superiors in the State Department to take positive action. The State Department, however, receiving no firm guidance from the Nixon administration, decided to consult with the House and Senate Immigration subcommittees before it submitted a formal proposal to the Immigration and Naturalization Service (INS) to establish a Chilean parole programme. Thus it was not until late April 1975 that the State Department formally proposed a group asylum programme for the Chileans to the Attorney General. It took Attorney General Edward Levi another two months to respond with qualified approval to the State Department's parole programme proposal. The programme which was finally approved was limited to 400 parole cases. The US indicated it would accept only those currently in prison for political offences and would not accept any persons outside of prison whose claims reflected only a fear of future persecution. It also announced that it would not consider under the programme any detainees or refugees found to be ineligible under the provisions of the Immigration and Naturalization Act because of membership in the Communist Party, in leftist revolutionary movements, 'or [in] other terrorist groups', or who had criminal records. Furthermore, all applicants would be required to undergo a 'rigorous' security screening and a 'detailed' medical examination.[60] Of all the resettlement countries involved in the Chilean programme, the US had the strictest admissions criteria.[61]

The Nixon and Ford administrations and Congress all resisted the establishment of a comprehensive parole programme to meet the humanitarian needs of Chilean refugees. Many members of Congress privately expressed misgivings about the parole programme for Chilean refugees, fearing that it would result in the admission of 'leftist radicals' into the United States or that it might burden the already existing unemployment situation.[62] This lack of Congressional consensus helps explain in great part the bureaucratic resistance within Department of State and the INS that occurred both prior to and after the implementation of the Chilean parole programme. Senator Edward Kennedy complained that

Foot-dragging and excuses have characterized our government's approach to the Chilean refugee program. We have heard a litany of promises but have seen very little action. For two years, letters from the Department of State, in response to my inquiries ... and the testimony of department officials before this subcommittee, have given assurances of an intent to provide generous parole for refugees from Chile. Those assurances were not fulfilled. Press releases were issued announcing a willingness to receive Chilean refugees. But that willingness has been contradicted by the lack of positive action. And then only when we were engaged in requesting those same international organizations and agencies for help in resettling Vietnamese, the red tape barriers suddenly were broken and the Chilean parole program was suddenly established in early June. (US Senate, *Refugee and Humanitarian Problems in Chile, Part 3*: 38–9).

Further delays occurred after the June 1975 establishment of the Chilean parole programme as the Executive Branch moved slowly on the processing of cases. Few Chilean refugees applied to the US parole programme because of their antipathy toward the US for having actively destabilized the Allende government and continuing to support Pinochet. Many were Communists or socialists and would not have been eligible for admission under US law. Nevertheless, it was not until more than four months after the initiation of the programme and only after hard-hitting hearings held by Senator Kennedy that the first Chilean parolee entered the United States on 17 October 1975. Even then, the screening process by INS officials was unprecedentedly long, and security screening exceptionally thorough.[63] Each Chilean parolee had to be personally approved by the Director of the INS.[64] It took months and sometimes years to secure INS approval, locate a sponsor for each refugee and his or her family, and receive an exit decree from the Chilean government. By January 1976, seven months after the programme began, only seventy-six people had been approved for the parole programme and only twenty-seven people had arrived in the United States. When the US finally did make good on its Chilean parole programme, it came too late to be of any real benefit.

Argentina's 'Dirty War' and the Abuse of Refugees

Perhaps the most difficult Latin American refugee problems confronting the UNHCR were those in Argentina. Not only refugees from Chile but also those from Bolivia, Brazil, Paraguay, and Uruguay had crowded into Argentina by the thousands. However, refugees found it increasingly difficult to obtain refugee status and permanent residence there. The economic situation in Argentina deteriorated rapidly and hyperinflation made employment prospects poor. By 1976, resettlement places became difficult to obtain for these refugees.[65] Some 8,000 refugees had settled in Argentina without UNHCR or NGO support of whom only 300 had been given refugee status by that country. Another 10,000 UNHCR mandate Latin American refugees awaited resettlement in 1976. The process of leaving Argentina was painfully slow. Only about 100 departures took place each month. For those who remained in Argentina, awaiting resettlement and depending entirely on daily allowances from the UNHCR and the assistance of several NGOs, the situation was extremely dangerous. In frustration refugees occupied the UNHCR branch office in Buenos Aires for 60 hours to protest their precarious situation.

The situation turned much more dangerous for refugees when, on 24 March 1976, the military ousted President Isabel Martinez de Peron and established a military dictatorship. The new junta embarked on an anti-terrorist campaign in which they collaborated with the secret police of other military regimes in the hemisphere, including Chile, Paraguay, and Uruguay. All these governments adhered to a rigid national security doctrine that identified all domestic opposition as terrorists and subversives. Right-wing vigilante groups and 'death squads' closely aligned to the new junta in Argentina initiated a dirty war which targeted leftists, including refugees. Their policy was to kidnap, detain, and execute opponents while denying any knowledge of their whereabouts. By such measures, the Argentine military hoped to avoid the international criticism and isolation that Chile had experienced when it had imprisoned and executed supporters of former President Allende.[66]

As the political situation in Argentina deteriorated in 1976 and political repression deepened, a number of refugees began to fear for their lives. In May, two former Uruguayan officials Hector Gutierrez Ruiz and Zelmar Michelini, and two other Uruguayan refugees were kidnapped, tortured, and shot. In June, armed men broke into the offices of the Argentine Catholic Commission (CCAI) and stole the personal files and records of almost all of the refugees under that agency's assistance. In July and September, about 60 Uruguayan refugees were abducted by Uruguayan intelligence agents with the co-operation of the Argentine security forces and forcibly returned to Uruguay. According to testimonies taken by the UNHCR,[67] the 'refugees were kept blindfolded and savagely tortured' after being kidnapped from their homes in Buenos Aires by Argentinian police in civilian clothes accompanied by Uruguayan officials. The refugees were tortured by 'la bandera' which consisted of 'electric shocks going through belt attached to naked body. Refugees had to stand on wet floor covered with salt so that electricity [would] pass better'. One of the refugees was killed by immersion in water, a torture method called 'submarine'. Later they were forcibly returned by air to Uruguay where they were detained, tortured again, and falsely accused of crimes carrying jail terms of 15 to 30 years. In another incident, heavily armed military men dressed in civilian clothes forced their way into residences for refugees run by NGOs for the UNHCR in Buenos Aires and took thirteen handcuffed refugees away to be tortured. According to testimony taken by the UNHCR:

The refugee was conducted into a dark room, where only one spotlight illuminated the victim. He was left hanging on his back bound by his hands and swinging from one side to the other. Electric poles were attached to his neck, wrists, waist and testicles. On the floor was a wet stone. When the hanging man tried to stand on this stone, the electric current went through the refugee's body. During the whole time, music was playing. The refugee was interrogated about his political activities in Chile and about his political affiliation. The interrogators were well informed and knew everything that they were asking the refugees. They asked for the personnel of the CCAI, the agency working for the UNHCR, and for the UNHCR Regional Office, and insulted these institutions. Finally they told the refugee that now would be the last chance to say something and put a cowl on his head. They put a cord around his head and lifted him up so that he was not able to say a word. This happened several times and finally the treatment ended. The cries of the tortured were taken in by tape-recorders, and played back afterwards, when the treatment was repeated. The victim was led to the room where the others were waiting and the next one was taken out to be tortured. (UNHCR Archives HCR/600/ARG, 20 July 1976).

The UNHCR faced an impossible situation in Argentina. Not only the refugees but also anybody collaborating with or representing the refugees—including the UNHCR, NGOs, lawyers or social workers—was in danger of being detained, kidnapped, tortured, or killed. Argentinian officials accused the UNHCR of politicization and left-wing infiltration.[68] In response to these attacks on refugees and to agencies protecting and assisting them, the UNHCR made several protests and diplomatic *demarches* to the Argentinian authorities. Alarmed at the disturbing cables that had been coming in from his officials in Buenos Aires, Sadruddin made several personal appeals on the refugees' behalf.[69] Argentine officials flatly dismissed these complaints as constituting unacceptable interference in their domestic affairs and a violation of their national sovereignty. In his opening remarks at the annual Excom meeting in Geneva, the High Commissioner expressed his frustration and dismay at events in Argentina:

Mr. Chairman, distinguished delegates. Once again we meet in the calm and peaceful atmosphere of Geneva to discuss human problems which stand in sharp contrast to the quiet environment. Let me illustrate through concrete examples: on 18 May in a Latin American country two refugees who were both well-known personalities in their country of origin were abducted from their residence very early in the morning by a non-identified armed group. Three days later their corpses were discovered along with those of two other refugees in an abandoned car. (From Sadruddin's opening statement to the UNHCR Executive Committee on October 4, 1976. Cited in Iain Guest, *Behind the Disappearances*: 110).

The Argentinian delegate to Excom responded angrily accusing the UNHCR of being linked to 'subversion and terrorism'.[70]

The situation appeared so desperate that for the first time ever, the UNHCR even considered submitting information it had collected on human rights abuses against refugees to the UN Human Rights Commission. The decision to provide information generated an intense discussion among the UNHCR's senior staff in Geneva. Some staff expressed the view that the discussions at the UN Human Rights Commission often led to politicized debates, 'which [the] UNHCR should not feed'. They also feared that confidential information would be leaked and that, if the Office agreed to report on Argentina, it would set a precedent that would require the UNHCR to report in the future on other countries as well. Finally, staff members felt that they had ways and means other than the Commission to make their position known, and to intervene on violations of human rights of refugees. Despite these reservations, the group decided that the UNHCR Statute permitted the agency to co-operate with other UN bodies and that 'the situation like the one the refugees are suffering in Argentina' made it necessary for the Office to prepare a paper for the Commission. It was decided that the information provided would be 'cold and factual' and would not involve the Office in a political debate.[71]

All of these efforts initially seem to have had little effect on the military regime. For a time, Argentina successfully prevented international condemnation of its human rights abuses.[72] The UNHCR did not follow up this first initiative on human rights reporting with additional submissions to the UN Human Rights Commission. Instead, the UNHCR focused its activities on obtaining visas to relocate refugees and to resettle them abroad as quickly as possible. Reluctance to criticize governments for their human rights policies or to co-operate closely with UN human rights bodies remained a cornerstone of UNHCR policy until the 1990s.

The situation in Argentina deteriorated further in August 1976 when the government issued decree 1483/76 requiring all persons residing illegally in Argentina, who were unable to return to their countries of origin because of fear of persecution, to register with the authorities before November. While in several cases this procedure resulted in the granting of new residence permits to some refugees, others were not accepted for permanent residence and had to leave the country. In their urgent quest for quick exits abroad, many of them crowded into the refugee reception centres. From July 1977, lists began to be issued by the Argentinian authorities indicating whether those who had complied with the decree were eligible for residence status. The remainder, along with those refugees who had refused to comply with the registration requirement were obliged to seek resettlement or, where feasible, voluntary repatriation. A wide variety of countries—some in Latin America itself, others as far as Sweden, France and Canada—responded to the High Commissioner's appeal. In the year after the 1976 military *coup*, the UNHCR resettled 5,500 refugees. The caseload gradually diminished further until there were fewer than a hundred refugees still waiting in reception centres in Argentina at the end of 1979.

The Latin American programmes had been immensely difficult and trying operations for the UNHCR. The military *coup* in Chile, along with the military takeovers in Uruguay in 1972 and in Argentina in 1976 and political repression in Bolivia, Brazil, and Paraguay, led to the increased involvement of the international refugee regime in the affairs of the Western Hemisphere. The Latin American crises spawned a worldwide diaspora as the exiles were resettled in forty-four different countries. This was done with the assistance of the UNHCR, which rapidly expanded its presence on the continent in order to respond to these developments. Prior to 1973, a single UNHCR Regional office in Buenos Aires covered all refugee problems south of the Rio Grande; by the end of the decade, it had offices in Brazil, Chile, Costa Rica, Honduras, Mexico, and Peru.

The UNHCR and Europe

During most of the Sadruddin era, the UNHCR had few problems in Western Europe. In the 1960s and 1970s, the UNHCR was still primarily a European agency with European values. The Office had great influence on the majority of the governments in the region. Most states demonstrated a generally liberal attitude toward asylum-seekers. In Europe the UNHCR's mastery on refugee issues derived from the legal authority it embodied and its control over information and technical expertise on refugee and asylum law and procedures. For most governments, the UNHCR was the guardian of refugee law. Its legal protection division interpreted the norms, rules, legalities, and procedures of refugee law and determined how these should be implemented by states. The UNHCR's legal authority made states willing to submit to UNHCR guidance and to allow them to oversee national and regional responses to refugees. Therefore, in Europe the UNHCR could focus on improving legal and social conditions for refugees. During the 1960s and 1970s, governments promulgated a series of measures—including work permits, social welfare benefits, and language training—that were relatively generous and fair. The UNHCR was also the repository of information and expertise about refugee and asylum matters. Its staff had specialized technical knowledge, training, and expertise that was not immediately available to the interior and justice ministries of many European states. Thus in Europe, unlike in the United States, the UNHCR played an active role in the refugee determination procedures of many states and exerted a considerable influence over government decisions.[73] The UNHCR's expertise also enabled it to shape state policies and to promote further expansion of refugee norms in Europe. Thus, throughout the 1960s and 1970s, European governments, through the Committee of Ministers and the Parliamentary Assembly of the Council of Europe and advised by the UNHCR, adopted various conventions, resolutions, and recommendations to strengthen the legal protection of refugees.[74]

The UNHCR's authority in Europe and elsewhere also derived from its claim to be an independent and neutral agent whose objective was simply to carry out the rules of the international community as laid down in the refugee instruments. Sadruddin frequently presented himself as the representative of an international humanitarian agency whose purpose was entirely non political. During most of his tenure as High Commissioner, he successfully maintained his image as the representative of the international community as embodied in the rules and resolutions of the United Nations and not as the instrument of the great powers. The claim to neutrality and apolitical decision-making coupled with its expert status and authority in refugee law enabled the UNHCR to exert great influence in Europe and elsewhere. Not surprisingly, it was during this period that the legal norms and rules became the *raison d'être* of the UNHCR. These permeated the culture of the UNHCR and greatly empowered the Division of Legal Protection over other parts of the organization.

Relatively liberal asylum policies in Western Europe were also facilitated by the fact that, until the early 1960s, nearly all the refugees who sought asylum in the region were generated by political repression and harsh economic conditions accompanying the transformation of eastern European states into Communist regimes. Throughout this period, Communist bloc refugees—Hungarians, Czechs, and East Germans among others—were accepted into the West with little scrutiny into their motives for departure. While the UNHCR concentrated on improving the legal and social conditions for refugees, it left the resettlement and transport of Communist bloc refugees to the American-led ICEM. By the early 1960s, this influx had largely subsided because fewer people were able to flee from behind the Iron Curtain and because the emerging political *détente* between East and West improved conditions in Eastern Europe.

The Warsaw Pact invasion of Czechoslovakia in 1968 and the subsequent refugee outflow reignited concern in Europe about East–West flows. The crisis resulted primarily from internal conditions in Czechoslovakia. Political liberalization under Alexander Dubcek alarmed neighbouring Eastern European regimes, particularly East Germany and Poland. Fearing that the 'Czechoslovakian disease' would spread, the leaders of these two hard-line Communist regimes—Ulbricht and Gomulka respectively—applied pressure on the Soviet Union to intervene in Czechoslovakia. On 20 August 1968, the Red Army invaded Czechoslovakia, with the support of smaller units from Bulgaria, East Germany, Hungary, and Poland. The invasion was justified by the 'Brezhnev doctrine' which stipulated that a socialist nation was duty bound to intervene in another socialist nation if socialism was threatened. The invasion produced fairly muted diplomatic reactions from the West. While the United States and most other Western powers disapproved of the invasion, they remained intent on continuing the policy of *détente*.

The Czech emergency, unlike the Hungarian crisis of 1956, did not confront the world with a major Cold War refugee crisis. Few people were killed and there was not an outpouring of people seeking refuge in neighbouring countries. At the time of the invasion some 80,000 Czech nationals were abroad, most of them were tourists or students visiting Austria, Italy, Switzerland, the UK, West Germany, and the US.[75] Most of these people did not seek to apply for asylum immediately but preferred to wait and see how the situation evolved in Czechoslovakia before deciding on a course of action. Host countries co-operated by adopting generous visa and employment policies so as to allow visiting Czechs to stay temporarily in order to carefully assess the situation back home. Neither the UNHCR nor host countries wanted to create 'an artificial refugee problem' by giving refugee status to tourists who might one day wish to return home and, therefore, were careful not to label the Czechs as refugees.[76] Nearly 43,000 returned home within two weeks of the invasion. There was little sense of crisis and the High Commissioner himself felt confident enough to be absent from Geneva for several weeks in September on mission to the Nordic countries and North Africa.

In September 1968, the new Czechoslovakian government urged its citizens to return home from abroad, promising that they would not be persecuted. Despite these assurances, increasing numbers of Czechs applied for refugee status over the next several months. Because most Czechs were highly educated and qualified, it was relatively easy for the UNHCR to find countries which would resettle them.[77] Not surprisingly, they were generally welcomed in Western Europe and were the recipients of resettlement offers from a number of other countries, including Australia, Canada, Iran, and South Africa. Although the US government established no special programme for them, American NGOs did bring some to the United States, and others found their own way there. Some 12,000 entered the US, but unlike the entry of the Hungarian freedom fighters twelve years earlier, their resettlement went virtually unnoticed.

The Czech crisis also led to an increased outflow to Western Europe of refugees from Bulgaria, Hungary, Poland, and Romania. In Austria, the total number of asylum-seekers from these countries reached 6,000 in 1968—double the number of the previous few years.[78] In addition, increasing numbers of Third World refugees arrived in Europe, many from previously dependent territories. By far the largest influxes into Western Europe during these years were primarily from countries with which it had earlier political and cultural links. In the early 1960s, for example, France had opened its doors to hundreds of thousands of Algerians and also to Tunisian Jews expelled during the 1967 Arab–Israeli war. Between 1961 and 1977 some 140,000 Cubans took advantage of air links maintained between Havana and Madrid to find asylum in Spain. In the mid-1970s, an estimated 600,000 returnees flooded into Portugal after independence was granted to Angola, Guinea Bissau, and Mozambique in what was proportionately the greatest post-colonial influx into any European state.

De facto Refugees and Quota Programmes in the 1970s

In addition, entirely new categories of asylum-seekers began to arrive in Europe from closely aligned Western states. Draft evaders and deserters from Greece, Portugal, and the United States who fled repressive regimes and unpopular foreign wars sought asylum in Western European countries.[79] These new asylum-seekers confronted European ministers with unusually difficult political problems. European governments were reluctant to grant full refugee status to these groups of asylum-seekers because they did not fulfil the strict criteria for refugee status as laid down in the 1951 Refugee convention. But Western policy-makers also feared that recognition of refugee status for these groups might lead to a deterioration in relations with the countries of origin who were close political and military allies. Despite these reservations, certain countries, especially in Scandinavia, considered it unacceptable to return war resisters to countries fighting wars considered unjust by the international community, or to military regimes violating human rights. In response, European governments created a special humanitarian status for persons in 'refugee-like situations', calling them *de facto* refugees.[80]

The UNHCR was divided on the question of *de facto* refugees and preferred to leave the initiative to governments. While the UNHCR advocated a liberal refugee recognition practice in European states, the Office was concerned that the creation of two separate refugee statuses would undermine the legal status of refugees as outlined in the 1951 Refugee Convention. There was particular concern that if European governments created a separate legal instrument regulating the status of *de facto* refugees, this would make the UNHCR's protection task more difficult:

. . . it would unavoidably result in the creation of two separate categories of refugees, one of which would benefit from a less favourable treatment than the other. It would be the task of the Office to insist that full-fledged refugees, i.e., 1951 Convention refugees, get the full benefits to which they are entitled. This would not be an easy task as there would certainly be a tendency, already observable in countries where so-called "B status" exists, to grant the refugees the minimum treatment. Remedial action would consist in trying to persuade governments to abide by their obligations in accordance with the 1951 Convention and drawing a clear distinction between the two categories of refugees. (UNHCR Archives, HCR/611, 2 October 1975, *De Facto Refugees*).

Some UNHCR staff members correctly foresaw that, as numerical and financial pressures on the European asylum system grew, governments would grant fewer asylum-seekers Convention status and greater numbers *de facto* status.

In addition to the arrival of *de facto* refugees, the second major development in Western European responses to refugee flows during this period was the adoption of quota programmes for specific refugee groups. Quota programmes were mainly motivated by public outcry about human rights abuses and by the pressures of public opinion on Western governments to take action and to 'do something' to save the victims of repressive regimes. Two groups in particular—the Chilean and Indo-Chinese refugees—benefited most from the quota programmes during the 1970s. In later years, the programmes were extended to Argentinians, Bolivians, Brazilians, and Central Americans.

In devising quota programmes, governments reserved a limited number of resettlement places for members of certain nationalities who required urgent resettlement because their lives were threatened. These determinations were made by governments in close consultation with the UNHCR and NGOs. They were automatically granted Convention status, often without close examination of their claim to refugee status, on the assumption that members of this specific group faced persecution in their homelands. Quota programmes were acceptable to governments because, unlike asylum-seekers who arrived spontaneously, refugees were specifically accepted for resettlement from abroad and arrived in an orderly manner.

Pressure for resettlement of Third World refugees was relieved by improved economic conditions in the 1950s and 1960s. During this period of rapid economic expansion, Western European nations needed labour and easily absorbed not only the hundreds of thousands of returning citizens from their former colonies and territories and the thousands of asylum-seekers from Eastern Europe and the developing world, but also the millions of actively recruited manual labourers. There were the so-called 'guest workers' and they came from former colonies in Africa, Asia, and the Caribbean and from Southern Europe.

As long as the economic situation remained generally buoyant and labour migration was clearly in the interest of the industrialized states, the feasibility of maintaining liberal refugee and labour migration policies in Europe was not seriously questioned. However, with the oil price shock of 1973, subsequent economic recession, and high unemployment in Europe, this welcoming attitude toward migrant workers and refugees began to change. With severely reduced demand for external labour in Western countries, most European governments introduced legislation that largely halted immigration flows. Western European governments had never intended the guest worker programmes of the 1960s to lead to long-term resettlement. With the onset of labour surpluses during the 1970s, they expected most of the guest workers to return home. Despite the withdrawal of the welcome mat and the offer of material inducements to leave, the majority of such workers stayed. Immigration levels actually increased during the rest of the decade, as immediate family members were brought over to join those who had entered as guest workers.

The immigration stop and the cessation of guest worker programmes in Europe coincided with the arrival of greater numbers of asylum-seekers from the Third World who came spontaneously and without prior screening. Most fled civil war, the consequences of natural disasters, economic decline, and external aggression as well as individual persecution. The nature of their arrival, by air and often without travel documents or with false ones, led to new government restrictions on asylum and to the rise of irregular movements and 'refugees in orbit'—those who are shunted from state to state.[81] The situation was further complicated when large numbers of economic migrants, who previously would have entered as guest workers, began to apply for refugee status in the hope of obtaining work and residence permits. The combination of all these factors would lead to an asylum crisis, widespread restrictionism, racial tension, and a considerable loss of authority and influence for the UNHCR in Europe during the 1980s and 1990s.

Sadruddin and the United States: An Anomalous Relationship

Throughout his 12 years as High Commissioner, Sadruddin had an anomalous relationship with the United States. The UNHCR was dependent on the US for financial assistance and funding and Sadruddin persistently sought greater American contributions for what he regarded as genuine refugee situations. Yet the High Commissioner was reluctant to get the UNHCR involved in crises which he considered were voluntary migrations disguised as legitimate refugee exoduses. Such were the 1965 exodus from Cuba to Florida, the mass displacements in South Vietnam during the war, and the early stages of the refugee outflow from Indo-China after the 1975 Communist victories.

Africa was one region where Sadruddin hoped for close UNHCR-US collaboration. He frequently reminded American policy-makers that the focus of the global refugee problem now centred on Africa and that the UNHCR played a useful role in contributing to overall US security objectives by promoting order and stability on the continent through responding to refugee problems.[82] While providing a useful stabilizing role in Africa, the UNHCR, in line with general UN policy at the time, also provided important support for Africa's national liberation movements. UNHCR support for Africa's liberation fighters was seen by the US as a useful conduit for keeping indirect contact with these groups.

Sadruddin also played an extremely useful and unpublicized role for the United States in the Middle East, acting as an intermediary in trying to persuade Middle Eastern governments to release some of the Jews and Christian minorities in Egypt, Iraq, and Syria. Some 100,000 Jews still lived in Arab countries. The High Commissioner made frequent trips to the Middle East and because of his family connections he had high-level contacts with policy-makers and ruling élites in the region. According to the State Department, Sadruddin described his missions in the following way:

Prince Sadruddin observed that he attempts to keep channels open to all sides in the highly charged Middle East atmosphere. In doing so he must move very cautiously and runs considerable risks not only for himself personally but also for the Office of the High Commissioner. He is discreetly keeping the Israelis fully informed of his efforts on behalf of Jews and thus risks losing the confidence of the Arabs. On the other hand, he is 'trying to bring justice to the Middle East' and thus runs the risk of losing the confidence of the Israelis. The Israelis, however, take pains to keep him informed about such matters as prisoner of war exchanges and general relations with the International Red Cross. Israeli Ambassador Kidron in Geneva is personally helpful in this discreet exchange of information. (US National Archives, Diplomatic Branch, REF 3, UNHCR, Box 3055, 19 November 1969).

The UNHCR also provided a channel for Jews exiting Middle Eastern countries to transit camps in Turkey and Europe on their way to permanent resettlement in Israel or other countries.[83] For example, at the end of the 1967 Arab–Israeli war, thousands of Jews fled from Libya to Italy and from Tunisia for France. Other Jews left Aden, Lebanon, Morocco, and the UAR for scattered European destinations. The Libyan Jews in Italy were in a particularly destitute condition. The United States believed the UNHCR to be politically neutral and therefore far less subject to attack from Arab or North African countries than an American NGO, and so authorized a special $125,000 grant to the UNHCR to assist these refugees.[84]

In spite of his obvious usefulness to American interests in the Middle East and Africa, the United States tried to keep Sadruddin on a short leash by not funding the UNHCR to the same extent it did other international refugee programmes. In 1968, for instance, while the US provided $600,000 to the UNHCR for its worldwide annual budget, it gave approximately $1.3 million to the ICEM for refugee and migrant programming, $700,000 for new refugees from Eastern European countries, and some $54 million in caring for Cuban refugees in the United States.[85] At times, Sadruddin was outspoken about the lack of US funding for his programmes. For example, speaking at a press conference in Luxembourg, the High Commissioner criticized governments for not adequately contributing to the UNHCR's Refugee Fund and listed some examples of cases where governments could use their funds for more worthy causes. Sadruddin pointedly noted that the loss of $20 million of electronic equipment aboard the downed US intelligence ship 'Pueblo' off the coast of Korea in early 1968 was sufficient to cover the UNHCR's Refugee Fund deficits for the next ten years. He then mentioned the four hydrogen bombs which the US had lost in Greenland, and said that the American government could have better used the money spent on those bombs by giving it to the Refugee Fund.[86] The High Commissioner felt that the US and NGO's focus on Eastern European refugees and other refugees fleeing Communist regimes discriminated against the UNHCR in favour of other humanitarian organizations.[87] This led to increasing tensions not only between Sadruddin and the US but also between the UNHCR and the ICEM. After an improvement in co-operation between the two agencies under Lindt and Schnyder, UNHCR relations with the ICEM deteriorated during the late 1960s.

US Asylum Policy and the UNHCR

During the late 1960s and early 1970s, US asylum policy remained directly tied to larger American foreign policy interests, principally in Europe but also in the Caribbean. Asylum decisions during these years continued to reflect the Cold War bias in American policy. For instance, in the three years from November 1970 to October 1973, the State Department issued advisory opinions on 1100 asylum applications, recommending in favour of asylum for all 110 applicants from Eastern Europe but for only 20 of the 990 asylum applicants from other areas.[88] Unlike in Western Europe, where UNHCR influence was great, the US deliberately kept the UNHCR out of all asylum decisions. And unlike the asylum policy promoted by the UNHCR–which required a commitment from all the signatories of the 1951 Refugee Convention that they would not return those genuinely fearful of persecution at the hands of any regime to their place of origin–the US approach to asylum-seekers was rooted in a clear anti-Communist ideology. In October 1965, the US had passed the *Immigration Reform Act*, which abolished the national origins quota system and provided special immigration opportunities for refugees fleeing 'Communist or Communist-dominated lands'. The 1965 Amendments to the *Immigration Act* had created a new 'seventh preference' status for entrants from the eastern hemisphere. This reserved 6 per cent of the visas made available under the new system for

aliens who . . . because of persecution or fear of persecution on account of race, religion or political opinion have fled . . . from any Communist or Communist-dominated country or area, or . . . from any country within the general area of the Middle East . . . or are persons uprooted by catastrophic natural calamities as defined by the President who are unable to return to their usual place of abode. (Section 1153(a)(7), Title 8, United States Code).[89]

By adopting an ideologically based refugee definition, the Congress thus institutionalized the American practice of admitting refugees according to Cold War preferences. Thus the 1965 amendments to the Immigration Act officially endorsed the practice, common since the late 1940s, of equating refugee with someone turning his or her back on Communism.

The new US immigration legislation coincided with a new wave of Cuban migration which began in October 1965. The boat influx to Florida was ushered in by two speeches. One was delivered in Havana by Fidel Castro inveighing against his domestic critics, inviting them to leave; the other was delivered by President Lyndon Johnson at the foot of the Statue of Liberty proclaiming the United States a land of freedom with room for all the Cubans who might seek to enter. Johnson declared, 'I have directed the Departments of State, Justice, and Health, Education, and Welfare to immediately make all the necessary arrangements to permit those in Cuba who seek freedom to make an orderly entry into the United States of America.'

During this period and until 1980, Cubans were welcomed without close examination into their motives for leaving Cuba. The United States made no effort to involve the UNHCR in its Cuban admissions programme. The 'freedom flights' served important symbolic purposes. Departure from Cuba was viewed as a demonstration of the economic and political repression of a Communist regime and was treated as a 'ballot for freedom'.[90]

However, for those whose entry to the United States served no Cold War purpose, but instead tended to embarrass American allies, there was no open-ended welcome. Over the years, a sharp double standard favouring Cuban 'anti-Communists' over Haitian entrants developed. Official US attitudes toward Haitian arrivals and the conditions they fled reflected progressively cozier relations between the United States and the government of Haiti who lent the US anti-Castro support at the price of increased tolerance of their human rights abuses.[91] The UNHCR's attempts to shift official American attention to the actual plight of particular Haitian boat people, and to the conditions in Haiti which brought them to the United States, were remarkably unsuccessful.

Haitians began to enter the United States in significant numbers in 1957 when Francois Duvalier transformed Haiti into a personal instrument of power, self-aggrandizement, and terror.[92] Those who resisted Duvalier's tyranny were systematically silenced, and tens of thousands of Haitians fled for their personal safety. Although never the beneficiaries of the strong rhetorical support which the Cubans received, the Haitians who arrived in the United States between 1957 and 1971 were generally tolerated. As a consequence, virtual refugee status was granted to Haitian entrants without any examination of individual persecution claims. However, none were ever officially categorized as refugees, and the formal steps to relax US immigration rules for Cubans, including the practice of waiving the visa requirement altogether, and the passage of legislation to grant earlier arrivals 'permanent resident' status were not taken for the Haitians. Consequently, even the most 'political' of the Haitians—active opponents of the Duvalier regime—were denied the certain asylum granted most Cubans. Unlike Cubans, Haitians were never characterized as voting with their feet against an oppressive regime, nor was there any US effort to portray the Duvalier regime as one of the most abusive in the world. It was not in the US national interest to characterize Haitians as victims of persecution. During much of this time, the UNHCR played no monitoring role and made no demands on the US to make a more searching evaluation of individual claims or to grant asylum.

Jean Claude Duvalier's accession to the presidency of Haiti in 1971 was marked by a significant increase in Haitian migration to the United States. Beginning in late 1972, a continuous flow of boatloads of Haitians seeking political asylum began to land in south Florida. In contrast to previous flows to the US, greater numbers of those arriving were poor, uneducated, and of rural origin. The increase in emigration did not result from a sudden worsening in political conditions. Instead, it reflected spreading dissatisfaction with every aspect of Haitian existence, grinding poverty, lack of opportunity, corruption, lack of political freedom, and failure to provide the average man or woman with any protection—legal or otherwise—against the avarice and the brutality of the state.[93]

In the eight years prior to the passage of the US *Refugee Act* of 1980, as many as 30,000 Haitians entered the United States by boat. Thousands sought asylum, but only fewer than fifty of these applicants were granted political asylum or its equivalent.[94] The rest were subjected to treatment totally unlike that afforded Cuban migrants, and totally inconsistent with the explicit terms and the underlying objectives of international refugee instruments. Initially, the INS denied 'excludable' Haitians the right to any formal hearing on their asylum claims. Excludable generally meant those apprehended in the high seas or immediately after reaching shore. Late in 1970, informal procedures were adopted.[95] Nevertheless, return to Haiti was automatic and immediate. New INS regulations adopted in 1974 provided for hearings but permitted the summary disposition of most asylum cases.

In 1969, the US had signed and ratified the 1967 Protocol on Refugees. By its accession to the Protocol, the United States had obligated itself not to expel those meeting the international refugee definition, provided they claimed asylum after reaching the US. It was not possible to determine which Haitians had a 'well-founded fear of persecution' without individually evaluating each case. The new streamlined US procedures, in contravention of standards promulgated by the UNHCR, were not tailored to produce careful evaluations or to give the benefit of the doubt to Haitian applicants.

After Haitians began arriving by boat in large numbers to claim political asylum, a conflict between the UNHCR and the US began to develop over eligibility determinations. This was well after the US took active steps to send Haitians back home and to prevent them from coming. UNHCR officials were generally reluctant to voice open criticism of US asylum policies. Yet, during Sadruddin's period, they did make behind-the-scenes efforts, sometimes with the support of American NGOs, to modify US policy regarding the forcible return of Haitian asylum-seekers. In March 1974, for example, the UNHCR protested about the suicide of a Haitian asylum-seeker detained in Dade City jail. The UNHCR reminded the State Department of the Office's concerns regarding the manner in which requests of asylum by Haitians were treated.[96] This protest was followed up by a meeting between the High Commissioner and US Ambassador Kellogg in New York.[97] Kellogg informed Sadruddin of assurances he had personally received from President Duvalier that there were no political prisoners in Haiti and that no returnees would be persecuted. In reply, Sadruddin stated that 'while we may get guarantees from any country', it was not always possible to check on the fate of those who are returned. The High Commissioner told Kellogg he needed to be vigilant, no less in relation to a Haitian than in relation to 'someone who might enter Finland from Estonia'. Sadruddin expressed his concern that those claiming to be refugees, whether from Haiti or anywhere else, be given a hearing as laid down in the Convention and Protocol. He stated that if there was the slightest risk to a person, then he should not be deported to his country of origin. The problem, according to the High Commissioner, was assuring that the occasional person who may indeed face a risk in returning be given the benefit of the doubt. In practice, this meant giving Haitian asylum-seekers an appropriate opportunity to have a hearing.

In order to gain independent information concerning the internal situation in Haiti, Sadruddin dispatched, one of his own staff, Dr Schlatter, to Port au Prince. Upon his return, Schlatter reported that although political prisoners existed in Haiti, he believed that systematic persecution for political reasons no longer occured there. He did believe, however, that people, who during their time abroad had been involved in an organization considered subversive by the Haitian authorities or had made derogatory statements to the press, could be subject to persecution upon return.[98] The UNHCR's position on Haitian asylum-seekers represented a middle ground between that of the INS and the Department of State, which collectively concluded that Haitians were, by and large, economic migrants and virtually no Haitians were genuine political refugees,[99] and that of concerned church groups and human rights NGOs, which concluded that conditions in Haiti were so universally bad that virtually all who departed, however much they hoped to improve their lot in the United States, were in fact fleeing persecution.[100]

US Congressional hearings held in 1975 and 1976[101] demonstrated that untrained American immigration officials systematically denied Haitian asylum-seekers any meaningful opportunity to present their claims or to receive individualized evaluation of their purported fear of persecution. They also revealed the primary role that the Department of State played in the asylum decision process. Although the INS had always been entrusted with the duty of evaluating individual asylum claims, prior to 1980 it was required to seek an advisory opinion from the State Department on doubtful cases and on those which the INS considered to be without substance. The hearings showed that State Department officials within the Office of Refugee and Migration Affairs (ORM) customarily rendered opinions on applicants whom they had never interviewed and whose files were woefully incomplete. They also demonstrated the key role played by the Haitian desk officer who automatically reviewed the applicant's claim before the State Department issued its advisory opinion. Such review was crucial because the applicant was required to demonstrate that his fear of persecution was due to political conditions inside Haiti and resulted from his activities or organizational affiliations. Yet the determinations of the desk officers were often based on the unexamined assumption that Haitian asylum claims were not valid. In very few instances were cases ever referred to the US Embassy in Port-au-Prince for further verification or investigation, nor was much effort expended to monitor returnees. Moreover, the Embassy had no guidelines for review of such asylum claims and did not have enough personnel to carry through a monitoring effort.[102] Thus decisions were made on the basis of considerations having little to do with individual fear of persecution and much to do with relations with a country considered to be an ally of the United States.

The problem with such procedures, and with the virtually certain deportation that followed, was that the US made it almost impossible for any individual Haitian to demonstrate that he or she was genuinely fearful of persecution. Thus a negative presumption, built into the summary asylum procedure itself, deprived particular applicants of the opportunity to prove that they had particular experiences or threats that had forced them to flee in fear of their lives or personal safety. The UNHCR frequently protested such procedures. In particular, it emphasized the need to establish a more credible practice in which asylum-seekers would not be detained for undue periods and would be authorized to seek employment while their applications were under consideration. It also pointed out that there was a need for more consistent follow-up on the treatment received by those who had been returned to Haiti.[103]

For the most part, however, the effect of UNHCR interventions on US asylum policy was marginal at best. The United States was able to take refuge in its very limited reading of the law to expel Haitians while it continued to admit Cubans. While the US tailored its refugee policy in this discriminatory fashion and paid little attention to its international obligations, the UNHCR remained essentially an outsider. Apart from reviewing a token number of cases, the Office was not invited to participate in asylum decision-making and was fearful of unduly antagonizing the United States. Thus, UNHCR had relatively little impact in securing better asylum treatment for Haitian asylum-seekers during the 1970s. Their influence would diminish further during the 1980s when large numbers of Central American and Caribbean refugees would seek entry to the United States.

Vietnam: The Roots of a Long-Term UNHCR Commitment

The UNHCR also had little influence in Indo-China. During the Vietnam War, an estimated half of South Vietnam's 20 million population was uprooted. Millions of Laotians and Cambodians—also caught up in violent and indiscriminate warfare—fled from the countryside into the cities and refugee camps. The population of Saigon swelled from 1.8 to 3.8 million; and by war's end the majority of the rural population of the three Indo-Chinese countries had moved into the cities for safety. The economic and social effects of these forced migrations were devastating to the rural economies; massive relief assistance was required just to keep people alive.

UN agencies did not give significant aid for the relief of Vietnam's war victims. The UNHCR considered the political impediments to initiating a major programme too great. The North Vietnamese government and the Provisional Revolutionary Government of South Vietnam (PRG) did not want UN involvement in the war zones. Moreover, Sadruddin initially took the position that the mass displacement in South Vietnam was a domestic problem and an American responsibility, but not a genuine refugee problem falling within his mandate. Nevertheless, pressures mounted on the UNHCR to take some action in the region. In 1967, the UNHCR channelled 100,000 Swiss francs from the Swiss Federal Government to the Cambodian authorities to aid Khmer refugees coming from South Vietnam.[104] In 1968, Virendra Dayal, a close adviser to Sadruddin, distributed a memorandum on South-East Asia within the Office. Noting the UNHCR's inaction in 1965 to Indonesia's massacres of its Chinese residents, Dayal complained that the UNHCR had 'hitherto, remained an onlooker in this region' and argued that 'this region is not receiving the attention which it should from this Office'.[105] Dayal's initiative led to the commissioning of a survey to examine the specific refugee problems of the region, the attitudes of governments to international involvement, and the extent to which the UNHCR could help achieve solutions to refugee problems in the area.[106] In 1969, a detailed survey was made of the refugee situations in the various South-East Asian countries and of the political difficulties governments had in agreeing to UNHCR intervention, but the Office took no formal position on expanding its presence in the region at that time.

No meaningful UNHCR involvement in the region took place until after March 1970 when Prince Sihanouk was overthrown by General Lon Nol. In April a combined US-South Vietnam military force intervened in Cambodia. During the next several months, anti-Vietnamese riots broke out in Cambodia and thousands of Vietnamese residents were attacked and killed. About 200,000 ethnic Vietnamese refugees fled Cambodia to South Vietnam. Since these were in fact refugees within the mandate of the High Commissioner, the Government of South Vietnam requested assistance from the UNHCR. Sadruddin allocated $50,000 each from his Emergency Fund to the South Vietnamese government and the Cambodian Red Cross, and sent a *Chargé de mission* to Saigon. The directives to the new *Chargé* made clear that the UNHCR presence in Saigon was required not only to assist the refugees from Cambodia but also to monitor 'the fluid situation in the Indochinese peninsula [which] may cause further movements of population which could be of direct concern to [the] UNHCR, either in the RVN or in neighboring countries'.[107] But it was also the case that the UNHCR continued to take an extremely limited view of its responsibilities in Indo-China. The new *Chargé* was informed, '[The] UNHCR cannot consider itself committed as a matter of principle to assist even those refugees in the RVN who come within the sphere of our competence, without a close scrutiny of numbers and financial means required.'[108]

UN interest in Indo-China began in earnest in 1973, following the Paris peace agreements on Vietnam and Laos. Realizing that the end of the Vietnam War would require a massive reconstruction programme in the region, the UNHCR, the UNICEF and other specialized UN agencies began actively to seek a share of the funding and programmes targeted for the region. Sensing the future importance of Indo-China to the UN, Sadruddin began to make overtures to all the parties on all sides of the Indo-China conflict, including Hanoi and the Vietcong, and offered humanitarian aid to the millions of people internally displaced by war. The UNHCR had opened an office in Bangkok in 1972. Further expansion took place in October 1974, when it established a regional office in Vientiane, Laos, and in November that year opened a branch office in Hanoi. The UNHCR developed a programme in 1974 for $12.5 million for assistance to the uprooted and displaced persons in North Vietnam, Laos, the territories of the Provisional Revolutionary Government in South Vietnam, and the territory of the Government of South Vietnam. A joint UNHCR/UNICEF Emergency Relief Operation collected over $17 million from donors for relief to Indo-Chinese war victims.

In 1975, while the UNHCR was preparing to further expand its presence in Indo-China, the pro-American regimes in Phnom Penh, Saigon, and Vientiane started to unravel as Communist forces mounted successful military offences against them. The fall of these governments precipitated an instantaneous refugee crisis which demanded immediate attention from the

United States. American policy-makers were presented with an emergency in which a large number of people with whom the US had been allied were threatened with harm. These potential victims of a Communist takeover vividly symbolized America's failed crusade in Vietnam and bore witness to the end of America's long, and frustrating involvement in Indo-China. The United States felt a profound sense of obligation to the Vietnamese and initiated an admissions programme that would rescue 130,000 of them.

The downfall of the South Vietnamese government and the speed with which the final collapse occurred were not anticipated. Many US government officials had expected the South Vietnamese army and the Saigon government to survive longer, despite US intelligence reporting to the contrary. But in March 1975, several South Vietnamese highland cities fell to a Communist military offensive, and panic ensued when President Thieu responded by ordering his army to retreat. Over 1 million refugees retreated from the highlands and headed southward and to the coast.

Until the last moment, the Ford administration worked hard to persuade Congress to approve its proposed aid package to Thieu to bolster the South Vietnamese regime and to prevent a military defeat and evacuation. It was only after the US Senate Armed Services Committee actually voted down the $722 million supplemental aid request which signalled the last hope for a military reversal in Vietnam that the administration belatedly called for an evacuation from South Vietnam. As originally planned, the Vietnamese were to be removed to neighbouring South-East Asian countries. However, the US Inter-agency Task Force in charge of the evacuation, sensing regional opposition to the granting long-term asylum, shelved this plan and decided instead to transport them directly to the United States. The decision to evacuate Vietnamese through US bases and Guam would make later efforts to internationalize the subsequent resettlement of Indo-Chinese refugees more difficult.

Most of the world perceived the refugees who where escaping Saigon as America's responsibility. Although the US Mission in Geneva had requested assistance from the UNHCR and the ICEM in locating third countries willing to accept refugees from Indo-China, there was little indication from the beginning of the crisis that efforts at internationalization, or burden sharing, would be successful.[109] Most of the UN, including the UN Secretary-General, Kurt Waldheim, and Prince Sadruddin, viewed the Indo-China crisis as an American problem and as the almost inevitable aftermath of years of American involvement. From a legal and political standpoint the UNHCR doubted that the Indo-Chinese were bona fide refugees. Rather it was the UNHCR's perception that the evacuations were American operations, and it was not UNHCR policy to take care of America's allies to the exclusion of other refugees.[110] The UNHCR also did not want to become too closely identified with the former Vietnamese client regime of the United States so as to offend the victorious Communist regimes in Indo-China. Sadruddin wanted to maintain good relations with Hanoi, apparently because he expected his Office to play a reconstruction and development role in the postwar era.

The US was also unsuccessful in getting its allies to resettle Vietnamese refugees. Although nearly all the South-East Asian nations had originally expressed a willingness to accept the Vietnamese, they had agreed to provide asylum on the condition that the refugees be admitted only temporarily and be resettled abroad as quickly as possible. Senior members of the US Inter-agency Task Force visited European capitals to solicit resettlement offers, but nearly every major nation except France viewed the Vietnamese refugees as an American responsibility. Thus, it was clear that if the US intended to rescue any Vietnamese, it had little choice but to admit most of the evacuees into the United States.

In addition to the 130,000 refugees who were resettled in the United States, approximately 60,000 Indo-Chinese refugees escaped to Thailand and some 12,000 scattered themselves throughout the region. In July 1975, the UNHCR signed an agreement with Thailand to provide temporary assistance to the new arrivals. The Thai authorities made no commitment to provide asylum, protection, or local settlement to the refugees. Neither Thailand nor any other Asian country was a signatory to the 1951 Refugee Convention or the 1967 Protocol and therefore acknowledged no obligation to provide asylum to arriving Indo-Chinese. To Bangkok, the only long-term solution was repatriation or resettlement to a third country.

Unlike the United States, which saw resettlement as the only possible solution for those fleeing the new Communist regimes in Indo-China, the UNHCR considered voluntary repatriation to be the most appropriate solution for these refugees.[111] In June 1975, the Provisional Revolutionary Government of Vietnam notified the UNHCR that it was willing, on a case by case basis, to take back 'those Vietnamese who had recently been induced to leave their country by false propaganda or who had been taken abroad against their will and who wished to be repatriated'. Sadruddin agreed to negotiate with the Communist authorities in Vietnam to arrange for voluntary repatriation and to send UNHCR personnel to Guam and to the US to interview Vietnamese indicating a desire to return home. Repatriation was a source of constant conflict between the UNHCR and the US. In the minds of many American military administering the camps on Guam and in the US, the idea that anyone would want to go back to Vietnam seemed incredible. The US also disagreed with the UNHCR over the possibility of repatriating Laotian refugees from Thailand.[112] UNHCR staff felt that many Laotians had fled their homes because of economic hardships and believed it might be possible to repatriate them in large numbers. But the Americans had just spent years fighting Communism in the region and large-scale repatriation was simply not in their interest. The US refused to believe that any Laotian could safely return home and therefore continued to push the UNHCR to find resettlement places for them. While some Laotians and about 1,500 Vietnamese refugees did finally repatriate, the UNHCR's negotiations with Vientiane and Hanoi proved extremely difficult and slow and Vietnamese approvals for repatriation were never given. In the end, it was apparent that repatriation was not popular with the refugees, with the United States, or with the new Communist regimes in the region.

The next best option in the view of the UNHCR was local settlement and it mounted programmes to rehabilitate families uprooted by war in Vietnam and Laos.[113] In efforts directed at assisting the internally displaced, the Office transported more than 35,000 people from Vientiane to their home areas in the Plain of Jars and provided them with the means to get through the next harvest. The UNHCR even sponsored agricultural, fishing, transport, and health projects for displaced people throughout Vietnam. However popular these programmes were in Laos and Vietnam, local settlement was not favoured by most non-Communist states in South-East Asia. Thailand, in particular, did not co-operate with the UNHCR's efforts to resettle refugees there. Sadruddin proposed a scheme under which the UNHCR would continue feeding the refugees if Thailand agreed to let them settle permanently. But Thai authorities steadfastly refused to agree to local integration for fear that this would only encourage a greater influx. The numbers of refugees in the Thai camps steadily climbed to over 100,000 by the end of 1977.

Only when repatriation and local settlement proved difficult, if not impossible, did the UNHCR consider the possibility of resettlement. The United States felt that the UNHCR failed to take the initiative in finding resettlement places for the refugees. Frustrated by the lack of UN efforts to internationalize the response to Indo-Chinese refugees, the United States pressured the Secretary-General to get the UNHCR to issue a worldwide appeal in May 1975 for countries to take Indo-Chinese refugees for resettlement. While some twenty countries responded to these appeals, most countries still viewed the refugee problem as Washington's special responsibility, not their own. By 1978, the world was also starting to wake up to another humanitarian disaster in Indo-China—the genocide and 'killing fields' in Cambodia under Khmer Rouge rule. Starting in 'Year Zero' on 17 April 1975, the Communist Party of Cambodia, the Khmer Rouge, had unleashed a bloody revolution that led to some 2 million deaths and several million displaced people. Despite the fact that the Khmer Rouge killings were possibly the worst to befall a people since the Nazi holocaust, there was remarkably little reaction among the UN member states and the major powers to what was happening in Cambodia. The UNHCR turned a blind eye to the massive killings and the human rights abuses there. In response to a letter by Leo Cherne, the Chairman of the International Rescue Committee, pleading for the High Commissioner to launch a humanitarian enquiry regarding Cambodia,[114] Charles Mace, the Deputy High Commissioner noted that 'it is not within the competence of the UNHCR to make enquiries to which you refer. Possibly the Human Rights Commission of the United Nations might be interested in the matter'.[115] The UN bodies involved in protecting human rights and providing emergency relief, including the UNHCR, did not step beyond their well-established and rigid organizational routines despite the well-known Khmer Rouge atrocities.

Perhaps even more disheartening was the fact that at the time the major powers all had geopolitical reasons for not pressing the issue publicly.[116] After an ignominious defeat, the Ford administration wanted to forget about Indo-China. The Carter administration, despite its general advocacy of human rights and its belief that humanitarian concerns should factor into the foreign policy calculus, proved to be more interested in supporting the government of Thailand, its principal ally in South-East Asia, and in wooing China, than it was in sounding an alarm about the situation in Cambodia. While it never condoned Khmer Rouge brutality, the US saw greater advantage in promoting Thailand's stability—which the Thai government sought through negotiations with the Pol Pot regime—and in achieving better relations with the Chinese government which was a strong supporter of the Khmer Rouge regime and opponent of the government in Hanoi. Thus for geopolitical reasons the US refrained from overt criticism of Khmer Rouge rule. Until 1978, Vietnam attempted to establish close relations with the Khmer Rouge and had no interest in damaging these relations by calling attention to human rights violations in Cambodia. In addition, television reporters had difficulty conveying the horrors in Cambodia. Hanoi refused journalists access to refugee camps in South Vietnam where some 120,000 Khmer and Chinese-Cambodian refugees had taken refuge by 1978. With the absence of visual images, the mass murder in Cambodia was not deemed newsworthy. Therefore, governments did not even discuss the genocide in Cambodia before the UN Human Rights Commission until 1978 when most of the killing was done. By December of that year, Vietnam had invaded Cambodia, routed the Khmer Rouge, driving them and their supporters to Thailand, and installed a client Khmer government in Phnom Penh. This government was made up of former Khmer refugees in Vietnam who had been trained by the Vietnamese and supplied with rice from the UNHCR and aid agencies in the refugee camps there.[117] These were the first in a long series of Khmer refugee warriors who would dominate refugee politics in Indo-China in later years.

From 1978 on, the Indo-Chinese refugee problem took on an entirely new dimension. A new phenomenon arose—that of the 'boat people'. As a result, the numbers of refugees in host countries in South-East Asia rose dramatically. Initially, the UNHCR resisted actively promoting resettlement to third countries because it believed such programmes would only open a migration channel to the West. In order to prevent refugees from being pulled out of Vietnam, the UNHCR thought it necessary to provide aid to displaced persons in Vietnam and Laos and maintain good relations with Hanoi. But as refugees piled up in Thailand and other countries, the new UN High Commissioner for Refugees, Poul Hartling, came under heavy pressure from South-East Asian governments and the United States to respond to the asylum crisis in the region with massive overseas resettlement. This would be the beginning of a seemingly endless international commitment to the resettlement of Vietnamese, Laotians, and Cambodians. It would dominate the attention and resources of the UNHCR until the mid-1990s and involve the resettlement of over 2 million people.

NOTES

1. US National Archives, Diplomatic Branch, Ref 3, Organizations and Conferences, UN, Box 3178, 27 August 1965.
2. US National Archives, Diplomatic Branch, Ref 3, Organizations and Conferences, UNHCR, Box 3178, 20 January 1966.
3. Prince Sadruddin Aga Khan, 'The New Geography of Political Refugees', *World Refugee Report, 1966-67* (Washington, DC: US Committee for Refugees, 1967): 11–14.
4. At the 1967 Executive Committee meetings, Sadruddin noted that although repatriation was one of the most important permanent solutions to the refugee problem, it was not possible to apply it to the great majority of the refugees, not only for political, but also for ethnic, demographic, and other reasons. He also emphasized that there were no grounds for over-optimism about the possibility of widespread repatriation and that it would be necessary to continue to devote substantial funds to local integration and resettlement. Gervase Coles, *Solutions to the Problem of Refugees and the Protection of Refugees: A Background Study* (Geneva: UNHCR, 1989): 149.
5. For a history of American involvement with displaced people in South Vietnam, see Louis Wiesner, *Victims and Survivors: Displaced Persons and Other War Victims in Vietnam: 1954–1975*, (Westport, CT: Greenwood Press, 1988).
6. US National Archives, Diplomatic Branch, REF and MIG, REF VIET, Box 3188, 10 November 1966. An earlier telegram gave the following policy guidance to US officers in South Vietnam: 'Instead of USAID-GVN refugee program being only a response to refugees when, as, and if they come in, I would urge that it also become part of planned and positive effort to systematize refugee flow in close coordination with military plans and psywar effort. . . . This helps deny recruits, food producers, porters, etc to VC, and clears battlefield of innocent civilians. Indeed in some cases we might suggest military operations specifically designed to generate refugees. . . . Measures to encourage refugee flows might be targeted where they will hurt the VC most and embitter people toward US/GVN forces least. . . . I suspect that we have not yet fully exploited refugee potential, and am prepared to support increased Chieu Hoi and Refugee programs, if necessary to meet above aims.' Telegram from R. W. Komer to Porter, American Embassy, Saigon, 3 September 1966. US National Archives, Diplomatic Branch, REF and MIG, REF VIET, Box 3188.

7. US National Archives, Diplomatic Branch, Ref 3, Organizations and Conferences, UNHCR, Box 3178, 26 February 1966.
8. US National Archives, Diplomatic Branch, REF and MIG, REF VIET, Box 3188, 9 December 1965.
9. US National Archives, Diplomatic Branch, Ref 3, Organizations and Conferences, UNHCR, Box 3178, 22 January 1966.
10. Interview with Gilbert Jaeger, former UNHCR senior staff member, Oxford, January 1989.
11. For background, see O. G. Roeder and a Special Correspondent, 'Tragedy of Errors', *Far Eastern Economic Review* (26 May 1966): 361–5.
12. UNHCR Archives, HCR/15/2/INDO, 19 January 1967.
13. Letter from Prince Sadruddin Aga Khan to Professor Herbert Jehle, 4 February 1970. UNHCR/1/NIG/GEN.
14. See Caroline Moorehead, *Dunant's Dream: War, Switzerland and the History of the Red Cross* (New York, NY: Harper Collins, 1998).
15. UNHCR Archives, HCR/1/7/75/SUD, 15 September 1966: 4.
16. UNHCR Archives, HCR/1/7/5/SUD, 10 October 1966.
17. Randolph Kent, *The Anatomy of Disaster Relief: The International Network in Action* (London: Pinter Publishers, 1987): 49–50.
18. UN General Assembly Resolution 2816 (XXVI) (December 1971).
19. Stephen Green, *International Disaster Assistance: Toward a Responsive System* (New York, NY: Council on Foreign Relations, 1977): 33.
20. *Report of the UN High Commissioner for Refugees*, General Assembly XXXIII, Supplement No 12 (A/33/12) (October 1978): 2.
21. US National Archives, Diplomatic Branch, REF 3 ICEM, Box 3002, 10 May 1973.
22. Interview with R. Jerrel, International Organization for Migration, Geneva, 1983.
23. US National Archives, Diplomatic Branch, REF 3 ICEM, Box 3002, 10 May 1973.
24. Interview with Bob Paiva, IOM, New York, July 2000.
25. US National Archives, Diplomatic Branch, REF3 UNHCR, Box 3002, 5 October 1973: 2.
26. State/AID Response to General Accounting Office's Draft to the Congress: 'Need to Build an International Disaster Relief Agency' Appendix 1, Comptroller-General of the United States, *Need for an International Disaster Relief Agency* (Washington, DC: GAO, 1976): 19.
27. Ibid: 3–4.
28. US National Archives, Diplomatic Branch, REF Burma, Box 3006, 23 February 1973.
29. UN General Assembly Resolution 2958 (XXVII) (12 December 1972).
30. UN General Assembly Resolutions 3454 (XXX) (9 December 1975) and 3460 (XXXIV), (1979).
31. UN General Assembly Resolution 1672 (XVI) (18 December 1961).
32. UN General Assembly Resolution 3271 (XXIX) (10 December 1974).
33. UN General Assembly Resolution 2956A (XXVII) (12 December 1972).
34. UN General Assembly Resolution 3143 (XXVIII) (14 December 1973).
35. UN General Assembly Resolution 3271 A (XXIX) (10 December 1974).
36. ECOSOC Resolution 2011 (LXI) (2 August 1976).
37. Ibid.

38. In a twelve-month period starting in March 1971, over $430 million was spent on the refugees, more than half of this amount coming directly from the Indian Government.

39. In a 20 July 1971 memorandum to the President of the UN Security Council, the Secretary-General expressed deep concern about the possible consequences of the situation, not only in the humanitarian sense but also as a potential threat to peace and security, and for its bearing on the future of the United Nations as an effective instrument for international co-operation and action. Noted in Gervase Coles, *Voluntary Repatriation: A Background Study* (Geneva: UNHCR, 1985): 87.

40. See Department of State Telegram, 'Presidential Letter to Prime Minister Gandhi', US National Archives, Diplomatic Branch, REF PAK/POL 15-1 US/Nixon 27 May 1971; and Department of State Telegram from American Embassy Islamabad to Secretary of State, 'Escalation of Indo/Pak Tensions: Refugees', US National Archives, Diplomatic Branch, REF PAK/Islamabad 4952, 20 May 1971.

41. R. E. Sisson and L. E. Rose, *War and Secession: Pakistan, India and the Creation of Bangladesh* (Berkeley, CA: University of California Press, 1990): 190, cited in UNHCR, *State of the World's Refugees 2000*.

42. UNHCR, *A Story of Anguish and Action: The United Nations Focal Point for Assistance to Refugees from East Bengal in India* (Geneva: UNHCR, November 1972): 79.

43. Interview with Nicholas Morris who was working in the High Commissioner's office at the time, March 2000.

44. See: 'The Problem of Militarized Refugee Camps', in UNHCR, *The State of the World's Refugees 2000*.

45. Cited in Coles, *Voluntary Repatriation*: 107.

46. Margaret Keck and Kathyrn Sikkink, *Activists Beyond Borders: Advocacy Networks in International Politics* (Ithaca, NY: Cornell University Press, 1998): 89–90.

47. Thomas Risse, Stephen Ropp, and Kathryn Sikkink, eds., *The Power of Human Rights: International Norms and Domestic Change* (Cambridge: Cambridge University Press, 1999): 21.

48. Donald Kommers and Gilburt Loescher, eds., *Human Rights and American Foreign Policy* (South Bend, IN: University of Notre Dame Press, 1979).

49. According to Sadruddin, many of those forcibly returned succeeded in boarding the next flight out of Uganda and ended up in transit camps in Italy or Austria. The High Commissioner did, however, formally protest to British authorities that this was *refoulement* in the worst sense, and that these refugees had every reason to fear all kinds of oppression and persecution in Uganda. See UNHCR Archives, HCR/1/GEN/ASI, 25 January 1973.

50. US National Archives, Diplomatic Branch, REF ASIA/XR REF 3 ICEM, Box 3002, 16 October 1972.

51. UNHCR Archives, HCR/1/UK/ASI, 13 August 1972.

52. UNHCR Archives, HCR/1/GEN/ASI/641/UGA, 9 January 1973.

53. For an account of these missions, see: UNHCR Archives, HCR/1/GEN/ASI, 25 January 1973.

54. UNHCR Archives, HCR/1/UK/ASI, 22 February 1973.

55. UNHCR Archives, HCR/1/GEN/ASI/641/UGA, 9 January 1973, 4.

56. Aristide Zolberg, Astri Suhrke, and Sergio Aguayo, *Escape from Violence: Conflict*

and the Refugee Crisis in the Developing World (New York, NY: Oxford University Press, 1989).

57. The following account of the international agencies' response to the refugee crises in Chile and Latin America is based in part on interviews with O. Haselman, UNHCR, Geneva, 1983; George Gordon Lennox, UNHCR, New York, 1983; Roberto Kojak, ICEM, Geneva, 1983; R. Jerrell, ICEM, Geneva, 1983; James Carlin, ICEM, Geneva, 1983; Lissen Schou, ICEM, Geneva, 1983; Jose Zalaquett, Amnesty International, London, 1983; and Judy Chavchavdze, Bureau of Refugee Programs, Department of State, Washington, DC, 1983.

58. UNHCR Archives, HCR/600/CHL/1/CHL/GEN, 9 September 1973.

59. For a chronological account of UNHCR's operation from September 1973 until the end of March 1974 see Ernest Schlatter, UNHCR Chargé de Mission, *Report on UNHCR Operation to Chile: 19 October 1973 - 29 March 1974* (29 March 1974). See also O. Haselman, UNHCR Regional Delegate for Latin America, *Situation des refugies et du HCR en Amerique Latine. et perspectives d'avenir* (28 November 1973). UNHCR Archives, HCR/1/CHL/GEN.

60. US Senate, Judiciary Committee, Subcommittee to Investigate Problems Connected with Refugees and Escapees, *Refugees and Humanitarian Problems in Chile, Part 3*, 94th Congress, 1st Session, (2 October 1975): 24–7.

61. Interview with Roberto Kojak, ICEM Chief of Mission, Chile, 1973–4, Geneva, 1983.

62. In the words of one analyst: 'State Department representatives went to great lengths trying to overcome these objections. They assured the doubters that the immigration act would be complied with and that no Communists or "subversives" would be admitted. There would be no "blanket admission" of Chileans. Finally, they argued that the number of admissions contemplated was only about 400 families—hardly enough to have a serious effect on the economy. In the end, though, congressional attitudes were still mixed: Chairman Eastland in the Senate . . . and . . . Edward Hutchinson, the ranking Republican on the House Judiciary Committee, appear to be opposed to a parole programme for those refugees in Chile and those in Peru. . . . Chairman Kennedy of the Senate Subcommittee enthusiastically supports a program of parole for both groups. . . . The House Subcommittee has indicated support for parole of refugees physically in Chile, but [has] declined to indicate support for those in Peru.' Christopher Hanson, 'Behind the Paper Curtain, Asylum Policy Versus Asylum Practice', *NYU Review of Law and Social Change*, 7 (Winter 1978): 107–41 at 113.

63. US Senate, *Refugee and Humanitarian Problems in Chile, Part 3*: 28–9.

64. Interview with Judy Chavchavdze.

65. UNHCR Archives, HCR/100/ARG/GEN/521/ARG, 11 March 1976.

66. See Lisa L. Martin and Kathryn Sikkink, 'U.S. Policy and Human Rights in Argentina and Guatemala, 1973-1980', in Peter Evans, Harold Jacobson, and Robert Putnam, eds., *Double-Edged Diplomacy: International Bargaining and Domestic Politics* (Berkeley, CA: University of California Press, 1993): 330–62; and Amnesty International, *Report of an Amnesty International Mission to Argentina* (London: Amnesty International, 1977).

67. UNHCR Archives, HCR/600/ARG, 8 February 1977.

68. Iain Guest, *Behind the Disappearances: Argentina's Dirty War Against Human Rights and the United Nations* (Philadelphia, PA: University of Pennsylvania Press, 1990): 110.

69. See for example: UNHCR Note for the File, *Visit to the High Commissioner of His Excellency Mr. Gabriel O. Martinez, Permanent Representative of Argentina in Geneva*. UNHCR Archives, HCR/100/ARG/GEN/600/ARG, 14 June 1976.

70. UN Doc. A/AC.96/Sr 274, 10; and cited in Guest, *Behind the Disappearances*: 110.

71. UNHCR Archives, HCR/600/ARG, 24 January 1977.

72. For a detailed history of Argentina's efforts to deter UN criticism, particularly of its policy of disappearances, see Guest, *Behind the Disappearances*.

73. Christopher Avery, 'Refugee Status Decision-making in Ten Countries', *Stanford Journal of International Law*, 17 (Winter 1984): 183–241; and Alexander Aleinikoff, 'Political Asylum in the Federal Republic of Germany and Republic of France: Lessons for the United States', *University of Michigan Journal of Law Reform*, 17 (Winter 1984): 183–241

74. All principal Western European countries have ratified or acceded to the 1951 Convention and the 1967 Protocol relating to the Status of Refugees. In addition, they are also parties to a range of other international instruments, the most notable of which are the European Convention for the Protection of Human Rights and Fundamental Freedoms—and the Protocols to this Convention—and the International Covenants on Civil and Political Rights, and on Economic, Social and Cultural Rights.

75. US National Archives, Diplomatic Branch, REF 3, UNHCR, Geneva 4600, 3 September 1968.

76. UNHCR, Archives, HCR/1/7/5/SCA, 24 September 1968.

77. UNHCR Archives, HCR/G XV/V/8/15/C (CSSR), N. 274, 9 December 1968.

78. UNHCR Archives, HCR/6/I AUS,. 4 December 1968.

79. Paul Weiss and Goran Melander, *De Facto Refugees* (Geneva: UNHCR, July 1974) examined in detail the nature and legal problems of *de facto* refugees. See also Paul Weiss, *The Legal Aspects of the Problems of De Facto Refugees* (Geneva: International Exchange Fund, 1974) and Anne Paludan, *The New Refugees in Europe* (Geneva: International Exchange Fund, 1974).

80. Johan Cels, 'European Responses to De Facto Refugees', in Gil Loescher and Laila Monahan, eds., *Refugees and International Relations* (Oxford: Clarendon Press, 1989): 187–215.

81. Goran Melander, *Refugees in Orbit* (Geneva: International Universities Exchange Fund, 1978).

82. US National Archives, Diplomatic Branch, REF 3, UNHCR, Box 3055, 24 November 1969.

83. US National Archives, Diplomatic Branch, REF 3, UN, Box 3054, 12 November 1968.

84. US National Archives, Diplomatic Branch, REF 3, UNHCR, Box 3054, 16 August 1967.

85. US National Archives, Diplomatic Branch, REF 3, UN, Box 3054, 19 November 1968.

86. US National Archives, Diplomatic Branch, REF 3, UN, Box 3054, 7 February 1968.

87. US National Archives, Diplomatic Branch, REF 3 UNHCR Box 3055, 24 November 1969.

88. US National Archives, Diplomatic Branch, REF3, UNHCR, Box 3002, 5 October 1973, *Refugee and Migration Affairs*, 3.

89. Repealed by the *Refugee Act* of 1980.

90. For an excellent treatment of the symbolic function of political migrations to the United States, see Silvia Pedraza-Bailey, 'Cubans and Mexicans in the United States: The Functions of Political and Economic Migration', *Cuban Studies*, 11/2 (July 1981) and 12/1 (January 1982): 79–97.

91. For a more detailed account of the history of US policy see Gilburt Loescher and John Scanlan, 'Human Rights, US Foreign Policy and Haitian Refugees', *Journal of Inter-American Studies and World Affairs*, 26/3 (August 1984): 313–56.

92. The characteristics of the Duvalier regime have been analysed and described in several studies. See Matts Lundahl, *Peasants and Poverty: A Study of Haiti* (London: Croom-Helm, 1979) and Robert Rotberg, *Haiti: The Politics of Squalor* (Boston, MA: Houghton Mifflin, 1978).

93. A report in 1973 by Amnesty International noted: 'Haiti's prisons are still filled with people who have spent many years in detention without ever being charged or brought to trial. Amnesty International remains seriously concerned with the continued repression of dissent in Haiti and the denial of human and legal rights. . . . The variety of torture to which the detainee is subjected is incredible. . . . In fact, those prisons are death traps . . . [and] find parallel with the Nazi concentration camps of the past but have no present day equivalent.' Cited in *Amnesty International Report* (London: Amnesty International, 1976). In 1975, Amnesty International saw little or no improvement in the Haitian government's treatment of its citizens: 'Arrests are carried out without warrants and often take the form of disappearances or kidnapping. . . . Prisoners are not allowed lawyers, nor contact with their families on arrest nor—with few exceptions—are they charged or brought to trial.' *Amnesty International Report*, 1976.

94. This estimate is based on newspaper reprints and Congressional testimony. No comprehensive record of asylum applications, approvals, and denials existed prior to 1980. The general accuracy of the estimate was confirmed in the author's interviews with INS Central Office personnel in May 1983.

95. Hanson, 'Behind the Paper Curtain'.

96. UNHCR Archives, HCR/600/USA/1/USA/HAI, 26 April 1974, (Telegram).

97. Ibid. (Note for the File).

98. UNHCR Archives, HCR/600/USA/1/GEN/HAI, 15 May 1974.

99. UNHCR Archives, HCR/600/USA/1/GEN/HAI, 19 April 1974.

100. See, for example, Letter from W. Sterling Cary, National Council of Churches in the USA to Kurt Waldheim, UN Secretary-General, UNHCR Archives, HCR/1/USA/HAI, 22 March 1974.

101. US House of Representatives, Subcommittee on International Organizations, *Human Rights in Haiti*, 94th Congress, 1st Session (18 November 1975); and Subcommittee on Immigration, Citizenship, and International Law, *Haitian Emigration*, 94th Congress, 2nd Session (July 1976).

102. US House, Subcommittee on Immigration, Citizenship and International Law, *Haitian Emigration*.

103. UNHCR Archives, HCR/100/USA/HAI/640/USA, 20 October 1977.

104. UNHCR Archives, HCR/15/82/27/3/23/SWI, 11 January 1967.

105. UNHCR Archives, HCR/15/SE Asia/GEN, 23 March 1968.

106. UNHCR Archives, HCR/15/SE Asia/GEN, 2/1/7, 10 April 1968.

107. UNHCR Archives, HCR/I.RVN/CAM, 8 February 1971.
108. Ibid.
109. Interview with James Carlin, former Director of ORM and ICEM, Geneva, 1983.
110. Interview with Gilbert Jaeger, Oxford, 1987.
111. This section relies extensively on Courtland Robinson, *Terms of Refuge: The Indochinese Exodus and the International Response* (London: Zed Books, 1998).
112. Interview with Martin Barber, former UNHCR official in Laos, 1975–7, London, 1983.
113. See UNHCR appeal to governments for UNHCR assistance in 1977 to displaced persons in the Socialist Republic of Vietnam and Lao People's Democratic Republic, 10 December 1976.
114. UNHCR Archives, HCR/100/CAM/GEN, 23 June 1975.
115. UNHCR Archives, HCR/100/CAM/GEN/7/2/3/CAM, 8 July 1975.
116. William Shawcross, *The Quality of Mercy: Cambodia, the Holocaust and Modern Conscience* (New York, NY: Simon and Schuster, 1984).
117. Robinson, *Terms of Refuge*.

7

The New Cold War and the UNHCR under Poul Hartling

Prince Sadruddin Aga Khan served as UN High Commissioner for Refugees for 12 years and resigned suddenly in 1977 in the middle of his third term. He was succeeded on 8 December 1977 by Poul Hartling, a 63 year-old former Danish Prime Minister and Minister for Foreign Affairs. Hartling, a clergyman and educator before turning to Danish politics, had aligned himself with the Liberal Party, blending conservatism with a progressive outlook on welfare, education, and other social issues. Hartling was the nominee of the Nordic group of countries, which were among the largest contributors and most loyal supporters of the High Commissioner's programme.

The younger and charismatic Sadruddin was a hard act to follow. Not only had Sadruddin overseen the global expansion of the UNHCR, but the Office had also developed autonomy and authority during his term. The UNHCR had established itself as an indispensable international actor in humanitarian crises and had developed a global agenda. Hartling was uneasy with Sadruddin's governing style. At the end of his tenure, Sadruddin had relied extensively on one or two trusted staff members for advice and his style of governance was frequently criticized for being 'imperial'. His closest advisers were accused of being arrogant and too powerful. Hartling, on the other hand, was unpretentious and had no exaggerated sense of self. He had been the leader of a small Nordic country and had presided over a coalition government of small political parties. Upon becoming High Commissioner, he established a cabinet style of management within the UNHCR. One of his first actions was to reassign Sadruddin's closest advisers to positions outside of Geneva.[1] As it turned out, Hartling himself came to rely on fellow Nordics, the 'Danish mafia', for some of his closest advice.

The new High Commissioner opened up several countries previously forbidden to the UNHCR. He visited the People's Republic of China and negotiated their 1980 entry into the UNHCR's Executive Committee. He also established working relations with other Communist states including the Soviet Union,

Nicaragua, and Ethiopia. Unlike Sadruddin, Hartling did not maintain a healthy independence from the United States. Given the important geopolitical purposes served by refugee aid, the UNHCR had little humanitarian space within which to function in high profile refugee settings. On highly politicised issues like Indo-China and Central America, the UNHCR toed the American line during the Hartling era. This cost the UNHCR the relative autonomy that it had developed during the Sadruddin era. In Europe, on the other hand, UNHCR criticism of government asylum politics alienated several major governments. In the developing world, refugees were in danger of being forced back to their own countries, of being attacked by pirates on the high seas, and of being bombarded in their camps and settlements. While the UNHCR did speak out publicly at times, Hartling frequently issued only muted protests, which found little support in the West. On sensitive human rights protection issues in countries closely aligned to the US, the High Commissioner often refused to take a stand, fearful that he would upset either his biggest donor, the United States, or the host states.

Hartling's most notable achievement was the rapid expansion of the Office's budget and resources. His first term coincided with a period of economic growth in the developed countries. It was also a high time in the history of refugee relief when the global refugee population expanded rapidly in Indo-China, South Asia, Africa, and Central America and resource-demanding care and maintenance programmes were established in near by asylum countries. The global refugee total tripled from 3 million in 1977 to over 10 million in 1982. Initially, donor governments were receptive to UNHCR appeals for assistance for this rapidly growing refugee population and the Office's budgets and programmes exploded. With the assistance of a Danish colleague, Ole Volfing, Hartling nearly quintupled annual government contributions to the UNHCR, raising the totals from $103 million in 1977 to $500 million in 1980. Volfing was so successful in raising funds that the Office could not spend all the funds that it was mobilizing. With carry-overs of $70 to $80 million per year, UNHCR staff were encouraged to spend more money than they were accustomed to doing. As a consequence, the UNHCR became increasingly operational, running more and more programmes by itself and offering a much greater variety of services for refugees.[2] Thanks to ample donor funding, the UNHCR began to give greater priority to material assistance than to protection. The emphasis on aid delivery and care and maintenance programmes also reflected the Western governments' desire to assist refugee warrior communities fighting Soviet-backed regimes. By the end of Hartling's second term, the Office could no longer sustain the huge expansion of responsibilities and the UNHCR had alienated several major donor governments.

Refugee Crises in Indo-China

The first crisis facing Poul Hartling was the exodus of the Vietnamese boat people. The exodus of refugees from Vietnam emerged slowly after 1975. Although no revenge killing or bloodbath took place there, the Communist Party relied on incarceration and indoctrination to bring the country under its control. Over 200,000 members of the former South Vietnamese government and military personnel and former members of political parties and organizations who were classified as reactionary after 1975 were imprisoned without trial for indefinite periods in 're-education camps'.[3] In 1976 the government also embarked on an unpopular programme of population relocation under which hundreds of thousands of Vietnamese were forcibly resettled on previously uncultivated land designated 'New Economic Zones'. Those who resisted these population transfers and those who were eventually released from re-education camps found themselves and their families with no legal status or means of livelihood in the new society. Large numbers of people soon became non-persons and had little choice but to try to leave Vietnam.[4] Little by little an exodus by boat began—mostly to southern Thailand, but also in smaller numbers to Malaysia, Hong Kong, the Philippines, Indonesia, Singapore, and even lands as far away as Brunei, Japan, Korea, and northern Australia.

Similar though less harsh political and economic developments occurred in neighbouring Laos.[5] The Hmong Lao were particularly vulnerable to persecution at the hands of the new Communist Pathet Lao government. The Hmong had been recruited by the United States during the Indo-China war as the CIA's 'secret army' to fight against the Pathet Lao. With the departure of the Americans, Hmong resistance collapsed and they began to flee in large numbers. During the next several years, poor human rights conditions, loss of personal freedoms, and desperate economic hardships led to the eventual flight of over 300,000 lowland Lao and Hmong—10 per cent of the country's population—across the Mekong River into Thailand.

Vietnamese boat people and Laotians captured much of the international attention given to refugees during this period. The terror in Cambodia which began in 1975 when the Khmer Rouge assumed power was not widely reported in the West and received little official attention until 1979, when hundreds of thousands fleeing Cambodia became part of the Indo-Chinese refugee problem. From 1978 on, Vietnamese and Laotian refugees progressively claimed more and more of the UNHCR's attention.

The Plight of Vietnamese Boat People

During 1978 and 1979, thousands of Vietnamese boat people drowned in an attempt to reach safety, and those who arrived in South-East Asia were met with hostility. Vietnamese refugees were not welcomed in neighbouring countries because they were viewed as a potential threat to economic and political security in the region.[6] Thai authorities, particularly the military, perceived the refugee influx as having an immense potential for disruption and as an increased security threat.[7] Malaysia was concerned that the flow of Vietnamese boat people, who were primarily ethnic Chinese, could upset the delicate domestic racial and political balance, particularly since they landed on the east coast of Malaysia where the population was overwhelmingly rural Malay, devotedly Islamic, and poor. The refugees were viewed as a subtle invasion force from Vietnam and as a potential fifth column for a renewed Communist insurgency.[8] Refugees in general were viewed as a domestic political liability throughout South-East Asia, and governments came under increasing pressure from local state, military, and political leaders to take a firmer stance against them.

The UNHCR was powerless to act on behalf of the boat people until they reached shore. Even then, it was hindered because Thailand, Malaysia, and Singapore were not signatories to the 1951 Refugee Convention or its 1967 Protocol and therefore, in the absence of strong commitments from those governments, the UNHCR lacked leverage for persuading them to provide temporary asylum to the Vietnamese. While the UNHCR was involved in channelling financial assistance to the host governments and in monitoring conditions in some of the refugee camps in the region, the Office had little leverage for exerting influence on the asylum policies of ASEAN governments. Government pledges to honour first asylum for the refugees were repeatedly broken and boats continued to be pushed off, thereby resulting in massive loss of life.

During the second half of 1978, there was a dramatic upswing in boat arrivals in South-East Asia. This was principally due to a series of economic decrees to nationalize private trade in Vietnam and the subsequent expulsion of Vietnam's Chinese minority. Economic restructuring affected the wealthy and middle class Vietnamese as well as the entire Chinese community who were the country's entrepreneurs. It made clear to these groups that there was no longer an economic future for them in Vietnam. A number of influential members of the Chinese community were subsequently arrested, creating fear of anti-Chinese persecution.[9] Political tensions between Vietnam and the People's Republic of China (PRC) intensified and more than 160,000 Vietnamese of Chinese origin travelled overland into China until July 1978, when the PRC closed the border. The number of refugees fleeing Vietnam to parts of Asia other than China reached dramatic proportions during the second half of 1978, setting a record every month. From 2,829 refugees who arrived by boat in other countries of South-East Asia from Vietnam in August 1978, the number leaped to 8,558 in September, to 12,540 in October, and to 21,505 in November. The number of boat arrivals in Thailand doubled from 1977 to 1978. It soon became evident that this exodus of refugees was not entirely spontaneous and was in fact being officially exploited by the Vietnamese government. By late 1978, a large-scale, well-organized scheme was established in which people wishing to leave Vietnam handed over their life savings, usually in gold bars, and were taken to small boats and thence to seagoing vessels. It was a very lucrative activity for the organizers. The trade in humans earned a high proportion of Vietnamese foreign exchange during a period when the country's economy was in ruins and its foreign currency reserves exhausted.[10]

With the arrival of freighters full of refugees in late 1978, South-East Asian sentiment hardened considerably against the boat people, and the policy of turning away overladen crafts was intensified. The tens of thousands of Vietnamese who managed to get ashore in South-East Asia were confined to crowded and inhumane camps. The international response to this evolving human tragedy in South-East Asia did not come readily or adequately at first. The United States had a strong interest in securing safe haven for these refugees. The refugee population included many who had supported the US military effort in South Vietnam and Laos, and in the wake of its humiliating defeat, it wanted to discredit the new Communist rulers in Indo-China. In addition, there were humanitarian concerns that exerted considerable pressure on American political leaders and policy-makers.[11] ASEAN governments, such as Thailand and Malaysia, sought to empty their refugee camps by obtaining agreement for resettlement to third countries such as the United States. But the US resisted large-scale resettlement believing it would be expensive and politically divisive. In the face of this growing refugee crisis, the UNHCR also was woefully unprepared. Prior to October 1978, for example, the UNHCR regional office in Thailand had only four field representatives to monitor fifteen camps in that country.[12] The policy from the UNHCR's Geneva headquarters was to encourage repatriation and to avoid open-ended resettlement.

In the face of this growing refugee crisis and the international reluctance to permit large-scale resettlement, Thailand and Malaysia resorted to deterrent threats and forced repatriation. On 28 November 1978, Thai Prime Minister General Kriangsak Chamanand declared that Thailand would not accept any more refugees. He said that unseaworthy boats would be repaired and sick refugees given treatment, but that Thailand would return them to the open sea. In Malaysia, military helicopters provided early warning of approaching refugee crafts, coastal patrols fired over their bows to deter them, and warships kept them away from the Malaysian shore.

By late 1978, the plight of the refugees and the reports of large numbers of drownings at sea began to attract international attention and concern. The need for more effective and dramatic action was underscored by the American press, which complained:

Isn't there someone—at the U.N. High Commission for Refugees, or in the world's civilized capitals—who has the will to cut through the baffling red tape that keeps these people penned up in fetid ships, starving and diseased, while the technicalities of maritime law are endlessly disputed? (*Washington Star*, 2 January 1979).

The US responded to the crisis and ASEAN threats by pressuring High Commissioner Hartling to convene an international consultation meeting in Geneva in December 1978 to which all governments interested in the problems of refugees in South-East Asia were invited. The ASEAN states dominated most of the discussion at the meeting, drew attention to the difficulties they faced, and called on the international community to provide them assistance, especially by providing immediate resettlement opportunities to the refugees. Unfortunately, the consultation meeting achieved few concrete commitments in regard to resettlement offers or more financial aid to UNHCR programmes in South-East Asia. The resettlement nations made pledges of only another $12 million and offered only about 5,000 new resettlement places. The Malaysian representative described these pledges as 'a drop in the ocean'. Furthermore, the ASEAN states received no assurances from Vietnam that the refugee flow would be curtailed. The Vietnamese representative, Vo Van Sung, denied that his government was involved in any way with the mass exodus and claimed that Hanoi was powerless to prevent it.

The pressure to involve the international community in the Indo-China refugee situation increased dramatically during the first half of 1979. The growing outflow of refugees began to directly affect many more countries in the region and the media began to depict the boat people as victims of an 'Asian holocaust'. By spring 1979, the number of new boat arrivals overwhelmed the South-East Asian asylum countries. The incidents of refugees from Vietnam arriving on large vessels increased and caused considerable paranoia throughout the region. The outbreak of war between China and Vietnam in February 1979 resulted in an even greater number of departures of Vietnamese citizens of Chinese descent to Malaysia, Thailand, Indonesia, and Hong Kong. From a March rate of 13,423, the numbers escalated to 26,602 in April, 51,139 in May, and 56,941 in June. The rate at which refugees were resettled in the West, however, failed to keep up with the pace at which they left Vietnam. While more than 51,000 Vietnamese arrived in South-East Asian countries in May, only about 8,500 left for resettlement in Western countries.

South-East Asian governments made it abundantly clear to the international community that their willingness to provide first asylum to the boat people depended entirely on firm commitments by Western countries to resettle the Vietnamese outside the region. When no new significant resettlement pledges were made by the West, ASEAN states took dramatic actions to deter boat people. Singapore admitted that if it had a heart, it was made of stone. Malaysian officials termed the refugees 'scum, garbage and residue' to be swept off the beaches and pushed back to sea, and threatened to shoot boat people on sight. The Malaysian navy systematically towed heavily laden boats back to sea even though they knew many were unseaworthy and would sink. Western refugee officials estimated that in February 1979 about 25 per cent of those who tried to land in Malaysia were pushed off, in April 50 per cent, and by mid-1979, 80 per cent. In the process, large numbers of Vietnamese died of starvation, thirst, or exposure and many drowned when their boats were capsized. Others were murdered by Thai pirates, who repeatedly and brutally attacked the refugee boats.

Only after such actions and after the foreign ministers of the ASEAN nations issued a comminiqué on 30 June 1979 declaring that 'their countries would no longer permit refugees to enter their borders and would take strong measures to send out those refugees then residing in the camps'[13] did a significantly strong sentiment for action emerge in the international community. In July 1979, with the crisis reaching alarming proportions, the United Nations held a conference in Geneva at which Vietnam agreed to impose a 'moratorium' on illegal departures. Simultaneously, Malaysia, Thailand, and other states in the region were persuaded to respect the refugees' right to asylum after the United States, Canada, Australia, France, and some thirty other nations embarked on a huge and costly resettlement programme that was to continue into the 1990s.

This *quid pro quo* led to the UNHCR having much greater resources and a higher international profile. The Indo-Chinese refugee programme involved the single largest permanent population transfer there has ever been between developing and industrialized countries, and was one of the most elaborate and expensive programmes in the UNHCR's history. It was also an example of the benefits of international burden sharing. By participating in the international refugee regime and establishing clear and consistent behaviour, both host and resettlement states reduced their transaction costs.

Throughout the 1980s, it was hoped that the Indo-Chinese states would eventually exhaust their stock of refugees before the resettlement countries ran out of admissions numbers or the asylum countries ran out of patience. However, the arrangement was unsustainable in the long term because it left the UNHCR on a treadmill and almost totally reliant upon the co-operation of the ASEAN states to maintain first asylum and the Western nations to resettle Vietnamese refugees indefinitely. Neither could be assured. Thailand and Malaysia continued to push boats back and eventually the West significantly reduced resettlement opportunities.

Throughout the 1980s, the generous assistance and preferential treatment for Indo-Chinese refugees had a magnet effect, attracting large numbers of people out of the embattled and impoverished countries of Indo-China. Pointing to the continuing migration of more than a million people six years after the collapse of pro-American governments of Indo-China, one UNHCR report[14] suggested that many of those leaving the Indo-Chinese states did so because of the magnetic attraction offered by large quotas announced by the United States and not because of a specific fear of persecution. The US programme was increasingly perceived by the UNHCR as being unduly influenced by people who had 'a strong personal and emotional interest in maintaining high quotas', and who believed 'a continuing exodus from Indo-China is a good thing' because 'it helps to prevent the stabilization of the communist regimes in Indochina, provides a useful source of information on the situation inside those countries, and appears to demonstrate to the world that Indochinese continue to vote with their feet'.[15] In view of mounting evidence that many Indo-Chinese could not be classified as refugees according to international criteria and that the programme itself was working as a magnet, senior regional UNHCR personnel argued that the UNHCR was 'in serious danger of being trapped into the continuing advocacy of resettlement programmes which were innovative—indeed, revolutionary—only two years ago but are now increasingly out of phase with the tenor of events. In particular, we need to revive our traditional emphasis on the support of genuine refugees rather than to be identified as co-sponsors with resettlement countries of a migratory process which is not our legitimate concern.'[16] In fact, the UNHCR was not able to get out of this trap, and it became extremely difficult to stem the flow from Indo-China.

By the early 1980s, the impetus for Western countries to sustain their large resettlement programmes diminished. In the United States, for example, the arrival of large numbers of Indo-Chinese coincided with the Mariel boatlift from Cuba and a huge influx from Haiti. From 1975 to 1980, the United States accepted as many refugees as did the entire rest of the world, and between 1975 and 1985 more than three quarters of a million Indo-Chinese refugees entered the US.[17] Such large admissions inevitably led to reductions in the number of overall quotas.[18] During the Reagan Administration, the proposed refugee allocations grew increasingly smaller, shrinking from 173,000 per annum in 1981–2 to 70,000 per annum in 1985–6.[19] Australia, Canada, and other resettlement countries soon followed suit.

'Compassion fatigue' hit Hong Kong and the ASEAN countries particularly hard. Western resettlement countries not only cut back their admissions quotas but also passed over certain Vietnamese, known as 'long-stayers', who did not fit their immigration criteria. The backlog, plus frustration over the protracted nature of the problem and concern with being left with tens of thousands of unwanted Vietnamese, led Hong Kong and the ASEAN countries to initiate a series of deterrent measures to discourage new and future arrivals.[20] Initially implemented against Cambodian refugees by Thailand, 'humane deterrence' became the policy adopted against all Indo-Chinese refugees throughout South-East Asia and in Hong Kong. As a steady stream of refugees continued to flow from Laos and Vietnam, Hong Kong and the ASEAN states took even more severe steps, including detention in closed camps,[21] forcible repatriation, and push-offs, which resulted in more drownings.

The UNHCR was powerless to act. The United States was implacably opposed to repatriation and refused to even discuss this option with Vietnamese authorities in Hanoi. Vietnam was equally adamant, refusing to accept the return of those who had fled the country. This standoff was not broken until the Comprehensive Plan of Action for Indo-Chinese Refugees was adopted at an international conference in 1989.

The UNHCR and the Survivors of the Khmer Rouge 'Killing Fields'

While the UNHCR endorsed the exodus from Vietnam, including many who were clearly not refugees, it did not play a forceful role in offering protection to many refugees fleeing from persecution and near-certain death by the Khmer Rouge in Cambodia. Not only was the Office slow in responding to forcible repatriation of Cambodian refugees but it also abandoned nearly a quarter of a million Cambodians on the Thai-Cambodian border, many of whom almost certainly would have qualified for protection under an expanded UNHCR mandate.

Before 1978, little news of the terrible suffering of the people of Cambodia reached the West. Information was fragmentary about the destruction of an entire people under Pol Pot's reign of terror. The only accounts available were a few dispatches for the handful of Western newsmen who retained access to Cambodia after the spring of 1975, and the stories of the few refugees who managed to escape across the heavily guarded borders. The newspaper accounts could not compete with the televised agony of the Vietnamese boat people, and the refugee stories generally were dismissed as exaggerations or anti-Communist propaganda. Only when the Vietnamese invaded Cambodia in late 1978, when tens of thousands of emaciated survivors crossed the border into Thailand and when mass graves were discovered, did the full horror begin to seep in.

For pure brutality the Khmer Rouge probably have had no equal in the postwar world. In three and a half years, from mid-1975 to the end of 1978, well over one million Cambodians died in executions or from malnutrition, disease, or exhaustion after forced marches and compulsory labour. The Cambodian experience was the worst to befall a people since the Nazi holocaust.

It was not until early 1978, nearly three years after the brutal seizure of power by the Khmer Rouge that the Western powers began to respond more aggressively to the situation in Cambodia. Public knowledge of Khmer Rouge atrocities had finally reached a point that no longer permitted the issue to be ignored. The Canadian Foreign Ministry compiled a dossier of human rights violations in Cambodia, and Britain asked for an enquiry into the situation in Cambodia at the UN Commission on Human Rights. Moreover, with the outbreak of open conflict between Vietnam and Cambodia, Vietnam, along with the Soviet Union, began for the first time to denounce Khmer Rouge atrocities.

The beginning of the international response to Cambodian refugees probably can be traced to the lightning offensive against the Pol Pot regime which the Vietnamese government launched late in December 1978. The effect of that strike was threefold. It drove Pol Pot and his inner circle into the remote jungle near the Thai border, it led to the establishment of a new pro-Vietnamese government headed by Heng Samrin, and it opened the Thai-Cambodian border for the first time since 1975. A year of unprecedented movement of people inside and outside Cambodia followed. Many Cambodians set out to return to their pre-1975 homes but found only devastation. Masses of people, undernourished and worn out by four years of slavery, criss-crossed the nation seeking reunion with their families. Stocks of rice, including seed rice, were eaten and food supplies ran low. Thousands, therefore decided to seek refuge, temporarily at least, on the Thai border.[22]

The Thais perceived the Cambodian influx, which began while large numbers of refugees continued to stream out of Vietnam and Laos, as having the potential for immense disruption. As a consequence, Thailand officially closed its border to the Cambodians and treated all those attempting to cross as illegal immigrants. Some were incarcerated in border camps; many were denied access to UNHCR investigating teams. At the same time, the UNHCR was under extraordinary pressure, particularly after Malaysia began pushing Vietnamese boats out to sea, to select those Vietnamese stranded in Malaysia first. Thai Prime Minister Kriangsak complained constantly that the Western world was interested only in the boat people, and did not care what happened along the Thai-Cambodian border. When the UNHCR and Western governments made few concrete assurances to Bangkok about increasing the numbers of Cambodian refugees to be resettled elsewhere,[23] Thailand took matters into its own hands.

From April 1979, the Thai army stepped up efforts to keep Khmers out of Thailand and began to push back into Cambodia entire groups of refugees who had congregated on the Thai side of the border.[24] Formal complaints about these forced repatriations were made to the Thai government by High Commissioner Hartling who wrote directly to Prime Minister Kriangsak. In May 1979, UN Secretary General Waldheim visited Thailand and raised the issue of asylum for the Cambodians with Kriangsak but his visit had no visible effect. Despite these protests, Kriangsak moved unilaterally to stop the Cambodian overland migration. In June 1979, the military rounded up 40,000 encamped Cambodians, then forced them by night across the border at gunpoint, pushing them along narrow trails on steep escarpments into heavily mined areas of Cambodia. Press reports stated that thousands died, from exploding mines when they tried to move forward and from Thai gunfire when they tried to return to Thailand. Many more succumbed during the following weeks in the immediate border area to malaria and starvation.

The UNHCR's response to this single largest forced repatriation since the Office was created in 1951 was totally inadequate. The UNHCR representative in Thailand hesitated to criticize Thai authorities openly, believing that external pressure would only embarrass the Thais and cause them to be even more restrictive. Lacking even a single protection officer for the period October 1978 to June 1979, the Bangkok office of the UNHCR was almost totally ineffective in the field and was powerless to prevent the forced repatriation of Cambodians or to provide decent camp facilities for the refugees who remained in Thailand.[25] Betraying a tension between its general function to offer protection to refugees and the necessity to work closely with the country of first asylum, the UNHCR headquarters in Geneva was also reluctant to irritate the Thai authorities by pressing too hard on protection problems in Thailand. The High Commissioner flatly refused a request by the Director of International Protection, Michel Mousalli, to publicly condemn the Thai action.[26] Instead, in a press statement released on 11 June, Hartling expressed 'deep concern' at the reports and urged the UNHCR Bangkok office to follow up with diplomatic missions in order to prevent further push-backs 'particularly of cases [with] a reasonable chance of resettlement'. 'This', wrote the UNHCR's Dennis McNamara, 'was to be the full extent of its official response . . . . UNHCR's remarkable failure to formally or publicly protest the mass expulsions of Cambodians from Thailand during 1979 must be seen as one of the low points in its protection history.'[27]

The UNHCR's early failures were obvious; yet its institutional capacity to ameliorate the situation in Thailand was limited. The success of the UNHCR's activities depended then as now on the willingness of national governments to co-operate with regional offices and the Geneva headquarters. The UNHCR can call attention to the legal obligations undertaken by governments that have adhered to the 1951 Refugee Convention and the 1967 Protocol, but it is without the power to change the course of a determined government that intends either to violate treaty commitments or to ignore the policies of the United Nations.[28] Thailand was not a signatory to the Refugee Convention and Protocol and was clearly unwilling to respect these treaties or co-operate with the UN.

Throughout the autumn of 1979, warnings of impending mass starvation in Cambodia emerged. The Cambodian crisis seized the conscience of the West. Pictures of emaciated and dying refugees were splashed across the world's newspapers and numerous editorials appealed for action. In September, having visited Cambodia, a UNICEF official reported that more than 80 per cent of Cambodian children were starving and that few under the age of five were still alive. Eyewitness accounts from Phnom Penh coincided with a US Embassy report from Thailand that

the physical conditions of newly arrived refugees over the past few days were among the worst we have witnessed. Assuming that only the strongest are able to make the trek into Thai territory, it appears that those still inside Cambodia are reaching the point where it is no longer possible for them to survive. (Unpublished US Embassy report in author's files).

At an international conference in November, $210 million in aid to be evenly distributed to Phnom Penh and the Thai-Cambodian border was pledged by participating nations. Compared with the response to similar and nearly simultaneous emergencies of Afghan refugees in Pakistan, Somalian, refugees in the Horn of Africa, and a famine in Uganda, the Cambodian crisis evoked an extraordinary outpouring of charitable giving in America and Europe.

However, Thailand insisted that Cambodians not be defined as refugees or granted first asylum. Rather, they would be considered illegal entrants and be placed in UMHCR-administered holding centres inside Thailand to await return to Cambodia when conditions there permitted. In the meantime, the Thais denied resettlement countries, including the US, access to refugees inside the holding centres. Bangkok did not want the Cambodians who had arrived in 1979 to be resettled in the West, since the Thais believed that a resettlement programme would only encourage more people to leave Cambodia.[29] The Thais feared that resettlement countries would not increase admissions quotas sufficiently to accommodate the large numbers of exiting Cambodians and that even partial resettlement would make the remaining Cambodians less willing to consider other alternatives. Of all the alternatives, voluntary repatriation of the refugees back to Cambodia seemed the most attractive to Thailand.[30]

After opening their doors to Cambodian refugees in October, the UNHCR holding centres for Cambodians inside Thailand were effectively closed to new arrivals by January 1980. By the middle of the year the situation in the holding centres and along the Thai-Cambodian border had stabilized. There were more than 160,000 Cambodian refugees in the UNHCR holding centres, about 200,000 straddling the Thai-Cambodian border, and more than 300,000 people still inside Cambodia who travelled regularly from the interior to the border to pick up food and medical supplies.[31] The Thais wanted to strengthen the resistance along the border and inside Cambodia, and so decided to make a concerted effort to reduce the holding centres' populations. In June 1980, concerned about the long-term impact of the Cambodians' presence, the Thai government announced a programme of voluntary repatriation. Despite the fact that Thai policy on return was driven by its military strategy against the Vietnamese and not by any promising political developments inside Cambodia, the UNHCR supported it. Subsequently, 9,000 Cambodian refugees—the majority of whom where Khmer Rouge supporters who had used the holding centres as rest and recuperation centres—were given hastily-arranged and summary interviews by the UNHCR, taken to the Thai-Cambodian border, and released. Not surprisingly, the Vietnamese perceived the repatriation as an attempt by the West to use the international agencies to return thousands of Khmer Rouge troops to the border to fight inside Cambodia. Within a week, Vietnamese troops retaliated by attacking several border camps, driving thousands of refugees back into Thailand and causing death and confusion. The repatriation programme was never resumed, although Zia Rizvi, who had been called back to UNHCR headquarters to become the Office's South-East Asia Regional Co-ordinator in October 1979, continued to try to negotiate a repatriation agreement until mid-1982.[32] The involvement of the UNHCR in this repatriation compromised the safety of the refugees under its protection. Security near the border was poor and returnees faced great dangers upon return. Moreover, conditions in Cambodia made it impossible for the UNHCR to monitor closely returning refugees or to provide reintegration assistance.

The UNHCR did not participate in relief efforts for Cambodians along the Thai-Cambodian border out of a concern that a large relief effort would encourage a further influx of Khmer seeking food and safety. As it turned out, refugees did not return home for nearly twelve years but remained pawns of Khmer military groups who used and abused the refugees at will.[33] Initially, border relief for the Cambodians was provided by the UNICEF and the ICRC. In 1982, the United Nations recognized the coalition of resistance movements on the border as the Cambodian government-in-exile. A new agency, the UN Border Relief Operation (UNBRO) was set up, though it did not provide protection for the refugees. Until it took over the UNBRO in late 1991, the UNHCR had relinquished its protection responsibilities for Cambodians stranded in border camps in favour of concentrating on resettling refugees from the holding centres to Western countries. Some 200,000 Cambodians were eventually resettled in the West. However, the absence of the UNHCR from the border and the virtual abandonment of Cambodians stranded there, many of whom constituted refugees and therefore fell under the UNHCR's mandate, was yet another major protection failure on the part of the Office regarding Cambodians.

The Second Cold War and New Refugee Flows

The Hartling era, which extended from the end of 1977 to the end of 1985, coincided with the renewal of East—West tensions, superpower rivalry, and manipulation of civil conflicts in the developing world. The Second Cold War generated regional conflicts across three continents from Afghanistan to Central America and forced millions of people to flee their homelands. The superpowers played an important role in these conflicts—whether by 'proxy' in an attempt to find regional allies, or by expanding local and ethnic conflicts into 'internationalized' civil wars. Backing either established regimes in the countries of origin or, more typically, exiled warriors seeking to overthrow those regimes, the superpowers exploited local conflicts to their own advantage and accelerated local arms races.[34]

During this time the UNHCR was totally preoccupied helping refugees fleeing violence in the developing world and trying to keep them alive in camps, instead of promoting durable solutions like repatriation. Huge sums of money were spent on large-scale material assistance programmes for the care and maintenance of millions of refugees in camps in Asia, Africa, and Central America.

The civil wars in Afghanistan, Angola, Cambodia, and Nicaragua are examples of the results of the so-called Reagan Doctrine. This shifted US foreign policy from containment of Communism to actively supporting insurgent movements fighting to overthrow Soviet-backed regimes in the developing world. Refugees themselves were increasingly used as so-called freedom fighters to intimidate revolutionary regimes into altering their political orientation and foreign policies. In regions of intense superpower conflict and competition—Afghanistan, Indo-China, Central America, the Horn of Africa, and Southern Africa—refugees were armed and their military struggles were supported both materially and ideologically. External support altered the balance of forces in civil conflicts, making conflict resolution difficult to achieve. Indeed, the competitive sale and provision of arms to Third World clients increased tension, exacerbated regional conflicts, and enlarged the flow of refugees from violence.

The military use of refugees also served the strategic and political interests of the West, in particular the United States. The demonstrable existence of freedom fighters symbolized popular rejection of Communist governments in these regions and served to legitimise the resistance movements. Thus, humanitarian support for refugees coincided with long-term Western objectives.

The use of refugee camps by combatants offered major advantages for them. Camps provided a relatively safe refuge from reprisals for combatants' families and supporters. The camps attracted humanitarian assistance, which became an important economic resource for refugee warriors. Combatants also used the administrative and political structures of refugee camps to maintain control over the civilian population and to legitimize their leadership on the international level.[35] The militarization of refugee camps placed the UNHCR and other aid agencies in anguished positions. On the one hand, they felt it was their duty to remain in the camps and to feed the needy. On the other hand, they disliked the fact that their humanitarian aid actually contributed to prolonging conflict. This tension and dilemma was at the centre of most refugee emergencies during the 1980s and 1990s.

The presence of refugees also accelerated conflicts within host countries. During the 1980s, for example, the proliferation of arms following the influx of 3 million Afghans into Pakistan brought about a resurgence of Pathan unrest. Palestinian refugees upset delicate domestic balances in Lebanon and Jordan. The emergence of organized groups of exiles in the developing countries compounded the refugee problem nearly everywhere. From Indo-China to the Middle East to Southern Africa to Central America, exiles agitated for changes in their home countries from within host countries. The presence of large armed groups of refugee warriors invited military retaliation, complicated relations with other states, and threatened the host states' security. As a result, host countries were often unwillingly drawn into conflicts with their neighbours. Thai-Vietnamese clashes over the issue of sanctuary for Khmer guerrillas, and the destruction wreaked on south Lebanon in Israeli reprisals for Palestinian raids were but two illustrations of the consequences for the security of host nations. Even where guerrillas operated within their own national territory—as in the case of Eritrean and Salvadoran rebels—they depended on sanctuary and supply routes in neighbouring countries, again aggravating interstate relations.

The issue of armed attacks on refugee camps became a major item of discussion at the UNHCR Executive Committee during the 1980s.[36] The former High Commissioner, Felix Schnyder, was appointed to study the problem. However, the issue polarized member states and heightened interstate tensions at the Excom sessions.[37] States which were host to militarized refugee camps and therefore subject to attack by the armed forces of the refugees' countries of origin advocated that these attacks should be condemned under all circumstances. Western governments, on the other hand, maintained that host countries had the responsibility to ensure the exclusively civilian nature of the refugee camps and that militarized refugee camps under some conditions could constitute a legitimate target of attack. The debate paralysed UNHCR attempts to forge a consensus in the Excom in favour of prohibiting attacks against refugee camps. The Conclusion reached in 1987 was a compromise that expressly recognized that attacks against refugee camps could not be justified, but was predicated on the assumption that refugee camps had an exclusively civilian and humanitarian character.[38]

Support for refugee warriors fighting the governments of neighbours also, on occasion, provided significant foreign policy benefits for host states. The Afghan war proved Pakistan's usefulness to the West and indirectly strengthened the Pakistani government. General Zia's international image was damaged by the 1979 execution of former Prime Minister Bhutto and by his poor human rights record. But it improved as Pakistan emerged as a bulwark against Soviet expansion on the subcontinent, as a channel for the free flow of weapons to the anti-Communist guerrillas, and as a safe refuge for 3 million Afghans. As Pakistan became a major strategic ally of the United States, Washington increased its military and economic assistance to Islamabad, and ceased its criticism of the late General Zia's repressive policies. In south-East Asia, Thailand became a front line state against an expansionist Vietnam, kept the Khmer resistance going, and provided a safe haven for Indo-Chinese refugees. In return, the United States supported the Thai military, and Bangkok became America's remaining ally on the South-East Asian mainland.

International Support for the West's 'Freedom Fighters'

The 3.2 million Afghan refugees who fled to Pakistan after 1979 formed a base for *mujahedin* resistance to Soviet and Soviet-backed control of Afghanistan. Military assistance to the insurgents came from the United States, the Arab states, and China. It was channelled through Pakistan, where a large international relief assistance programme run by the Pakistani government and the UNHCR—and largely funded by the United States—had been established to aid the *mujahedin* and their supporters. Pakistan gained handsomely from the UNHCR relief. During the 1980s, over sixty international NGOs and at least as many Afghan NGOs had grown up around the massive inflow of international humanitarian aid. In 1982, international relief assistance for Afghan refugees peaked at $192 million. However, international generosity to Pakistan stood in stark contrast to the miserly international assistance given to Iran, which hosted more Afghan refugees than Pakistan. Between 1979 and 1997, the UNHCR spent over one billion US dollars on Afghan refugees in Pakistan but only $150 million on those in Iran because Muslim fundamentalist-ruled Iran was a pariah state to the West after the fall of the Shah.[39] Despite the benefits of massive international aid, the long-term cost to Pakistan and to the refugees was high. The massive influx of Pashtun people tilted the tribal balance in the north-west of Pakistan and Peshawar became a centre for gun-running, narcotics trafficking, and crime.

The UNHCR and most of the NGOs operated programmes for Afghan refugees in Pakistan with little or no pretence of neutrality. The vast majority of the agencies, including the UNHCR, worked through the Pakistani administration and the seven Pakistani-based resistance movements. The UNHCR and most NGOs had no presence on the Kabul side of the conflict but tolerated the *mujahedin* use of the refugee camps inside Pakistan. Pakistan refused to recognize the Kabul regime and facilitated the political organization of the resistance. It required that all refugees register with one of the seven resistance parties and permitted the Afghan movements complete control over the civil and political affairs of the Afghan community in exile in Pakistan. The parties, in turn, acted with impunity to quash dissent and to maintain absolute control over the civilian Afghan population.[40] During the 1980s, intimidation, assault, and the assassination of dissidents, women speaking out on gender issues, and political opponents of the various resistance parties in Pakistan, were commonplace. The parties maintained their own prisons within the camps and justice was administered harshly. In striking blindness to refugee protection problems, the UNHCR and the NGOs stood by and made no effort to monitor widespread human rights abuses that regularly took place in the camps. The human rights and physical security of refugees were completely overshadowed by traditional Afghan norms, the excesses of fundamentalist Islam, and the imperatives of the political movements.

The refugee camps provided a cover for military activities and the international attention focused on the refugees reduced the chances of retaliatory attacks by the Soviet forces. Some of the refugee camps were highly militarized. One UNHCR official reported seeing anti-aircraft weapons in the midst of civilian settlements and warriors with AK-47s were a common sight in many camps.[41] The refugee camps provided a shield behind which Pakistan could channel military aid and training to the *mujahedin* fighters. Even humanitarian aid had military purposes. By distributing food through local Afghan middlemen, the UNHCR and the World Food Programme had no way of ensuring that food went exclusively to non-combatants, since the camps were used by the *mujahedin* as headquarters between military raids. Forcible recruitment was widespread, and even relief officials were harassed by fundamentalists among the refugees. Despite the blatant violation of UNHCR safeguards, there were no protests from the UNHCR or from major Western governments, such as the United States, who pursued a policy of the ends justifying the means.[42] The US was far more interested in wholeheartedly supporting the Afghan jihad and war effort against the Soviet occupation in Afghanistan than in curbing abuses among the refugees.

Feeding the Perpetrators of Cambodia's Killing Fields

As in Afghanistan, relief for the Cambodians along the Thai-Cambodian border served Western political and military objectives by sustaining the Khmer rebel forces. Following Vietnam's invasion of Cambodia in late 1976, China, Thailand, and the United States were determined to rebuild the Khmer Rouge into a fighting force capable of unseating the Vietnamese client regime in Phnom Penh and as a way of maintaining pressure on the Soviet Union's client, the Vietnamese government. Refugee camps provided sanctuary for the Khmer Rouge and non-Communist forces; refugees were sources of new military recruits and helped finance the war economy.

For Thailand, Cambodian refugees had strategic value as a buffer against Vietnamese incursions along the border and as a source of support and cover for the re-emerging resistance movement. As a country hosting hundreds of thousands of Cambodian refugees, Thailand played a central role in support-ing the resistance forces opposing the Vietnamese-installed regime in Phnom Penh. Thailand provided territory on which the Cambodian factions built military bases; it facilitated the flows of arms and finance to the armed groups; it provided international legitimacy of the resistance by hosting the Coalition Government of the Democratic Kampuchea—CGDK, the Cambodian government-in-exile—on Thai soil. These functions were made possible by the existence of several hundred thousand refugees in camps along the Thai-Cambodian border.

As in Pakistan, the relief aid provided by international agencies sustained the resistance and contributed to the war economy. Food aid was diverted by camp leaders and sold on the black market or channelled to nearby military camps of the resistance groups. The revenue gained from the diversion of aid was supplemented by the taxation and extortion levied on refugees. In addi-tion, the camps' medical and training facilities performed valuable support functions for the refugee warrior communities.

Protection for the refugees along the border was non-existent. The UNHCR refused to get involved and all other agencies hesitated to challenge openly, either the misuse of aid or the abuse of refugees for fear of being expelled by the Thai authorities. Real power lay in the hands of the resistance movements and the Thai military units who patrolled the camps. The Khmer Rouge treated residents in their camps in much the same way as they had treated the population of Cambodia during the Killing Fields period. All able-bodied men were forcibly recruited into military service and women and children were engaged as porters, carrying war material to the front lines. In non-Khmer Rouge camps, political intimidation, imprisonment, and disappearances were employed to silence dissent. Thai Rangers used violence and extortion to maintain control in the camps, especially after nightfall when international aid personnel were required to leave the camps.[43] Despite flagrant violations of human rights in the refugee camps, the agencies turned a blind eye and remained silent. The United States, as the largest single donor of the border programme, had significant leverage over the Thai government. However, during the 1980s, supporting the anti-Vietnamese and Khmer resistance movements through the aid programme was a primary objective of the Reagan administration. Thus, Cambodian refugees remained pawns in the larger geopolitical struggle in South-East Asia.

The Politicization of Refugee Programmes in Central America

While the situation along the Pakistani and Thai-Cambodian borders constituted some of the most blatant political uses of humanitarian aid, refugee programmes in Central America were also highly politicized.[44] From the late 1970s to the end of the 1980s, Central America was the scene of mass refugee movements. Military repression, human rights abuses, and internationalized civil wars in El Salvador, Guatemala, and Nicaragua drove millions from their homes to become internally displaced or refugees in neighbouring countries. Host states saw refugee settlements as security threats and as sanctuaries for freedom fighters and guerrillas. Refugees were a frequent source of interstate conflict. The Guatemalan military attacked refugee camps in Chiapas, Mexico and the Salvadoran army made raids against refugee camps in Honduras. Costa Rica harassed Salvadoran refugees but permitted Nicaraguan contra forces to train on its soil.

The most politicised refugee programmes were in Honduras which hosted both Nicaraguan and Salvadoran refugees.[45] Refugee camps in Honduras provided a military sanctuary for both Nicaraguan and Salvadoran refugee warriors. The United States and Honduras supported Nicaraguan contras in their guerrilla war against the socialist Sandinista government in Managua. Salvadoran refugees, on the other hand, were viewed as supports of the leftist Salvadoran rebels—Farabundo Marti National Liberation Front (FMLN)—who were fighting to overthrow an American supported regime in El Salvador. Honduras treated the two refugee groups unequally. Refugee camps for Nicaraguan refugees in Honduras remained relatively open throughout the 1980s and refugees enjoyed freedom of movement and employment opportunities, while camps for Salvadorans remained closed and ringed by hostile Honduran armed forces.

The UNHCR was caught in the middle of these political and ideological battles and had to tread a perilous path between trying to ensure protection for refugees and respecting the political interests of the US and Honduran governments. The UNHCR made efforts to relocate refugees away from the border and to protect them and the aid distribution system from the political and military agendas of the Nicaraguan opposition. However, Nicaraguan contra groups forcibly recruited refugees out of UNHCR camps and their leaders took charge of the relief supplies provided by the UNHCR. The Salvadoran camps in Honduras also provided a source of food and medical supplies for the insurgents and a refuge for the families of FMLN fighters.[46] FMLN political committees controlled the aid distribution systems within the camps enabling them to exert influence over the refugee population. In contrast to the Nicaraguan camps, the Honduran military surrounded the Salvadoran camps and harassed the refugees. Since Honduras treated refugees primarily as a political-security problem, the UNHCR was in a weak position to protect refugees. The fact that Honduras, like Thailand, had not ratified the 1951 Refugee Convention—and did not do so until 1992—further limited the UNHCR's formal protection role there. The UNHCR depended on Honduras for permission to run its programmes there and therefore felt obliged to mute its criticism of the Honduran military's maltreatment of Salvadoran refugees or of Honduran tolerance of contra human rights abuses. In 1981 Honduras and the US put pressure on the UNHCR to move Salvadoran refugees from the militarized border to camps further inland where the pro-FMLN refugees could be more tightly controlled. The refugees, backed by the FMLN, vehemently opposed relocation. Nevertheless, believing the refugees could be better protected away from the border, the UNHCR proceeded with the relocation and employed coercive measures to force the refugees to move. The UNHCR informed refugees that the only alternative to relocation was repatriation, and agency staff withheld food supplies from refugees refusing to be part of the relocation. During the poorly planned operation, many refugees were injured and killed. Conditions in the new camps were as bad as in the abandoned ones. Concerned about the safety of their families who were in the camps, the FMLN compelled a large number of refugees to return to guerrilla controlled territory in El Salavdor.[47] The relocation greatly strained the UNHCR's relations with human rights NGOs who perceived the Office to be in collusion with the Honduran and US governments.

The UNHCR in Honduras was greatly constrained by its financial dependence on the United States, which contributed about one-third of the agency's regional budget.[48] The US used this leverage to exert pressure on the agency to improve conditions in UNHCR camps for Nicaraguans and to relocate or repatriate Salvadoran refugees. The US invested heavily in ensuring that Honduras served as a bulwark against the spread of Communism in the region, and the contra war against the Sandinistas was chiefly directed from Honduras. Nicaraguan refugees constituted an important symbol of Sandinista oppression and were used by the US to generate support for the contra war effort with Congress and the American public. In this highly politicized context, refugees became pawns and the US subjugated humanitarian concerns to foreign policy interests. Despite the protection problems it caused for refugee communities, many of the relief NGOs working with both Nicaraguan and Salvadoran refugees permitted aid to serve the political agendas of the refugee warriors, host governments, and the United States.

The UNHCR was caught up in this vortex and was unable to provide effective protection. Given that it needed funds from the US to finance its programmes and permission from Honduras to maintain camps in its territories, the Office had limited leverage in persuading the host government to protect refugees. Effective protection required operational independence, but setting up camps, generating assistance efforts, and raising money necessitated dependence on national governments.

This placed the UNHCR in a situation of structural disharmony. The better-funded and more expansive the UNHCR's organization of physical care became, the more heavily it relied on national governments for money and for authorization to advance assistance efforts and the weaker its position became in the neutral pursuit of protection. No refugee agency can be simultaneously independent for the purpose of protection and dependent for the purpose of relief.

Africa's Post Independence Struggles

Africa presented the UNHCR with many new refugee problems arising from post-independence civil wars and repressive regimes. The conclusion of the first civil war in Sudan in 1972 and the attainment of independence by Portugal's African colonies in 1975 took more than half of Africa's refugees off the UNHCR rolls. Within a few years new ones arose to take their places. Masses of people fled brutal regimes in the Central African Republic, Equatorial Guinea, and Uganda. In Burundi, the Tutsi embarked on a genocidal massacre of Hutus, thereby generating a huge outflow of refugees and laying the basis for ethnic cleansing in the African Great Lakes region in the 1990s. Chad became involved in a protracted conflict between Muslim and non-Muslim populations that resulted in the flight of Chadians to Sudan, the Central African Republic, Cameroon, and Nigeria. In North Africa, war between the Polisario Front—a movement fighting for the independence of the Western Sahara—and the combined armies of Morocco and the Mauritania, subjected the Saharawi people to military attack and precipitated their mass flight to Algeria. By 1980, Africa's refugee population stood at over 4 million.

Foreign and strategic policy concerns of host countries greatly affected the treatment of refugees in Sudan and Ethiopia. Under the successive governments of Ja'far Numeiri and Sadiq el-Mahdi, Sudan's relations with the government of Colonel Mengistu Haile Miriam in Ethiopia were hostile. Sudan opposed the Marxist orientation of the regime in Addis Ababa and deeply resented Mengistu's support for the Sudanese People's Liberation Army (SPLA). Sudan strongly backed the liberation movements which were fighting the Ethiopian central government, including the Eritrean Liberation front (ELF), Ethiopian People's Liberation Front (EPLF), and the Tigray People's Liberation Front (TPLF). Sudan treated refugees from Ethiopia and Eritrea favourably and provided members of the EPLF, ELF, and TPLF with logistical and political support in conducting their military operations against Ethiopia. Not only were the liberation fronts active among the refugee camps in Sudan, but Sudan permitted the fronts' relief organizations, such as the Eritrean

Relief Association and the TPLF Relief Society to conduct cross-border feeding operations from Sudan into Eritrea and Tigray provinces inside Ethiopia. In turn, Ethiopia supported the SPLA and permitted the rebel movement to control the operation of the UNHCR-serviced camps in western Ethiopia. The Sudanese refugee population in Ethiopia, many of whom were family members of SPLA fighters, were generously supported by the Mengistu regime.

The conflicts in the Horn of Africa proved to be the most difficult and costly operations for the UNHCR. In Sudan, the UNHCR established refugee settlements for some 130,000 refugees from Eritrea and northern Ethiopia and several hundred thousand others settled on their own in local communities without UNHCR assistance. In 1984 a famine developed in Eritrea, Tigray, and Wollo provinces in Ethiopia in which nearly a million people died. When the Ethiopian government refused NGOs access to the famine affected areas under TPLF and EPLF control, the liberation front organizations organized a cross-border relief effort. UN agencies, including the UNHCR, were not willing to take part in this effort because they did not have the permission of the Ethiopian government. However, at the end of 1984, over 200,000 of the emaciated famine victims fled across the border to Sudan. The UNHCR was not prepared for the scale and speed of the mass influx and death rates among the severely malnourished refugees were extremely high. Consequently, the UNHCR was severely criticized, particularly by the United States, for its lack of preparedness and late response to the famine crisis. By this time too, the international media gave massive attention to the famine, which generated an outpouring of concern and donations in the West. In 1985, donor governments gave $76 million for the UNHCR's programme in Sudan alone.[49] While many of the Tigrayans returned to Ethiopia in 1986, most of the Eritreans stayed in Sudan. At the same time, hundreds of thousands of Sudanese and Somali refugees fled to Ethiopia.

While many of the armed conflicts and secessionist movements in the Horn of Africa could be traced to long-standing religious and ethnic rivalries and other internal factors, the roots of internal and regional tension there must also be seen within a broader international context. Because the Horn was perceived as having geopolitical significance, the superpowers and some Middle Eastern states became involved in these regional struggles by supporting one faction or one government over another. As in other regional conflicts, humanitarian assistance was used for political purposes both by host governments and by guerrilla groups. For example, following the defeat of Somalia in the Ogaden at the hands of Ethiopia, hundreds of thousands of Ogadani Somalis fled to Somalia. The Siad Barre regime appealed to the UNHCR for assistance in 1979 and in subsequent years UNHCR camps grew so large that they became larger than most Somali cities. No one knew for sure how many refugees there were but the Somalian government had an interest in inflating the numbers of refugees it was hosting in the hope of obtaining more assistance from the international community. In the mid-1980s, international humanitarian assistance represented approximately one-quarter of the country's gross national product.[50] Somalia's inflated figures were accepted by donor states because it was at the time the major client state of the United States in the geo-politically important Horn of Africa. The UNHCR largely complied with donor states' interests. Its massive assistance programmes to camps in remote regions throughout the Horn of Africa kept large numbers of refugees alive, even as the camps themselves came under armed attack and some of their inhabitants were forcibly conscripted into government or rebel armies.

Refugee Warriors and Regional Conflicts

Apart from the meddling of the two superpowers, military intervention in local Third World conflicts by other outside powers increased as well. Among those seeking to take advantage of the situation were South Africa, Cuba, Israel, Vietnam, China, Syria, Iraq, Iran, Saudi Arabia, and India. In attempting to preserve and establish their own regional security interests and objectives, even developing countries became heavily involved in internal conflicts. Pakistan supported the Afghan mujahedin; Nicaragua supplied arms to Salvadoran insurgents; the Vietnamese occupied Cambodia; India intervened in Sri Lanka. The South African military used proxies against frontline states in southern Africa—especially Angola and Mozambique—to destabilize neighbouring countries, resulting in the creation of large-scale refugee movements. Sudan assisted guerrilla groups in northern Ethiopia; Ethiopia and Libya supported the Sudan People's Liberation Army's insurgency in southern Sudan. Libya, Egypt, and Sudan became involved on different sides in Chad; Somalia supported the guerrilla activities of Ethiopian liberation movements and allowed them considerable freedom of movement within its borders. Such interventions transformed local wars into complex and intransigent international confrontations, with direct implications for refugee flows.

Third World conflicts became extremely difficult to resolve quickly, not only because of external involvements, but also because governments and opposition movements frequently saw themselves locked in life-or-death struggles with each other. In the eyes of most governments, secessionist struggles threatened the physical survival of the state and presented serious risks to central government. For example, successive regimes in Ethiopia believed that according self-government to the Eritreans would cut off its access to the Red Sea. Similarly, Iraq opposed granting autonomy to its Kurds for fear of losing control over the country's oil reserves and causing tensions with neighbouring Iran and Turkey.

Religious issues also contributed to the violence and civil conflict in many parts of the developing world. Islamic fundamentalism reasserted itself not only in the Middle East but in regions as far apart as South-East Asia, South-West Asia, and North Africa. Religious revivalism was the direct cause of several major refugee movements during the decade. In Sudan, for instance, demands by northerners for the adoption of Islamic laws alarmed southern Sudanese Christians and animists and fuelled the renewal of the insurgency in South Sudan led by the Sudanese Peoples Liberation Army.

The UNHCR and the Forced Return of the Rohingya Muslims to Burma

In mid 1978, some 200,000 Rohingya Muslims fled their homes in Arakan state in Burma as a consequence of widespread ethnic discrimination and violence at the hands of the Burmese military. The refugees arrived in neighbouring Bangladesh in desperate condition. Initially, Bangladesh mounted basic relief programmes and set up improvised and rudimentary camps for the newcomers. But the magnitude of the refugee situation grew rapidly, making it necessary for Dhaka to request assistance from the UN Secretary-General. The UNHCR was asked to co-ordinate the international response and appealed for aid.

From the beginning of the crisis, however, Bangladesh made it clear that only temporary asylum would be provided and that it was in their national interest to see the Rohingya repatriated as soon as possible. Burma also had an interest in seeing that the Rohingya return. Rangoon officials believed that the adverse publicity arising from the exodus of Rohingyas would damage their international legitimacy and their hopes for greater international development assistance. Burma was also informed by UN officials that 'the high daily cost to the international community of keeping refugees could well jeopardize contributions to the development projects of both countries—the implication being that Burma would suffer most'.[51] On 9 July, a repatriation agreement was reached between the two countries despite the fact that the conditions within Burma which had led to the flight of the Rohingya had not changed. The UNHCR did not have a role in the agreement and there were also no provisions in the agreement guaranteeing the voluntary nature of the return. Essentially this was a bilateral repatriation arrangement which stemmed not from the interests of the refugees but from a convergence of the two states' national interests.[52]

Not surprisingly, the refugees fiercely resisted repatriation under these conditions. In response, Bangladeshi troops stepped up pressure on the refugees to return, primarily through intimidation tactics and restricting food supplies to the refugees. Conditions in the camps were appalling and by the end of 1978, some 10,000 refugees died of epidemic illnesses and malnutrition.[53] Nevertheless, the UNHCR, believing that conditions were unlikely to improve in Bangladesh, sanctioned the repatriation. The UNHCR felt it had little leverage as both countries were not signatories to the international refugee instruments and there was little interest on the part of major donor countries in preventing the repatriation of Rohingya. Faced with deprivation and death in the camps, the Rohingya decided to return home, and by the end of 1979 nearly 190,000 had done so. No meaningful actions were taken by the UNHCR to ensure that the Rohingya were not at risk after they returned. Indeed, in 1980, Burma passed a new citizenship law which created two categories of citizen, the second being those outside Burmese indigenous ethnic groups, such as the Rohingya. As second class citizens, the Rohingya were excluded from the military, elected government office, and from certain key economic activities. Continued discrimination and persecution would lead to another mass outflow of Rohingya in the early 1990s. The fact that the UNHCR sanctioned this forced repatriation and did nothing to assure a safe future for the returnees constituted a major protection failure for the Office.

Long-Term Exile for Most Refugees

The politicisation of refugee problems during the 1980s precluded an easy solution to the refugee dilemma by the UNHCR. The UNHCR's three traditional solutions—resettlement, local settlement and integration, and repatriation—no longer proved adequate. With the exception of the Indo-Chinese, there were no compelling political or ideological reasons for Western states to resettle large numbers of Third World refugees. And by the mid-1980s, even the Indo-Chinese were discovering that the doors to overseas resettlement were rapidly closing. Moreover, outside Central America and Indo-China, there was no evidence that any sizeable number of refugees ever wanted to abandon their countries and settle permanently elsewhere. The second traditional solution, local settlement leading to naturalization, was perceived by most countries of first asylum to be politically and economically infeasible. Given the volatile security situation and lack of social stability and cohesion in most host societies, successful local settlement was very much the exception, rather than the rule. Finally, with the exception of the return of the Rohingya to Burma, neither donor governments nor most countries of origin had any interest in promoting repatriation. As long as refugees were engaged in guerrilla warfare against enemy countries, the US showed little interest in the large-scale return of refugees.

Likewise, countries of origin were in no hurry to facilitate repatriation, particularly when the refugee population consisted of enemies or guerrilla resistance movements.[54] Because repatriation operations were expensive and required donor support, donor governments, particularly the US, were in a strategic position to oppose repatriations. This was clearly reflected in one of the conclusions of the UNHCR's Executive Committee in 1980 which emphasized the risks to refugees' safety in repatriation rather than the opportunities. Thus, repatriation to countries where conflicts still raged was extremely difficult for the UNHCR to negotiate, as well as being dangerous for refugees.

The failure to provide any kind of viable alternatives for the world's refugees meant that majority of them were given temporary asylum in camps, with no prospect of effective long-term solutions. Despite the futility of providing relief assistance without any permanent solution in sight, a variety of political interests converged to maintain camps almost indefinitely. The donor countries, particularly the US, generously funded most of these camps, especially those that provided refuge for 'refugee warrior groups' and their families. There was no political will on the part of the superpowers for much of the decade to seek political solutions to the long-standing regional conflicts. The confinement of refugees to remote border encampments removed any sense that there was an urgent need on the part of the various governments involved to address the root causes and press for political solutions. Rather, much like the early 1990s, generous Western support for the UNHCR and for refugee assistance programmes provided an excuse for political inaction on the diplomatic front and contributed to the political stalemate between the superpowers and their clients. Host governments, concerned about the security risks of hosting refugees from neighbouring countries and about the enormous strains on local economic, political and physical resources, viewed refugee camps as the most convenient way to segregate refugees and to limit their impact on the local community. UNHCR and NGO officials believed that by assembling refugees in one place they could better supply them with food, shelter, clean water, sanitation, and health care on which their survival depended. Refugee camps also came to be perceived as an unequalled fund-raising tool. Refugee camps focused donor governments' attention and demonstrated a tangible proof of a need. Even the refugees' own political leaders recognized the advantages of a camp life as a way of keeping their cause before the world. Furthermore, the refugee warriors of Cambodia, Central America, the Horn of Africa, Southern Africa, Afghanistan, and Palestine all maintained political solidarity in exile through the tight leadership structures possible in the refugee camps.

The Search for New Approaches: Refugee Aid and Development and the 'Root Causes' Debate

By the early 1980s, donor governments began to grow tired of funding the UNHCR's care and maintenance operations and sought ways to limit their overseas aid expenditures. The explosion of refugees in the 1980s and the protracted nature of refugee camps greatly strained the UNHCR's administrative and financial structures. The global refugee total surpassed 10 million in the early 1980s and grew steadily to 17 million by the end of the decade. In the early 1980s, this surge in refugee numbers was matched by government contributions to the UNHCR, but contributions soon failed to keep pace with the growing refugee numbers. Part of the problem of resourcing the UNHCR lay in the restrictions that had originally been placed on the Office's ability to raise funds. Each October, the Office's Executive Committee approved the UNHCR's general administrative budget but governments made no commitment to actually fund it. The money came in over the following year, often in fits and starts. Donor governments, primarily Western states, had their own political priorities and budget cycles. Many governments earmarked certain refugee programmes, which meant that some UNHCR programmes were inadequately funded leading to great disparities between regions. For example, it was easy to raise money for the high profile Indo-Chinese and Afghanistan refugee programmes but almost impossible to fund development-oriented integration programmes in Africa. Consequently, the UNHCR found it increasingly difficult to continue to raise the money to keep up with the growing numbers of refugees. Between 1980 and 1989, the UNHCR's funding per refugee fell by more than 50 per cent in constant US dollars.[55]

African leaders complained bitterly that Hartling had spent too much time and resources on refugees from Afghanistan and Indo-China while neglecting the four million refugees in Africa. African states stressed the need for greater international burden sharing so that they could better manage the adverse impact of refugees on their economies and environments. To respond to this situation, Hartling held a series of meetings in the early 1980s that spelled out the UNHCR's 'refugee aid and development strategy'.[56]

In 1981, the first International Conference on Assistance to Refugees in Africa (ICARA I) was held in Geneva where Hartling tried to win funds for UNHCR projects to promote substantial development rather than open-ended relief for Africa's refugees. At ICARA I, African governments requested $1.15 billion in integration assistance. In the end, only $69 million was allocated to emergency relief and almost all the $560 million offered by donor governments was earmarked for projects and allocated to favoured nations. Very few funds went to especially hard hit nations like Ethiopia and other countries in the Horn of Africa.

In August 1983, Hartling convened a meeting of experts to study how a development approach to refugee situations could contribute to a solution of the problem. The group formulated a refugee aid and development strategy, which was discussed at follow-up meetings and finally endorsed by the UNHCR Executive Committee in 1984.[57] A second International Conference on Assistance to Refugees in Africa (ICARA II) was held in Geneva in July 1984. African governments were particularly interested in winning additional resources to be used for repairing the damage to the environment caused by refugees and for developing infrastructures needed in areas accommodating them. Some 163 projects of this type, requiring approximately $430 million of external aid, were presented at ICARA II.[58] This amounted to more than the UNHCR's total global expenditure the previous year.

ICARA II was no more successful that ICARA I. As one UNHCR report[59] later pointed out, the African countries tried to win funds for development projects under the guise of refugee emergency relief. They were more interested in being compensated for the burden of hosting refugees than they were in using these funds to promote local integration. But the donor governments were less interested in compensation and international burden sharing than they were in finding lasting solutions to refugee problems. In addition, drought and famine and the resulting refugee crises ravaged many African countries in 1984 and 1985, and major donor governments used whatever funds they had earmarked for ICARA II projects for large-scale emergency relief projects. There were a limited number of inter-agency projects involving the UNHCR and the World Bank in Pakistan and Sudan that benefited both refugees and host governments. Apart from these, the concept of refugee aid and development was never fully supported by the donor community and the idea died after the departure of Hartling.

While the UNHCR was promoting its refugee aid and development strategy, a debate was initiated at the United Nations in 1980 to address the root causes of refugee movements.[60] Unlike during the Cold War, the UN now became quite active in the area of human rights and began to draw the connection between human rights violations and refugee movements. Governments held discussions on these issues in the UN's Special Political Committee and a group of governmental experts issued a report on averting refugee flows. A second report entitled *Study on Human Rights and Massive Exoduses* by the former UN High Commissioner for Refugees, Sadruddin Aga Khan,[61] identified both international human rights abuses and global structures of inequality as the root causes underlying the political violence and upheaval generating refugee movements. The 'root causes debate' led to the unambiguous conclusion that if governments wanted to find lasting solutions to the refugee problem, they had to develop a comprehensive regional and international strategy that addressed conflict, human rights abuses, and poverty. At the time, the UNHCR avoided participation in this wide-ranging debate, although the themes and findings of these reports would influence UNHCR thinking a decade later.

Asylum Crises in the Industrialized Countries and Confrontation with States

Despite stiff opposition from African states who backed a Sudanese candidate as their own regional candidate, Hartling was re-elected for a shortened 3-year term as High Commissioner in 1982. During his second term, the UNHCR came under strong criticism not only from the developing world but also from Western donor governments. As the global refugee crisis intensified in the Third World during the 1980s, greater numbers of people travelled to North America and Western Europe to claim political asylum. When Western governments adopted a series of restrictionist policies to deter new arrivals of asylum-seekers, the UNHCR exerted pressure on them to change their policies. When the UNHCR did intervene on behalf of asylum-seekers or challenge governments on their asylum policies, this frequently led to a direct confrontation. Both the US and Western European governments responded to such pressures with frequent and overt criticisms of both High Commissioner Hartling and his Office.

The 1980s rudely shook the industrialized countries out of their old notions of insularity from the world's refugee problems. Apart from the occasional ballet dancer, rocket scientist, or merchant marine seaman from the Soviet bloc, political asylum had been an exceptional event for the West. Most refugees fled well-publicized persecution in Communist countries. Western governments never envisaged large-scale population movements from the Third World. The developed world was simply too distant, and jet-age travel too uncommon, for most Third World nationals to reach it. Particularly disturbing to Western governments was the fact that, in contrast to the past, asylum applicants increasingly bypassed established refugee-processing channels. Unlike the millions who endured the rigours of camp life throughout the Third World, the new refugees either independently took the initiative to secure safety in the West or turned to immigrant-trafficking organizations to purchase false documents that enabled them to travel to industrialized countries to apply for asylum.

Asylum-seekers from El Salvador

Western governments regarded such activities as illegal and branded these people as opportunists, bogus refugees, and queue jumpers. Although some asylum applicants clearly attempted to enter the West by subterfuge, in reality many were genuinely in search of a safe havens. This was particularly true for the Salvadorans whose close relatives had 'disappeared' or who had been terrified by roaming 'death squads' and by the violence of the civil war in El Salvador, and who had streamed northward toward the US border.[62] The targets of the death squads included students, teachers, labour leaders, peasants suspected of harbouring guerrillas, elected officials, priests, and leftist politicians. Early in the decade, the UNHCR had established camps for Salvadoran refugees in Honduras, Costa Rica, and Nicaragua, but these camps were small, understaffed, remote and able to take only a tiny fraction of the hundreds of thousands of people who fled.[63] Moreover protection in the region was precarious. Many refugees were targets of periodic attacks, forced recruitment, harassment, and abuse.[64] As early as 1980, in response to such conditions, many attempted to enter the United States, further swelling both the illegal immigration population and the number of asylum applicants.

The United States almost uniformly denied asylum to all of the Salvadorans who applied for such status. A general determination was made in the State Department that almost all Salvadorans who entered the United States did so either because they feared 'generalized violence' rather than 'persecution', or were economically motivated.[65] This determination was made despite the fact that from 1979 to 1990 about 50,000 civilians were killed in El Salvador. Over one million people—about a quarter of the population—were displaced from their homes, and the UNHCR argued that Salvadorans should have a *prima facie* right to political asylum. The best available evidence indicates that in 1980, no Salvadorans were granted asylum, and nearly 12,000 were deported.

Salvadorans were frequently turned back at the border with no practical opportunity to submit asylum claims. Those not turned back were detained in holding facilities a few miles from the Mexican border. Legal representation was discouraged; INS officials frequently coerced Salvadorans into leaving the country 'voluntarily' within hours after their arrival. This avoided the necessity of protracted asylum and deportation hearings. Still others were forcibly deported, either via Mexico, or on direct flights to El Salvador. Deportations continued even after it was demonstrated that some of those involuntarily returned had since been murdered. Asylum requests were processed slowly and almost always turned down.[66]

The UNHCR protested regularly about the US policy of deporting Salvadorans back to a country where human rights abuses were widespread and death squads were operating freely. In June 1981, the UNHCR protection division in Geneva criticized American policy in an *aide-mémoire* to the US mission in Geneva. It followed up with another aid *aide-mémoire* in September arguing that the Salvadorans 'should be given permission to remain in the United States until such time as conditions in El Salvador improved'.[67] That same month two officials from the Washington liaison office of the UNHCR visited several detention centres for Salvadoran asylum-seekers in the American southwest. Their report detailed how the US created a disincentive for Salvadorans to enter and pursue asylum claims by the use of high bond, denial of work authorization, pressure from the INS to sign 'voluntary departure' forms, summary hearings, and long detention. The officials noted that 'though in theory any Salvadoran illegal entrant may apply for asylum, there appears to be a systematic practice designed to secure the return of Salvadorans, irrespective of the merits of asylum claims'.[68] The officials' final recommendation was that the

UNHCR continue to express its concern to the U.S. government that its apparent failure to grant asylum to any significant number of Salvadorans, coupled with continuing large-scale forcible and voluntary return to El Salvador, would appear to represent a negation of its responsibility assumed upon its adherence to the Protocol. (Report of the United Nations High Commissioner for Refugees Mission to Monitor INS Asylum Processing of Salvadoran Illegal Entrants—September 13–18, 1981, reprinted in *Congressional Record*, 11 February 1982, S827–831).

These concerns continued to be voiced exclusively through private diplomatic channels and so irritated US policy-makers in the Office of the US Coordinator for Refugee Affairs that they reportedly suggested that the UNHCR Washington office be closed.[69] The US rejected all UNHCR criticisms of its asylum policy, and the UNHCR was unable to exert significant pressure on the US to change its policy regarding Salvadorans. Salvadorans continued to be denied asylum,[70] and deportations continued at a monthly rate of 300 to 500 individuals.

Haitian Boat People

The UNHCR enjoyed even less success in exerting pressure on the US to change it policy regarding Haitian asylum-seekers. The UNHCR was in a weak position to be an advocate for the protection of refugees and asylum-seekers. The agency's growing reliance on major donor governments for financial resources to fund its huge care and maintenance programmes for the millions of refugees warehoused in camps throughout the developing world made the Office hesitant to openly criticize Western governments' asylum policies no matter how discriminatory and inhumane they were. Such concerns underlay Hartling's reluctance to criticize US policy toward Haitian asylum-seekers.

In 1977, the newly elected American administration of Jimmy Carter placed a greater priority on human rights in US foreign policy. A National Security Council (NSC) Presidential Review Memorandum urged President Carter to 'demonstrate a generous humanitarian policy of providing refuge to victims of repression'.[71] The NSC policy memorandum continued:

Specifically, we believe that the Attorney-General and the INS in considering applicants for parole into the United States should be more forthcoming with respect to victims of authoritarian regimes. Such a change in policy would be a concrete demonstration of the sincerity of our commitment to human rights . . . Dissidents in repressive countries, to the extent that they may be able to proceed to free countries, should generally be considered as refugees. Most such dissidents would qualify as refugees under the new definition of refugees contained in the pending legislation that we support. (Presidential Review Memorandum/NSC 28: *Human Rights* (15 August 1977): 27–8).

These developments led to the passage of new US legislation—the *Refugee Act* of 1980—which abolished the former requirement in US law that refugees come from Communist countries, and committed the US unequivocally to the same definition and standards contained in the international refugee legal instruments.

Despite the human rights commitment of the Carter administration, US refugee and asylum decision-making remained highly politicised and not amenable to meaningful supervision by the UNHCR. The Congressional investigations and hearings in 1975 and 1976 had cast doubt on the adequacy and fairness of US actions. Nevertheless, the immigration service launched a programme in 1978 that had as its objective the expulsion of all Haitian asylum-seekers. Asylum hearings were expedited, depriving applicants of effective representation. INS operating instructions that afforded Haitians the opportunity to fight their deportation were ignored. The hearings themselves were summary and their results automatically negative. In 1980, in a lengthy and angry opinion on the Haitian programme, Judge Lawrence King stated:

Those Haitians who came to the United States seeking freedom and justice did not find it. Instead, they were confronted with an Immigration and Naturalization Service determined to deport them. The decision was made among high INS officials to expel Haitians, despite whatever claims to asylum individual Haitians might have. A program was set up to accomplish this goal. The program resulted in wholesale violations of due process, and only Haitians were affected. This program, in its planning and executing, is offensive to every notion of constitutional due process and equal protection. (*Haitian Refugee Center v. Civiletti*, 503 F. Supp. 442. (S.D. Fla. 1980) affirmed 676 F. 2nd 1023 (11 Cir. 1982)).

The UNHCR frequently expressed its concerns about the treatment accorded Haitians. In August 1976, the State Department requested that the UNHCR provide advisory opinions as to the eligibility for refugee status of Haitians seeking asylum in the United States.[72] During 1977, the UNHCR reviewed some 169 cases out of 337 referred to the Office for advisory opinions.[73] On the basis of the files submitted, the UNHCR recommended the granting of asylum in only a few instances. In public statements defending its asylum policy, the State Department interpreted this result as approval of its own negative findings. The UNHCR, however, objected strongly, asserting that its approval rate primarily reflected the large numbers of files that were so incomplete that no inferences, positive or negative, could be drawn from them. The UNHCR also questioned the State Department's willingness to grant asylum in the instances where positive recommendations had been made.[74] Finally, whatever the merits of the asylum claims, the UNHCR expressed concern that Amnesty International, the National Council of Churches, the Haitian exile community, and most of the asylum applicants believed that returnees would be severely punished or even killed.[75] Consequently, UNHCR officials believed that the 'UNHCR has a humanitarian obligation not to agree to Haitians being forcibly returned to Haiti from the U.S. until the position as to the human rights situation in the country has been clarified'.[76] They argued that the UNHCR should extend its 'good offices' to assist Haitian refugees and displaced persons and to protect them from being returned to their country of origin just as the Office had done in the past for Eastern Europeans and Vietnamese boat people—the majority of whom had been assessed by the UNHCR as not falling within the strict refugee definition.[77] These views had no noticeable effect on US policy either then or later, and the United States continued to evaluate Haitian claims in a manner consistent with its own geopolitical interests. Even after the passage of the 1980 *Refugee Act*, the US made no serious attempt to apply the standards of international law to the decision-making process.

In April 1980, an asylum crisis of unparalleled dimensions in US history profoundly affected American asylum policy during the 1980s. Within only a month of the passage of the *Refugee Act* of 1980, the first wave of boats that would eventually bring 130,000 Cubans to Florida over a five-month period, hit American shores. The asylum system was completely swamped. By the end of 1980, these Cubans had been joined by over 11,000 Haitian boat people and by an indeterminate number of Iranians, Nicaraguans, and Ethiopians seeking political asylum. Perhaps 150,000 to 160,000 aliens with potential asylum claims entered the United States in 1980. According to a high INS official at the time, 'within six months after the passage of the Refugee Act, more than 100,000 individual claims for asylum had been filed'.[78]

The domestic backlash and public resentment resulting from the sudden and chaotic arrival of Cubans in Florida jeopardized the principle of asylum and refugee welcome in the United States. The US government agencies charged with regulating refugee flow and determining asylum claims were completely overwhelmed. The INS lacked the personnel to interview and evaluate each applicant properly. According to the Assistant Director of the INS at the time, 'overnight the U.S. had become a country of first asylum. No machinery had been assembled to handle this workload. And no serious thinking or planning had been done to analyze the implications of the U.S. as a country of both first asylum and resettlement'.[79]

The arrival of Cubans and Haitians reached crisis proportions at the same time the refugee flow from Indo-China peaked at nearly 200,000. In 1980 alone, 800,000 immigrants and refugees—more than those entering all the other countries in the world combined—entered the United States legally while hundreds of thousands of Mexicans and others entered illegally. The problem of asylum-seekers and refugees came to be linked in the public mind with the problem of illegal aliens and thus fanned the public fear of hordes of uncontrolled illegal immigrants crossing US borders almost at will.

As the asylum system became hopelessly blocked and as resettlement problems grew, the mood of the American public shifted, first in Florida and then in the nation as a whole. The widespread perception was that the government was totally unable to control its borders and that the asylum process was 'a dagger pointed at the throat of the American immigration process'. This belief played indelibly on the public mind and figured critically in the shape of the policy responses of the Ronald Reagan administration which assumed office in 1981. In order to reduce the number of asylum claims from the Caribbean and Central America, the new administration adopted a number of restrictive measures and deterrents, including interdiction, widespread use of detention, denial of due process, and swift deportation. In September 1981, an interdiction campaign was launched against Haitian boat people, who were seized in international waters by the US Coast Guard, towed back to Haiti, and delivered up to Haitian authorities. Those fortunate enough to reach the United States were subjected to a harsh detention regime designed specifically to discourage the illegal entry of all Haitians, whatever their reasons for arrival. An internal UNHCR memorandum of 29 October 1981, noted:

Whether or not the measures can be challenged from a legal point of view is not certain. The newly introduced interdiction measures, of course, deprive asylum-seekers at sea of access to counsel and of the appeal possibilities which they would have had had they entered the USA . . . the new interdiction measures could certainly constitute an undesirable precedent for other areas of the world (e.g., South East Asia) where UNHCR has sought to prevent asylum seekers being towed out to sea. (Cited in William Shawcross, *The Quality of Mercy*: 326–7).

Moreover, many UNHCR officials believed that the interdiction policy directly contravened US obligations under the international refugee instruments and the 1980 *Refugee Act*. However, these officials were not only incapable of changing US policy, they had grave difficulty in getting initial support from the High Commissioner, Poul Hartling, who was afraid of upsetting his Office's main financial backer. On a mission to the US in October and November 1981, Hartling failed to take up these matters forcefully with the US government. Asked at a press conference about the Reagan administration's claim that the Haitians and Salvadorans were 'economic migrants', not refugees, he replied that a prospective host country should make decisions on eligibility. Moreover, he said he was satisfied that the United States' interviews of Haitians on the high seas 'adhered to the absolutely fair and fine [US] tradition to treat asylum-seekers in a right and generous way'.[80]

Hartling's remarks provoked a storm of protest in the ranks of the UNHCR.[81] Ultimately, the UNHCR exerted more pressure on the US to change its policy. During spring 1982, a UNHCR mission to the US looked specifically at the Haitian interdiction programme. According to sources in the UNHCR and the INS, the only concession made by the US was a promise to afford Haitians intercepted on the high seas adequate shipboard asylum hearings. From September 1981 to March 1985, some 3,000 Haitians were intercepted by the US Coast Guard. Not one Haitian was found by US authorities to have presented a valid claim to asylum, and not one Haitian was taken to the US to have his claim more carefully examined.[82] So although the US was supposed to have changed INS guidelines regarding the interdiction programme, actual decision-making regarding Haitian asylum-seekers did not change in any way. Selective and quiet UNHCR efforts to halt deportations continued but the US refused to alter its policies.[83]

Asylum and Migration Pressures in Europe

The 1980s also put additional pressures on the political asylum systems of Western Europe. Previously, Western Europe generally demonstrated a liberal attitude toward asylum-seekers but by the 1980s the welcome mat in Europe was quickly being withdrawn. The number of applicants in European countries suddenly rose from approximately 20,000 in 1976 to 158,500 in 1980.[84] The steep rise in European unemployment combined with high immigration levels gave rise to increasing concern about being flooded by foreigners. Governments reacted by tightening border controls, but such deterrent measures did not work for long. The numbers reached over 450,000 per annum by 1990.[85] From 1983 to 1989, some 60 per cent of the 1.3 million asylum-seekers in Europe came from the Third World. They were driven by political crises and armed conflicts in Africa, Asia, and the Middle East[86]— one-third originated from the Middle East; 15 per cent from the Indian subcontinent; 10 per cent from Africa; and over 20 per cent from Eastern Europe. The Gulf War between Iran and Iraq generated 150,000 asylum applicants, civil wars in Sri Lanka brought 100,000 Tamils, and the war in Lebanon brought some 50,000 Lebanese to Europe.

The influx included many people who, although they could not return to their countries of origin where their lives were at risk, did not meet the criteria of the 1951 Convention. Growing numbers of economic migrants also tried to use the asylum system to enter Europe. The unexpected arrival in the West of large numbers of people with a variety of claims to asylum severely jolted existing practices and overtaxed the procedural systems for handling refugee determinations. Once in the West, the majority of asylum-seekers stayed, sometimes for several years, working through appeal procedures up to and including judicial review. In Germany, for example, despite the introduction of accelerated procedures for some applicants, it often took many years for a final determination to be made. In other countries it took 18 months or longer. The substantial backlog of claims resulted in claimants remaining even longer in Western countries and requiring additional material assistance, thus putting a considerable strain on reception and integration facilities.

It was not only the magnitude, but also, more importantly, the nature of contemporary asylum movements that alarmed European policy-makers. Western officials became increasingly sceptical of the genuineness of many of the asylum claims and viewed the influx of refugees as part of a mass attempt by foreigners to enter their societies illegally in search of employment and social welfare. Furthermore, they believed that foreigners were simply taking advantage of the work permits and social service benefits that had been provided to asylum applicants. It was argued that most of their claims were spurious, thinly disguising economic migrants as political refugees. Not surprisingly, West European governments sought to reduce the number of asylum-seekers by applying a rigorous standard in judging whether they should grant an individual refugee status. The UNHCR countered governments' alarm over 'irregular' asylum-seekers by pointing out that these individuals were in fact only persons who had failed to comply with 'structured international efforts to provide appropriate solutions. . .'. They were people who, sensing themselves to be in jeopardy dared to take their fate into their own hands and moved on 'without the proper consent of national authorities'.[87] Indeed, as the UNHCR noted, nothing in the international refugee instruments indicated that asylum-seekers who found neither security nor means of subsistence in the country where they first arrived should not be allowed to proceed to another country where their situation might be more secure.[88] The UNHCR consistently urged nations to construe the language of the 1951 Refugee Convention generously, so as not to exclude vast numbers of people. The Office maintained that large groups of asylum-seekers who did not fulfil the strict criteria of the refugee definition were nevertheless in need of protection and should not be returned to their countries of origin. But with the upsurge in asylum claims, European governments were not as willing to submit to the UNHCR's authority and leadership as they had been previously.

Governments believed that the most effective way to limit asylum-seekers was to prevent them from arriving in Europe in the first place. Consequently, Western European governments began to build barriers, firstly by revising immigration laws and asylum regulations and procedures, and secondly by adopting restrictive practices and deterrent measures to curb new arrivals. By the mid-1980s, nearly all Western European governments had introduced legislation to make access to their asylum procedures more difficult. As part of their deterrence strategies, governments also began to withdraw most social benefits and work permits from asylum-seekers and to detain them in crowded, austere centres in order to discourage others from trying to seek asylum.

The UNHCR responded to these developments by increasing its monitoring of the asylum policies of Western European governments and issuing critical reports of its findings. This led to increasing tensions between governments and the Office. This is perhaps best illustrated in the case of West Germany where the pressures presented by large flows of asylum-seekers were the greatest in the region. In the early 1980s, West German media and international human rights organizations had reported attempted suicides by asylum-seekers, internment in psychiatric wards, harsh punishment, and malnutrition. In June 1983, the head of the UNHCR's European regional division, Candida Toscani, visited accommodation and detention centres in West Germany and wrote a devastating critique of conditions for asylum-seekers there. Her report criticized the German authorities for allowing only limited freedom of movement for asylum-seekers, for providing insufficient social aid and limited medical and psychiatric care, and for requiring obligatory labour from them. Toscani also reported rumours of malnutrition among refugees and staff hostility towards them. The report pointed out that there was disregard and contempt for the cultural and religious backgrounds of asylum-seekers, including the serving of pork meals to Muslims. Toscani concluded that these measures and conditions had been designed to make life so miserable for asylum-seekers that they would consider returning home. Toscani maintained that these measures 'set a dangerous precedent in Europe which may be imitated by other countries unless the High Commissioner remains vigilant and intervenes in time'.[89]

The Toscani Report was leaked to the press, leading to a direct confrontation between the UNHCR and West Germany. A German interior ministry spokesman bitterly criticized the UNHCR report as unfair and as wrongly creating the impression that Germany was again operating concentration camps. In protest, the German Minister for the Interior refused to receive Poul Hartling. Since the German government had effectively withdrawn its invitation to the High Commissioner to visit the country, Hartling cancelled his planned trip to Bonn. During the following months, no substantial improvements were made in the accommodation centres for asylum-seekers in Germany.

Tensions between the UNHCR and West European governments reached a critical point in the mid-1980s over disagreements regarding the treatment of Tamil asylum-seekers fleeing civil war in Sri Lanka. The Dutch and Swiss governments took a firm stance against the granting of refugee status to the Tamils, claiming that they did not qualify for refugee status as they fled civil war and not individual persecution. Moreover, both governments believed Tamils could be returned to the south of Sri Lanka and deported groups of them in 1984 and 1985. UNHCR officials interviewed Tamils and concluded that most did indeed have a 'well-founded fear of persecution' as required by the 1951 Convention. The UNHCR thought that it was unsafe for Tamils to return, especially for young Tamil males who faced a threat from both Sri Lankan security forces who perceived them as enemies and Tamil guerrilla fighters who wanted to forcibly recruit them.[90] But fearing a backlash by the European governments, the UNHCR did not push them to grant full refugee status for the Tamils. Instead, the UNHCR contended that the Tamil asylum-seekers should be treated as extra-Conventional refugees, who may not be entitled to receive the status provided for under the Refugee Convention, but who must receive protection until it was safe for them to return home.[91]

The UNHCR's concessions to European governments did not increase the agency's leverage with states nor did it improve protection for Tamil asylum-seekers. Governments opposed the Office's claim that Tamils were of legiti-mate concern to the Office and accused the UNHCR of 'taking over the sovereign state's function of deciding whether or not asylum outside the Convention should be granted'.[92] Governments felt that 'such action by UNHCR inhibited the normal (and proper) functions of immigration control and de facto enlarged the effective limitation of the refugee definition in the 1951 Convention'.[93]

By the mid-1980s, European governments and the UNHCR no longer had converging interests, and states were concerned that the Office might reduce their autonomy and power over immigration policy. Consequently, the UNHCR was no longer perceived by governments to be the sole authority and source of legitimacy on refugee and asylum matters. Information and exper-tise did not give the UNHCR the power and influence it had enjoyed previ-ously in Europe. Governments had developed their own asylum administrative arrangements and were determined to reclaim sole authority over their borders and admissions policies.

Not only did Western European governments bristle at what they perceived as UNHCR interference, they also sought to exclude the Office from interstate discussions about their asylum policies. In 1984, the Swiss and Dutch governments arranged a series of informal meetings among European states to discuss the phenomenon of irregular movements of asylum-seekers and the possibility of co-ordinating action and developing common policies to combat these. These meetings gave little consideration to protection issues and the UNHCR was not even invited to observe the meetings. Alarmed by these moves to exclude the UNHCR, Poul Hartling tried to regain face and legitimacy for the Office by initiating a series of formal consultations with states on asylum-seekers and refugees in Europe. The first meeting was convened in Geneva in May 1985 and was chaired by the High Commissioner.

In his opening statement to the consultations, Hartling criticized European governments for making such a fuss about the arrival of so few refugees compared with the burden developing countries had to carry. He reminded governments that only 3 per cent of the world's refugees had sought asylum in the West, and he referred to the asylum-seekers as victims rather than abusers, 'spending weeks at European air terminals, tossed around like ping-pong balls from airport to airport, thrown into orbit'.[94] In direct criticism of government policies, Hartling noted that,

States which have been the champions of human rights are now finding it difficult to grant some of these basic rights to asylum seekers; peoples who have in the past opened their doors and their hearts to refugees are now showing signs of greater reserve and even intolerance *vis-à-vis* asylum-seekers and refugees. (Consultations on the Arrivals of Asylum-Seekers and Refugees in Europe. *Opening Statement by the United Nations High Commissioner for Refugees* UNHCR/CAE/85/1 (Geneva, 28–31 May 1985): 2).

Most governments did not take kindly to Hartling's remarks and the meeting had very mixed results. In his final remarks to the conference, Hartling implied that a compromise had been reached with European governments. The governments had agreed that asylum-seekers like the Tamils, 'should be treated humanely and, in particular, should not be returned to areas where they may be exposed to danger'. In return, the UNHCR agreed that asylum-seekers in Europe 'who left their countries of origin in order to escape from severe internal upheavals or armed conflicts', like the Tamils, were not refugees under the 1951 Convention.[95] However, subsequent treatment of Tamils and other groups of asylum-seekers by European governments proved this to be a bad compromise for refugee protection results. Governments did not fundamentally change their asylum policies as a result of the discussion. Deportations of Tamils continued, particularly in the later 1980s, despite an escalation of the fighting in Sri Lanka.

The May meeting, however, did lay the foundations for subsequent informal and *ad hoc* consultations between the UNHCR and governments and these consultations became the Office's most important line of communication between them. The initial objectives of these consultations were, in the first stage, to co-ordinate European asylum policies and later to conclude multilateral agreements with countries of transit and origin. This dialogue created problems with NGOs who were not participants in the exchanges and who suspected that governments were using the consultations both as a way to exclude them and to get the UNHCR to endorse states' strategy of detention and deterrence in Europe.[96]

European discussions surrounding the creation of a 'Single Europe' left the UNHCR even more marginalized. The removal of internal borders and the creation of a common external border in the new European Union (EU) had considerable bearing on refugee and asylum policy. Consequently, several new regional and intergovernmental groups focused on the asylum issue and drew up new agreements regulating asylum and immigration policies and practices. Most of these groups, however, were closed to outside observers, including the UNHCR, reflecting the growing restrictionism in the region. In bypassing the UNHCR and acting collectively through the EU, European states gained legitimacy for their restrictive policies which otherwise would have been criticized. By the late 1980s, the UNHCR was almost totally excluded from asylum policy discussions by Western European governments and its own authority and legitimacy sank to a new low point.

The Search for a New, Operation-Minded High Commissioner

The confrontation between the UNHCR and its donors reached a critical point in 1985. Not only were European governments impatient with Hartling's handling of the asylum crisis there, but donor governments had tired of funding massive resettlement programmes for the Indo-Chinese and expansive relief operations in the Third World. It was clear that these protracted operations would not end soon. As one report noted, '[i]t made little difference that Hartling—and the UNHCR—had been victim to events beyond their control, particularly the Cold War. Nor was there any sympathy for the way the increase in refugees had overwhelmed the UNHCR's capacity . . . .'[97] The US severely criticized the UNHCR's emergency response to the influx of Tigrayan refugees into Sudan in late 1984. The UNHCR's failure to anticipate the crisis and its mishandling of relief logistics revealed the limits of the Office's capacity to play an operational role in a humanitarian emergency.[98] The US felt that the UNHCR was too legalistic. What was needed, according to the Americans, was a High Commissioner who was more operational and able to handle refugee emergencies. In the search for a solution to the problem, governments turned to the most operational humanitarian agency, the ICRC and its director of operations, Jean-Pierre Hocke.

NOTES

1. According to one UNHCR official, Hartling called Zia Rizvi, Sadruddin's right-hand man, into his office and pointed to several places on a world map. Hartling said, 'You can go here, here or here. You choose.' Rizvi chose Rome. Interview with UNHCR official, Geneva, January 2000.
2. Sometimes this resulted in excesses. For example, when one UNHCR official visited a Laotian refugee camp, he noted that the camp canteen was serving Peking Duck for lunch! Some of the medical facilities at Indo-Chinese refugee camps were so sophisticated that the doctors could perform open heart surgery. Interview with Zia Rizvi, UNHCR, New York, 1983.
3. See Jean and Simone Lacouture, *Vietnam Voyage a Travers une Victoire* (Paris: Seuil,

1976); and Theodore Jacqueney, 'Vietnam's Gulag Archipelago', *New York Times* (17 September 1976).

4. Interviews with David McAree, Amnesty International, London, August 1983; William Shawcross, London, July 1983; and Vietnam Desk Officer, US Department of State, Washington, DC, March 1979. See also: Nguyen Long with Harry H. Kendall, *After Saigon Fell: Daily Life Under the Communists* (Berkeley, CA: Institute of East Asian Studies, University of California, 1981).

5. The description of events in Laos is based on authors' interviews with Martin Barber, UNHCR official in Laos and Thailand from 1973 to 1981, London, July and August 1983; and in Martin Stuart-Fox, ed., *Contemporary Laos* (London: University of Queensland Press, 1983).

6. See US Congress, Joint Economic Committee, *Indochinese Refugees: The Impact on First Asylum Countries and Implications for American Policy* (Washington, DC: Government Printing Office, 1980).

7. Thailand had hosted Vietnamese refugees well before the late 1970s. Tens of thousands of refugees from Vietnam and Laos had taken refuge in Thailand as a result of Vietnam's war of independence against France in the 1950s and subsequent conflicts in the region. The great majority of these refugees had never repatriated and hence the Thai authorities were particularly sensitive to 'the potential danger of long-term responsibility for refugees'. See John Rogge, 'The Indochinese Diaspora: Where Have All the Refugees Gone?', *The Canadian Geographer*, 29: 66, cited by Lester Zeager in *The Role of Threat Power in Refugee Resettlement: The Indochinese Crisis of 1979* (Greenville, NC: East Carolina University, Department of Economics, 30 April 1999).

8. For a Malaysian view see Zakaria Haji Ahmed, 'Vietnamese Refugees and ASEAN', *Contemporary Southeast Asia*, i (Singapore: May 1979): 66–74.

9. Amnesty International, *Submission to the Government of the Socialist Republic of Vietnam on Amnesty International's Current Concerns* (London: Amnesty International, April 1983). See also US State Department cable from Ambassador Morton Abramowitz to Secretary of State, 'Socialist Transformation in South Vietnam', August 1978, in author's files.

10. Barry Wain, *The Refused: The Agony of the Indochinese Refugees* (New York, NY: Simon and Schuster, 1981).

11. For an account of effective domestic lobbying on behalf of the Indo-Chinese refugees, see: Gil Loescher and John Scanlan, *Calculated Kindness: Refugees and America's Half-Open Door*, 1945 to Present (New York, NY: The Free Press, 1986).

12. Interview with Martin Barber, former UNHCR official, August 1983.

13. Valerie Sutter, *The Indochinese Refugee Dilemma* (Baton Route, LA: Louisiana State University Press, 1990): 95.

14. Martin Barber, 'Resettlement of Indochinese in 1981–82', UNHCR internal memorandum, Bangkok, 22 April 1981.

15. Ibid. 10.

16. Ibid. Cover note by A. J. F. Simmance, UNHCR Regional Representative for Western South Asia to R. Sampatkumar, Chief, South and South-East Asian Regional Section, UNHCR Headquarters.

17. US Department of State, *Report of the Indochinese Refugee Panel* (Washington, DC: US Department of State, 18 April 1986).

18. Norman Zucker and Naomi Zucker, *The Guarded Gate: The Reality of American Refugee Policy* (New York, NY: Harcourt Brace Jovanovich, 1987) and Gil Loescher and John Scanlan, *Calculated Kindness*.

19. See Nadine Cohodas, 'Refugee Entries Up in 1984, Same Levels Expected in 1985', *Congressional Quarterly Weekly Report*, 42 (8 December 1984): 3077 (Table—'United States Refugee Admissions, Fiscal Years 1981–85).

20. Dennis McNamara, 'The Origin and Effects of "Humane Deterrence" Policies in South-east Asia', in Gil Loescher and Laila Monahan, eds., *Refugees and International Relations* (Oxford: Clarendon, 1989): 123–33.

21. The author visited closed refugee centres in Hong Kong in 1983 and witnessed the squalid, inhumane conditions prevalent there.

22. Author's interviews with Lionel Rosenblatt, Washington, DC, December 1982. See also William Shawcross, *The Quality of Mercy, Holocaust and Modern Conscience* (New York, NY: Simon and Schuster, 1984), and Linda Mason and Roger Brown, *Rice, Rivalry, and Politics* (South Bend, IN: University of Notre Dame Press, 1983).

23. Interviews with Morton Abramowitz and Lionel Rosenblatt.

24. Interview with Martin Barber, former UNHCR official in Thailand, London, July 1983.

25. Interviews with Martin Barber, Abramowitz Shawcross, and Lionel Rosenblatt, December 1982; Mark Malloch-Brown, UNHCR, Geneva, June 1983; and numerous UNHCR and NGO staff in Geneva and Bangkok, June 1983 and January 1984. See also Shawcross, *The Quality of Mercy*.

26. Interview with Dennis McNamara, UNHCR Director of International Protection, London January 1999.

27. Dennis McNamara, 'The Politics of Humanitarianism: A Study of Some Aspects of the International Response to the Indochinese Refugee Influx (1975–1985)', unpublished manuscript: Section II, 47 and Section V, 21, cited in Courtland Robinson, *Terms of Refuge: The Indochinese Exodus and the International Response* (London: Zed Books, 1998): 49.

28. Thailand expelled the ICRC Head of Delegation in Bangkok after he complained about the mass *refoulement* at Preah Vihear and dismissed the criticism because it was considered 'only Thailand's business, done to protect its national interest'. Courtland Robinson, *Double Vision: A History of Cambodian Refugees in Thailand* (Bangkok: Institute of Asian Studies, Chulalong Korn University, 1996): 55.

29. Interviews with Morton Abramowitz, Lionel Rosenblatt, Martin Barber, Zia Rizvi, John Crowley, and Sheppard Lowman.

30. Ibid.

31. Interview with Lionel Rosenblatt.

32. Initially, the UNHCR opposed the resettlement option. Rizvi believed that if the West offered broad resettlement opportunities to Cambodians, it would, in effect, magnetize the border and create a pole of attraction for farmers who might more profitably stay inside their own country. Making resettlement more readily available might also discourage those refugees in holding centres who would otherwise seek to be repatriated. The UNHCR believed that substantial numbers of Cambodians in the holding centres would be ready to return to their home villages if a safe means of transport could be found. The UNHCR, therefore, discouraged the US from admitting large numbers of Cambodians until the results of repatriation

negotiations with the Vietnamese authorities in Phnom Penh could be determined. Author's interview with Zia Rizvi, Martin Barber, and Mark Malloch-Brown, UNHCR staff members, New York, London, and Geneva, 1983.

33. Josephine Reynell, *Political Pawns: Refugees on the Thai-Kampuchean Border* (Oxford: Refugee Studies Program, 1989).

34. Gil Loescher, *Refugee Movements and International Security* Adelphi Paper 268 (London: Brasseys, for the International Institute for Strategic Studies, 1992); and Aristide Zolberg, Astri Suhrke, and Sergio Aguayo, *Escape from Violence: Conflict and Refugee Crises in the Developing World* (New York, NY: Oxford University Press, 1989).

35. Jean-Christophe Rufin, *Le Piege Humanitaire suivi de Humanitaire et Politique depuis le Chute du Mur* (Paris: Jean-Claude Lattes, 1994) cited by Fiona Terry, 'Condemned to Repeat? The Paradoxes of Humanitarian Action'. Ph.D. dissertation (Canberra: Australian National University, 2000): 24.

36. Elly-Elikunda Mtango, 'Military and Armed Attacks on Refugee Camps', in Loescher and Monahan, *Refugees and International Relations:* 87–121.

37. *Informal Meeting on Military Attacks on Refugee Camps and Settlements in Southern Africa and Elsewhere* (Geneva: EC/SCP/27, Sub-committee of the Whole on International Protection, UNHCR Executive Committee, 6 June 1983): 109–11.

38. No. 48 (XLVII) 1987: 'Military or Armed Attacks on Refugee Camps and Settlements', in UNHCR, *Conclusions on the International Protection of Refugees Adopted by the Executive Committee of the UNHCR Program* (Geneva: UNHCR, 1991): 61.

39. UNHCR, *State of the World's Refugees: Fifty Years of Humanitarian Action* (Oxford: Oxford University Press, 2000).

40. The US allegedly placed strong pressure on the UNHCR to avoid criticizing Pakistani support of the resistance parties and not to interfere in Pakistani policy. See H. Baitenman, 'NGOs and the Afghan War: The Politicization of Humanitarian Aid', *Third World Quarterly*, 12/1 (1990): 68.

41. Interview with Anders Johnson, UNHCR, Geneva, 1988. The militarization of Afghan refugee camps was also evident to the author when he visited these camps in Pakistan in 1988.

42. Robert Oakley, US State Department and former American Ambassador to Pakistan, comments at an MIT conference, October 1999.

43. The author visited the Khmer camps along the Thai-Cambodian border in 1983.

44. Gil Loescher, 'Humanitarianism and Politics in Central America' in Bruce Nichols and Gil Loescher, eds., *The Moral Nation: Humanitarianism and U.S. Foreign Policy Today* (South Bend, IN: University of Notre Dame Press, 1989): 154–91. The author visited refugee camps in Honduras, Costa Rica, Nicaragua, and Mexico in 1986.

45. The author visited refugee camps for Salvadoran and Nicaraguan refugees in Honduras in 1986.

46. Interview with FMLN leader, Facundo Guardado Guardado, New York, July 2000.

47. Ibid.

48. US Comptroller General, *Central American Refugees: Regional Conditions and Prospects and Potential Impact on the United States*, Report to the Congress of the United States (Washington, DC: GAO/NSIAD–84–106, US General Accounting Office, 20 July 1984).

49. UNHCR, *Refugees*, 27 (Geneva: UNHCR, March 1986): 22.

50. Jeff Crisp and Nick Cater, 'The Human Consequences of Conflict in the Horn of Africa: Refugees, Asylum and the Politics of Assistance'. Paper presented at International Institute o Strategic Studies Regional Security Conference, Cairo, Egypt (27–30 May 1990): 6.

51. United Nations, *Quarterly Economic Review of Thailand, Burma*, 4th Quarter (1978): 11. Cited in Tony Reid, 'Repatriation of Arakanese Muslims from Bangladesh to Burma, 1978–79. "Arranged" Reversal of the Flow of the Ethnic Minority'. Unpublished paper (Oxford: Documentation Centre, Refugee Studies Centre, Oxford University): 15.

52. Reid, 'Repatriation of Arakanese Muslims': 22.

53. Cato Aall, 'Disastrous International Relief Failure: A Report on Burmese Refugees in Bangladesh from May to December 1978,' *Disasters*, 3/4 (1979): 429.

54. Barry Stein, 'Ad Hoc Assistance to Return Movements and Long-Term Development Programmes', in Timothy Allen and Hubert Morsink, eds., *When Refugees Go Home* (Trenton, NJ: Africa World Press, 1994): 50–70.

55. *World Refugee Survey* (Washington, DC: US Committee for Refugees, 1989).

56. Interview with Jacques Cuenod; Jacques Cuenod, 'Refugees: Development or Relief' in Loescher and Monahan, *Refugees and International Relations*: 219–53; and UNHCR, *The State of the World's Refugees 2000*.

57. United Nations General Assembly, Doc. A/AC.96/645, 28 August 1984, 'Refugee Aid and Development', annex 1.

58. United Nations General Assembly, Doc. A/Conf.125/2 of 23 March 1987 and Addendum no. 1 of 8 November 1984, 'Detailed Description of Needs, Project Outlines, and Background Information on the Refugee Situation'.

59. UNHCR, Central Evaluation Section, *Returnee Aid and Development* (Geneva: UNHCR, 1994).

60. For a wider discussion see Zolberg, Suhrke, and Aguayo, *Escape From Violence*.

61. Sadruddin Aga Khan, *Study on Human Rights and Massive Exoduses*, ECOSOC doc. E/CN4/1503, 1981.

62. Amnesty International, Americas Watch, United Nations and OAS reports all documented widespread human right violations in El Salvador during the 1980s.

63. The author visited refugee camps for Guatemalans, Salvadorans, and Nicaraguans in Mexico, Honduras, Costa Rica, and Nicaragua in 1986.

64. Gil Loescher, 'Humanitarianism and Politics in Central America', *Political Science Quarterly*, 103 (Summer 1988): 295–320.

65. The standard set for a Salvadoran asylum-seeker was much higher than for other nationalities. The INS noted in an internal report: 'For an El Salvadoran national to receive a favourable asylum advisory opinion, he or she must have "a classic textbook case".' See INS, 'Asylum Adjudications: An Evolving Concept and Responsibility for the INS' (Internal Memorandum, June and December 1982): 59.

66. In 1981, the INS granted asylum to 2 Salvadorans, denied asylum to 154 and remained undecided about 6,043 applicants. INS statistics provided to the author by the UNHCR.

67. UNHCR aide-mémoire, 23 September 1981.

68. Report of the United Nations High Commissioner for Refugees Mission to Monitor INS Asylum Processing of Salvadoran Illegal Entrants—September 13–18, 1981,' reprinted in *Congressional Record*, 11 February 1982, S827–831.

69. Interview with Joachim Henckel, UNHCR, Washington, DC, 1983.
70. In 1982, 69 Salvadorans were granted asylum, 1,178 were denied asylum, and 22,314 cases were left pending; in 1983, 328 Salvadorans were granted asylum and 13,045 were denied.
71. Presidential Review Memorandum/NSC 28: *Human Rights* (15 August 1977): 27–8.
72. This was the first institutional involvement of the UNHCR with eligibility determination of asylum-seekers in the US. See: UNHCR 100.USA.HAI, Memorandum, *Haitians Seeking Asylum in the U.S.* (23 February 1978).
73. Ibid.
74. Ibid.
75. There were reports of returnees 'going missing' or of being imprisoned, tortured, and killed. Amnesty International reported in 1976 that Haiti had the highest prisoner mortality rate in the world, that the rule of law was effectively suspended in Haiti, and that the judicial system did not operate.
76. UNHCR. 100.USA.HAI. John Kelly, Regional Representative, UN Headquarters, New York from Dennis McNamara, Assistant Regional Representative, *Question of Return to Haiti of Haitians in the United States*, 1 September 1978.
77. Ibid.
78. Doris Meissner, 'Central American Refugees: Political Asylum, Sanctuary and Humanitarian Policy', in Nichols and Loescher, *The Moral Nation*: 126.
79. Ibid: 127.
80. Shawcross, *The Quality of Mercy*: 326–7.
81. The *Guardian*, 'Refugee Law Violated', (10 December 1981).
82. Interview with UNHCR officials, Washington, DC, March 1985.
83. Ibid.
84. The huge increase in asylum applications at the beginning of the 1980s was largely the result of three factors: 1) political and economic unrest in Poland; 2) the refusal by Germany and other governments to grant citizenship to a substantial number of immigrant workers, mostly Turks, who, after quite long periods of residence in Western Europe, claimed asylum to avoid deportation to Turkey where harsh military rule was imposed in 1980; and 3) the sharply worsening conditions of physical security in certain parts of the Third World which led many young people, particularly Iranians, who upon completing studies in Europe, to try to extend their stay by seeking refugee status. See: Philip Rudge, 'Fortress Europe' in *World Refugee Survey: 1986 in Review* (Washington, DC: US Committee for Refugees, 1987): 5–12.
85. The character of migration to Europe also changed during the 1980s. Until the oil crisis of the 1970s, about 70% of immigration involved foreign workers. From the mid-1980s, the number of asylum-seekers entering Europe annually exceeded the number of foreign workers. By 1989, over 80% of legal immigration has involved people admitted on social and humanitarian grounds, mainly cases of family reunion and refugees. See Jonas Widgren, 'Europe and International Migration in the Future', in Loescher and Monahan, *Refugees and International Relations*: 49–61.
86. For example, in addition to the larger numbers of persecuted people in need of protection, there was a dramatic rise in the number of applicants from Bangladesh, Ghana, India, Pakistan, Turkey, and Yugoslavia with no or very weak asylum claims. By 1988, moreover, the flows from chronic refugee-generating countries

such as Sri Lanka, Iran, Lebanon, and Ethiopia had stabilized or decreased, while flows from countries on the periphery of Western Europe increased—in particular from Turkey, Poland, and Yugoslavia which comprised over 40 per cent of the asylum applications in Europe just before the collapse of Communist regimes in Eastern Europe.

87. UNHCR, Executive Committee, EC/SCR/40, 1985, cited in James Hathaway, 'Burden Sharing or Burden Shifting? Irregular Asylum Seekers: What's All the Fuss?', *Refuge* 8 (December 1988): 1.

88. Michael Petersen, *Asylum in Europe at a Crossroads*, UNHCR 600 GEN (25 February 1986); and Gilbert Jaeger, *Study of Irregular Movements of Asylum Seekers and Refugees* (Geneva: UNHCR, 1985).

89. UNHCR internal report, Candida Toscani, *Mission to the Federal Republic of Germany, June 6–10, 1983* (Geneva: 1 July 1983).

90. Interviews with Dennis McNamara and Shamshul Bari who led two UNHCR to Sri Lanka in 1984 and 1986, Geneva, December 1986.

91. The UNHCR strongly criticized government asylum policies toward Tamils, Palestinians, and Iranians, and argued that in cases of large-scale influxes of asylum-seekers it might 'be necessary to find an intermediate solution for the group as a whole, e.g., by regularizing the situation of the group on a temporary basis until individual screening can be carried out, or by resorting from the outset to a so-called *prima facie* group determination of refuge status'. Executive Committee of the High Commissioner's Programme, Sub-Committee of the Whole on International Protection, Follow-up on earlier Conclusions of the sub-Committee, The Determination of Refugee Status, *inter alia*, with reference to the role of the UNHCR in National Refugee Status Determination Procedures, Geneva, 1982.

92. This was the view of a British minister who participated in the debates at the time. Roy McDowall, 'Coordination of Refugee Policy in Europe', in Loescher and Monahan, *Refugees and International Relations*: 186.

93. Ibid.

94. UNHCR/CAE/85/1. Consultations on the Arrivals of Asylum-Seekers and Refugees in Europe. *Opening Statement by the United Nations High Commissioner for Refugees* (Geneva, 28–31 May 1985): 4.

95. Ibid: *Summing-Up by the United Nations High Commissioner for Refugees.*

96. Interview with Philip Rudge, European Council on Refugees and Exile, London, July 1985.

97. Lawyers Committee for Human Rights, *The UNHCR at 40: Refugee Protection at the Crossroads* (New York, NY: Lawyers Committee for Human Rights, 1991): 27.

98. Ibid: 26–7.

8

The UNHCR's 'New Look', Financial Crisis, and Collapse of Morale under Jean-Pierre Hocke and Thorvald Stoltenberg

By the end of 1985, there was a general lack of government confidence in the UNHCR. The world's most powerful governments, particularly the United States, were unhappy with the UNHCR and felt that the Office needed vigorous leadership and new thinking. Western donor governments perceived the UNHCR to be too focused on protection issues in Europe and North America and too little concerned with managing refugee programmes in the developing world. The United States, in particular, criticized the Office's 'legalistic' approach and campaigned strenuously for a new High Commissioner who would be more 'operational' and have a 'hands-on' approach to refugee problems. By the mid-1980s, UNHCR-run refugee camps in Africa, Central America, Indo-China, and Pakistan were filled beyond capacity, and the US perceived many of these camps to be important refuges and sources of support for 'freedom fighters' against Soviet or Soviet-backed rule.[1] There was no question that the UNHCR at that time was more valued by the US and many donor governments for its relief operations than for its protection of refugees.

Jean-Pierre Hocke, the Swiss director of Operations at the International Committee of the Red Cross (ICRC) in Geneva seemed to many to fit the description of an operations-oriented manager and was consequently strongly supported by the United States and many Third World governments to succeed Hartling as High Commissioner. Hocke was a car salesman before joining the ICRC to help in the Biafran conflict. He became director of operations of the ICRC in 1973. In that position, he pushed the ICRC into the global limelight by making the organization more professional and internationally minded, thereby drawing the support of the media and donor governments. Under his leadership, the logistics of handling major relief programmes were vastly improved and the number of ICRC delegations around the world doubled between 1978 and 1983.[2] Consequently, the ICRC moved to the forefront of humanitarian affairs in the 1980s and Hocke earned the reputation of being a strong, direct, and decisive leader. He was not an intellectual but a pragmatic operator who preferred to act alone rather than to plan carefully and consider all options. His style of management was sometimes abrasive and inconsiderate of others. He made many enemies and had few close allies. He preferred to take decisions and to act without consulting others beforehand. However, in the homogeneous and close-knit world of ICRC, his ambitious, confident, and daring style seemed to be effective. The United States was clearly enamoured of the ICRC director and almost single-handedly won him the post of High Commissioner: and three years later managed Hocke's re-election for a second term.

The UNHCR's 'New Look' under Hocke

When Jean-Pierre Hocke took up the position of High Commissioner on 1 January 1986, he was determined to 'get rid of dead wood' in the UNHCR and to give the Office a new face and a new purpose.[3] He believed that he was given a mandate by donor governments to change past practice and make the organization more relevant to the contemporary refugee problem. In a speech at Oxford University in October 1986, Hocke outlined his views on the directions the UNHCR should take in the future.[4] The High Commissioner criticized Hartling's willingness to let millions of refugees sit idle for years in camps without any hope of solution:

Consider the fact that there are some 3 million refugees in Pakistan, 2 million in Iran, over a million in Sudan, hundreds of thousands in Somalia, and tens of thousands in various other countries in Asia, Africa, and Central America. Unlike the not too distant past when most refugees had the opportunity to integrate into and become useful and productive members of their host societies, today's refugees often find themselves confined in overcrowded refugee camps and settlements. For many people this has become the normal way of life. Its perpetuation crushes human dignity and reduces the human capacity for hope and regeneration. (Jean-Pierre Hocke, 'Beyond Humanitarianism: The Need for Political Will to Resolve Today's Refugee Problem', in Loescher and Monahan, eds., *Refugees and International Relations*: 37–8).

In words reminiscent of van Heuven Goedhart, the first High Commissioner, when speaking about the displaced persons camps in Europe in the 1950s, Hocke called the long-term confinement of millions of refugees in refugee camps in the 1980s 'a blot on the human conscience'.[5] The High Commissioner also noted that the global refugee problem had grown to such large dimensions that it could no longer be treated in a legalistic manner nor in isolation from the larger context of international relations. In his view the traditional means and approaches of the Office would no longer work.

Everything had changed. The 1951 Refugee Convention was outdated and the majority of refugees no longer corresponded to the formal definition of refugee in that Convention. Rather, the High Commissioner believed that refugees now belonged to 'the wider category of persons who leave their countries because of danger to their lives and security emanating from armed conflict or other forms of violence or danger'.[6] While these people had to be given international protection, including temporary asylum and humane treatment, the refugee crisis could only be adequately addressed by approaching the problem in its broad international political context and by seeking comprehensive political and diplomatic as well as legal solutions. According to Hocke, this strategy required involving not only asylum governments in negotiations, as the UNHCR was traditionally inclined to do, but also countries of origin. He also believed the Office had to be involved in discussions of the 'root causes' of the refugee exoduses. In particular, the High Commissioner identified voluntary repatriation as 'the only realistic alternative to indefinite subsistence on charity'.[7]

This analysis of the refugee crisis and the UNHCR's role was far-sighted and presaged many of the policies and practices that the Office would try to put into operation in the post-Cold War period of the 1990s. However, Hocke's ideas were clearly too far ahead of the time. Throughout most of the 1980s, Cold War politics continued to paralyse diplomatic initiatives to break the deadlock of regional conflicts in most of Africa, Asia, and Central America and hence most refugees were destined to remain trapped in camps for most of the decade. Moreover, Hocke's style of management was terribly divisive. He was stubborn and refused to take advice. He criticized the Protection Division as élitist in its attitude towards other bureaux within the Office and sought to redirect the focus of protection away from UNHCR headquarters in Geneva towards the field.[8] Rather than promoting a greater sense of teamwork within the Office, his policies tore apart the UNHCR, drastically lowered morale, and subjected the Office to international humiliation and unprecedented external scrutiny. Hocke's term would end abruptly in disgrace in 1989 before the Cold War officially ended.

The Downgrading of Protection and the UNHCR's Legal Culture

Hocke's mode of operation had serious implications for both the direction and reputation of the Office. The protection of refugees was considered by many both within and without the organization to be the bedrock of the UNHCR mandate. However, Hocke's priority was to raise the profile of operations in the field, not protection. One of Hocke's most controversial decisions involved reorganizing the Office to emphasize the new orientation towards operations. Previously the Director of Protection had overall authority and responsibility for protection work in the field. Hocke downgraded the protection division to a unit servicing the regional bureaux and renamed it the division of 'Refugee Law and Doctrine', a term he took from the ICRC.[9] In place of the Director of Protection issuing instructions to the field, Hocke ordered that each regional bureau appoint a protection officer whose job it was to report protection problems to the regional bureau heads. These organizational changes essentially sidelined the former protection division and caused it to lose its pre-eminence inside the UNHCR.

In making these decisions, Hocke acted alone and did not consult staff or governments. The High Commissioner made no attempt to explain or justify these decisions and hence these changes provoked great controversy both within the Office and among NGOs. Many UNHCR staffers believed this restructuring reflected a de-emphasis of protection and a triumph of expediency over principle. NGOs complained that the new UNHCR had lost its 'soul' by reorienting its priorities from protection to operations.

Placing protection in the field rather than in Geneva did not have the effect Hocke desired. Because of limited resources and the resistance of staff in the field to take human rights initiatives, an operational link to protection did not develop. As a result Hocke weakened the UNHCR's long-standing protection regime without strengthening it elsewhere in the UNHCR system. Morale within the UNHCR sank like a rock and the High Commissioner began to lose the confidence of NGOs and some governments.

The High Commissioner also made several controversial personnel changes and appointments. In a very visible sign of downgrading the import-ance of protection, Hocke removed Michel Moussalli, who had been a widely respected Director of Protection under Hartling, and replaced him with Ghassan Arnaout, a Syrian, who was not known as an advocate for refugee protection. He also appointed Antoine Noel, an Ethiopian, as the director of the Africa bureau. Both men had strongly lobbied Third World governments to secure Hocke's election and re-election. They were widely perceived as political appointments that smacked of patronage. Consequently an inordinate amount of time was spent on politicking within the Office and little time on protection. In another controversial move, Hocke appointed Jonas Widgren, a former Swedish Deputy Minister of Immigration, to take over the co-ordination of the UNHCR's informal consultations with European governments. Hocke felt that Hartling had mishandled European governments over the asylum issue and in order to calm their hostility he selected Widgren, one of their own kind, to be his point man. Hocke believed that this appointment would increase his leverage with governments and thereby strengthen asylum procedures. However, UNHCR officials perceived this as a deliberate under-mining of the Europe bureau and as a sign of the Office's capitualation to European governments. Coming on top of the UNHCR's loss of influence and legitimacy in Europe over the asylum issue there, this marked a new low point for the Division of Refugee Law and Doctrine.

One incident, in particular, illustrates the decline in protection priorities during Hocke's tenure. In January 1988, Hocke was infuriated when he learned that the UNHCR's *Refugees* magazine was about to run an article that was critical of West Germany's detention policies. He had just met with the German Minister of Interior in an effort to restore relations with Bonn which were still poor after the critical 1983 Toscani report. Hocke ordered the entire stock of the *Refugees* issue on Germany pulled from circulation and burned. This incident, more than just about any other, caused widespread disaffection among staff. It also almost completely disillusioned NGOs who felt that the High Commissioner's efforts to restore dialogue with European governments were at the direct cost of refugees and asylum-seekers. It was not long into his term that some of Hocke's senior staff began to ask to be reassigned to other positions within the Office and governments began to hear about the quarrelling.

A New Focus on Repatriation

Hocke had assumed his position as High Commissioner at a time when millions of refugees were stranded in camps and were being assisted by costly long-term care and maintenance programmes. There were no serious political negotiations underway to end the regional conflicts that had created these problems. Western governments had already cut back on resettlement programmes and Third World host governments were reluctant to offer refugees the opportunity to integrate with local populations. Suffering compassion fatigue, donor governments were not keen to continue funding refugee camps indefinitely and put pressure on the UNHCR to come up with solutions to the global refugee problem.

The High Commissioner shared the view that solutions other than expensive and debilitating refugee camps had to be found. In his 1986 Oxford speech, Hocke had noted:

It must be recognized that the longer a refugee problem is allowed to stagnate, the more difficult the solutions are going to become. It has been observed in many refugee situations that over a period of time the refugees themselves become an integral part of the overall political problem, and thus may impede any solution. If human problems are not solved, there exists the real danger of exacerbating political tension. If humanitarian issues are ignored, states will only pay a higher price at a later date. (Hocke, 'Beyond Humanitarianism': 48).

For Hocke, repatriation was the 'only viable alternative' to the current situation and he vigorously began to promote return as the solution to protracted care and maintenance. In this effort, he had the backing of the Executive Committee which, during its October 1985 session, had adopted a conclusion that encouraged the High Commissioner to look for opportunities to promote repatriation.[10] These initiatives included promoting dialogue, acting as an intermediary, and facilitating communication between governments and refugees, but also actively pursuing return where there were appropriate conditions. The Executive Committee also noted that because refugees might be returning home to situations of unresolved conflict and uncertainty the UNHCR would have to continue to play a protection role after their repatriation. Excom also noted that the Office should provide reintegration assistance where appropriate and should have unhindered access to returnees, in order 'to monitor fulfillment of the amnesties, guarantees or assurances on the basis of which the refugees have returned'.[11] Hocke, therefore, had the legislative mandate to exploit political openings to promote repatriation, even into conflict situations. This implied a major expansion of the agency's mandate. But repatriation under these conditions was uncharted territory for the UNHCR and the Office proceeded on a basis of trial and error.

Hocke took advantage of the thaw in East–West relations in the mid-1980s and began to seek out repatriation possibilities, particularly in the horn of Africa and Central America. Repatriation movements during these years highlighted a number of controversial issues for the UNHCR. In particular, the promotion of repatriation in the Horn of Africa and Central America caused problems because refugees in both regions were returning to situations of either on-going conflict or of political tensions. The UNHCR encouraged these returns but the Office's involvement raised questions about the information it was giving refugees regarding conditions in the countries of origin, the use of coercion or active encouragement by the UNHCR in promoting repatriation, the cessation or revocation of refugee status, and the means of securing the protection and security of returnees.[12]

In the Horn of Africa, for example, repatriation was complicated by the lack of information regarding conditions in the countries of origin. During 1985, the UNHCR began to promote the return of tens of thousands of Chadian refugees in South Sudan to Ouaddai, their home province in Chad. However, uncertainty about the conditions in Chad, the unwillingness on the part of many of the refugees to return, and a perception that repatriation was being encouraged by methods designed to make continued stay in neighbouring host countries more difficult, led many NGOs to criticize the UNHCR programme.[13] The repatriation of Ethiopian refugees from Djibouti in 1986 and 1987 also illustrated how easy it was to use indirect and direct pressures on refugees to coerce them to return home. In July 1986, the government of Djibouti issued a circular encouraging all refugees in the country to return home. It declared that it was now safe for refugees to return to Ethiopia and that the UNHCR would ensure that their security was guaranteed. The circular also stated that those who did not return voluntarily would have their refugee status re-examined and those who lost their status would also have to leave Djibouti and would lose all international assistance. In the view of many refugees and NGOs, this amounted to outright coercion and created a furore.[14] The UNHCR assisted those who elected to return by organizing transit by rail to Ethiopia and establishing reception facilities there. The controversial nature of this repatriation was fuelled by a separate incident when five Ethiopians died of suffocation in a train returning some 125 illegal immigrants. Although this was not a UNHCR repatriation train, the incident demonstrated for many the forced and involuntary nature of the repatriation.[15] The UNHCR also tried to encourage voluntary repatriation of Ethiopians in the south of Somalia by setting up a tripartite commission with the two governments in 1989 but repatriation was hindered by debilitating civil conflict and a collapsing state in Somalia.

In Central America, the UNHCR initially resisted the forced repatriation of Salvadoran and Guatemalan refugees from Honduras and Mexico. Both countries were still undergoing brutal civil wars that drove peasants out of rural areas of guerrilla resistance. Nevertheless, host governments, such as Honduras, perceived refugees as security risks and were anxious to see them leave. Most refugees lived in closed camps and were viewed with extreme hostility by local authorities. In 1985, for example, the Salvadoran camp at Colomoncagua was attacked by the Honduran army and several refugees were killed, wounded, or seized.[16] Consequently, large numbers of refugees in camps along the Honduran–Salvadoran border realized that they could not expect local protection. They also realized that, although the conflict would not end any time soon, repatriation presented the only hope for them to return to a normal way of life. Most importantly, the Farabundo Marti National Liberation Front FMLN, concerned about their families' safety in the refugee camps, pushed for repatriation.[17]

The election of centrist president José Napoleon Duarte in El Salvador provided an opportunity for the UNHCR to drop its opposition to return and to actively promote repatriation. In April 1986, Hocke encouraged the governments of Honduras and El Salvador to establish a tripartite commission with the UNHCR to facilitate repatriation. Hocke also used his ICRC contacts in El Salvador and persuaded the Salvadoran Catholic Church to assist refugees returning from Honduras. After a December 1986 visit of the High Commissioner to Central America, several thousand Salvadoran refugees at the Mesa Grande camp on the border announced their intention to return to their former settlements in the north of El Salvador in October 1987. Duarte was concerned about his country's international image. He believed that the repatriation of refugees would signal to the rest of the world that El Salvador was a democratic country where human rights were respected. The fact that El Salvador had been a signatory of the so-called Arias Peace Plan of 7 August 1987 was also a significant factor in Duarte's decision to eventually accept repatriation. The peace plan required governments in the region to 'facilitate in the repatriation (when it is "voluntary and individually expressed"), [and] resettlement' of refugees.[18] Although President Duarte had approved the repatriation, the Salvadoran armed forces viewed the pro-FMLN refugees as their mortal enemies and refused to give the go-ahead for the operation to begin. The army believed that the return of thousands of guerrilla sympathizers to the same areas from which they had fled would impede their efforts to isolate and defeat the guerrillas. Consequently, the UNHCR came into direct conflict with the Salvadoran government and armed forces. The UNHCR was unable to break this deadlock and threatened to withdraw from the tripartite commission unless the repatriation proceeded. Finally, the refugees forced the issue themselves by dismantling the huts in Mesa Grande and beginning their trek to the border on their own. Within hours, the Duarte government relented to the inevitable and handed the logistics for the repatriation over to the UNHCR.

Over the next two years, more than 10,000 Salvadorans returned to their homes in four mass movements organized by the UNHCR. Once the returnees resettled in El Salvador, they became functionally indistinguishable from the hundreds of thousands of internally displaced in the countryside. Thus, in the course of trying to provide protection to the returnees, the UNHCR found itself indirectly struggling to assist the displaced as well. The repatriation and the UNHCR presence provoked the immediate suspicion and hostility of the army. The army perceived the UNHCR's presence as a challenge to the country's national sovereignty and made the UNHCR's resettlement and protection efforts extremely difficult. The army largely excluded the UNHCR from the resettlement villages. Because thousands of repatriates possessed no identification documents, they were subjected to frequent arrest, intimidation, and detention. One of the UNHCR's most important tasks, therefore, was to assist the returnees in obtaining documents. But the army resisted the Office's documentation efforts not only by denying agency staff acess to resettlement sites but also by hindering the issuance of documents. In an effort to prevent the repatriates from giving aid to the FMLN, the armed forces put the returnee settlements under virtual siege, allowing delivery of only the most basic necessities. Under these circumstances, the UNHCR was unable to give adequate protection and played a role that was heavily circumscribed by the security concerns and military tactics of the Salvadoran military.[19]

Another controversial UNHCR repatriation programme involved Sri Lankans returning from India. Tens of thousands of Tamils had fled to Tamil Nadu in southern India to escape the violence and ethnic persecution that had erupted in Sri Lanka since 1983. Initially, India welcomed the Tamils but on 29 July 1987, India and Sri Lanka signed the Indo-Sri Lankan Peace Accord which provided for an Indian peacekeeping force in Sri Lanka and for the repatriation to Sri Lanka of Tamils who had sought refuge in India. However, the peace accord was opposed by the Tamils who felt that it undermined their struggle and by the Sinhalese who came to regard the Indian troops as an occupying force. Within months, the violence worsened and thousands of Sri Lankans, both Tamils and Sinhalese were killed in the fighting.

Despite the continued violence, High Commissioner Hocke viewed the peace accord as a basis for returning Tamils to Sri Lanka, first from India and later from Europe. Under the accord, India was to register the Tamils in India and transport them back to Sri Lanka, where the UNHCR would provide them with assistance and protection, thus serving to legitimize the repatriation. In August, the UNHCR agreed to assist the returning Tamils as part of a broad plan to rehabilitate 430,000 internally displaced in Sri Lanka and $2 million was immediately released from a special emergency fund. However, it was soon evident that not all Tamils were returning voluntarily to Sri Lanka. In October, the Indian government withdrew food rations and stipends for the Tamils in India and announced that any Tamils who did not register for repatriation would be treated as illegal aliens and deported. India, moreover, did not permit UNHCR officials to be present in the camps in India and therefore the Office could not ensure that the returns were voluntary. All India would permit was a single UNHCR Official crossing with the boats from India to Sri Lanka. Thus, the UNHCR was not in a position to guarantee the safety of the returnees.

In 1988, the UNHCR attempted to follow up the repatriation from India with a similar pilot project for the return of Tamil asylum-seekers from Europe.[20] In April of that year, the UNHCR decided that rejected asylum-seekers could safely be returned to Mannar and Colombo. European governments were only too pleased to have the UNHCR support their effort to return Tamils. In European eyes, Tamil asylum-seekers had bypassed seeking refuge in Tamil Nadu in nearby India in order to obtain greater economic benefits in the West. Deeply suspicious of the motives of Tamil asylum-seekers and believing that none of them qualified as refugees under the 1951 Convention, European governments used all means of coercion to get rid of them. By 1988, European governments stepped up the deportation of rejected Tamil asylum-seekers, a practice that had been begun in 1985. NGOs protested that the UNHCR could not possibly ensure the safety of returnees under the violent conditions then prevalent in Sri Lanka[21] and lobbied hard to change UNHCR and government policy. A year and a half later, European governments' assertion that Tamils were not refugees under the 1951 Convention was rejected in an important lawsuit in Britain. A British adjudicator found that five Tamils who qualified as refugees under the 1951 Convention had been wrongfully returned to Sri Lanka where they had been detained and interrogated.[22] By the time returns were stopped, however, large numbers of Tamils had already been repatriated from India and Europe.

Hocke's Achievements: Anticipating the End of the Cold War

Jean-Pierre Hocke accomplished two particular achievements during his term. The first was to exploit improvements in the international political environment by building bridges to the Soviet Union and its East European allies. During the Cold War, the Communist states had seen the UNHCR as an instrument of the West. However, the political reforms initiated first in the Soviet Union in 1985 and later in Eastern Europe provided the catalyst for improving East–West relations. Given that most refugee-generating conflicts had been fuelled by the involvement of the two superpowers, the end of the East–West conflict also improved the prospects for the resolution of long-standing refugee problems in the developing world. Hocke quickly realized that, since most refugees had fled from Communist or Communist-backed regimes, the UNHCR could not seek solutions to most refugee problems in the Office remained isolated from contact with these goverments. The High Commissioner's first opportunity to reach out to the Communist bloc occurred when Budapest appealed to the UNHCR to assist the thousands of Romanians from Transylvania who had arrived in 1987. Hocke responded positively and, after a visit to Budapest by Ghassan Arnaout, Hungary became the first country in the region to accede to the 1951 Refugee Convention.

In the mid-1980s, Soviet leader Mikhail Gorbachov began to relax internal political controls in the USSR, releasing ethnic tensions and nationality disputes, which had been largely suppressed by decades of Communist rule. The Soviet leadership was suddenly confronted by massive new internal population movements. At the same time, with the increasing difficulty of seeking asylum in Western Europe, larger numbers of foreign asylum-seekers were congregating in Moscow. The Soviet Union did not have the administrative machinery to deal with these populartion movements and so turned to the UNHCR for assistance. Initially, discussions focused on how the Soviet Union could integrate itself into the international refugee regime. In 1990, the Soviet Union and Poland sent observers to the UNHCR Executive Committee meetings in Geneva. These developments paved the way for most of the major Eastern European governments' joining the UNHCR and signing the international refugee legal instruments a few years after the departure of Hocke. Following Hungary's lead, the governments of Poland, the Czech and Slovak Federal Republics, Romania, and Russia signed the 1951 Refugee Convention. By 1992, an entire new region encompassing over one-sixth of the world, which had previously been completely isolated from the international refugee regime, was opened to the UNHCR.

Beyond Eastern Europe and the Soviet Union, the improvements in East–West relations made possible new diplomatic initiatives in resolving protracted conflicts in the developing world. Hocke positioned the UNHCR for possible political settlements in Afghanistan, Cambodia, and Nicaragua. For example, as early as 1985, the Soviet Union had signalled a desire to withdraw from Afghanistan. Since the settlement of the Afghan conflict would involve the return of millions of refugees, the Soviet Union recognized the usefulness of co-operation with the UNHCR. The High Commissioner readied the Office for these new opportunities. Shortly after taking office, Hocke set up a special unit within the UNHCR and drew up a contingency plan to stockpile food and materials in Pakistan to take advantage of any breakthrough in diplomatic negotiations regarding the war in Afghanistan. Hocke visited Moscow in late 1987, and raised the issue of Afghanistan with the Russians. This angered the United States because the High Commissioner had not cleared this initiative with Washington ahead of time and the US did not want the UNHCR to take any action that might legitimize the Soviet regime in Kabul. After the signing in April 1988 of the Geneva Accords on Afghanistan, Hocke tried to have the UNHCR declared the lead agency in the UN relief programme for that country. But Secretary-General Perez de Cuellar initiated Operation Salaam and appointed Prince Sadruddin Aga Khan as its head. As it turned out, repatriation of Afghans occurred in fits and starts. While Soviet troops withdrew in 1989 from that country, the Soviet Union and the US continued to fuel the civil conflict, making large-scale repatriation impossible. It was not until after the superpowers cut arms supplies to their Afghan clients in 1992 that an estimated 1.8 million Afghan refugees finally returned home. The reduction of superpower involvement also led to the eventual resolution of long-standing conflicts and refugee repatriations in Cambodia, Central America, the Horn of Africa, and Southern Africa. Even though many of these events took place after the departure of Hocke, the fact that he foresaw some of these developments and tried to position his Office to take advantage of them is testament to his political vision and drive.

Building Regional Responses in Central America and Indo-China

The other major achievement of the UNHCR during Hocke's period involved the adoption of comprehensive regional approaches to resolving the two complex refugee problems in Central America and Indo-China. In the Central American case, the UNHCR attempted to resolve the situations of forced migrants who had lived in displacement for some time. In the Indo-Chinese case, the Office sought to stem the outflow of migrants who used the asylum system because no other migration channels were open to them. Both cases involved the participation of countries of asylum, resettlement, and origin as well as donor governments and international organizations such as the UNHCR and the UN Development Programme (UNDP) and NGOs. Though initiated under Hocke, these comprehensive regional plans did not come to fruition until the early 1990s and only then did they lead to the large-scale repatriation of Central Americans and Indo-Chinese.

The mass displacement that occurred throughout Central America in the 1980s affected not only the countries of origin but also the host countries in the region. It was evident from the beginning of the Central American peace negotiations that a successful resolution of the region's conflicts would involve not only the end of war but also large-scale assistance in the wake of wide social and economic disruption that the wars produced, including the displacement of peoples. Hence, the Esquipulas II peace agreement of 1987— the Arias Peace Plan—signed by the five Central American presidents, took the position that a lasting peace could not be achieved without initiatives to solve the problems of refugees, displaced persons, and returnees throughout the region.[23] In September 1988, the Central American presidents called upon the UN Secretary-General, the UNHCR, and the UNDP to convene an international conference to address the problems of refugees as well as displaced persons and returnees. In May 1989, and International Conference on Central American Refugees (CIREFCA) was convened in Guatemala City and the Plan of Action drawn up there linked the solutions for refugees and displaced people to national reconciliation and the attainment of peace and democracy.

Most importantly, CIREFCA aimed at bringing about a co-ordinated regional process to identify projects and mobilize resources from donor governments for the reintegration of uprooted people in Central America. One of the major results of this activity was greater collaboration between UNHCR and the UNDP. This was no mean achievement. Institutional constraints between UN agencies had traditionally inhibited co-operation on development projects. The UNHCR had no development mandate and institutionally was geared to only working for refugees. The UNDP, on the other hand, had a longer-term development mandate and was not limited to any single category of beneficiaries. Yet it was extremely difficult for the UNDP to undertake development activities for refugees and the displaced because it normally worked through governments and lacked experience in direct field operations. While collaboration between the UNHCR and the UNDP was not always smooth, the UNHCR sought to involve the UNDP in CIREFCA programmes to a far greater extent than had been the case anywhere else before. The UNDP initiated the Development Programme for Displaced Persons, Refugees, and Repatriates (PRODERE) which worked with local communities and NGOs in development-related projects to help reintegrate uprooted peoples. The UNHCR also contributed to the CIREFCA process by documenting tens of thousands of returnees and creating quick impact projects (QIPs) which were designed to fill short-term development needs that had to be met if the return of refugees and displaced peoples were to succeed.[24] Donor governments made available funding for CIREFCA projects because the development work was part of a political framework of reconciliation and an integrated approach to aiding the large numbers of displaced people in Central America.[25]

Perhaps the best example of the UNHCR's new commitment to repatriation and other long-term solutions under Hocke was the vigorous way in which the Office tried to reverse the exodus of Vietnamese boat people and to resolve one of the most protracted refugee problems in history.[26] The Indo-Chinese refugee problem had bedevilled the UNHCR since 1975. In 1979, the international community had devised a comprehensive burden-sharing mechanism to respond to the crisis. In exchange for the co-operation of first asylum countries in South-East Asia, and West promised blanket refugee status to the Indo-Chinese refugees and virtually automatic settlement for those in UNHCR camps. After 1979, international resettlement commitments maintained a fragile equilibrium in the South-East Asia camps, slightly outpacing new arrivals but not by so much as to trigger new outflows. The promise of eventual resettlement preserved asylum in South-East Asia for most of the 1980s.

By the mid-1980s, however, both the UNHCR and resettlement countries were seeking alternatives to open-ended resettlement while preserving asylum. A 1985 UNHCR study of Vietnamese boat people arriving in the mid-1980s challenged the presumptive eligibility of refugee status that all Vietnamese asylum-seekers had enjoyed since 1979. The report concluded that somewhat less than two-thirds of arrivals at the time had no claim on refugee status, had no claim to international protection, did not need resettlement, and yet could not be returned to their home country. The UNHCR's Anders Johnsson, the author of the report, argued that a solution to the Vietnamese problem could only be achieved by a global approach involving Vietnamese-receiving countries in the region, and resettlement countries, and that 'such an approach should also . . . include a screening procedure, deportation arrangements for non-refugees and a strengthening of the Orderly Departure Program'. High Commissioner Hartling, however, was not in a mind to take any new initiatives on Vietnam in 1985. Knowing that the government of Vietnam remained unwilling to take back rejected asylum-seekers and that the US would not countenance involuntary returns to Communist Vietnam, Hartling rejected any proposals to 'screen' out the boat people and to return non-refugees to their home countries.

Resistance to repatriation began to crack in 1987 and 1988, when after a five year decline, arrivals of Vietnamese boat people in South-East Asia began to surge again. The number of Vietnamese asylum-seekers arriving in Thailand was three times the number in the previous year. In Hong Kong the numbers climbed from 3,400 in 1987 to over 18,000 in 1988. By April 1989 the refugee caseload in Malaysia had risen past 20,000 for the first time in ten years. Alarmed at the increasing numbers of asylum-seekers and seeing no end to the situation, Thailand, Malaysia, and Hong Kong all adopted harsher policies towards the boat people. As a result they suffered inhumane detention, push-offs, and increased piracy attacks. The asylum countries were no longer willing to offer open-ended asylum, just as resettlement countries were no longer willing to maintain open-ended resettlement.

Hocke found this situation to be highly unsatisfactory and underlined the need to put into place a new conprehensive system for burden-sharing among host and resettlement countries, for screening asylum-seekers, and for managing the returns of the Vietnamese and Laotians who did not qualify for refugee status. Opportunities for breaking the Vietnam refugee deadlock soon presented themselves. By the end of 1988, Vietnam's principal patron, the USSR had cut aid to Vietnam and had pressed Hanoi to withdraw its troops from Cambodia. Taking advantage of Vietnam's isolation and evident desire to achieve international legitimacy, the UNHCR won an agreement from Vietnam to permit voluntary repatriation of its citizens, to expand and accelerate the Orderly Departure Program, and to allow the UNHCR access to the returnees.[27] Sergio Vieira de Mello, head of the UNHCR's Asia Bureau, along with several colleagues from the Office's Refugee Law and Doctrine Division, moved quickly and determinedly to achieve an international consensus on the Vietnamese refugee problem.

In March 1989, a preparatory meeting was held in Kuala Lumpur to draft a comprehensive plan of action (CPA) for the upcoming second international conference on Indo-Chinese refugees held in Geneva on 13–14 June 1989. The CPA resulting from the Geneva conference had several components. There was agreement that it was no longer appropriate to grant blanket admission followed by nearly automatic resettlement to asylum-seekers from Indo-Chinese countries. Instead, states decided to establish a regional system of 'screening' throughout South-East Asia to identify refugees and non-refugees. The host countries in the region also recommitted themselves to preserving temporary first asylum for the boat people. The resettlement countries, in turn, agreed to resettle all the refugees in UNHCR camps who had arrived before an announced cut-off date in 1989—1988 for Hong Kong—and they would continue to resettle abroad those refugees who were screened in or given refugee status. Finally, the Orderly Departure Program (ODP) would be strengthened, thereby expanding the possibilities for legal departures from Vietnam.

The CPA's major shortcoming was that governments were unable to agree on measures to ensure the return to Vietnam of screened-out asylum-seekers who were unwilling to return voluntarily. It was hoped that rejected asylum-seekers would agree to return to Vietnam voluntarily. However, if voluntary repatriation did not work, the CPA called for the examination of 'alternatives' to voluntary repatriation, which implied forced repatriation. The US declared unequivocally that it was opposed to the forced repatriation of asylum-seekers and was supported in this position by Vietnam. The British Foreign Secretary, Sir Geoffrey Howe, on the other hand, threatened to introduce mandatory repatriation if insufficient numbers of boat people opted for voluntary return. The 'voluntary' character of the CPA was also undermined when governments in the region took steps almost immediately to forcibly return boat people to Vietnam. The harshest policy was instituted by Hong Kong and the UK. The UK under Prime Minister Margaret Thatcher initiated secret bilateral negotiations with Vietnam that allowed for the return of boat people from Hong Kong and attempted to implement a forced return policy in late 1989. In one incident, on 31 October 1989, Hong Kong security officials forcibly removed screened-out Vietnamese from one of their detention centres in a pre-dawn operation and returned them to Vietnam. A second incident occurred 12 December 1989, when without informing the UNHCR, heavily armed Hong Kong security guards forcibly deported to Hanoi 51 screened-out Vietnamese refugees: 17 women, 8 men, and 26 children.

From 1989 until the CPA formally ended in June 1997 when Hong Kong reverted to the Peoples' Republic of China, the UNHCR found itself being pushed to support compulsory returns.[28] The UNHCR trained governments in refugee status determination and monitored the screening of refugees by governments. In September 1990, the UNHCR and the governments of Britain, Hong Kong, and Vietnam agreed on measures to return 'non-refugees' from the camps of Hong Kong to Vietnam. The UNHCR's Chief of Mission in Hong Kong underlined the Office's attitude at the time: 'The solution will remain voluntary repatriation, but this [the repatriation deal] is sending a clear signal into the camps for people to wake up and stop wasting their lives here—they have to return one way or the other.'[29]

To promote the repatriation of the screened-out asylum-seekers, the UNHCR eliminated educational programmes above primary level in its camps, cut back on medical and counselling services, imposed new restrictions on freedom of movement in and around some camps, reduced employment opportunities and eliminated income-generating activities, and limited the receipt of remittances from overseas. NGOs sharply criticized the UNHCR for what they perceived to be a serious abrogation of its responsibilities. Eventually, most of the host countries in the region signed orderly return programme agreements with Vietnam and the UNHCR. In many instances, the returns were involuntary.

When the CPA formally came to an end in mid-1997, the programme's costs had exceeded $500 million over seven years. In eight years time, about 110,000 Vietnamese returned home, more than 400,000 people left Vietnam safely and legally via the ODP, and nearly 125,000 refugees were resettled out of the first asylum camps, including more than 80,000 Vietnamese and 44,000 Laotians. Most importantly, for the first time in over 20 years, the refugee camps that were once scattered throughout South-East Asia were closed and the asylum flow from Indo-China had been almost completely stopped. This was a monumental achievement but, for many human rights NGOs, the forced repatriations of screened-out Vietnamese non-refugees tarnished the UNHCR's reputation as the protector of refugees. The CPA brought to an end one of the largest, longest, and most politically significant refugee crises of the Cold War. For the UNHCR it demonstrated the importance of pursuing comprehensive approaches to refugee problems involving countries of origin, countries of asylum, and the donor and resettlement status. The UNHCR would use this method of reaching political solutions to refugee problems again and again in the 1990s.

The UNHCR's Management and Financial Crisis and Hocke's Resignation

In late 1988, Jean-Pierre Hocke was re-elected as High Commissioner for a second three-year term. However, many governments gave him only a lukewarm endorsement. They were concerned by what they saw as his high-handedness, disinclination to follow advice or direction, lack of consultation, and arbitrary management of his agency.[30] Hocke originally had been elected High Commissioner to improve the management of the UNHCR's operational and relief services. Many donor governments were particularly upset that during Hocke's first term, the staff and budget of the UNHCR grew substantially at a time when the United Nations system as a whole was under pressure to downsize its programmes, staff, and expenses. From the time that Hocke had taken over as High Commissioner, the UNHCR staff had grown almost 30 per cent and the budget by some 27 per cent. The NGOs were concerned that the UNHCR was weakening its ability to protect refugees as a result of the priority emphasis on operational effectiveness and relief. Inside the UNHCR, Hocke had run roughshod over many of his staff. Although he was an incredibly energetic and capable High Commissioner who had solid knowledge of the field, Hocke failed either to inspire others or to create a common ethos and institutional vision within the Office. Instead, he made disastrous personnel appointments, which encouraged factionalism within the UNHCR and lowered morale within the staff. Thus, when Hocke was elected for a second term, apart from the US, he had few allies and supporters, and the need for effective leadership of the UNHCR was greater than ever.

Early in 1989 it was evident that there would be a deficit in the UNHCR's annual budget. The reasons for the deficit were understandable. The number of refugees worldwide had increased dramatically during Hocke's first term as a result of conflict in Somalia, Mozambique, and Sudan and continuing outflows from Afghanistan, Iran, and Vietnam. In addition, the UNHCR had promoted expensive large-scale repatriation programmes in Namibia, Nicaragua, and Sri Lanka, which included not only refugee emergency relief but also reintegration and development projects. Another reason for the deficit was that under Hocke the UNHCR had discontinued a policy of exaggerating the budget needs every year, which previously had given the UNHCR a valuable financial cushion enabling it to respond to unexpected crisis.

Donor governments, led by the United States, seized on this shortfall to bring the High Commissioner and his Office under their direct financial control. Even the US, which had been Hocke's strongest supporter, turned on him. No compromise solution was sought and there was a complete breakdown of confidence between the donors and the UNHCR. Donors refused to cover the deficit and insisted that the UNHCR base its operations on the funds that were available instead of refugee needs. The financial situation worsened during the year. By October 1989 there was a shortfall of more than $100 million between the funds that donors had actually provided to the UNHCR and the budget amount that had been approved by the Executive Committee a year earlier. The UNHCR cut spending by $70 million during the year, but that still left a deficit of some $40 million. The Office faced an unprecedented financial crisis.

The last straw for donor states came on the eve of the 1989 Executive Committee meetings when news of a financial scandal involving the High Commissioner was made public. Apparently Hocke and his wife had travelled first class and on Concorde on business trips, using a special slush fund that had been established by the Danish government for former High Commissioner Hartling. The adverse publicity caused by this news further weakened Hocke's ability to stand up to donor governments. The Executive Committee forced through a humiliating budget for 1990 and established a working group composed of Excom and UNHCR representatives to scrutinize every aspect of the Office's administration and programmes. Excom refused to approve the annual UNHCR budget. Instead they only authorized a semi-annual budget instalment of $170 million which was a reduction of 18 per cent compared with assessed real needs. It also permitted a carry-over of $40 million in 1990 to cover the deficit. For the UNHCR, however, the creation of a working group to oversee management of the funds was the most humiliating development. Donor governments required that every UNHCR programme, no matter how minute, be scrutinized by the working group. They also authorized that an extraordinary session of Excom be convened in May 1990 to review the fundings of the working group and to determine 'the level of UNHCR obligation for the second half of 1990 so as not to exceed the realistic level of contribution likely to become available that year.'[31] For most people at the UNHCR this was the lowest moment in the Office's history. The UNHCR had lost control of its management and was publicly humiliated.

Even in the early 1950s under van Heuven Goedhart, the Office had had greater support from donor governments.

With no governmental support and under strong pressure from Secretary-General Perez de Cueller, Hocke reluctantly resigned as High Commissioner shortly after the end of the October 1989 Executive Committee meetings. The new High Commissioner, Thorvald Stoltenberg, Norway's representative at the UN in New York, did not assume office until mid-January 1990. Thus, at a time when the Office was financially and politically handicapped and demoralized, the UNHCR was leaderless. Between November 1989 and March 1990, the Excom working group subjected the UNHCR to relentless and cricial scrutiny, making staff justify every penny of the Office's expenditures. In a further blow to the Office's pride and self-confidence, Secretary General Perez de Cuellar dispatched a senior official from New York, Kofi Annan, to take over the management of human resources at the UNHCR.

Thorvald Stoltenberg and the Painful Rebuilding of Confidence in the UNHCR

Thorvald Stoltenberg was a highly respected European policy-maker who had considerable authority among the donor community. He was a political person and formerly had been Norway's Foreign and Defence Minister. Stoltenberg was an open and unpretentious person who quickly gained the confidence and loyalty of his staff. He required all these skills to turn around the dire situation in which the UNHCR found itself in 1990. The new High Commissioner faced the unenviable task of not only putting the UNHCR's financial house in order again but also restoring the Office's morale and authority.

Stoltenberg's efforts to cope with the UNHCR's financial crisis and to restore government confidence in the Office constituted his greatest achievement during his short time at the UNHCR. From the start of his term, he realized his most important task was to improve the Office's relations with Excom members and to win back their confidence and financial support. He did so with surprising alacrity but not without considerable pain for the UNHCR and for refugees worldwide. At their May 1990 Extraordinary meeting, Exective Committee members told the High Commissioner that he would have to tailor his spending to available funds, as opposed to need, and they approved a budget of $550 million for 1990. This represented a shortfall of approximately $150 million over projected needs for 1990. In his opening address to the Excom, Stoltenberg stated that the UNHCR 1990 General Programme budget represented a reasonable balance between the needs of refugees and the income that the UNHCR could reasonably expect to have at its disposal. However, the High Commissioner also noted that these cuts made it necessary for the Office to make significant reductions worldwide that severely affected the welfare of refugees as well as the prospects for or solutions to refugee problems.[32] But swallowing these cuts was the price the UNHCR had to pay to restore donor government confidence. By the October 1990 Executive Committee meetings, Stoltenberg had managed to re-establish both the credibility of the Office and a working relationship with donor governments. In fact, he was the first High Commissioner to receive a standing ovation at an Executive Committee meeting.

The events surrounding the UNHCR's 1989–90 financial crisis highlighted the most significant institutional weakness of the Office, namely its dependence on voluntary governmental contributions to carry out its programmes. Less than 2 per cent of the UNHCR's annual expenditures are covered by the UN Regular Budget; the remainder of the Office's resources comes mainly from the governments of industrialized nations. During most of the 1990s, its assistance activities were broadly divided into General and Special Programmes. Each year the UNHCR Executive Committee approved a General Programme budget that covered emergency relief, repatriation, integration into host societies, and resettlement. It also covered appeals to all UN members for the resources to pay for the programme year. In addition to its General Programme budget, the UNHCR, at the request of the Secretary-General or the UN General Assembly, undertook Special Programmes. These included major and unforeseen emergency operations and rehabilitation assistance for returnees. Special Programmes were the subject of specific fund raising appeals to interested governments and were financed from trust funds framed by particular purposes and conditions. Because of this arrangement, the UNHCR had to raise funds for each new refugee problem.

The financial support offered to the UNHCR often fell short of the Office's real needs. During the Hocke years, donor contributions for refugee assistance generally did not keep pace with the growth in refugee numbers. During 1985–9, for example, US financial support for the UNHCR declined consisently, despite the fact that America had been Hocke's most steadfast supporter. The American share of the UNHCR's total expenditure dropped from 30 per cent in 1982 to 22 per cent in 1989, during a period when the number of refugees under UNHCR protection increased by 50 per cent.[33] Moreover, accurate prediction of resource requirements for refugees is inherently difficult, and UNHCR programmes often require rapid adjustment by field and headquarters staff in the course of their implementation. Because the problems faced by the UNHCR and refugees are often unpredictable and usually urgent, response cannot be postponed to some future programme cycle if resources are not immediately available. The UNHCR must constantly request additional contributions in order to meet chronic shortfalls. Although Hocke as the High Commissioner had available an emergency fund of $25 million, a single refugee emergency could easily swallow this up.

The problem is exacerbated by the fact that donor governments often do not fulfil their financial pledges until the end of the fiscal year, thereby making it impossible for the UNHCR to plan its programmes and to meet its commitments to host governments regularly and effectively. Governments also increase restrictions on the UNHCR by earmarking funds for certain refugee groups or programmes or exerting direct and indirect political pressure to guide their use. Stoltenberg protested about these constraints in his opening statement to the Executive Committee in October 1990. He noted that the 'unstable and unpredictable nature of funding our activities' had a crippling effect on the UNHCR and made the Office 'a much less responsible and effective organization'.[34] While imposing drastic cuts on the UNHCR, the Executive Committee took no action to resolve the underlying causes of the Office's outdated funding mechanisms or financial problems or to develop a more efficient means of funding refugee relief and protection programmes.[35]

Stoltenberg also took immediate steps to restore the self-confidence and raise the morale of UNHCR staff members. One of his first actions upon assuming office in January 1990 was to set up an *ad hoc* review group within the Office to examine the overall structure of the UNHCR and to reassess the role of the Office in the light of the end of the Cold War. Staff were encouraged to think for themselves and to come up with an overall plan of action to overcome the UNHCR's institutional crisis. This exercise improved self-confidence and morale at the UNHCR and laid the groundwork for policy changes that would be adopted later. The report of the Ad Hoc Review Group[36] identified the challenges confronting the Office in the 1990s, including both the changes in transnational migration flows and the dramatic shift in the international political environment with the winding down of the Cold War. The report argued that in the future the UNHCR should be less reactive and more proactive and assertive in the political arena. It identified many of the central themes and issues that would come to dominate UNHCR thinking and action in the years ahead—issues such as early warning and work in countries of origin, internally displaced persons, and the need to strengthen asylum protection by emphasizing a liberal interpretation of refugee status. Stoltenberg also partially restored the prominent role of the protection division within the Office. In an extremely popular move, the High Commissioner renamed the Division of Refugee Law and Doctrine as the Division of International Protection, upgraded it to the level of the five regional bureaus, and brought back Michel Moussalli to serve as its director. However, Stoltenberg did not follow through on the recommendation of the Ad Hoc Review Group to restore to the Protection Division the overall authority and responsibility for protection in the field it had enjoyed before the restructuring under Hocke.[37]

Stoltenberg was able to resolve the institutional crisis at the UNHCR in a remarkably short time partly because there were no new major refugee crises during the short time he was in office. The most dramatic forced migration crisis in 1990 occurred in the Middle East as a result of Iraq's invasion of Kuwait on 2 August 1990. Some 2 million migrants returned to their countries of origin.[38] Hundreds of thousands of migrant workers from India, Bangladesh, and Pakistan who had worked in Kuwait before the attack, took shelter in Jordan and sought to return to their home countries. Many of them were in desperate physical condition and in need of immediate assistance. Despite the fact that these people were not refugees in the legal sense of the term, the High Commissioner felt he had no choice but to offer the services of his Office to the UN Secretary General. However, Perez de Cuellar turned down Stoltenberg's offer and made the International Organization for Migration the lead agency instead.

Stoltenberg's time as High Commissioner also coincided with the sudden and dramatic collapse of Communist regimes in Easter Europe, including the Soviet Union. There was enormous fear within the West that the changes and instability generated by the end of the Cold War would trigger new mass movements of people from the former Communist bloc to Western Europe. Indeed, in 1989 the flood of refugees from East to West Germany had brought down the Berlin Wall, had expedited the unification of the two German states, and had generated the most significant transformation in international relations since World War II. Throughout 1990 there was widespread concern that masses of new refugees would flee the disintegration of Communism in the East and seek asylum in the West. *The Economist* news magazine ran an alarming front page entitled 'The Russians are Coming' and Moscow warned Western Europe to expect an influx of as many as three million Russians once the government eased restrictions on departure.[39] Western policy-makers were terrified at the prospect of new mass flows from the East, particularly at a time when asylum-seekers from political crises and armed conflicts in the Third World were increasing. Ironically, within months of the tearing down of the Berlin Wall, European governments began to erect new barriers to keep out those they had welcomed as refugees for over 40 years.

As a European, Stoltenberg reflected these fears and concerns. In 1989, he had lost his parliamentary seat following an electoral backlash against foreigners in Norway. He knew from personal experience how strongly many European governments felt about uncontrolled migration. Stoltenberg believed that if the UNHCR was to play a significant role in Europe and secure admissions for genuine refugees, it had to deal not only with refugees but also with the broad issue of migration from the developing countries and from Eastern Europe. One of Stoltenberg's main objectives upon assuming office was to put the refugee issue 'on the political agenda' of states. He told Excom members that it was 'increasingly evident that the issue of refugees and migration at large is bound to be one of the threats to the broad concept of international, regional and national security in the decade ahead of us'.[40] In his view, the real problem driving migration was poverty and not persecution.[41] Stoltenberg also believed that there was widespread abuse of the asylum system by 'bogus refugees'. In light of this, the High Commissioner believed that the UNHCR had to be more responsive to the security concerns of governments concerning migrants. Despite serious misgivings from his staff, he wanted the UNHCR to spearhead a new global approach to the problem of migration which included helping governments transport non-refugees back to their homes and initiating programmes of early warning and increased development aid aimed at preventing future migration flows.

Many UNHCR staff strongly disagreed with the High Commissioner's views on the Office's future priorities. By extending the UNHCR concern from refugees to a much broader category of migrants, there was a danger that the Office's mandate, and the core definition of what a refugee is, could be diluted. For many, this seemed an overextension of the UNHCR's energies at a time when the agency was already weakened by the financial crisis it had just weathered. As it turned out, Stoltenberg never had the opportunity to implement these ideas.

In November, 1990, within a month of introducing these concepts to his Executive Committee, Stoltenberg resigned as High Commissioner. He wanted to return to Norwegian politics and seized the opportunity to become Foreign Minister in the new Norwegian government of Gro Bruntland. The announcement came as a complete surprise and shock to the UNHCR. Many staff were extremely disappointed and felt angry and personally betrayed by Stoltenberg. After finally recovering from the humiliation of the financial and institutional crisis of the previous year, many felt that the Office would once again plunge into crisis and might lose the hard-won confidence of governments. At a time of unprecedented change in international relations, the UNHCR had to mark time until the arrival in February 1991 of yet another new and untested High Commissioner. The post-Cold War era was to generate massive new numbers of refugees and to pose a variety of new challenges for the UNHCR and the international community.

NOTES

1. The US Co-ordinator for Refugee Affairs in the Reagan Administration argued that '. . . the fact that from Vietnam and Cambodia, to Afghanistan and Ethiopia, to Cuba and Nicaragua, the tyrannies spawning refugees today all bear the Marxist-Leninist label should galvanize us into a better understanding of the need to stand together in the promotion of political liberty. . . . Such a policy must counter soviet expansion—limit soviet option—everywhere our real interests are threatened. It must work to wean away client states from soviet domination and to unmask the

ideologues of Marxism-Leninsim before they gain power wherever that is threatened.' H. Eugene Douglas, 'The Problem of Refugees in Strategic Perspective', *Strategic Review* (Autumn 1982): 20.

2. For background on Hocke and the ICRC see: Caroline Moorehead, *Dunant's Dream: War, Switzerland and the History of the Red Cross* (New York, NY: Harper Collins, 1998).

3. Interview with Jean-Pierre Hocke, Geneva, October 1987.

4. Jean-Pierre Hocke, 'Beyond Humanitarianism: The Need for Political Will to Resolve Today's Refugee Problem', in Gil Loescher and Laila Monahan, eds., *Refugees and International Relations* (Oxford: Clarendon Press, 1989): 37–48. Many of these ideas reflected the thinking of Gervase Coles, an Australian diplomat who worked in the Protection Division of the UNHCR.

5. Hocke, 'Beyond Humanitarianism': 37–8.

6. Ibid: 43.

7. Ibid: 48.

8. Interviews with Jean-Pierre Hocke, October 1987, Dennis McNamara and Michel Moussalli, January 1999, Geneva and London.

9. In choosing this name for the protection division, Hocke simply borrowed from the ICRC where 'doctrine' was almost synonymous with 'action'. This new title was widely perceived to indicate a dilution of protection within the UNHCR. See Lawyers' Committee for Human Rights, *The UNHCR at 40: Refugee Protection at the Crossroads* (New York, NY: Lawyers' Committee for Human Rights, 1991).

10. Conclusion 40 (XXXVI) on voluntary repatriation. Text in UNHCR, *Conclusions on the International Protection of Refugees*: 86–8. In 1980, the Executive Committee had encouraged the UNHCR to facilitate repatriation. The encouragement to promote repatriation implied a more proactive stance on the part of the Office.

11. See Guy Goodwin-Gill, 'Voluntary Repatriation: Legal and Policy Issues', in Loescher and Monahan, *Refugees and International Relations*: 255–91.

12. Ibid.: 275; and Jeff Crisp, 'Refugee Repatriation: New Pressures and Problems', *Migration World*, 14/5 (1986): 18.

13. Hiram Ruiz, *When Refugees Won't Go Home: The Dilemma of Chadians in Sudan* (Washington, DC: US Committee for Refugees, 1987).

14. Goodwin-Gill, 'Voluntary Repatriation': 277–81.

15. 'Reluctant Refugees Return to Ethiopia', the *Guardian* (9 December 1986) and 'Deaths in a Boxcar: Who Cares About Ethiopian Refugees?', *Wall Street Journal* (10 August 1987).

16. The author visited Colomoncagua refugee camp in February 1986. See Gil Loescher, 'Humanitarianism and Politics in Central America', *Political Science Quarterly*, 103 (Summer 1988): 295–320.

17. Interview with FMLN leader, Facundo Guardado, New York, July 2000.

18. 'The Central American Peace Plan', *Current History*, 86/524 (December 1987): 436.

19. Interview with Patricia Weiss-Fagen, former head UNHCR office in El Salvador, South Bend, Indiana, February 1999.

20. Interview with Jonas Widgen, Geneva, 1990.

21. Fact finding visits to Sri Lanka in 1988 by the World Alliance of YMCAs, Amnesty International, the Danish Refugee Council, and the Swiss Government confirmed that conditions in Sri Lanka were not safe for returns.

22. European Commission of Human Rights, *Reports of the Commission*, Appl. Nos. 13153/87, 13164/87, 13165/87, 13447/87 and 13448/87 (8 May 1990): 24.

23. For background see: Patricia Weiss-Fagen, 'Peace in Central America: Transition for the Uprooted', *World Refugee Survey 1993* (Washington, D.C.: US Committee of Refugees, 1993): 30–9.

24. See UNHCR memorandum to L. Mebtouche, Regional Bureau for Latin America and the Caribbean, from Jenifer Otsea, 'Returnee Aid and Development' (Geneva: UNHCR, 14 January 1992).

25. The total contributions to CIREFCA from 1989 to the end of 1992 were $238 million, not counting the $122 million for PRODERE, mainly through the Italian government. Patricia Weiss-Fagen, 'Peace in Central America': 38.

26. The best history of the Comprehensive Plan of Action for Indo-Chinese refugees (CPA) is contained in Courtland Robinson, *Terms of Refuge: The Indochinese Exodus and the International Response* (London: Zed Books, 1998).

27. Memorandum of Understanding between the Socialist Republic of Vietnam and the United Nations High Commissioner for Refugees, Geneva (13 December 1988).

28. Alex Cunliffe, 'The Refugee Crisis: A Study of the United Nations High Commissioner for Refugees', *Political Studies*, 43/2, June 1995: 287.

29. Ibid.: 288, citing J. Cheng and P. Kwong, eds., *The Other Hong Kong Report* (Hong Kong: Chinese University Press, 1992): 114.

30. See Nicholas Morris, 'Refugees: Facing Crises in the 1990s—A Personal View from within UNHCR', *International Journal of Refugee Law*. Special Issue (September 1990): 38–58.

31. Report of the 40th Session of the UNHCR Executive Committee: UN doc. A/AC.96/733 (19 October 1989), para. 30(j).

32. See Report of the UNHCR Executive Committee Extraordinary Meeting: UN doc. A/AC.96/747, 1 June 1990.

33. See Testimony of Hiram Ruiz, US Committee for Refugees, before a Joint Hearing of the House Committee on Foreign Affairs, Subcommittees on International Operations and Africa, 101st Congress, 2nd Session, 10 May 1990.

34. Opening statement of the High Commissioner, UNHCR Executive Committee, 1 October 1990: 4.

35. At the beginning of 2000, the UNHCR introduced a new unified budget system that merged the General Programme with Special Programmes. While the integration of the two former major parts of the UNHCR budget would lead to a more flexible and transparent system, the politicization and earmarking of governmental allocation of resources to the agency continued throughout 2000. Raimo Vayrynen, 'The Dilemma of Voluntary Funding: Political Interests and Institutional Reforms', *International Migration Review* (forthcoming).

36. UNHCR, *Report of the Ad Hoc Review Group on the Role and Structure of UNHCR* (Geneva: UNHCR, 6 March 1990).

37. While the Ad Hoc Review Group recommended restoring the Division of Protection to the dominant role it had played with the Office before the reorganization under Hocke, the directors of the regional bureaus strongly resisted any attempts to be made subordinate to the Division of International Protection.

38. Nicholas Van Hear, 'Mass Flight in the Middle East: Involuntary Migration and the Gulf Conflict 1990–1991', in Richard Black and Vaughn Robinson, eds., *Geography*

and Refugees: Patterns and Processes of Change (London: Belhaven Press, 1992): 33–51.

39. 'Moscow Warns EC of Mass Migration', the *Independent* (25 September 1990).
40. Thorvald Stoltenberg, Opening Address to 40th Executive Committee, 1 October 1990.
41. Lawyers' Committee for Human Rights, *The UNHCR at 40: Refugee Protection at the Crossroads* (New York, NY: Lawyers' Committee for Human Rights, 1991): 52.

9

The Post-Cold War Era and the UNHCR under Sadako Ogata

In December 1991, Sadako Ogata, a Japanese professor of International Relations, was elected the eighth UN High Commissioner for Refugees. Ogata was the first woman and the first East Asian to hold the post. The election of a Japanese citizen as High Commissioner reflected Japan's increasing interest in playing an active international role at the United Nations, particularly in the development and humanitarian fields. After the debacle of the late 1980s, donor governments wanted the UNHCR in a safe pair of hands that would consolidate the financial restructuring that had been imposed on the Office. Japan was a good fund-raising country and Ogata was American-educated and fluent in English.

Ogata grew up in a cosmopolitan environment and was encouraged by her family in her education and personal pursuits. Unlike many Japanese women, she had international experiences from an early age. Granddaughter of a Japanese Foreign Minister and daughter of a career diplomat, Ogata spent several years as a child in the United States and China. She did graduate work in the United States, earning a Master's degree in International Relations from Georgetown University and a Doctorate in Political Science from the University of California, Berkeley. Upon returning to Japan, she married Shijuro Ogata who embarked on a prominent career in the Bank of Japan. She became active in academic and public life, serving in the Permanent Mission of Japan to the United Nations and as chairperson of the UNICEF Executive Board during a period of residence in New York in the late 1970s. Returning to Japan again in 1980, Ogata became Professor of International Relations at Sophia University in Tokyo and later served as dean of the Faculty of Foreign Studies. During the 1980s, she was the Japanese government's representative on the UN Human Rights Commission, was a member of the Trilateral Commission and the Independent Commission on Humanitarian Issues, and served as Special Rapporteur for the UN Human Rights Commission for Burma.

Apart from a trip to the Thai-Cambodian border in 1979 as the head of the Japanese Government Mission to Extend Relief Measures to Cambodian

Refugees, Ogata had no direct experience with refugees before taking up her post as High Commissioner in early 1991. But she brought to her new position in Geneva the skills that she had acquired in her dual roles as an academic and diplomat. As an international relations scholar, Ogata was familiar with international political and security issues and with the dynamics of political currents within the UN. She felt that, in order to be effective, UN agencies had to be a step ahead of governments, anticipating changes in world politics and the demands and expectations of states.[1] Nevertheless, in her initial weeks at the agency, Ogata was cautious and tentative, feeling that she needed to understand the organization and the nature of refugee problems before committing herself and her Office to bold new steps. During her first days at the job, she was briefed by each division. Staff members were impressed both by her curiosity about the workings of the UNHCR and by the incisiveness of her questioning.

During her time as High Commissioner, Ogata proved to be an enterprising entrepreneur and showed a sophisticated awareness of the political opportunity structures within which the UNHCR operated. Under her leadership, the UNHCR's staff expanded rapidly and its budget increased threefold to well over $1 billion within her first two years. The Office became heavily involved in a variety of complex emergencies in which the delivery of relief assistance was emphasized. As the UNHCR was drawn into the intense political struggles accompanying these emergencies, it lost its focus on protection along with some of its autonomy and independence.

The 1990s: Old Certainties Give Way to New Complexities

The luxury of slowly immersing herself in the details of the UNHCR came to an abrupt end within weeks of taking office. In April 1991, in the aftermath of the Gulf War, Iraqi forces attacked the Iraqi Kurdish population, forcing hundreds of thousands of Kurdish civilians to flee to the mountains and seek asylum in Turkey and Iran. The new High Commissioner was suddenly and unexpectedly thrust into the first major post-Cold War refugee crisis. In succeeding months, refugee crises in Bangladesh, Bhutan, Bosnia, Somalia, and the former Soviet Union repeatedly tested the new High Commissioner and stretched the capacities of the UNHCR to the limit. As international action on behalf of refugees became intricately involved with high politics and military force, the international community encouraged and authorized the UNHCR to take action on behalf of ever-growing numbers of refugees and internally displaced people.

The early 1990s was a dramatic period in the history and growth of the

UNHCR. The range of issues facing the High Commissioner became vast and complex, with old certainties and old definitions of *refugee* seeming very inadequate to the realities of people whose situations of displacement were generated by violence, human rights abuses, ethnic, communal, and religious conflicts, underdevelopment, and ecological disasters. Ogata believed that the traditional legal approach to refugee protection was too dominant in the Office. She felt that refugee law was not the solution for the daunting dilemmas that the UNHCR faced. In situations like Bosnia warring parties widely disregarded international humanitarian and refugee law. According to the High Commissioner, the UNHCR could not protect people in the midst of conflicts using only legal arguments. She told her immediate staff: 'The real problem is saving peoples' lives. We can't protect dead people'.[2]

Ogata was a realist who believed that political and government support, especially from the US, Japan, and European states, was essential to the UNHCR's effective functioning. She thought that by leveraging powerful states and appearing useful, if not indispensable to them, the UNHCR could gain influence far beyond its ability to impact state practices directly. She perceived that in high-profile operations like Bosnia, states needed the services of the UNHCR as much as she needed them.[3] Her objective, therefore, was to maintain a dialogue with governments and to avoid direct confrontation. Ogata did not believe in lecturing governments or directly accusing them of bad behaviour.[4] When Michel Moussalli—Director of Protection when Ogata arrived— urged the High Commissioner to exert her moral authority on asylum issues with European governments, Ogata strongly disagreed. She felt it was more important to be politically astute than morally right when dealing with governments.[5] Ogata was a pragmatic High Commissioner who sought to make her Office useful to governments and to seek compromise when conflicting forces clashed. She believed the UNHCR to be essentially a service organization. In her own words, her proudest achievement as High Commissioner 'was to make the UNHCR relevant in world politics'.[6]

The Implosion of the Soviet Union

One of the most dramatic developments in international relations in the early 1990s was the spectacular implosion of the Soviet Union. It spanned over one-sixth of the earth's surface and its breakup resulted in vast population displacements and caused Western Europe's first major refugee crisis since the 1956. The numbers of asylum applications lodged in West European states shot up from just over 65,000 in 1983 to more than ten times that level in 1992. Whereas initially during this period most of the asylum-seekers originated from Africa, Asia, and the Middle East, from 1989 on, approximately two-thirds came from the former Soviet bloc states. In addition, the EU states provided temporary protection to some 700,000 persons fleeing ethnic cleansing and conflict in the former Yugoslavia. During the 1990s, Western policy-makers were totally preoccupied with breakup of the Soviet Union and the fear that Western Europe would be overrun by masses escaping poverty rather than fear of Communist persecution.

While massive East–West population movements did not materialize, there was considerable internal displacement within the former Soviet Union resulting from ethno-political conflicts, economic dislocation, increased competition for economic resources, and the resurgence of extreme national-ism in the post-Communist states.[7] After 1991, millions of former Soviet citi-zens migrated within and between the fifteen successor states of the USSR. During Soviet rule, huge numbers of people had been forcibly transferred or induced to move from one part of the country to another. The formation of post-Communist states in non-Russian republics threatened the maintenance of nationality rights for substantial numbers of people resident in the new states. This was a particular concern for the 25 million Russians who had long resided in other Soviet republics. Between 1992 and 1996, some 3 million refugees and forced migrants, primarily Russian and almost all Russian-speak-ing, had fled to Russia. Russian legislation passed in June 1992 granted all refugees the right to choose a place of residence and job, and guaranteed them housing, food, and medical care. However, this influx caused numerous problems for a Russian government already taxed with finding room for tens of thousands of demobilized soldiers from Eastern Europe. Major population displacements also took place in Central Asia and the south Caucasus during the early 1990s and in the north Caucasus in the late 1990s.

In Central Asia, most countries had territorial claims on each other, thereby increasing the risk of region-wide conflicts and major refugee flows. In 1992, a civil war erupted in Tajikistan, the poorest of all the former Soviet Republics, which left most areas without basic commodities. As fighting intensified between the Government and the various opposition groups, the country spiralled into civil war, and 600,000 people—about 10 per cent of the total population of Tajikistan—were reportedly displaced.[8] Another 250,000 refugees crossed into Russia, and other neighbouring states and into northern Afghanistan where some groups became embroiled in a war by proxy between various Afghan Islamic groups, including mujahedin groups affiliated with Hezbi-i Islami. Although the civil war effectively ended in 1993 and a peace agreement was signed in 1997, sporadic fighting continued throughout the 1990s. Nevertheless, most of the refugees and IDPs returned home by the late 1990s. By 2000, the peace settlement was under threat, with the government retreating from its power-sharing commitments and unable to bring the opposition into the administration. Consequently, violence and local conflicts increased throughout the country, causing further internal displace-ment. Elsewhere in Central Asia, during the decade, many tens of thousands of Uzbeks, Kirgiz, and others became internally displaced or refugees.

Ethnic conflicts in the Caucasus also generated large refugee movements, as the autonomous territories of Abkhazia and South Ossetia began to press for secession from Georgia. The conflict in Abkhazia, which broke out in 1992, displaced 270,000 people, while a further 80,000 fled to Russia and other Commonwealth of Independent States (CIS) states. By the end of 1992, the situation began to stabilize although the majority who had been displaced by the conflict did not return home. In 1998, renewed fighting between Georgia and Abkhaz separatists provided a further setback to peacemaking efforts. The conflict in nearby South Ossetia, which began in 1989, created some 36,000 internally displaced and generated over 120,000 refugees who fled to North Ossetia, Russia, and Georgia. The conflict between Georgia and South Ossetia was eventually resolved in 1997, permitting the repatriation of large numbers of refugees. In addition to the conflicts in Georgia, the struggle between Armenia and Azerbaijan over the enclave of Nagorno-Karabakh displaced an estimated 1.6 million people. A cease-fire was negotiated in May 1994, but a political settlement to resolve the future status of Nagorno-Karabakh had not yet been achieved by 2000. Most of those who had been uprooted by the conflict were not able to return home and remained hostages to the political stalemate between Armenia and Azerbaijan. Other areas of conflict where ethnic tensions were high included the Dniester region of Moldavia where ethnic Romanians and Slavs clashed and the Chechen-Ingush Autonomous Republic. In 1995 and again in 1999, armed conflict between Russian forces and Chechen guerrilla fighters displaced well over a million people, many of whom fled to neighbouring autonomous territories of the Russian Federation.

Nationalism in many of the fifteen newly independent republics not only encouraged secessionist movements but also led to widespread discrimination against minorities. The more than 25 million Russians who lived outside the Russian Federation in the independent republics were particularly targeted. In the Baltic states, for example, new laws threatened more than one million Russians with statelessness. Similar problems occurred elsewhere as the new states felt compelled to satisfy historic grievances against minorities by adopting legislation which failed to protect minority rights. Consequently, the pressures for mass migration within the former Soviet Union grew and three million Russians and Russian speakers returned from the Baltics, Caucasus, and Central Asia to the Russian Federation. In total, over nine million persons were uprooted in the former Soviet Union during the years 1989–96.[9] At the same time, the ability of the former republics to contain these pressures was extremely limited. There was a need for a massive and comprehensive international response to the growing migration crisis in the former Soviet Union.

The initial international response to these forced population movements was to establish UN offices in Moscow and in several of the newly independent republics, and to draft comprehensive plans for humanitarian relief for the CIS both by the UN Department of Humanitarian Affairs and by the UNHCR. This response also included the dispatch of United Nations needs-assessment missions to Armenia, Azerbaijan, Kirghizstan, Tajikistan, Turkmenistan, Uzbekistan, the Russian Federation, and the Baltic States. In addition, consolidated appeals for funds for emergency relief were launched for Armenia, Azerbaijan, Georgia, and Tajikistan. Most of these appeals, however, were underfunded as Western donor governments were reluctant to commit adequate resources for the development of a comprehensive strategy for the former Soviet Union that could anticipate and mitigate future mass migrations. Moreover, the UNHCR was already stretched to the limit by responding to humanitarian emergencies in other parts of the world.

The international community, particularly Western Europe, feared further migrations from the former Communist bloc and took preventive policy actions to stabilize the populations within the former Soviet Union. In particular, Western governments felt it necessary to adopt policies that tried to structure and regulate any future flows from the former Soviet Union in a way that did the least damage to the countries of origin, the receiving countries, and the displaced people themselves. Believing that would-be migrants were motivated primarily by economic hardship or by the hope of a better standard of living, Western European states tried to exercise some control over the flows in the short term. In the early 1990s, there was a plethora of intergovernmental meetings held at the Council of Europe, the International Labour Organization, the Organization for Economic Co-operation and Development, and elsewhere which stressed the necessity of a co-ordinated policy approach to East–West migration that involved receiving and sending states and regional and international institutions. There were also limited efforts to give some order to existing and potential migration flows. Germany and other Western European governments signed bilateral agreements with some of the Eastern European states for labour exchange programmes. Germany carried out development policy projects with a view to controlling migration of ethnic Germans from Eastern Europe and the former USSR. There were various European programmes targeting employment and training opportunities designed to facilitate economic reform in the East. Italy provided food aid to Albania in order to stabilize the situation there and prevent mass outflows of boat people from that poorest country in Europe. The International Organization for Migration and the UNHCR initiated information campaigns in Romania and Albania, which provided realistic assessments of the circumstances in which those leaving these countries would find themselves in the West. The UNHCR opened offices throughout the region to offer training and advice in the implementation of immigration and refugee laws.

The breakup of the Soviet Union in late 1991 opened up an entirely new region for the UNHCR. Ogata initially was reluctant to become involved there. Not only did the scale and complexity of the problems in the region appear daunting but the UNHCR was concerned about the operational and financial implications of greater involvement. This part of the world was completely uncharted territory for the UNHCR as the vast expanse of the USSR had been largely closed to the outside world for some 70 years. The Soviet Union had not signed the 1951 Convention and the UNHCR had no presence in the country prior to 1991. None of the former Soviet republics knew anything at all about the UNHCR or the international refugee regime. Therefore, the Office had to work in an entirely new political and operational environment. UNHCR staff were completely unfamiliar with its languages, cultures, climates, and political and legal systems.[10] Some of the biggest handicaps confronting the UNHCR involved the lack of institutional capacity to respond to mass displacements and the unreliable physical infrastructure, particularly outside of Moscow and other major cities.

The outbreak of conflicts and mass displacements in the South Caucasus and Central Asia within months of the December 1991 collapse of the Soviet Union led Ogata to review her approach to the region. During subsequent years, the Office came to establish a presence throughout the former Soviet Union. It also developed a comprehensive approach, which not only included the provision of emergency relief but also the building of local institutions to help prevent further forced displacement in the region. One of the Office's most comprehensive programmes was in Tajikistan. In early 1993, the UNHCR along with the ICRC initiated operations that were conducive to the return of refugees and IDPs. The UNHCR set up a unit on the Tajik-Afghani border to prepare for an early repatriation programme. It also provided emergency assistance to large numbers of internally displaced persons and established a shelter programme that provided materials for repairing houses destroyed in the Tajik conflict. Staff members also investigated the refugees' complaints and mediated between them and Tajik authorities and local populations. As a result of the short-term improvement in the security situation in the country, the great majority of refugees and IDPs returned home by mid-1995. Despite these initial successes, security conditions deteriorated considerably in 1996 and the situation remained difficult because of the widespread destruction and economic collapse in the country. Pro-government militias continued to harass returnees and large numbers of people were displaced once again, leaving thousands of people in precarious circumstances.

In the Caucasus, the brutality, complexity, and tenacity of the ethnic conflicts threatened to overwhelm the UNHCR. In co-operation with other international and regional agencies, the Office did play an active role in promoting repatriation of refugees from Georgia to Abkhazia and South Ossetia, but had to drop plans for the large-scale repatriation of ethnic Georgians to their former homes in Abkhazia because of a stalemate in political negotiations there. Similarly, in Armenia and Azerbaijan, a UNHCR emergency programme launched in 1993 had to be indefinitely extended because of the lack of any progress in ending the conflict over Nagorno-Karabakh and the absence of any prospect for repatriation. In Chechnya in 1995, the UNHCR launched the first UN humanitarian operation to be carried out on Russian territory. Working alongside the ICRC and other agencies, the UNHCR provided emergency assistance to masses of IDPs and war victims. These programmes helped contain the conflict and refugee crisis largely to Chechnya, thereby helping to prevent destabilization in neighbouring Daghestan and Ingushetia. In addition to trying to contain and manage refugee movements in the new post-Soviet republics, the UNHCR also initiated programmes of institution building and training, which included advice on drafting laws and institutions based on respect for human rights and minority rights and backed with effective human rights monitoring.

It became evident to the UNHCR that the problems of forcible displacement were intertwined and that issues such as citizenship and return of peoples to their ancestral homes could only be tackled by means of an integrated regional approach. It was also obvious that the UNHCR could not solve this problem alone. In December 1993, at the initiative of the Russian Federation, the UN General Assembly approved a resolution to hold a UN conference on the problems of refugees, returnees, and migrants.[11]

Two and a half years later, in May 1996, the UNHCR, IOM and the Organization for Security and Co-operation in Europe (OSCE) convened an international conference in Geneva. While the intention was to devise a comprehensive strategy at the national, regional, and international levels to deal with population displacements in the region, the conference itself only generated a very general statement of principles and objectives which remained largely unrealized long after the conference ended. In addition, the conference objective of focusing the attention of donors on the region did not succeed as donor states failed to respond to the UNHCR/IOM fund-raising appeal to support new programmes outlined in the 1996 conference action proposal. NGOs were also limited in the role they could play in the conference follow-up process. To many NGOs, the dearth of concrete implementation activities undertaken by the UNHCR represented a missed opportunity to address the problems of forced migration and displacement in the Commonwealth of Independent States (CIS) and to take an active preventive role in that region.[12] Indeed, during the remainder of the 1990s, most of the major conflicts within the CIS remained unresolved. By 2000, many of the cease-fire and peace agreements that had been negotiated earlier were under threat and domestic and foreign political forces were mobilized to exploit new outbursts of popular or separatist discontent, particularly in Central Asia.[13] Popular expectations for more pluralistic politics or for representative governments were frustrated and the standard of living for large sections of the populations of the CIS countries continued to decline. It was widely expected that the region would experience major new displacements in future years.

Despite the problems of implementation, the CIS conference did help raise the consciousness of the states in the region about the importance of adhering to international norms and practices regarding refugees and IDPs. As the 'teacher of refugee norms', the UNHCR helped the new CIS states train national refugee bureaucracies to comply with the international norms about state responsibility for refugees. By extending these values to new regions of the world, the UNHCR also enhanced its own legitimacy in the CIS and expanded the reach of the international refugee regime. In the follow-up to the conference, the Office was also able to extend its activities to new groups of displaced populations, particularly formerly deported peoples. This benefited the Crimean Tatars and Meskhetian Turks in particular. The UNHCR and the OSCE High Commissioner on National Minorities co-operated to facilitate the repatriation and reintegration of both groups in their homelands.

The 1990s: The Decade of Repatriation

Continuing a policy direction begun under Jean-Pierre Hocke, Ogata also made repatriation a primary objective of the organization. Indeed, in 1991 she declared that the 1990s would be 'the decade of voluntary repatriation' and massive numbers of refugees and IDPs returned to their homes during that time. According to the UNHCR, from 1991 to the beginning of 1996, more than 9 million refugees repatriated, a substantial increase over the period from 1985 to 1990 when about 1.2 million refugees repatriated.[14] In 1996, an additional two million refugees returned to their home countries. During the first half of the 1990s, the Office's annual spending on repatriation programmes grew substantially, increasing from an average of just two per cent of the agency's total budget prior to 1984 to some 14 per cent in the period 1990–7. In 1996 alone, the UNHCR allocated $214 million to reintegration programmes, almost twice as much as its 1994 expenditure.[15]

The dramatic increase in the number of repatriations in the early 1990s was largely due to the resolution of several protracted conflicts that originated in the Cold War. Once the superpowers had ended their rivalry and cut the lifeline to their clients in the developing world, many of the political obstacles to settling conflicts and to encouraging refugees to return home diminished considerably. As had been anticipated by Jean-Pierre Hocke, the political transformations taking place in the developing nations after the end of the Cold War gave the international community an unprecedented opportunity to empty many of the world's refugee camps. In late 1991, the UNHCR requested funding for twenty possible repatriations worldwide that it foresaw might occur in the years ahead.

Indeed, many refugees did return home in succeeding years. In Namibia, more than 42,000 refugees returned from exile following a UN-brokered peace settlement. After years of war and famine, up to one million refugees, primarily from Djibouti, Somalia, and Sudan returned to Ethiopia and Eritrea after the change of government in Addis Ababa in 1991. In 1992 and 1993, approximately 370,000 Cambodians repatriated from camps in Thailand, where many had been living since 1979. Between 1992 and 1996, some 1.7 million Mozambican refugees returned to their homeland from Malawi and five other neighbouring states. Despite the outbreak of civil conflict in Afghanistan and the absence of a central government, more than 2.7 million Afghans repatriated from Pakistan and Iran during 1992 and 1996. Not all Cold War conflicts were easily resolved, however, as continuing conflict and other political and economic obstacles proved insurmountable. In Angola, for example, UNHCR plans for the return and reintegration of Angolan refugees from Zaïre, Zambia, and Congo-Brazzaville had to be abandoned as fighting broke out again between UNITA and the Angolan government.

Two of the largest and most expensive repatriations with which the UNHCR was involved in the early 1990s were in Cambodia and Mozambique. Both countries had experienced protracted bloody conflicts that had killed millions of civilians, had generated a similar number of refugees and IDPs, and had left most of both countries in ruins. These conflicts were readily resolved once the Cold War had ended and superpower rivalry had ceased. The international peace agreements that ended these two conflicts had specific provisions regarding the return of refugees and IDPs. The UNHCR played an integral role in the comprehensive peace plan operations undertaken by the United Nations in both countries. In particular, the UNHCR ensured that refugees were repatriated in time to participate in the nationwide elections that were central to the comprehensive peace settlements. The Office also embarked on reintegration and rehabilitation projects in regions to which the refugees returned, thus helping to stabilize communities struggling to absorb the new arrivals.

Repatriation to Cambodia

The return of some 370,000 Cambodians was one of the largest logistical operations ever undertaken by the UNHCR.[16] The October 1991 Paris Peace Accords stipulated that the return of refugees should take place in time for them to be registered to vote in the May 1993 elections in Cambodia. The return not only had to be conducted in a relatively short timeframe but also in very difficult circumstances. Most of the refugees had been confined to refugee camps in Thailand for twelve or more years and many were returning to a land they feared was no longer familiar to them. Cambodia had been devastated by decades of war and much of the domestic infrastructure had been destroyed. As the refugees were primarily peasant farmers, the UNHCR decided to return them to the region around Battambang where the agency could provide them with between one and two hectares of arable land each. However, because much of this land had been heavily mined or was near Khmer Rouge-occupied territory, this plan had to be abandoned early in the repatriation and other options including cash payments instead of land were provided to the refugees. Despite these problems, the repatriation proceeded on schedule. By April 1993, all but a handful of the refugees were safely returned to Cambodia. In addition to ensuring the provision of land for the returnees, the UNHCR, in collaboration with UNDP, embarked on a series of quick impact development projects in an effort to help reintegrate the returnees while simultaneously helping the local population. Despite the outbreak of violence and intimidation by the Khmer Rouge and Hun Sen's forces, the elections were held on time, and, after further difficult negotiations, a new coalition government was formed. By late 1993, the UN along with the UNHCR, pulled most of its staff out of Cambodia, leaving a very fragile political and economic infrastructure behind. Despite the fact that many observers considered the repatriation programme a success, the political and security situation in Cambodia remained precarious for the remainder of the decade.

Repatriation to Mozambique

In Mozambique, some 1.7 million refugees from six neighbouring asylum countries and some 4 million IDPs returned home between 1992 and 1996. The October 1992 agreement between the Frelimo-ruled Mozambican government and the armed opposition movement (RENAMO) opened the way for the UNHCR to undertake the largest organized repatriation ever in Africa. As in Cambodia, the conflict had devastated the country's economy and social infrastructure. The repatriation and reintegration assistance carried out by the UNHCR was meant to dovetail with UN peace-building efforts and with long-term reconstruction and development programmes by the UNDP, the Food and Agricultural Organization (FAO), and the World Bank.

The economic dislocation and continuing distrust between the government and RENAMO delayed various aspects of the peace process, making the repatriation plan especially difficult to implement. With limited funds available for the repatriation operation, the UNHCR encouraged most of the refugees to organize their own return. Given the scale of the devastation within Mozambique, the UNHCR had to initiate reintegration and rehabilitation programmes along with the repatriation operation. The UNHCR completed hundreds of community-based rehabilitation projects in returnee-impacted areas in an effort to stabilize the situation and to enable the refugees to re-establish themselves. The projects were also intended to benefit other groups, including IDPs, demobilized soldiers and their families, and the local population. As in Central America and Cambodia, quick impact projects aimed at increasing food production, repairing transport infrastructure, promoting income-generating activities, and restoring basic water supplies, health care, and education were initiated in Mozambique. The Mozambican repatriation, like the one in Cambodia, was considered to be one of the UNHCR's successes despite the fact that Mozambique remained vulnerable to economic and political setbacks for the remainder of the decade.

Repatriation and Changing UNHCR Doctrine

The UNHCR became increasingly involved in managing repatriations during this time not only as a result of international peace agreements and under the umbrella of multidimensional UN peacekeeping missions, but also as a consequence of its own initiatives. Ogata was willing to exercise her mandate in a liberal and expansionist manner. Consequently UNHCR thinking and policy doctrine on repatriation and reintegration changed significantly under her.

Until the mid-1980s, repatriation had played a relatively small part in the organization's programmes. Many of the world's refugees had fled from Communist countries to which return was unthinkable. Nevertheless, some major repatriations did occur in Algeria, Bangladesh, Sudan, and other African countries. Many of these returns took place in the context of successful wars of national liberation. Moreover, the timing of the UNHCR's involvement in voluntary repatriation programmes was determined largely by refugees themselves. To a large extent they decided when to return and under what conditions and until they chose to return they received UNHCR assistance in host countries.

It was not until the end of the mid-1980s that states began to encourage the UNHCR to promote repatriation. The UNHCR under Hocke began to play a more proactive role in repatriation and consequently developed new thinking about repatriation and refugee protection. The agency's repatriation policies became more flexible and based more on pragmatic considerations and less on protection principles. Within the Office, there was a growing view that, with resettlement and asylum no longer realistic as solutions, refugees could not be satisfactorily protected in camps where they were increasingly exposed to physical harm and were unwanted by host governments. Rather, protection required freeing refugees from camps and finding a way for them to return to their home countries as quickly as possible, even if that occurred under less than ideal circumstances.[17] The UNHCR Executive Committee discouraged the Office from waiting any longer for opportunities but rather encouraged it to create the conditions that made repatriation possible. In the late 1980s, the UNHCR actively promoted the repatriations of Tamils to Sri Lanka and of Salvadorans to El Salvador despite the fact that these policies posed considerable risks for returnees because those who did go home returned to extremely violent civil wars.

By the 1990s, the UNHCR shifted its policy priorities even further in the direction of repatriation. In order to facilitate the return of refugees, the UNHCR acquired new means for considering repatriation under less demanding standards. The Office developed terminology and concepts like 'safe return' which stipulated that conditions in the home country did not have to improve 'substantially' but only 'appreciably' so that there could be a 'safe' return.[18] The UNHCR had come a long way from its traditional position that repatriation had to be a strictly voluntary decision by refugees. Rather, it would now be the UNHCR who would make the assessment as to whether conditions presented a threat to their safety. Moreover, there was a growing view that refugee safety did not necessarily always outweigh the security interests of states or broader peace-building and conflict resolution goals.[19]

A more proactive policy on repatriation also required that the UNHCR become involved in countries of origin, supplementing its traditional protection activities with work in the reintegration, rehabilitation, and development processes of returnee areas. Since a growing number of refugees were repatriating under some form of pressure into situations of social unrest and political instability, the UNHCR felt there was need for an international presence to monitor the welfare of the returnees and to facilitate their reintegration back into their home societies. Moreover, there was international concern that since most refugees were returning to areas that had been devastated by decades of conflict, they would be unable to support themselves and might once again be displaced. But economic development was not part of the UNHCR's traditional range of activities, and international development and financial institutions were not disposed to develop programmes in returnee-populated areas.

To fill this gap, Ogata encouraged her Office to develop a new strategy of 'returnee aid and development'.[20] This strategy envisioned the UNHCR providing short-term assistance to promote reintegration and that this would be followed up with long-term development assistance supplied by the international development agencies. Even though the UNHCR proved to be institutionally ill-equipped for the task of reintegration and its activities generally proved to be an ineffective bridge to rehabilitation and development, a great deal of the Office's energy and resources were devoted to promoting post-conflict reintegration.

The UNHCR and the Repatriation of Rohingyan Refugees to Burma

An early test case for the UNHCR's new thinking and policy on repatriation and reintegration was the 1994–5 return of Rohingyan refugees to Burma.[21] Between 1991 and 1992, about 270,000 people fled from the Rakhine State of

Burma to neighbouring Bangladesh. Almost all of the refugees were a Muslim minority group (Rohingyas) living in a predominantly Buddhist country. The Rohingya had been denied citizenship rights by the Rangoon government and had been persecuted by the Burmese military. Refugees reported that they had been subject to forced conscription and forced labour, rape, torture, and execution. This was the second mass exodus of Rohingya to Bangladesh in 12 years. In 1978, some 200,000 had fled across the border, only to be forcibly repatriated by Bangladeshi authorities using physical coercion and food cutbacks as weapons of intimidation.[22]

The Bangladesh government responded in similar ways to the 1991–2 influx. Beginning in autumn 1992, on the basis of a memorandum of understanding with the government of Burma, Bangladesh began to deport thousands of refugees and denied the UNHCR access to the camps where the refugees were accommodated. In response to the UNHCR's public protests about the forcible repatriation, the government of Bangladesh signed an agreement with the Office in October 1992 permitting the UNHCR to verify the voluntary nature of the repatriation. Despite the agreement, the UNHCR was denied a monitoring role and subsequently withdrew from the refugee camps and the repatriation programme at the end of December 1992. A mass repatriation of more than 10,000 Rohingya in early 1993 elicited an international protest and caused the government to call a halt to it.

Ogata, had a special interest in Burma, having served as Special Rapporteur on Burma for the UN Human Rights Commission before coming to the UNHCR. She perceived herself to have a special relationship with the Burmese authorities and to have a unique knowledge of the country. In May 1992, following the High Commissioner's trip to Dhaka, a memorandum of understanding was signed between the government of Bangladesh and the UNHCR that permitted the Office access to the camps and the right to interview the refugees independently in order to determine whether their decisions to repatriate were indeed voluntary. In return, the UNHCR agreed to promote repatriation once an international presence in Burma was established that could verify the existence of reasonable conditions for the returnees. The UNHCR then concluded a memorandum of understanding with Burma in November 1993 which permitted the refugees the right to return to their places of origin and allowed the UNHCR access to all returnees in order to monitor their safe reintegration. Human rights NGOs criticized these agreements on the grounds that they failed to state explicitly that the refugees could repatriate only after the human rights and security situation in Rakhine state had changed substantially. They feared, quite correctly as it turned out, that the UNHCR was about to promote a repatriation programme for which conditions in the home country were unsafe and in which the principles of voluntary repatriation would not be strictly adhered to. In 1994, after many false starts, the UNHCR began to actively promote the repatriation of the

Rohingya. Although human rights conditions in Burma had not changed, the Office determined that refugees could be better served by returning as soon as possible while their return and reintegration could be monitored.[23] Not only had the situation in Burma not changed, but the UNHCR manipulated information and provided financial incentives to the refugees in order to get them to return voluntarily. UNHCR officials repeatedly told the refugees that life had improved but these claims were highly exaggerated. According to international human rights organizations, there was little evidence that the security situation in Burma had improved substantially.[24] The Rohinga were promised that now that the Office had a presence in the country, it had the capacity to protect returnees from persecution and discrimination at the hands of the Burmese military. In addition, returning refugees were offered financial inducements to repatriate, including assistance packages and cash payments. By the end of 1995, all but 20,000 of the Rohingya had been returned to Burma.

The UNHCR expedited its repatriation campaign even though some of those who had recently repatriated, again fled Burma.[25] The UNHCR no longer sought out refugee preferences regarding repatriation but instead gave them the right to notify the UNHCR if they did not want to return, and refugees were no longer interviewed on an individual basis before being returned *en masse*. UNHCR staff also cautioned the refugees that if they returned to Bangladesh after being repatriated they risked being arrested for illegal departure by the Burmese authorities. So determined was the UNHCR to push repatriation that most of the refugees were not aware that they had the right to refuse to return if they so chose. The UNHCR's capacity to monitor the returnees in Burma was also highly questionable because of the significant geographical and logistical constraints faced by field staff. The Rakhine State of Burma is an inaccessible region with few paved roads and transportation links. UNHCR officials were frequently accompanied on their visits to returnees by Burmese military officials and so it was difficult, if not impossible, to get an accurate account of the difficulties returnees faced.[26] Moreover, the UNHCR staff were reluctant to challenge openly Burma's treatment of the Rohingyas, fearing that this might risk their ability to remain in Burma and undermine the Office's ability to claim that a safe return was possible.[27] Given the continued instability and human rights violations in Burma, it seemed unlikely that the mere presence of the UNHCR there would be sufficient either to provide the Rohingya Muslims with greater long-term security or to avert further future mass outflows of refugees.

The UNHCR as the International Community's Firemen

The UNHCR's biggest challenge in the 1990s was in responding to large-scale humanitarian emergencies. The end of the Cold War brought about major changes in the general pattern of refugee emergencies and posed considerable challenges to the agency. Most new operations were in reply to complex emergencies combining political instability, ethnic tensions, armed conflict, economic collapse, sharp socio-economic inequalities, human rights abuses, widespread availability of high-powered weaponry, and the disintegration of civil societies. Refugee movements frequently aggravated existing problems— such as growing competition for scarce resources—and were seldom confined to single countries but often affected entire regions. These refugee movements were usually the result of internal conflicts, in which questions of ethnic and religious identity were predominant in both the objectives and methods of the adversaries. In such conflicts, civilians were commonly used as weapons and targets of war, while large-scale population displacements were used to claim and exert control over territory.

During the early 1990s, the UNHCR's budget, staffing level, and international presence all expanded at an unprecedented rate. The nature of the Office's work also underwent a significant transformation in many parts of the world. Previously the UNHCR's programmes had been concentrated on refugees in the relatively safe and stable environment provided by countries of asylum. In the 1990s, however, a large proportion of the Office's operations took place within countries of origin, in zones of active conflict, and in close association with UN-mandated peacekeeping forces. At the same time, the organization provided assistance to broader categories of forcibly displaced people including the internally displaced, war-affected populations, the victims of mass expulsions, and returnees, as well as its traditional beneficiaries—refugees and asylum-seekers. The UNHCR in many senses was transformed from a refugee organization into a more broadly based humanitarian agency.

A notable feature of multilateral responses to the 1990s conflicts was that donor governments frequently used humanitarian assistance as a substitute for political and military intervention. The international community was all too often content to provide support to the UNHCR and to non-governmental organizations rather than to actively engage in seeking political solutions to internal wars. In place of a more proactive approach to armed conflict and to the underlying human rights causes of refugee movements, the international community focused on providing humanitarian relief rather than protection in civil wars, principally as a means of containing the outpouring of refugees and the destabilization of regions.

Intervention as a Means to Contain Refugee Movements in Iraq

Reliance on providing material assistance to war-affected populations rather than on protecting their human rights was most evident in the cases of Northern Iraq, Bosnia, and Rwanda, the post-Cold War's most publicized humanitarian crises. During the 1990s, most humanitarian interventions were undertaken within the UN framework and were justified by a flexible definition of the phrase 'threats to international peace and security', thereby permitting the UN Security Council to act under Chapter VII of the UN Charter. The first explicit use of UN enforcement action to contain refugee crises was in Northern Iraq. Following the end of the 1991 Gulf War, Iraqi suppression of widespread revolt in northern Kurdish areas had created fears that the entire Kurdish population would be uprooted. In late March 1991, some 2 million Iraqi Kurds fled to the Turkish border and into Iran. This posed a particularly grave prospect for neighbouring Turkey. Turkish officials argued that the Kurdish refugees would have an inflammatory effect on Turkey's own restive Kurds and could destabilize the country. Turkey closed the border and stated that the only solution to the crisis was to create a safe haven for the Kurds in northern Iraq. When television viewers around the world saw the desperate plight of Kurdish women and children struggling through the snow in inaccessible mountain passes along the Iraqi-Turkish border, Western leaders felt pressure to take international action.

Confronted with her first major refugee crisis, the new High Commissioner, flew to northern Iraq in early April to assess the situation herself. Upon her return to Geneva, Ogata called her Senior Management Committee together to discuss whether the UNHCR should assist the fleeing Kurds on the Turkish or Iraqi side of the border. The Director of International Protection argued that the High Commissioner had to stand up to Turkey's violation of international refugee law and doubted whether the Kurds could be adequately protected in Iraq. Overruling this advice, Ogata decided to treat the Kurds as internally displaced persons in Iraq rather than as refugees in Turkey. For some within the agency, this signalled the end of the era of asylum. The High Commissioner felt she had no choice. The NATO powers refused to force Turkey to accept the Kurds and had already announced that they were preparing a safe zone in northern Iraq.[28] The UNHCR was declared the lead agency in northern Iraq but the Kurdish crisis caught the agency unprepared. At the outbreak of the Kurdish crisis, the agency had no presence in northern Iraq and was not equipped to respond quickly and effectively to a humanitarian emergency of this size. It took almost two weeks after the Kurdish outflow for the UNHCR to become at all evident in the mountains in northern Iraq.[29]

It quickly became apparent that the UN alone could not mobilize resources and transport displaced people and materials in the short time available. The international community quickly turned to the Allied military forces to provide a solution. UN Security Council resolution 688 of April 5, 1991 provided the basis for intervention in northern Iraq by allied coalition forces. The Security Council noted that it was gravely concerned by the repression of the Iraqi civilian population in many parts of Iraq, including most recently in Kurdish populated areas, which led to a massive flow of refugees towards and across international frontiers and to cross-border incursions, which threaten international peace and security. (UN Security Council Resolution 688 of 5 April 1991).

UN Security Council action was made possible in this case because Iraq had just lost a war and could not counter such interference. In addition, this resolution was in fact rather limited. Although international forces were subsequently deployed to northern Iraq to carve out 'safe areas' for Kurds and Iraqi forces withdrew from these areas under pressure, the call for humanitarian action was limited to the provision of assistance within Iraq. Moreover, Resolution 688 offered no international redress to the 'repression' other than to express 'the hope for an early dialogue' among the parties to the conflict.[30] It was clear that international assistance and protection for Kurds in Iraq was intended to stem their movement into Turkey, a NATO member state and close Western ally. The security of Kurdish populations within Iraq was far from guaranteed. This region continued to be unsafe and prolonged Western military engagement was required to sustain the arrangement.

During the 1991 crisis, the UNHCR dispatched emergency response teams to the region, but it lacked the resources and emergency capacity to meet the acute needs of the Kurdish refugees. Allied military forces led the relief effort and provided the means to carry out Operation Provide Comfort and to establish camps in northern Iraq. The military had greater capacity to mobilize and deploy resources—particularly in the logistics sector—and unrivalled access to a range of material and logistical resources in transportation, communications, and medical services that was simply not available to the UNHCR. The allied forces met the immediate needs of the Kurds and saved the day for the UNHCR in northern Iraq by protecting relief shipments, creating a safety zone, and evacuating and relocating civilians from the mountains. It was only after UN 'humanitarian centres' were established and the UN had signed a Memorandum of Understanding with Baghdad that the UN took over the relief operation for Kurdish refugees.

Reforms of Emergency Relief Mechanisms at the UNHCR and the UN

The enormous challenges posed by Operation Provide Comfort provided many lessons for the UNHCR. The Kurdish emergency revealed weaknesses in the agency's emergency response capacity and taught the High Commissioner how important it was to be properly prepared for unexpected refugee emergencies by having a system in place for responding immediately to such crises. The experience also taught her the importance of good public relations and the centrality of refugee movements to the future conduct of international relations in the post-Cold War era. In the autumn 1991, Ogata took a number of corrective measures. A structure of emergency response teams was introduced and arrangements made to pre-position and stockpile relief supplies to be drawn upon in future emergencies. To enable the agency to move with greater flexibility and speed in the future, standby arrangements were made with the Danish and Norwegian Refugee Councils and the UN Volunteers for quick deployment of staff to emergency operations in any part of the world.

The Kurdish refugee crisis also made Ogata aware of the importance of the media and particularly its portrayal of the UNHCR. Media coverage of the plight of the Kurds in 1991 and of widespread starvation in Somalia in 1992 provoked massive responses at public and political levels and redirected the attention of the West to these humanitarian tragedies. The High Commissioner realized the significance of the impact of media coverage on public opinion and the impact, in turn, of public opinion on political processes and leaders. Ogata was also aware that, without a high profile, it would be difficult to raise money for bigger operations. She had long admired UNICEF and the public identification of that agency with children. She wanted the UNHCR too to have a highly recognizable niche and for the public to identify her Office with humanitarian emergencies.[31] She, therefore, set about reforming the UNHCR's public information activities in order to mobilize greater funds for refugee assistance and to arouse public sympathy and support. Ogata felt that the Office could only succeed in the new international environment through a combination of more effective operational capacity and more aggressive public information. For Ogata, the UNHCR not only had to develop better emergency response mechanisms but the agency also had to be perceived by the media as being more operational and effective.

Ogata hired Sylvana Foa to head the Public Information Office and several new news wire agency staff to project the right image of the Office. The incorporation into the UNHCR of professional news people who had broad contacts with the media and who knew how to package information and get it out quickly transformed the public information capacity of the agency.[32] The upgrading of public information coincided with growing UNHCR involvement in Bosnia and other humanitarian emergencies. As the UNHCR took on greater operational responsibilities and its vehicles were seen delivering assistance on the front lines of conflicts around the world, its prestige and reputation soared. Suddenly the UNHCR was on the world political map. It grew from being an obscure humanitarian agency with no emergency relief profile, to become a well-known international humanitarian assistance agency.

Foa set out deliberately to attract press attention and to reach a broader audience. In Bosnia in the early 1990s, the UNHCR placed considerable importance on the provision of information and its relations with the media.

Jose Marie Mendiluce was the UNHCR's first representative in the field there. He had previously been in fund raising and knew the importance of public information. The UNHCR was in fact, the only relief agency in Bosnia with a public information spokesperson in the field. It quickly cultivated a reputation for credibility with the media and packaged information in a timely and dramatic way to attract press notice. The world's media came to rely on the Office for immediate coverage of atrocities against civilians and attacks on relief convoys. Consequently, the press often portrayed the UNHCR as more capable than it really was.[33] Sylvana Foa reportedly quipped that the 'world's media had actually started to believe what we tell them'.[34] The UNHCR became the world's good guys and could do no wrong. *Time* magazine praised 'Ogata's Angels' for their courageous action in the field and asserted that 'to other members of the extended United Nations family, one agency stands out as something of a paradigm of what the organization could and should be: the United Nations High Commissioner for Refugees.'[35] Pictures of Ogata visiting refugees and displaced people on the battlegrounds in the Balkans and Africa were splashed across the front pages of the *New York Times* and other major newspapers. The world's press and media idolized her. The British press called her the 'Diminutive Giant of Japan' and *Vogue* magazine ran a story on 'Mrs. Ogata: The Chief Surgeon in the world's Emergency Room'. From being a much-maligned agency in 1989, the UNHCR suddenly became one of the most valued and esteemed of all UN agencies.

At about the same time that the UNHCR was retooling its emergency response capacity and restoring and reinvigorating its public image, the institutional framework for international humanitarian action at the United Nations also changed. The Gulf War and its aftermath had highlighted the problems of co-ordinating a rapid and effective emergency humanitarian operation. In part due to the dissatisfaction of governments with UN performance during the Gulf crisis in December 1991, the UN General Assembly adopted resolution 46/182 to strengthen the co-ordination of emergency humanitarian assistance. In March 1992, the Secretary-General created the Department of Humanitarian Affairs (DHA) and appointed the UN's first humanitarian assistance co-ordinator at the level of Under-Secretary-General. The UN resolution that established the DHA also stipulated that humanitarian aid was to be provided, with 'the *consent* of the affected country',[36] rather than at its *request*, as was the case in the past. The Kurdish refugee crisis had highlighted the plight of displaced people around the world whom the international community had had difficulty in reaching. Generally, providing assistance to refugees and internally displaced people had been contingent upon invitation from host or home governments. In many cases, international organizations and NGOs had delayed assistance to people whose lives were at risk, either because governments had not asked for it or because no central authority existed to authorize outside aid. During the Cold War, various *ad hoc* measures were adopted that permitted intervention by the international community on behalf of refugees and displaced people. 'Corridors of tranquility', through which relief convoys were allowed to pass without interference and 'humanitarian cease-fires', 'zones of peace', and 'safe havens', that allowed humanitarian assistance into conflict zones, were pragmatic mechanisms used by some international agencies and NGOs in such places as Angola, Ethiopia, Iraq, Sri Lanka, and Sudan.

The creation of the DHA was perceived by some as an important first step toward creating modalities to ensure freer humanitarian access to vulnerable populations and to improve the UN emergency response capacity.[37] At the same time, the Inter-Agency Standing Committee (IASC) was established to facilitate inter-agency co-ordination in humanitarian emergencies. However, larger UN agencies like the UNHCR, saw no clear benefit to themselves in co-ordination. The UNHCR, while not opposed to informal sharing of information and responsibilities, rejected external control and did not wish to see inter-agency co-ordination specifically defined. As the lead agency and the vehicle for vast sums of relief money, resources, and materials in many of the major humanitarian emergencies, the UNHCR was particularly opposed to the successful functioning of the DHA. The UNHCR with its high public profile, independent moral authority, and a specific and well-defined mandate was well positioned to undermine the DHA. Moreover, many UN agencies were wary that the DHA might become increasingly active in the field, directly competing with their own authority and programmes. Because the DHA was never given adequate authority over other agencies or adequate funding to carry out its responsibility, the UNHCR and other humanitarian organizations successfully undermined it. In 1997 the DHA was eliminated in a major restructuring of the UN system under Secretary-General Kofi Annan.

The 1997 UN reforms revealed underlying tensions among the international humanitarian agencies and deep-seated resentment against the UNHCR. Annan had asked Maurice Strong, a long-time UN hand, to study the UN response to humanitarian emergencies and to come up with suggestions for improved co-ordination among UN agencies. Strong recommended either an amalgamation of all the agencies into one super agency or the assignment of a co-ordinating role to one of the existing agencies. He considered the UNHCR to be the most suitable agency to take on either of these roles. Before the Secretary-General had time to consider Strong's proposals, Ogata instructed key aides to devise a plan. They proposed to restructure the UNHCR, keeping its traditional refugee mandate and office in Geneva and creating a new humanitarian affairs department at the UN in New York that would be responsible for co-ordinating complex emergencies. When news of this report leaked out to the other humanitarian agencies, all hell broke loose in New York and at other UN agency headquarters, particularly at the World Food Program and UNICEF. The UNHCR's proposal was widely perceived as an attempt by the UNHCR to completely take over the humanitarian assistance field. These events left bitter feelings towards the UNHCR among several of the major UN humanitarian agencies. Ogata called this 'one of my most painful experiences as High Commissioner'.[38]

In the end, Annan established a new position of Under-Secretary-General for Humanitarian Affairs (USG) and re-named the DHA the Office for the Co-ordination of Humanitarian Affairs (OCHA).[39] The USG acts as both the head of OCHA and as the Emergency Relief Co-ordinator who chairs the IASC. In addition, he serves as the chairperson of the Executive Committee for Humanitarian Affairs which provides a means to integrate the various components involved in humanitarian emergencies: humanitarian relief, human rights, political affairs, and peacekeeping.

Debates over Internally Displaced Persons

The Kurdish emergency had also underlined the extreme vulnerability of IDPs, who were emerging as a central issue in the post-Cold War period. There was widespread recognition that there was a need to develop a coherent and effective legal basis for protecting IDPs and to establish a new international agency to provide them protection and assistance. But governments remained reluctant and existing agencies, including the UNHCR, perceived such possible developments as a threat to their vested interests. In order to highlight this problem, the UN Human Rights Commission proposed that the Secretary-General appoint a Representative for IDPs. In 1991, the UN Secretary-General appointed Francis Deng, a former Sudanese diplomat, to become the Secretary-General's Representative for IDPs. Over the course of several years, Deng took a series of incremental steps to increase the international visibility of the problem of IDPs.

Ogata herself was interested in IDPs both because of her background in human rights and because of the high political profile of several of the IDP emergencies in the early post-Cold War period. The High Commissioner thought that the Office had too passive an approach to displacement and felt that the UNHCR could no longer wait for refugees to cross borders before it took action.[40] She was intrigued by the success of cross-border relief activities and pushed for more imaginative approaches to the problem of internal displacement. But within the UNHCR itself there was little enthusiasm for expanding the organization's mandate to include the internally displaced. The Office's involvement with IDPs in the northern Iraq and the former Yugoslavia made senior staff members aware of the political and operational difficulties that such an initiative might create for the organization. Some maintained that such an expansion of the UNHCR's mandate would divert attention and resources from the Office's traditional activities and weaken its ability to protect and assist refugees. Others feared that the organization would find itself overwhelmed by the proliferation of international conflicts and the massive movements of IDPs which such wars were likely to create. But during the early 1990s, the High Commissioner was under international pressure to become involved with IDPs. In 1992, the UN General Assembly welcomed

efforts by the High Commissioner, on the basis of specific requests from the Secretary-General or the competent principal organs of the United Nations and with the consent of the concerned state, to undertake activities in favor of internally displaced persons, taking into account the complementarities of the mandates and expertise of other relevant organizations. (UN General Assembly Resolution 47/105 of 1992).

Nevertheless, Ogata turned down requests to become involved with IDPs in Cambodia and Zaïre in 1992 because she felt the Office did not have sufficient capacity to take on these problems. The growing international interest in IDPs precipitated a flurry of discussions and reports within the UNHCR. In the past, decisions concerning the UNHCR's involvement with IDPs were taken on an *ad hoc* basis, and with an emphasis on assistance rather than protection activities. Consequently, Ogata felt that the organization should develop a more systematic and comprehensive approach to the issue. At the same time, she wanted to maintain almost complete freedom of action regarding IDPs.

In April 1993, the High Commissioner published a set of guidelines concerning the organization's activities on behalf of IDPs.[41] The guidelines indicated that the UNHCR's involvement with IDPs should be contingent upon a specific request emanating from the General Assembly, the Secretary-General, ECOSOC, or another UN organ, that it should be with the consent of the concerned state, and dependent upon the availability of resources.[42] The guidelines also suggested that the UNHCR should take primary responsibility for IDPs only in situations where there were clear links with activities undertaken on the basis of the organization's regular mandate. This would be the case in situations where IDPs were mixed with returnee populations or were found in areas to which refugees might be returning, where the same causes have produced both internal displacement and a refugee flow, or where there was a risk that the internal displacement might become a refugee movement.

The criteria set by the UNHCR to guide its work with IDPs were purposely broad and flexible. Ogata wanted to avoid a formal commitment to IDPs but also wanted the flexibility to get involved in IDP emergencies she considered appropriate or politically important to address. At the same time, the guidelines gave the High Commissioner the leeway to reject involvement in any emergencies presenting legal or operational difficulties. While the April 1993 guidelines were helpful in establishing a general framework for the UNHCR's approach to IDPs, they did not resolve the problem of how the international community should deal with IDPs nor did they clarify the scale, scope, or duration of the UNHCR's operational involvement. The UNHCR's ambivalence towards IDPs also had the effect of making the Office further dependent on major donor governments. While the UNHCR intervened in high profile IDP emergencies such as Northern Iraq and Bosnia where donor states guaranteed generous funding to undertake operations, the High Commissioner kept a cautious distance in numerous other humanitarian emergencies involving IDPs where donors tended to underplay or disregard the problem.[43] Later, under pressure from the US Ambassador to the UN, the UNHCR took measures to enhance and to make more predictable its response to IDPs.

Making the UNHCR Relevant and the Failure of Preventive Protection in Bosnia

Apart from its work with Kurdish IDPs in Northern Iraq, the UNHCR's first major involvement with IDPs was in the former Yugoslavia. Despite the fact that intervention in the Balkans meant open-ended involvement in on-going internal conflicts, Ogata perceived UNHCR engagement there as an opportunity to make the agency relevant to the international community's most powerful actors.[44] When she first became High Commissioner, the UNHCR was recovering from the worst financial crisis in its recent history. It was on extremely poor terms with European governments regarding their treatment of asylum-seekers and it was trying to restore its image as an effective relief organization after it had been battered by its inability to play a prominent role in responding to the population displacements after the Gulf War. The breakup of the former Yugoslavia was a high-profile, strategic crisis on the edge of Western Europe. Not only would this initiative revitalize the organization and enable it to enhance its influence and prestige with governments—particularly UN Security Council member states—but it would also restore the confidence of European governments in the UNHCR.[45] At the October 1991 UNHCR Executive Committee meeting, the Yugoslav delegate requested UNHCR intervention and subsequently approached UN Secretary-General Perez de Cuellar. On 14 November 1991, the High Commissioner did not hesitate to accept the request by the UN Secretary-General to assist refugees from the warring republics of the former Yugoslavia and to act as the lead UN agency for the delivery of humanitarian assistance there.

As the former Yugoslavia was disintegrating into violence, the UNHCR was launching a huge repatriation operation in Cambodia. Initially therefore, the UNHCR started on a small scale in the former Yugoslavia, distributing family parcels and other assistance to the displaced in co-ordination with the ICRC. But that role expanded quickly in early 1992 when the conflict within the former Yugoslavia extended into Bosnia-Hercegovina. After Bosnia proclaimed independence in March 1992, fighting intensified and large numbers of Muslims were displaced and forcibly expelled into neighbouring Croatia. According Jose Mendiluce, who was the High Commissioner's representative there at the time, it soon became obvious to the UNHCR that civilian displacement—what came to be known as 'ethnic cleansing'—was not a consequence but an objective of the war.[46] The ICRC withdrew for Bosnia after the killing of one of its delegates, effectively leaving the UNHCR to fill the gap. The Office commenced food distributions to displaced and besieged persons inside Bosnia from Sarajevo in April and later from Mostar and Banja Luka. From Sarajevo beginning in July 1992 the agency co-ordinated what became the longest running humanitarian airlift in history. By the end of 1992, UNHCR convoys were providing relief to more than 1.6 million people or about one-half of the population trapped in besieged cities and regions inside Bosnia, and to 1.4 million people in the rest of the former Yugoslavia. By 1995, out of a pre-war population of 4.3 million, an estimated 900,000 had become refugees in neighbouring countries and Western Europe, while a further 1.3 million had become internally displaced. Governments came to view the UNHCR as an indispensable actor in their efforts to keep the aid flowing into Bosnia. The prestige of the High Commissioner soared as she had access to the world's political leaders and regularly briefed the UN Security Council on developments in Bosnia.

Bosnia transformed the UNHCR into the world's largest relief agency but the relief effort there overwhelmed it. By the end of the war, the organization became badly overextended in the former Yugoslavia, inevitably at the expense of other crises, particularly in Africa. The UNHCR-directed operation mushroomed into a huge multidimensional effort involving over 250 international humanitarian organizations.[47] Throughout most of the conflict, the UNHCR committed approximately one-quarter of its staff and one-third of its total resources worldwide to providing assistance in the Balkans.[48] The UNHCR assisted virtually the entire Bosnian population. According to Ogata she had become 'the desk officer for former Yugoslavia'.[49]

The UNHCR's involvement in the former Yugoslavia became part of a comprehensive policy doctrine that Ogata encouraged her Office to develop in 1992. The High Commissioner felt that in the changing international political environment after the Cold War, international refugee problems could no longer be managed simply by aiding refugees after the fact. She believed that traditional concepts of protection were changing and that there were reduced opportunities for conventional asylum in both the industrialized states and the developing countries.[50] Moreover, the UN Security Council had started to reassert its authority in international security and humanitarian issues and to undertake new forms of collective action to which the UNHCR had to adapt. In 1992, the new UN Secretary-General Boutros-Ghali issued his *Agenda for Peace* [51] which emphasized preventive diplomacy and signalled that 'the time of absolute and exclusive sovereignty . . . has passed,' thus opening the way for international intervention against repressive regimes of the kind that historically had been the major cause of refugee movements. Inspired by these developments, Ogata believed that refugee policy must include attention to prevention as well as to solutions. Believing that, if the UNHCR did not meet this challenge, the Office's relevance and future would be put in doubt, the High Commissioner mandated an internal UNHCR working group to come up with 'new responses which were innovative and realistic, balancing humanitarian concerns with political realism and States' interests with the rights and needs of refugees'.[52] She wanted a policy doctrine that reflected the growing activity of the UNHCR in conflict areas.

The Working Group report set out an agenda for the UNHCR for the 1990s that focused on in-country protection, prevention, and solutions. It outlined the following tasks:

In terms of specific activities which the Office should undertake in the area of prevention, particularly as a catalyst, it was agreed that early warning, preventive diplomacy, human rights promotion, economic and social development and protection of internally displaced persons were all areas appropriate for specific UNHCR activities. (UNHCR, 'Report of the UNHCR Working Group on International Protection' (Geneva: UNHCR, 6 July 1992): 1).

The group's report argued that the UNHCR should involve itself in a broad range of policies touching on issues formerly considered domestic and therefore too 'political'. In essence, the working group argued that protection, which was the core activity of the High Commissioner's mandate, could take many forms, including the provision of relief assistance to civilians caught in conflicts. This constituted a dramatic expansion of the Office's functions, which would be sorely tested in the former Yugoslavia. The Office's new concepts and the principal points of the report were set out in a paper to the Executive Committee of the UNHCR in 1992[53] and were formally endorsed by Excom in October 1993.

This new policy doctrine had been previously introduced at a July 1992 ministerial-level conference in Geneva that the High Commissioner had convened to mobilize support for a comprehensive response to the humanitarian crisis in the former Yugoslavia. In a major policy statement,[54] Ogata outlined the elements of this policy which involved the Office in several phases of the conflict from prevention to the return of refugees. The most innovative and controversial element was 'preventive protection' which was intended to make flight unnecessary for most of the war victims. In the former Yugoslavia, preventive protection—in theory—included human rights measures to reduce violence on the ground and protection and assistance to those who might otherwise feel compelled to move. The other novel element was the request for states to assure temporary protection for those who were externally displaced while preparing for their eventual return.

As the conflicts intensified in the former Yugoslavia, it became evident that the UNHCR had an over-optimistic assessment of what preventive policies could realistically deliver given the fact that the agency was operating for the first time in a war zone and under severe political and logistical constraints.[55] While the UNHCR was able to deliver large quantities of humanitarian supplies, it was much less successful in carrying out its protection mandate. The UNHCR found it difficult in practice to ensure the protection of human rights and the physical security of war-affected populations. It had hoped that by establishing a presence on all sides of the conflict, it would be able to monitor human rights abuses and carry out its protection activities. However, warring parties often prevented the UNHCR from visiting areas where ethnic cleansing was taking place and staff were unable to prevent harassment of minorities, evictions, expulsions, and human rights abuses.[56] On 11 August 1992 UNHCR internal note on preventive protection admitted that:

. . . any humanitarian action aimed at prevention and at improving the situation on the ground has its limits, especially in a context so emotionally charged, dangerous and volatile as is currently the case in the Republic of Bosnia-Hercegovina where the displacement of civilians is often the objective of armed hostilities. Without an immediate cease fire, the shelling or destruction of civilian targets and other violations of the laws of war are unlikely to stop, despite their international exposure and wide-spread condemnation. Without a negotiated settlement, addressing the political root causes of the conflict, efforts of prevention of ethnic persecution and of other human rights abuses risk to have only limited effect. (UNHCR Internal Note, 'Preventive Protection', unpublished document in author's files, 11 August 1992: 1).

In view of its powerlessness to prevent harassment and expulsions, the UNHCR was faced with the dilemma of whether to continue to counter ethnic cleansing or to evacuate displaced and vulnerable civilians and uphold their right to seek asylum. UNHCR staff on the ground were reluctant to engage in mass evacuation because they feared that this would only contribute to and encourage further ethnic cleansing. Rather they hoped to buy time for displaced persons by extending protection to them as close to their homes as possible through its strategy of preventive protection. However, this approach failed in the face of the combatants' extreme brutality and utter disregard for humanitarian principles. In Bosnia, the organization was confronted with a stark choice: either collaborate in ethnic cleansing by helping those in need of protection to cross borders or leave these defenceless civilians to be killed.[57] According to Mendiluce, 'We decided to help people survive. We chose to have more displaced persons or refugees than more bodies'.[58]

The UNHCR's work in countries of origin differed substantially from the its traditional work in countries of asylum. In the past, the UNHCR had worked primarily with people who had fled across borders to neighbouring countries. The organization had protected and assisted refugees in association with the host government, on the general assumption that following a resolution of the situation generating the original displacement, the refugees would return home. In Bosnia, by contrast, the UNHCR was called upon to meet the needs of displaced people who lived amidst conditions of inter-communal violence and on-going conflict. The organization's staff members found themselves working not only with governments but also with opposition groups, guerrilla forces, political factions, and clan leaders, as well as with UN peacekeepers and military intervention forces. This work was very different from that which they had done in countries of asylum. In addition to conventional protection and assistance activities, the UNHCR's role expanded in the former Yugoslavia to include functions such as protecting civilians against attack and forced displacement, relocating and evacuating civilians from conflict areas, and assisting besieged populations who were unable or unwilling to move from their homes. Despite the expenditure of massive resources, UNHCR protection officers were often too inexperienced and too few in number to fulfil an adequate protection role. The organization was simply not well-enough equipped to respond to the needs of internally displaced people in Bosnia. The UNHCR was caught up in massive and unconventional humanitarian operations that required a high level of inventiveness and innovation on the part of the organization and its personnel. There were many courageous acts on the parts of individual staff members but most UNHCR staff were neither recruited nor trained to work in the crossfire of internal conflicts where soldiers and guerrillas view the internally displaced and returnees as the enemy, and UN assistance as favouring one side to the disadvantage of the other.

The UNHCR's operational effectiveness was also hampered by the fact that the agency was part of an overall UN effort including both political-military and humanitarian functions. After the war broke out in Bosnia in April 1992, the humanitarian assistance programme came to be the basis of the multilateral response to the Balkans crises and remained virtually the sole substitute for an overall approach to the political problem there.[59] Unwilling to take sides in the conflict and unable to agree on ways to end the bloodshed, the international community concentrated largely on the humanitarian relief operation led by the UNHCR. When the UN Security Council authorized the deployment of a UN Protection Force (UNPROFOR) on 7 April 1992,[60] it stipulated that UNPROFOR's original mission in Bosnia was to facilitate the delivery of UNHCR's assistance and not to secure a cease-fire or settlement of the conflict. Moreover, UN Security Council member states determined that UNPROFOR should maintain the established principles of consent, impartiality, and minimal use of force in achieving this objective. While the Security Council later authorized UNPROFOR to carry out 'all necessary means' to ensure delivery of assistance,[61] it was never equipped with sufficient force to carry out this threat. UNHCR staff had to negotiate access to displaced people with the very authorities who were causing the forced displacement. As a consequence, the Bosnian Serbs were able to obstruct the delivery of humanitarian aid and blackmail UNPROFOR and the UNHCR for assistance almost at will throughout most of the conflict.[62]

The focus of UN activity remained humanitarian relief and not protection of civilians caught in the crossfire of war. Yet the very purpose of war in the former Yugoslavia was to consolidate and legitimize territorial control on the basis of ethnic homogeneity.[63] While Security Council resolutions condemned concentration camps, attacks on non-combatants, and ethnic cleansing, and the Special Rapporteur for the UN Commission on Human Rights requested that the Security Council send troops to counter human rights violations, the international community never provided UNPROFOR with adequate force and mandate to address ethnic cleansing and other atrocities.[64] Similarly, UN human rights monitors sent to the former Yugoslavia had extremely limited resources and mandate and there were never enough UNHCR protection officers in the field to stop the attacks on civilians and the expulsion of refugees. In spite of the cynical disregard for all prior agreements and the flagrant abuses of human rights by the warring parties, states and the UN Secretary-General exerted pressure on the UNHCR to continue operations. For example, when the High Commissioner decided to suspend UNHCR operations in Bosnia in February 1993 in protest against the blockage of the safe passage for humanitarian supplies to displaced people, Boutros-Ghali quickly overturned the action. Consequently, the UNHCR lost any limited capacity it had to take independent decisions or to exert its own pressures on the warring parties. The agency was left with trying to make the best of an impossible job thus damaging its reputation as an autonomous actor.

The international community was more interested in ensuring the continuation of the aid operation in Bosnia than in protecting the displaced. The worst protection failures in Bosnia occurred when access to asylum in nearby countries was closed and displaced people were compelled to remain in their own country at the mercy of those intent on persecuting them.

Western countries did not want increased numbers of Bosnian refugees and asylum-seekers. They instituted stiffer visa requirements, forbade UNPROFOR to escort Bosnians abroad, and compelled the UNHCR to deliver assistance to those who remained in Bosnia. The agency became a major instrument for the Western policy of 'containment' of refugee problems in the Balkans. In effect, the UNHCR actually undermined the right of Bosnians to seek asylum.[65] Even the establishment of 'safe areas' in Bosnia in the spring of 1993[66] could not save the Bosnians. Hundreds of thousands of people became dependent on humanitarian assistance, particularly in the besieged Muslim enclaves of Sarajevo, Srebrenica, Zepa, Gorazde, and Bihac. Although UNPROFOR provided humanitarian actors with vital security and logistics support, it was singularly unsuccessful in improving access for the UNHCR to the government enclaves, which were besieged by Bosnian Serb forces. Furthermore, international efforts to provide local protection through such means were limited. There was never any intention to take the measures that were necessary to defend the safe areas. The 34,000 soldiers needed to guard those places never materialized and ethnic cleansing continued unabated. The over-running of the so-called safe areas of Srebrenica and Zepa in the summer of 1995 by Bosnian Serb forces, the subsequent withdrawal of all UNPROFOR troops from eastern Bosnia, and the massacre of large numbers of men and boys from Srebrenica marked the final humiliation of UNPROFOR.[67]

Famine, Civil War, and 'Failed States' in Africa

During the early 1990s, war and anarchy prevailed in several African countries and this resulted in a steady increase in the numbers of refugees and internally displaced populations throughout the region. The end of the Cold War brought to an abrupt end external aid and legitimacy for many African regimes that had been clients of one or the other of the superpowers. Without external support, long-time strong men and dictators were overthrown by warlords and armed factions. Angola, Liberia, and Somalia had been flooded with weapons during the Cold War, and after the superpowers withdrew support to their clients, warlords and their followers used these weapons to try to gain control of their country's resources.[68] In the wake of these brutal conflicts, state political and economic structures collapsed, leading Western analysts to term most of Africa's warring states as 'failed states'. In some places, internecine fighting so badly damaged the physical environment and agriculture that famines occurred. In these circumstances, civilians were targeted and masses of refugees and internally displaced persons were driven from their homes.

Liberia was one of these so-called failed states.[69] After the overthrow of the Liberian regime of Samuel Doe by the National Patriotic Front of Liberia (NPFL) headed by Charles Taylor, law and order disintegrated as at least half a dozen armed factions fought each other for control of the country's territory and resources. From 1990 to 1995, more than 800,000 of the country's 2.4 million citizens were forced into exile. A similar if not greater number of Liberians were internally displaced. The civil war in Liberia caused very difficult problems for the international humanitarian agencies. Warlords respected very few international humanitarian norms and seldom observed agreements. Hence, because the lives of relief workers were constantly put at risk by the internecine fighting, NGOs repeatedly withdrew their staff from Liberia.

The Liberian refugees spilled over into five neighbouring West African states: Guinea and the Ivory Coast had refugee populations of around 400,000 and 360,000 respectively by 1995 and Sierra Leone, Ghana, and Nigeria had a combined refugee population of some 35,000. The disorder generated by the Liberian conflict spread throughout the region, provoking further violence and population displacements. In Sierra Leone, Liberian NPFL forces backed the Revolutionary United Front of Sierra Leone to overthrow the country's government. Subsequently, the level of brutality and violence increased in Sierra Leone as armed factions sought control of the diamond and ore producing areas of the country.[70] More than 300,000 Sierra Leoneans fled the country—120,000 to Liberia and 190,000 to Guinea—and some 600,000 were internally displaced. In both Sierra Leone and Liberia, civilian populations were frequently attacked and hundreds of thousands non-combatants were killed or brutally maimed by having their arms or legs hacked off. Adolescent boys were routinely drafted into the armies of the conflicting factions and forced to commit unspeakable atrocities.

The principal international response to these conflicts and humanitarian tragedies came from intervention by the multinational military force of the Economic Community of West African States (ECOWAS). While the UN Security Council endorsed the regional peacekeeping initiatives in Liberia and Sierra Leone, it did not provide them sufficient political attention and military resources. The regional peacekeeping force, known as ECOMOG, had limited means for imposing peace on the various parties to the conflicts. Although the UNHCR had a presence in the region and operated camps for refugees fleeing the conflicts, the level of international attention and humanitarian assistance provided to the region's refugees and displaced people was minuscule compared to other high-profile conflicts. The difference in international resources allocated to humanitarian activities in the Balkans and in West Africa and Somalia was particularly glaring, leading Boutros-Ghali to characterize Bosnia as 'a rich man's war'.[71]

Warlords, Famine, and UNHCR Cross-Border Relief in Somalia

Somalia became an early test case for how the international community would respond to Africa's humanitarian emergencies during the post-Cold War era. As in Liberia, the outbreak of conflict and a humanitarian crisis in Somalia had its roots in the Cold War. For years the Somali regime of Siad Barre was supported by one or the other superpower. When external aid ceased, the Barre regime disintegrated and fell only to be replaced by warlords and clans competing for territorial control of the country. Inter-clan fighting and repeated droughts disrupted the harvest and famine threatened to kill massive numbers of Somalian citizens. By mid-1992, several thousand people were dying every day and hundreds of thousands were internally displaced. About 285,000 people crossed the border into north-western Kenya. The arrival of refugees was accompanied by an influx of weapons, bandits, and combatants who posed a security risk for the host state and destabilized the region.

Initially, the international community was indifferent to the mounting catastrophe in Somalia. In stark contrast to the Cold War period, Somalia no longer attracted the political and strategic attention of the international community. Without a strong patron to rally support for it and with the UN Security Council focused on Bosnia and other issues of greater strategic importance, the international community at first took little action to prevent the fighting and famine that ravaged Somalia. However, widespread media coverage of starving women and children finally turned policy-makers' attention to the disaster. In April 1992, the UN Security Council called for international intervention on the grounds that 'the magnitude of human suffering' in Somalia constituted a threat to international peace and security.[72] Although a Special Representative of the Secretary-General and a UN peacekeeping mission (UNOSOM I) were established at this time, the forces deployed to provide security for the delivery of humanitarian assistance was woefully underequipped and could not prevent looting of supplies by warring factions. Starvation continued in Somalia. Under threat from warlords, the UNHCR withdrew its staff from Somalia and effectively closed down its programme there.

The UNHCR was concerned that if nothing was done to stabilize the food situation in Somalia, Kenya would be faced with even more massive numbers of refugees. The Office was also worried that it would be unable to adequately protect and assist large numbers of Somalis where the problem was compounded by local violence. In an effort to deal with this problem, the UNHCR launched a cross-border assistance programme from Kenya in an effort to stabilize famine-related population movements in southern Somalia and to slow the momentum of refugee flows across the Kenyan border.[73] Cross-border relief programmes were not new to the international community. They had been employed by NGOs in the 1980s to reach needy populations in the Horn of Africa and in Afghanistan. But for the UNHCR this was a new approach to humanitarian assistance. Previously the agency had adopted a passive approach to similar developments and had waited for the refugees to cross borders before taking action.[74] The UNHCR reasoned that most of the 285,000 Somalis who fled to Kenya did so not only to escape from violence but also because the armed conflict had destroyed their livelihoods and their traditional survival strategies. In addition, a large proportion of displaced Somalis came from a nomadic background where movement was the way of life and where international boundaries had little or no meaning. In such situations, it was not possible to determine whether a person was a refugee, an IDP, a returnee, or a member of the local population. Thus, the UNHCR abandoned the traditional distinctions between these groups and decided to support all those in need in southern Somalia and northern Kenya.[75]

The UNHCR shared, or 'crossed', its mandate with other UN agencies and NGOs in a co-operative effort to address the needs of the entire community affected by conflict. The cross-mandated operation involved importing assistance from Kenya into 'preventive zones' in southern Somalia. The primary objective was to discourage mass movements of people by providing assistance in specific areas from which people might have been forced to move because of food shortages. A second objective was to create conditions conducive to the eventual repatriation of refugees from camps in Kenya.[76] To promote such stability in Somalia, the UNHCR, in co-operation with other organizations, initiated Quick Impact Projects[77] to rehabilitate the social infrastructure which included schools and clinics, and to encourage self-sufficiency in agriculture and herding. The Office hoped that such programmes would enable some Somalis to avoid becoming refugees and would enable others who had fled their homes to return.

The UNHCR's preventive strategy was given a boost in late November 1992 when US President George Bush, moved by repeated images on television of starving and emaciated Somalis, indicated that the US military was willing to lead a multilateral task force to bring humanitarian assistance to Somalia. In December the UN Security Council authorized the Secretary-General and member states 'to use all necessary means to establish as soon as possible a secure environment for humanitarian relief operations in Somalia'.[78] Under the American-led UNITAF, US marines entered Somalia on 8 December 1992, as the first contingent of some 44,000 troops from 21 different countries. With the arrival of UNITAF there was better security and improved control of relief distribution. For the most part, the task force succeeded in accomplishing the objective of delivering humanitarian assistance to the most devastated parts of Somalia's interior.[79]

In March 1993, the UN Security Council created UNOSOM II which inherited UNITAF's enforcement powers. In creating UNOSOM II, the Security Council also greatly expanded the military mission beyond the provision of security for the delivery of humanitarian assistance to include the disarmament of the warlords and clans and 'other assistance to the people of Somalia in rehabilitating their political and economic institutions and promoting political settlement and national reconciliation'.[80] One of the most important militia leaders, Mohamed Aideed, rejected the expanded UN mandate as unacceptable interference,[81] and in early June 1993 clashes occurred between Aideed's followers and members of the Pakistani contingent of UNOSOM II, resulting in the death of 24 Pakistani soldiers. In retaliation, the UN, with US troops in the lead, sought to restore order and initiated a search for Aideed. The search culminated in a bloody battle in October 1993 in the streets of Mogadishu that left hundreds of Somalis and 18 Americans dead. Television cameras captured the images of dead American soldiers being dragged through the streets by jeering Somali crowds. The impact of this battle on the US government was dramatic. Faced with a public outcry over the loss of American lives in Somalia, the Clinton administration withdrew its troops from Somalia. But the long-term effects of this incident were much more significant. The Mogadishu battles caused the US to fundamentally reassess its involvement in future UN peacekeeping missions. In May 1994, while mass killings were taking place in Rwanda, President Clinton signed Presidential Decision Directive 25[82] setting new and much tighter post-Somalia criteria for US participation in, and payment to support, UN peacekeeping operations.

The international involvement in Somalia in 1992–3 represented the culmination of the interventionist impulse of the international community in the early 1990s. The major lesson drawn from Somalia, particularly by the United States, was that the interventions of the early 1990s had overextended the UN and that in the future interventions should be much more limited and essentially restricted to the most strategically important areas of the world. During the next several years, therefore, support for international military involvement in humanitarian operations lost momentum as the US sharply curtailed its participation in such interventions.

Failure to Stop Genocide in Rwanda

The retrenchment could not have come at a worse time for hundreds of thousands of Rwandan victims of genocide. Bruised by their failure to restore stability in Mogadishu, the world's major governments and the UN chose to do nothing in the face of wanton mass killings in Rwanda in 1994. The early warning signs that the extremist Hutu forces were planning a systematic programme of genocide were tragically ignored. Half a million people were killed in mass slaughter in Rwanda in 100 days, most in the first four weeks. The critical issue of genocide was not addressed by the UN and the major powers and no substantive measures were taken to counter the killings, thereby sending a message to the killers that they could carry on with impunity.[83] Possible responses in the form of international support for regional initiatives to tackle the crisis, the application of diplomatic pressures, or support for a more rapid domestic military solution to the crisis were not tried. Later, when over two million Hutu refugees fled to neighbouring Zaïre, the international community also failed to do all that it could to help resolve some of the security and political problems at the refugee camps in Zaïre. Under these circumstances voluntary repatriation proved impossible until military developments forced the return of many of the Hutu refugees to Rwanda in late 1996. After 1996, the world again abandoned several hundred thousand refugees who had fled into the dense forests of eastern Zaïre after their camps had been attacked. Large numbers of refugees starved to death or were murdered before international agencies could reach them.

The conflicts between Hutus and Tutsis in the central African states of Rwanda and Burundi date back many generations. The international community, particularly the UNHCR, had been deeply involved in assisting previous generations of refugees in the Great Lakes region of Africa as far back as the 1960s. There were many forewarnings of this tragedy. In April 1993, the UN special rapporteur on extrajudicial, summary, or arbitrary executions strongly warned the international community of potential genocide in Rwanda[84] but UN member states took little notice. In August 1993, the Hutu leadership in Rwanda and the Rwanda Patriotic Front (RPF), an armed Tutsi force in exile in Uganda, signed the Arusha Peace Agreement. Following the Arusha Accord, the UN Security Council authorized the establishment of the UN Assistance Mission for Rwanda (UNAMIR) with a limited mandate to carry out traditional peacekeeping functions there.[85] No attention was paid to the Special Rapporteur's warnings and recommendations to establish a human rights monitoring mechanism in Rwanda. After the Arusha Accord was signed, UNAMIR sent strong warnings to UN headquarters of growing violence. By early 1994, the commander of UNAMIR, General Romeo Dallaire, was alerting Boutros-Ghali to the Hutu preparations that were being made for genocide in the event that the Arusha Accords were implemented.[86] Neither Kofi Annan, then head of UN Peacekeeping, nor Boutros-Ghali passed this information on to the Security Council.[87] The UN leadership perceived that governments were reluctant to become involved in a peacekeeping operation in another civil war in Africa so soon after the Somalia debacle. This was a major abdication of responsibility on the part of the UN.

On 6 April 1994, the airplane carrying the Hutu presidents of Rwanda and Burundi was shot down, and both leaders were killed.[88] Within hours of the downing of the aircraft, a highly organized killing machine went into operation in Rwanda.[89] The army, gendarmerie, and the extremist militia—the Interahamwe—as well as ordinary citizens went on a rampage first in Kigali and then in the countryside, murdering Tutsis and moderate Hutu leaders. Although UNAMIR forces initially protected thousands of civilians, they were not empowered either to put up a strong resistance or to try to stop the killings. When ten Belgian peacekeepers were captured, they were tortured and killed in the most heinous way. Consequently, Belgium withdrew its troops from UNAMIR, leaving the force mainly comprised of poorly equipped contingents from Bangladesh and Ghana spelling doom for both the peacekeeping operation and hundreds of thousands of innocent civilians in Rwanda.

Without the support of Security Council member states, the UN simply did not have the institutional capacity to respond to the genocide. The Secretary-General argued that UNAMIR should either be increased substantially or be reduced to a symbolic size. The US and practically all UN Security Council states perceived that no vital interests were at stake and therefore strongly opposed intervention. Western governments also felt that the UN was already stretched thin with too many peacekeeping missions deployed around the world. They were also influenced by the botched peacekeeping operations in Somalia and Bosnia and felt that it would be impossible for UN troops to honour the principles of neutrality and impartiality in the chaotic situation existing in Rwanda. The Security Council was unwilling to assume any responsible leadership on human rights and instead chose inaction. Governments and the UN were more concerned about protecting their peace-keepers in an increasingly frayed and dangerous operation than in saving the lives of Rwandan civilians. On 21 April, the Security Council voted to cut UNAMIR from 2500 to 250 personnel and instructed UNAMIR to stand aside and not to intervene. Not only the Security Council but also the Secretary-General and his staff at the UN Secretariat in New York were indifferent and indecisive in the face of genocide in Rwanda. It was not until mid-May that the Security Council reluctantly passed a resolution which would increase the force level of UNAMIR to 5,000 personnel and would expand its mandate to contribute to the security and protection of displaced persons, refugees, and civilians at risk, including the establishment and maintenance of secure humanitarian areas, and to provide security for the distribution of human-itarian assistance.[90] But it would be several months later before the Secretary-General received sufficient troop commitments for the operation and deployment to Rwanda was complete. By this time, estimates of the death toll in Rwanda had reached well over half a million persons. Finally, in mid-June, France belatedly indicated its intention to intervene militarily for humanitar-ian purposes. Despite French sympathy for the former Hutu regime and antipathy to the Tutsi-led RPF, the UN Security Council supported the French deployment of forces in south-west Rwanda in late June 1994 'to contribute to the security and protection of displaced persons, refugees and civilians at risk'.[91]

The French Operation Turquoise established a safe zone in south-west Rwanda where some one million Hutu IDPs had fled the Tutsi-led RPF advances. The French intervention had the effect of stabilizing the situation inside Rwanda long enough to permit the Hutus to escape the wrath of the invading Tutsis. In fact, France and Zaïre facilitated the escape into exile of the Hutu leadership who had launched and carried out the genocide. In one five-day period in mid-July in an organized evacuation ordered by Hutu lead-ers, slightly fewer than a million Hutu refugees crossed the border, mostly from north-west Rwanda, into northern Kivu province in Zaïre. Other outflows crossed into southern Kivu and Burundi and into Tanzania, bringing the total number of Hutus outside Rwanda to about two million. The outflow would have been even greater if hundreds of thousands had not remained internally displaced in the French protected zone inside Rwanda.

This was the largest humanitarian crisis of the 1990s and the UNHCR was caught almost completely unprepared. During July and August 1994, UNHCR staff suffered from a lack of co-ordination from Geneva. Despite considerable early warning of this disaster, the UNHCR did not anticipate the scale and rapidity of this refugee outflow. The relief effort involved so much air transport and was so immense that airline traffic throughout all of Africa was paralysed for several weeks because of a lack of fuel. The UNHCR did not have sufficient transportation to move refugees and failed to provide adequate reception facilities and clean water for this mass influx. The lack of preparedness helped precipitate an outbreak of cholera, which killed over 2,000 refugees per day.

When the situation was finally stabilized in September, it was clear to the UNHCR that the exiled Hutu leadership intended to remain temporarily in Zaïre to gather strength and to eventually return to Rwanda to regain power there. In the meantime, the former leaders took almost total control of the population in the camps. It was also evident that international aid was helping to refuel the Hutu military machine.[92] The UNHCR and NGOs were faced with the dilemma of whether to continue to assist everyone, including the genocidaire, or to pull out of Zaïre. NGOs reported that not only did former Rwandese authorities use the distribution of relief items to reinforce their position but they also resorted openly to force and intimidation to stop refugees who were inclined to return to Rwanda.[93] In November 1994, a number of NGOs threatened to withdraw from the refugee camps in Goma, stating that:

Under present conditions the UNHCR is prevented from fulfilling its mandate of protecting and assisting refugees.

The work of humanitarian organizations is largely compromised due to the current power structure within the camps. When aid workers attempt to intervene on behalf of the victims of discriminatory practices, their lives are threatened.

The relief operation is unsustainable. Refugees are denied the right to return to their homes, equal access to humanitarian aid, protection, and the guarantee of basic human rights. They remain hostages. (Ian Martin, 'Human Rights and Political Failures in Rwanda,' in Jonathan Moore, ed., *Hard Choices: Moral Dilemmas in Humanitarian Intervention* (Boston, MA: Rowman and Little Field Publishers, 1998): 157–76.).

Despite its inability to provide protection and to separate genuine refugees from the armed killers, the UNHCR stayed on in the camps, subcontracting most of the assistance work to NGOs. Ogata felt she had no choice: 'To do otherwise would mean abandoning the refugees to the Hutu extremists'.[94] UNHCR staff were worried, however, because protection under these circumstances proved impossible. A consensus developed within the UNHCR staff there that in order to break the leaders' hold on the refugees, the majority of them would need to return to Rwanda sooner or later. But there were sharp divisions within the Office about the timing of such a return.[95] Some felt that the longer the refugees remained in exile, the harder the return would be since the refugees would be increasingly perceived by Kigali as supporting those responsible for the genocide. It would also be more difficult to reclaim lost property after a prolonged absence. The UNHCR also feared that the leaders would use the refugee population as a shield against any attempt to have them arrested and tried for genocide. Finally, the refugee presence aggravated the complex ethnic problem already existing in the Kivu region in Zaïre and threatened to further destabilize that country. Others argued that a premature return to Rwanda would endanger the lives of the refugees. There was concern that the security situation inside Rwanda prevented a more forceful support to a return movement. This concern was supported by early reports from Rwanda of RPF and other Tutsi persecution and revenge-killing of both Hutu residents and Hutu returnees. Moreover, the Rwandan government sent mixed signals about repatriation and reconciliation to the Hutu exiles and to the UNHCR. The dominant Tutsi faction within the government appeared more interested in consolidating the new regime and resolving the deteriorating security position on the border than in promoting and encouraging returns. The destabilizing impact of the camps and the threats to refugees posed by the thousands of genocidal killers who had reasserted their control over the population had to be weighed against the mixed signals received from Rwanda and the uncertain security situation prevailing in that country.[96] Such a situation did not lend itself to a clear, straightforward policy on the part of the UNHCR. Consequently, during 1994–6, the Office wavered between encouraging or facilitating repatriation and suspending these activities because of deteriorating security conditions in Rwanda. For the most part, there were very few returns to Rwanda during this period. The different perceptions of the situation within the UNHCR and the alternating policies on repatriation also limited the High Commissioner's capacity to influence decision-makers within the international community.

In the absence of any real progress on repatriation, the UNHCR tried unsuccessfully to improve the security situation in the camps. Without the presence of international security forces in the refugee camps, there was very little the UNHCR could do to break the hold of the Hutu militants in the camps and to alleviate some of the concerns of NGOs and their staff members who had to work under extremely dangerous conditions. The UN Secretary-General put several options to the Security Council for separating the armed forces from the refugee population and for addressing the issue of security in the Zaïre camps. One option proposed the establishment of a peacekeeping force of 10,000 to 12,000 soldiers to provide the dual function of separating out the former political leaders as well as maintaining security in the camps. Another much scaled-down option combined the deployment of peacekeeping forces with the training of local security forces to police the camps. Only Bangladesh offered to contribute troops to this second option. The Security Council perceived that the militarization of the refugee camps was an intractable problem and simply refused to authorize the deployment of military forces to 'neutralize' the refugee camps.[97] Instead, Boutros-Ghali delegated the problem to the UNHCR to solve. In a letter to the Zaïrian Prime Minister, the UN Secretary-General admitted that under the circumstances, 'I believe that the best way for the United Nations to help improve security in the refugee camps is for UNHCR to address this issue under its refugee protection and humanitarian assistance programs'.[98]

Having the problem of security thrown back into its lap, the UNHCR subcontracted the Zaïre government to provide a contingent of élite troops to provide security in the camps. While this arrangement initially stabilized the camps and brought a degree of security to the aid workers, it proved to be a fatally flawed decision that convinced the government in Rwanda that the camps had to be overrun. The UNHCR was not able to convince the Zaïrian forces to arrest the former Hutu leaders who continued to intimidate the refugees. Neither did the Zaïrian forces halt their flow of arms to the genocidaires or cross-border incursions into Rwanda.[99] The Hutu rebels in the camps had the support of President Sese Seko Mobuto of Zaïre who sought the overthrow of the Tutsi government in Rwanda and the return to power of the exiled Hutus. The Rwandan government accused the UNHCR of supporting the genocidaires and their sponsor, the Mobutu regime. Rwanda warned that the agency's incapacity to regain political and military control of the camps would enable the Hutu army in exile to launch a new invasion.

In the absence of a forcible separation of Hutu extremists and combatants from Hutu civilians in the refugee camps, the UNHCR and over 100 NGOs continued to feed the refugees and the Hutu forces. This was one of the largest humanitarian operations in the world, with costs in excess of one million dollars a day. The UNHCR also took steps to encourage voluntary repatriation through cross-border visits and an information campaign designed to counter propaganda from the former Hutu leaders declaring returnees would be killed. Militant Hutus actively discouraged returns and intimidated those who wished to repatriate. The human rights situation inside Rwanda also steadily deteriorated, making it extremely difficult to counter the widespread fear among refugees of arbitrary arrest and retribution upon return to Rwanda.[100] A UNHCR report carried out in August and September 1994 had alleged the continuing practice of atrocities carried out against Hutus in parts of Rwanda. The findings of this report were given substance in April 1995 when thousands of internally displaced Hutus were killed by Rwandan forces during the forcible closure of the Kibeho camp. To make matters worse, the massacre was carried out in the presence of UNAMIR troops who were mandated to contribute to the security and protection of internally displaced persons. In addition, tens of thousands of Hutus suspected of carrying out the 1994 genocide were imprisoned in grossly overcrowded and inhumane prisons inside Rwanda. These events fed the fears of Hutu refugees who believed that any refugee returning home would become a target for revenge-killing or prolonged imprisonment in atrocious conditions.

By 1996, the Great Lakes region was rife with instability. In July, a Tutsi seized power in Burundi, leading to an increase in violence between Hutus and Tutsis and the death of tens of thousands of people. By mid-year, regional pressure had built up for seeking a military solution to the security problem posed to Rwanda by the Hutu refugee camps.[101] Hutu insurgents were operating in larger groups, and a pattern of attacks on local officials and Tutsi civilians inside Rwanda became evident. The Kigali government became convinced of the need to eliminate this source of danger either by isolating the camps with a buffer zone or by dissolving them entirely. In September 1996 conflict broke out in Kivu province in Zaïre between the Zaïrian army and the Zaïrian Tutsi known as the Banyamulenge. The Banyamulenge rebellion gave Rwanda the chance to attack the Hutu refugee camps and to destroy the power base of the Hutu Interahamwe. When the camps in Zaïre came under attack, the UNHCR and its partner agencies suspended their operations and evacuated their expatriate staff. In the ensuing mêlée, tens of thousands of Hutu militia and refugees were killed and hundreds of thousands of refugees scattered in all directions across North and South Kivu. The fighting and destruction of the camps set off a massive return of some 500,000 refugees into Rwanda. But the Hutu militia, army, and some 300,000 to 500,000 civilians retreated and scattered further into Zaïre. The Banyamulenge militia and those fighting with them—The Alliance of Democratic Forces for the Liberation of Congo-Zaïre, led by Laurent Kabila and backed by Rwanda and Uganda—regarded the Hutus as their enemy. Many of the refugees who took flight into Zaïre would subsequently die of starvation and disease or be killed by Kabila's troops as they marched through Zaïre to topple Sese Seku Mobuto.[102]

The massive return home of refugees from Zaïre in November 1996 encouraged Tanzania to take the initiative to force the repatriation of Rwandan refugees on its soil as well. In December, Tanzania, long a traditional African host state, announced its intention to return immediately all Rwandan and Burundian refugees regardless of individual wishes. The UNHCR could have distanced itself from events and criticized the forced return. The Division of International Protection supported this course of action and appealed over the Head of the Africa Bureau directly to Ogata.[103] But the High Commissioner and the Africa Bureau felt that this stance would have left the refugees completely at the mercy of the situation. Instead, the UNHCR effectively condoned this forcible repatriation of 500,000 refugees. It co-signed a statement with the Zaïrean government setting an imminent deadline, with no reference to any process for considering the cases of those who feared return. The Office argued that without political support from the international community it was in no position to oppose this and decided not to abandon the refugees on their way home.[104] It was soon evident that conditions inside Rwanda were not conducive to a safe return. Despite the fact that the initial reception of the returnees was monitored by both the UNHCR and the UN Human Rights Field Operation in Rwanda, thousands of the returnees from Burundi, Tanzania, and Zaïre were detained and at least 100 returnees were killed by members of the local population or soldiers in the first few weeks of the repatriation. In early 1997, UN monitoring was severely restricted after the murder of five UN staff, the killings of expatriates, and the worsening of the security situation in Rwanda. The major international human rights organizations severely criticized the UNHCR for this abject failure of protection and for permitting refugees to return home where some would be killed or made victims of other human rights violations.[105]

The abandonment by the international community of hundreds of thousands of Hutu refugees who fled into the dense rainforests of eastern Zaïre also constituted a dramatic failure of refugee protection. In the chaos caused by the military attacks on refugee camps in Kivu, the UNHCR had lost track of the majority of refugees as they fled eastwards. Amid concern that another major humanitarian crisis had begun, the UN Security Council authorized a Canadian-led multinational force to be launched to take humanitarian aid to those at risk in eastern Zaïre. It soon became clear, however, that the international force risked being drawn into the local conflicts raging in Zaïre. As massive numbers of refugees returned to Rwanda, the governments of Rwanda and the United States maintained that practically all refugees formerly in Zaïre had returned, that only a minuscule number of refugees remained in eastern Zaïre, and that the refugee issue had been resolved. With little international support and fearful of being overwhelmed by the conflict to overthrow Mobuto in Zaïre, the Canadian-led mission was aborted. Consequently, the UNHCR was left to monitor, protect, and assist the Hutu refugees who had been driven into eastern Zaïre without any international political or military support.

In a belated effort to rescue the refugees in eastern Zaïre, the UNHCR mounted efforts to locate the refugees, to assist them, and to return them to Rwanda. However, the UNHCR and NGOs found themselves dependent on Kabila and his forces for access to the hundreds of thousands of refugees stranded in desperate conditions in remote areas. The UNHCR was forced to negotiate with armed groups who had little respect for the UNHCR and the protection principles which form its core mandate. In April 1997, UNHCR staff reached some 80,000 refugees who were fleeing ahead of Kabila's forces.

The UNHCR established two temporary camps for them and prepared to airlift them back to Rwanda. Before the evacuation operation could take place, however, Kabila's forces arrived. They immediately closed off the camps, prevented UNHCR access to the refugees, and killed huge numbers of unarmed men, women, and children. Because humanitarian aid was used to lure refugees out of the forests to their deaths, the UNHCR was criticized for not strongly standing up for its protection principles. Confronted with the dilemma of whether to protest and withdraw or to remain and save as many they could, the UNHCR continued its rescue operation until late 1997. Those refugees whom the UNHCR was able to reach were given no other choice but to return to a perilous situation in Rwanda. Eventually, over 260,000 refugees were transported back to Rwanda either by truck or aircraft.

The Rwandan crisis was a colossal failure for the United Nations, the UNHCR, the US, and the rest of the international community. The failure to halt the genocide in 1994, the failure to halt the militarization of refugee camps in Zaïre in 1994–6, and the failure to protect and assist the Rwandan refugees driven into eastern Zaïre from late 1996 onward, constituted a major dereliction of responsibility and moral negligence.

The Failure of International Responses to Mass Killings and Human Rights Abuses in Civil Conflicts

The UNHCR's high-profile relief efforts in Northern Iraq, Bosnia, and Rwanda during the first half of the 1990s underlined dramatically the inadequacy of providing protection in humanitarian relief programmes in the midst of on-going civil conflicts. Protection failures in these operations also provoked an anguished debate among relief agencies as to whether relief aid actually helped the displaced and other victims or harmed them by prolonging the conflicts. The international community was all too often content to provide support to the UNHCR and other humanitarian organizations rather than to actively engage in seeking political solutions in intrastate wars. In each of these operations, the international community and the UNHCR favoured assistance over protection.[106] The Office remained largely reactive to events and failed to address the direct links between human rights abuses, violence, and humanitarian emergencies. These operations also demonstrated that as long as the underlying causes of conflict were not addressed, relief risked serving a mere palliative to human suffering, or even worse, a means of prolonging it.

Until the early 1990s, the UNHCR did not get much help on refugee protection issues from the UN Human Rights Centre in Geneva. The UN human rights machinery was reluctant to engage in human rights protection work for refugees, and forcibly displaced people did not figure prominently in the activities of the UN Human Rights Centre or the UN Human Rights Commission. In the 1990s this longstanding neglect of refugee issues within the UN human rights regime began to change. In the early 1990s, the Commission convened exceptional sessions to discuss urgent human rights situations in the former Yugoslavia and Rwanda, and after 1991 regularly discussed the protection needs of internally displaced persons and the problems involving minorities.

At the same time, the UN Human Rights Centre, through its Advisory Services, became closely associated with a number of UN peacekeeping or peace enforcement missions. The Centre provided significant technical assistance to the UN human rights presence in the field in El Salvador, Guatemala, Haiti, Somalia, and Rwanda to name a few. A new position of UN High Commissioner for Human Rights was created. These events underscored both the key potential role of the UN human rights machinery and the growing involvement of the Security Council in humanitarian matters. They demonstrated that the promotion and protection of the human rights of refugees, returnees, and the internally displaced constituted an integral part of UN peacemaking.

While these were encouraging developments, many of the traditional constraints on the international human rights regime did not disappear with the passing of the Cold War. The UN human rights programme remained grossly understaffed and underfunded. During the early 1990s when billions of dollars were poured into emergency relief programmes and peacekeeping operations, virtually no extra funds were provided for the UN human rights regime despite its potential to strengthen civil society, to promote democratic and pluralistic institutions and, thereby, to prevent human rights abuses and subsequent mass displacements.

The other major international initiative undertaken to counter human rights violations in brutal civil wars during the early 1990s, was the establishment of international war crimes tribunals to investigate, indict, and try the individuals who carried out genocide and atrocities in former Yugoslavia and Rwanda. These tribunals had the potential to set an important legal precedent, namely to affirm that those who commit atrocious crimes against civilians in war risk serious punishment. By the end of 1996, however, it was clear that the tribunals had not fulfilled the tasks the international community had set for them. In particular, the capture of leading war criminals in former Yugoslavia, such as Radovan Karadzic and Ratko Mladic, collided with the Western powers' more urgent interests in seeing the Dayton Peace Accords hold and in ensuring that conflict did not break out once again in Bosnia. In Rwanda, initial lack of international support for the tribunal and distrust of external judicial interference by the Tutsi government in Kigali meant that the tribunal made very little headway in its early years. The states that created the tribunal seemed reluctant to take any steps that could provide it or any other UN human rights programmes for Rwanda with any long-term institutional independence. For example, totally inadequate funding was provided for the operation of the international criminal tribunal, the international programme of assistance to Rwanda's justice system, and the UN human rights field operation in Rwanda.

The conflict between the goal of achieving justice by prosecuting war criminals and the objective of ending bitter intrastate conflicts by reaching agreements among contending forces resulted in emasculated legal proceedings in the former Yugoslavia and Rwanda. Lack of support for the tribunals damaged the long-term prospect for reconciliation and peace in both countries. Without a strong tribunal, the political process in the former Yugoslavia was dominated by extremist nationalist parties and the promise of the Dayton agreements to reverse ethnic cleansing and to create a multicultural, democratic society in Bosnia was not realized.

After the mass return of refugees to Rwanda in late 1996, the prosecution of war crimes there was not pursued effectively enough to foster a culture of accountability and to promote long-term peace and reconciliation. The issues of institution-building, development, and human rights protection within Rwanda itself were not adequately addressed and domestic instability exacerbated ethnic tensions. As long as a fair judiciary process was not restored in Rwanda and justice was not perceived to have been accomplished, there was no end to ethnic separation and hatred. As a consequence, another genocide in the Great Lakes region of Africa in the future cannot be discounted.

Another policy that was introduced in the early 1990s was the concept of temporary protection.[107] In 1992, as the number of asylum-seekers appearing on the doorsteps of Western European states reached an all-time high, substantial numbers of people fleeing from the bloody conflicts in the former Yugoslavia began to arrive in the region claiming political asylum. By mid-1992, most EU states had imposed a visa regime restricting Bosnians' access to their territories. Ogata was aware that these refugees put heavy pressure on the asylum procedures of EU states. At the July 1992 International Conference on the Former Yugoslavia she urged governments to grant temporary protection to asylum-seekers from former Yugoslavia, pending their return home after the war. She realized that if the European states did not provide this protection, the role of the international refugee regime would be seriously undermined. The UNHCR believed that the provision of temporary protection would not only provide immediate security to people forced to flee the Balkans but also would relieve states of the need to examine thousands of individual asylum applications, thereby permitting governments to be more generous than they might otherwise be. As the High Commissioner was to explain later: 'Temporary protection is an instrument which balances the protection needs of people with the interests of states receiving them.'[108]

From April 1992 until the end of 1996, over half a million people benefited from receiving temporary protection, mostly from European states with Germany taking by far the largest number, followed by Austria, Sweden, and Switzerland. As important as temporary protection was for providing short-term security for people whose lives were at risk, it was not in itself a solution to the refugee problem in the former Yugoslavia.[109] Many of the people granted temporary protection might very well have qualified for refugee status if they had been able to apply for it on an individual basis. Many human rights NGOs felt that temporary protection would be used as a substitute for asylum for those refugees meeting the international standard of a well-founded fear of persecution. Temporary protection for refugees from the former Yugoslavia was premised on the assumption that return would occur when it was safe to do so. Yet soon after the 1995 Dayton Peace Accord was signed, some governments withdrew temporary protection status from Bosnians in order to encourage early repatriation. The UNHCR came under tremendous pressure from some European governments to endorse forcible returns despite the continuation of ethnic division and hatred in Bosnia.

Asylum Crises and Restrictionism in the Industrialized States

During the early 1990s, increasing international action to respond to humanitarian emergencies coincided with a weakening of traditional protection and asylum mechanisms in most states. During the period 1983–92, there was a rapid increase in the number of asylum applicants in industrialized countries.[110] In 1983, less than 100,000 people requested asylum in Europe, North America, Australia, and Japan. By 1992, the number had risen to over 891,000. In total, approximately 3.7 million asylum applicants were recorded in the North during the decade 1983–92. Germany was the most seriously affected by the sharp increase, with the number of asylum-seekers rising from 121,000 in 1989 to 438,000 in 1992. As a result, huge backlogs of asylum cases and rising costs exceeding $7–8 billion per year put heavy strains on the asylum systems in industrialized states. This rapid increase in asylum applications combined with high structural unemployment in most Western European states increased xenophobia and anti-refugee sentiments throughout Europe. In response to these growing asylum pressures, the advanced industrialized states became increasingly reluctant to let people enter their countries to apply for political asylum. Most Northern states concluded that preventing entry of asylum-seekers by imposing visa requirements on the nationals of refugee-producing states, fining airlines for bringing refugees into their countries, and forcibly interdicting refugees at frontiers and in international waters was the best way to reduce both the numbers and the costs of asylum applications.

In a climate of national restrictionism, EU states started a process of harmonization, which led to a regional regime of exclusionary controls and agreements.[111] From the late 1980s on, EU states created a plethora of fora in which to discuss common concerns and plan strategies regarding refugees, asylum-seekers, and migrants. For example, Western European states drafted several agreements to formalize intensified co-operation on asylum-seekers and related issues, the central pillars of which were the Schengen Agreement of 1985 and the Schengen and Dublin Conventions of 1990. Together these two European instruments constituted a framework for policy which permitted asylum-seekers to lodge an application only in one state and allowed information about applicants to be extensively shared among member states. In addition, EU states adopted the principle of 'manifestly unfounded' claim, permitting governments fast track mechanisms for screening-out applicants suspected of making spurious asylum claims. These regional policies were established outside the framework of the European Union. The development and implementation of the Schengen and Dublin Conventions took place primarily in the EU's Ad Hoc Group on Immigration, which met regularly and made recommendations to the Ministers of Immigration for final approval by the Council of Ministers. The fact that the European Parliament, the European Commission, and the European Court of Justice—as well as the UNHCR—were largely bypassed in this process resulted in the evolution of a regional approach which was essentially restrictionist and secretive.

In the early 1990s, the Ad Hoc Group and the Council formulated two concepts of 'safe country' designed to permit states to return asylum-seekers without strictly violating the *non-refoulement* provision in international refugee law.[112] According to this procedure, nationals of a state judged to be a 'safe country of origin' *ipso facto* had 'manifestly unfounded' claims to asylum and could be excluded from the asylum process in EU states. The criteria for defining 'safe' were at best uncertain and mostly controversial. Germany after 1993 defined a 'safe state of origin' as a country 'where it was safe to assume that neither political persecution nor inhumane or degrading practices take place'. Britain put Sri Lanka and Nigeria on its list of safe countries of origin in late 1995.

Potential refugees could also be excluded from the EU states' asylum procedures if on their journey to Europe they transited a so-called 'safe third country'. Under this procedure, governments assumed the right to refuse admission to an asylum-seeker if he or she had arrived via a country where their claim to refugee status might have been submitted. Thus, because Germany declared all of its neighbours to the east to be either safe countries of origin or safe third countries, it effectively renounced responsibility for considering the asylum request of most persons arriving in the country by land without a valid visa. Critics argued that the safe third country concept fundamentally compromised refugee protection because it withheld due process and lacked other basic safeguards to ensure that refugees would in fact have access to a comprehensive and fair asylum procedure somewhere. Moreover, the safe third country procedure failed to distinguish *bona fide* refugees from those with spurious claims. A person's travel route into exile, rather than the reasons behind his or her flight, became the overriding factor in deciding whether protection would be granted. Finally, many of the countries considered safe either implemented safe third country laws of their own, or routinely deported asylum-seekers to fourth countries without reviewing their cases. Thus, the ultimate danger for refugees was that safe country policies could cause 'chain deportations' whereby no country assumed responsibility for examining a specific asylum request and an asylum-seeker was bounced from one country to the next, either to countries with no means to protect them adequately, or worse, to the countries where they were persecuted.[113] Such cases of 'refugees in orbit' occurred with increasing frequency in the 1990s.

UNHCR advocacy for asylum-seekers in Europe was weakened because the Office did not speak with one voice on this issue.[114] While the Director of International Protection promoted a proactive and interventionist approach with European governments, the European Bureau cautioned restraint and preferred to maintain working relations with EU states. The High Commissioner sided with the European Bureau. Having won back the confidence of Western states by her active involvement in Bosnia, Ogata did not want to risk losing it again by upsetting governments. Consequently, NGOs began to harshly criticize the High Commissioner for being weak on protection. In the mid-1990s in an effort at 'damage control', Ogata began to give higher profile in her speeches to the importance of protection in the work of the UNHCR. But the rhetoric was not often matched with protection action in the Agency's operations in the field.

The cumulative effect of the restrictive measures undertaken by EU states during the 1990s was to drastically limit the numbers of asylum-seekers arriving on their territory and applying for asylum. Starting in 1993, asylum applications in many industrialized states fell considerably. After the introduction of new asylum regulations in Germany, for example, the number of asylum applications there declined from 438,000 in 1992 to 95,110 in 1999. In the United States, the number fell from 150,700 in 1992 to 31,740 in 1999.[115] Overall, the numbers of asylum applicants in the industrialized countries fell from a high of 848,630 in 1992 to 537,650 in 1999.[116]

There is some evidence that, far from resolving the asylum problem, these measures merely diverted the problem elsewhere. For example, in 1994, a 60 per cent drop in the number of asylum applications submitted in Germany was matched by a 50 per cent increase in the number of asylum claims in neighbouring Netherlands. In 1998 and 1999, when asylum applications in Germany continued to decline from their 1992 high, asylum applications in neighbouring Austria, Belgium, Luxembourg, and Switzerland increased as did numbers of cases in Italy and the United Kingdom.[117] With the introduction of stricter EU policies, the countries on the periphery of Western Europe began to experience a substantial increase in the number of asylum-seekers arriving from other continents. According to some estimates, at the end of the 1990s, there were around 700,000 illegal and transit migrants in the Commonwealth of Independent States (CIS), of whom 500,000 were to be found in the Russian Federation alone.

At the end of the 1990s, the EU stood at a crossroads in its approach to asylum and refugees. The 1997 Amsterdam Treaty on European Union mandated the European governments to bring asylum policy under EU control and to involve the European Parliament and the European Court of Justice in this process. It gave the EU power to pass binding legislation on asylum and laid out a plan leading to greater harmonization of asylum policy among EU states to replace the divergent, and sometimes contradictory, laws, policies, and practices of individual EU states. Soon after the treaty became effective in mid-1999, EU political leaders met in Tampere, Finland to set priorities and to provide political support to implement the Treaty of Amsterdam. While the Tampere summit strongly endorsed the goal of 'establishing a Common European Asylum System, based on the full and inclusive application of the Geneva [Refugee] Convention',[118] the future direction of asylum policy in Europe still remains uncertain. Should EU legislation on asylum continue to require the unanimous agreement of the member states it is likely that future efforts at harmonization will gravitate to the lowest standards practiced among European states. In the five-year transition period to 2004 for implementing the Amsterdam Treaty, EU leaders have to find a way to balance the right to asylum with the right to control their borders. Failure to accomplish this objective could result in EU states continuing to deny asylum-seekers access to their territories and asylum procedures.

During the 1990s, there was also an increase in asylum applications and intensification of the asylum debate in the United States. From about 17,000 claims in 1985, the total rose to 149,000 in 1995.[119] On top of these asylum claims, some 125,000 refugees, 700,000 legal immigrants, and hundreds of thousands of illegal migrants entered the US annually. During the decade, immigration to the United States was at its highest levels since the beginning of the twentieth century. Immigration also became significantly more diverse in terms of national origin and ethnic and cultural background. As a result, immigration assumed a visibility and prominence in the life of the United States not evident since the early 1900s.

The impact of the new immigration rapidly became an important political issue in the US. In the early 1990s, there was a growing sentiment among some sectors of the population that the influx of too many foreigners to the US threatened America's social cohesion and national identity. In states like

California where large numbers of refugees and immigrants had settled, discriminatory legislation was passed that made undocumented migrants ineligible for most social services.

These initiatives sparked a debate within the US Congress on immigration in general, including refugees and asylum-seekers. In 1996, responding to what it perceived as an increasing and widespread abuse of the US asylum system and fears of new influxes of foreigners and terrorists, US legislators passed the *Illegal Immigration Reform and Immigrant Responsibility Act* (IIRIRA). The legislation created 'expedited removal' which permitted the Immigration and Naturalization Service (INS) to automatically detain and place into a fast-track deportation process any persons arriving in the US without documentation or with false identification. The 1996 Act also expanded the definition of 'aggravated felony' in US domestic law to include offences that by international standards might be considered minor, such as shoplifting or disorderly drunken behaviour. Thus, the INS was required by law to detain 'convicted felons' who could not apply for asylum whatever the underlying circumstances of the case. The law was also applied retroactively and caught people who had already been convicted, served their sentences and been released, but now were detained again and subsequently deported. The UNHCR Division of International Protection pointed out the unjustness of these restrictive provisions and lobbied hard against the legislation but to no avail.[120]

These stricter measures inevitably led to an escalation in the number of asylum-seekers who were held in detention throughout the US, often in prisons along with criminal offenders. Vulnerable women and hundreds of unaccompanied minors were also put in common prisons. Detainees were frequently abused and conditions were atrocious at some places. In a scathing 1999 report Amnesty International claimed: 'Asylum seekers have often been treated like criminals, stripped and searched, shackled and chained, sometimes verbally or physically abused.'[121] In another report, the Lawyers' Committee for Human Rights claimed that asylum-seekers were not represented by lawyers and were not provided with interpreters.[122] UNHCR staff visited detention centres but were unable to bring about major changes in US asylum policy during the 1990s.

Other restrictive measures against asylum-seekers were also introduced in the US including removing the right for asylum-seekers to work immediately upon arrival. Thus, while most European governments continued to grant either work eligibility or social assistance, asylum-seekers in America received neither government welfare nor had the ability to support themselves by working legally. As a result of these restrictive measures and stricter enforcement by the INS at US borders, the numbers of asylum applicants declined significantly, from 149,000 in 1995 to just 31,740 in 1999.[123]

The reduction of asylum applications in the US and the EU was viewed as a successful effort. However, it was not clear to what degree the new border control and other restrictive measures acted as a deterrent for fraudulent asylum-seekers. It was questionable whether these actions simply deterred *bona fide* asylum-seekers, merely shifted refugee flows to other countries, or resulted in an expansion of migrant trafficking, illegal immigration, and organized crime in the industrialized states. Some experts believed that greater controls meant that more people simply 'went underground' and entered countries illegally. In other words, the restrictive asylum practices introduced by Western states converted what was a visible flow of asylum-seekers into a covert movement of irregular migrants that was even more difficult to count and control. At the end of the 1990s, irregular migration represented one-quarter of the total yearly inflow into the United States and as much as one-half of that in Europe. At the global level some $7 billion was channelled every year into human trafficking.[124]

The covert nature of migrant trafficking almost inevitably meant that international criminal syndicates got involved, making huge profits on the stealing and forging of travel documents, passports, work and residence permits. The migrants themselves were subjected to constant physical insecurity and financial exploitation. In June 2000, British customs officers at the port of Dover discovered 54 dead Chinese men and women who had suffocated in a sealed container truck in their failed attempt to secretly enter the United Kingdom.[125] Those more fortunate migrants who managed to reach their destinations often found that they had to turn to crime to pay off their debts to traffickers. Increasingly, illegal migrants were forced to transport or sell drugs for criminal organizations or engage in prostitution or other criminal activities. Thus, an unintended consequence of the restrictive measures of EU and North American states was to further expand the marginalized, excluded, and criminalized underclass in Western societies. The association with organized crime also made it more difficult for some refugee groups to seek asylum in the West. Thus, despite having the most advanced asylum and migration control systems, the EU and the US deterrent and control policies have proved increasingly inadequate to deal with the problem of asylum-seekers

Donor Fatigue and Its Effect on African Refugees

By the mid-1990s, there was not only a crisis in refugee protection but also a crisis in assistance funding. International assistance overall dropped 21 per cent from 1992 to 1997.[126] Donor governments also grew increasingly tired of funding refugee emergencies and protracted stays in host countries. From 1995 on, the failure of donor governments to provide adequate support for refugees became a chronic problem, resulting in several years of steady budget decline at the UNHCR. In 1997–8, donors provided only $320 million for the UNHCR's general programme budget, a decline of $31 million from 1996 and a shortfall of $65 million compared to the Office's 1997 requirements. In following years, continuing funding shortfalls caused the Agency for the first time in many years to reduce its general programmes for refugees. The reductions were partly a correction to the high budget levels associated with the Office's operation in Bosnia in the early 1990s but it seriously affected the UNHCR's ability to mobilize resources for new unanticipated humanitarian emergencies. Consequently, the UNHCR initially had difficulty responding quickly and effectively to the mass exodus from Kosovo in 1999.

The principal loser in these shortfalls was Africa. Not only did international development aid flows to Africa decline during the decade, but donor responses to UN requests for humanitarian emergency programmes in Africa also dropped precipitously. The World Food Program curtailed its feeding programmes for two million people uprooted in Sierra Leone, Liberia, and Guinea after receiving less than 20 per cent of the requested funding. The UNHCR programmes in Africa were seriously underfunded, making it impossible for the Office to provide consistent and timely assistance there. By one estimate, in 1999 the UNHCR spent about $0.11 per refugee per day in Africa, and spent ten times that amount—an average of $1.23 per refugee per day—in the Balkans.[127] Before the 1990s, many African governments had policies that encouraged self-reliance and local integration. However, with the international neglect of Africa's refugee populations and in the absence of international assistance to support local integration programmes, most African governments adopted practices and policies that forced refugees to live in confined camps. Harassment and mistreatment of refugees and forced repatriation became commonplace practices throughout Africa. Partly because of resource constraints, the UNHCR gave into these restrictive government actions, fearing that to protest would endanger the continuation of its programmes and its access to refugees.

Fewer resources also meant that long-staying refugee populations were denied funding for local integration and income generating projects. Entire groups have been kept in protracted camp situations where their morale and welfare have suffered. For example, since 1991, over 100,000 Nepalese-speaking Bhutanese have been warehoused in remote UNHCR camps in eastern Nepal awaiting the time when they can return home. The UNHCR has run these camps in emergency mode with very little provision for building local capacities and developing refugees self-reliance. The Bhutanese and similar groups in Africa and elsewhere are effectively being ignored by the international community.

The UNHCR's Expansion into Post-Conflict Reintegration

During the second half of the 1990s, the UNHCR became much more involved in 'post-conflict reintegration' operations. However, the transition from war to peace proved to be more difficult than it had in the early part of the decade. The UN peace agreements and repatriations in countries like Cambodia, Mozambique, or Namibia were more easily implemented. While these countries experienced various setbacks during the late 1990s, none of them plunged back into full-scale conflict. On the other hand, reintegration programmes for returnees after international peace agreements in the Balkans, in the Caucasus, and in Africa proved much more difficult, if not impossible, to implement. In the late 1990s, the United Nations was increasingly asked to pick up the pieces and to help rebuild countries after bitter and destructive civil wars. But the UN had few tools for rebuilding states. It often lacked the resources and structural capacity to deal with governance issues like establishing civil administration, police forces, and judicial systems or rebuilding economies through reconstruction and rehabilitation programmes.[128] Since successful repatriation and reintegration programmes depended on these broader developments, the UNHCR experienced great difficulties in its post-conflict reintegration operations.

The UNHCR repatriation operation in Bosnia and Hercegovina illustrates the kinds of problems that confronted the Office. Annex 7 of the Dayton Peace Agreement signed in 1995 was intended to undo the consequences of ethnic cleansing and to restore the multi-ethnic composition of Bosnia and Hercegovina by facilitating the return of refugees and displaced persons to their original homes. The UNHCR faced enormous difficulties in trying to implement this provision of the Agreement. Coming hard on the heels of ethnic and communal conflicts and with no visible signs of reconciliation among bitter communal enemies, it was not surprising that reintegration proved so difficult. The parties to the conflict refused to fulfil their commitments either to permit Bosnian refugees and IDPs to return to their homes in eastern Bosnia—the scene of some of the war's worst atrocities—or to allow Serbian refugees to return to Muslim-dominated Sarajevo. Many people were simply blocked from returning by opposing communities; others were physically attacked when they tried to return to areas where they were an ethnic minority; in some instances, houses and other property were deliberately destroyed to prevent minority returns.

A major obstacle to the return of displaced Bosnians was the shortage of accommodation. Some 60 per cent of Bosnia's housing had been destroyed or damaged during the conflict. Reconstruction in Bosnia was estimated to cost billions of dollars, but the international community was reluctant to provide the needed funds in the absence of co-operation among the ethnic groups. While the UNHCR initiated a number of confidence building measures and programmes, including a shelter programme, the deep-seated social and economic tensions existing among the divided communities made reintegration an enormously difficult undertaking. While changes in property laws introduced in 1998 eliminated some of the local obstructions and small numbers of refugees began to return spontaneously to their pre-war homes, most returnees relocated away from their original homes in areas controlled by members of their own ethnic group. Ethnic groups remain divided and separated in Bosnia and Herzegovina. General elections held in Bosnia in November 2000 reconfirmed the strength of nationalist parties and the difficulties of recreating a multi-ethnic state.

'Project Delphi': Restructuring of the UNHCR and the Downsizing of Protection

Beginning in 1996, the UNHCR underwent an intensive internal review of its operations, priorities, and organizational structure.[129] 'Project Delphi'—or the 'confused oracle' as some staff called it—was clearly influenced by the cutbacks in funding experienced by the Office in the mid-1990s and by the perception that more cuts were still to come. According to the Assistant High Commissioner, 'it was better for the UNHCR itself to reduce spending and to lay off personnel than to have downsizing imposed from outside the agency'.[130]

The review was also motivated by a desire to improve the UNHCR's efficiency in the delivery of assistance by decentralizing and delegating authority to the field. Ogata believed that, by decentralizing the operations of the Office, policy decisions 'could be shifted from headquarters in Geneva to the field where the UNHCR interacted with refugees'.[131] In its efforts to streamline the UNHCR's operations to respond more quickly to the immediate physical needs of refugees, the Delphi Plan of Action shifted much of the responsibility for the planning and oversight of daily field activities away from headquarters to regional based 'situation managers'.[132] These field managers had almost complete authority over policy and practice.

The Protection Division (DIP) was effectively sidelined in the planned restructuring of the Office. Unlike Operations, the DIP did not have a role in overall policy formation.[133] Rather than giving the Director of International Protection central oversight of UNHCR's protection activities, protection was to be decentralized to the field. But the DIP was concerned that when confronted with refugee emergencies most field managers would place logistical or assistance needs ahead of the UNHCR's protection function.[134] This had, after all, been the trend in the Office's response to the major emergencies of the 1990s. Thus, instead of main streaming protection within the organization as was the objective of the Delphi reform, protection was effectively downsized.

The fact of the matter was that protection no longer figured prominently in the overall orientation of the Office. In a frank memorandum to Ogata in August 1998,[135] the Director of International Protection, Dennis McNamara noted , 'We can advise and suggest—or even criticize—but [we] have no independent authority to act, even on the most important and key protection issues.'[136] Without a close link between the protection division and field operations, he continued, it was not possible to 'ensure consistency and compatibility in our protection activities globally'.[137] He also noted that within the UNHCR there was considerable resistance to any oversight or monitoring role by the DIP. In fact many senior managers at headquarters and in the field did not accept that protection should be given a status equal to operations. McNamara also pointed out that his division lacked the essential human resources to ensure a basic level of protection for refugees worldwide. In Geneva, for example, the DIP had some 50 staff compared to a total of over 1000 headquarters staff. The situation in the field was even more desperate. McNamara noted that

in some cases, protection posts are being cut or reclassified to non-protection functions without any consultation with the Division of International Protection and irrespective of our assessment that concerted focus and resources devoted to protection continue to be required. . . . In other cases, key protection posts have been left unfilled for months, and due to staff shortages, inexperienced local lawyers are used for difficult protection work, including refugee status determination, without adequate training or supervision. (UNHCR PR00/98/118, 'Protection Management', 26 August 1998).

The downgrading of protection was also noted in a number of internal reviews of the Office's operations carried out at the time by the UNHCR's Inspection and Evaluation Unit. For example, in a July 1998 report on Bosnia-Hercegovina, the Inspector's team found that the UNHCR operation there suffered from a serious lack of leadership and strategy in the protection field during the crucial post-Dayton Agreement period in 1996 and 1997. Not only was the post of Assistant Chief of Mission for Protection in Bosnia vacant for nine months in 1997 but there was also a lack of adequate field staff to monitor protection issues, particularly in areas of return. The report emphasized the need for all staff to be better informed on basic protection issues. In a May 1998 report on Rwanda, the inspection team found serious gaps in protection staffing at the senior level at headquarters and in the field with almost two-thirds of all protection posts in the country having been vacant for a considerable period of time at the end of 1997. The report also identified a lack of training and briefings on protection to staff in the field. A November 1997 report on the UNHCR operation in Tanzania found that more consistent UNHCR statements on protection issues would have significantly strengthened protection management. The October 1997 report on Iraq stated that the UNHCR was unable to provide even minimal protection coverage to caseloads of concern. It also reported that there was very little cumulative knowledge or experience within the senior management of the Baghdad office on the UNHCR's established practices and approaches to protection. Other Inspection and Evaluation reports in the Middle East pointed to the fact that there was no management authority to ensure consistency in the Office's global approach to protection issues. This led to, among other things, wide discrepancies in different countries in refugee status determination procedures conducted by the UNHCR.

Despite these critical reports, the UNHCR leadership took no meaningful steps to rectify the situation. Consequently, protection remained almost entirely subservient to the pragmatic priorities of operations.

The Delphi restructuring exercise took almost two years to accomplish and was deeply resented by many staff as 'an unpleasant downsizing of the Office without benefit to staff'.[138] For months, Project Delphi meetings totally preoccupied the Office and disrupted work.[139] Despite an inordinate amount of time given over to this exercise, few of the major structural reforms envisioned in the Delphi Plan of Action were fully implemented. While the UNHCR headquarters was restructured into four divisions for operations, protection, resource management, and communications and information, power and influence were not evenly distributed. One of the key recommendations of the Delphi Plan of Action was to appoint two Assistant High Commissioners—one for operations and one for protection—thereby placing protection and operations at the same level within the power hierarchy of the UNHCR. But the High Commissioner proposed to the Secretary-General the appointment of an Assistant High Commissioner for Operations only, solidifying the UNHCR's transition from a refugee protection agency to a humanitarian agency.

The UNHCR and New Refugee Emergencies at the End of the Century

Despite the efforts to improve its response capacity, the UNHCR was woefully unprepared for two of the most dramatic upheavals of the decade: Kosovo and East Timor. Neither Kosovo nor East Timor had overriding geopolitical or strategic importance for the more powerful Western states. Western states had to decide whether to remain on the sidelines or to challenge state sovereignty and intervene on explicitly humanitarian grounds to save victims of persecution.

After initial hesitation and under heavy public pressure to do something, the international community chose to intervene. They did so with minimal risk to themselves. In stark contrast to Kosovo and East Timor, the West purposely distanced itself from the conflict in Chechnya. The claims of sovereignty by a permanent member of the UN Security Council kept the international community completely out of the conflict there. The war in Sierra Leone and the atrocities carried out against civilians there and in other African conflicts stirred little international attention among the major Western powers, primarily because they had no strategic interests in these countries.

NATO's 'Humanitarian War' and the UNHCR's Role with Kosovar Refugees

The political repression and mass exodus of the bulk of the Albanian Kosovar population from Serb-ruled Kosovo should have come as no surprise to the international community. The crisis had been widely anticipated throughout the 1990s.[140] The seeds of the refugee crisis in Kosovo can be traced back many decades, even centuries. By the late 1980s, in an estimated population of 1.9 million, ethnic Albanians outnumbered Serbs by a ratio of around nine to one. In 1989 Serbian leader Slobodan Milosevic inflamed Serbian nationalistic passions by revoking Kosovo's autonomous status and set the stage for a showdown between the two groups. Between 1989 and 1998, as Serbian repression of Albanians in Kosovo escalated, some 350,000 Albanian Kosovars sought refuge in Europe. Widespread fighting between Serbian security forces and the Kosovo Liberation Army (KLA) erupted in March 1998. Within months several hundred thousand more civilians were displaced inside the province or fled abroad.

In September 1998, a cease-fire was negotiated and monitors from the Organization for Security and Co-operation in Europe (OSCE) were stationed in Kosovo to verify compliance with the agreement. During this time—and until it was obliged to abandon Kosovo in March 2000—the UNHCR was also active inside Kosovo assisting some 400,000 internally displaced people. In January 1999, following the KLA murder of several Serb policemen, 45 Kosovo Albanians were massacred by Serb forces at Racak. International mediation efforts to contain the conflict were stepped up. Although further fighting and displacement of civilians continued, it was hoped that peace talks in Rambouillet, France would produce a settlement. Rather than accept a humiliating political defeat, Slobodan Milosevic chose to challenge Western leaders over Kosovo.

Political negotiations failed to resolve the crisis and on 24 March 1999, without obtaining specific authorization from the UN Security Council, NATO launched a 78-day air war over Serbia and Kosovo. Almost immediately, Milosevic unleashed the Serb army, police, and paramilitary forces on Kosovo's ethnic Albanians, turning hundreds of thousands of them into refugees within days. Serbian militias moved from village to village and from house to house searching for members of the Kosovo Liberation Army. Draft-aged men were separated from women, children, and the elderly and were detained or were taken away at gunpoint to be executed. Masses of civilians were forced onto roads leading to Albania while tens of thousands of others were packed onto trains for the journey to Macedonia. Houses were turned into piles of rubble after being deliberately torched and then bulldozed. In the Serbian rampage across Kosovo over one-quarter of all buildings were destroyed or badly damaged.

By forcing Albanians out of Kosovo, Milosevic attempted to systematically depopulate the province and to destabilize the region. Over the 10-week bombing campaign, a total of 795,000 Albanians fled or were expelled, including 426,000 to Albania, 228,000 to Macedonia, and 45,000 to Montenegro. Several hundred thousand more people were displaced within the province, hiding in the mountains or trekking from village to village, sheltering for weeks in basements and barns.

The most dramatic aspect of the Kosovo crisis was the sudden and huge exodus of desperate refugees to neighbouring Albania, Macedonia, and Montenegro. The outflow of people was staggering. They did not simply flee; they were forcibly expelled from their homes in a brutal ethnic cleansing. The regional repercussions of the conflict and refugee crisis were immense. Serbia itself was crippled by the effects of the bombing campaign and became a virtual international outcast. Bosnia hosted more than 20,000 Kosovars and political events there remained sensitive to regional developments. But the greatest effects were felt in the major host countries in the region.

Within three days of the beginning of NATO bombing, ethnic Albanians began to arrive in the neighbouring states of Albania, Macedonia, and Montenegro, causing serious security problems in all three countries. Albania, the poorest country in Europe, hosted the majority of refugees. Kukes, a border town of just 28,000 people, handled a sudden influx of destitute and terrified refugees of around sixteen times the size of its own population. Most refugees eventually moved away from the sensitive border zone to places further inside Albania. Many other Kosovars lived with local families or in the camps on the fringes of Kukes. Despite Albania's generosity, the massive influx of refugees seriously destabilized the country. The Kosovo Liberation Army actively recruited among the refugees and the Albanian border was constantly shelled by Serbian forces.

The political situations in Macedonia and Montenegro were particularly fragile. In the largest 24 hour exodus during the crisis, an estimated 45,000 refugees arrived in Macedonia on 2 April. The Macedonian government, fear-ful that a massive influx of ethnic Albanians could destabilize its own finely tuned ethnic balance of Macedonian Slavs and Albanians, kept tens of thou-sands of new arrivals stranded in an open field at Blace on the Kosovo-

Macedonia border. These refugees had virtually no medical assistance, little food, and limited access to the UNHCR or the humanitarian aid agencies. At one point, the Macedonian authorities suddenly and forcibly cleared the field of refugees without the knowledge of the UNHCR. They bundled some 15,000 people onto flights to Turkey and shipped others to Albania and to nearby hastily-constructed camps. After the Skopje government made it clear that it could not absorb any more people, nearly 92,000 refugees were airlifted from Macedonia to 29 countries outside the region for temporary safety as part of an international humanitarian evacuation programme. Although the numbers of refugees crossing into the Yugoslav republic of Montenegro were small compared to those going to Albania and Macedonia, the Kosovars represented over 10 per cent of the tiny republic's population and were added to an estimated 30,000 refugees who had fled there from the previous wars in Croatia and Bosnia. The arrival of Albanian refugees was deeply resented by the local population and there was widespread concern that their presence would create ethnic instability and worsen the economic crisis brought on by the war. Of special concern to the Montenegrin leadership was their fear that the Yugoslav military would use the presence of refugees as an excuse to unseat them and replace them with more pliant politicians.

The Kosovo emergency was as difficult and complex as any that the international community had faced in the 1990s. Despite several early warnings that conflict was inevitable, no one, including the UNHCR, had anticipated a deliberate, well-planned policy to virtually cleanse the entire province of Albanian Kosovars. In addition to not forecasting the exodus, the UNHCR was also widely criticized for not being well prepared once the influx began and being unable to deliver emergency supplies or to build camps quickly enough. Prior to the crisis, the UNHCR had made contingency plans for the region and had stockpiled emergency supplies for about 100,000 refugees. Initially, the influx overwhelmed the response capacity of the UNHCR. The Office had few personnel and resources in the region and had inadequate senior staff who had the experience and authority to lead operations in the field. Because of the Delphi restructuring exercise, the UNHCR had downsized by over 1,000 staff at the end of 1998. The majority of workers eventually deployed were new to the organization and hired on short-term contracts. Finally, despite being designated the lead agency in the Kosovo refugee emergency, the UNHCR failed to co-ordinate the international response. Regional governments preferred to work with military over humanitarian actors.[141] Rather than using the UNHCR to co-ordinate refugee relief, Macedonia and Albania dealt bilaterally with donor governments and their armed forces. Throughout the crisis, the UNHCR was dominated by NATO's military and strategic priorities and any pretense of humanitarian neutrality and independence by the UNHCR was shattered.[142]

The NATO air campaign represented 'the first major bombing campaign intended to bring a halt to crimes against humanity being committed by a state within its own borders'.[143] Yet from the start of the NATO campaign, it was clear that the bombing could not stop ethnic cleansing. The bombing exacerbated rather than stopped the Serb attacks against Kosovar civilians. Refugees soon became the centrepiece of the conflict. Consequently, for political as well as humanitarian reasons, the principal NATO war objective became the mass return of refugees.

NATO was also compelled to provide direct assistance to the refugees. When it became evident that the UNHCR and the NGO aid agencies were not equipped to handle independently the mass outflows, NATO quickly stepped into the breach. On 2 April, NATO Secretary-General Javier Solana offered to assist the UNHCR and requested that the agency become involved in joint planning.[144] Albania had already called for NATO aid to refugees and Macedonia had insisted that refugees on its border be housed in military-built camps as a *quid pro quo* for granting them temporary asylum. On 3 April, Ogata accepted NATO support for the humanitarian relief operation, but she sought to preserve the civilian character of assistance.[145] After the UNHCR and NATO met in Brussels, a second exchange of letters on 21–2 April confirmed arrangements. NATO recognized the leading role of the UNHCR and agreed to focus on the areas of logistics, camp construction, refugee transport, and road repairs.[146] NATO military forces subsequently built refugee camps in Macedonia and organized the air evacuation programme from Macedonia to third countries. In the eyes of many observers, since NATO was a party to the conflict, the close co-operation between the UNHCR and NATO compromised the impartiality and independence of both the Office and the humanitarian operation.[147]

UN appeals for assistance to confront the Kosovo emergency were met quickly by governments. They donated $70.8 million for 350,000 refugees on 1 April, $138.4 million for 650,000 refugees on 5 April, and $265.4 million for 950,000 refugees on 22 April.[148] It was one of the highest *per capita* levels of international relief for a refugee population ever provided. However, very little of this money was channelled through the UNHCR. Because of the high profile nature of the relief operation and the media attention and publicity focused on the refugees, donor governments channelled most of their financial contributions through their own national NGOs or directly to the host governments. Nearly 300 government agencies and NGOs clamoured for some of the publicity and media attention and competed for a share of the humanitarian funding. For many, their own visibility had a much higher priority than inter-agency co-operation. Some governments and agencies simply bypassed the UNHCR and set up their own programmes and camps without notifying the Office. Consequently, the UNHCR had a difficult time in carrying out its lead agency co-ordination role.

The practical and political problems of assistance and lack of co-ordination were huge, but there were also major human rights protection headaches, such as the virtual abandonment of refugees in open fields by the Macedonian authorities and by the UNHCR. In Montenegro, Kosovar Albanians were harassed and intimidated by Yugoslav security forces. In both Albania and Macedonia, the UNHCR was dependent on the governments' consent for its continued access to refugees and its presence on their territories and so was severely restricted in its interventions. The UNHCR's situation was particularly difficult in Macedonia where NATO, in need of Skopje's cooperation to conduct military operations, pressured the UNHCR to mute its criticism of the government.[149] The US in particular was adamant that any criticism of Macedonia on refugee protection issues might destabilize the country and endanger the war effort.

In early June 1999, a cease-fire accord was signed, ending the fighting in Kosovo and precipitating a rapid exodus in reverse. In less than a month, over 500,000 of the refugees returned home in one of the swiftest and largest repatriations in modern history. As the Albanian Kosovars streamed home, over 170,000 Serbs and Gypsies who feared violent retribution fled Kosovo, generating yet another crisis of forcible displacement.

Refugees returned to a completely destroyed society where there was no functioning administrative or judicial system. The widespread destruction of houses, schools, and health centres, as well as the absence of the availability of food because of the halt in agricultural production during the war, made the international reconstruction and rehabilitation effort extremely difficult. The Secretary-General appointed the UNHCR to lead the humanitarian relief effort. Within a few weeks of the end of the war, the UNHCR had a field presence throughout Kosovo and led a massive humanitarian assistance operation, involving other UN agencies, the ICRC, and an enormous number of NGOs. While two Kosovo donor conferences resulted in pledges in excess of $3 billion, the UN remained underresourced and with inadequate expertise for most of the post-conflict operation. Delays by governments in committing funds and other bureaucratic and logistical hurdles prevented a rapid start-up of the reconstruction effort. About one-half of the province's 1.4 million people lacked adequate shelter because so many homes were destroyed by the Serbs. The UNHCR and other agencies established a large-scale rehabilitation programme and distributed shelter materials and food assistance to hundreds of thousands of returnees.

The biggest problem confronting Kosovo in the first year and a half after the war ended was the continuing Albanian violence against non-Albanian minorities in Kosovo, especially remaining Serbs and Gypsies. The magnitude and importance of this problem was not recognized for months. Because of widespread sympathy for the Albanians there was no real effort by the UN civilian leadership or the NATO peacekeeping forces to try to deal with the violence. The KLA and gangs of organized criminals beat up and killed Serbs and Gypsies with impunity. Warnings and admonitions to Albanians to stop the violence were not followed up by any action. In the first year of the post-conflict operation, there was not a single conviction of any perpetrator of an ethnically motivated crime. The criminal justice system did not function and foreign governments were slow to send adequately trained police officers to keep law and order. UNHCR and other humanitarian staff were intimidated and at times assaulted and attacked. UN vehicles were burned and UN agency offices were ransacked. These incidents drew little serious response from the UN in New York or in Kosovo.[150] According to the UN special Envoy for humanitarian affairs in Kosovo, the international community was not prepared to invest as much political effort and resources in winning the peace in Kosovo as it did in fighting the war.[151]

In an effort to counter these trends, the UNHCR and the OSCE human rights staff initiated activities in Kosovo to assist the minority communities of Serbs and Gypsies, promote their safety, and persuade NATO troops to ensure their physical protection.[152] The Office also tried to encourage the return of minority groups who had fled at the end of the war. But, for the most part these efforts were unsuccessful. The UNHCR faced a dilemma similar to the one it confronted in Bosnia in the early 1990s. In an effort to prevent persecution and attacks on Serbs, the agency ended up assisting further evacuations of minority populations from Kosovo. By the end of 2000, there was little evidence that the conflict and subsequent reconstruction of Kosovo would lead to the rebuilding of a multi-ethnic society there.

Mass Terror and Displacement in East Timor

While the NATO bombing campaign against Yugoslavia was still in full force, a new crisis was brewing in East Timor in the Indonesian archipelago. In 1975, after the Portuguese colonial authorities left the island, Indonesia invaded East Timor and then forcibly annexed it the next year.[153] Although the major Western powers had not formally recognized Indonesia's annexation and both the UN Security Council and the General Assembly had called for Indonesia's withdrawal, no meaningful political or economic measures were taken to force Jakarta to comply. Rather, the Western powers generously supplied the regime of General Suharto with arms and regarded Indonesia as a strategically important ally in South-East Asia. Indonesia was therefore left free to rule East Timor with an iron hand and to try to force integration by military repression.

After nearly two and a half decades of terror, intimidation, and the deaths of some 250,000 East Timorese—about one-third of the population—events in East Timor suddenly took an encouraging turn at the end of the 1990s. In May 1998, General Suharto was forced to resign in the midst of an economic and political crisis. Consequently, the central government's hold on its outlying provinces, including East Timor, weakened. In January 1999, under pressure to reform both from within and outside Indonesia, Suharto's successor, B. J. Habibie, agreed to a UN-monitored referendum on 30 August 1999 to give the East Timorese the choice between independence or remaining within Indonesia with some form of autonomy. Indonesia refused to permit foreign troops into East Timor to monitor the voting and insisted that security would remain in the hands of the Indonesian army and police. However, the Indonesian military and paramilitary militias in East Timor opposed the referendum and initiated a campaign of intimidation. Despite the escalation of violence and the displacement of more than 50,000 people before the voting began, the referendum was held on schedule. Over 98 per cent of registered East Timorese voters went to the polls and overwhelmingly rejected autonomy—78.5 per cent of them voted in favour of independence.

After the result was announced on 4 September, rampaging militias supported by elements of the Indonesian Army and police terrorized the civilian population and local UN officials in East Timor. Within three weeks, over one-half of the country's 800,000 population was forcibly displaced from their homes. Approximately 250,000 East Timorese fled or were forced at gunpoint to West Timor where militias separated out men and boys and either killed them or sent them to more distant locations on other islands. The remaining refugees were in the grip of the paramilitary gangs and the international aid agencies were unable to protect them from intimidation and abuse. Another 200,000 terrified civilians took refuge in East Timor's mountainous interior. They were without adequate food and survived on foraged roots. Most of the capital, Dili, was reduced to rubble and ashes by the lawless militiamen. Even the United Nations mission in Dili was attacked and the UN compound was looted after its staff was forced to withdraw.

In mid-September, after East Timor had been laid waste, Indonesia bowed to international pressure and permitted an international peacekeeping force led by Australia—who had an interest in preventing a wave of refugees—to restore order. In October, the Indonesian Parliament ratified the referendum in East Timor that had called for its independence. In response, the UN Security Council authorized the dispatch to East Timor of approximately 10,000 UN peacekeeping troops and police forces called the International Force in East Timor (INTERFET), and civilians administrators called the UN Transitional Administration in East Timor (UNTAET), to run the country until an East Timorese government could take control of the new nation.

During the crisis, the UNHCR and most other humanitarian agencies were prevented from gaining access to the displaced. Hence, refugees were not protected and were completely at the mercy of their persecutors. After the arrival of INTERFET forces, humanitarian agencies were given sufficient protection to be able to provide emergency relief, first to those in Dili, and then to those in other major towns. By late October 1999, most of the internally displaced had returned to their homes and the UNHCR was assigned the lead role in providing shelter assistance to the returnees.

The situation in West Timor was incomparably worse than that in East Timor.[154] Refugees lived in appalling conditions in makeshift camps from which the UNHCR was almost totally excluded. The UNHCR and the International Organization for Migration focused on registering refugees to determine how many wanted to return home and on organizing a repatriation programme. But this was no easy task as refugees were held as bargaining chips by the paramilitary units who remained opposed to independence in East Timor. They still thirsted for revenge and sought to destabilize East Timor through guerrilla operations against UN civilians and peacekeepers. The militia gangs used the refugee camps in West Timor as bases for cross-border incursions and attacks. Although Indonesia had agreed in a Memorandum of Understanding with the UNHCR to provide security for humanitarian workers in West Timor, the Indonesian military failed to control the militias operating in the camps. No attempt was made to disarm or demobilize these groups. UNHCR staff were frequently harassed and attacked. Despite the continuing problems of gaining access to the camps and the widespread intimidation by the militia of refugees who expressed an interest in returning to East Timor, the UNHCR organized repatriation flights and ferry journeys from West to East Timor from early October 1999. A year later, over half of the refugees in West Timor had been repatriated.

In September 2000, the UNHCR faced a new crisis in West Timor. Rampaging militia trapped three UNHCR workers inside the Office's compound in West Timor, beat, stabbed, and hacked them to death, and burned their bodies. Desperate appeals for help to the local Indonesian military went unanswered. Subsequently, the UNHCR evacuated its staff and the repatriation programme was terminated. These incidents, coming on top of similar attacks on humanitarian aid personnel in other parts of the world during the past decade, underscored the importance of protecting UN staff and of establishing a comprehensive and credible response to violent actions against them.

In East Timor, the UN experienced extreme difficulties ensuring a steady transition to East Timorese rule. The UN's task was complicated by the fact that the country had been laid to waste and had no economic resources with which to rebuild. There were also few experienced civil servants among the East Timorese and no institutions of governance. Unlike in Kosovo—where NATO troops provided security—the East Timor operation was purely a UN programme. Working in an environment where there was no functioning state, UNTAET constituted the sole sovereign authority in East Timor. Its power was absolute. East Timorese leaders frequently complained that they were neither consulted about issues of governance nor were they offered positions in the new UN-ruled East Timor.[155] By the middle of 2000, East Timor had become a test case for the ability of the United Nations to administer territories in transition.

African Refugee Problems Neglected

While the international community focused attention and resources on the crisis in Kosovo and East Timor, conflict and displacement in Africa were virtually ignored. For senior international policy-makers, Africa continued to be strategically unimportant. Humanitarian disasters dominated developments in Africa and hundreds of thousands of new refugees took flight throughout that continent. For example, during 1999 and 2000, an estimated 600,000 Angolans were in acute need and there were fears for up to 3 million more whose condition could not be ascertained because they lived beyond the range within which UN agencies were able to operate. In Sudan hundreds of thousands of southern Sudanese became newly uprooted—adding to the nearly 4 million people already displaced from their homes—and chronic malnutrition threatened to turn into a full-scale famine. While the international community poured hundreds of millions of dollars of humanitarian aid into southern Sudan, there was no unified international diplomacy to address the crisis. In Somalia 300,000 people faced starvation and another 1 million were in a rapidly deteriorating condition. Conflict between Ethiopia and Eritrea resulted in large numbers of deaths and in displacements of an estimated 1.5 million people. Cease-fire agreements in Lome and Lusaka in 1999 sought to bring peace to Sierra Leone and the Democratic Republic of Congo. However, peace continued to be a mirage for the half-million refugees in Sierra Leone who still lived in camps in Guinea and Liberia and for the 300,000 to 600,000 persons who were internally displaced as of mid-2000 after nearly 10 years of war. And despite the deployment of UN peacekeepers in Sierra Leone, violence broke out again in 2000, pushing at least 150,000 Sierra Leoneans from their homes. In Central Africa, coalitions of defeated and disbanded armed groups caused the outbreak of smaller, violent sub-conflicts. An estimated half-million Congolese became newly uprooted in 2000, bringing the total of displaced persons to 1.4 million. Burundi, Congo-Brazzaville, Guinea-Bissau, Rwanda, Tanzania, and Uganda also faced serious humanitarian need.

Donor governments continued to give vastly disproportionate amounts of aid to a few well-known crises and trivial amounts of aid to dozens of other hidden humanitarian emergencies. In 1999, international humanitarian organizations criticized governments for neglecting refugee problems in Africa while pumping billions of dollars into the refugee crisis in Kosovo. Faced with a severe cutback in funds for humanitarian relief during 1999 and 2000, the UN cut food aid and other essentials to millions of refugees. For example, by mid-1999, the UN had received from governments less than half the $800 million it had sought for urgent help for 12 million displaced people in Africa. In August 1999, Ogata complained that her office had received only a little more than half of its requests for refugee programmes in sub-Saharan Africa. In October 1999, the World Food Program had to cut emergency aid to more than 1.8 million refugees in Sierra Leone, Liberia, and Guinea because international donors had provided less than one-fifth of the $106 million needed to feed refugees and displaced people in those countries. By mid-2000, donor governments largely ignored the pleas of international aid agencies for assistance to Congo-Brazzaville, the Democratic Republic of the Congo, and Uganda despite serious needs on the part of displaced people in those countries. By the end of 2000 the financial crisis had deepened.

Reluctance to get Involved in Chechnya

Armed conflict broke out again in Chechnya in mid-1999. After Chechnya-based rebels invaded neighbouring Daghestan in August and September 1999, displacing some 33,000 people, the Russian armed forces attacked Chechnya. In a particularly brutal offensive, Russian planes and artillery launched wave after wave of strikes on the secessionist republic, causing mass displacement and widespread misery and hunger among the civilian population. Over 200,000 Chechens fled to neighbouring Ingushetia, Georgia, and other neighbouring republics where they found lodging with the local population. The exodus of refugees into neighbouring republics resulted in shortages of housing, growing unemployment, and rising crime rates, which threatened the delicate balance within the ethnically diverse northern Caucasus region. The cross-border movement of criminal gangs and the uncontrolled accumulation of arms in host states constituted major threats to regional security. Tens of thousands of other Chechens were trapped in a war zone in their own country and forced to live in the open, often without food or water, as the temperatures plummeted. In a particularly brutal move, Russian troops sealed the border with Ingushetia, causing thousands of women, children, and the elderly to be stranded on the Chechen side of the border.

From the beginning of the conflict, the major Western powers tempered their criticism of Russia's atrocities against Chechen civilians. Moscow condemned any international criticism of its actions on the grounds that the war was purely a domestic matter in which the international community had no right to interfere. Unlike in Kosovo and East Timor, Russian claims of sovereignty and non-intervention kept the international community at arm's length from the conflict. The Western states had little interest in directly challenging a major power and a veto-wielding permanent member of the UN Security Council.

When armed conflict broke out in mid-1999, there were virtually no international humanitarian agencies present on the ground. After the murder of six ICRC workers in Chechnya in December 1986, most NGOs pulled out of the province. The UNHCR redeployed its staff out of the region after the head of its office in Ingushetia was kidnapped in January 1998. Finally, in December 1998, continued kidnappings and violence forced the OSCE, then the only international organization left in Chechnya, to evacuate its international staff. The Russian onslaught in Chechnya, therefore, had a terrible impact on the refugees and Chechen civilians caught in the conflict. After Secretary-General Annan intervened with the Russian Prime Minister, Vladimir Putin, High Commissioner Ogata was permitted to visit the refugee camps in the region, and was able to increase deliveries of tents and other emergency supplies. The UNHCR did not criticize Russian policies in Chechnya for fear of being refused permission to mount a relief operation there. International relief and development aid to the region remained extremely limited, however, largely because of security concerns for staff of the UNHCR and other humanitarian organizations and because of Russia's lack of receptiveness to outside involvement. Throughout the crisis, the international community remained extremely deferential to the idea of sovereignty and non-intervention in another country's internal affairs, particularly in this case which involved one of the world's most powerful countries.

The UNHCR in the 1990s: A Balance Sheet

The refugee crises of the 1990s severely challenged the UNHCR. As High Commissioner, Ogata tried to address the refugee problem in its totality—from initial flight to return and reintegration—through a strategy that emphasized emergency preparedness and response, the pursuit of solutions, and the development of preventive activities. As the UNHCR reoriented its activities and dramatically expanded its agenda, the Office assumed institutional responsibility far beyond the parameters set for the agency 50 years ago by its founders. The Office became involved with new actors in a vast range of new activities, including co-operating with UN human rights mechanisms, working with UN agencies to provide economic development for repatriation and reintegration, and collaborating with UN peacekeeping forces to try to secure the protection and security of people displaced and threatened with displacement. As a result, the UNHCR was launched into new and largely untested waters in countries of origin. In addition to its more traditional role it found itself providing humanitarian aid, building civil societies and engaging in other forms of rehabilitation aid in war-torn countries, and trying in specific cases to monitor human rights violations in hopes of stemming population flows before they began.

The UNHCR's in-country and preventive strategies coincided with the emergence of a more assertive UN Security Council. Reacting to a public alarmed by images of refugees and other helpless victims of war splashed across Western television screens, the international community developed a series of experimental measures, including a number of humanitarian interventions, for responding to refugee crises. These initiatives included the offer of temporary protection rather than full refugee status, the establishment of safe havens, cross-border deliveries of assistance, and the use of military resources for the delivery of humanitarian assistance. They were not derived from any clearly defined strategy but were developed in an *ad hoc* fashion. These non-traditional methods of assistance and protection not only failed to protect refugees and internally displaced people caught up in brutal conflicts but they also seemed to exacerbate or prolong their suffering in many cases. While the UNHCR scored some major operational successes, it became clear by the mid-1990s that if refugee problems were to be resolved then the international community would have to become active well beyond the mandate of the UNHCR. As seemingly intractable conflicts continued in the Balkans, Africa, and within the former Soviet Union, it became evident that states lacked the will to initiate effective enforcement for maintaining peace and security, for empowering human rights mechanisms, or for promoting sustainable development in crisis regions. Powerful states had only minimal interest in most countries with internal conflicts and humanitarian crises, and they became increasingly reluctant to offer traditional forms of protection and asylum to persecuted peoples. Rather than provide a realistic alternative to asylum these new forms of response often seemed intended to evade the obligations of states to provide international protection on their own territories. Many of the new ways of reacting to refugee flows were aimed at deflecting rather than protecting threatened people.

The pitfalls of the UNHCR's new approach to refugees soon became evident. In adopting a holistic approach to refugee problems, the UNHCR spread its capacities too thinly. Given its statutory responsibility as an independent actor representing the interests of refugees, many questioned whether the Office should be engaged in such a broad range of activities and whether it was the most appropriate agency to carry out all these programmes.[156] At the same time, the place of protection within the UNHCR's decision-making hierarchy was downgraded.

The High Commissioner's aspirations to transform the UNHCR into a humanitarian emergency agency diluted the Office's focus as the main international actor responsible for promoting asylum and providing legal protection for refugees. In the new international political environment, the UNHCR was no longer willing to make decisions solely on the basis of the international legal norms that had been the guide for its work in the past. The UNHCR claimed that it increasingly had to choose between adhering to its mandate and principles—which the High Commissioner feared would decrease her influence and marginalize the Office—or adopting politically pragmatic approaches aimed at securing the 'best bargain' for refugees under the circumstances. As a result, the UNHCR had many protection failures during the 1990s. Among them were Turkey's closure of its border with Iraq in 1991, the forcible repatriation of Rohingya to Burma, the UNHCR's signing of a return agreement without safeguards with Tanzania in 1996, and numerous instances of negligence with regard to protection concerns in the Great Lakes and the Balkans.

The international community, including the UNHCR, frequently pursued policies that were less than ideal from the perspective of refugees. As a result, the UNHCR's image as the protector of refugees was seriously tarnished. Refugees faced increasingly limited choices of where to seek protection and when to return home. A new set of rules and practices emerged in the 1990s that stressed more state control over refugee and asylum admissions, that limited access to asylum procedures, that emphasized humanitarian aid over protection, and that eroded refugee rights.[157] Because the UNHCR had willingly accepted responsibility for dealing with complex humanitarian emergencies and had accepted, and in some cases endorsed, most of the experiments in refugee protection and humanitarian response, it was not in a strong position to protest the worldwide decline in refugee protection. Indeed, the Office became complicit in many of the refugee protection failures of the decade.

In recent years, the UNHCR achieved a higher profile in world politics and greater access to international statesmen. But a higher profile did not readily translate into increased leverage with governments, particularly on protection issues. On a number of occasions the Office was forced out on a limb by governments, and consequently became a more overt instrument of state policies and interests. Many observers complained that, in its desire to become relevant in world politics through spectacular emergency operations, the UNHCR had lost sight of its traditional protection principles. As a result, the Office lost influence and some of its autonomy during the 1990s. The most important challenge facing the UNHCR in the twenty-first century is to redress the imbalance that has evolved between protection and operations.

In January 2001, Ruud Lubbers, a former Dutch Prime Minister, became the ninth United Nations High Commissioner for Refugees. Among his major challenges include countering the decline in the willingness of states to provide asylum to refugees, securing a strong and permanent basis for financing the UNHCR's activities, and reforming the agency to make it a more effective and accountable organization. Under Lubbers and future High Commissioners, the UNHCR will evolve steadily just as the organization has done over the past 50 years. One thing is certain. Refugee problems will remain a central issue of our time.

NOTES

1. Interview with Sadako Ogata, UNHCR, Geneva, August 2000.
2. Ibid.
3. Ibid.
4. In a speech, the High Commissioner stated, 'Humanitarian action must remain broadly non-judgemental. . . .' Sadako Ogata, Human Rights, Humanitarian Law and Refugee Protection'. Speech at the Graduate Institute of International Studies, Geneva, 16 March 1995.
5. Interview with Irene Kahn, UNHCR, Geneva, January 1999.
6. Interview with Sadako Ogata, 2000.
7. See: Stephen Van Evera, 'Primed for Peace: Europe after the Cold War', *International Security*, 16/4 (1990/1991): 2–57; US Agency for International Development, *Population Movements in the Former Soviet Union* (Washington, DC: The Emergency Humanitarian Assessment Team in the New Independent States, June 1992); and Anatoli Vishnevsky and Zhanna Zayonchkovskaya, *Internal and International Migrations in the Former Soviet Space* (Moscow: Institute for Employment Studies, Russian Academy of Sciences, June 1992). Janie Leatherman notes that in 1988 Nagorno-Karabakh was the only armed conflict in the USSR. Between 1988 and 1991, more than 150 such conflicts broke out. See Janie Leatherman, 'The Challenge of Ethnic Conflict in the Post Cold War: How Effective is the CSCE Response?'. Unpublished paper, International Studies Association Meeting, 23–7 March 1993.
8. Author's interviews with UNHCR staff, Geneva, March 1993.
9. This does not include illegal migrants or displacements after 1996, including the conflict in Chechnya. IOM, *CIS Migration Report* (Geneva: Technical Cooperation Center for Europe and Central Asia, 1997).
10. Interviews with UNHCR staff, Geneva, 1993.
11. UN General Assembly Res. 48/113 (20 December 1993).
12. 'Tepid Response at CIS Conference Steering Group Meeting', *Forced Migration Monitor* (New York, NY: Open Society Institute, July 1997): 1.
13. Gareth Evans, 'Central Asians Need Help Now to Head Off Conflict', *International Herald Tribune* (16 August 2000).
14. UNHCR, *The State of the World's Refugees: A Humanitarian Agenda* (Oxford: Oxford University Press, 1997): 143.
15. Jeff Crisp, 'Mind the Gap! UNHCR, Humanitarian Assistance and the Development Process', *International Migration Review* (forthcoming).
16. In March and April 1992, the author visited both the camps along the Thai-Cambodian border and the reception centres near Battambang in Cambodia and interviewed UNHCR officials.
17. UNHCR, 'Note on International Protection', (Geneva: UNHCR, 15 July 1986). See also Marjorleine Zieck, *UNHCR and Voluntary Repatriation of Refugees: A Legal Analysis* (The Hague: Martinus Nijhoff, 1997).
18. Michael Barnett makes this point in 'Humanitarianism with a Sovereign Face: UNHCR in the Global Undertow', *International Migration Review* (forthcoming).
19. In 1992, the UNHCR noted: 'Criteria for promotion and organization of large

scale repatriation must balance protection needs of the refugees against the political imperative towards resolving refugee problems . . . the realization of a solution in a growing number of refugee situations today is most likely when the solution is made an integral part of a 'package' which strikes a humane balance between the interests of affected states and the legal rights, as well as humanitarian needs, of the individuals concerned.' UNHCR, *Note on International Protection*, UN doc. A/AC.96/799 (1992), paras.38 and 39.

20. UNHCR, 'Bridging the Gap Between Returnee Aid and Development: A Challenge for the International Community' (Geneva: UNHCR, 1992).

21. This section draws upon C. R. Abrar, 'Repatriation of Rohingya Refugees', unpublished manuscript (1995); Michael Barnett, 'UNHCR and Involuntary Repatriation: Environmental Developments, the Repatriation Culture, and the Rohingya Refugees', unpublished paper presented at International Studies Association meeting, Los Angeles (20 March 2000); and on interviews with UNHCR and Bangladeshi officials and Rohingyan refugees in refugee camps near Teknaf-Cox's Bazar, Bangladesh, February 1998.

22. Tony Reid, 'Repatriation of Arakanese Muslims from Bangladesh to Burma, 1978-79: "Arranged" Reversal of the Flow of an Ethnic Minority'. Unpublished paper from the International Research and Advisory Panel Conference, Oxford, 5–9 January 1994 (Oxford: Documentation Centre, Refugee Studies Centre, Oxford University); and Cato Aall, 'Disastrous International Relief Failure: A Report on Burmese Refugees in Bangldesh from May to December 1978', *Disasters*, 3/4 (1979): 429.

23. Interviews with Milton Moreno and Irene Kahn, UNHCR, Geneva, March 2000.

24. Human Rights Watch, *Burma: The Rohingya Muslims Ending a Cycle of Violence?* (New York, NY: Human Rights Watch, September 1996); and US Committee on Refugees, *The Return of Rohingyan Refugees to Burma: Voluntary Repatriation or Refoulement?* (Washington, DC: US Committee on Refugees, March 1995).

25. This was still the case in early 1998. Interviews with newly arrived Rohingya refugees, near Teknaf-Cox's Bazar, Bangladesh, February 1998.

26. Ibid.

27. David Petrasek, 'Through Rose-Colored Glasses: UNHCR's Role in Monitoring the Safety of the Rohingya Refugees Returning to Burma'. Unpublished paper (1999).

28. Interview with Sadako Ogata, 2000.

29. Interviews with Soren Jessen-Petersen and Irene Kahn, UNHCR, Geneva, January 1999.

30. UN Security Council Resolution 688 (5 April 1991).

31. Interview with Sadako Ogata, 2000.

32. Interviews with Kris Janowski, UNHCR, Geneva, March 2000 and Ron Redmond, UNHCR. Geneva, August 2000.

33. Interview with Soren Jessen-Petersen, UNHCR, Geneva, January 1999.

34. Interview with Ron Redmond.

35. John Elson, 'Ogata's Angels', *Time* (23 October 1995): 67.

36. UN General Assembly Resolution A/Res/46-182, 19 December 1991 (my emphasis).

37. John Borton, 'Recent Changes in the International Relief System', *Disasters*, 17/3 (1993): 187–201.

38. Interview with Sadako Ogata, 2000.

39. Kofi Annan, *Renewing the United Nations: A Programme for Reform*, U.N. doc. A/51/950, New York, NY: United Nations, July 1997; and John Borton, *The State of the International Humanitarian System* (London: Briefing Paper, Overseas Development Institute, March 1998).

40. Interview with Sadako Ogata, 2000.

41. UNHCR, IOM-FOM 33/93 of 28 April 1993 on 'UNHCR's Role with Internally Displaced Persons'.

42. In 1997, the UNHCR modified these criteria by stating that in cases where IDPs and refugees shared a common area and when the UNHCR's activities arose as a natural extension of its mandate, the High Commissioner is not required to obtain formal permission from either the UN or the concerned state to undertake programmes on behalf of IDPs. See UNHCR, IOM-FOM 91/97 of December 1997.

43. This situation is well described by Andreas Feldman, 'The UNHCR and Internal Displacement: Rational Ambivalence?'. Conference paper, International Studies Association, Los Angeles (March 2000).

44. Interviews with Soren Jessen-Petersen and Irene Kahn.

45. Ibid.

46. Jose-Maria Mendiluce, 'War and Disaster in the Former Yugoslavia: The Limits of Humanitarian Action', *World Refugee Survey—1994* (Washington, DC: US Committee for Refugees, 1995): 10–19.

47. For an overview, see Mark Cutts, 'The Humanitarian Operation in Bosnia, 1992–95: Dilemmas of Negotiating Humanitarian Access', *New Issues in Refugee Research*, Working Paper No. 8 (Geneva: UNHCR, May 1999).

48. Interviews with UNHCR staff, Geneva, April 1993.

49. Interview with Sadako Ogata, UNHCR, Geneva, 1993.

50. Interview with Sadako Ogata, 2000.

51. *An Agenda for Peace: Preventive Diplomacy, Peacemaking and Peace-keeping* (New York, NY: Report of the Secretary-General pursuant to the statement adopted by the Summit Meeting of the Security Council on 31 January 1992, United Nations, 1992).

52. UNHCR, 'Report of the UNHCR Working Group on International Protection' (Geneva: UNHCR, 6 July 1992): 1.

53. A/AC.96/799. *Note on International Protection,* Executive Committee of the High Commissioner's Programme, 25 August 1992.

54. See *A Comprehensive Response to Humanitarian Crises in the Former Yugoslavia,* HCR/IMFY/1992/2 (Geneva: International Meeting on Humanitarian Aid for Victims of Conflict in the former Yugoslavia, 29 July 1992).

55. Mikhael Barutciski, 'The Reinforcement of Non-Admission Policies and the Subversion of UNHCR: Displacement and Internal Assistance in Bosnia-Herzegovina (1992–1994)', *International Journal of Refugee Law*, 8/1/2 (1996): 49–110; Nicholas Morris, 'Protection Dilemmas and UNHCR's Response: A Personal View from within UNHCR', *International Journal of Refugee Law*, 9/3 (1997): 492–9; Erin Mooney, 'Presence, ergo Protection? UNPROFOR, UNHCR and the ICRC in Croatia and Bosnia and Herzegovina', *International Journal of Refugee Law*, 7/3 (1995): 407–35; and Alex Cunliffe and Michael Pugh, 'The Politicization of the UNHCR in the Former Yugoslavia', *Journal of Refugee Studies*, 10/2 (1997): 134–53.

56. Wilbert van Hovell, 'New Concepts of Protection in Conflict: "Safe Keeping" Interventions in Iraq, Bosnia and Rwanda', unpublished manuscript, 26 July 1995.

57. UNHCR field staff were encouraged to uphold the right of asylum above all else. See Wilbert van Hovell, 'Yugoslav Emergency', *Update on Protection Issues* (Geneva: UNHCR, 12 September 1992).

58. Mendiluce, 'War and Disaster in the former Yugoslavia'.

59. Eric Morris, *The Limits of Mercy: Ethno-political Conflict and Humanitarian Action* (Cambridge, MA: MIT Center for International Studies, 1997).

60. UN, Security Council Resolution 749 (7 April 1992).

61. UN, Security Council Resolution 770 (13 August 1992).

62. Mark Cutts, 'The Humanitarian Operation in Bosnia'.

63. David Rieff, *Slaughterhouse: Bosnia and the Failure of the West* (New York, NY: Simon and Schuster, 1995).

64. Misha Glenny, *The Fall of Yugoslavia: The Third Balkan War* (New York, NY: Penguin, 1992) and Laura Silber and Allan Little, *The Death of Yugoslavia* (London: Penguin, 1995).

65. David Forsythe, 'The Mandate of the UNHCR: The Politics of Being Non-Political'. Unpublished paper (2000).

66. UN Security Council Resolution 836 (4 June 1993).

67. David Rohde, *Endgame: The Betrayal and Fall of Srebrenica, Europe's Worst Massacre Since World War II* (New York, NY: Farrar, Strauss and Giroux, 1997); and United Nations General Assembly Document A/54/549, *Report of the Secretary-General pursuant to General Assembly resolution 53/35: The fall of Srebrenica* (New York, NY: UN, November 1999).

68. David Keen, *The Economic Functions of Violence in Civil Wars*, Adelphi Paper 320 (London: International Institute for Strategic Studies, June 1998); and Aristide Zolberg, 'The Specter of Anarchy', *Dissent*, 39 (Summer 1992): 303–11.

69. Stephen Ellis, *The Mask of Anarchy: The Destruction of Liberia and the Religious Dimension of an African Civil War* (New York, NY: New York University Press, 1999).

70. Paul Richards, *Fighting for the Rain Forests: War, Youth and Resources in Sierra Leone* (Oxford: James Currey, 1996).

71. Michael Ignatieff, *The Warrior's Honor: Ethnic War and the Modern Conscience* (London: Chatto and Windus, 1998)

72. UN Security Council Resolution 751 (24 April 1992).

73. UNHCR, 'A New Approach in the Horn of Africa: The Preventive Zone Concept', unpublished document in author's files, July 1992 and UNHCR PSBF/132/92, 'Preventive Zones', 1 October 1992.

74. Interview with Sadako Ogata, 2000.

75. UNHCR, 'A New Approach in the Horn of Africa'.

76. Ibid.

77. Quick impact projects are small-scale economic and social projects aimed at improving access to water, transport, education, agricultural services, and health care. Results are meant to be achieved quickly thereby achieving short-term stability and laying the groundwork for longer-term development projects.

78. UN Security Council Resolution 794 (3 December 1992).

79. John Hirsch and Robert Oakley, *Somalia and Operation Restore Hope* (Washington, DC: United States Institute of Peace Press, 1995).
80. UN Security Council Resolution 814 (26 March 1993).
81. Mohamed Sahnoun, *Somalia: The Missed Opportunities* (Washington, DC: United States Institute of Peace Press, 1994).
82. Presidential Directive 25, 4 May 1994.
83. Alison Des Forges, *Leave None to Tell the Story* (New York, NY: Human Rights Watch, 1999).
84. In his report he described mass killings of civilians that could constitute genocide; the involvement of extremist political militias; the existence of a 'second power' alongside that of the government officials; and the 'pernicious' role of Radio Rwanda in instigating several massacres. To avert future killings, he recommended that a mechanism for the protection of civilian populations against massacres be set up, including international teams of human rights observers and a civilian police force. UN document E/CN.4/1997/7/Add. 1, 'Report by the Special Rapporteur on Extrajudicial, Summary or Arbitrary Executions on his Mission to Rwanda, 8–17 April 1993', 11 August 1993.
85. UN Security Council Resolution 872 (5 October 1993).
86. Romeo Dallaire, 'The End of Innocence: Rwanda 1994', in Jonathan Moore, ed., *Hard Choices: Moral Dilemmas in Humanitarian Intervention* (Boston, MA: Rowman and Littlefield, 1998): 71–86; and Joint Evaluation of Emergency Assistance to Rwanda, *The International Response to Conflict and Genocide: Lessons from the Rwandan Experience*, Study 2, 'Early Warning and Conflict Management' (Copenhagen: Steering Committee of the Joint Evaluation of Emergency Assistance to Rwanda, 1996).
87. United Nations, *Report of the Independent Inquiry into the Actions of the United Nations during the 1994 Genocide in Rwanda* (New York, NY: United Nations, 15 December 1999).
88. It was rumoured that the Hutu President of Rwanda was close to agreeing to a power-sharing arrangement with the Tutsis.
89. For background to the genocide and refugee crisis see Philip Gourevitch, *We Wish To Inform You That Tomorrow We Will Be Killed With Our Families: Stories from Rwanda* (New York, NY: Farrar Straus and Giroux, 1998); Philip Gourevitch, 'The Continental Shift', *The New Yorker*, 4 (August 1997): 42–55; Howard Adelman and Astri Suhrke, eds., *The Path of Genocide: The Rwandan Crisis from Uganda to Zaire* (New Brunswick, NJ: Transaction Publishers, 1999); Gerard Prunier, *The Rwanda Crisis: 1959-1994: History of a Genocide* (London: Hurst and Co., 1995) and *Update to End of March 1995* (London: Writenet, May 1995); Michael Ignatieff, *The Warrior's Honor*; William Shawcross, *Deliver Us From Evil: Peacekeepers, Warlords and a World of Endless Conflict* (New York, NY: Simon and Schuster, 2000); Joint Evaluation of Emergency Assistance to Rwanda, *The International Response to Conflict and Genocide: Lessons from the Rwandan Experience*.
90. UN Security Council Resolution 918 (17 May 1994).
91. UN Security Council Resolution 929 (22 June 1994).
92. Amnesty International, *Rwanda: Arming the Perpetrators of the Genocide* (London: Amnesty International, June 1995) and Human Rights Watch, *Rwanda/Zaire:*

Rearming with Impunity. International Support for the Perpetrators of the Rwandan Genocide (New York, NY: Human Rights Watch, May 1995).

93. Interview with UNHCR staff, 1997 and 1998.

94. Interview with Sadako Ogata, 2000.

95. For background and analysis about the UNHCR's role and thinking, see: Joel Boutroue, *Missed Opportunities: The Role of the International Community in the Return of Rwandan Refugees from Eastern Zaire*, The Rosemarie Rogers Working Paper Series, Working Paper 1 (Cambridge, MA: MIT Inter-University Committee on International Migration, June 1998).

96. Ibid: 19–25.

97. The Security Council was also paralysed by a clash of interests between France and the US over their respective interests and influence in the Great Lakes region.

98. Letter dated 17 January 1995. *The United Nations and Rwanda, 1993–1996* (New York, NY: UN Department of Public Information, 1996) cited in Boutroue, *Missed Opportunities*: 43.

99. Martin, 'Human Rights and Political Failures in Rwanda': 161.

100. Interviews with UNHCR staff, Geneva, 1997 and 1998.

101. For a summary of events leading to the military operations in Zaire in late 1996 see Gerard Prunier, 'The Geopolitical Situation of the Great Lakes Area in Light of the Kivu Crisis', *Refugee Survey Quarterly*, 16 (1997: 1–25) and 'The Great Lakes Crisis', *Current History*, 96/610 (May 1997): 193–9.

102. David Rieff, 'Realpolitik in Congo: Should Zaire's Fate Have Been Subordinate to the Fate of the Rwandan Refugees?', *The Nation* (7 July 1997): 16–21.

103. Interview with Dennis McNamara, former Director of International Protection, Oxford, August 2000.

104. 'The UN's African Refugee Dilemma', *International Herald Tribune* (10 March 1997).

105. Amnesty International, *Rwanda: Human Rights Overlooked in Mass Repatriation* (London: Amnesty International, January 1997), and *Great Lakes Region Still in Need of Protection: Repatriation, Refoulement and the Safety of Refugees and the Internally Displaced* (London: Amnesty International, 24 January 1997); Human Rights Watch, *Uncertain Refuge: International Failures to Protect Refugees* (New York, NY: Human Rights Watch, April 1997).

106. Bill Frelick, 'Preventing Refugee Flows: Protection or Peril?', *World Refugee Survey 1993* (Washington, DC: US Committee for Refugees, 1993); Andrew Shacknove, 'From Asylum to Containment', *International Journal of Refugee Law*, 5 (1993): 516–33.

107. Temporary protection was not an entirely new concept. Mass protection without individual determination of eligibility had been a UNHCR practice in situations of mass influx for Hungarian refugees in the late 1950s and in developing countries since the 1960s. Moreover, mechanisms for coping with large influxes of persons not meeting the Convention criteria in Europe had been developed in the 1970s with the emergence of *de facto* humanitarian statuses, such as B-status, humanitarian status, and 'exceptional leave to remain'. Dennis Gallagher, Susan Forbes Martin, and Patricia Weiss-Fagen, 'Temporary Safe Haven: The Need for North American-European Responses', in Gil Loescher and Laila Monahan, eds., *Refugees and International Relations* (Oxford: Clarendon Press, 1989): 333–54.

108. Sadako Ogata, 'Statement at the Intergovernmental Consultations on Asylum,

Refugee and Migration Policies in Europe, North America and Australia' (Washington, DC, May 1997). Cited in UNHCR, *The State of the World's Refugees: A Humanitarian Agenda* (Oxford: Oxford University Press, 1997): 209–10.

109. Joanne Thorburn, 'Transcending Boundaries: Temporary Protection and Burden-sharing in Europe', *International Journal of Refugee Law*, 7/3 (1995): 459–79.

110. The following are figures provided by the Inter-Governmental Consultations on Migrations based in Vienna. Cited in Gil Loescher, *Beyond Charity: International Cooperation and the Global Refugee Crisis* (New York, NY: Oxford University Press, 1993). More recent figures come from UNHCR, *Refugees and Others of Concern to UNHCR: 1999 Statistical Overview* (Geneva: UNHCR, 1999).

111. Danielle Joly, *Haven or Hell? Asylum Policies and Refugees in Europe* (London: Macmillan, 1996).

112. R. Byrne and Andrew Shaknove, 'The Safe Country Notion in European Asylum Law', *Harvard Human Rights Journal*, 9 (Spring 1996): 78–98.

113. European Council on Refugees and Exiles, *Safe Third Countries: Myths and Realities* (London: ECRE, 1996).

114. Interviews with UNHCR officials, Geneva, March 1996 and January 2000.

115. UNHCR, *Refugees and Others of Concern to UNHCR*: 88.

116. Ibid.

117. Ibid.

118. Steven Edminster, 'The High Road or the Low Road: The Way Forward to Asylum Harmonization in the European Union', in US Committee for Refugees, *World Refugee Survey 2000* (Washington, DC: US Committee for Refugees, 2000): 58.

119. UNHCR, *Refugees and Others of Concern to UNHCR*: 88.

120. Interview with Dennis McNamara.

121. Cited in Ray Wilkenson, 'Give Me Your Huddled Masses . . .', *Refugees*, 2/119 (2000): 15.

122. Lawyers' Committee for Human Rights, *Slamming the 'Golden Door': A Year of Expedited Removal* (New York, NY: Lawyers' Committee for Human Rights, April 1998).

123. UNHCR, *Refugees and Others of Concern to UNHCR*: 88.

124. Bimal Ghosh, *Huddled Masses and Uncertain Shores: Insights into Irregular Migration* (The Hague: Martinus Nijhoff, 1998).

125. 'The Last Frontier', the *Economist* (24 June 2000): 63–4.

126. Karen De Young, 'Generosity Shrinks in an Age of Prosperity', *Washington Post* (25 March 1999): A11.

127. John Vidal, 'Blacks Need, but Only Whites Receive: Race Appears to be Skewing the West's Approach to Aid', *Guardian* (12 August 1999).

128. See Kimberly Maynard, *Healing Communities in Conflict: International Assistance in Complex Emergencies* (New York, NY: Columbia University Press, 1999) for a discussion of some of these problems.

129. UNHCR, EC/46/SC/CRP, 'Project Delphi: Plan of Action', a Conference Room Paper for the Standing Committee's Fourth Meeting, 4 September 1996.

130. Interview with Sergio Vierra de Mello, UNHCR, Geneva, March 1996.

131. Interview with Sadako Ogata, 2000.

132. UNHCR, 'Delphi Project: Plan of Action'.

133. UNHCR, Memorandum, Dennis McNamara, 'Project Delphi Recommendations' (15 May 1996).

134. Interview with Dennis McNamara.

135. UNHCR PR00/98/118, 'Protection Management', 26 August 1998.

136. Ibid.

137. Ibid.

138. Interview with UNHCR staff, Geneva, UNHCR, 1996.

139. The author was a senior consultant at UNHCR headquarters in Geneva during the time of the Delphi Project discussions.

140. For background see: Michael Ignatieff, *Virtual War: Kosovo and Beyond* (New York, NY: Henry Holt and Co., 2000).

141. Interview with Neill Wright, UNHCR, Geneva, March 2000.

142. UNHCR, *The Kosovo Crisis: An Independent Evaluation of UNHCR's Emergency Preparedness and Response* (Geneva: UNHCR, 2000).

143. Adam Roberts, 'NATO's "Humanitarian" War over Kosovo', *Survival*, 41/3, Autumn 1999: 102–23.

144. This correspondence in reproduced in Larry Minear, Ted Van Baarda, and Marc Sommers, *NATO and Humanitarian Action in the Kosovo Crisis*, Occasional Paper 36 (Providence, RI: Watson Institute of International Studies, 2000): 161–8.

145. UNHCR, *The Kosovo Crisis: An Independent Evaluation*.

146. Minear, Van Baarda, and Sommers, *NATO and Humanitarian Action*: 14.

147. Michael Pugh, 'Civil-Military Relations in Kosovo', *Security Dialogue*, 31/2 (June 2000): 229–42.

148. Roger Winter, 'The Year in Review', *World Refugee Survey 2000* (Washington, DC: US Committee for Refugees, 2000): 17.

149. Interview with Neill Wright.

150. Dennis McNamara, 'Humanitarian Activities in Kosovo: End of Mission Report'. Unpublished document (July 2000).

151. Interview with Dennis McNamara.

152. Dennis McNamara, 'Humanitarian Activities in Kosovo'.

153. For a definitive account of this period by the Australian Consul in Dili in 1975, see James Dunn, *Timor: A People Betrayed* (Sydney: ABC Books, 1996).

154. Interview with Milton Moreno, UNHCR, Geneva, March 2000.

155. Jarat Chopra, 'The UN's Kingdom in East Timor', *Survival*, 42/3 (Autumn 2000): 27–40.

156. Guy Goodwin-Gill, 'Refugee Identity and Protection's Fading Prospect', in Frances Nicholson and Patrick Twomey, eds., *Refugee Rights and Realities: Evolving International Concepts and Regimes* (Cambridge: Cambridge University Press, 1999): 220–52; and S. Alex Cunliffe and Michael Pugh, 'UNHCR as Leader in Humanitarian Assistance: A Triumph of Politics over Law?' in Nicholson and Twomey, *Refugee Rights*: 200–19.

157. Kathleen Newland, 'The Decade in Review', *World Refugee Survey 1999* (Washington, DC: US Committee for Refugees, 1999): 21.

10

Toward the Future: The UNHCR in the Twenty-First Century

From uncertain beginnings in 1951, the UNHCR has demonstrated quite an extraordinary capacity for perpetuation and growth. The resilience of the UNHCR indicates that it is greatly needed and that it is very adaptive to its international environment and to new challenges. A large, complex, international organization such as the UNHCR did not spring up overnight nor was it designed and built in one piece. The Office evolved gradually in a complicated historical process in which state interests have been extremely significant. At the same time, the history of the UNHCR demonstrates that it is not simply a passive mechanism of states. Rather, its growth and evolution is a result of the Office having initiated and capitalized on international political developments and having expanded its scope and authority both operationally and geographically.

Of all the international organizations created this century to deal with refugees it is the only one charged with protection and, since the mid-1950s, with assistance functions. Moreover, it has a global mandate, encompassing all but the Palestinian refugees, and has repeatedly been empowered by both the United Nations General Assembly and Security Council to deal with broader classes of forced migrants. Finally, it has frequently taken on the role of catalyst and co-ordinator of other humanitarian and development organizations. Since its inception in 1951, the UNHCR has sustained remarkable growth in its budget, staff, and expansion of its mandate. This expansion has been a consequence of the Office's striving, first for institutional survival and more recently, for institutional pre-eminence among humanitarian organizations. Its rapid growth has also resulted from the need to respond to a progressively more complex refugee phenomenon than when UNHCR came into existence.

Scholars and practitioners of international relations have been slow to recognize that the UNHCR has played a significant role in world politics during the past half-century. The Office has tried not only to influence policy outcomes but also to advocate and instigate changes in the behaviour of states and in the very terms and nature of major developments in international relations. At times, some states, especially powerful ones, have not been willing to be constrained by the UNHCR, but on many occasions, states have been willing to work through the office because this legitimized the state's behaviour both domestically and internationally. While some High Commissioners have been more successful than others in working with states, the UNHCR has steadily increased its role as a relevant participant in policy debates and, when it has been successful, it has played an important part in changes in world politics. The history of the agency demonstrates that international organizations matter in international relations.

Political and Resource Limitations

While the UNHCR has assumed several new responsibilities, many of the political problems facing the Office have remained the same as those that existed during the Cold War. The agency was designed to appear to be non-political and strictly humanitarian, a strategy employed to receive permission to work in host countries and to secure funding from donor governments. The UNHCR's actions are limited by the practices of states concerning sovereignty, particularly those norms which preclude intervention in the domestic affairs of these states. The attachment to the principle of state sovereignty remains strong, especially among several of the most powerful Western states, and others like Russia, China, India, Iran, and many developing and non-aligned states. The major powers, including the United States, have been highly selective about whether and to what extent to get involved in political crises and humanitarian emergencies. By statute, the authority of the High Commissioner does not extend to addressing the factors that are likely to generate refugee flight. The UNHCR is not mandated to intervene politically against governments or opposition groups, even where there is clear evidence of human rights violations that result in forcible displacement. In civil war situations, UNHCR staff are often unfamiliar with human rights and humanitarian law and are uncertain of how governments and opposition groups will react to their interventions using these protection norms. Increasingly, the organization finds itself out of its depth and faced with security and political issues that it has neither the mandate nor the resources to deal with.

The UNHCR is an intergovernmental organization and remains dependent on states which fund and advise it. About 98 per cent of the Office's funding comes from voluntary contributions from governments: and most of this from a small number of the major industrialized states which inevitably exercise a disproportionate amount of influence on the organization. For example, in 1999, the United States, Japan, and the European Union accounted for

94 per cent of all government contributions to the UNHCR.[1] Governments exert leverage on the Office by earmarking funds for programmes that are of particular political interest to them. In 1999, 80 per cent of contributions were earmarked, the highest percentage in the agency's history.[2] Some emergencies are favoured over others. Donor governments give vastly disproportionate amounts of aid to a few well-known cases and correspondingly trivial aid to dozens of other less well-publicized refugee emergencies. UNHCR refugee programmes in Africa, for example, have been seriously underfunded in recent years. In 2000, the per capita expenditures for Kosovar refugees were ten times higher than they were for African refugees. Because the total budget of the UNHCR decreased from $1.256 billion in 1996 to $911.6 million in 1999,[3] the UNHCR has had to cut back on education, health care, and other basic services for long-staying refugees in countries such as Somalia and Sudan. The absence of an autonomous resource base for the UNHCR and the limited mandates and competencies of the organization continue to limit its response to future refugee crises just as they have done for the past 50 years. States also influence the UNHCR through their membership on the Office's Executive Committee, which oversees the agency's budget and advises it on policy issues. Finally, the UNHCR is not independent of the political organs of the United Nations. Like all other UN bodies, it is subject to the decisions of the Security Council, requests by the Secretary-General and to the formal control of the General Assembly, to which it is obliged to report back each year on issues relating to refugees.

In spite of the UNHCR's characterization of its activities as non-political, the Office is a highly political actor and is clearly shaped by the interests of major governments. In mounting massive relief operations, the UNHCR is often at the mercy of its donors and host governments. The agency can only carry out its enormous emergency and maintenance programmes if it receives funding from the industrialized states. It can only operate in the countries into which refugees move if host governments give it permission to be there. Thus, the UNHCR is in a weak position to challenge the policies of its funders and hosts, even if those policies fail to respond adequately to refugee problems.

Financial vulnerability and reliance on powerful donor governments as well as host states also impede the UNHCR in carrying out its principal function of providing protection to refugees. Response to refugee emergencies is absorbing most of the limited funds available for international assistance. To meet its huge financial and relief responsibility, the UNHCR sometimes feels compelled to remain silent about human rights protection problems. In recent years, in order to demonstrate its 'relevance' to states the UNHCR has regularly co-operated in the containment of the internally displaced within countries of origin and in the enforcement of repatriation programmes that are often less than voluntary. Such instances of 'humanitarian pragmatism' as well as the rapid expansion of the UNHCR's mandate and programmes have caused widespread concern. Many observers fear that in becoming a general humanitarian agency and a more overt instrument of state policy, the UNHCR has diluted its primary function of protecting refugees.

The Crisis of Refugee Protection

Current trends do not paint a particularly positive picture for refugee protection in the years ahead. Increasingly refugees are perceived as destabilizing to national, regional, and international security and as triggers for regional instability. Everywhere pernicious laws now exist to turn away refugees and restrict their rights. This situation is a significant departure from state practice in the Cold War when—largely for political purposes—attitudes towards refugees were far more tolerant and welcoming.

The traditionally favoured solutions of third country and local resettlement are no longer viewed by states as adequate. Since resettling the Indo-Chinese refugees in the late 1970s and 1980s, many Western countries have largely refused to accept permanent settlers. Overseas resettlement is generally viewed as too costly in terms of expenses and cultural adjustment on the part of host societies and refugees alike. Even traditional first asylum countries in Africa and Asia are increasingly reluctant to give asylum to people from neighbouring countries, much less to accept them as permanent citizens. The treatment of asylum-seekers everywhere has been marked by exclusion and expulsion and there exists a worldwide asylum crisis. Most states now favour repatriation. But the persistence of violence and economic devastation in countries of return frequently makes voluntary return under safe conditions difficult if not impossible. Despite the risks involved, refugees are being returned to increasingly precarious and dangerous situations.

Alongside government pressure for return at any cost, Western states have introduced an array of measures designed to prevent asylum applications from being lodged in their countries. Although states still profess a commitment to uphold the 1951 Refugee Convention, governments have initiated a series of legal and political manoeuvres that *de facto* extend their frontiers into refugee-producing countries. In theory, asylum-seekers are supposed to be protected by international refugee law as soon as they cross national frontiers to seek refuge in another country. The primary protection is contained in Article 33 of the Refugee Convention, which provides for *non-refoulement* of refugees: no state 'shall expel or return [*refouler*] a refugee...to the frontiers of territories where his life or freedom would be threatened'.[4] Therefore, asylum-seekers cannot be sent back home or expelled against their will, at least until their cases are examined. The UNHCR's mandate is to promote liberal asylum policies and to protect asylum-seekers against forcible repatriation. This includes the treaty

criteria of *non-refoulement* for those who have a well-founded fear of persecution upon return to their home countries. However, governments disagree
over the exact obligations that the principle of *non-refoulement* impose on
states. For example, the principle of *non-refoulement* is interpreted by the
United States and many other Western governments to apply only to persons
who meet the Convention persecution standard. Accordingly, people fleeing
generalized violence from civil war and intercommunal strife—such as
Haitians or Tamils—have customarily not been protected by *non-refoulement*,
despite the fact that the UNHCR and many international legal authorities
contend that they should be.[5] In the current restrictionist climate, many
national policy-makers also claim that *non-refoulement* does not apply to
persons seeking asylum if they are encountered before they actually enter a
state's territory. The US and other Western governments have taken the position that interdiction of refugees on the high seas and a variety of visa restrictions and sanctions against airlines and shipping companies for carrying
undocumented persons do not contravene *non-refoulement*. In addition, off-
shore processing of asylum applicants and pre-selection of those to be admitted as refugees are designed primarily to avoid or deter uninvited arrivals
rather than to enhance protection. Thus, in practice the UNHCR is often
unable to provide full protection because states retain the discretion to determine who is and who is not a refugee. It is also the states' own business just
how much material assistance and legal aid they provide refugees. As long as
states are the sole arbiters of status and protection of refugees, it is difficult to
see how international standards can be applied more even-handedly.

In the hope of deterring all prospective entrants—migrants and asylum-
seekers alike—the industrialized states are continually developing newer
control measures, contributing to a cycle of more and more restrictive
measures. Substantial resources have been expended in high tech border
control, including technical assistance to developing countries for more
effective management of their borders. However, the evidence suggests that
enforcement measures alone are not sufficient to deal with the problem nor
that such measures produce any significant reduction in the number of those
arriving spontaneously. In countries where conditions are desperate, people
continue to seek to emigrate by any means possible. The majority of asylum-
seekers now resort to traffickers or smuggling rings because of more daunting
obstacles to entry. The advent of well-organized criminal trafficking organizations make state controls effective for shorter periods of time as these
organizations have the resources to rapidly shift tactics to ensure continued
access and penetration. Not only are the national systems for controlling
borders and entry in most developed states not very effective but they are also
extremely expensive, especially relative to the worldwide needs of refugees.
For example, a medium sized country like Canada that had an annual intake
of some 13,000 asylum-seekers in 1999 spends about $300 million each

year—or ten times its annual contribution to UNHCR for worldwide assistance and protection activities—to control their borders.[6]

Gaps in Institutional Mandates and Lack of Co-ordination

Many of the humanitarian organizations existing today were created after World War II. Despite the close connections between the refugee problem and the related issues of human rights, economic development, and security, the international community maintained a sharp distinction between these issues. For the past fifty years, separate agencies focused only on their specific areas of concern. Currently, the international response arrangements to refugee crises constitute a vast, often uncoordinated melange of multilateral, national, and non-governmental institutions and initiatives. Each of these agencies independently raises funds from donor governments, implements its own programmes either directly or more often in sub-contractual arrangements with NGOs, and has its own governing board made up of representatives from states. In humanitarian emergencies each agency contributes its specialized resources to respond to the needs of the crisis, while also pursuing independent agendas.

The transaction costs of each actor pursuing independent actions are great and contribute to considerable duplication of efforts and operational inefficiency. For example, for many emergencies, the UNHCR conducts its own separate assessment missions, negotiations with local governments, funding proposals to donors, registration and distribution procedures, and transportation arrangements. These tasks are repeated by each agency involved in the humanitarian emergency, leading not only to inefficiency but also to needless and sometimes destructive competition for donor funds and for access to the affected populations. There is also little transparency and agencies are seldom held accountable for lapses in performance in humanitarian emergencies.

The more logical strategy would be for agencies to consolidate their functions to avoid duplication and redundancy and to co-ordinate their activities and resources in order to increase overall efficiency and effectiveness of programmes. Better co-ordination mechanisms would theoretically reduce the costs. Information could be shared and labour divided. There now exists a consolidated appeals process (CAP) that covers complex emergencies. The CAP theoretically reduces the burden of separate appeals on the donors and makes them more willing to provide regular funds on a predictable basis. However, the CAP does not cover all appeals for humanitarian emergencies.

With the end of the Cold War, the international community has begun to question the capacity of these post-World War II institutions to deal effectively with the more complex problems of humanitarian emergencies today. Consequently, the issue of better co-ordination has been at the top of policy-makers' agendas in recent years. While the formal framework for co-ordination of international humanitarian action has evolved considerably, there are still many challenges and problems to overcome. Most agencies still resent co-ordination from above and the interaction among these institutions remains far from harmonious. The reality is that institutions perceive co-ordination to threaten their interests. More often than not, humanitarian organizations function without reference to, and in competition with each other. Paradoxically, the strategies that enable the UNHCR to survive in the humanitarian marketplace also limit the possibilities for co-ordination with other agencies.[7] Because an increasing number of organizations are attempting to survive off a shrinking pool of donor resources, it is in the interest of the UNHCR to maximize its funding intake relative to its competitors. Since donor governments determine who gets funding by each organization's image and identity, the UNHCR like all organizations, perceives that co-ordination blurs its individual visibility and identity, thereby reducing its ability to generate external funds. This constitutes a powerful reason for the UNHCR not to fully participate in international co-ordination efforts. Most emergencies are marked, not by co-operation, but by intense competition among agencies for publicity in order to raise funds and gain recognition. The UNHCR seeks to be involved in high-profile operations where the Office can demonstrate to donor governments tangible results of humanitarian relief. The UNHCR wants to lead and not to be led or otherwise constrained in its activities.

The Gap in Protection and Assistance for Internally Displaced Persons

The lack of co-ordination among humanitarian agencies also reveals serious gaps of coverage in the international system, especially for the protection and assistance of internally displaced persons (IDPs). A critical weakness of the international humanitarian system is that at present there is no special international organization to protect and assist the world's estimated 20 to 30 million IDPs. While there is a clear mandate for the protection and the provision of humanitarian assistance to refugees, there is a lack of clarity within existing international instruments regarding the allocation of responsibilities and mechanisms for addressing the immediate needs of IDPs.

One of the major gaps in the international response system for the internally displaced is a lack of predictable response. No UN agency can be counted upon to respond automatically when there is a crisis involving massive internal displacement. Agencies choose the situations in which they will become involved in the light of their mandates, resources, and interests. The selectivity and conditionality of the response often results in limited and inconsistent coverage for the internally displaced leaving large numbers with little or no protection or assistance. The 1999 Kosovo emergency was a case in point. The UNHCR and other international agencies were heavily involved in assisting refugees who fled the country. But practically no international attention was directed to the victims of ethnic cleansing and the internally displaced within the country during the NATO bombing campaign, largely because it was not safe for international agencies to be there.[8] In the absence of a single organization within the UN system for the internally displaced, reliance has been placed on a system-wide approach. From 1991, DHA theoretically co-ordinated responses to IDP emergencies. In1998, OCHA was formally designated the international community's focal point for IDPs. In the past, this collaborative approach has often been constrained by delays, duplication of effort and programmes, neglect of protection issues, and insufficient political and financial support for reintegration and post-conflict development efforts. UN resident co-ordinators who have been assigned to co-ordinate assistance to internally displaced populations frequently have had no operational capacity, little experience in dealing with the internally displaced, and minimal understanding of protection concerns. In his programme for reform of the UN in July 1997, Secretary-General Annan recognized the challenge of providing protection, assistance and reintegration, and development support for internally displaced persons, and cited this area as an example of a humanitarian issue that falls between the gaps of existing mandates of the different agencies.[9] In 1998, governments urged the UNHCR and other agencies to develop 'frameworks of co-operation' to provide protection, assistance, and development for IDPs, by appointing focal points within these organizations for these matters.[10]

In January 2000,the UN Security Council discussed the issue of IDPs in some detail. US Ambassador Richard Holbrooke stated his belief that the UNHCR would be the most effective lead agency, especially in cases where protection is the main issue. In March 2000, he set out a series of recommendations:

First, the UN should designate a lead agency for each specific internal refugee emergency, and define much more clearly lead agency responsibilities.

Second, in order to facilitate cooperation throughout the UN system, we must encourage all UN humanitarian agencies to designate a point of contact on internal refugees . . .

Third, we must improve our understanding and monitoring of internal refugee emergencies. One possibility would be for the Secretary-General to provide regular, comprehensive reports to the UN General Assembly and the Economic and Social Council on the state of the world's displaced and the nature of the UN's response on a country-by-country basis . . .

Fourth, we must be as clear as we are for refugees, that protection and advocacy are essential elements of assisting internal refugees. Some humanitarian and development agencies still do not see that as part of their mandate, or do not implement sufficiently in the field. (Statement by Ambassador Richard Holbrooke, US Permanent Representative to the UN. Press release of 28 March 2000).

Numerous interagency meetings were held during 2000 to discuss the respective responsibilities of individual agencies to IDPs. The UNHCR resisted the expansion of its mandate to include IDPs, arguing that the magnitude of the problem of internal displacement dwarfed the capacity and resources of any one existing agency. Rather, the Office indicated that it was willing to play an expanded role when the links between refugees and IDPs are strong and when serious protection problems requires the Office's expertise.[11] Finally, the Inter-Agency Standing Committee incorporated a mechanism to identify a senior official in each humanitarian agency who would be accountable for marshalling a response from within the UN system to deal with the needs of IDPs. It would then be this person's responsibility to collaborate with other agencies and organize a response among UN agencies and NGOs to IDP emergencies. While this may improve the current situation, there still exists a serious gap in the way the international community organizes responses to IDPs. Only a weak and incoherent arrangement at the international level is in place at present. Whatever organizational structure emerges, lack of sufficient resources will remain a major impediment to a more effective international policy. Governments are generally less willing to fund IDP emergencies than refugee emergencies. International agencies would be more effective if donor governments were less selective in their funding and were more willing to find political and other long-term solutions to IDP problems.

The Gap between Humanitarian Relief and Development

Another often noted gap in the international humanitarian system concerns post-conflict situations where emergency relief operations have ended and development and institution-building projects have yet to be established. The UNHCR has been concerned for decades about the lack of co-ordination between relief and development agencies in refugee emergencies. In recent years, the Office has become increasingly aware of a similar gap which exists during post-conflict situations when refugees are returned and reintegrated into their home societies after costly and debilitating wars. In his *Agenda for Development*[12] the former UN Secretary-General Boutros-Ghali called attention to the need to assist 'countries emerging from crisis situations in the rehabilitation phase' and to the widely accepted conclusion that without reconstruction and development following conflict, 'there can be little expectation that peace will endure'. Indeed, rebuilding war-torn societies is one of the most urgent tasks currently facing the international community. Over half the low income countries in the world today have been at war during the 1990s and these trends are likely to continue in the future.

Building close relationships between humanitarian and development agencies in post-conflict situations involves a number of institutional and funding constraints that have so far proved impossible to overcome. Although the UNHCR can be a catalyst in initiating small scale development assistance through quick impact projects, it is not a development agency like the UNDP or the World Bank. Co-ordination between the UNHCR and development agencies has been difficult to arrange because each has specialized functions that require it to proceed in different time and policy frameworks. The planning and implementation machinery of international development and financial agencies are geared toward long-term development, and projects funded by them are subject to laborious scrutiny before being implemented. These agencies give priority to long-term programmes, chiefly invest in areas with economic potential, and work in close co-operation with host governments. They are not inclined to fund projects in the more distant and marginal border areas typically affected by refugee and returnee movements. Unlike development agencies, the UNHCR operates on a short-term annual programme basis, even when administering long-term solutions. Moreover, the Office's refugee reintegration programmes have normally been undertaken in remote areas which have been unable to attract significant international development assistance. This divergence in priorities and operational calendars has inhibited progress in achieving co-operation between development and financial institutions and the UNHCR.

In 1999, the UNHCR launched yet another initiative to formulate new international institutional arrangements and funding systems to 'bridge the gap' in the realm of reintegration and development. In conjunction with the World Bank in the so-called 'Brookings process', the two agencies proposed the establishment of a post-conflict fund with up to $100 million to address the problem. Donor governments have so far opposed the idea and have insisted instead that 'the priority should be to improve and rationalize the co-ordination of agencies implementing post-conflict assistance programs'.[13]

How Effective is the UNHCR? Cultural Constraints and Lack of Accountability

The UNHCR, like most international organizations, has its own institutional culture that greatly affects its operating procedures and effectiveness. Some aspects of its culture are positive. For example, human rights values and principled ideas are central to the mandate and *raison d'être* of the organization and some members of staff daily risk their lives to protect refugees. Other aspects of the UNHCR's culture are less positive and prevent the agency from fulfilling its mandate. The UNHCR possesses a self-contained culture that focuses largely on protecting the agency's reputation and cultivating the largesse of its patrons—the donor and host state community. The Office is jealous and protective of its turf. It is extremely sensitive to external criticism and it is largely unaccountable to the populations it is mandated to protect. It also suffers from a lack of internal openness and defensiveness on the part of senior management. The UNHCR's culture of defensiveness impedes learning and innovation in the policy process. It also causes the Office to make the same costly mistakes repeatedly, sometimes doing more harm than good to refugee populations. Some individual staff members are preoccupied with their own career advancement, which leads to conservative, risk-averse behaviour. As a consequence of these factors, the UNHCR does not find institutional change an easy task and is sometimes not as effective as it might be.

The Office competes with other agencies for funds and media attention. It feels pressure to preserve public trust and the confidence of donor governments. Hence, the UNHCR discourages open discussion about its failures or the negative consequences of some of its actions and policies. When confronted with criticism, the UNHCR frequently rationalizes its actions and eschews blame by claiming that it is an operational and humanitarian agency delivering food and supplies in extremely complex and difficult situations to refugees and war victims. 'Pragmatic idealism' is encoded into the culture of the organization. It is both a way of coping with the failure to fulfil its mandate, and explaining and excusing it. Ironically it is also a way of maintaining a conviction of the rightness of the Office's cause. Therefore, the UNHCR sometimes acts as if it is above criticism and normal measures of accountability. Resistance to external criticism not only stifles argument and debate but also ultimately inhibits the ability of the Office to learn from past mistakes, to make substantive changes, and to fulfil many of its core objectives.

The UNHCR is primarily an operational agency with only very limited analytical or 'thinking' capacity. While the organization has initiated a number of important policy and programme improvements in recent years such as increased attention to evaluation, policy analysis, and selective input from external researchers,[14] the Office is still woefully underprepared and understaffed in these areas. Staff members have little time for genuine reflection even after complex and stressful humanitarian emergencies. There are still not enough opportunities for staff members to reflect on lessons of past operations and to log their experiences so that past mistakes are not repeated in future operations. For most staff, there is great pressure to simply move on to the next emergency.

In general, the UNHCR does not nurture intellectual growth or the development of critical research capacity among its staff members. Only a select few UNHCR staff members have been offered the opportunity of study leaves in university or policy research centres and then only for very brief periods. Staff do not perceive intellectual and research skills as useful to job promotion and career advancement within the agency. Among most senior managers and staff, as well as government delegates to the UNHCR's Executive Committee, the general feeling is that the priority of the agency should focus on its operations in the field, not on research, even if this activity might improve overall operational effectiveness. As a consequence, the UNHCR has had an extremely difficult time in recent years identifying staff members to fill the few policy research positions that are available. Thus, essential learning is stifled and opportunities to improve innovation in the process of policy design, implementation, and evaluation are missed.

Independent external research has had little impact on UNHCR policies or operations.[15] Communication and information from outside observers are not systematically incorporated into the decision-making and policy-making processes within the organization. The institutional culture is generally distrustful of critical comment from researchers and academics, particularly when it is viewed as damaging to the agency's external image. The UNHCR is resistant to bringing in outsiders because it fears external input will complicate decision-making, will challenge the existing sources of authority, and might undermine loyalty within the organization. Senior UNHCR staff, therefore, have a stake in limiting the intake of outside researchers as well as in not making them part of the bureaucracy. Criticism from outside the Office is often dismissed out of hand as naïve and unhelpful on the grounds that external researchers do not know the UNHCR's unique problems. Yet, the need for independent, critical assessments of the rapidly changing international political and humanitarian environment and the role of UNHCR in it has never been greater.

In an attempt to resolve these some of these shortcomings the UNHCR recently established an evaluation and policy analysis unit. This unit appears committed to facilitating the feedback of information into the policy process and to producing independent and transparent assessments of the agency's operations. The UNHCR is particularly proud of an independent evaluation of its Kosovo operation which it commissioned. This change in attitude towards external evaluations of its activities needs to be consolidated and strengthened. However, recognizing the need for independent and open evaluations is one thing. Linking the findings of evaluations to actual changes in practice and operations is another thing altogether. The UNHCR has numerous evaluation reports from past years but has often failed to actually use the recommendations in these studies to make policy changes and to effect learning within the agency. Consequently, many of the problems confronting the

UNHCR remain unaddressed and the difficult task of improving operational practices by applying the lessons learned from evaluations and independent studies remains undone.

The Effects of Personnel Problems and Adverse Working Conditions on the UNHCR's Brief

Like all UN agencies, the Office recruits personnel from all regions of the world. The staff of the UNHCR represent more than 120 nationalities. It is a multicultural and multilingual organization, and its members have diverse educational backgrounds. Despite the multinational makeup of the agency, in many respects the UNHCR is a closely-knit organization characterized by close bonds and personal loyalties built around common experiences often forged when working together in refugee emergencies.

While the UNHCR has many highly committed and professional staff members, it is not a meritocracy.[16] Despite repeated attempts to improve the personnel system, staff are generally not hired and promoted only on the basis of individual accomplishment or merit. People often get desirable postings or promotions through their personal networks rather than because of competence. Appointment and recruitment policies are also unduly influenced by governments, each of whom want to see their nationals appointed, particularly to senior positions. While some High Commissioners tried to make changes in personnel selection and promotion, there has been little significant improvement in career management.

Many of the UNHCR's regional bureaux are heavily staffed with nationals from the same regions. This is an unhealthy development that increases patronage within the Office. The regionalization of the UNHCR has exacerbated the baronial power of individual directors of the regional bureaux and other divisions of the Office. The governing style of some directors has been hierarchical and authoritarian, if not dictatorial, providing little room for free expression of opinions or democratic discourse. Hierarchical power and decision-making structures and concern for rank and privilege create barriers and disincentives to innovation and new thinking. It is not uncommon for headquarters staff to suppress or filter information or requests from the field if reports are too negative or if they require action that is considered to be either impossible or undesirable.[17] Senior managers are likely to insist on orthodoxy and to resist policy innovation if such initiatives are perceived as challenging either traditional methodologies or their own personal control and authority. It is an ethos that stifles debate or dialogue. Strong opinions are frequently perceived as disloyal and uncooperative and are suppressed by the bureaucratic hierarchy. Under such working and decision-making conditions, individual staff members either leave the organization or simply choose to remain apathetic to organizational policies and do their jobs unquestioningly.[18] This can only mean that the real potential of a talented workforce is lost.

UNHCR staff labour under very difficult and arduous conditions on the front lines of many of the world's most brutal conflicts. Most UNHCR duty stations are now in remote and insecure regions where relief workers themselves are targets and where it is impossible to take families. During the 1990s, 24 members of its staff were killed in the field. Hundreds of employees were subjected to rapes and sexual assaults, armed robberies, attacks on relief convoys, carjackings, arrests, and detentions. The decline in physical security has had a major impact on UNHCR morale. In recent years staff have been placed in dangerous situations without sufficient security support. Working in extremely tense and violent environments and experiencing prolonged separation from partners and families causes greatly increased emotional and psychological stress among UNHCR personnel. The agency also has a strict rotation policy whereby every few years staff members rotate to new positions, often where they have had no prior experience or specific knowledge.[19]

Adverse and hazardous working conditions have negatively affected organizational performance. This has resulted in particular in the flight of middle and senior managers from the UNHCR to other agencies where work is less stressful and more family-friendly. As a result, there now exists a serious lack of sufficiently experienced senior staff to take leadership positions in responding to refugee emergencies. At present, the senior and middle professional ranks within the UNHCR are so thin that the Office must call upon the same few people as each new emergency occurs. At the time of the Kosovo emergency, for example, there were only 15 UNHCR staff members who had sufficient experience and training to be placed on the senior emergency roster.[20]

In addition to increased physical and emotional hardships, UNHCR staff have less job security than most other agencies. Because the number of UNHCR staff regularly expands and contracts with each new emergency and funding crisis, most personnel are now hired on short-term contracts. Fear of not having their contracts renewed inhibits new staff from voicing criticisms of policy problems and encourages conservative, risk-averse behaviour. Taken together, these factors stifle the expression of critical or unpopular views within the Office and limit the degree of innovation and learning necessary for improvement in policies and programmes.

While significant advances have been made in introducing training programmes for UNHCR personnel, training remains one of the agency's weakest elements.[21] In recent years, the Office has launched a series of training programmes in emergency management, protection, 'people-oriented planning', and other areas, but not everyone has had the formal training.[22] Until recently, the UNHCR had a tradition of on-the-job training by senior staff in the field. However, with the departure of so many senior people, it is no longer possible to supervise and informally train young staff in this way.

The UNHCR's shift to working directly in countries of origin and in conflict zones requires specialized training and professional development. Working in countries of origin differs substantially from work in countries of asylum. In countries of origin, the UNHCR must work with governments as well as opposition movements and guerrilla factions, often in the context of collapsing states and where population displacements are among the central objectives of war. The UNHCR is ill-equipped to respond to the needs of internally displaced people and returnees who live amid conditions of intercommunal violence and on going conflict. UNHCR staff are now engaged alongside UN peacekeeping forces in anarchic and unstable countries which lack viable local and national structures. Their activities include protecting civilians against reprisals and forced displacement, relocating and evacuating civilians from conflict areas, and assisting besieged populations who choose not to move from their homes. Frequently, however, the UNHCR lacks any firm institutional and legal basis for this work. Until recently, protection at the UNHCR focused on issues arising during refugee status adjudication or where there was a legal threat of *refoulement*. Protection now involves securing the physical safety of forced migrants, particularly those in conflict zones. Most UNHCR staff are neither recruited nor adequately trained to work in the crossfire of internal conflicts. In situations like Bosnia, Kosovo, the Caucasus, Tajikistan, or West Timor, the UNHCR uses humanitarian and legal interventions similar to those used by the ICRC, but frequently without the necessary training, preparedness, or back-up support to carry out these tasks effectively. Addressing the physical protection needs of refugees and IDPs requires a more rigorous type of training than UNHCR staff have been accustomed to receiving.

The organizational culture of the UNHCR also permits the Office to be largely unaccountable to the refugee populations it is mandated to protect. Thus, the agency has at times pursued policies that have been at odds with the interests of its major consituency.[23] For example, the UNHCR has at times repatriated refugees prematurely to contexts of violence and famine, where they are uncertain whether adequate protection or resources necessary for successful return will be provided. In other situations, UNHCR staff found themselves working in highly militarized and politicized situations such as was found in the Great Lakes region of Africa after the Rwandan genocide[24] or in the Balkans during the Bosnia and Kosovo operations.

Despite these failures of policy, there exists no mechanism, internal or external, to monitor either the UNHCR's behaviour or the extent to which the agency's programmes and policies satisfy its clients, namely refugees and other forced migrants. The agency too infrequently has structured dialogue and communication with refugee populations or their leadership. Thus, the principal consumers of the UNHCR's services, the refugees themselves, have little or no means of influence or recourse in cases where the Office's programmes and policies may be unsatisfactory or may even lead to increased suffering or even death in some situations.

The Shift from Protection to Emergency Assistance

Perhaps the most significant change in the UNHCR's organizational culture in recent years has been the shift in the agency's focus from legal protection to material assistance. Since 1951, the protection of refugees reflected the core values and practices of the Office and gave the UNHCR special meaning, identity, and coherence. As its operational activities gained precedence over protection from the mid-1980s on, the UNHCR's culture of protection declined. The Division of International Protection was sidelined in favour of the more pragmatic and operational regional bureaux. This shift in identity has accelerated in recent years as humanitarian emergencies came to be perceived chiefly in terms of logistics and as the UNHCR became identified with providing massive relief to refugees. Moreover, the major humanitarian emergencies of the 1990s spawned a new cadre of logistics personnel and managers whose priorities are effectiveness of aid delivery rather than protection. The lack of a human rights culture within the UNHCR, coupled with the infusion of pragmatic managers and the departure of mid-career and senior staff from the agency, have deeply affected the organizational values, recruitment policies, socialization of staff, and policy guidelines of the UNHCR.

The new culture of the organization is rapidly being established. Recent personnel have little or no knowledge or memory of institutional history and lack appropriate experience or awareness to learn from the UNHCR's pre-1990s policies or programmes. This is unfortunate because UNHCR staff face difficult political and moral dilemmas, often without the benefit of knowledge about either the underlying nature of refugee disasters or about the success or failure of past UNHCR interventions in similar situations. For UNHCR staff, the general tendency is to perceive emergencies in terms of logistics and not as failures of politics, the development process, or ethnic relations. The UNHCR's objectives are increasingly pragmatic—to do the best in difficult circumstances and to implement options with the least negative impact—and not chiefly to uphold universal principles.

Today the UNHCR is not mainly concerned with preserving asylum or protecting refugees. Rather, its chief focus is humanitarian action.[25] The UNHCR is primarily about assistance—the delivery of food, shelter, and medicine—to refugees and war-affected populations. Successes and failures of humanitarian action are judged primarily in terms of technical standards of aid delivery and in fulfilling the material needs of refugees and threatened populations. With the UNHCR, as with most organizations today, success is measured quantitatively—how much relief can be delivered how quickly. The central importance of human rights protection of displaced and threatened populations is frequently neglected. This is a qualitative aspect of the agency's work and less easily measured and less easily sold to donor nations as worthy of funding. While the UNHCR and other humanitarian organizations are able to deliver large quantities of humanitarian supplies under extremely difficult conditions, they are much less successful in protecting civilians from human rights abuses, expulsions, and ethnic cleansing.[26]

The Way Forward: New Strategies and Advocacy

Many foreign policy and strategy experts believe that the humanitarian and military crises of the 1990s in the Balkans, the Caucasus, Central and West Africa, and Indonesia may simply be the precursor to similar new emergencies in the beginning of the twenty-first century. The costs of past failures in humanitarian crises have been great, both to millions of refugees and other forced migrants but also to national and regional stability. A sense of frustration with the international humanitarian system has been mounting in recent years. Redundancy of effort, unclear lines of authority, slow and inadequate responses to crises, inadequate staff, and poor planning have all contributed to this disillusionment. The future success of international responses will depend on more proactive and comprehensive policies and on new and improved mechanisms for international co-ordination. The problem, in short, is not one that can be faced and resolved solely by the UNHCR. While the UNHCR is likely to continue to play a central role, to be fully effective, the Office will have to overcome some of the legal, political, and bureaucratic ambiguities and limitations that still impede the agency in its daily operations. These ambiguities have led the UNHCR over recent years to assume powers beyond the scope of its original charter. They have also engendered an *ad hoc* approach to problem solving, leading to contradictions and confusions concerning the legitimate role of the UNHCR. As we enter a new century, with its spectre of refugee 'system overload', the need for a general review of the mandate, organization, and operations of the UNHCR would appear to be justified.

There is no quick fix for the future of the UNHCR but it is possible to identify several policy initiatives which the international community might take to strengthen the UNHCR's current approaches to refugee and asylum problems. A coherent action programme for the UNHCR in the future would address the following interrelated problems:

(1) well-planned and focused advocacy that more adequately spells out the responsibilities of states in providing asylum and in dealing with refugee problems;
(2) more effective co-ordination with other agencies;
(3) strong financial support; and
(4) a coherent and more accountable institutional culture and staff system.

The Need to Reverse the Erosion of Refugee Protection

There is an acute need to reverse the worldwide erosion of refugee protection. This probably can best be achieved by more proactive advocacy with states by both the UNHCR and NGOs. The global refugee problem is manageable and does not need drastic measures to be handled more effectively. As noted by a former UNHCR Director of International Protection,

Refugees have always (and by definition) entered countries illegally—often without proper documents, and with the help of traffickers. None of these acts detract from their refugee status—on the contrary, they may in fact confirm it.

Economic migration (and trafficking of migrants) is not new—and attempts by would-be migrants to use asylum channels for entry (in the absence of migration programmes) do not invalidate the asylum process.

Over 90% of refugees stay in their (developing) regions—only a very small percentage make it to Western countries. The large bulk of the refugee and asylum burden continues to be borne in the South.

A narrow interpretation of the refugee definition is applied exclusively by developed states (led by Western Europe)—those in the south are expected to (and generally do) apply a much broader definition, as in the OAU Convention. Unsuccessful asylum-seekers are not all bogus—many are victims of this restrictive interpretation.

. . . Asylum systems in Western countries are clogged up mainly from a long-term failure to invest adequate resources in prompt and fair adjudication and review processes, with the speedy recognition of those needing protection and the early return of those not qualifying. (Dennis McNamara, 'Refugees, Politics and the Press', Keynote Address to British Refugee Council, Annual General Meeting, London, 6 November 2000).

The UNHCR should take a liberal yet realistic perspective on the possibility for change. While the role of the UNHCR is significant, for the foreseeable future it seems that states will continue to guard their borders jealously and will never accept a wide-open asylum door.[27] Any new approach to refugee protection must acknowledge that states still hold the key to asylum and to finding and implementing solutions to refugee problems. By explaining the nature and extent of the global refugee problem to policy-makers, the media and press, and the public, the UNHCR could help lower the political temperature of much of the asylum and refugee debate and could focus on more realistic responses.

Some Western governments argue that the 1951 Refugee Convention has outlived its usefulness and should be radically revised but its age does not invalidate its key role in refugee protection. Watering down the UN Convention is not the answer to present problems. Neither is drawing up a list of safe countries from which no application will be accepted. If the Convention is to be reformed, changes should not aim to weaken the protection mechanism but rather to strengthen it. The priority should be to broaden the definition of refugee to recognize vicitims of civil wars, to ensure voluntary repatriation, and to formally recognize the right to seek asylum and obtain it. Since these developments are unlikely to occur—despite the professed human rights commitment of most Western states—it is essential to re-emphasize that the 1951 Convention, properly applied, remains the essential underpinning of the refugee protection system.

To date, the focus of state action has been on domestic and unilateral responses that dwell on controls to entry. Policy-makers need to turn their attention away from controls and towards the much more difficult tasks of improving their asylum adjudication systems and devising both burden sharing arrangements for refugees and new immigration programmes for migrant workers and their families.

Western states need to improve their asylum adjudication systems and quickly sift out those not entitled to the benefits of refugee status. Maintenance of a proper distinction in approach and process between migrants and forcibly displaced persons is essential to gain the confidence of all concerned. Adjudicators need to be trained and adequately funded to speed up processing. Refugees should be admitted quickly and illegal migrants who don't qualify should be returned as soon as possible. The UNHCR and NGOs should monitor these procedures to be sure they are carried out fairly and humanely.

The UNHCR can also make a case for some form of institutionalized sharing of responsibilities—for international arrangements to spread the burden of refugees among affected states. Responsibilities could be shared within the Caribbean Basin, the Mediterranean region, East and Central Europe, southern Africa, Central America, and South-East Asia. While it is important for states to meet their international responsibilities for refugees, irrespective of their countries of origin, governments could also agree to redistribute refugees on a regional or subregional basis. Thus, intergovernmental arrangements conceivably could be negotiated to promote regional consultations, which would establish minimum standards and organized sharing. The principal argument in favour of a sharing scheme is that the protection of refugees is a global problem whose solution goes beyond the capacity of any one state. When states confront problems that they cannot resolve alone, they seek to co-operate in order to realize joint gains or to avoid mutually undesirable outcomes. By reaching long-term agreements to share responsibility for all refugees likely to affect their region, individual states would not only escape unfair burdens but would also diffuse the adverse effects of the overall refugee problem over time.[28]

Currently, there is little co-operation in sharing the costs of assisting refugees and asylum-seekers. Certain states continue to receive the bulk of asylum-seekers in their region while other states receive disproportionately fewer applicants and do not share responsibility in the international refugee regime. Since most refugees remain in or near their own home countries, a few developing countries are left hosting a majority of the world's refugees, often under extremely difficult conditions. The present imbalance in the international distribution of refugees is also evident in the developed countries. In Europe, for example, Germany received well over 50 per cent of the region's asylum-seekers for many years. Consequently some European states have been able to shirk their responsibilities. International co-operation and collective action through resettlement sharing would benefit both states and refugees. For states, it would introduce clarity, consistency, and lower transaction costs, and 'the equivalent of an insurance against any one state becoming sole host to a massive inflow of asylum seekers'.[29] For refugees, resettlement sharing could conceivably introduce more certainty and more reliable assistance and protection, provided that the scheme is based on international legal standards of refugee rights and not on restrictive interpretation of these standards.

In addition to new sharing arrangements for refugees, many of the responses that states may make will be facilitated if governments, particularly Western European states, expand existing immigration programmes, guest worker arrangements, and migration quotas to relieve pressures on already overburdened asylum systems. It is increasingly evident that most industrialized countries have low birthrates and rapidly ageing populations and many may have to import labour in the future anyway. Greater efforts should also be made to integrate immigrants. In the absence of increased immigration programmes, hopeful migrants will continue to try the asylum route as the only way into Western countries. And without offering a path to citizenship for newcomers, immigrants become marginalized, creating the potential for racial tension and social conflict.

The UNHCR also has an important role to play in convincing states that it is in their own national interests to find satisfactory solutions to refugee problems. The task ahead is formidable, particularly at a time when political leaders are reluctant to take positions that they feel might expose them to electoral risks. Being the international 'watch dog' on asylum and balancing the protection needs of refugees with the legitimate concerns of states requires courage and a willingness to confront governments when necessary. As the guardian of international refugee norms, the UNHCR has a role to play in reminding liberal democracies of their own identity as promoters of international human rights.

Refugee and human rights norms enjoy a special status among Western states because they help define the identities of liberal states.[30] They are also important to non-Western states because adherence to these norms constitutes a crucial sign to others of their membership in the international community of law-abiding states. Most states are not proud of practices and policies that contradict international refugee norms. The most powerful, liberal democratic states are particularly sensitive to the criticism they have received for not providing the leadership role on these humanitarian principles. Political leaders are floundering in their search for effective responses to refugee movements and are looking for intellectual and political leadership and guidance on this policy issue. The UNHCR and other refugee rights advocates have a unique opportunity to insert human rights ideas into the contemporary policy debate about refugees. The UNHCR needs to help states transform their perceptions of their national interests and alter their calculations of the costs and benefits of their refugee and asylum policies. While individual governments may feel uncomfortable being criticized, the UNHCR will gain greater respect in the long term for speaking up for refugee protection principles than remaining silent.

The UNHCR needs to develop a well-considered and consistent policy on refugee advocacy. Presently, the extent to which agency officials engage in attempts to criticize and pressure governments depends more on personalities and individual initiatives than on Office-wide policies. The role and example of the High Commissioner is key. If the High Commissioner chooses to utilize the moral authority and prestige of the Office, it sets a positive tone and example for the entire agency. While public statements and pressures may prove ineffective in the short term in bringing about improvements for refugees, persistent and well-founded advocacy may well achieve desired change in the long term.[31] A proactive protection policy has the added benefit of contributing to the UNHCR's reputation for integrity which is vital to its long term influence.

The Need for a Broader, More Effective Co-ordinated International Response

If the international community wants to resolve future refugee problems, it must develop a policy action agenda that extends beyond humanitarian action into broader policy realms that address the problems that generate forced migrants. This is not a task for the UNHCR. Indeed, in its recent efforts to contribute to peacekeeping and peace enforcement missions in internal conflicts and to reintegration and post-conflict reconstruction, the UNHCR has assumed responsibilities that more rightly belong to other agencies and actors. The Office has raised expectations that it cannot possibly hope to fulfil. In the future, responses to forced migration cannot proceed solely within the mandate of international humanitarian organizations, such as the UNHCR. These tasks will inevitably involve greater government support not only for the traditional international refugee and relief organizations and also political and financial backing for more active involvement of international development agencies, human rights networks, and peacekeeping and conflict resolution mechanisms in global and regional refugee matters.

One of the greatest challenges confronting the international community in the years to come will be to link the task of refugee protection to the broader defence of human rights. Political realism demands that higher priority be given to combating human rights violations because of their propensity to cause regional and international instability and hence refugee movements. This will require incorporating, in current re-evaluations of state security doctrine, greater international attention to human rights violations. It should also include the development of foreign policy tools and mechanisms aimed at the prevention and reversal of forced migration.

During the 1990s, the international community has begun—albeit haltingly—the process of establishing the principle that policies of forced expulsion are unacceptable, and of routinizing the pressures and sanctions against such policies. Refugee movements are perhaps the clearest example of the principle that 'once the consequences of a policy enacted for domestic purposes become external, the policy itself is open to international comment and action, with proclamations of "sovereign rights" being no defense against outside interference'.[32] As summarized in the words of Myron Weiner, 'A country that forces its citizens to leave or creates conditions which induce them to leave has internationalized its internal actions. . . . If a people violate the boundaries of a neighboring country, then they and their government should expect others to intervene in their internal affairs.'[33]

This connection is not simply an accidental one in which humanitarian intervention is fortuitously justified by the presence of refugees. The link is organic, in that 'refugees are human rights violations made visible', in the words of a former US Co-ordinator of Refugee Affairs.[34] Refugees also serve as an index of internal disorder and as *prima facie* evidence of the violation of human rights and humanitarian standards. No other issue, perhaps, provides such a clear and unassailable link between humanitarian concerns and legitimate international security issues. This suggests the necessity of establishing a framework of general principles to guide the international community in deciding when, because of its potential to involve other states, a domestic human rights situation warrants action by the Security Council or by regional organizations.

International security also depends on protecting minorities and displaced people threatened by communal violence, protecting the delivery of humanitarian relief and of humanitarian personnel, monitoring human rights violations, overseeing cease-fire and demobilization agreements after civil wars, building civil and legal institutions, and enforcing sanctions. An international police force is also needed to demilitarize refugee camps, to separate military from civilian populations in camps, to control the distribution of aid in these situations, and to protect international aid personnel. The UN needs to replace its makeshift arrangements for providing security for its staff with more predictable and robust mechanisms. The UNHCR's shortcomings in responding to the Kosovo exodus also highlight the need for the international community to have in place an efficient and effective rapid response system when faced with an emergency refugee crisis.

If the international community hopes to respond more effectively to the global problem of refugees and internal displacement, it must also strengthen the UN's capacity to monitor developments in human rights issues and to intercede on behalf of forced migrants. Governments must guarantee a meaningful funding base to the specialized human rights bodies of the UN and withdraw the financial and political constraints on human rights action.

The creation of the Office of the UN High Commissioner for Human Rights in 1993 brought higher profile to human rights within the UN system and stepped up the monitoring of protection concerns in major crises.[35] There has also been an increase in the presence of the UN Human Rights Office staff in the field and increased activities by special rapporteurs appointed by the UN Human Rights Commission to document human rights violations in certain countries and to report back to the Commission. A key to strengthening UN capacity to monitor human rights in the future is enhancing its capacity to undertake a protection role in the field. Nevertheless, as in the past, major weaknesses continue to exist in the UN human rights system. Countries can and often do stonewall any new initiatives by refusing entry to human rights officials and monitors. And despite considerable improvements, inter-agency co-ordination and the institutional division of labour regarding human rights within the UN remain problematic.

UN member states should also support the newly created permanent international criminal tribunal. Such a mechanism is a potentially extremely important and effective innovation in situations where there have been intrastate conflict, genocide, human rights abuses, and forcible displacement. Institutions and individuals who are responsible for the human rights abuses that provoke forced population displacements must know they cannot act with impunity. An international tribunal could create consistent expectations of accountability for violations of human rights. As such, it would serve as a deterrent as well as a vehicle for reconciliation in societies torn apart by violent conflict.

Until that time when the capacity of the UN human rights regime is fully developed, NGOs—especially human rights NGOs—will have to assume a larger share of responsibility for ensuring the protection of forcibly displaced people. Protection of refugees and other displaced people requires a readiness on the part of human rights agencies to act on observed human rights abuses. In order to accomplish this, human rights NGOs need to establish a continuous presence in regions experiencing conflict.[36] NGOs provide a basis for consciousness-raising regarding humanitarian norms and democratic principles within regions, and they could enable local organizations to assume responsibility for monitoring, intervening, and managing humanitarian programmes without major external involvement. Human rights organizations, like Human Rights Watch and Amnesty International, fill some of this gap. Yet most of these organizations have their headquarters in the West, where their constituency base and funding are the strongest. There is an urgent need to support NGO efforts to train and place independent human rights monitors in regions where they can provide liaison with local organizations interested in the problem, and to assess the protection needs of refugees, asylum-seekers, and the internally displaced. These Refugee Watch organizations could record and publicize human rights violations without jeopardizing operational relief agency services. UN agencies could also contribute to this development through programmes aimed at strengthening the capacity of NGOs to work in the human rights field.

Relief NGOs, likewise, have an essential protection role to play. Many NGOs today are far more willing and able to address protection issues than they have been in the past. Their presence in most civil war situations makes them important sources of information which is crucial for human rights monitoring, early warning of conflicts and refugee crises, and preventive diplomacy. Humanitarian organizations that operate in conflict situations should institutionalize procedures to manage and report information on human rights abuses by their own personnel in the field. Efforts should also be made to improve both the channels of communication and the readiness to act on human rights information at high political levels. At a minimum, NGOs, with the assistance of UN agencies, should train their staff regarding human rights principles and protection techniques to be used in the field.

Moreover, because NGOs have a central role in securing access to the civilian victims of conflicts and are often in close contact with both governments and opposition movements, they can play a significant role in conflict resolution. As a result of working with disenfranchised populations, NGOs are also often able to gain an understanding of the underlying tensions causing the conflict. Such information is crucial to conflict resolution processes, particularly in societies where on-going human rights violations have become part of the spectrum of issues to be resolved in any comprehensive settlement. NGOs' presence within communities at war and their ability to move among civilian populations and armed forces are characteristics not shared by UN agencies and donor governments. Thus, NGOs are well placed to engage in a new comprehensive form of humanitarian action, encompassing assistance and protection, mediation, and conflict resolution.[37]

In countries where central government itself is weak or non-existent and therefore unable to protect its citizens, the key issue will be not only how to bring together contending groups but how to build institutions of governance. In such situations, economic development and social stability are inseparable. Rehabilitative relief and development activities must be accompanied by support for civil society[38] in order to be effective. Sustainable progress can only be achieved if built on a strong civil foundation that allows the gains made to be consolidated throughout society. Without this foundation, relief and development activities will constitute a one-time consumption of resources that will result in little long-term change. The development of civil society is also related to the avoidance of violence. Violent political conflict generally can be avoided only in a context in which the citizenry is able to participate meaningfully in the political decisions that affect their lives by holding the persons and institutions that exercise power over them accountable for their actions.[39] Finally, local communities need to be encouraged to develop their own religious, cultural, and institutional means to ensure security and to prevent the resurgence of conflict.[40]

In the future, there will have to be a growing focus on co-operation at the international and local levels, particularly in achieving peace and greater security, without which there will be no end to refugee movements. Future threats to national and regional stability will essentially be transnational in nature and will not be countered solely by unilateral or international action. Advocacy programmes that promote the cause of refugees and asylum-seekers at the local level and mobilize public support for these groups can have a very immediate impact on the world's displaced. The strengthening of democratic institutions and civil society are among the major preventive actions against future conflict and refugee migration.

The supply of small arms and anti-personnel mines to all sides in intrastate conflicts will continue to play a major role in the formation of refugee migration. As long as small arms are widely available, conflicts will continue to be protracted and cause mass displacement. International attention needs to focus on reducing the level of violence associated with future conflicts by the imposition of limits on the level and kinds of weapons that are readably available. Many developing countries, however, continue to divert limited resources from development to buy arms, which is stimulating an increase in the multibillion dollar arms trade, particularly in small arms and other light weapons. It will be difficult to control small weapons trade because of the surplus stocks of such weapons dating from the Cold War, the large numbers of producers of small arms, the existence and growth of black market channels, and the difficulties of monitoring and controlling the transport and sales of these goods. Nevertheless, the international community should try to control future arms trade. It should also explore other possibilities to control the transfer of small weaponry, such as supporting regional organizations in efforts to enforce embargoes on weapons trade in areas of conflict.

A Comprehensive Approach

The current refugee regime has a number of important gaps in institutional mandates, with the result that entire groups of forced migrants are neglected. The international response to forced migration can no longer be run on the basis of existing rules and institutions that are too fragmented and outdated in the face of a host of new challenges. A high priority should be given to closing the gaps in the sequence, and coverage in protection and assistance to forcibly displaced persons.

The problem of internal displacement and the plight of war-affected populations will undoubtedly acquire increasing humanitarian and strategic importance for the international community. Given the continuing intrastate violence in many parts of the world, coupled with the growing readiness of states to close their doors to asylum-seekers, the number of people forcibly displaced and trapped within their own countries can only be expected to increase. In addition to the problem of refugees, more attention will have to be given to the question of how to provide in-country protection and assistance to IDPs. More resources and international political attention should also be given to post-conflict situations. Despite a virtually universal consensus that peace agreements must be consolidated by investments that improve the security and economic well-being of the former adversaries and victims of conflict, it is still the case that too little funding is invested in post-conflict rebuilding. International funding invariably declines soon after cease-fires are in place and elections are held. Moreover, the assistance given to countries emerging from war is conditioned in ways that emergency relief funds are not, with major impacts on humanitarian and social initiatives. In the future, greater resources must be devoted over longer periods of time to catalyse sustainable forms of development and to create conditions that will prevent refugee movements from re-occurring.[41]

In order for the humanitarian agencies to achieve these objectives either the various agencies will have to consolidate into a super humanitarian agency or they will have to collaborate and co-ordinate more closely. Given the institutional resistance to consolidation, humanitarian organizations, including the UNHCR, are going to have to develop better mechanisms for co-ordination themselves and undertake internal reforms to overcome cultural impediments to co-operation. The UNHCR should co-operate more closely with the UN Inter-Agency Standing Committee, the UN Office for the

374 Towards the Future

Co-ordination of Humanitarian Affairs, and the Resident/Humanitarian Co-ordinator in countries where there are emergency relief programmes. It also needs to promote support for the international refugee protection system through closer collaboration with other agencies such as the Office of the UN High Commissioner for Human Rights. However, even with the best will of the UNHCR and other agencies, international co-ordination will not be easy or smooth. There is a need to develop a model of co-operation that incorporates the designation of specific roles and co-ordination among humanitarian agencies.

A Renewed, More Effective UNHCR

A key challenge for the UNHCR will be to maintain a core mission and identity in the face of changing world politics. The Office will be faced with increasing opportunities and pressures to become engaged in in-country protection and assistance programmes involving developmental and peace-building objectives that could risk further compromising the Office's core refugee protection mandate. While upholding core principles and instruments, the Office must, at the same time, be innovative and imaginative in order to be effective in responding to a rapidly moving international environment.

International organizations need to keep pace with the changes around them. Their ability to learn and adapt sets the general course of institutional growth and evolution and pushes the organization towards improved performance. Above all else, the UNHCR needs to become aware of the organizational cultural dynamics and values that influence the agency's behaviour and actions. By taking active steps to modify its organizational culture, the UNHCR will become a more effective and reinvigorated humanitarian organization with the capacity to approach refugee protection with a clearer perspective and in a more realistic and deliberate manner.

One of the UNHCR's strengths is that it fulfils a legitimation function in global politics. International order is founded not only on a stable balance of power among states but also on a set of shared norms or legitimation principles.[42] As the guardian of international refugee norms, the UNHCR, must be seen to promote and uphold these norms. Unlike politicians who are held accountable during elections or private sector organizations for which the market place is the ultimate evaluator, there is very little external scrutiny of the UNHCR. The legitimacy of the UNHCR is badly weakened by its secretiveness and its inconsistent policies on disclosure about operational failures and shortcomings. The Office must be held accountable when it acts in a self-interested or expedient manner, abuses its position, or does not live up to its principles. Kofi Annan set an important precedent for UN agencies by commissioning independent, critical reports of the UN failures in the Srebrenica massacre and the Rwanda genocide. However, despite the gravity of the mistakes made by the UN, including by Kofi Annan himself, no individuals were held directly responsible. No officials resigned on a matter of principle. Without individual accountability, real improvements in future behaviour and performance are unlikely to happen. There is a need for an institutionalized, countervailing force that can pressure the UNHCR to honour its norms and more effectively carry out its mandate. An external ombudsman for the UNHCR should be established and annual external protection and management audits should be undertaken of the UNHCR's activities so that the Office will have to account publicly for policy failures resulting in risk to refugees. Greater transparency and openness to external scrutiny would do much to strengthen the UNHCR's legitimacy and restore the High Commissioner's authority to deal with states and NGOs. The UNHCR also needs to learn from past mistakes and failures. An independent external evaluation mechanism should be established. The regular publication of externally conducted and independent evaluations of the agency's programmes would foster open discussion and follow-up of the findings and recommendations of these reports. The UNHCR must also generate and channel information and policy analysis to senior management more effectively than it has in the past. Not only must research analyse how changes in the international environment affect refugee movements but it should also examine the implication of changing international events and refugee situations on the UNHCR and its programmes. Given the Office's limited intellectual and research resources, any High Commissioner must draw upon external research to receive the kind of input needed to make well-informed policy decisions.

The UNHCR must necessarily develop closer relations with external research communities. This requires opening up the organization to outside expertise through creating new opportunities for short-term assignments in UNHCR for external researchers and for a greatly expanded exchange and sabbatical programme in outside research centres and universities for UNHCR staff. Such changes would more than pay for themselves in the resulting overall improved efficacy and strategic thinking of the organization. At present, there is too little interaction between the UNHCR, UN agencies and NGOs. The Office needs to establish an institutionalized framework with other agencies within which information and evaluations can be exchanged. Finally, ways should be found to include refugees themselves, who are, after all, the UNHCR's principal clients, in the external review process from the start. There should be increased emphasis on freedom of the refugees to choose the solution—repatriation, local integration, or third country resettlement—that best suits their needs, with the UNHCR acting to ensure implementation of that choice.[43] The UNHCR should adopt the practice of listening and taking in the views of others and not just pronouncing its own positions and opinions.

The Executive Committee (Excom) of the UNHCR, consisting of many of the donor and host governments, and combining many different interests and perspectives on the world, does not now effectively shape UNHCR policy.[44] The current Executive and Standing Committees are large and cumbersome bodies. Committee members include those who have not signed the international refugee instruments or are themselves the cause of refugee flows. This sometimes results in discussions getting waylaid by national interests and makes it increasingly difficult to achieve consensus.[45] Not only are there too many participants but the issues are complex and numerous and meetings are not really a forum for organizational guidance. Individual donor governments and some key host states—not Excom— establish the priorities that guide the UNHCR's programme direction.

Excom member states and the UNHCR need to streamline the agency's governance arrangements by making Excom a more assertive advisory body with serious oversight functions and a capacity for organizational guidance. As states scrutinize the UNHCR, they need also to become more self-critical of their own roles in refugee protection and assistance. Excom should reaffirm the core principles of refugee protection through the work of its standing committees, and member states should not undermine the UNHCR by adopting policies that violate the international refugee norms and set undesirable precedents for refugee protection elsewhere. An independent monitoring mechanism or ombudsman should be established to provide oversight of state activities in refugee protection and assistance. In addition to monitoring the critical area of refugee protection, this new oversight unit should critically assess donor governments' increasing tendency to earmark their contributions to the UNHCR for particular programmes and geographical areas. It also should stimulate a debate about the need for a regular UNHCR budget to overcome some of the problems attending the uncertainty of financial contributions and to enable the Office to plan ahead. There needs to be more predictability of UNHCR budgetary resources through such mechanisms as contributions negotiated for longer time-periods than one year and more equitable burden-sharing.

A key issue for the UNHCR is to raise the protection profile of the agency. While relief operations provide for the physical security of refugees and give UNHCR staff a presence with which to monitor protection developments in the field, material assistance operations must not dominate the Agency's policies to such an extent that traditional protection of refugees and asylum-seekers is undermined. Protection issues do not figure consistently as a real priority in the UNHCR's management culture. Currently the role of the Department of International Protection (DIP) on operational issues is marginal and the Director of Protection has no independent authority to act, even on the most pressing protection crises. UNHCR staff now see job experience in operations, not in protection, as the way to advance their careers and ensure regular promotions. The sidelining of protection within the Office not only damages the traditional protection ethos of the organization but also severely limits the staff expertise needed to pursue a vigorous protection policy. The most significant step that the High Commissioner could take to redress this imbalance between protection and operations would be to restore a close link between DIP and field operations with an oversight capacity and authority for the Director of Protection. At the same time, operations managers should be held accountable for shortcomings and failures in protection activities as for assistance. Without adequate authority given to DIP and the necessary priority given to protection issues, the UNHCR will be unable to ensure consistency in its approach to the worldwide protection of refugees.

The DIP not only needs to be given greater authority but it also needs the essential human resources to upgrade the role of protection. Adequate resources are required for the comprehensive protection training of UNHCR staff at all levels, and particularly at the management level. Although progress has been achieved in recent years to improve professional development, the Office needs to ensure that all staff receive regular training of all kinds. Recent humanitarian emergencies in Kosovo and elsewhere have revealed a serious shortage of senior staff capable of assuming leadership roles on short notice. A future priority should be that heads of missions be trained on how to handle emergencies.

Since 1986 the UNHCR has undergone several restructuring exercises in an effort to break the cycle of organizational dysfunction and improve the efficacy of the Office. However, these efforts have demonstrated that structural re-engineering alone will not solve the problems. The UNHCR needs to direct its attention to changing institutional behaviour and culture. Policies that focus on stimulating staff and rewarding openness and innovation are likely to produce more durable benefits.

Most importantly, the UNHCR should make performance a central part of its organizational culture and take steps to ensure that staff are held accountable on the basis of their performance. This means that personnel would be recruited and selected on the basis of their potential for performance and that the UNHCR would invest heavily in its employees through performance-driven training and career development. Changes in the way staff are recruited, hired, and promoted would improve morale at both headquarters and in the field.

One of the most important changes that could be made is in the selection process of the High Commissioner. Presently, the High Commissioner is hand picked by the UN Secretary-General after close consultation with governments and then presented to the UN General Assembly for approval. The selection is done in secret in a completely undemocratic, non-transparent process. The High Commissioner's post is not advertised. There is no job description, no indication of the skills and experience required of the successful candidate, and no mission statement. There is no public scrutiny of the candidates and no open debate about the kinds of personal and professional qualifications needed for this very demanding job. Typically, each new High Commissioner is selected by the most powerful governments in the world in 'consultation' with the Secretary-General. Governments veto certain candidates either because they are not nationals of a major UNHCR donor country or don't speak French or for some other political precondition. The successful candidate who emerges from this arcane procedure is often an 'acceptable compromise' rather than the best-qualified and most dynamic leader. Frequently in the past the High Commissioner has been a national of a key donor state—a Nordic country, Switzerland, or Japan—with the post of Deputy High Commissioner reserved for a US national. Oftentimes the new High Commissioner is indebted to major government supporters and therefore starts the job with a lack of legitimacy and autonomy.

The selection process needs to be revamped and made more rigorous and professional. The post of High Commissioner is a particularly demanding job that requires exceptional qualities on the part of the successful candidate—diplomatic skills, fund-raising abilities, and the capacity to manage and lead a large and complex international organization. Above all, the candidate should be a highly motivated individual with an unwavering commitment to the protection of refugees. Candidates should be measured against these and other criteria and objectives in an open and transparent process. Governments should not impose any political preconditions or exercise a veto on any candidate. The independence, prestige, and authority of the UNHCR will be best assured if the General Assembly selects the High Commissioner in an open election rather than consigning the choice to the Secretary-General. The adoption of a new selection procedure would inspire greater confidence in the UNHCR at a time when the agency requires exceptional leadership.

The UNHCR should also give high priority to the retention of personnel and investment in their experience. In the past, the Office had a tradition of senior staff training entry-level personnel in the field. Staff members were socialized over a period of years into the norms and workings of the organization. With the rapid disappearance of senior staff, apprentice learning has all but disappeared within the UNHCR. Such experience cannot be substituted by offering more training courses. Every effort should be made to preserve the extraordinary human qualities that made training unique within the UNHCR. In order to accomplish this, the UNHCR must adopt measures to retain a greater proportion of its staff, particular at middle and senior levels. First of all, security needs to be improved, working conditions need to be humanized and psychological support provided where needed. The UNHCR, with the backing of the UN, needs to adopt measures to ensure the physical security of staff working in dangerous and insecure environments. While there may be good reasons to continue to regularly rotate staff, allowances need to be made for personal circumstances and family considerations. Psychological problems resulting from work in emergency situations, such as stress, physical exhaustion, or sexual or physical harassment, should be given special attention. The UNHCR also should give staff more opportunities to voice their dissent and frustrations, and to offer suggestions about how to improve policies and programmes. Such measures will considerably improve morale and give personnel more a sense of working for an organization that cares about their welfare.

Finally, at times the Office lacks a well-focused self-identity and is confused about the role it plays in the international system. The UNHCR sometimes acts as if it were independent—almost like the ICRC—with little connection to the other parts of the UN system. At other times, it works alongside UN peacekeeping and peace enforcement troops and other UN agencies as part of a broad UN-led effort. The Office's overall mission combines international protection and seeking durable solutions with an expanded mandate centred on 'persons of concern to UNHCR'. However, the limits to the UNHCR's practical work are not clear. Increasingly the organization has taken on more general humanitarian and development assistance tasks and expanded the roster of its clients to include many different kinds of forced migrants. Not only is it questionable whether the UNHCR has the necessary resources or expertise to take on such a broad range of activities, but the ambitious but ambiguous nature of its expanded mandate and programmes leads to confusion and loss of autonomy, particularly when there have been so few clear policy statements about its overall responsibilities.

A key to making its institutional structure stronger and more unified is to identify a particular niche for the Office in humanitarian affairs. One of the UNHCR's strengths is its clear original mandate. Only the UNHCR has the legitimacy from its Charter to protect refugees and to promote solutions to refugee problems. Because of this, the Office is indispensable and deserves the fullest support of governments. But the UNHCR loses authority and autonomy when it steps outside of its mandate to take on tasks that other agencies or governments do better. The advantage of reaffirming and clarifying its original protection mission would be to convey to personnel what is important and to provide them with a sense of overall purpose. A distinctive niche would also provide the external public with a strong message about the UNHCR commitment and focus and would build up trust and confidence in the authority of the organization.

The UNHCR is not a static organization but has constantly changed and evolved over the past 50 years. The Office must seize the opportunities to break the cycle of organizational dysfunction and to improve its efficacy. It is far better for the UNHCR to initiate these changes than for radical transformation to be imposed from outside.

Refugees and the Promotion of Open Societies

During the past fifty years, a central tenant of open societies and liberal democracies has been the moral imperative to preserve the right to escape persecution and violence and to seek asylum. The UNHCR and international refugee law were created with these principles in mind. There may be greater overlap of state interest and respect for the principles of refugee law and protection than is the current perception of most governments today. It is simply not possible in an age of globalization to wall out the world's dispossessed. Placing unduly harsh restrictions on the movement of people will simply lead to greater isolation and deprivation and pose yet new threats to regional and international security. It is also the case that if states remain indifferent to the plight of the world's refugees, the social and political fibre of their own societies will suffer. The way states deal with refugees speaks volumes about their human rights health and their tolerance for ethnic and racial minorities.

Sustainable solutions to refugee problems can only be achieved if built on a strong civil foundation. Without this foundation, humanitarian policies will result in little long-term change and will provide no guarantee that refugee movements will not reoccur. Thus, how states respond to refugees, and how refugee policies develop and are implemented by the UNHCR, matter greatly because both are essential to the preservation and functioning of open societies around the globe and to international security in the twenty-first century.

NOTES

1. UNHCR, *UNHCR Global Report 1999* (Geneva: UNHCR, 2000): 32.
2. Ibid: 33.
3. Ibid: 32.
4. 'The 1951 United Nations Convention Relating to the Status of Refugees', *United Nations Treaty*, 184/2545 (July 28, 1951): 137.
5. Guy Goodwin-Gill, 'Non-refoulement and the New Asylum Seekers', in David Martin, ed., *The New Asylum Seekers: Refugee Law in the 1980s* (Dordrecht: Martinus Nijhoff, 1988), 103–22.
6. John Scratch, 'Closing the Back Door. The Limits of Unilateral Action'. Paper for

workshop 'Alternative futures: Developing an Agenda for Legal Research on Asylum', Oxford, Refugee Studies Centre, 1–3 June 2000.

7. Mark Walkup, 'Policy and Behavior in Humanitarian Organizations: The Institutional Origins of Operational Dysfunction'. Ph.D. dissertation, University of Florida (1997).

8. For a critique of UNHCR's operation in Kosovo, including its neglect of the internally displaced there during the conflict, see United Kingdom, House of Commons, International Development Committee, 'Kosovo: The Humanitarian Crisis' (15 May 1999).

9. UN Secretary-General's Report to the General Assembly, July 1997 (A/51/950, para. 186).

10. UN Doc. E/CN/1998/50, 1998. UN Resolution 1998/50.

11. UNHCR, 'Internally Displaced Persons: The Role of the United Nations High Commissioner for Refugees' (Geneva: UNHCR, 6 March 2000).

12. Boutros Boutros-Ghali, *Agenda for Development* (New York, NY: United Nations, 1994).

13. Internal information note on the round table discussion on the gap between humanitarian assistance and long-term development, UNHCR, Geneva, January 1999. Cited in Jeff Crisp, 'Mind the Gap! UNHCR, Humanitarian Assistance and the Development Process', *International Migration Review* (forthcoming).

14. During the 1990s, the UNHCR strengthened its emergency management capacity, increased its training programmes for staff, updated its handbooks on standards in emergency response and protection of refugees, and made initial attempts to improve its policy analysis and evaluation capacities.

15. While the UNHCR had in recent years set up an Academic Advisory Committee as a vehicle for increasing interaction with external researchers on some of these issues, this group met too infrequently and irregularly to be of much use. Too often, the meetings were occasions for the UNHCR to make presentations about policy developments rather than opportunities for the Office to listen to and learn from external researchers. Perhaps the most useful function of this interaction with academics has been the external input provided to the UNHCR's *State of the World's Refugees*. Even here little serious dialogue has occurred between academics and the UNHCR's policy-makers.

16. Article 101 of the UN Charter stipulates that 'the paramount consideration in the employment of staff and in the determination of the conditions of service shall be the necessity of securing the highest standards of efficiency, competence, and integrity'. But the same article also stipulates: 'Due regard shall be paid to the importance of recruiting the staff from as wide a geographical distribution basis as possible.' More often than should be the case, efficiency has given way to geographical balance in the UNHCR's hiring and promotion practices.

17. This point is also made by Randolph Kent, *Anatomy of Disaster Relief* (London: Pinter Publishers, 1987): 151. Cited in Mark Walkup, 'Policy Dysfunction in Humanitarian Organizations: The Role of Coping Strategies, Institutions, and Organizational Culture', *Journal of Refugee Studies*, 10/1 (1997): 37–60.

18. Walkup, 'Policy Dysfunction in Humanitarian Organizations': 43.

19. The rotation policy is based on the assumption that UNHCR personnel need to be generalists and not specialists, particularly in responding to refugee emergencies.

Other UN agencies are moving away from cultivating a cadre of generalists to hiring people with specialized skills.

20. Interview with Irene Kahn, UNHCR, Geneva, March 2000.

21. Ibid. On training see Susan Martin, 'Forced Migration and Professionalism', *International Migration Review*, Special UNHCR 50th Anniversary issue (forthcoming).

22. This is true even for staff with several years' experience with UNHCR. Interview with Mark Cutts, UNHCR, Geneva, March 2000.

23. This point has been made in terms of international organizations generally by Michael Barnett, 'Bringing in the New World Order: Liberalism, Legitimacy and the United Nations', *World Politics*, 49 (July 1997): 526–51.

24. Philip Gourevitch, *We Wish to Inform You That Tomorrow We Will Be Killed with Our Families: Stories from Rwanda* (New York, NY: Farrar, Straus, Giroux, 1998). See also: Joel Boutroue, *Missed Opportunities: The Role of the International Community in the Return of the Rwanda Refugees from Eastern Zaire*. Rosemary Rogers Working Paper 1 (Cambridge, MA: MIT Inter-university Committee on International Migration, June 1998); Gerard Prunier, 'The Great Lakes Crisis', *Current History*, 96 (May 1997): 193–9; and Ian Martin, 'Hard Choices after Genocide: Human Rights and Political Failures in Rwanda', in Jonathan Moore, ed., *Hard Choices: Moral Dilemmas in Humanitarian Intervention* (Lanham, MA: Rowman & Littlefield Publishers, 1998): 157–76.

25. This shift in focus within the UNHCR to humanitarian action is reflected in the subtitles of the last two editions of the UNHCR's *The State Of the World's Refugees*: 'A Humanitarian Agenda' and 'Fifty Years of Humanitarian Action'.

26. David Rieff, *Slaughterhouse: Bosnia and the Failure of the West*, (New York, NY: Simon and Schuster, 1995) and Michael Ignatieff, *The Warrior's Honor: Ethnic War and the Modern Conscience* (New York, NY: Henry Holt and Company, 1997).

27. Julie Mertus, 'The State and the Post-Cold War Refugee Regime: New Models, New Questions', *International Journal of Refugee Law*, 10/3 (1998): 321–48.

28. A major effort to develop possibilities for burden-sharing has been carried out by James Hathaway of the University of Michigan law school. See: James Hathaway, ed., *Re-conceiving International Refugee Law* (The Hague: Martinus Nijhof, 1997).

29. For fuller development of the limitations and potential gains of international burden-sharing regarding refugees see: Astri Suhrke, 'Burden-sharing During Refugee Emergencies: The Logic of Collective versus National Action', *Journal of Refugee Studies*, 11/4 (1998): 396–415.

30. Thomas Risse, Stephen Ropp, and Kathryn Sikkink, eds., *The Power of Human Rights: International Norms and Domestic Change* (Cambridge: Cambridge University Press, 1999); and Margaret Keck and Kathryn Sikkink, *Activists Beyond Borders: Advocacy Networks in International Politics* (Ithaca, NY: Cornell University Press, 1998).

31. David Forsythe, *Human Rights in International Relations* (Cambridge: Cambridge University Press, 2000).

32. John Chipman, 'The Future of Strategic Studies: Beyond Even Grand Strategy', *Survival*, 34/1(Spring 1992): 112.

33. Myron Weiner, ed., *International Migration and Security* (Boulder, CO: Westview Press, 1993): 25–6.

34. Jonathan Moore, 'Refugees and Foreign Policy: Immediate Needs and Durable Solutions', Lecture at Harvard University (6 April 1987).

35. As part of a UN-wide effort to give a higher priority to the integration of human rights into the various activities and programmes of the UN, the High Commissioner is now a member of the four Executive Committees which orchestrate the UN's work in humanitarian affairs, peace and security, economic and social affairs, and development.

36. Diane Paul, *Beyond Monitoring and Reporting: The Field-level Protection of Civilians Under Threat* (New York, NY: Jacob Blaustein Institute for the Advancement of Human Rights and the Center for the Study of Societies in Crisis, 2000).

37. Kimberly Maynard, *Healing Communities in Conflict: International Assistance in Complex Emergencies* (New York, NY: Columbia University Press, 1999).

38. 'Civil Society' refers to non-state community-based groups, such as religious associations, advocacy groups focusing on human rights, democracy or the environment, civic associations, business and professional associations, labour unions, women's groups, co-operatives, academic institutions, and student groups.

39. Jochen Hippler, *The Democratisation of Disempowerment: The Problem of Democracy in the Third World* (London: Pluto Press, 1995) and Marc Howard Ross, *The Management of Conflict: Interpretations and Interests in Comparative Perspective* (New Haven, CT: Yale University Press, 1993).

40. Paul Richards, *Fighting for the Rain Forest: War, Youth and Resources in Sierra Leone* (Oxford: James Currey, 1996). Richards makes a number of suggestions regarding the mobilization of local institutions and means to deal with conflict including 'smart relief', more creative use of the local radio, and greater involvement of local communities in analysing why conflicts occur and how they can be prevented.

41. Patricia Weiss-Fagen, *Peace Making as Rebuilding War Torn Societies*, War Torn Societies Project (Geneva: UNRISD, 1996).

42. Barnett, 'Bringing in the New World Order'; Martha Finnemore, 'Constructing Norms of Humanitarian Intervention', in Peter Katzenstein, ed., *The Culture of National Security: Norms and Identities in World Politics* (New York, NY: Columbia University Press, 1996).

43. This is a recommendation of 'The UNHCR Note on International Protection You Won't See', *International Journal of Refugee Law*, 9/2 (1997): 267–73.

44. United Kingdom Department for International Development, 'United Nations High Commissioner for Refugees: Interim Strategy Paper', (London: Department for International Development, June 2000).

45. An example of the politicization of Excom took place in October 1997 when the Democratic Republic of Congo accused the UNHCR of enticing refugees out of Rwanda and of starving thousands of them to death. This caused the Director of Protection to heavily criticize governments for their lack of support for UNHCR and for undermining refugee norms across the world. Dennis McNamara, 'The Future of Protection and the Responsibility of the State', (statement to the 48th Session of the UNHCR Executive Committee, 16 October 1997), in *International Journal of Refugee Law*, 10/1/2 (1998): 230–5.

BIBLIOGRAPHY

Manuscript Collections

Acheson, Dean. Papers. Harry S. Truman Library, Independence, Missouri.
British Public Records Office. Foreign Office Files, London.
Betts, T. F. Papers. Refugee Studies Centre, University of Oxford, Oxford.
Cabinet Collection. Dwight D. Eisenhower Library, Abilene, Kansas.
Cambodia Crisis Center. Papers. University of Notre Dame, South Bend, Indiana.
Dulles, Allen. Papers. Seeley G. Mudd Library, Princeton University, Princeton, New Jersey.
Dulles, John Foster. Papers. Dwight D. Eisenhower Library, Abilene, Kansas.
—— Papers. Seeley G. Mudd Library, Princeton University, Princeton, New Jersey.
Eisenhower, Dwight D. Papers. Dwight D. Eisenhower Library, Abilene, Kansas.
Hulten, Charles. Papers. Harry S. Truman Library, Independence, Missouri.
International Collection. Dwight D. Eisenhower Library, Abilene, Kansas.
International Organization for Migration, Archives, Geneva.
International Rescue Committee. Citizens' Commission for Indochinese Refugees Collected Papers, New York.
Jackson, C. D. Papers. Dwight D. Eisenhower Library, Abilene, Kansas.
Kennedy, John F. National Security Files. John F. Kennedy Library, Boston, MA, Massachussets.
Kennedy, John F. President's Office Files. John F. Kennedy Library, Boston, MA, Massachussets.
Lloyd, David D. Papers. Harry S. Truman Library, Independence, Missouri.
Refugee Studies Centre. Collected Papers. Oxford University, Oxford.
Rosenfield, Harry N. Papers. Harry S. Truman Library, Independence, Missouri.
United Nations Archives. Departmental Archive Group, New York.
United Nations High Commissioner for Refugees, Archives, Geneva.
US National Archives. Diplomatic Branch, College Park, Maryland.
US National Archives. National Security Council Policy Paper Files, Washington, DC.
Warren, George. Papers. Harry S. Truman Library, Independence, Missouri.
Weiss, Paul. Papers. Refugee Studies Centre, Oxford University, Oxford.

Articles, Books, Journals, Magazines, Newspapers, Reports, and Unpublished Materials

Aall, Cato, 'Disastrous International Relief Failure: A Report on Burmese Refugees in Bangladesh from May to December 1978', *Disasters*, 3/4 (1979): 429.
Acheson, Dean, *Present at the Creation* (New York, NY: Norton, 1966).
Adelman, Howard, 'Palestinian Refugees, Economic Integration and Durable Solutions', in Anna Bramwell, ed., *Refugees in the Age of Total War* (London: Unwin-Hyman, 1988).
—— and Suhrke, Astri, eds., *The Path of Genocide: The Rwandan Crisis from Uganda to Zaire* (New Brunswick, NJ: Transaction Publishers, 1999).

Aga Khan, Sadruddin, Speech by Deputy High Commissioner at OAU Conference (27 October 1965).

—— 'The New Geography of Political Refugees', *World Refugee Report, 1966-67* (Washington, DC: US Committee for Refugees, 1967): 11–14.

—— *Legal Problems Related to Refugees and Displaced Persons* (The Hague: Academy of International Law, 1976).

—— *Study on Human Rights and Massive Exoduses*. ECOSOC document E/CN4/1503 (1981).

Aguayo, Sergio, and Weiss-Fagen, Patricia, *Central Americans in Mexico and the United States: Unilateral, Bilateral and Regional Perspectives* (Washington, DC: Georgetown University, 1988).

Ahmad, Zakaria Haji, 'Vietnamese Refugees and ASEAN', *Contemporary Southeast Asia*, 1 (Singapore: May 1979): 66–74.

Aleinikoff, Alexander, 'Political Asylum in the Federal Republic of Germany and Republic of France: Lessons for the United States', *University of Michigan Journal of Law Reform*, 17 (Winter 1984): 183–241.

Allen, Timothy, and Morsink, Hubert, eds., *When Refugees Go Home* (Trenton, NJ: Africa World Press, 1994): 50–70.

Amnesty International, *Amnesty International Report* (London: Amnesty International, 1976).

—— *Report of an Amnesty International Mission to Argentina* (London: Amnesty International, 1977).

—— *Submission to the Government of the Socialist Republic of Vietnam on Amnesty International's Current Concerns* (London: Amnesty International, April 1983).

—— *Rwanda: Arming the Perpetrators of the Genocide* (London: Amnesty International, June 1995).

—— *Great Lakes Region Still in Need of Protection: Repatriation, Refoulement and the Safety of Refugees and the Internally Displaced* (London: Amnesty International, 24 January 1997).

—— *Rwanda: Human Rights Overlooked in Mass Repatriation* (London: Amnesty International, January 1997).

Angenendt, Steffen, ed., *Flucht und Migration: Aufgaben und Strategien für Deutchland, Europa und die Internationale Gemeinschaft* (Bonn: German Federal Agency for Political Information, 1997).

Anker, Deborah and Posner, Michael, 'The Forty Year Crisis: A Legislative History of the Refugee Act of 1980', *San Diego Law Review*, 19 (Winter 1981): 9–89.

Annan, Kofi, *Renewing the United Nations: A Programme for Reform*. UN doc. A/51/950 (New York, NY: United Nations, July 1997).

—— 'Two Concepts of Sovereignty', *The Economist* (18 September 1999): 19–21.

Arendt, Hannah, *The Origins of Totalitarianism* (New York, NY: Harcourt Brace Jovanovich, 1958).

Avery, Christopher, 'Refugee Status Decision-making in Ten Countries' *Stanford Journal of International Law*, 17 (Winter 1984): 183–241.

Awad, Mohamed, 'Refugees from the Sudan', in Hugh C. Brooks and Yassin El-Ayouty eds., *Refugees South of the Sahara: An African Dilemma* (Westport, CT: Negro Universities Press, 1970).

Baitenman, H., 'NGOs and the Afghan War: The Politicization of Humanitarian Aid', *Third World Quarterly*, 12/1 (1990): 68.

Barber, Ben, 'Feeding Refugees or War? The Dilemma of Humanitarian Aid', *Foreign Affairs*, 76/4 (1997): 8–14.

Barnett, Michael, 'Bringing in the New World Order: Liberalism, Legitimacy and the United Nations', *World Politics*, 49 (July 1997): 526–51.

—— 'Humanitarianism with a Sovereign Face: UNHCR in the Global Undertow', *International Migration Review* (forthcoming).

—— and Finnemore, Margaret, 'The Politics, Power, and Pathologies of International Organizations', *International Organization*, 53/4 (1999): 699–732.

Barutciski, Mikhael, 'The Reinforcement of Non-Admission Policies and the Subversion of UNHCR: Displacement and Internal Assistance in Bosnia-Herzegovina (1992–1994)', *International Journal of Refugee Law*, 8/1/2 (1996): 49–110.

Beigbeder, Yves, *Le Haut Commissariat des Nations Unis pour les Refugies* (Paris: Universitaires de France, 1999).

Berdal, Mats and Keen, David, 'Violence and Economic Agendas in Civil Wars: Some Policy Implications, *Millennium: Journal of International Studies*, 26/3 (1997): 795–818.

—— and Malone, David, *Greed and Grievance: Economic Agendas in Civil Wars* (Boulder, CO: Lynne Reiner, 2000).

Bethell, Nicholas, *The Last Secret: Forcible Repatriation to Russia, 1944-47* (London: Andre Deutch, 1974).

Betts, T. F., 'Zonal Development in Africa', *Journal of Modern African Studies*, 7 (1966): 149–53.

—— *Integrated Rural Development: Reports 1–4* (Geneva: International University Exchange Fund, 1969).

—— 'Evolution and Promotion of the Integrated Rural Development Approach to Refugee Policy in Africa', *Africa Today*, 31 (1984): 7–24.

Black, Richard and Koser, Khalid, eds., *The End of the Refugee Cycle: Refugee Repatriation and Reconstruction* (New York, NY: Berghahn Books, 1999).

—— and Robinson, Vaughn, eds., *Geography and Refugees: Patterns and Processes of Change* (London: Belhaven Press, 1992).

Blaschke, Jochen, *East-West Migration in Europe and International Aid as a Means to Reduce the Need for Emigration* (Geneva: ILO/UNHCR, 1992).

Bohning, W. R., 'Integration and Immigration Pressures in Western Europe', *International Labour Review*, 130 (1991): 445–58.

Borton, John, 'Recent Changes in the International Relief System', *Disasters*, 17/3 (1993): 187–201.

—— *The State of the International Humanitarian System* (London: Briefing Paper, Overseas Development Institute, March 1998).

Boutros-Ghali, Boutros, *Agenda for Development* (New York, NY: United Nations, 1994).

Boutroue, Joel, *Missed Opportunities: The Role of the International Community in the Return of Rwandan Refugees from Eastern Zaire*. The Rosemary Rogers Working Paper Series, Working Paper 1 (Cambridge, MA: MIT Inter-University Committee on International Migration, June 1998).

Bower, Tom, *The Pledge Betrayed: America, Britain and the De-Nazification of Postwar Germany* (Garden City, NY: Doubleday, 1982).

Bramwell, Anna, ed., *Refugees in the Age of Total War* (London: Unwin Hyman, 1988).

Brooks, Hugh and El-Ayouty, Yassin, eds., *Refugees South of the Sahara: An African Dilemma* (Westport, CT: Negro Universities Press, 1970).

Brown, Francis, ed., *Refugees*, Special issue of *Annals of American Academy of Political and Social Science*, 203 (1936).

Brown, Michael, ed., *Ethnic Conflict and International Security* (Princeton, NJ: Princeton University Press, 1993).

Buehrig, Edward, *The United Nations and the Palestinian Refugees: A Study in Non-Territorial Administration* (Bloomington, IN: Indiana University Press, 1971).

Byrne, R. and Shacknove, Andrew, 'The Safe Country Notion in European Asylum Law', *Harvard Human Rights Journal*, 9 (Spring 1996): 78–98.

Canadian International Development Agency, 'CIDA Evaluation of UNHCR Synthesis Report' (Montreal: Universalia Management Group, 8 September 1992).

Carey, J. P. Clark, 'Displaced Populations in Europe in 1944 with Partial Reference to Germany', *Department of State Bulletin* (25 March 1945): 491.

Cels, Johan, *A Liberal and Humane Policy for Refugees and Asylum Seekers: Still a Realistic Option?* (London: European Council on Refugees and Exiles, 1986).

—— 'The European Refugee Regime', Ph.D. dissertation, University of Notre Dame, South Bend, Indiana (1989).

—— 'European Responses to De Facto Refugees', in Gil Loescher and Laila Monahan, eds., *Refugees and International Relations* (Oxford: Clarendon Press, 1989).

Center for Migration Studies, *International Migration Review* (Staten Island, NY: CMS, Quarterly).

Chambers, Robert, 'Rural Refugees in Africa: What the Eye Does Not See', *Disasters*, 3 (1979): 381–92.

—— 'Hidden Losers? The Impact of Rural Refugees and Refugee Programs on Poorer Hosts', *International Migration Review*, 20 (1986): 245–63

Cheng, J. and Kwong, P. eds., *The Other Hong Kong Report* (Hong Kong: Chinese University Press, 1992).

Chesnais, Jean-Claude, *Migration from Eastern to Western Europe, Past (1946–1989) and Future (1990–2000)* (Strasbourg: Council of Europe, 1990).

—— *The USSR Emigration: Past, Present and Future* (Paris: Organization for Economic Co-operation and Development, 1991).

Childers, Erskine, and Urquhart, Brian, *Strengthening International Response to Humanitarian Emergencies* (New York, NY: Ford Foundation, 1991).

Chimni, B. S., 'The Meaning of Words and the Role of UNHCR in Voluntary Repatriation', *International Journal of Refugee Law*, 5 (1993): 442.

—— 'The Geopolitics of Refugee Studies: A View from the South', *Journal of Refugee Studies*, 11/4 (1998): 350–75.

Chipman, John, 'The Future of Strategic Studies: Beyond Even Grand Strategy', *Survival*, 34/1 (Spring 1992): 112.

Chopra, Jarat, 'The UN's Kingdom in East Timor', *Survival*, 42/3 (Autumn 2000): 27–40.

—— and Weiss, Thomas, 'Sovereignty Is No Longer Sacrosanct', *Ethics and International Affairs*, 6 (1992): 95–117.

Claude, Inis, *National Minorities: An International Problem* (Cambridge, MA: Harvard University Press, 1955).

Clay, Jason, *Politics and the Ethiopian Famine, 1984–1985* (Cambridge, MA: Cultural Survival, 1986).

Coate, Roger, ed., *United States Policy and the Future of the United Nations* (New York, NY: Brookings Institution Press, 1994).

Cobban, Alfred, *Nationalism and Self–Determination* (London: Oxford University Press, 1969).

Cohen, Roberta, *Human Rights Protection for Internally Displaced Persons* (Washington, DC: Refugee Policy Group, 1991).

—— and Deng, Francis, *Masses in Flight: The Global Crisis of Internal Displacement* (Washington, DC: Brookings Institution Press, 1997).

—— —— *The Forsaken People: Case Studies of the Internally Displaced* (Washington, DC: Brookings Institution Press, 1998).

Cohodas, Nadine, 'Refugee Entries Up in 1984: Same Levels Expected in 1985', *Congressional Quarterly Weekly Report*, 42 (8 December 1984).

Coles, Gervase, *Our Role and Responsibility for the Solution of the Refugee Problem* (Geneva: UNHCR, 1983).

—— *Voluntary Repatriation: A Background Study* (Geneva: UNHCR, 1985).

—— *Solutions to the Problem of Refugees and the Protection of Refugees: A Background Study* (Geneva: UNHCR, 1989).

—— 'Approaches to the Refugee Problem Today', in Gil Loescher and Laila Monahan, eds., *Refugees and International Relations* (Oxford: Clarendon Press, 1989).

Collinson, Sarah, *Europe and International Migration* (London: Pinter Publishers for Royal Institute of International Affairs, 1993).

Conquest, Robert, *The Great Terror: Stalin's Purge of the Thirties* (Harmondsworth: Penguin Books, 1971).

Copeland, Emily, 'Paths to Influence: NGO Networks and Refugees', unpublished conference paper for International Studies Association meeting, Washington, DC (1999).

Crisp, Jeff, 'Voluntary Repatriation Programmes for African Refugees: A Critical Examination', *Refugee Issues*, 1/2 (December 1984).

—— 'Uganda Refugees in Sudan and Zaire: The Problem of Repatriation', *African Affairs*, 85/339 (April 1986): 163–80.

—— 'Mind the Gap! UNHCR, Humanitarian Assistance and the Development Process', *International Migration Review* (forthcoming).

—— 'Refugee Repatriation: New Pressures and Problems', *Migration World*, 14/5 (1986): 18.

—— and Cater, Nick, 'The Human Consequences of Conflict in the Horn of Africa: Refugees, Asylum and the Politics of Assistance'. Paper presented at International Institute of Strategic Studies Regional Security Conference, Cairo, 27–30 May 1990.

Cuenod, Jacques, 'The Problem of Rwandese and Sudanese Refugees', in Sven Hammel, ed., *African Refugee Problems* (Uppsala: The Scandinavian Institute of African Studies, 1966): 345–53.

—— *Report on Refugees, Displaced Persons and Returnees*, UN Economic and Social Council, E/1991/109/Add. (1 June 1991).

Cunliffe, Alex, 'The Refugee Crisis: A Study of the United Nations High Commissioner for Refugees', *Political Studies*, 43/2 (June 1995): 287.

—— and Pugh, Michael, 'The Politicization of the UNHCR in the Former Yugoslavia', *Journal of Refugee Studies*, 10/2 (1997): 134–53.

—— —— 'UNHCR as Leader in Humanitarian Assistance: A Triumph of Politics over Law?', in Frances Nicholson and Patrick Twomey, eds., *Refugee Rights and Realities:*

Evolving International Concepts and Regimes (Cambridge: Cambridge University Press, 1999): 200–19.

Current History, Reproduction of 'The Central American Peace Plan', 86/524 (December 1987): 436.

Cutts, Mark, 'The Humanitarian Operation in Bosnia, 1992-95: Dilemmas of Negotiating Humanitarian Access', *New Issues in Refugee Research,* Working Paper No. 8 (Geneva: UNHCR, May 1999).

Dacyl, Janina, 'Between Compassion and Realpolitik', Ph.D. dissertation, University of Stockholm (1992).

Dallaire, Romeo, 'The End of Innocence: Rwanda 1994', in Jonathan Moore, ed., *Hard Choices: Moral Dilemmas in Humanitarian Intervention* (Boston, MA: Rowman and Littlefield, 1998).

Damrosch, Lori Fisler, ed., *Enforcing Restraint: Collective Action in Internal Conflicts* (New York, NY: Council on Foreign Relations Press, 1993).

Des Forges, Alison, *Leave None to Tell the Story* (New York, NY: Human Rights Watch, 1999).

Demars, William, 'Waiting for Early Warning: Humanitarian Action after the Cold War', *Journal of Refugee Studies*, 8/4 (1995): 390–417.

Dennett, Raymond, and Johnson, Joseph, eds., *Negotiating with the Russians* (Boston, MA: Little, Brown, 1951).

—— and Turner, Robert K., *Documents on American Foreign Relations 1947* (Princeton, NJ: Princeton University Press, 1949).

de Waal, Alex, *Famine Crimes: Politics and Disaster Relief Industry in Africa* (Oxford: James Currey, 1997).

De Young, Karen, 'Generosity Shrinks in an Age of Prosperity', *Washington Post* (25 March 1999): A11.

de Zayas, Alfred, *Nemesis at Potsdam: The Anglo-Americans and Expulsions of the Germans* (London: Routledge and Kegan Paul, 1979).

Dinnerstein, Leonard, *America and the Survivors of the Holocaust, 1941–1945* (New York, NY: Columbia University Press, 1982).

Divine, Robert, *American Immigration Policy, 1924–1952* (New Haven, CT: Yale University Press, 1957).

Donnelly, Jack, 'International Human Rights: A Regime Analysis', *International Orgnization,* 40 (Summer 1985): 249–70.

Douglas, H. Eugene, 'The Problem of Refugees in Strategic Perspective', *Strategic Review* (Autumn 1982): 20.

Dowty, Alan, *Closed Borders: The Contemporary Assault on Freedom of Movement* (New Haven, CT: Yale University Press, 1987).

—— and Loescher, Gil, 'Refugee Flows as Grounds for International Action', *International Secruity,* 21/1 (Summer 1996): 43–71.

—— —— 'Changing Norms in International Responses to Domestic Disorder', in Raimo Vayrnen, ed., *Global Governance and Enforcement* (Latham, MA: Rowman and Littlefield, 1999): 199–223.

Druke, Louise, *Preventive Action for Refugee-Producing Situations* (Frankfurt: Peter Lang, 1990).

Duffield, Mark, 'Complex Emergencies and the Crisis of Developmentalism', IDS Bulletin, 25/4 (1994): 37–45.

Duffield, Mark, 'The Symphony of the Damned: Racial Discourse, Complex Political Emergencies, and Humanitarian Aid', *Disasters*, 20/3 (1996): 173–93.

Dunn, James, *Timor: A People Betrayed* (Sydney: ABC Books, 1996).

Dunne, Tim and Wheeler, Nicholas, eds., *Human Rights in World Politics* (Cambridge: Cambridge University Press, 1999).

Economist, 'The Last Frontier' (24 June 2000): 63–4.

Edminster, Steven, 'The High Road or the Low Road: The Way Forward to Asylum Harmonization in the European Union', in US Committee for Refugees, *World Survey 2000* (Washington, DC: US Committee for Refugees, 2000): 58.

Eduards, Krister, Rosen, Gunnar, and Rossborough, Robert, *Responding To Emergencies: The Role of the UN in Emergencies and Ad Hoc Operations* (Stockholm: Nordic UN Project, September 1990).

Elliot, Mark, *Pawns of Yalta* (Champaign, IL: University of Illinois Press, 1982).

Ellis, Stephen, *The Mask of Anarchy: The Destruction of Liberia and the Religious Dimension of an African Civil War* (New York, NY: New York University Press, 1999).

Elson, John, 'Ogata's Angels', *Time* (23 October 1995): 67.

European Commission of Human Rights, *Report of the Commission*. Appl. Nos. 13163/87, 13164/87, 13165/87, 13447/87, and 13448/87 (8 May 1990).

European Council on Refugees and Exiles, *Safe Third Countries: Myths and Realities* (London: ECRE, 1996).

Evans, Gareth, 'Central Asians Need Help Now to Head Off Conflict', *International Herald Tribune* (16 August 2000).

Evans, Peter, Jacobson, Harold, and Putnam, Robert, eds., *Double-Edged Diplomacy: International Bargaining and Domestic Politics* (Berkeley, CA: University of California Press, 1993).

Fagen, R. F., Brody, R. A., and O'Leary, T. J., *Cubans in Exile: Disaffection and the Revolution* (Stanford, CA: Stanford University Press, 1968).

Feingold, Henry, *The Politics of Rescue: The Roosevelt Administration and the Holocaust, 1938-45* (New Brunswick, NJ: Rutgers University Press, 1970).

Feldman, Andreas, 'The UNHCR and Internal Displacement: Rational Ambivalence?' Conference paper, International Studies Association, Los Angeles (March 2000).

Ferris, Elizabeth, ed., *Refugees and World Politics* (New York, NY: Praeger, 1985).

—— *Central American Refugees and the Politics of Protection* (New York, NY: Praeger, 1987).

—— *Beyond Borders: Refugees, Migrants, and Human Rights in the Post Cold War Era* (Geneva: World Council of Churches Publications, 1993).

Finnemore, Martha, 'Constructing Norms of Humanitarian Intervention', in Peter Katzenstein, ed., *The Culture of National Security: Norms and Identities in World Politics* (New York, NY: Columbia University Press, 1996).

—— 'Norms, Culture, and World Politics: Insights from Sociology's Institutionalism', *World Politics*, 1/2 (Spring 1996): 325–48.

Forbes Martin, Susan, 'Emigration, Immigration and Changing East–West Relations', (Washington, DC: Refugee Policy Group, November 1989).

Ford Foundation, Final Report on Ford Foundation Program for Refugees, Primarily in Europe (July 1968): 40–68.

Forsythe, David, 'UNRWA, the Palestinian Refugees, and World Politics', *International Organization*, 25 (Winter 1971): 26–45.

—— 'The Palestine Question: Dealing with a Long-Term Refugee Situation', *Annals of the American Academy of Political and Social Sciences*, 468 (May 1983): 89–101.

—— 'The United Nations and Human Rights, 1945–1985', *Political Science Quarterly*, 100 (Summer 1985): 249–70.

—— *Human Rights in International Relations* (Cambridge: Cambridge University Press, 2000).

Frelick, Bill, 'Preventing Refugee Flows: Protection or Peril?', *World Refugee Survey 1993* (Washington, DC: US Committee for Refugees, 1993).

—— 'Refugee Rights: The New Frontier of Human Rights Protection', *Buffalo Human Rights Law Review*, 4 (1998): 261–74.

Frohardt, Mark, Paul, Diane, and Minear, Larry, *Protecting Human Rights: The Challenge to Humanitarian Organizations*. Occasional Paper 35 (Providence, RI: Watson Institute for International Studies, Brown University, 1999).

Gallagher, Dennis and Diller, J., *CIEREFCA: At the Crossroads between Uprooted People and Development in Central America* (Washington, DC: The Refugee Policy Group, 1990).

—— Forbes Martin, Susan, and Weiss–Fagen, Patricia, 'Temporary Safe Haven: The Need for North American-European Responses', in Gil Loescher and Laila Monahan, eds., *Refugees and International Relations* (Oxford: Clarendon Press, 1989): 333–54.

Garvey, Jack, 'Toward a Reformulation of International Refugee Law', *Harvard International Law Journal*, 26 (1985): 483–500.

Ghosh, Bimal, *Huddled Masses and Uncertain Shores: Insights into Irregular Migration* (The Hague: Martinus Nijhoff, 1998).

—— ed., *Managing Migration: Time for a New International Regime?* (Oxford: Oxford University Press, 2000).

Gibney, Mark, ed., *Open Borders? Closed Societies? The Ethical and Political Questions* (Westport, CT: Greenwood Press, 1988).

Glenny, Misha, *The Fall of Yugoslavia: The Third Balkan War* (New York, NY: Penguin, 1992).

Goedhart, G. J. van Heuven, *The Problem of Refugees* (Leiden: A. W. Sijthoff, 1953).

—— *Refugee Problems and Their Solutions* (Geneva: UNHCR, 1955).

Goodwin–Gill, Guy, *International Law and the Movement of Persons Between States* (Oxford: Clarendon Press, 1978).

—— 'Non–refoulement and the New Asylum Seekers', in David Martin, ed., *The New Asylum Seekers: Refugee Law in the 1980s* (Dordrecht: Martinus Nijhoff, 1988).

—— 'Voluntary Repatriation: Legal and Policy Issues', in Gil Loescher and Laila Monahan, eds., *Refugees and International Relations* (Oxford: Clarendon Press, 1989).

—— 'Different Types of Forced Migration Movements as an International and National Problem', in Goran Rystad, ed., *The Uprooted: Forced Migration as an International Problem in the Post-War Era* (Lund: Lund University Press, 1990).

—— *The Refugee in International Law* (Oxford: Clarendon Press, 1996).

—— 'Refugee Identity and Protection's Fading Prospect', in Frances Nicholson and Patrick Twomey, eds., *Refugee Rights and Realities: Evolving International Concepts and Regimes* (Cambridge: Cambridge University Press, 1999): 220–52.

—— 'UNHCR and Internal Displacement: Stepping into the Legal and Political Minefield', *World Refugee Survey 2000* (Washington, DC: US Committee for Refugees, 2000): 26–31.

Gordenker, Leon, *Refugees in International Politics* (London: Croom Helm, 1987).

Gorman, Robert, *Coping with Africa's Refugee Burden: A Time for Solutions* (Dordrecht: Martinus Nijhoff, 1987).

—— *Historical Dictionary of Refugee and Disaster Relief Organizations* (Metuchen, NJ: The Scarecrow Press, 1994).

Gourevitch, Philip, 'The Continental Shift', *The New Yorker*, 4 (August 1997): 42–55.

—— *We Wish to Inform You That Tomorrow We Will Be Killed with Our Families: Stories From Rwanda* (New York, NY: Farrar, Strauss and Giroux, 1998).

Gowlland-Debbas, Vera, ed., *The Problem of Refugees in the Light of Contemporary International Law Issues* (The Hague: Martinus Nijhoff, 1996).

Grahl-Madsen, Atle, *The Status of Refugees in International Law*, 2 vols. (Leiden: A. W. Sijthoff, 1966, 1972).

—— *Territorial Asylum* (Dobbs Ferry, NY: Oceana Publications, 1980).

Green, Stephen, *International Disaster Assistance: Toward a Responsive System* (New York, NY: Council on Foreign Relations, 1977)

Greenfield, Richard, 'The OAU and Africa's Refugees', in Yassin El-Ayouty, ed., *The OAU after Twenty Years* (New York, NY: Praeger, 1984): 85–115.

Grose, Peter, *Operation Rollback: America's Secret War Behind the Iron Curtain* (Boston, MA: Houghton Mifflin Co., 2000).

Guardian, 'Refugee Law Violated', (10 December 1981).

—— 'Deaths in a Boxcar: Who Cares About Ethiopian Refugees?', (9 December 1986).

Guest, Iain, *Behind the Disappearances: Argentina's Dirty War Against Human Rights and the United Nations* (Philadelphia, PA: University of Pennsylvania Press, 1990).

Gungwu, Wang, ed., *Global History and Migrations* (Boulder, CO: Westview Press, 1997).

Gurr, Ted Robert, 'Ethnic Warfare and the Changing Priorities of Global Security', *Mediterranean Quarterly*, 1 (1990): 82–98.

Hakovirta, Harto, *Third World Conflicts and Refugeeism: Dimensions, Dynamics and Trends of the World Refugee Problem* (Helsinki: Finnish Society of Sciences and Letters, 1986).

—— *An Ethical Analysis of Refugee Aid and the World Refugee Problem* (Amsterdam: Workshop on Duties Beyond Borders, April 1987).

—— *The World Refugee Problem* (Tampere: Hillside Publications, 1991).

Hambro, Edvard, *The Problem of Chinese Refugees in Hong Kong* (Leiden: A. W. Sijthoff, 1955).

Hammel, Sven, ed., *African Refugee Problems* (Uppsala: The Scandinavian Institute of African Studies, 1966).

Hansen, Art, 'Managing Refugees: Zambia's Response to Angolan Refugees, 1966–1977', *Disasters*, 3 (1979): 375–80.

—— and Smith, D., eds., *Involuntary Migration and Resettlement: The Problem and Responses of Dislocated People* (Boulder, CO: Westview Press, 1982).

Hanson, Christopher, 'Behind the Paper Curtain: Asylum Policy vs. Asylum Practice', *New York University Review of Law and Social Change*, 7 (Winter 1978): 107–41.

Harding, Jeremy, *The Uninvited: Refugees at the Rich Man's Gate* (London: Profile Books, 2000).

Harff, Barbara, and Gurr, Ted Robert, 'Toward Empirical Theory of Genocides and Politicides: Identification and Measurement of Cases Since 1945', *International Studies Quarterly*, 32 (1988): 359–71.

Harrell-Bond, Barbara, 'Humanitarianism in a Strait–Jacket', *African Affairs*, 334 (1985): 3–13.

—— *Imposing Aid: Emergency Assistance to Refugees* (Oxford: Oxford University Press, 1985).

—— 'Repatriation: Under What Conditions Is It the Most Desirable Solution for Refugees? An Agenda for Research', *African Studies Review*, 31 (1988): 41–69.

Hathaway, James, 'Burden Sharing or Burden Shifting? Irregular Asylum Seekers: What's All the Fuss?', *Refuge* 8 (December 1988): 1.

—— 'A Reconsideration of the Underlying Premise of Refugee Law', *Harvard International Law Journal*, 31 (1990): 129–83.

—— 'Reconceiving Refugee Law as Human Rights Protection', *Journal of Refugee Studies*, 4 (1991): 113–31.

—— *The Law of Refugee Status* (Toronto: Butterworths, 1991).

—— ed., *Re–conceiving International Refugee Law* (The Hague: Martinus Nijohff, 1997).

Hausermann, Julia, *Root Causes of Displacement: The Legal Framework for International Concern and Action* (London: Rights and Humanity, 1986).

Heisbourg, Francois, 'Population Movement in Post-Cold War Europe', *Survival*, 33 (1991): 31–43.

Helton, Arthur, 'Political Asylum Under the 1980 Refugee Act: An Unfulfilled Promise', *University of Michigan Journal of Law Reform*, 17 (1984): 243.

Hippler, Jochen, *The Democratisation of Disempowerment: The Problem of Democracy in the Third World* (London: Pluto Press, 1995).

Hirsch, John and Oakley, Robert, *Somalia and Operation Restore Hope* (Washington, DC: United States Institute of Peace Press, 1995).

Hitchcox, Linda, 'Vietnamese Asylum Seekers', Ph.D. dissertation, St. Anthony's College, Oxford University (1990).

—— *Vietnamese Refugees in Southeast Asian Camps* (Basingstoke: MacMillan, 1990).

Hocke, Jean-Pierre, 'Beyond Humanitarianism: The Need for Political Will to Resolve Today's Refugee Problem', in Gil Loescher, and Laila Monahan, eds., *Refugees and International Relations* (Oxford: Clarendon Press, 1989).

Holborn, Louise, *The International Refugee Organization: A Specialized Agency of the United Nations, Its History and Work, 1946-1952* (London: Oxford University Press, 1956).

—— *Refugees: A Problem of Our Time: The Work of the United Nations High Commissioner for Refugees,* 2 vols. (Metuchen, NJ: Scarecrow Press, 1975).

Holbrooke, Richard, Statement by Ambassador Holbrooke, US Permanent Representative to the UN at Cardozo Law School, New York (28 March 2000).

Human Rights Quarterly (Baltimore, MD: Johns Hopkins University Press, Quarterly).

Human Rights Watch, *The Lost Agenda: Human Rights and UN Field Operations* (New York, NY: Human Rights Watch, 1993).

—— *Rwanda/Zaire: Rearming with Impunity. International Support for the Perpetrators of the Rwandan Genocide* (New York, NY: Human Rights Watch, May 1995).

—— *Burma: The Rohingya Muslims Ending a Cycle of Violence?* (New York, NY: Human Rights Watch, September 1996).

—— *Uncertain Refuge: International Failures to Protect Refugees* (New York, NY: Human Rights Watch, April 1997).

Humphrey, Derek, and Ward, Michael, *Passports and Politics* (London: Penguin Books, 1974).

Huntington, Samuel, *Political Order in Changing Societies* (New Haven, CT: Yale University Press, 1968).

Ignatieff, Michael, *The Warrior's Honor: Ethnic War and the Modern Conscience* (London: Chatto and Windus, 1998).

—— *Virtual War: Kosovo and Beyond* (New York, NY: Henry Holt and Co., 2000).

Independent, 'Moscow Warns EC of Mass Migration', (25 September 1990).

Independent Commission on International Humanitarian Issues, *Modern Wars: The Humanitarian Challenge* (London: Zed Books, 1986).

—— *Refugees: The Dynamics of Displacement* (London: Zed Books, 1986).

Intergovernmental Committee for Migration, and Research Group for European Migration Problems, *International Migration*. Review on the role of migratory movements in the contemporary world, in English, French, and Spanish. (Geneva: ICM, Quarterly).

International Bibliography of Refugee Literature (Geneva: International Refugee Integration Resource Center, 1985).

International Herald Tribune, 'The UN's African Dilemma', (10 March 1997).

International Journal of Refugee Law (Oxford: Oxford University Press, quarterly).

——'The UNHCR Note on International Protection You Won't See', 9/2 (1997): 267–73.

International Organization for Migration, *CIS Migration Report* (Geneva: Technical Cooperation Center for Europe and Central Asia, 1997).

Interpreter Releases. Information service on asylum, immigration, naturalization, and related matters (Washington, DC: Federal Publications, weekly).

International Refugee Organization, *International Refugee Organization Constitution*, Articles 1(c) and 2 (1948).

Jacqueney, Theodore, 'Vietnam's Gulag Archipelago', *New York Times* (17 September 1976).

Jaeger, Gilbert, *Status and International Protection of Refugees* (San Remo: International Institute of Human Rights, 1978).

—— *Study of Irregular Movements of Asylum Seekers and Refugees* (Geneva: UNHCR, 1 August 1985).

Jambor, Pierre, *Indochinese Refugees in Southeast Asia: Mass Exodus and the Politics of Aid* (Bangkok: Ford Foundation, 1992).

Joint Evaluation of Emergency Assistance To Rwanda, *The International Response to Conflict and Genocide: Lessons from the Rwandan Experience*, Study 2, 'Early Warning and Conflict Management' (Copenhagen: Steering Committee of the Joint Evaluation of Emergency Assistance to Rwanda, 1996).

Joly, Danielle, *Haven or Hell? Asylum Policies and Refugees in Europe* (London: Macmillan, 1996).

—— and Cohen, Robin, *Reluctant Hosts: Europe and Its Refugees* (Aldershot: Gower, 1987).

—— with Nettleton, Clive, *Refugees in Europe* (London: Minority Rights Group, October 1990).

Katzenstein, Peter, ed., *The Culture of National Security: Norms and Identities in World Politics* (New York, NY: Columbia University Press, 1996).

Keck, Margaret, and Sikkink, Kathryn, *Activists Beyond Borders: Advocacy Networks in International Politics* (Ithaca, NY: Cornell University Press, 1998).

Keely, Charles, 'Filling a Critical Gap in the Refugee Protection Regime: The Internally Displaced', *World Refugee Survey 1991* (Washington, DC: US Committee for Refugees, 1991): 22–7.

Keen, David, *The Economic Functions of Violence in Civil Wars*. Adelphi Paper 320 (London: International Institute for Strategic Studies, June 1998).

Kennedy, David, 'International Refugee Protection', *Human Rights Quarterly*, 8 (February 1986): 9–69.

Kenny, Karen, 'When Needs are Rights: An Overview of UN Efforts to Integrate Human Rights in Humanitarian Action'. Occasional Paper 38 (Providence, RI: Watson Institute for International Studies, Brown University, 2000).

Kent, Randolph, *The Anatomy of Disaster Relief: The International Network in Action* (London: Pinter Publications, 1987).

Kibreab, Gaim, *Reflections on the African Refugee Problem: A Critical Analysis of Some Basic Assumptions* (Uppsala: Scandinavian Institute of African Studies, 1983): 123–40.

—— 'Local Settlements in Africa: A Misconceived Option?', *Journal of Refugee Studies*, 2 (1989): 468–90.

—— *The State of Art Review of Refugee Studies in Africa* (Uppsala: Uppsala Papers in Economic History, 1991).

Kenneth, John, *Orphans of the Cold War* (Washington, DC: Public Affairs, 1999).

Koehn, Peter, *Refugees from Revolution: U. S. Policy and Third World Migration* (Boulder, CO: Westview Press, 1991).

Kommers, Donald and Loescher, Gilburt, eds., *Human Rights and American Foreign Policy* (South Bend, IN: University of Notre Dame Press, 1979).

Kritz, Mary, ed., *U. S. Immigration and Refugee Policy: Global and Domestic Issues* (Lexington, MA: D. C. Heath, 1983).

—— Lim, Lin Lean, and Zlotnik, Hania, eds., *International Migration Systems: A Global Approach* (Oxford: Clarendon Press, 1992).

Kulischer, Eugene, *Europe on the Move: War and Population Changes 1917–1947* (New York, NY: Columbia University Press, 1948).

Kuper, Leo, *Genocide: Its Political Uses in the Twentieth Century* (New Haven, CT: Yale University Press, 1981).

Lacouture, Jean, and Lacouture, Simone, *Vietnam Voyage à Travers une Victoire* (Paris: Seuil, 1976).

Lake, Anthony, ed., *After the Wars: Reconstruction in Afghanistan, Indochina, Central America, Southern Africa and the Horn of Africa* (New Brunswick, NJ: Transaction Publishers, 1991).

Lama, Mahendra, *Managing Refugees in South Asia* (Dhaka: Refugee and Migratory Movements Research Unit, University of Dhaka, 2000).

Larkin, Mary Ann, Cuny, Frederick, and Stein, Barry, *Repatriation Under Conflict in Central America* (Washington, DC: Georgetown University, 1991).

Lawless, Richard, and Monahan, Laila, eds., *War and Refugees: The Western Sahara Conflict* (London: Pinter, 1987).

Lawyers' Committee for Human Rights, *Refugee Refoulement: The Forced Return of Haitians Under the U.S.-Haitian Interdiction Agreement* (New York, NY: Lawyers' Committee for Human Rights, 1990).

—— *The Implementation of the Refugee Act of 1980: A Decade of Experience* (New York, NY: Lawyers' Committee for Human Rights, 1990).

—— *Uncertain Haven* (New York, NY: Lawyers' Committee for Human Rights, 1991).

—— *The UNHCR at 40: Refugee Protection at the Crossroads* (New York, NY: Lawyers' Committee for Human Rights, 1991).

Lawyers' Committee for Human Rights, *General Principles Relating to the Promotion of Refugee Repatriation* (New York, NY: Lawyers' Committee for Human Rights, 1992).

—— *Slamming the 'Golden Door': A Year of Expedited Removal* (New York, NY: Lawyers' Committee for Human Rights, April 1998).

League of Nations, *Treaty Series*, cxcviii/4634 (19 January 1939).

—— *Treaty Series*, clix/3363 (28 October 1933).

Lemarchand, Rene, *Rwanda and Burundi* (London: Pall Mall Press. 1970).

Loescher, Gil, 'Power Politics In Indochina', *The Yearbook of World Affairs* (London: Stevens and Sons for the London Institute of World Affairs, 1983).

—— 'Humanitarianism and Politics in Central America', *Political Science Quarterly*, 103 (Summer 1988): 295–320. Also in Bruce Nichols and Gil Loescher, *The Moral Nation: Humanitarianism and U.S. Foreign Policy Today* (South Bend, IN.: University of Notre Dame Press, 1989).

—— 'The European Community and Refugees', *International Affairs* (Autumn 1989): 617–36.

—— ed., *Refugees and the Asylum Dilemma in the West* (University Park, PA: Pennsylvania State University Press, 1992).

—— *Refugee Movements and International Security*, Adelphi Paper 268 (London: Brasseys, for the International Institute for Strategic Studies, 1992).

—— *Beyond Charity: International Cooperation and the Global Refugee Crisis* (New York, NY: Oxford University Press, 1993).

—— 'Forced Migration within and from the Former USSR: The Policy Challenges Ahead'. Rand Corporation Policy Paper, DRU–564–FF (Santa Monica, CA: November 1993).

—— 'The United Nations, the High Commissioner for Refugees, and the Global Refugee Problem', in Roger Coate, ed., *United States Policy and the Future of the United Nations* (New York, NY: Brookings Institution Press, 1994): 139–66.

—— 'Les mouvements de refugies dans l'apres-guerre froide', *Politique Etrangère* (Paris: Insitut Français des Relations Internationales, Autumn 1994): 707–17.

—— 'The International Refugee Regime', *The Journal of International Studies*, 47/2 (Winter 1994): 139–66.

—— 'Wanderungsbewegungen und internationale Sicherheit', in Steffen Angenendt, ed., *Flucht und Migration: Sufgaben und Stategien für Deutchland, Europa und die Internationale Gemeinschaft* (Bonn: German Federal Agency for Political Information, 1997).

—— 'Refugees: A Global Human Rights and Security Crisis', in Timothy Dunne and Nicholas Wheeler, eds., *Human Rights in World Politics* (Cambridge: Cambridge University, 1999): 233–58.

—— and Loescher, Ann Dull, *The Global Refugee Crisis: A Reference Handbook* (Santa Barbara, CA: ABC CLIO, 1994).

—— and Monahan, Laila, eds., *Refugees and International Relations* (Oxford: Clarendon Press, 1989).

—— and Scanlan, John, eds., *The Global Refugee Problem: U. S. and World Response*. Special issue of *Annals of American Academy of Political and Social Science*, 467 (1983).

—— —— 'Human Rights, U. S. Foreign Policy and Haitian Refugees', *Journal of Inter-American Studies and World Affairs*, 26 (August 1984): 313–56.

—— —— *Human Rights, Power Politics, and the International Refugee Regime: The Case of U.S. Treatment of Caribbean Basin Refugees* (Princeton, NJ: Princeton University Center for International Studies, World Order Studies Occasional Paper Series, No. 14, 1985).

—— —— *Calculated Kindness: Refugees and America's Half-Open Door, 1945 to Present* (New York, NY, and London: The Free Press and Macmillan, 1986).

Loftus, John, *The Belarus Secret* (New York, NY: Alfred A. Knopf, 1982).

Long, Nguyen, with Kendall, Harry H. *After Saigon Fell: Daily Life Under the Communists* (Berkeley, CA: Institute of East Asian Studies, University of California, 1981).

Lundahl, Matts, *Peasants and Poverty: a Study of Haiti* (London: Croom-Helm, 1979).

Lyons, Gene M., *Military Policy and Economic Aid: The Korean Case* (Columbus, OH: Ohio University Press, 1961).

MacAlister-Smith, Peter, *International Humanitarian Assistance: Disaster Relief Organizations in International Law and Organization* (Dordrecht: Martinus Nijhoff, 1985).

Macartney, C. A., *National States and National Minorities* (New York, NY: Russell & Russell, 1968).

Macrae, Joanna and Zwi, Anthony, eds., *War and Hunger: Rethinking International Responses to Complex Emergencies* (London: Zed Books, 1994).

McDowall, Roy, 'Coordination of Refugee Policy in Europe', in Gil Loescher and Laila Monahan, eds., *Refugees and International Relations* (Oxford: Clarendon Press, 1989).

McNamara, Dennis, 'The Origin and Effect of "Humane Deterrence" Policies in Southeast Asia', in Gil Loescher and Laila Monahan, eds., *Refugees and International Relations* (Oxford: Clarendon Press, 1989): 123–34.

—— 'The Future of Protection and the Responsibility of the State', *International Journal of Refugee Law*, 10/1/2 (1998): 230–5.

Mainz, Beatrice, *Refugees of a Hidden War: The Aftermath of Counterinsurgency in Guatemala* (Albany, NY: State University of New York Press, 1988).

Makinda, Samuel, *Security in the Horn of Africa*. Adelphi Paper 269 (London: Brasseys for International Institute for Strategic Studies, 1992).

Malkki, Liisa, *Purity and Exile: Violence, Memory, and National Cosmology among Hutu Refugees in Tanzania* (Chicago, IL: University of Chicago Press, 1995).

Marrus, Michael, *The Unwanted: European Refugees in the Twentieth Century* (New York, NY: Oxford University Press, 1985).

Martin, David, ed., *The New Asylum Seekers: Refugee Law in the 1980s* (Dordrecht: Martinus Nijhoff, 1988).

Martin, Ian, 'Hard Choices after Genocide: Human Rights and Political Failures in Rwanda', in Jonathan Moore, ed., *Hard Choices: Moral Dilemmas in Humanitarian Intervention* (Lanham, MA: Rowman and Littlefield Publishers, 1998): 157–76.

Martin, Lisa and Sikkink, Kathryn, 'U. S. Policy and Human Rights in Argentina and Guatemala, 1973–1980', in Peter Evans, Harold Jacobson, and Robert Putnam, eds., *Double-Edged Diplomacy: International Bargaining and Domestic Politics* (Berkeley, CA: University of California Press, 1993).

Martin, Susan, 'Forced Migration and Professionalism', *International Migration Review* (forthcoming).

Mason, Linda, and Brown, Roger, *Rice, Rivalry and Politics* (South Bend, IN: University of Notre Dame Press, 1983).

Mayall, James, *Nationalism and International Society* (Cambridge: Cambridge University Press, 1990).

Maynard, Kimberly, *Healing Communities in Conflict: International Assistance in Complex Emergencies* (New York, NY: Columbia University Press, 1999).

Medecins Sans Frontieres, *World in Crisis: The Politics of Survival at the End of the 20th Century* (London: Routledge, 1997).

Meissner, Doris, 'Central American Refugees: Political Asylum, Sanctuary and Humanitarian Policy', in Bruce Nichols and Gil Loescher eds., *The Moral Nation: Humanitarianism and U. S. Foreign Policy Today* (South Bend, IN: University of Notre Dame Press, 1989).

—— 'Managing Migrations', *Foreign Policy* (Winter 1992): 66–83.

Melander, Goran, *Refugees in Orbit* (Geneva: International Universities Exchange Fund, 1978).

—— *The Two Refugee Definitions* (Lund: Raoul Wallenberg Institute, 1987).

Mendiluce, Jose-Maria, 'War and Disaster in the Former Yugoslavia: The Limits of Humanitarian Action', *World Refugee Survey-1994* (Washington, DC: US Committee for Refugees, 1995): 10–19.

Mertus, Julie, 'The State and the Post-Cold War Refugee Regime: New Models, New Questions', *International Journal of Refugee Law*, 10/3 (1998): 321–48.

Mills, Kurt, 'United Nations Intervention in Refugee Crises in the Post–Cold War World'. Paper for Annual Meeting of the International Studies Association, Toronto, Canada (18–22 March 1997).

Millwood, David, ed., *The International Response to Conflict and Genocide: Lessons from the Rwanda Experience*, i–iv (Odense: Steering Committee of the Joint Evaluation of Emergency Assistance to Rwanda, March 1996).

Minear, Larry, 'Civil Strife and Humanitarian Aid: A Bruising Decade', *World Refugee Survey-1989 in Review* (1989): 13–19.

—— Van Baarda, Ted, and Sommers, Marc, *NATO and Humanitarian Action in the Kosovo Crisis*. Occasional Paper 36 (Providence, RI: Watson Institute of International Studies, Brown University, 2000): 161–8.

—— Weiss, Thomas, and Campbell, Kurt, 'Humanitarianism and War: Learning the Lessons from Recent Armed Conflicts'. Occasional Paper 9 (Providence, RI: Watson Institute for International Studies, Brown University, 1991).

—— Chelliah, U., Crisp, Jeff, Mackinlay, John, and Weiss, Thomas, *United Nations Coordination of the International Humanitarian Response to the Gulf Crisis, 1990-1992*. Occasional Paper 13 (Providence, RI: Watson Institute for International Studies, Brown University, 1992).

Mooney, Erin, 'Presence, Ergo Protection? UNPROFOR, UNHCR and the ICRC in Croatia and Bosnia and Herzegovina', *International Journal of Refugee Law*, 7/3 (1995): 407–35.

Moore, Jonathan, ed., *Hard Choices: Moral Dilemmas in Humanitarian Intervention* (Boston, MA: Rowman and Littlefield, 1998).

Moorehead, Caroline, *Dunant's Dream: War, Switzerland and the History of the Red Cross* (New York, NY: Harper Collins, 1998).

Morris, Benny, *The Birth of the Palestinian Refugee Problem* (Cambridge: Cambridge University Press, 1987).

Morris, Eric, *The Limits of Mercy: Ethno-political Conflict and Humanitarian Action* (Cambridge, MA: MIT Center for International Studies, 1997).

Morris, Nicholas, 'Refugees: Facing Crises in the 1990s—A Personal View from within UNHCR', *International Journal of Refugee Law*. Special issue (September 1990): 38–58
—— 'Protection Dilemmas and UNHCR's Response: A Personal View from within UNHCR', *International Journal of Refugee Law*, 9/3 (1997): 492–9.

Mtango, Elly–Elikunda, 'Military and Armed Attacks on Refugee Camps', in Gil Loescher and Laila Monahan, eds., *Refugees and International Relations* (Oxford: Clarendon Press, 1989): 87–122.

Munz, Rainer and Weiner, Myron, eds., *Migrants, Refugees, and Foreign Policy* (Providence, RI: Berghahn Books, 1997).

Murphy, Robert, *Diplomat Among Warriors* (Garden City, NY: Doubleday, 1964).

Nanda, Ved, ed., *Refugee Law and Policy* (Westport, CT: Greenwood Press, 1989).

Netherlands Institute of Human Rights, *Report of the International Conference 'Refugees in the World: The European Community's Response', The Hague, 7–8 December 1989* (Utrecht: Netherlands Institute of Human Rights; and Amsterdam: Dutch Refugee Council, 1990).

Newland, Kathleen, 'The Decade in Review', *World Refugee Survey 1999* (Washington, DC: US Committee for Refugees, 1999): 21.

Newman, Larry, 'Locke Sees Reds Playing Cosy Game in the Middle East', *The Daily Star* (Beirut: 2 December 1952): 1.

New York Herald Tribune (10 May 1957).

New York Times 'Parley on Agency Set' (24 August 1951).
—— Articles on refugees in editions (6 August 1957) and (23 April 1953).

Nichols, Bruce, *The Uneasy Alliance: Religion, Refugee Work, and U. S. Foreign Policy* (New York, NY: Oxford University Press, 1988).
—— and Gil Loescher, eds., *The Moral Nation: Humanitarianism and U. S. Foreign Policy Today* (South Bend, IN: University of Notre Dame Press, 1989).

Nicholson, Frances, and Twomey, Patrick, eds., *Refugee Rights and Realities: Evolving International Concepts and Regimes* (Cambridge: Cambridge University Press, 1999).

Ogata, Sadako, 'Statement at the Intergovernmental Consultations on Asylum, Refugee and Migration Policies in Europe, North America and Australia', Washington DC, May 1997.

Organization for Economic Co-operation and Development, *The Future of Migration* (Paris: OECD, 1987).
—— *International Conference on South–North Migration* (Paris: OECD, 1991).
—— *SOPEMI: Continuous Reporting on Migration* (Paris: OECD, Annual).

Paludan, Anne, *The New Refugees in Europe* (Geneva: International Exchange Fund, 1974).

Paul, Diane, *Beyond Monitoring and Reporting: The Field-level Protection of Civilians Under Threat* (New York, NY: Jacob Blaustein Institute for the Advancement of Human Rights and the Center for the Study of Societies in Crisis, 2000).

Pedraza-Bailey, Silvia, 'Cuban Americans in the United States: The Functions of Political and Economic Migration', *Cuban Studies*, 11/2 (July 1981) and 12/1 (January 1982): 79–97.

Penrose, Edith, 'Negotiating on Refugees and Displaced Persons, 1946', in Raymond Dennett and Joseph Johnson, eds., *Negotiating with the Russians* (Boston, MA: Little Brown, 1951): 144–67.

Pitterman, Shelly, 'Determinants of Policy in a Functional International Agency: A Comparative Study of UNHCR Assistance in Africa, 1963-1981', Ph.D. dissertation, Northwestern University (1984).

—— 'International Responses to Refugee Situations: The United Nations High Commissioner for Refugees', in Elizabeth Ferris, ed., *Refugees and World Politics* (New York, NY: Praeger, 1986): 43–81.

—— 'Determinants of International Refugee Policy: A Comparative Study of UNHCR Material Assistance to Refugees in Africa, 1963-1981', in John Rogge, ed., *Refugees: A Third World Dilemma* (Totowa, NJ: Rowman & Littlefield, 1987): 15–36.

Plender, Richard, *International Migration Law* (Leiden: A. W. Sijthoff, 1989).

Porter, B., *The Refugee Question in Mid-Victorian Politics* (Cambridge: Cambridge University Press, 1970).

Proudfoot, Malcolm, *European Refugees, 1930–1952: A Study in Forced Population Movement* (London: Faber and Faber, 1957).

Prunier, Gerard, *The Rwanda Crisis: 1959–1994: History of a Genocide* (London: Hurst and Co., 1995).

—— *Update to the End of March 1995* (London: Writenet, May 1995).

—— 'The Geopolitical Situation of the Great Lakes Area in Light of the Kivu Crisis', *Refugee Survey Quarterly*, 16 (1997): 1–25.

—— 'The Great Lakes Crisis', *Current History*, 96 (May 1997): 193–9.

Pugh, Michael, 'Civil-Military Relations in Kosovo', *Security Dialogue*, 31/2 (June 2000): 229–42.

—— and Cunliffe, Alex, 'The Lead Agency Concept in Humanitarian Assistance: The Case of the UNHCR', *Security Dialogue*, 28 (1997): 17–30.

Read, James, 'The United Nations and Refugees—Changing Concepts', *International Conciliation*, 537 (New York, NY: Carnegie Endowment for International Peace, March 1962).

Rees, Elfan, 'Century of the Homeless Man' *International Conciliation*, 515 (New York, NY: Carnegie Endowment for International Peace, November 1957).

Refugee Documentation Project, *Refugee*. Forum for discussion of Canadian and international refugee issues (Toronto: York University, Refugee Studies Centre).

Refugee Policy Group, *Migration in and from Central and Eastern Europe: Addressing the Root Causes* (Washington, DC: Refugee Policy Group, June 1992).

Refugee Studies Programme, *Journal of Refugee Studies*. Academic exploration of forced migration and national and international responses (Oxford: Oxford University Press, Quarterly).

Reid, Tony, 'Repatriation of Arakanese Muslims from Bangladesh to Burma, 1978–79: "Arranged" Reversal of the Flow of an Ethnic Minority'. Unpublished paper. (Oxford: Documentation Centre, Refugee Studies Centre, Oxford University).

Reynell, Josephine, *Political Pawns: Refugees on the Thai-Kampuchean Border* (Oxford: Refugee Studies Programme, 1989).

Richards, Paul, *Fighting for the Rain Forests: War, Youth and Resources in Sierra Leone* (Oxford: James Currey, 1996).

Rieff, David, *Slaughterhouse: Bosnia and the Failure of the West* (New York, NY: Simon and Schuster, 1995).

—— 'Realpolitik in Congo: Should Zaire's Fate Have Been Subordinate to the Fate of the Rwandan Refugees?', *The Nation* (7 July 1997): 16–21.

Risse, Thomas, Ropp, Stephen, and Sikkink, Kathryn, eds., *The Power of Human Rights: International Norms and Domestic Change* (Cambridge: Cambridge University Press, 1999).

Roberts, Adam, *Humanitarian Action in War*. Adelphi Paper 305 (Oxford: Oxford University Press, 1996).

—— 'More Refugees and Less Asylum: A Regime in Transformation', *Journal of Refugee Studies*, 11/4 (1998): 375–95.

—— 'NATO's "Humanitarian" War over Kosovo', *Survival*, 41/3 (Autumn 1999): 102–23.

Robinson, Courtland, *Burmese Refugees in Thailand* (Washington, DC: US Committee for Refugees, 1990).

—— *Double Vision: A History of Cambodian Refugees in Thailand* (Bangkok: Institute of Asian Studies, Chulalong Korn University, 1996).

—— *Terms of Refuge: The Indochinese Exodus and the International Response* (London: Zed Books, 1998).

Robinson, Nehemiah, *Convention Relating to the Status of Refugees: Its History, Contents and Interpretation* (New York, NY: Institute of Jewish Affairs, 1953).

Roeder, O. G. and a Special Correspondent, 'Tragedy of Errors', *Far Eastern Economic Review* (26 May 1966): 361–5.

Rogers, Rosemarie and Copeland, Emily, *Forced Migration: Policy Issues in the Post-Cold War World* (Medford, MA: The Fletcher School of Law and Diplomacy, Tufts University, 1993).

Rogge, John, 'The Indochinese Diaspora: Where Have All the Refugees Gone?, *The Canadian Geographer*, 29.

Rohde, David, ed., *Endgame: The Betrayal and Fall of Srebrenica, Europe's Worst Massacre Since World War II* (New York, NY: Farrar, Strauss and Giroux, 1997).

—— .*Refugees: A Third World Dilemma* (Totowa, NJ: Rowman & Littlefield, 1987).

Ross, Marc Howard, *The Management of Conflict: Interpretations and Interests in Comparative Perspective* (New Haven, CT: Yale University Press, 1993).

Rotberg, Robert, *Haiti: The Politics of Squalor* (Boston, MA: Houghton Mifflin, 1978).

Rubin, Gary, *Refugee Protection: An Analysis and Action Proposal* (Washington, DC: US Committee for Refugees, 1983).

Rudge, Philip, 'Fortress Europe', *World Refugee Survey–1986 in Review* (1987): 5–12.

—— 'Europe in the 1990s: The Berlin Wall of the Mind', *World Refugee Survey–1989 in Review* (1989): 20–4.

Rufin, Jean-Christophe, *Le Piege Humanitaire suivi de Humanitaire et Politique depuis le Chute du Mur* (Paris: Jean-Claude Lattes, 1994).

Ruiz, Hiram, *When Refugees Won't Go Home: The Dilemma of Chadians in Sudan* (Washington, DC: US Committee for Refugees, 1987).

Russell, Sharon Stanton, and Teitlebaum, Michael, *International Migration and International Trade* (Washington, DC: World Bank Discussion Paper 160, 1992).

Ruthstrom-Ruin, Cecelia, *Beyond Europe: The Globalization of Refugee Aid* (Lund: Lund University Press, 1993).

Rystad, Goran, ed., *The Uprooted: Forced Migration as an International Problem in the Post-War Era* (Lund: Lund University Press, 1990).

Sahnoun, Mohamed, *Somalia: The Missed Opportunities* (Washington, DC: United States Institute of Peace Press, 1994).

Salomon, Kim, *Refugees in the Cold War: Toward a New International Refugee Regime in the Early Postwar Era* (Lund: Lund University Press, 1991).

Sayigh, Yezid, *Confronting the 1990s: Security in the Developing Countries*. Adelphi Paper 251 (London: Brasseys for International Institute, 1990).

Scanlan, John, and Loescher, Gil, 'Mass Asylum and Human Rights in American Foreign Policy', *Political Science Quarterly*, 97 (Spring 1982): 39–56.

—— —— 'U. S. Foreign Policy, 1959-1980: Impact on Refugee Flow from Cuba', in *The Annals of the American Academy of Political and Social Science* (May 1983): 116–37.

Scarritt, James, and Gurr, Ted Robert, 'Minority Rights At Risk: A Global Survey', *Human Rights Quarterly*, 11 (1989): 375–405.

Schatten, Fritz, *Communism in Africa* (New York, NY: Praeger, 1966)

Schechtman, Joseph, *European Population Transfers 1939–45* (New York, NY: Oxford University Press, 1946).

—— *Postwar Population Transfers in Europe 1945-1955* (Philadelphia, PA: University of Pennsylvania Press, 1962).

—— *The Refugee in the World: Displacement and Integration* (New York, NY: A. S. Barnes, 1963).

Scheinman, Ronald, 'The Office of the United Nations High Commissioner for Refugees and the Contemporary International System', Ph.D. dissertation, University of California, Santa Barbara (1974).

Schmeidl, Suzanne, 'Comparative Trends in Forced Displacement: IDPs and Refugees, 1964–1996', in Janie Hampton, ed., *Internally Displaced People: A Global Survey* (London: Earthscan, 1998): 24–33.

Schnyder, Felix, Statement to the Third Committee of the UN General Assembly (19 November 1962).

—— 'Les Aspects Juridiques Actuel du Probleme des Refugies', *Recueil*, 114 (Leiden: Academie de Droit International, 1965).

Scratch, John, 'Closing the Back Door: The Limits of Unilateral Action'. Unpublished paper for workshop 'Alternative futures: Developing an Agenda for Legal Research on Asylum', Minster Lovell, UK (1–3 June 2000).

Shacknove, Andrew, 'From Asylum to Containment', *International Journal of Refugee Law*, 5 (1993): 516–33.

Shakya, Tsering, *The Dragon in the Land of Snows* (London: Pimlico/Random House, 1999).

Shawcross, William, *The Quality of Mercy: Cambodia, the Holocaust and Modern Conscience* (New York, NY: Simon and Schuster, 1984).

—— *Deliver Us From Evil: Peacekeepers, Warlords and a World of Endless Conflict* (New York, NY: Simon and Schuster, 2000).

Silber, Laura and Little, Allan, *The Death of Yugoslavia* (London: Penguin, 1995).

Silk, James, *Despite a Generous Spirit: Denying Asylum in the United States* (Washington, DC: US Committee for Refugees, 1986).

Simpson, John Hope, *The Refugee Problem* (London: Oxford University Press, 1939).

Sisson, R. E. and Rose, L. E., *War and Secession: Pakistan, India and the Creation of Bangladesh* (Berkeley, CA: University of California Press, 1990).

Sjoberg, Tommie, *The Powers and the Persecuted: Refugee Problem and the Intergovernmental Committee on Refugees, 1938–1947* (Lund: Lund University Press, 1991).

Skran, Claudena, 'Profiles of the First Two High Commissioners', *Journal of Refugee Studies*, 1 (1988): 277–96.

—— *Refugees in Inter-War Europe: The Emergence of a Regime* (Oxford: Clarendon Press, 1995).

Slim, Hugo, 'Doing the Right Thing—Relief Agencies, Moral Dilemmas, and Moral Responsibility in Political Emergencies and War', *Disasters*, 21/3 (1997): 342–52.

Smith, Anthony, *The Ethnic Origin of Nations* (Oxford: Basil Blackwell, 1986).

Smyser, William, 'Refugees: A Never Ending Story', *Foreign Affairs*, 64 (Fall 1985): 154–68.

—— *Refugees: Extended Exile* (New York, NY: Praeger, 1987).

Stein, Barry, 'Ad Hoc Assistance to Return Movements and Long-Term Development Programme', in Timothy Allen and Hubert Morsink, eds., *When Refugees Go Home* (Trenton, NJ: Africa World Press, 1994): 108–29.

—— and Cuny, Fred, 'Repatriation Under Conflict', *World Refugee Survey 1991* (1991): 15–21.

—— and Tomasi, Sylvano, eds., 'Refugees Today', *International Migration Review*, 15 (Spring-Summer 1981): 331–93.

Stewart, Barbara McDonald, *United States Government Policy on Refugees from Nazism, 1933–1940* (New York, NY: Garland Publishing, 1982).

Stewart-Fox, Martin, ed., *Contemporary Laos* (London: University of Queensland Press, 1983).

Stoessinger, John, *The Refugee and the World Community* (Minneapolis, MN: University of Minnesota Press, 1956).

Strategic Survey (London: Brasseys for International Institute for Strategic Studies, Annual).

Suhrke, Astri, *Towards a Comprehensive Refugee Policy: Conflict and Refugees in the Post-Cold War World* (Geneva: ILO/UNHCR, 1992).

—— 'Uncertain Globalization: Refugee Movements in the Second Half of the Twentieth Century', in Wang Gungwu, ed., *Global History and Migrations* (Boulder, CO: Westview Press, 1997).

—— 'Burden-sharing During Refugee Emergencies: The Logic of Collective versus National Action', *Journal of Refugee Studies*, 11/4 (1998): 396–415.

—— and Zolberg, Aristide, 'Beyond the Refugee Crisis: Disengagement and Durable Solutions for the Developing World', *Migration*, 5 (1989): 69–120.

Sutter, Valerie, *The Indochinese Refugee Dilemma* (Baton Rouge, LA: Louisiana State University Press, 1990).

Tabori, Paul, *The Anatomy of Exile* (London: George C. Harrap, 1972).

Teitelbaum, Michael, 'Immigration, Refugees and Foreign Policy', *International Organization*, 38 (Summer 1984): 429–50.

Terry, Fiona, 'Condemned to Repeat? The Paradoxes of Humanitarian Action', Ph.D. dissertation, Australian National University, Canberra (2000).

Tolstoy, Nikolai, *The Silent Betrayal* (New York, NY: Scribners, 1977).

—— *Victims of Yalta* (London: Hodder & Stoughton, 1977).

Tomasi, Lydio, *In Defense of the Alien* (New York, NY: Center for Migration Studies, Annual since 1983).

Toscani, Candida, *Mission to the Federal Republic of Germany, June 6-10, 1983*. UNHCR internal report. (Geneva: 1 July 1983).

Tucker, Robert, Keely, Charles, and Wrigley, Linda, eds., *Immigration and U. S. Foreign Policy* (Boulder, CO: Westview Press, 1990).

United Kingdom, Department for International Development, 'United Nations High Commissioner for Refugees: Interim Strategy Paper', (London: Department for International Development, June 2000).

United Kingdom, House of Commons, International Development Committee, 'Kosovo: The Humanitarian Crisis', (15 May 1999).

United Nations, *Report of the Independent Inquiry into the Actions of the United Nations during the 1994 Genocide in Rwanda* (New York, NY: United Nations, 15 December 1999).

United Nations General Assembly, Charter, Article 101 (1945).

—— Sixth Session, Document E/2036/Add.1 (13 November 1951).

—— The 1951 United Nations Convention Relating to the Status of Refugees', *United Nations Treaty*, 184/2545 (28 July 1951): 137.

—— Sixth Session, Third Committee, 382nd Meeting (10 January 1952).

—— Resolution 538B (VI) (1952).

—— Advisory Committee (IV), A/AC.36/32 (29 January 1954).

—— Resolution 1006 (ES11) (9 November 1956).

—— Official Records, Session II, Plenary Meeting 578 (21 November 1957).

—— Resolutions 1166 and 1167 (XII) (26 November 1957).

—— Resolution 1039 (XI) (23 January 1957).

—— Resolution 1286 (XIII) (5 December 1958).

—— Resolution 1388 (XIV) (20 November 1959).

—— Resolution 1672 (XVI) (18 December 1961).

—— Resolution 2039 (XX) (1965).

—— Resolution 2816 (XXVI) (December 1971).

—— Resolution 2958 (XXVII) (12 December 1972).

—— Resolution 2956A (XXVII) (12 December 1972).

—— Resolution 3143 (XXVIII) (14 December 1973).

—— Resolution 3271 (XXIX) (10 December 1974).

—— Resolution 3454 (XXX) (9 December 1975).

—— *Quarterly Economic Review of Thailand, Burma*, 4th Quarter (1978).

—— *Report of the UN High Commissioner for Refugees*, 33rd Session, Supplement No 12 (A/33/12) (October 1978): 2.

—— Resolution 3460 (XXXIV) (1979).

—— UN Secretary-General's Report to the General Assembly, A/51/950, paragraph 186 (July 1997).

United Nations Security Council, Resolution adopted on 9 June 1961, S/4835 (9 June 1961).

—— *Quarterly Economic Review of Thailand, Burma* (4th Quarter 1978).

UNHCR, UN Refugee Emergency Fund Advisory Committee, 4th Session, Documents A/AC.36/SR.26 and SR.27 (3 March 1954).

—— UN Refugee Emergency Fund Executive Committee (31 January 1957).

—— *A Story of Anguish and Action: The United Nations Focal Point for Assistance to Refugees from East Bengal in India* (Geneva: UNHCR, November 1972).

—— 'Report of the United Nations High Commissioner for Refugees Mission to Monitor INS Asylum Processing of Salvadoran Illegal Entrants—September 13–18, 1981'. Reprinted in *Congressional Record* (11February 1982): S827–31.

—— *Informal Meeting on Military Attacks on Refugee Camps and Settlements in Southern Africa and Elsewhere* (Geneva: EC/SCP/27, Sub-committee of the Whole on International Protection, UNHCR Executive Committee, 6 June 1983).

—— *Refugees*, 27 (Geneva: UNHCR, March 1986).

—— 'Note on International Protection', (Geneva: UNHCR, 15 July 1986).

—— Report of the 40th Session of the UNHCR Executive Committee. UN doc. A/AC.96/733 (19 October 1989).

—— *Report of the Ad Hoc Review Group on the Role and Structure of UNHCR* (Geneva: UNHCR, 6 March 1990).

—— Report of the UNHCR Executive Committee Extraordinary Meeting. UN doc. A/AC.96/747 (1 June 1990).

—— 'Opening statement of the High Commissioner. UNHCR Executive Committee Meeting (1 October 1990).

—— *Excom in Abstracts* (Geneva: UNHCR, The Centre for Documentation on Refugees, October 1990).

—— *Conclusions on the International Protection of Refugees* (Geneva: UNHCR, 1991).

—— 'Returnee Aid and Development' (Geneva: UNHCR, 14 January 1992).

—— 'Report of the UNHCR Working Group on International Protection' (Geneva: UNHCR, 6 July 1992).

—— 'Bridging the Gap Between Returnee Aid and Development: A Challenge for the International Community' (Geneva: UNHCR, 1992).

—— *Note on International Protection*, UN doc. A/AC.96/799 (1992).

—— *The State of the World's Refugees: The Challenge of Protection* (Geneva: UNHCR, 1993)

—— *UNHCR's Operational Experience with Internally Displaced Persons* (Geneva: UNHCR, Division of International Protection, September 1994).

—— Central Evaluation Section, *Returnee Aid and Development* (Geneva: UNHCR, 1994).

—— *The State of the World's Refugees: In Search of Solutions* (Geneva: UNHCR, 1995).

—— *Collection of International Instruments and Other Legal Texts concerning Refugees and Displaced Persons*, 2 vols. (Geneva: UNHCR, 1995)

—— *The State of the World's Refugees: A Humanitarian Agenda* (Oxford: Oxford University Press, 1997).

—— 'Resourcing the Managing a Unified Budget'. Consultations on the UNHCR's Budget Structure (New York, NY: UNHCR, 13 January 1999).

—— *Refugees and Others of Concern to UNHCR: 1999 Statistical Overview* (Geneva: UNHCR, July 1999).

—— *New Issues in Refugee Research* 1–30 (Geneva: UNHCR, May 1999–September 2000).

—— *The State of the World's Refugees: Fifty Years of Humanitarian Action* (Oxford, Oxford University Press, 2000).

—— *The Kosovo Crisis: An Independent Evaluation of UNHCR's Emergency Preparedness and Response* (Geneva: UNHCR, 2000).

—— 'Internally Displaced Persons: The Role of the United Nations High Commissioner for Refugees' (Geneva: UNHCR, 6 March 2000).

US Agency for International Development, *Population Movements in the Former Soviet Union* (Washington, DC: The Emergency Humanitarian Assessment Team in the New Independent States, June 1992).

US Committee for Refugees, *World Refugee Survey* (Washington, DC: US Committee on Refugees, 1989).

—— *The Return of Rohingyan Refugees to Burma: Voluntary Repatriation or Refoulement?* (Washington, DC: US Committee on Refugees, March 1995).

—— *World Refugee Survey 2000* (Washington, DC: US Committee for Refugees, 2000).

US Comptroller General, *Need for an International Disaster Relief Agency* (Washington, DC: General Accounting Office, 1976): 19.

—— *Central American Refugees: Regional Conditions and Prospects and Potential Impact on the United States.* Report to the Congress of the United States. (Washington, DC: GAO/NSIAD–84–106, US General Accounting Office, 20 July 1984).

US Congress, *Central Intelligence Act* (July 1949).

—— *Refugee Relief Act* (7 August 1953).

—— Joint Economic Committee, *Indochinese Refugees: The Impact on First Asylum Countries and Implications for American Policy* (Washington, DC: Government Printing Office, 1980).

—— *Congressional Record* (11 February 1982): S827–31.

US House of Representatives. Committee on Foreign Affairs, *Hearings on Palestine Refugees*, 81st Congress, 2nd Session (16 February 1950).

—— Judiciary Committee, *Migration and Refugee Assistance*, 87th Congress, 1st Session (3 August 1961): 39.

—— Judiciary Committee, *Study of Population and Immigration Problems* (Washington, DC: US Government Printing Office, 1963): 38.

—— Subcommittee on International Organizations, *Human Rights in Haiti*, 94th Congress, 1st Session (18 November 1975).

—— Subcommittee on Immigration, Citizenship, and International Law, *Haitian Emigration*, 94th Congress, 2nd Session (July 1976).

—— Committee for Refugees. Testimony of Hiram Ruiz before Joint Hearing of the House Committee of Foreign Affairs, Subcommittees on International Operations in Africa, 101st Congress, 2nd Session (10 May 1990).

US Immigration and Naturalization Service, 'Asylum Adjudications: An Evolving Concept and Responsibility for the INS'. INS internal memorandum. (June and December 1982): 57.

US Library of Congress, 'Chronology of the Hungarian Refugee Program', Typescript (14 May 1975).

US Mission to the UN, Press Release. Statement by Ambassador Holbrooke (28 March 2000).

US Senate. Senate Report 950, Appendix, 80th Congress, 2nd Session (1948).

—— Committee on Foreign Relations, *Migration and Refugee Assistance Act of 1961*, 87th Congress, 1st Session (11 September 1961): 11–12.

—— Judiciary Committee, Subcommittee to Investigate Problems Connected with Refugees and Escapees, *Refugees and Escapees*, 87th Congress, 2nd Session (6 June 1963): 7.

—— Judiciary Committee, Subcommittee to Investigate Problems Connected with Refugees and Escapees, *African Refugee Problems*, 89th Congress, 1st Session (21 January 1965): 38–9 and 41–2.

—— Judiciary Committee, Subcommittee to Investigate Problems Connected with Refugees and Escapees, *Refugees and Humanitarian Problems in Chile, Part 3*, 94th Congress, 1st Session (2 October 1975): 24–7.

US State Department, 'Refugees and Stateless Persons', *Foreign Relations of the United States* (Washington, DC: UGPO, 1950).

—— *The US Government and Refugee Relief*. Mimeo (August 1972).

Van Evera, Stephen, 'Primed for Peace: Europe after the Cold War', *International Security*, 16/4 (1990/1991): 2–57.

Van Hear, Nicholas, 'Mass Flight in the Middle East: Involuntary Migration and the Gulf Conflict 1990–1991', in Richard Black and Vaughn Robinson, eds., *Geography and Refugees: Patterns and Processes of Change* (London: Belhaven Press, 1992): 33–51.

—— *New Diasporas: The Mass Exodus, Dispersal and Regrouping of Migrant Communities* (London: University College of London Press, 1998).

van Hovell, Wilbert, 'Yugoslav Emergency', *Update on Protection Issues* (Geneva: UNHCR, 12 September 1992).

van Selm Thorburn, Joanne, *Refugee Protection in Europe: Lessons of the Yugoslav Crisis* (The Hague: Martinus Nijhoff Publishers, 1998).

Vayrynen, Raimo, *Global Govenance and Enforcement* (Latham, MA: Rowman and Littlefield, 1999).

—— 'The Dilemma of Voluntary Funding: Political Interests and Institutional Reforms', *International Migration Review* (forthcoming).

Vernant, Jacques, *The Refugee in the Post-War World* (New Haven, CT: Yale University Press, 1953).

Vidal, John, 'Blacks Need, but Only Whites Receive: Race Appears to Be Skewing the West's approach to Aid', *Guardian* (12 August 1999).

Vishnevsky, Anatoli and Zayonchkovskaya, Zhanna, *Internal and International Migrations in the Former Soviet Space* (Moscow: Institute for Employment Studies, Russian Academy of Sciences, June 1992).

Wain, Barry, *The Refused: The Agony of the Indochinese Refugees* (New York, NY: Simon and Schuster, 1981).

Walkup, Mark, 'Policy and Behavior in Humanitarian Organizations: The Institutional Origins of Operational Dysfunction'. Ph.D. dissertation, University of Florida (1997).

—— 'Policy Dysfunction in Humanitarian Organizations: The Role of Coping Strategies, Institutions, and Organizational Culture', *Journal of Refugee Studies*, 10/1 (1997): 37–60.

Wall Street Journal (10 August 1987).

Warner, Daniel, 'Forty Years of the Executive Committee: from the Old to the New', *International Journal of Refugee Law*, 2/2 (1990): 238–51.

Warren, George, *The Development of United States Participation in Inter-governmental Efforts to Resolve Refugee Problems* (Mimeo, 1967).

Weiner, Myron, *Security, Stability and International Migration* (Cambridge, MA: Center for International Studies, 1991).

—— ed., *International Migration and Security* (Boulder, CO: Westview Press, 1993).

—— *The Global Migration Crisis: Challenge to States and to Human Rights* (New York, NY: Harper Collins, 1995).

—— 'Bad Neighbours, Bad Neighbourhoods: An Enquiry into the Causes of Refugee Flows', *International Security*, 21/1 (1996): 5–42.

Weis, Paul, *The Legal Aspects of the Problems of De Facto Refugees* (Geneva: International Exchange Fund, 1974).

—— *Travaux Preparatoires of the Convention Relating to the Status of Refugees of 28 July 1951* (Geneva: UN Institute for Training and Research, 1991).

—— and Melander, Goran, *De Facto Refugees* (Geneva: UNHCR, July 1974).

Weiss, Thomas, ed., *Humanitarian Emergencies and Military Help in Africa* (New York, NY: St. Martin's Press, 1990).

—— *Military-Civilian Interactions* (Lanham, MD: Rowman & Littlefield Publishers, 1999)

Weiss-Fagen, Patricia, 'Peace in Central America: Transition for the Uprooted', *World Refugee Survey 1993* (Washington, DC: US Committee for Refugees, 1993): 30–9.

—— *Peace Making as Rebuilding War Torn Societies*. War Torn Societies Project (Geneva: UNRISD, 1996).

—— and Martin, Susan Forbes, *Safe Haven Options in Industrialized Countries* (Washington DC: Refugee Policy Group, 1987).

Wheeler, Nicholas, *Saving Strangers: Humanitarian Intervention in International Society* (Oxford: Oxford University Press, 2000).

Widgren, Jonas, 'International Migration and Regional Stability', *International Affairs*, 66 (October 1990): 749–66.

—— 'Europe and International Migration in the Future', in Gil Loescher and Laila Monahan, eds., *Refugees and International Relations* (Oxford: Clarendon Press, 1989): 49–62.

Wiesner, Louis, *Victims and Survivors: Displaced Persons and Other War Victims in Vietnam, 1954–1975* (Westport, CT: Greenwood Press, 1988).

Wilkenson, Ray, 'Give Me Your Huddled Masses . . . .', *Refugees*, 2/119 (2000): 15.

Winter, Roger, 'The Year in Review', *World Refugee Survey 2000* (Washington, DC: US Committee for refugees, 2000): 17.

Woodbridge, George, *The History of UNRRA* (New York, NY: Columbia University Press, 1950).

Woodward, Susan, *Balkan Tragedy: Chaos and Dissolution after the Cold War* (Washington, DC: The Brookings Institution, 1995).

World Council of Churches, *Refugees* (Geneva: WCC, Monthly).

Wyman, David, *Paper Walls: America and the Refugee Crisis, 1938–1941* (Amherst, MA: University Of Massachusetts Press, 1968).

—— *The Abandonment of the Jews: America and the Holocaust, 1941–45* (New York, NY: Pantheon Books, 1984).

Zarjevski, Yefime, *A Future Preserved: International Assistance to Refugees* (Oxford: Pergamon Press, 1988).

Zeager, Lester, *The Role of Threat Power in Refugee Resettlement: The Indochinese Crisis of 1979* (Greenville, NC: East Carolina University, Department of Economics, 30 April 1999).

Zieck, Marjorleine, *UNHCR and Voluntary Repatriation of Refugees: A Legal Analysis* (The Hague: Martinus Nijhoff, 1997).

Zolberg, Aristide, 'The Formation of New States as a Refugee Generating Process', in Gil Loescher and John Scanlan, eds., *The Global Refugee Problem: US and World Response*. Special issue of *Annals of the American Academy of Political and Social Science*, 467 (May 1983): 24–38.

—— 'The Specter of Anarchy', *Dissent*, 39 (Summer 1992): 303–11.

—— Suhrke, Astri, and Aguayo, Sergio, *Escape from Violence: Conflict and the Refugee Crisis in the Developing World* (New York, NY: Oxford University Press, 1989).

Zucker, Norman and Flink Zucker, Naomi, *The Guarded Gate: The Reality of American Refugee Policy* (San Diego, CA: Harcourt Brace Jovanovich, 1987).

—— *Desperate Crossings: Seeking Refuge in America* (Armonk, NY: M. E. Sharpe, 1996).

INDEX